Handbook of Clinical Health Psychology

Handbook of Clinical Health Psychology

Edited by
Theodore Millon
Catherine Green
Robert Meagher
University of Miami, Coral Gables, Florida

PLENUM PRESS • NEW YORK AND LONDON

Library of Congress Cataloging in Publication Data

Main entry under title:

Handbook of clinical health psychology.

Includes bibliographical references and index.
1. Medicine, Psychosomatic. I. Millon, Theodore. II. Green, Catherine, Date-   . III.
Meagher, Robert. [DNLM: 1. Attitude to health. 2. Disease — Psychology. 3. Psychology, Clinical.
4. Psychophysiologic disorders — Therapy. WM 90 H236]
RC49.H325 1982   616'.001'9   82-11236
ISBN 0-306-40932-1

©1982 Plenum Press, New York
A Division of Plenum Publishing Corporation
233 Spring Street, New York, N.Y. 10013

Printed in the United States of America

To the memory of a wise, warm, and witty colleague

PARK DAVIDSON

Whose untimely death has deprived
clinical health psychology of one of its
most distinguished contributors

Contributors

James L. Alexander, *Department of Rehabilitation, Behavioral Ecology Programs, Baylor College of Medicine, Waco, Texas*

Laurence H. Baker, *Department of Psychology, University of Connecticut, Newington, Connecticut*

Theodore X. Barber, *Department of Supportive Services, Cushing Hospital, Framingham, Massachusetts*

Cheryl S. Brischetto, *Department of Medical Psychology, Oregon Health Sciences University, Portland, Oregon*

Alvin G. Burstein, *Department of Psychiatry, University of Texas Health Science Center at San Antonio, San Antonio, Texas*

Timothy P. Carmody, *Department of Medical Psychology, Oregon Health Sciences University, Portland, Oregon*

Sonja L. Connor, *Department of Medicine, Oregon Health Sciences University, Portland, Oregon*

William E. Connor, *Department of Medicine, Oregon Health Sciences University, Portland, Oregon*

James C. Coyne, *Department of Psychology, University of California, Berkeley, California*

Park Davidson, *Late of the Department of Psychology, University of British Columbia, Vancouver, British Columbia, Canada*

Jerald F. Dirks, *Division of Psychobiology, National Jewish Hospital and Research Center, and Department of Psychiatry, University of Colorado School of Medicine, Denver, Colorado*

Barbara Snell Dohrenwend, *Division of Sociomedical Sciences, School of Public Health, Columbia University, New York, New York*

Bruce P. Dohrenwend, *Social Psychiatry Research Unit, Department of Psychiatry, Columbia University, New York, New York*

Martin Falletti, *Miami Jewish Home and Hospital for the Aged, Miami, Florida*

Steven G. Fey, *Department of Rehabilitation Medicine, University of Washington, Seattle, Washington*

Wilbert E. Fordyce, *Department of Rehabilitation Medicine, University of Washington School of Medicine, Seattle, Washington*

Catherine J. Green, *Department of Psychology, University of Miami, Coral Gables, Florida*

Kenneth Holroyd, *Department of Psychology, Ohio University, Athens, Ohio*

Mardi J. Horowitz, *Department of Psychiatry and Center for the Study of Neuroses, Langley Porter Psychiatric Institute, University of California, San Francisco, California*

Jan Howard, *Behavioral Medicine Branch, National Cancer Institute, National Institutes of Health, Bethesda, Maryland*

Nelson F. Jones, *School of Professional Psychology, University of Denver, Denver, Colorado*

William H. Kaplan, *Department of Psychiatry, University of Chicago, Chicago, Illinois*

Chase P. Kimball, *Division of Biological Sciences and College of the University of Chicago, Chicago, Illinois*

Robert A. Kinsman, *Division of Psychobiology, National Jewish Hospital and Research Center, and Department of Psychiatry, University of Colorado School of Medicine, Denver, Colorado*

Henry M. Levine, *Department of Psychology, University of Washington, Seattle, Washington*

Sandra M. Levy, *Behavioral Medicine Branch, National Cancer Institute, National Institutes of Health, Bethesda, Maryland*

Sandra Loucks, *Department of Psychology and Center for Personal and Educational Development, Trinity University, San Antonio, Texas*

James E. Maddux, *Department of Psychology, Texas Tech University, Lubbock, Texas*

Joseph D. Matarazzo, *Department of Medical Psychology, Oregon Health Sciences University, Portland, Oregon*

Robert B. Meagher, Jr., *Department of Neurological Surgery, University of Miami School of Medicine, Miami, Florida*

Theodore Millon, *Department of Psychology, University of Miami, Coral Gables, Florida*

Rudolf H. Moos, *Social Ecology Laboratory, Department of Psychiatry and the Behavioral Sciences, Stanford University and VA Medical Center, Palo Alto, California*

Diane K. Pierce, *Department of Medical Psychology, Oregon Health Sciences University, Portland, Oregon*

Michael C. Roberts, *Department of Psychology, University of Alabama, University, Alabama*

Barbara R. Sarason, *Department of Psychology, University of Washington, Seattle, Washington*

Irwin G. Sarason, *Department of Psychology, University of Washington, Seattle, Washington*

Gary Sexton, *Department of Medicine, Oregon Health Sciences University, Portland, Oregon*

Franklin C. Shontz, *Department of Psychology, University of Kansas, Lawrence, Kansas*

Jeffrey R. Soloman, *Altro Health and Rehabilitation Services, 345 Madison Avenue, New York, New York*

Jeffrey C. Steger, *Department of Rehabilitation Medicine, University of Washington School of Medicine, Seattle, Washington*

James J. Strain, *Mount Sinai School of Medicine, New York, New York*

Rebecca M. Warner, *Department of Psychology, University of New Hampshire, Durham, New Hampshire*

Herbert Weiner, *Department of Psychiatry and Neuroscience, Albert Einstein College of Medicine, and Department of Psychiatry, Montefiore Hospital and Medical Center, New York, New York*

Edwin P. Willems, *Department of Psychology, College of Social Sciences, University of Houston, Houston, Texas*

Logan Wright, *Institute of Health Psychology for Children, Oklahoma City, Oklahoma*

Sandy K. Wurtele, *Department of Psychology, University of Alabama, University, Alabama*

Steven Yunik, *Douglas Gardens Community Mental Health Center of Miami Beach, Miami Beach, Florida*

Preface

We seek to throw down the gauntlet with this handbook, challenging the hegemony of the "behavioral medicine" approach to the psychological study and treatment of the physically ill. This volume is not another in that growing surfeit of texts that pledge allegiance to the doctrinaire purity of behavioristic thinking, or conceptualize their subject in accord with the sterility of medical models. Diseases are not our focus, nor is the narrow band of behavioral assessment and therapy methodologies. Rather, we have sought to redefine this amorphous, yet burgeoning field so as to place it squarely within the province of a broadly-based psychology—specifically, the emerging, substantive discipline of health psychology and the well-established professionalism and diverse technologies of clinical psychology. The handbook's title—*Clinical Health Psychology*—reflects this reorientation explicitly, and Chapter 1 addresses its themes and provides its justifications more fully.

In the process of developing a relevant and comprehensive health assessment tool, the editors were struck by the failure of clinical psychologists to avail themselves of the rich vein of materials that comprise the psychosocial world of the physically ill. Perhaps more dismaying was the observation that this field was being mined—less than optimally—by physicians and nonclinical psychologists. As valuable as their tools and expertise may be for their respective subject areas, neither discipline possesses the scientist-professional blend that characterizes the coordinated research *and* services training of the clinical psychologist. Physicians exemplify the standard for professional attitudes and clinical skills, but they are often, at best, novices when it comes to grasping the complex relationships between "psyche" and "soma". Similarly, nonclinical psychologists bring a rich background of knowledge and scientific methodology to their realms of study, but only rarely do they have the requisite grounding and service expertise called for in direct patient care. As a consequence of their respective strengths and shortcomings, a symbiotic, if peculiar hybrid has emerged—a unit composed of physician and experimental psychologist. It seems time to us for the third and perhaps most essential member to join this health care team—the clinical psychologist. It is hoped that this handbook will activate an increased involvement on their part.

THEODORE MILLON
CATHERINE J. GREEN
ROBERT B. MEAGHER, JR.

Coral Gables, Florida

Contents

PART II. THE CLINICAL SETTINGS OF HEALTH PSYCHOLOGY 173

Chapter 9. The Psychologist as Health Care Clinician   175

ALVIN G. BURSTEIN AND SANDRA LOUCKS

*Chapter 10. Pediatric Psychology: Health Care Psychology
for Children*   191

MICHAEL C. ROBERTS, JAMES E. MADDUX, SANDY K. WURTELE, AND
LOGAN WRIGHT

Chapter 11. The Psychologist as Geriatric Clinician   227

JEFFREY SOLOMON, MARTIN FALETTI, AND STEVEN YUNIK

Chapter 12. Collaborative Efforts in Liaison Psychiatry   251

JAMES J. STRAIN

Chapter 13. The Psychologist as Social Systems Consultant — 277

REBECCA M. WARNER

Chapter 14. Behavioral Cardiology with Emphasis on the Family Heart Study: Fertile Ground for Psychological and Biomedical Research — 301

JOSEPH D. MATARAZZO, WILLIAM E. CONNOR, STEVEN G. FEY,
TIMOTHY P. CARMODY, DIANE K. PIERCE, CHERYL S. BRISCHETTO,
LAURENCE H. BAKER, SONJA L. CONNOR, AND GARY SEXTON

Chapter 16. Assessing the Impact of Life Changes   *377*

IRWIN G. SARASON, HENRY M. LEVINE, AND BARBARA R. SARASON

Chapter 17. Behavioral Indicators of Client Progress after Spinal Cord Injury: An Ecological-Contextual Approach   *401*

EDWIN P. WILLEMS AND JAMES L. ALEXANDER

Chapter 18. Issues in Patient Compliance   *417*

PARK O. DAVIDSON

Chapter 19. Psychomaintenance of Chronic Physical Illness: Clinical Assessment of Personal Styles Affecting Medical Management

435

ROBERT A. KINSMAN, JERALD F. DIRKS, AND NELSON F. JONES

Chapter 20. Behavioral Health Care in the Management of Chronic Pain

JEFFREY STEGER AND WILBERT FORDYCE

Chapter 21. Cognitive Behavior Therapy in Health Psychology   499

ROBERT B. MEAGHER, JR.

Chapter 22. Hypnosuggestive Procedures in the Treatment of
Clinical Pain: Implications for Theories of Hypnosis and
Suggestive Therapy   521

THEODORE X. BARBER

Chapter 23. Patient-Centric Technologies: A Clinical-Cultural Perspective   561

Sandra M. Levy and Jan Howard

On the Nature of Clinical Health Psychology

Theodore Millon

A major error in professional health care training and practice, one founded on a misconceived and primitive mind–body dualism, is undergoing serious reexamination today. This chapter seeks to contribute to these reflections by arguing for a broadened conception of the role of the clinical psychologist. This chapter not only fosters the view that clinical psychology should move beyond its conventional—albeit well-founded—attention to the "mentally" disordered but also demonstrates specifically that there is both a need and a justification for psychologists to assume an active role in the assessment and management of the "physically" disordered.

Psychologists are especially well suited to understand "illness behavior" and to aid patients in coping with the emotional and psychosocial consequences of medical disease. Relevant also to the increased need for the skills of the clinical psychologist is the changing character and prevalence of physical disorders in contemporary Western society. Today, humanity is at the mercy of virulent infectious diseases to a considerably lesser extent than in the past. We suffer now from progressive and insidious disorders that slowly devastate our bodies. These largely chronic cardiovascular, respiratory, and metastatic diseases are in great measure the consequence of simple aging and destructive behavioral life-styles (e.g., too little physical activity and too much eating, smoking, and stress). In effect, major medical problems today result from misguided psychological habits and attitudes, in many cases to an even greater extent than from invading microbes and aging. Given origins such as these, it can be argued that a growing

THEODORE MILLON • Department of Psychology, University of Miami, Coral Gables, Florida 33124.

proportion of so-called physical disorders require the preventive, diagnostic, and rehabilitative attentions of psychologists at least as much as they do the reparative talents of physicians and surgeons. Seen in this light, psychology as a profession is not merely justified but obligated to apply its knowledge and methods to those who succumb to modern-day "physical" ailments.

1. Some Historical and Philosophical Reflections

Before characterizing the content, functions, and training that I foresee for clinical health psychology, it may be useful to discuss a number of issues that will provide a perspective and context within which to view these prospects.

1.1. Historical Notes

Psychologists have recently shown impressively increased interest in physical disorders, but this attention is not new. Although in a scattered and piecemeal manner, psychologists have worked with physicians on problems of health and illness for close to a century. An early professor–student association between Wilhelm Wundt and Emil Kraepelin in the last quarter of the 1800s strongly shaped the systematic and experimental outlook evident in Kraepelin's later studies; a similar and notable joint enterprise between G. Heymans and E. Weirsma at the turn of the century in Holland was also exceptionally fruitful in synthesizing psychological and medical perspectives. Although both of these collaborations focused primarily on the "mental" rather than the "physical" aspect of disorders, both sought to resolve the traditional and often sharply drawn mind–body dichotomy.

Efforts in the United States to coordinate the perspectives of physicians and psychologists in matters of general physical health began in earnest in the second decade of this century. One early group of collaborators sought ways to infuse the principles of psychology into the training of medical students, hoping thereby to make the education of the fledgling physician more "holistic" (Franz, 1912; Meyer, 1912; Prince, 1912; Southard, 1912). Among the proponents of this suggestion was John Watson (1912), soon to be known for his vigorous espousal of behaviorism. Despite this early effort, few psychologists were added to medical school faculties during the first third of the century. In the 1930s, a small group of psychologists were drawn to university medical centers because of opportunities to work on basic and applied projects in neurological and psychophysiological research (Watson, 1953). Despite this growth, the total number of research psychologists employed in health settings remained rather modest until the 1960s.

A major reason for the paucity of opportunities for psychologists was that medical schools supported few of their faculty on university funds. For the most part, faculty ranks were filled with volunteer private practitioners and those whose salaries depended on the clinical fees they could generate. Except for research grants, few funds were available to salary non-fee-producing Ph.D. psychologists. Psychologists began to gain significant entree into the medical and health establishment when they were able to duplicate the clinical functions of the physician, that is, when they became integral members of a fee-generating service. This began, albeit slowly, in the late 1950s and mushroomed rapidly in the late 1960s and early 1970s (Matarazzo, Lubin & Daniel, 1957; Matarazzo, Lubin, & Nathan, 1978; Mensh, 1953; Wagner & Stegeman, 1964; Witkin, Mensh, & Cates, 1972). It occurred primarily in university departments of psychiatry, where the functions of the psychiatrist and clinical psychologist were, in large measure, interchangeable. It was not until the mid-1970s that psychologists began to be seen not as psychiatry's surrogate but as independent colleagues and consultants to physicians who worked in nonpsychiatric health settings.

This latest and most autonomous of roles, that of psychologist-professional in general medical as opposed to psychiatric settings, arose as a consequence of three factors. First, psychologists demonstrated a wide range of skills that were not to be found among other medical specialties, for example, in preventive education, biofeedback training, and family therapy. Second, there was a growing awareness among physicians that an increasing number of ailments seen in everyday practice reflected the ravaging effects not of infectious agents or ordinary bodily decay but of pernicious styles of life and habits of behavior. Third, health care professionals began to recognize that the psychodynamic concepts and treatment prescriptions of their psychiatric colleagues were not only often obscure and tangential to the issues with which they dealt but frequently proved less than practical as guides to action.

The deepening involvement of psychologists in problems of general health is nowhere better evident than in the recent emergence of formal organizations, national conferences, and professional journals. As is well known by now, the late 1970s saw the establishing of the Society of Behavioral Medicine, formed by the joining of health professionals from both psychology and medicine; the approval of a Division of Health Psychology within the American Psychological Association; and the publication of periodicals such as the *Journal of Behavioral Medicine*, and the journals of *Health Psychology* and *Rehabilitation Psychology*. Each of these indicates that a scientific foundation is being built to undergird the professional practice of the health psychologist. Moreover, this impressive expansion, as well as the parallel acceptance of psychologists as clinicians in *general* health, suggests that psychology has finally crossed the rigid boundaries set by a mind–body dualism.

1.2. Bridging the Mind–Body Dichotomy

It is clear that a new conceptual and training model is called for in clinical psychology, one that seeks to implement a synthesis of both mind and body and that views these traditional polarities as complementary facets of a single, integrated unity. Until scientific formulations and clinical activities bridge this arbitrary distinction, efforts to devise progressively more effective solutions to problems of illness and disease will be stymied. Advances in this sphere depend greatly on the contributions of the psychologist, as suggested in the following (American Psychological Association, 1976):

> No other discipline is better suited and equipped than psychology to discover, delineate, and demonstrate the organismic nature of humans and to encourage an ever-broad-

ening realization that humanity's total functional health is threatened whenever either side of the interactive mind-body equation is neglected. Any program for health care and illness management can achieve comprehensiveness and integration only as there is respect for the functional unity of the individual. (p. 271)

More recently, DiMatteo and Friedman (1979) have argued that the "holistic approach" goes beyond the mere training of physicians to be increasingly sensitive to their patients' emotions and needs. They contend not only that social, cultural, and psychological factors are an intrinsic part of illness and its treatment but that it is the psychologist alone who possesses special expertise in each of these realms.

It should not be overlooked in our effort to work toward a mind–body synthesis that significant research gains were achieved by early investigators who separated their studies into these two realms. Insofar as effective health service is concerned, however, the separation proved less than satisfactory. The contrasting benefits for clinical service versus research of adhering to the traditional Cartesian dualism is noted well by Scofield (1979):

> it is a conceptual convention that has facilitated scientific inquiries more than it has encouraged a truly comprehensive medicine. . . . Specialization and focus on body *or* mind has made for effective and progressive programmatic research. A small number of illnesses have been viewed as "psychosomatic" and only a very few physicians and psychologists have been attracted to the complex interface of the physical and the mental. Recent years have seen an increasing appreciation for the need to study the reciprocity between psyche and soma as there has been growing awareness that the individual's health status is a personal gestalt to which situational/environmental and mental/emotional conditions contribute in a complex interactive fashion. (p. 450)

Many clinical psychologists may resist a broadened conception of their role, preferring to strengthen their embrace of the "mental" to the exclusion of the "physical." Having long been second-class citizens in the house of psychiatry, psychologists are beginning to "feel their oats" as highly competent, fully recognized, and—perhaps most significantly—independent health practitioners. Why should they take a step backward, some will say, and invite the "inferior" status of being handmaidens again, this time to nonpsychiatric physicians? We will refer later to the justified concerns that are represented in this "is it good for psychology?" view. The questions we will address for the moment are: "Does it make conceptual sense to distinguish the processes of the mind from those of the body?" and "Is it good health care practice for the patient to be segmented into physical and psychic components?"

The answer to both these questions, this handbook contends, is definitely no! And to the extent that current practices will continue to follow the traditional dualism, we would conclude that both clinical psychology and clinical medicine remain in crisis, each adhering to a different aspect of a single discipline that divides the patient illogically and deleteriously. Although presented as a challenge to his physician colleagues, the views expressed in Engel's incisive critique of the "medical model" (1977) are applicable also to the traditional "mental" or "behavioral" models of psychologists. Engel voiced his concerns thus:

> Medicine's crisis stems from the logical inference that since "disease" is defined in terms of somatic parameters, physicians need not be concerned with psychosocial issues which lie outside medicine's responsibility and authority. (p. 129)

If we substitute the words *clinical psychology* for medicine, *behavior disorder* for disease, *psychologists* for physicians, and reverse the terms *somatic* and *psychosocial*, then we have as cogent an indictment of psychology as we do of medicine. A close reading of Engel's thoughtful analysis will go far in leading the reader to appreciate both the scientific and clinical utility of what he terms the *bio-psychosocial model*.

2. Problems of Boundary and Definition

What shall this newly evolved field of psychological science be called—medical psychology, health care psychology, behavioral medicine, health psychology, psychological medicine, behavioral health? Will its practitioners be best referred to simply as clinical psychologists, despite their new settings and expanded functions, or should a new descriptive term be coined?

Psychology has always had greater difficulty than other disciplines in describing the scope of its activities and in delimiting or defining its subspecialities. Both a science and a profession, it struggles between its identity as a lofty and dispassionate academic discipline, on the one hand, and an applied profession concerned with matters of public recognition, as well as methods for improving human welfare, on the other. In both spheres, science and profession, its boundaries spread across into other disciplines, into the scholarly realms of the biologist and sociologist and into the service functions of the professional educator and physician (Millon, 1975). It is at its boundary with medicine that psychology's newly evolved interests interface most significantly and most sensitively. Shall its scope and formal designation be sharply delimited, and should it be defined as a discipline independent of medicine? The label chosen to represent the field is of no minor import; it will certainly shape its focus as a research realm and its viability and character as a service profession. For these reasons, then, it may be useful to examine several descriptive terms that have been employed in recent years to characterize this emerging field.

2.1. Psychosomatic Medicine

The first of the modern labels applied to the study of mind–body relationships was *psychosomatic medicine*. Despite this discipline's historical role in sensitizing physicians and psychologists to the interplay of emotions and physical disorders, its exclusive concern with matters of illness (and not those of health), its strong roots in psychodynamic theory, and its attention to only a limited subset of physiological disorders that ostensibly are activated by obscurely symbolized intrapsychic repressions makes it too restricted in scope and focus to represent the breadth and orientation of the new field we are discussing. That one of the descriptive terms comprising its title is *medicine* further limits its appropriateness as designating an area of psychology.

2.2. Medical Psychology

Another label, which has had a long and prominent history since the turn of the century, is *medical psychology;* it is, however, often viewed as synonymous with *psychiatry* (e.g., one of England's major psychiatric publications is called the *British Journal of Medical Psychology*). It too suffers from the adjective *medical*, with its implicit association with disease processes only; this association is diluted in part by the presence of *psychology* as the prime subject of its title. Despite the tacit medical orientation of this label, Asken (1975, 1979) has championed it as the most appropriate one to encompass the wide spectrum of topics and activities that characterizes the field. In his definition of medical psychology, Asken writes:

> Medical psychology is the study of psychological factors related to any and all aspects of physical health, illness and its treatment at the individual, group, and systems level. Medical psychology represents no particular theoretical orientation; the problems of medical psychology can be conceptualized from any desired orientation. Medical psychology further involves, as its foci, all areas of scholarly interests—research, clinical intervention, and application and teaching. (1979, p. 67)

Although Asken's definition and suggestions may be appealing in support of the *medical psychology* title, it appears that its time to achieve recognition as the most suitable designation has passed.

2.3. Rehabilitation Psychology

Another early term, *rehabilitation psychology*, remains an apt designation to represent a significant realm of activities, particularly those oriented to the restoration of functions consequent to physical trauma or disability. As with other terms, however, the focus of rehabilitation is narrow in scope and the population served by these activities is too circumscribed in light of the breadth and variety of persons encompassed by the new field.

2.4. Health Care Psychology

The label *health care psychology* also addresses the service-provision facet of the field. It is much broader, however, than *rehabilitation psychology* in that its focus is on systems of activity, including those of disease prevention, health maintenance, and health service. Within its broad purview are studies of epidemiology, cross-cultural comparisons, and the economics of large-scale intervention programs, each of which is a legitimate and valuable sphere of research. However, many of these extend well beyond psychology's more limited province of knowledge and competence. Some aspects of its larger schema do mirror psychology's interests well, as noted in the following quote from the American Psychological Association's task force report on health research (1976):

> Health care delivery involves more than the treatment of illness. The goal is to minimize the need for treatment of disease through positive and proactive programs of health maintenance. . . . Health maintenance includes, but extends far beyond, the prevention of infectious disease. It includes early detection and correction of defects, reduction

in the severity of chronic disease processes through early diagnoses and treatment, and education in positive health practices that reduce the need for subsequent treatment. (p. 265)

This description comes close to depicting major aspects of the new field, but its boundaries are too wide, encompassing, as they do, issues, skills, and activities that reach outside the realm of psychological study and service.

2.5. Behavioral Medicine

Perhaps the best known and most frequently employed label of the day is *behavioral medicine*. It is represented in one of the major organizations in the field (the Society of Behavioral Medicine) and appears on the masthead of the first of several recent journals to concentrate exclusively on the subject (*The Journal of Behavioral Medicine*). At a conference sponsored by the National Academy of Science, the following definition and description was adopted:

> Behavioral Medicine is the interdisciplinary field concerned with the development and integration of the behavioral and biomedical science knowledge and techniques relevant to health and illness and the application of this knowledge and these techniques to prevention, diagnosis, treatment and rehabilitation. (Schwartz & Weiss, 1978, p. 250)

Broad in scope as this definition may be—including as it does behavior and biology, health and illness, as well as prevention, diagnosis, treatment, and rehabilitation—the work and orientation of those who identify themselves as specialists in behavioral medicine tend to be much narrower in focus than the definition suggests. Most who identify their activities with the designation *behavioral medicine* are largely research-oriented and often limit their service work to helping patients to modify habits associated with stress, obesity, and smoking. Almost to the exclusion of all other methods, their "clinical" techniques are variants either of biofeedback, relaxation procedures, or simple operant conditioning. Perhaps this focus stems from the fact that many of its early leaders had rather narrow behavioral-learning and psychophysiological backgrounds, inclining them, therefore, to utilize only those principles and techniques congenial to their training. Whatever the source, the dominant belief system that characterizes those who hold vigorously to the label *behavioral medicine* is often a dogmatic one that typically is prejudiced against the more cognitive and psychodynamic approaches of most diagnosticians and therapists who carry out the majority of clinical psychological services. Somewhat related, and of no lesser significance, is the fact that the label *behavioral medicine* itself may misdirect the future growth and character of the field. The term *behavioral* represents a single and doctrinaire "school" of psychological thought among several equally relevant schools. No single point of view should gain preeminence in a field that must remain open to diverse perspectives and methodologies if it is to flourish. Second, and as noted earlier, the term *medicine* not only narrows its focus on illness but is misleading as a descriptor for scientific and clinical enterprises that are essentially psychosocial in rationale and technique. In sum, this new field is neither behavioral nor medicine.

2.6. Behavioral Health

For reasons other than those just noted, Matarazzo (1980) has proposed the use of the term behavioral health, which he defines as:

> A new interdisciplinary subspecialty within behavioral medicine specifically concerned with maintenance of health and the prevention of illness and dysfunction in currently healthy persons. (p. 807)

What is distinctive in Matarazzo's proposal is psychology's role in fostering programs of prevention in which individuals assume responsibility for their own health through improved life-styles. Matarazzo's emphasis on health and his suggestion that psychology encourage methods of personal responsibility are excellent proposals. The label he suggests, however, as well as the view that behavioral health should be seen as a subfield of behavioral medicine, is troubling. As noted earlier, the labels we employ to represent a subject will, sooner or later, affect its character as a science and as a profession. Designations such as *behavioral* reflect a doctrinaire bias. Although interpreted more broadly by physicians than by nonbehavioral psychologists, the appelations that Matarazzo proposes for the emerging field are as likely to appear as repugnant to non-behaviorists as descriptors such as *cognitive medicine* or *psychodynamic health* would be to behaviorists.

2.7. Health Psychology

Where, then, do we go in an attempt to orchestrate the many themes presented thus far, so that they can blend and be represented by a single unifying designation? The resolution that appears most successful is the label *health psychology* (Stone, Cohen, & Adler, 1979). In contrast with the interdisciplinary character of many of the descriptive terms previously suggested, it stands distinctly within the boundaries of psychology. Although every science interfaces and relates with others, each must limit its scope and define its province so that it can be explored in its fullest depth and in all its subtleties. In terms of gaining a clear disciplinary identity, then, *health psychology* is the most appropriate if not ideal designation. That it includes the term *health*, rather than *illness* or *medicine*, is another step in the right direction. The definition provided by Matarazzo (1980) is close to the mark and deserves repeating here.

> *Health psychology* is the aggregate of the specific educational, scientific, and professional contributions of the discipline of psychology to the promotion and maintenance of health, the prevention and treatment of illness, and the identification of etiologic and diagnostic correlates of health, illness, and related dysfunctions. (p. 815)

2.8. Clinical Health Psychology

Assuming that the definitions and distinctions made thus far have been helpful in clarifying relevant issues, it may be useful next to separate the several elements that comprise this emerging field. Having drawn the boundaries and prime dimensions of the rather broad-ranging subject of health psychology, we must begin to recognize that there are a number of differentiations among its adherents in their orientation and focus. To illustrate: Stone and his associates (1979) have provided thoughtful essays on the larger domain of health psychology as a field; their orientation, if any can be spoken of as their special perspective, would best be characterized as a social or systems approach. Other recent books in the field have been written from what may be described as a physiological viewpoint (Schwartz & Beatty, 1977; Selye, 1976; Weiner, 1977); others still are best characterized by their application of learning models (Brady & Pomerleau, 1979; McNamara, 1979; Melamed & Siegel, 1980). With but few exceptions, and these have taken the form of isolated papers or essays (e.g., Scofield, 1969; 1979; Wirt, 1980), what is missing most among current publications is the significant relationship between health psychology and clinical psychology.

As noted previously, it can be argued that these two major areas of applied psychology are essentially one and the same. Clinical psychology was misguided in its evolution when it followed a dualistic mind–body model and thereby limited itself to ministering to the "mentally" disordered. Health psychology came into being in great measure as an antidote to the deficits and imbalance this created. Located outside the pale of clinical psychology, the problems and needs of the "physically" disordered fell to the growing provinces of applied learning, physiological psychology, and social psychology. That the knowledge and skills of these subfields of basic psychological science are relevant and useful in understanding and treating the physically impaired cannot be questioned, no less so than that they are valuable sources of thought and methodology in the management of the mentally ill. However (and it may appear to be quibbling at first), when psychological knowledge and techniques from any and all aspects of our science are applied professionally to the assessment and treatment of individuals in distress, we refer to and identify these activities as those of *clinical psychology*. Clinical psychology is not so much a content area of our science as it is a professional attitude that seeks to apply the principles and methods derived from the content areas of psychology, such as learning, social, developmental, and so on. Clinical psychology differs from other applied spheres of psychology in that its primary attentions and skills are oriented to helping patients in distress. That is, the feature that distinguishes the clinician from his or her colleagues in psychology is a focus on the needs of specific individuals whose suffering either stems from or can be relieved by psychological influences.

If we overlap the newly emergent content field of health psychology with the traditional focus and professional attitudes of clinical psychology, we will have constructed a subspecialty of psychology that is both applied (clinical) and substantive (health), one that may best be described by the designation *clinical health psychology*. Encompassing both mental *and* physical disorders within its purview, clinical health psychology may be defined as:

> The application of knowledge and methods from all substantive fields of psychology to the promotion and maintenance of mental *and* physical health of the individual and to the prevention, assessment, and treatment of all forms of mental *and* physical disorder in which psychological influences either contribute to or can be used to relieve an individual's distress or dysfunction.

3. The Domain of Clinical Health Psychology

We appear to be at an important crossroads in the historical evolution of a "new" discipline. Be it the times in general, the increasing availability of simple solutions to "purely physical" diseases, the growing concern of the public with matters affecting the quality of life, or what have you, there has been a developing awareness on the part of the physically ill themselves, their families, and those who minister to them of the importance of psychosocial considerations in the care of medical illness. As a consequence, persons from all walks of life are increasingly alert to the inadequacies in both traditional and current approaches to patient treatment and management. Moreover, it has become evident that conventional medicine is ill equipped to deal with the vast proportion of patients whose disorders are essentially psychological in origin and whose course and treatment are highly susceptible to psychosocial influences.

The opportunity for psychologists to meet these recognized health service needs are unparalleled today. Psychologists are not only finding themselves increasingly accepted as members of the health team but their participation is being actively sought by physicians who have come to appreciate the significant contributions they can make to a variety of diverse problems that range from presurgical counseling to posthospital medication compliance. Although there has been a long history of cooperation between psychiatry and psychology in providing clinical services, these collaborations have begun to diminish in recent years. By contrast, relationships between psychology and other medical specialities have increased significantly. The specialties of internal medicine—especially cardiology and gastroenterology, obstetrics and gynecology, rehabilitation and physical medicine, pediatrics, family medicine, oncology, and surgery—have been adding psychologists to their service teams at a rapid rate. Hospital-affiliated pain clinics—typically associated with department of anesthesiology, neurological surgery, or orthopedics—almost invariably include a psychologist as an integral therapy team member, and these clinics have recently surged in number throughout the nation. Health psychologists no longer find themselves adjuncts to liaison-consultation psychiatrists; they have become autonomous health-care professionals and are often the key figures in both planning and executing treatment programs. Promising as this growth may be, psychologists are only just beginning to cross the threshold of their many opportunities. They must actively communicate with their health service colleagues to the effect that they have an extensive body of knowledge and skills that can be effectively utilized to increase both the quality and humanistic character of patient care.

What is contained in the body of knowledge of clinical health psychology, and what comprises the armamentarium of the clinical health psychologist's skills? These can only be briefly noted here. Although the remainder of this handbook will provide more detailed illustrations, it too must be seen as a beginning, a first approximation of a storehouse of information and skills that will continue to be filled over the years.

In searching out the literature of the field for an earlier project (Millon, Green, & Meagher, 1979), the author uncovered a rather confusing and seemingly contradictory array of concepts and findings. On closer examination, it became evident that many of these ostensibly conflicting ideas and data pointed in the same directions; they differed largely in the labels they employed and in the theoretical approaches they took to reach essentially similar conclusions. Two major themes were extracted in efforts to synthesize and collate this literature. By no means are they exhaustive, nor would it be correct to claim them to be the most useful schema for diverse endeavors in this field. It does appear, however, that they encompass two of the basic spheres of knowledge that comprise *clinical* health psychology as distinct from other realms of health psychology. For didactic purposes they have been termed *personality: the styles of coping* and *psychogenic attitudes: objective and subjective stressors*.

3.1. Personality: The Styles of Coping

Although there are many syndromes of psychopathology with which the general clinical psychologist is acquainted, most are not relevant to understanding and managing the physically ill. One syndromal realm is pertinent, however: that subsumed under terms such as *personality* and *coping*. Clinicians do not deal here with the dramatic or severe forms of psychiatric disturbance but with the milder problems of ordinary life. Personality styles characterize the more or less everyday manner in which people approach the events of their lives. It is these typical ways of coping that the clinical psychologist understands well, especially those attitudes and behaviors that may contribute to illness and the manner in which individuals deal with it (Kahana, 1972; Lipowski, 1977). In a particularly illuminating paper, Cohen and Lazarus (1977) described what they termed *anticipatory coping*, that is, the characteristic ways in which the individual not only adapts to but also shapes his or her environment. To them, coping represents more than just a response to confrontations or stress. It is an ongoing "personality" process, a habitual style of relating to events and structuring life.

What are the salient styles of personality and coping that have been described in the literature? In the following section we will briefly note the major "types" to illustrate this sphere of clinical knowledge and its implications for health psychology (Leigh & Reiser, 1980; Lipowski, 1970; Millon, 1969, 1977, 1981; Millon, Green, & Meagher, 1982).

3.1.1. Introversive Style

According to Millon *et al.* (1982), these patients are rather colorless and emotionally flat, tending to be quiet and untalkative. Often unconcerned about their problems, they typically are vague and difficult to pin down concerning symptoms and may be passive with regard to taking care of themselves. Lipowski (1970) describes patients such as these as employing a cognitive coping style termed *minimization*, characterized by a tendency to ignore, deny, or rationalize the personal significance of information input. Borrowing from profiles suggested earlier by Kahana and Bibring (1964), Leigh and Reiser (1980) prefer to label these patients as "seclusive and aloof," noting that their main concern is a "desire not to be intruded upon by others." To them, as well as to Millon *et al.*

(1982), these personalities tend to be oblivious to the implications of their illness and indifferent to medical procedures that normally arouse anxiety.

3.1.2. Inhibited Style

These personalities are characteristically shy and ill at ease; they expect to be hurt, are disposed to feel rejected, and are overly concerned about whether others will think well or ill of them (Millon *et al.*, 1982). Fearing that they will be taken advantage of, they are inclined to keep their problems to themselves. Lipowski refers to personalities similar to these as seeing illness as "punishment." They typically interpret this form of punishment as both expected and just; as a consequence, they are likely to offer little resistance to what they see as the inevitable and often adopt a rather fatalistic attitude toward illness. Leigh and Reiser (1980) touch upon similar features in their description of "guarded and suspicious" patients, who are ever watchful about the possibility that harm may be done them. Prone to worry about the ulterior motives of others, they are extraordinarily sensitive to criticism and anticipate being exploited.

3.1.3. Cooperative Style

Millon *et al.* (1982) note the eagerness with which these personalities seek to attach themselves to supportive persons and their willingness to follow advice religiously as long as they need assume little or no responsibility for themselves. According to Lipowski (1970), patients such as these may be disposed to see illness as "relief," that is, a welcome respite from the demands and responsibilities of being well. Leigh and Reiser (1980) saw these individuals as "dependent, demanding" patients. Their underlying striving is a "regressive wish to be cared for as if by an idealized, nurturant mother." This need for reassurance and care is unusually exaggerated among these people and the sick role is quickly adopted as an opportunity to return to a state of infantile dependency.

3.1.4. Sociable Style

Described by Millon *et al.* (1982) as outgoing, talkative and charming, these individuals are often undependable, highly changeable in their likes, more concerned with appearances than substance, and disinclined to deal with serious matters or personal problems. To Lipowski (1970), illness is seen by such patients as a "strategy" to secure attention, support, and compliance from others. Leigh and Reiser (1980) label these individuals "dramatic, emotional" types. Their major goal is the wish to be attractive and desirable, often leading them to be concerned more with their masculinity or femininity than with their health.

3.1.5. Confident Style

In a brief description of this type, Millon *et al.* (1982) note their characteristic calm and somewhat supercilious manner. Despite their narcissistic airs of superiority, they fear bodily harm and are often highly motivated to regain a state of well-being. It is typical of these personalities both to seek and to expect to be given special treatment; they are also likely to take unjust advantage of others. This portrayal is reinforced by the descriptions provided by Lipowski and by Leigh and Reiser. Lipowski (1970), referring to an "avoiding" behavioral style, notes that it is observed most often among individuals for whom acceptance of the sick role signifies a severe threat to the self-image as independent, masculine, and invulnerable. Characterizing this type as "superior and special," Leigh and Reiser (1980) portray them as behaving like VIPs whether or not such behavior is justified. They are snobbish, self-confident, even grandiose at times. Often displaying arrogance and a disdain of others, they occasionally precipitate competitive struggles for status, even with medical personnel who are in a position to treat them well or badly.

3.1.6. Forceful Style

Similar in certain respects to the foregoing type, these individuals are more overtly aggressive and hostile in their behavior (Millon *et al.*, 1982). Acting in a domineering and tough-minded fashion, they often go out of their way to be intimidating and to undermine the efforts of others. Their behavioral coping style, according to Lipowski (1970), might be termed *tackling,* that is, an unwillingness to accept the sick role and a disposition to go on the attack in dealing with the challenges and limitations posed by a disability. This coping attitude would be seen most dramatically in tendencies to fight illness at any cost, such as insisting on using a traumatized body part as if it were intact. A similar pattern has been termed the *impulsive* type by Leigh and Reiser (1980). Here, they note the characteristic lack of deliberation of these patients and their inability to tolerate sustained frustration.

3.1.7. Respectful Style

These individuals are overly responsible and conforming, usually going out of their way to impress others with their self-control, discipline, and serious-mindedness (Millon *et al.*, 1982). To Lipowski (1970), a major element in the behavior of these types is their inclination to see illness as weakness, that is, as a failure on their part and a shameful loss of personal control. Also characteristic is their strong desire to deny or conceal any problem that might prove publicly humiliating. When such denial is impossible, they become "model" patients. Leigh and Reiser (1980) speak of similar types as "orderly and controlling." They can usually be identified by the complete, precise, and dispassionate way in which they describe their symptoms. The sick role is a difficult one for them to assume since illness disrupts their rigid routines and their adherence to inflexible daily schedules.

3.1.8. Sensitive Style

These are unpredictable and moody types who are often displeased or dissatisfied with much in their life (Millon *et al.*, 1982). Lipowski (1970) describes patients similar to these as seeing illness as possessing "value" in the sense that "sickness makes health pleasant." Referred to as "long-suffering, self-sacrificing" persons by Leigh and Reiser (1980), they can often be diagnosed simply by the tone of their first words. Frequently speaking in a wailing and complaining voice, they report a history replete with medical misdiagnoses and complicated surgical procedures. They act as if they were "born to suffer" and, in fact, many have suffered. Needless to say, they are typically seen by health personnel as problem patients, since they react negatively to reassurance and typically report that efforts to minister to them have produced more rather than less trouble.

3.2. Psychogenic Attitudes: Objective and Subjective Stressors

The concept of stress has lost much of its early usefulness, having come to represent too diverse a range of events and reactions. Unspecific in its meaning, it subsumes nothing less than all matters that are experienced as burdensome, taxing, or harrassing. Little more is gained by labeling and categorizing them as *stressors, significant life events,* or *stressful life changes.* It may be useful, nevertheless, to separate the objective features of these events from their subjective impact or phenomenological meaning to an individual. Obviously, not everyone perceives events in the same way; to rephrase an old cliché, "one man's poison may be another man's meat." Depending on prior experience, health status, and personality disposition, one individual may interpret a series of potentially troublesome circumstances as a positive challenge rather than as a disruption that portends danger. In essence, objective "stress" means nothing unless the person apprehends it as such. It is the individual's phenomenological interpretation (Millon, 1967) or cognitive appraisal (Lazarus, 1966) that translates events and thereby determines their impact.

In the following paragraphs we will briefly describe six areas of subjective outlook or phenomenological set that appear relevant as psychogenic attitudes that either increase the susceptibility of individuals to illness or aggravate the course or intensity of an existent illness. Different facets of psychic stress are tapped by the first pair: *chronic tension,* which refers to internally felt and often self-induced pressures, and *recent life stress,* which relates to the perceived impact of essentially transient external events. The second pair of dimensions, *premorbid pessimism* and *future despair,* pertains to the tendency to interpret either past, current, or future events subjectively as more negative and troublesome than they objectively were or are likely to be. The third set refers to specific content areas of relevance to illness behavior and outcome, those of *social alienation* and *somatic anxiety.*

3.2.1. Chronic Tension

This is a well-studied area of research, most frequently associated with investigations into the "coronary-prone behavior pattern" (Friedman & Rosenman, 1974; Jenkins, 1976, 1978). It suffices to say that research strongly links this attitudinal and behavioral trait to an increased risk of angina and myocardial infarction (Rosenman, Brand, Jenkins, Friedman, Straus, & Wurm, 1975).

Distinctive to this constellation is an ostensive chronicity in self-induced tension, reflected in persistent or excessive competitive drives, an impatience with persons and events, an unyielding sense of time urgency, and ceaseless demands placed on oneself.

3.2.2. Recent Life Stress

The earliest research on this precipitant of illness onset was carried out by Holmes and Rahe (1967). The prime hypothesis was that objective events that called for changes in the individual's life routine would be experienced as stressful. A wide range of life events were assigned weights as a means of quantifying the extent to which they were judged disruptive. Cumulative life–change scores were obtained to determine whether they would "predict" an increased incidence of illness. Early findings provided support for the investigators' expectations, but subsequent studies indicate that only undesirable events contributed significantly to negative outcomes (Liem & Liem, 1976; Yunik, 1980). A further criticism is the aforementioned note that people give highly divergent interpretations to identical events. Thus, in her thoughtful review of both theoretical and methodological issues in this research area, Cohen (1979) notes:

> It is both theoretically and practically important to determine whether it is the actual *occurrence* of life changes, both positive and negative, or the person's *reporting* of or negative evaluation of such life changes, that is linked to either increased treatment-seeking behavior or incidence of illness. (p. 94)

Despite difficulties in identifying the precise mechanisms that mediate whatever relationships do exist, our speculation is that the "real" linkage, probably one of moderate proportions, is largely a function of the individual's personal interpretation of the stressful character of events.

3.2.3. Premorbid Pessimism

No other factor is likely to reflect a negative attitudinal set more powerfully than what we have termed *premorbid pessimism*. Derived in part from work on depression as both a contributor to and exacerbator of illness (Engel, 1968; Engel & Schmale, 1967; Schmale, 1972; Schmale & Engel, 1967; Schmale & Iker, 1966, 1971), the concept may be seen to parallel "chronic tension" (i.e., the Type A or coronary-prone coping pattern). However, rather than representing internal time-urgency pressures, competitiveness, and self-imposed achievement demands, as in the Type A pattern, the premorbid pessimistic attitude represents internal tendencies to complain and to be discontent, to display a persistently negative outlook toward life events, and to anticipate and interpret experiences as troublesome and discomforting. Perhaps the suggestion is a bit facile, but in line with the appelations *Type A* and *Type B*, it might be suitable to label this pattern *Type C*, signifying thereby the complaint tendencies of these individuals. What is notable in Type C individuals is that actual occurrences of objective stress are significantly less important than the characterologically negative and discontented attitude of the patient. Events that do occur in reality—good, bad or indifferent—are transformed phenomenologically by Type C patients so as to be experienced as stressful.

3.2.4. Future Despair

Similar in certain respects to premorbid pessimism, this dimension focuses specifically on future outlook. Those disposed characterologically to be pessimistic will, of course, darken their future perspectives as well as those of the past and present. The distinction that is drawn here recognizes that one need not be premorbidly pessimistic in order to feel depressed, especially in relation to one's future prospects. Faced with the reality of a serious or life-threatening disease, many well-integrated and content individuals may gradually succumb to a process that has been termed *giving up* (Engel, 1968; Schmale, 1972). Anticipating an inexorable downward course, such individuals will no longer be inclined to look forward to a long and productive life free of persistent discomfort and inevitable deterioration. Despairing of one's future prospects not only foreshadows a less favorable prognosis (Wright, 1960) but calls for the most skillful and sympathetic care.

3.2.5. Social Alienation

Despite some inconsistencies in the data, there appears to be a reasonably good empirical base for the view that people who believe they possess a strong social support network do better than others during times of stress. Many experience fewer ailments, survive illnesses longer, are less subject to somatic complications and, in general, exhibit a high level of morale (Berkman, 1969; Cassell, 1976; Cobb, 1976; Comstock & Partridge, 1972; Gore, 1973; Moss, 1973; Pinneau, 1975). Epidemiologists have shown that there is a close relationship between the overall extent of interpersonal involvement and morbidity; this is seen most dramatically in the increased incidence of severe illness and death among the recently bereaved (Lynch, 1977). It is unclear whether feelings of alienation or loss are themselves sources of stress, whether they allow the impact of other stressors to be magnified, or whether they simply diminish the desire to cope or to "bother" seeking medical attention.

3.2.6. Somatic Anxiety

A major thesis in this chapter is that all forms of objective stress can be reduced or intensified by the way an individual perceives and interprets events. Reality, then, is merely grist for each person's phenomenological mill. Whereas *chronic tension* represents a cognitive assumption that one *must* strive ceaselessly and *premorbid pessimism* reflects an equally immutable assumption that life has been and will be troublesome and unjust, *somatic anxiety* conveys yet another persistent assumption that something is wrong or will soon go wrong with one's body. At this time it can only be hypothesized that this hypersensitivity to physiological functioning does, in fact, lead to either an increased incidence of illness or an exacerbation of existent illnesses (Lipowski, 1970; Weiner, 1977). There is little question, however, that individuals so disposed do overreact to both the possibility and reality of illness. That patients such as these comprise a significant portion of those seen in medical offices, clinics, and hospitals is also self-evident. Only further research will enable us to tease out whether their somatic concerns actually mediate and foster real increments in illness or just illness behaviors.

The body of this handbook will elaborate many of the themes that have been and will be touched on only briefly in this introductory chapter. For example, the first section of the text, Part I, includes seven chapters that provide in-depth discussions concerning what we have termed the *knowledge domain* of clinical health psychology. Part I parallels the preceding section of this chapter, in which the author sought to outline a number of themes, notably personality coping styles and psychogenic attitudes. These were formulated because they appear to have significant health care implications; they are, however, only two of a number of alternative conceptual models for ordering the domain of clinical health psychology. Others will be detailed in the chapters that comprise Part I. The subject materials for Parts II and III of this handbook cannot be approached by way of alternative conceptual models. These parts address matters that are relatively tangible or functional. In contrast with Part I—which poses the essentially abstract or theoretical question, "What is it that we know?"—Part II simply asks "Where do clinical health psychologists work?" and Part III queries "What do clinical health psychologists do?" Because these last questions are answered better by fact than by theoretical formulation, it would seem wisest to let those who work in the field describe both the health settings within which they practice and the clinical activities they carry out. A few introductory notes should suffice to furnish the reader with a précis of what to anticipate.

4.1. The Clinical Settings of Health Psychology

The first chapter in Part II outlines problems and issues that arise in general hospital settings. Although clinical health psychologists are new to the broadly medical, as opposed to the specifically psychiatric, hospital environment, it is quite likely that this locale will be the one in which the profession will find its major niche in the future. The chapter by Burstein and Loucks provides the reader with a thoughtful as well as realistic appraisal of both the opportunities and difficulties that are inevitable in this setting.

The two chapters that follow—one by Roberts, Maddux, Wurtele, and Wright and the other by Solomon, Falletti and Yunik—focus on age-related populations that have become primary concerns of the health care system. As infectious diseases have come to constitute a decreasing proportion of illnesses, medical attention has turned to both the developmental anomalies and dysfunctions of the young and the degenerative and chronic ailments of the old. Accordingly, health psychologists are being called on to apply a disproportionately greater segment of their clinical skills to the needs of both populations. The two chapters devoted to the special problems of these patient groups illustrate well both the issues and opportunities involved in work with them.

In the final chapters comprising Part II, each of the contributors has sought to describe one of the major collaborative roles played by psychologists in carrying out their work in clinical health settings. The chapter by Strain focuses on the liaison role and outlines the joint contributions made by psychiatrists and psychologists as well as other members of the health team. Strain gives greater authority to the physician team member than might be optimal from the perspective of other disciplines, but his is nevertheless both a fine analysis as well as one of the more "equalitarian" and psychosocial models of collaborative liaison work. In Warner's contribution we are offered a richly developed presentation of social systems theory, with particular reference to its applications to health systems analysis and consultation. Whether so disposed or not, clinical health psychologists are often called on to assess and propose policies that relate to the very context within which they carry out these services; similarly, the behaviors of patients with whom they work are in great measure a product of the same health system context as well as the larger cultural environment from which they come. In an entirely different vein, Matarrazo, Conner, Fey, Carmody, Pierce, Brischetto, Baker, Connor, and Sexton furnish us with a detailed illustration of the health psychologist as clinical researcher. A more complete, collaborative investigatory team than that involved in Matarrazo's project would indeed be difficult to find, including as it does cardiologists, biostatisticians, nutritionists, psychologists, and so on. The chapter is especially useful in that it illustrates the frequent necessity of extensive collaborations when studies of serious or definitive clinical significance are being undertaken; equally valuable are the highly original data reported in this major NIH-sponsored project.

4.2. The Clinical Functions of the Health Psychologist

Seriously lacking in this emerging field is the array of assessment instruments that clinical psychologists have been accustomed to including in their armamentarium of *mental* health tools. In the initial chapter of Part III, Green has set out to provide a comprehensive review and systematic appraisal of diagnostic tests employed to assess psychosocial factors among the physically ill. She finds those instruments developed primarily for psychiatric diagnoses to be seriously lacking. This should not be surprising, given their orientation to clinical psychopathology and their failure to include the many psychometric and normative considerations that are required to develop a population-relevant instrument. Her examination of instruments designed specifically for assessing the physically disordered finds these tools to be appreciably more relevant to the needs of the health psychologist, but they are also shown to be quite divergent both in the range of populations for which they are suitable and the scope of psychological traits they encompass. The chapter by Sarason, Levine, and Sarason marks the move from the psychodiagnostic assessment of individual traits to the assessment of stressful life events. Sarason, Levine, and Sarason present a well-reasoned analysis of the issues and instruments that have been employed in this area. Whereas Green's primary focus is on instruments designed to gauge "inner psychological traits" and that of Sarason *et al.* is on the appraisal of significant "external situational events," Willems and Alexander concern themselves with procedures for gauging "functional behavioral changes," especially those that relate to rehabilitative progress. To Willems and Alexander, the major goal of assessment in clinical health psychology is a pragmatic one, that of appraising the extent to which patient recovery is adaptive and relevant to the functional requirements of home and work environments.

The next two chapters deal with issues of compliance and noncompliance.

In addition to a cogent review of the research literature, Davidson provides an incisive and theoretically astute analysis of both the elements and the interactive dimensions that comprise the process of adherence to medical regimens. The authors of the second of these chapters, Kinsman, Dirks, and Jones, elaborate compliance themes more from the perspective of "psychological resistance" than of "social transactions," as does Davidson. Here attention is directed to what the authors label *psychomaintenance*, that is, psychological and behavioral factors that maintain and increase both the perceived severity and the medical intractability of an already present illness. Together, these two chapters provide what we believe to be among the most thoughtful presentations of both theory and data associated with the problem of medical compliance.

The next three chapters have as their common theme the treatment of pain, perhaps the most frequent activity that clinical health psychologists carry out today. These chapters are the only contributions in the text that have as their primary objective the presentation of issues and techniques of therapy. As a means of enabling the reader to compare three ideologically different approaches—one behavioral, one cognitive, and one intrapsychic—each of the chapters addresses the same clinical problem, that of pain. First, Steger and Fordyce present a carefully developed rationale that explicates the behavioral (operant) model of pain management. Second, Meagher sketches the logic of the cognitive approach to therapy and furnishes an illustration of how it can fit well into a comprehensive medical-psychological intervention program. Last, Barber has written a thorough and scholarly yet highly practical exposition that elucidates the elements of hypnosuggestive therapy and its application to diverse sources of the pain complaint.

As is evident from the foregoing, this handbook deviates significantly from the perspectives that dominate almost every other text in the field—those informed by a "behavioral" orientation—with their doctriinare adherence to the same slender band of treatment techniques (e.g., habit extinction, relaxation training, biofeedback). We have taken a clear and strong stand in favor of a much broader conception of health psychology's clinical applications, one in which the so-called behavioral perspective and technology are set into what we judge to be their proper place as representing only one of a number of equally fruitful, alternative approaches to psychological assessment and treatment. The final chapter of this handbook goes one step further in taking a view that is critical of the presumptions and arrogance of *all* health care professionals and orientations—be they physicians, or psychologists, of a behavioral persuasion, or a cognitive one, or what have you. In an illuminating and forward-looking chapter, Levy and Howard argue vigorously for the role that patients themselves can and should play in their own treatment. What they term *patient-centric* (as opposed to *doctor-centric*) technologies beautifully illustrates the important "domains of patient power."

5. Training Clinical Health Psychologists

As noted earlier, clinical psychology has had as its primary mission the assessment and treatment of patients with emotional problems. This work has been carried out in mental health centers, psychiatric clinics, private offices, and state hospitals. Psychologists who have been asked to work for the first time in comprehensive health settings, such as general medical hospitals, are often ill prepared for the new populations with which they must deal, and for the goals, terminology, and procedures that characterize these settings.

5.1. Need for Formal Training

It is the unusual psychologist who begins his or her responsibilities in a general medical setting fully acquainted with the distinctive features and complications associated with diverse physical illnesses. Not trained to be cognizant of the typical emotional precursors, concomitants, and sequelae commonly associated with these disorders, the psychologist may be unable to provide informed and appropriate interpretations of patient behaviors or to formulate well-targeted recommendations for their psychosocial management. Moreover, many psychologists will find themselves in environments that are hostile toward patients evidencing emotions which complicate their illness and its treatment. Nor may they be prepared to be seen by their health care colleagues either as saviors or as interlopers—frequently both. Few will have the luxury of extended interactions with patients or the opportunity to administer a comprehensive assessment battery and reflect leisurely on its meaning. In physical health settings, psychologists are often asked to provide almost instant diagnostic judgments and decisions as well as to assume management responsibilities for patients, and they are expected to do so without benefit of data on patients' prior psychological histories or the time to achieve the goals of treatment in any but the briefest of periods. These are not impossible tasks, but they do call for different attitudes, expectancies, and knowledge than clinicians have had to employ in their work in the past. As the author and his coeditors have written elsewhere (Millon *et al.*, 1979):

> The burgeoning responsibilities associated with these roles do not call for discarding familiar skills and techniques, nor do they require transforming oneself into a totally new professional. The task that faces the psychologist is to intelligently and creatively refine and extend previously acquired skills to fit these new responsibilities. (p. 529)

Continuing education and specialized workshops are likely to be helpful to those who have been thrust into these new roles without prior preparation. However, given the rapid emergence of the profession of clinical health psychology, there is a clear need to develop an appropriate preprofessional curriculum, a formal Ph.D. training program that will prepare fledgling health psychology clinicians to assume these new tasks with relevant knowledge and skills.

5.2. Problems in Program Development

There are several difficulties facing those who seek to establish clinical health psychology as a professional discipline with a formal doctoral curriculum. These problems derive largely from matters relating to intra- and interprofessional rivalries.

One group, clinical psychologists of more or less traditional leanings, are likely to resist any incursion into their training programs, particularly recommendations that may necessitate reductions among long-established course requirements. Much must be done to persuade those in charge of clinical training curricula of the need to broaden their perspectives. As touched on earlier in the chapter, clinical psychological knowledge must not be limited to patients who suffer only from mental health problems. The emotional precipitants and psychosocial concomitants of illnesses that are primarily physical in nature are also the proper subject of the clinical psychologist. By a judicious pruning, the infusion of physical health content into existent clinical courses, and the selective addition of relevant new topics and practica, clinical students can readily be inculcated with the principles and tools they need to work skillfully with the psychosocial dimensions of physiologic diseases and illness behaviors.

Other difficulties in program development may arise among nonclinical psychologists, especially those of a behavioral persuasion, who have recently achieved a significant measure of recognition in medical settings. Here, there will be the formidable task of persuading them to forego much of the hard-won status they have acquired. This is a task of no mean proportions, since many are convinced that their orientation and technology is not only the best of alternatives but is sufficient in itself to deal with the clinical problems facing health psychologists. Antagonistic as many are to those who employ more traditional psychodynamic philosophies and tools, they are likely also to resist efforts to develop programs that require a "foundation" in these alien perspectives. Much must be done to persuade them also that the ability to function effectively in diverse clinical settings will demand a broader array of technical skills than the mere behavioral and that their students must acquire a sensitivity to the psychological complexities that often underlie what appear ostensibly to be "simple"behaviors.

It would be most naive for those planning training programs in clinical health psychology to overlook the negative valuations and prejudices that some health care professionals have toward psychologists. Moreover, as a consequence of psychology's less than optimal recent relationship with psychiatry, psychologists themselves are often disposed to approach their role in medical settings somewhat ambivalently and with a not unrealistic anticipation of being cast as second-class citizens. Uncertain of professional boundaries and unclear as to how their roles will evolve over the next decade, psychologists planning program curricula today must carefully weigh several alternative models so that trainees will be able to deal flexibly with both current ambiguities and future role changes. Since neither we nor our colleagues in other health professions know fully what to expect from each other, psychology has an unexcelled opportunity at this time to shape its future by training its fledgling clinical health psychologists to be indispensable agents in optimizing health care delivery.

5.3. General Training Goals

This section is not organized in accord with the usual format that many of our educational colleagues suggest; that is, it does not offer formal statements of goals, explicit objectives, procedures for their implementation, criteria for appraising the acquisition of skills, and so on. A few discursive paragraphs will suffice in light of the limited extent to which our programmatic efforts have progressed.

Any rough curriculum blueprint should contain courses covering the basic scientific knowledge of our discipline or what is often called the "core" or "foundation" of a graduate program. Second, the fundamental clinical content and tools of our discipline must be thoroughly conveyed also, as well as opportunities for appropriate practicum and apprenticeship experiences that will develop essential clinical skills. Built on the foundation of the prior two units, the program must provide both formal didactic coursework and experiential opportunities that refine and give a special health focus to the curriculum. In this latter regard, both dissertation and internship should be directed toward the end of strengthening and maturing this specialization. A few additional words elaborating a number of these themes may be useful before we go on to outline the Ph.D. curriculum of a recently developed clinical health psychology program.

As far as the core of basic psychological study is concerned, it is quite possible to present both the content of a field and, at the same time, highlight its applications to issues of health and illness. No substantive area of psychology lacks aspects relevant to health matters. For example, a course in psychophysiology can be taught with illustrations and applications that trace the pathogenesis of various impairments, such as coronary artery disease or the behavioral sequelae of lesions in one or another cerebral region; no less fruitful would be the study of basic physiological processes with reference to such dysfunctions as insomnia, pain, stress, and so on. Similarly, a core social psychology course could exemplify its basic principles by reviewing topics such as ethnic differences in health-seeking behavior, group dynamics among health team members, and the organizational structure of health delivery systems.

The second goal of such a program, that of building the foundations of clinical psychology as both a domain of knowledge and an applied profession, can illuminate not only the disorders of "mind" but also those of the body. For example, a psychopathology course can include within its purview the newly conceived "psychosomatic" disorders of the DSM-III (American Psychiatric Association, 1980), topics such as stress disorder and pain, the psychogenesis of cardiovascular dysfunction, and the susceptibility of different personality types to physical illness as well as the distinctive mechanisms they employ in coping with them. Similarly, traditional psychotherapy courses may be broadened to include techniques that promote weight loss and the cessation of smoking as well as techniques of a psychodynamic or cognitive nature oriented to personality change. Supervised practica and clinical role-modeling at this basic level are best geared to the *in vivo* learning of fundamental observational and interviewing skills.

Practical experiences, apprenticeship opportunities, and in-depth didactic training build in a health psychology specialization in order to fulfill the third goal of the program: that is, a level of expertise that goes beyond what all well-trained beginning clinicians are prepared to undertake. As a means of further deepening the trainee's understanding and potential as a contributor to health psychology, research on both theses and dissertations should be oriented to health psychology issues. For similar reasons, the internship year should expose the trainee to relevant role models in the clinical health field during nonpsychiatric clerkships.

5.4. University of Miami Clinical Health Track

There can be no "ideal" training program for clinical health psychology at this time; it is a growing field with changing expectancies for the practitioner and an evolving body of knowledge and technique that must be progressively incorporated into a developing curriculum. Despite this fluidity, the clinical faculty at the University of Miami Department of Psychology found the three goals enumerated above to be useful guidelines in developing their "clinical health track." The program is briefly described below, as are some aspects of the rationale and content of its typical course sequence.

5.4.1. First Year

This is an intense didactic period, serving as a comprehensive introduction to basic clinical concepts and tools as well as the techniques of psychology in general, its health-related applications, and methods of research design and statistics. Of particular relevance to our interests here is that each of the department's four "foundation" courses (Psychopathology, Biopsychology, Developmental Psychology, and Social Psychology) was redesigned to address and illustrate its principles with health-related topics and research findings. Each clinical student registers for one foundation course in each of his or her first four semesters. Next, a full year prepracticum course entitled Introduction to Clinical Methods is taken by students who have not had prior extensive clinical experience. Among its aims are "experientially-oriented" sessions designed to increase self-knowledge and interpersonal sensitivity. Its skill-oriented aims take the form of rudimentary apprenticeship roles in clinical interviewing, intake procedures, and psychological test administration. Students with prior clinical training or work experiences usually skip the prepracticum and go directly to relevant practicum settings. The typical first year curriculum is: *fall semester*, psychopathology, assessment I, introduction to clinical methods I, research design and statistics I, directed research; *spring semester*, developmental psychology, assessment II, introduction to clinical methods II, research design and statistics II, directed research.

5.4.2. Second Year

Following the academic orientation of the first year, the focus of the second year is clearly directed toward experiential learning. At this time the typical student will be exposed to a variety of *in vivo* clinical activities, participating under full supervision at least one day a week in one or two mental health facilities either in the community or at the university. In addition to the department's own clinic, the practicum facilities that have been selected provide close supervision and permit students to participate in all facets of the agency's work, for example, individual therapy, diagnostic evaluations, short-term crisis or consultation, group and family therapy, and intake and assessment interviewing as well as walk-ins, phone inquiries, and emergencies. The key aspect of this year is the acquisition of a modicum of clinical skill across a variety of settings and situations, all of which are closely monitored and supervised. Weekly departmental clinic case conferences are attended by all graduate students as a means of broadening each trainee's exposure to issues and problems in settings other than the one in which his or her practicum is held. Second-year practica are general in focus, that is, designed to develop basic clinical skills. Second-year students who have selected a specialty "track" are expected, however, to pursue their research with topics and populations consonant with their track. Those opting for the clinical health track usually design and carry out their second-year or thesis project in a "real" clinical setting, frequently in collaboration with fellow students and faculty mentors who comprise an ongoing health research group. The usual clinical second-year curriculum, fairly uniform regardless of track, is: *fall semester*, biopsychology, psychotherapy I, clinical research methods, practicum I (general), directed research; *spring semester*, social psychology, psychotherapy II, advanced assessment (projectives), practicum II (general), directed research.

5.4.3. Third Year

As noted earlier, the third year has a specialization focus, that of providing several alternative or overlapping tracks that students may pursue depending on their particular interests or career goals. Composed of formal seminars and relevant practicum placements, these tracks seek to blend both general clinical skills and those of a specific substantive area, such as health psychology. Students in the health track will already have taken the department's four health-related foundation courses. During the third year of their training, they are free to choose from departmental courses, seminars in other departments (e.g., Sociology, Health Administration), and practicum placements in settings that serve the needs of those who are primarily physically ill (e.g., the pain clinic in the Department of Neurological Surgery, the University's Comprehensive Cancer Center, the Medical School's Rehabilitation Institute, the County's major renal dialysis units, as well as the Department of Psychology's own health-oriented research and training clinic). A typical third-year program taken by a clinical health student would be: *fall semester*, behavioral medicine, psychological assessment in health settings, experimental psychopathology and psychosomatics, advanced practicum I (health), dissertation research; *spring semester*, social psychology of health behavior, psychological intervention in health settings, seminar on aging, advanced practicum II (health), dissertation research.

5.4.4. Fourth Year

The majority of students undertake their internship during the fourth year. Many do so with an approved dissertation proposal in hand and frequently far enough under way to be carried to its completion during or shortly after the internship year. Students are strongly encouraged to select an internship that will enrich the health specialization they have chosen. With the background of their specialty track as a base, the health psychology student should be able to assume the internship role with a secure feeling, a reasonable identity as a clinician, and a firm conviction in his or her professional preparedness and developing maturity.

6. References

American Psychiatric Association. *Diagnostic and statistical manual of mental disorders* (DSM-III). Washington, D.C.: American Psychiatric Association, 1980.

American Psychological Association, Task Force on Health Research. Contributions of psychology to health research: Patterns, problems, and potentials. *American Psychologist*, 1976, *31*, 263–274.

Asken, M. J. Medical psychology: Psychology's neglected child. *Professional Psychology*, 1975, *6*, 155–160.

Asken, M. J. Medical psychology: Toward definition, clarification and organization. *Professional Psychology*, 1979, *10*, 66–73.

Berkman, P. L. Spouseless motherhood, psychological stress, and physical morbidity. *Journal of Health and Social Behavior*, 1969, *10*, 323–334.

Brady, J., & Pomerleau, O. (Eds.). *Behavioral medicine: Theory and practice*. Baltimore: Williams & Wilkins, 1979.

Cassell, J. The contribution of the social environment to host resistance. *American Journal of Epidemiology*, 1976, *104*, 107–123.

Cobb, S. Presidential address—1976: Social support as a moderator of life stress. *Psychosomatic Medicine*, 1976, *38*, 300–314.

Cohen, F. Personality, stress, and the development of physical illness. In G. C. Stone, F. Cohen, & N. E. Adler (Eds.), *Health psychology: A handbook*. San Francisco: Jossey-Bass, 1979.

Cohen, F., & Lazarus, R. S. Coping with the stresses of life. In G. C. Stone, F. Cohen, & N. E. Adler (Eds.), *Health psychology: A handbook*. San Francisco: Jossey-Bass, 1979.

Comstock, G. W., & Partridge, K. B. Church attendance and health. *Journal of Chronic Diseases*, 1972, *25*, 665–672.

DiMatteo, M. R., & Friedman, H. S. (Eds.). Interpersonal relations in health care. *Journal of Social Issues*, 1979, *35*, 1–206.

Engel, G. L. A life setting conducive to illness: The giving up–given up complex. *Bulletin of the Menninger Clinic*, 1968, *32*, 355–365.

Engel, G. L. The need for a new medical model: A challenge for biomedicine. *Science*, 1977, *196*, 129–136.

Engel, G. L., & Schmale, A. H. Psychoanalytic theory of somatic disorder. *Journal of the American Psychoanalytic Association*, 1967, *15*, 344–363.

Franz, S. I. The present status of psychology in medical education and practice. *Journal of the American Medical Association*, 1912, *53*, 909–911.

Friedman, M., & Rosenman, R. H. *Type A behavior and your heart*. New York: Knopf, 1974.

Gore, S. *The influence of social support and related variables in ameliorating the consequences of job loss*. Unpublished doctoral dissertation, University of Michigan, 1973.

Holmes, T. H., & Rahe, R. H. The Social Readjustment Rating Scale. *Journal of Psychosomatic Research*, 1967, *11*, 213–217.

Jenkins, C. D. Psychological and social risk factors for coronary disease. *New England Journal of Medicine*, 1976, *294*, 987–994.

Jenkins, C. D. Behavioral risk factors in coronary artery disease. *Annual Review of Medicine*, 1978, *29*, 543–562.

Kahana, R. J. Studies in medical psychology: A brief survey. *Psychiatry in Medicine*, 1972, *3*, 1–22.

Kahana, R. J., & Bibring, G. Personality types in medical management. In N. Zinberg (Ed.), *Psychiatry and medical practice in a general hospital*. New York: International Universities Press, 1964.

Lazarus, R. S. *Psychological stress and the coping process*. New York: McGraw-Hill, 1966.

Leigh, H., & Reiser, M. F. *The patient.* New York: Plenum Press, 1980.

Liem, J. H., & Liem, R. *Life events, social supports, and physical and psychological well-being.* Paper presented at the American Psychological Association annual meeting, Washington, D.C., 1976.

Lipowski, Z. J. Physical illness, the individual, and the coping process. *Psychiatry in Medicine,* 1970, *1,* 91–102.

Lipowski, Z. J. Psychosomatic medicine in the seventies: An overview. *American Journal of Psychiatry,* 1977, *134,* 233–244.

Lynch, J. J. *The broken heart: The medical consequences of loneliness.* New York: Basic Books, 1977.

Matarazzo, J. D. Behavioral health and behavioral medicine. *American Psychologist,* 1980, *35,* 807–817.

Matarazzo, J. D., & Daniel, R. S. The teaching of psychology by psychologists in medical schools. *Journal of Medical Education,* 1957, *32,* 410–415.

Matarazzo, J. D., Lubin, B., & Nathan, R. G. Psychologists' membership on the medical staff of university teaching hospitals. *American Psychologist,* 1978, *33,* 23–29.

McNamara, J. R. (Ed.). *Behavioral approaches to medicine.* New York: Plenum Press, 1979.

Melamed, B. G., & Seigel, L. J. *Behavioral medicine: Practical applications in health care.* New York: Springer, 1980.

Mensh, I. N. Psychology in medical education. *American Psychologist,* 1953, *8,* 83–85.

Meyer, A. The value of psychology in psychiatry. *Journal of the American Medical Association,* 1912, *53,* 911–914.

Millon, T. (Ed.). *Theories of psychopathology.* Philadelphia: Saunders, 1967.

Millon, T. *Modern psychopathology: A biosocial approach to maladaptive learning and functioning.* Philadelphia: Saunders, 1969.

Millon, T. (Ed.). *Medical behavioral science,* Philadelphia: Saunders, 1975.

Millon, T. *Millon Clinical Multiaxial Inventory Manual.* Minneapolis: National Computer Systems, 1977.

Millon, T. *Disorders of personality: DSM-III: Axis II.* New York: Wiley–Interscience, 1981.

Millon, T., Green, C. J., & Meagher, R. B. The MBHI: A new inventory for the psychodiagnostician in medical settings. *Professional Psychology,* 1979, *10,* 529–539.

Millon, T., Green, C. J., & Meagher, R. B. *The MBHI Manual; Third edition.* Minneapolis: National Computer Systems, 1982.

Moss, G. E. *Illness, immunity, and social interaction.* New York: Wiley, 1973.

Pinneau, S. R. *Effects of social support on psychological and physiological strains.* Unpublished doctoral dissertation, University of Michigan, 1975.

Prince, M. The new psychology and therapeutics. *Journal of the American Medical Association,* 1912, *53,* 918–921.

Rosenman, R. H., Brand, R. J., Jenkins, C. D., Friedman, M., Straus, R., & Wurm, M. Coronary heart disease in the Western Collaborative Group study: Final follow-up experience of 8.5 years. *Journal of the American Medical Association,* 1975, *233,* 872–877.

Schmale, A. H. Giving up as a final common pathway to changes in health. *Advances in Psychosomatic Medicine,* 1972, *8,* 20–40.

Schmale, A. H., & Engel, G. L. The giving up–given up complex illustrated on film. *Archives of General Psychiatry,* 1967, *17,* 135–145.

Schmale, A. H., & Iker, H. P. The affect of hopelessness and the development of cancer: I. Identification of uterine cervical cancer in women with atypical cytology. *Psychosomatic Medicine,* 1966, *28,* 714–721.

Schmale, A. H., & Iker, H. P. Hopelessness as a predictor of cervical cancer. *Social Science and Medicine,* 1971, *5,* 95–100.

Schwartz, G. E. & Beatty J. (Eds.). *Biofeedback: Theory and research.* New York: Academic Press, 1977.

Schwartz, G. E., & Weiss, S. M. Behavioral medicine revisited: An amended definition. *Journal of Behavioral Medicine,* 1978, *1,* 249–251.

Scofield, W. The role of psychology in the delivery of health service. *American Psychologist,* 1969, *24,* 565–584.

Scofield, W. Clinical psychologists as health professionals. In G. C. Stone, F. Cohen, & N. E. Adler (Eds.), *Health psychology: A handbook.* San Francisco: Jossey-Bass, 1979.

Selye, H. *The stress of life* (Rev. ed.). New York: McGraw-Hill, 1976.

Southard, E. E. Psychopathology and neuropathology: The problems of teaching and research contrasted. *Journal of the American Medical Association,* 1912, *53,* 914–916.

Stone, G. C., Cohen, F., & Adler, N. E. (Eds.). *Health psychology: A handbook*. San Francisco: Jossey-Bass, 1979.

Wagner, N. N., & Stegeman, K. L. Psychologists in medical education: 1964. *American Psychologist*, 1964, *19*, 689–690.

Watson, J. B. Content of a course in psychology for medical students. *Journal of the American Medical Association*, 1912, *58*, 916–918.

Watson, R. I. A brief history of clinical psychology. *Psychological Bulletin*, 1953, *50*, 321–346.

Weiner, H. *Psychobiology and human disease*. New York: American Elsevier, 1977.

Wirt, R. D. Clinical psychology and health psychology: The application of clinical psychology to health-care practice. In M. Jospe, J. Nieberding, & B. D. Cohen (Eds.), *Psychological factors in health care*. Lexington, Mass.: Heath, 1980.

Witkin, H. A., Mensh, I. N., & Cates, J. Psychologists in medical schools. *American Psychologist*, 1972, *27*, 434–440.

Wright, B. A. *Physical disability: A psychological approach*. New York: Harper & Row, 1960.

Yunik, S. *The relationship of personality variables and stressful life events to the onset of physical illness*. Unpublished doctoral dissertation, University of Miami, 1980.

I

The Knowledge Domain of Clinical Health Psychology

Psychobiological Factors in Bodily Disease

HERBERT WEINER

Psychosomatic medicine is based on the axiom that there are no diseases *per se* but only sick persons. Psychosomatic medicine is not a subspecialty of medicine dedicated to the investigation of one bodily organ or bodily system, nor is it defined by a special technology with which to examine diseased organs or cells. Finally, is is not confined to the study of a small number of diseases (von Uexküll, 1979; Weiner, 1977).

Psychosomatic medicine is concerned with the social and psychobiological factors that antecede disease or are associated with its onset rather than with the pathophysiology and pathological anatomy of diseased organs (and their cells) or bodily systems after onset. Yet even this claim is overstated, because the impact and meaning of disease or of being ill on individuals, their families, and their social groups have also been a vital and major concern of those interested in the psychosomatic approach. In short, it is believed by those who hold to this approach that social and psychological factors play some role in the predisposition to, initiation of, response to, and maintenance of every disease.

But psychosomatic medicine has, like other conceptual approaches to disease, had little to say about health. Health is not merely the absence of disease. Health may be defined as successful psychobiological adaptation even in those who may be predisposed to a specific disease but do not fall ill with it. Successful psychobiological adaptation has hardly been studied, yet some evidence is beginning to accrue that diverse factors contribute to such adaptation—for example, genetic (Notkins, 1979) and psychological ones (Vaillant, 1977).

HERBERT WEINER • Department of Psychiatry and Neuroscience, Albert Einstein College of Medicine, and Department of Psychiatry, Montefiore Hospital and Medical Center, New York, New York 10467.

Health care, health maintenance, or disease prevention do not usually fall within the purview of the medical profession. Midwives deliver babies. Sanitary officers enforce the distribution of clean water and pasteurized milk, fresh meats and vegetables, and the disposal of garbage and offal. The ideal of eliminating poverty, with which so many diseases are associated, has been upheld by many enlightened governments. Vaccination, immunization, and the suppression of insect vectors of disease have been instrumental in the virtual elimination of many dreaded infectious or parasitic diseases. In fact, preventive measures have been far more successful in averting disease, disability, and death than has the treatment of diseases after their onset by physicians. Yet physicians—for complex historical reasons—are largely concerned with the therapeutic, not the preventive approach. Usually but not always, a knowledge of the antecedents of disease allows one to carry out preventive measures. It is a curious fact that most of the commonest and potentially most disabling diseases of Western society are today understandable in terms of the complex interaction between psychobiological predisposition and social, economic, occupational, and personal factors that are potentially preventable.

This last statement needs further qualification, however. There has been a traditional assumption in medicine that a disease can be defined by its characteristic anatomical configuration, with which the patient's symptoms and signs are then correlated. Until recently, it was assumed that this anatomical configuration had a single invariant predisposition, pathogenesis, and pathophysiology; but this assumption has proved to be incorrect. As our medical knowledge has grown, multiple subforms of many diseases have been discovered, and heterogeneity of disease has turned out to be the rule, not the exception. Thus the characteristic anatomical lesion may come about in a variety of different ways. Heterogeneity (as this chapter will emphasize) manifests itself in the predisposition to, pathogenesis of, and pathophysiology of every disease defined in the traditional manner. Therefore, caretakers engaged in the prevention of disease and the care of diseased individuals must recognize the subform with which they are dealing.

1. The Development of Psychosomatic Concepts

If one subscribes to the point of view that individuals have diseases, it follows logically that one might ask whether certain kinds of people become hosts to particular ones. This approach reached its height in the modern era in the work of Dunbar (1943), who correlated the traits, attitudes, and habits of people with a variety of diseases and found that each disease was characterized by rather consistent personal features. Thus Dunbar described hypertensive patients, for example, as shy, perfectionistic, reserved, and self-controlled but also at times given to "volcanic eruptions of feeling" when in conflict with authority.

Yet Dunbar's approach to the role of the psychological factors in disease did not address itself either to the question of how hypertension is initiated in such a person and the mechanisms set into operation at its onset or to that of what factors maintain the elevation of blood pressure. In addition, the origin of the different personal characteristics that she found in persons with different diseases remained unstudied. Nevertheless, the description of a patient's traits may have a practical value; many patients these days do not comply with advice and treatment. In fact, the issue of patient compliance is a major one when physicians attempt to avert the complications of a variety of diseases.

The second major figure in psychosomatic medicine in the past fifty years was Alexander (1950). (In fact, the psychosomatic approach to disease and his name are virtually synonymous in the minds of most people). In Alexander's work, we find the point of view that specific, dynamic, unconscious constellations of conflicts characterized patients with the diseases he studied. These constellations were not, in his view, unique to those with these diseases, but they differed in individuals with different diseases and were, therefore, specific to the disease. The patient with a peptic duodenal ulcer has an unconscious wish to be fed and to receive. Being ashamed of this wish, he or she becomes excessively independent. Patients with essential hypertension fear their own agressive assertiveness, which they inhibit or repress, often from fear of retaliation. The child with bronchial asthma wishes to be enveloped and protected by the mother. In some children that wish is expressed in a cry for the mother's protection, but the cry is inhibited for fear that the mother will repudiate the child. In other children, the wish to be protected and enveloped is imagined to be dangerous; in these children the asthmatic attack can be averted by separating the child from its mother.

Much controversy has surrounded Alexander's formulations about specific psychological conflicts. While this controversy was raging, his other statements were forgotten. His concept of these diseases was actually tripartite: (1) the specific conflict predisposed patients to certain diseases, but only in the presence of other (at his time, undetermined) genetic, biochemical, and physiologic X factors; (2) in certain specific life situations to which the patient was sensitized by virtue of his or her key conflict, the conflict was activated and enhanced; (3) strong emotions accompanied the activated conflict; through autonomic, hormonal, or neuromuscular channels, they produced changes in structure and function.

Alexander made the most comprehensive statements about the several factors that play a role in the etiology and pathogenesis of disease. His concepts contain statements about the (multiple) predisposition to, onset, and initiation of a finite number of diseases (incorrectly called the only "psychosomatic" ones). Furthermore, Alexander also specified the developmental-experiential origins of the psychological conflicts and how they were habitually handled. When not handled, they aroused strong emotions.

His concepts are heuristically powerful because they separate the predisposition to disease from the context in which it began and the (presumed) mechanisms that produced it.

By specifying different psychological conflicts in different bodily diseases, Alexander abjured studying the psychological characteristics that patients with these and other diseases shared. These features were specified by Marty and de M'Uzan (1963), McDougall (1974), Nemiah and Sifneos (1970), and Ruesch (1948). Ruesch, in particular, stressed the age-inappropriate behavioral and psychological features of adult patients that made them particularly unadapted to and unable to cope with their environments. He listed these features as impaired or arrested social learning, a reliance on imitating others, a tendency to express thought and feeling in direct physical action, dependency on others, passivity, childlike ways of thinking, lofty and unrealistic aspirations, difficulties in assimilating and integrating life experiences, a reliance on securing love and affection from others, and—above all—an inability to master changes in their lives or to learn new techniques for overcoming the frustration of their wishes. The other writers describe features, which they call *alexithymic*, whose central aspects are (1) a failure of such patients to be aware of their own emotions (which serve as signals of personal distress) and to resort to constructive imagination in solving problems and (2) a preoccupation with the concrete specifics rather than the meaning of events in their lives.

Ruesch, and many other writers since his time, have stressed these patients' adaptive incapacities and the reliance on others. This notable shift from a preoccupation with intrapsychic conflicts, stressed by Alexander, to maladaptive psychological features is further supported by and implicit in the work of Engel (1968), Greene (1954), and Schmale (1958), who have stressed that many diseases begin in a setting of separation or bereavement for people who are particularly reliant on others and cannot cope without their support and help. The consequence of such separations and bereavements ("losses") is a state of adaptive failure, signaled by helplessness, hopelessness, and giving up. Conversely, the consequences of "losses" can be averted by making available to the stricken person supportive measures that are usually provided by families, friends, nurses, physicians, or other health workers.

This brief summary of the history of some of the concepts of psychosomatic medicine is designed to highlight a shift away from a preoccupation with intrapsychic conflict to a study of psychological adaptation and the key role that personal relationships between patients and others play in health and disease.

1.1. Behavioral Factors in Disease

However, other features of patients as well as the environment also play a role in disease. Clearly, psychosomatic medicine has failed until recently to pay much attention to the *behaviors* and *personal habits* of patients in predisposing to, initiating, and sustaining disease and disability.

Many serious and prevalent health problems—industrial and automobile accidents; the consequences of violence; alcohol, tobacco, and drug abuse; excessive food and salt intake; lack of exercise; and coronary artery disease—stem in part from individual behaviors.

Some of these behaviors—particularly the excessive use of alcohol, tobacco smoking, the abuse of addictive drugs, overeating, and lack of exercise—are at present virtually intractable. Alcohol intoxication has diverse, dire consequences, including automobile accidents and family disruption; its excessive abuse often presages a variety of neurological and psychiatric syndromes as well as liver and cardiac disease. Smoking is also a risk factor in a number of diseases, such as cancer of the mouth, larynx, and lung; obstructive pulmonary diseases; coronary heart disease; and peptic duodenal ulcer.

The two conditions that have received the most attention from behavioral scientists are obesity and coronary artery disease. Many of the factors that lead to obesity remain unknown; nonetheless, it is fairly certain that juvenile-onset obesity is associated with excessive food intake and adult-onset obesity with lack of exercise. Obesity is, in turn, a hazard predisposing to late-onset diabetes mellitus, and it contributes to elevated blood pressure levels, cholelithiasis, gout, osteoarthritis, the Pickwickian and sleep-apnea syndromes, and very likely to carcinoma of the breast and of the uterine endometrium in women (DeWaard, 1975; Mirra, Cole, & MacMahon, 1971; Wynder, Escher, & Mantel, 1966).

The behavior of some patients with coronary artery disease is known as Type A. (Other patients—especially those over 65 years of age—with coronary artery disease show Type B behaviors. And still other patients with this disease show neither form of behavior.) Type A people are driven, impatient, and ambitious, with a sense of having to complete tasks—most of which they set themselves. In addition, these people show a variety of physiological and bio-chemical variations which, together with their behavior, predisposes them to the disease.

1.2. Social Factors in Disease

Until recently, psychosomatic medicine had also failed to incorporate into its research and theory the role of the social (not only the human) environment (Eisenberg, 1977; Engel, 1977; Weiner, 1977, 1978, 1981). This neglect of social factors in disease could only have come about because of the preoccupation in the field with intrapsychic conflict. But as soon as the conceptual framework shifted to an adaptational one, environmental—that is social—factors, to which an adaptation had to be made, began to be taken into account.

Social factors clearly play a role in every aspect of health care and of disease. The poor have notoriously less access to health care. Low socioeconomic status has been associated with shorter life expectancy, an increased risk for mental disorders and alcoholism, a higher infant mortality and incidence of birth com-plications, the social and nutritional deprivation of infants and children, and obesity.

Therefore, it is not only the behavior of persons that leads to obesity, because excess weight is unevenly distributed in the various social classes; it decreases with increasing socioeconomic status. And the social class of the obese subject's origins is almost as closely linked to obesity as is his or her own social class (Goldblatt, Moore, & Stunkard, 1965).

The behavior of the Type A personality is a risk factor (along with high blood pressure, smoking, raised cholesterol levels, and glucose intolerance) in coronary artery disease and, therefore, potentially of myocardial infarction (MI); on the other hand, social order, stability, and traditional religious and secular ways—that is, a predictable environment—protect against death from MI. A longitudinal study on MI mortality (Bruhn, Chandler, Miller, Wolf, & Lynn, 1966; Stout, Morrow, Brandt, & Wolf, 1963) was carried out in 1964 and 1966 in Roseto, Pennsylvania, a community of southern Italian immigrants who have retained their traditional patriarchal ways and have trusting and cohesive relationships. Mutually supportive, the rules and the roles of the members of this community are well defined. The typical diet of these people contains 41% fat and the average individual is 9.1 kg overweight. By contrast, the population of Bangor, an adjacent town, is of mixed English, German, and Italian stock. Families there are less gregarious and religious, and their roles are less clearly defined. The death rate from MI in Roseto was half of that in Bangor. By 1976, however, as the younger inhabitants of Roseto were leaving and entering the mainstream of American life, the incidence of MI in younger age groups was increasing.

There have been studies contrasting Japanese and Japanese-Americans, American Benedictine priests working in the community and members of a cloistered religious order, nomadic Bedouins and Bedouin settlers in villages in Israel; they all come to similar conclusions (Caffrey, 1966; Marmot, 1975; Marmot & Syme, 1976; Matsumoto, 1970).

A stable social environment is by definition unchanging and predictable and imposes a minimum of adaptive demands and tasks on its members. Conversely, poverty, social and family discord, and a frightening, unpredictable environment may be conducive to raised blood pressure (Harburg, Erfurt, Hauenstein, Chase, Schull, & Schork, 1973).

These are but a few examples of environmental factors in disease. Other features of the human environment have been linked to disease; they include economic hardship, exposure to natural or other disasters (such as war and famine), technological changes, occupational stress, social customs, and political and social change (Weiner, 1981).

2. The Current Status of Psychosomatic Concepts

The review just carried out has emphasized a paradigmatic shift in psychosomatic concepts. For many years, it was held that psychological conflict (along with unspecified physiological factors) played a prepotent role in the predisposition to certain model diseases as well as in their initiation and pathogenesis. Gradually, a shift has occurred and the onset of disease is seen as an aspect of the individual's failure to adapt to his or her (changing) human and nonhuman environment (that may also elicit conflict). The disease with which this person falls ill is determined by complex and multiple predisposing factors (Weiner, 1977, 1978) that include psychological vulnerabilities. These are in part determined by an excessive reliance on others as well as cognitive deficits that express themselves in an inability to utilize information and overcome change and frustration.

This change in concept makes psychosomatic medicine a form of human biology (Weiner, 1977, 1978; von Uexküll, 1979). Yet the new theory must also avoid overemphasizing the role of psychological and social factors in disease, because every disease is multifactorially determined *and* heterogeneous in nature (Weiner, 1979).

The multifactorial nature of disease was exemplified in the foregoing discussion of the factors involved in coronary heart disease and obesity. The heterogeneous nature of disease has many implications for prevention and treatment. Heterogeneity is manifested at every phase of disease—in its predisposition, onset conditions, initiation, and maintenance; in fact, the factors that predispose to disease are not necessarily or even usually the same as those that set it off or that maintain it. These assertions are exemplified by the syndrome of peptic duodenal ulcer. It is recognized that a duodenal ulcer may be anteceded by gastrinomas, extensive resection of the small intestine, alcoholic cirrhosis of the liver, chronic renal failure, or chronic obstructive lung disease; it may also be associated with a syndrome that occurs in families and consists of limb tremors, congenital nystagmus, and a disturbance of consciousness reminiscent of narcolepsy (Neuhäuser, Daly, Magnelli, Barreras, Donaldson, & Optiz, 1976).

When these antecedents to duodenal ulcer are not present, we are still faced with a predicament, because not every patient with this disorder has an elevated serum pepsinogen level, nor does each have the psychological profile that Alexander described.

Recently the study of the risk factors in peptic duodenal ulcer disease has become even more complex; at the same time, however, many of the issues that previously confounded this field of investigation have been clarified (Ackerman & Weiner, 1976; Rotter & Rimoin, 1977; Weiner, 1977). The new thrust of these investigations derives from the fact that human pepsinogens can be separated immunochemically into two main groups—pepsinogen I (PG-I) and pepsinogen II (PG-II) (Samloff, 1971a, b; Samloff & Liebman, 1974). Elevated levels of PG-I are found in about two-thirds of all unrelated patients with peptic duodenal ulcer (Samloff, Liebman, & Panitch, 1975). The remaining third have normal levels of PG-I. The distribution of PG-I is bimodal in patients but not in control subjects.

PG-II levels are also greater in patients with peptic duodenal ulcer, in whom PG-I levels are elevated, than in hospitalized control patients (Samloff, 1977). But we still do not know whether PG-II levels are elevated in patients whose PG-I levels are within the normal range.

Two groups of patients with peptic duodenal ulcer have, therefore, been identified—those with elevated PG-I (and possibly, PG-II levels) and those with normal PG-I levels.

Elevations of PG-I levels are inherited as an autosomal dominant trait, because about half of the offspring of parents with such elevations also own the trait (Rotter, Sones, Richardson, Rimoin, & Samloff, 1977; Rotter, Sones, Samloff, Richardson, Gursky, Walsh, & Rimoin, 1979) and none of the children of parents without the trait manifest it. Yet the enhanced PG-I level is not invariably associated with duodenal ulcer disease; 42% of those with it had the disease, the rest did not. Based on other studies carried out by Rotter and Rimoin (1977), it is now possible to calculate that in those patients with raised PG-I levels, the trait accounts for 25% of the etiologic variance of this form of duodenal ulcer disease.

These observations also lay to rest a long-standing doubt that the raised levels of PG (or PG-I) are inherited and are not merely a result of age, gastric mucosal damage, eating meals, or the diminished excretion of the enzyme due to renal damage.

Patients with normal pepsinogen levels also develop duodenal ulcer, as do their siblings, in a small percentage of whom PG-I levels may be elevated. The incidence of duodenal ulcer among siblings of patients with normal PG-I levels is almost as great as in the siblings of patients with raised PG-I levels (Rotter, Rimoin, Gursky, & Samloff, 1977; Rotter, Rimoin, Gursky, Terasaki, & Sturdevant, 1977). However, the mode of inheritance in the former has not been worked out, nor is it known how the genes express themselves as markers of risk for this subform of the disease.

In duodenal ulcer disease, additional genetic markers have been found. Individuals who have blood type O and who do not secrete the blood group antigens ABH, which are secreted into the saliva and gastric juice, have higher incidences of both gastric and duodenal ulcer (Hanley, 1964; Marcus, 1969; Sievers, 1959; Vesely, Kubickova, & Dvorakova, 1968). The blood group and nonsecretor factors account for about 2.5% to 3% of the etiologic variance of peptic ulcer disease. Stated in other terms, people of blood type O who do not secrete ABH antigens are 25% to 35% more likely to develop peptic ulcer than are individuals of blood type A, B, or AB who do secrete these antigens.

But the mechanisms by which these etiologic contributions are made is unclear. It has been suggested that blood type O may be related to high serum pepsinogen levels (Hanley, 1964; Sievers, 1959). Furthermore, blood group antigens are related to the mucoprotease fraction of gastric mucin, whose production may be genetically regulated (Glass, 1968). But the role of the genes in controlling ABH secretion remains unknown. One possibility is that genes do not play a role in causing the disease; rather the genes that control blood group O may help determine the severity of duodenal ulcer.

Finally, still another genetic marker has been described for this disease—that is, the ability of a person to taste or not to taste dilute solutions of phenylthiocarbamide (PTC) (Vesely et al., 1968). This ability is determined by simple Mendelian principles of heredity. Interestingly, the PTC taste sensitivty has been found to be more prevalent among patients with duodenal ulcer than among controls. This may, then, be another genetic marker of susceptibility—provided, of course, the presence of duodenal ulcer does not in itself influence the ability to taste PTC.

The human lymphocyte antigen (HLA) B5 also occurs more frequently in patients with duodenal ulcer than in normal controls; white males possessing the HLA-B5 antigen are 2.9 times as likely to develop duodenal ulcer than those who do not (Rotter, Rimoin, Gursky, Terasaki, & Sturdevant, 1977). By contrast, the relative risk for the same disease in a person with blood group O is 1.3; for one with blood group nonsecretor status, it is 1.5 (Langman, 1973; McConnell, 1963). The risk when both blood group O and nonsecretor status are combined is 2.5.

The studies on these genetic markers did not take into account the heterogeneity of peptic ulcer disease. We do not know whether the three serologic markers are associated differentially with normal or raised PG-1 levels.

Additional risk factors for peptic duodenal ulcer have been identified: Men in our society are more prone to develop it than women. Habits such as cigarette smoking, the presence of a gastric ulcer, and prior coffee consumption all play additional predisposing roles: their effects appear to be cumulative.

One might conclude from the previous discussion that peptic duodenal ulcer consists of two forms, one of which is characterized by elevated and the other by normal PG-I levels. However, this conclusion is not warranted. A variety of regulatory disturbances are found in patients with peptic ulcer disease. They may show an increased proclivity to secrete gastric acid and pepsin and to produce hydrochloric acid when stimulated by gastrin, a postprandial hypergastrinemia, an increased rate of gastric emptying, an impaired feedback inhibition of gastrin secretion by acidification of the gastric antrum, or an impaired release of prostaglandin E (an inhibitor of gastric acid secretion) when hydrochloric acid is released by vagal stimulation (Cheun, Jubiz, Moore, & Frailey, 1975; Grossman, 1978, 1979).

But these deviations are seen after the onset of disease; therefore, one may not assume they are present prior to it. Yet these abnormalities characterize different patients with the disease; they are not present in all patients. Nor do we know whether they are correlated with high or low PG-I levels except in patients in whom elevated levels of PG-I and acid occur together. We also need to know whether patients with elevated PG-I levels differ from those with normal levels. In fact, we need "psychophysiological profiles" of patients with the various subforms of peptic duodenal ulcer.

The obvious questions that these observations raise are: Do patients with elevated PG-I levels differ psychologically from those with normal PG-I levels? Why do some persons with elevated PG-I levels develop a peptic duodenal ulcer and others do not? We have no complete answer to either of these questions.

Yet data from the study of female patients with rheumatoid arthritis suggest that the difference between similarly predisposed siblings, one of whom is ill and the other is not, is that the latter is functioning well in her everyday life and the former is not. Solomon and Moos (1965) compared the nonarthritic female relatives of patients (matched on a number of social and personal variables) on the basis of whether or not their sera contained rheumatoid factors. The authors caution that it is not possible from their study to tell whether the rheumatoid factors were the same as those found in the disease. Employing the MMPI, they reported that those relatives whose sera contained the factors scored significantly higher on inhibited aggression; on concern about the social desirability of their actions and about socioeconomic status; on compliance, shyness, conscientiousness, and morality; and on the capacity for successful defense and adaptation. In some ways they resembled and in others they did not resemble patients with rheumatoid arthritis (Moos & Solomon, 1965; 1966). But in contrast to patients with the disease, they were functioning well in their everyday lives. Interestingly enough, the relatives whose sera did not contain rheumatoid factors or contained them only in low titers scored high on those items that indicated obsessive compulsive traits and rituals: fears, anxiety, and guilt feelings; indecisiveness; self-critical attitudes; and bodily complaints. They also had a reduced capacity for successful "defense" against impulses. They complained of more psychiatric symptoms; they dissimulated, accepted themselves less, and felt alienated from others. They scored higher on dependency and inner maladjustment scales. The study suggested that in order to develop rheumatoid arthritis, one must not only be able to develop rheumatoid factors but have certain psychological problems that one cannot contain or cope with.

These observations suggest that individuals with rheumatoid arthritis differ from their siblings only by virtue of their inability to adapt to the vicissitudes of their everyday lives and to function well. Therefore, neither the presence of rheumatoid factors nor the psychological predisposition to the disease need manifest itself in rheumatoid arthritis provided that the individual is compensated in his or her everyday functioning.

The implications of this study are readily apparent. An appreciation of the predisposition to a disease would allow those interested in health maintenance to do preventive work. They could identify those at risk for that disease and help maintain their adaptation to their personal environments. Such an endeavor would have to be based on an appreciation of the personal sensitivities of the subject; a complete knowledge of the social, human, and occupational environment in which he or she lives; and a grasp of how this environment is coped with. However, since the predisposition to the disease may not be uniform, a knowledge of what subform of that disease the person is predisposed to would also be necessary.

4. The Onset and Initiation of Disease

The next question—one that has been a central focus of psychosomatic investigations for the past twenty years—is why a predisposed person falls ill at a particular time of life and not at another (or why recurrences of the illness arise at a particular time after a remission).

The answer to this third question has been approached by clinical and more systematic studies that deal with changes in a person's environment: for example, Engel's studies (1968) on bereavement and separation as a general onset condition of many diseases and the studies by Holmes and Rahe (1967) of life change.

The Holmes and Rahe studies have provoked incredulity and considerable criticism. They have been criticized for the following reasons:

1. Do some patients overreport their experiences? Conversely, because human memory is fallible, underreporting may occur if the life changes took place weeks or months before the onset of symptoms.
2. Do patients seek reasonable but *post hoc* explanations for their illnesses?
3. How reliable are retrospective reports?
4. Do investigators search diligently for events in the sick?
5. What is the directionality of the relationship between the illness and event? Symptoms may occur without disease and disease without symptoms. Also, subclinical disease may impair psychological adaptation to events and alter the way in which they are experienced.
6. Is the illness real? Or does the subject merely report that he or she is sick?

There are, of course, additional problems with the Holmes-Rahe scale, whose categories are not well defined: for example, how does the reporter define major illness, or what family members should be included? We also know that the test–retest reliability varies from .9 to .26 in various studies and that the total score is either produced by one major event or many minor ones. Finally, high scores and high rates of illness may say more about the reporter's attitudes about illness than about life changes or real illnesses. And, in actuality, the correlation between high illness rates and high scores is of the order of .3.

Despite these many reservations, this work contains an important grain of truth that confirms what every wise physician can observe every day in his or her patients. Yet the association of life changes and illness onset is, once again, too linear. It fails to take into account other variables such as:

1. The perception of the life change as distressing or not is a critical variable in the association (Lundberg, Theorell, & Lind, 1975), and the successful or unsuccessful psychological adaptation to the changes is critical as well.
2. The presence or absence of social supports play crucial intervening roles in modifying the effects of life changes (DeFaire & Theorell, 1975).

We are now more on psychological territory. Clearly, life changes alone do not determine disease onset: as Hinkle (1974) showed, healthy people frequently tend to be contented in their personal lives and occupations, and contentment can insulate them from change. Other data suggest that social change is not directly pathogenetic; it does not act directly on the individual. The change must be perceived and appraised—activities that in turn are influenced by past experience as well as role and status relationships (Lazarus, 1966).

To summarize the pathogenetic role of life experience:

1. Life experiences may be overwhelming: for example, living in London during the blitz, fighting in Stalingrad, or being exposed to explosions. The former experience led to increased perforation of the duodenum, the two latter to high blood pressure.
2. The meaning of the experience may idiosyncratically be perceived as portentous or as excessively dangerous, leading to a "paralysis" of appropriate coping measures.
3. The significance of the experience may be denied or responded to inappropriately, or no attempt may be made to deal with it. In other people the signals of distress or danger fail or they are not as clearly perceived (Nemiah & Sifneos, 1970).
4. The person may be vulnerable because the event mobilizes specific unmastered personal problems with their own antecedents in that individual's history.
5. Some people (children, the mentally defective, the dependent, the widowed, the elderly) have limited adaptive capacities or do not have the education, skills, social supports, or information to cope with the events and solve the personal problems the events create.

Many psychological and psychiatric studies of medically ill patients have also described their poor adaptive and coping capacities, dependency, and primitive defensive measures, which result in adaptive failure and are signaled by helplessness and finally lead to giving up (Engel, 1968; Ruesch, 1948; Vaillant, 1977; Weiner, 1977). In other words, in every population there are a number of individuals predisposed to a given disease, but only a certain number fall ill when losses or life changes occur. Those who fall are usually psychologically and biologically maladapted. Certain characteristics are common to many of the ill; they have been outlined earlier in this chapter (pp. 33–34).

Conversely, effective coping is determined by a combination of psychological skills—intelligence, the capacity to use information and solve problems, familiarity with the task, self-reliance and a commitment to face it. But the task is made easier when the environment is relatively stable and predictable.

The work of Engel (1968) suggests that bereavement and separation is a general onset condition of a variety of diseases whose specific nature is determined by other factors. The work of Holmes and Rahe, on the other hand, lead one to believe that quantitative factors—the number or severity of changes—determine disease onset. However, additional observations suggest that in some diseases at least, no uniform event determines disease onset. For example, primary anorexia nervosa may begin in a variety of settings. In some young women, the disease begins when they leave home; in others, it begins when they diet because of peer pressure to be thin, because they are overweight at puberty, or because thinness is a prerequisite to professional success; in still others, the disease begins after a sexual temptation or adventure. It may also begin after a young woman stops taking oral contraceptive medication (Fries & Nillius, 1973).

In fact, every disease has its onset in different contexts; or the meaning of the same setting—a bereavement or separation—may be interpeted differently by different patients.

But a knowledge of the onset conditions can have major preventive and therapeutic implications. Most patients are quite unaware of the fact that changes and events in their lives, and their reactions to them, are related to the onset of their illness. Making the patients aware of the association of these events to their illness is a first step in rehabilitating them and teaching them to avoid or cope with the particular situations and events to which they are sensitive. There are also some bereaved patients who, because of their remarkable lack of adaptive capacities and their fragility, are not ever able to cope and may need a long-term surrogate for the departed person.

5. Initiating Mechanisms of Disease

We do not know the mechanisms by which bereavement or life changes set off a train of events leading to bodily disease. Implicit in all past and current psychosomatic theory is the belief that the brain, which regulates every bodily process, mediates in an undisclosed manner the changes that lead to physiological disturbances in bodily systems or to structural changes in organs and their constituent cells. And, in fact, there is a growing body of experimental evidence suggesting that the brain participates at some stage in diseases as diverse as anorexia nervosa, bronchial asthma, and essential hypertension (Chalmers, 1975; Weiner, 1977; Weiner, Hofer, & Stunkard, 1980).

But there is also a growing body of evidence suggesting that the initiating mechanisms of illness are not uniform. This statement is illustrated by describing the pathogenesis of three major illnesses: essential hypertension, myocardial infarction, and diabetes mellitus.

There are no established ways of identifying people at risk for the development of essential hypertension. Two strategies have, therefore, been devised in the past several years. The first is to classify hypertensive patients according to physiological patterns that consist of deviations of cardiac output, plasma renin activity, or plasma volume (Julius, Randall, Esler, Kashima, Ellis, & Bennet, 1975; Laragh, Baer, Brunner, Buhler, Sealey, & Vaughan, 1972; Tarazi, Dustan, Frohlich, Gifford, & Hoffman, 1970). The second strategy is to study patients very early in the disease process, before the appearance of (mal)adaptive changes in response to the raised blood pressure itself. Many patients early in the disease are said to have borderline or labile essential hypertension.

Not all patients with borderline, essential hypertension go on to essential hypertension. Groups of patients with borderline hypertension tend to have some increase in cardiac output as well as increased cardiac contractility and heart rate. Their plasma catecholamine levels are likely to be higher and their urinary excretion of catecholamines is excessive on standing. Stress produces exaggerated catecholamine and blood pressure responses. Ganglionic blocking agents produce a fall in blood pressure that closely correlates with a fall in plasma norepinephrine levels (DeQuattro & Miura, 1973; Julius *et al.*, 1975; Kuchel, 1977; Lorimer, McFarlane, Provan, Duffy, & Lawrie, 1971; Louis, Doyle, Anavekar, & Chua, 1973).

Patients with borderline hypertension differ as a group (but not necessarily as individuals) from normotensive subjects. But the patients also differ from each other. Not all patients with borderline hypertension have an elevated cardiac output; in 30% the cardiac output is 2 standard deviations beyond the mean for normal, age-matched subjects. In this subgroup of patients, the total peripheral resistance is inappropriately normal at rest (it should be decreased when increased tissue perfusion is brought about by the increased cardiac output). In other patients with borderline hypertension in whom a normal cardiac output and heart rate are found, the total peripheral resistance is increased at rest, possibly owing to increased alpha-adrenergic vasoconstrictor tone. Blood volume is unevenly distributed in the circulation (mainly in the cardiopulmonary bed) in borderline hypertension, but only in those patients with an increased cardiac output. In about 30% of all patients with borderline hypertension, plasma renin activity and norepinephrine concentration are elevated. Other patients increase their plasma renin activity excessively with postural changes. Yet the increased plasma renin activity does not seem to maintain the heightened blood pressure levels through its effect on angiotension II and aldosterone production. The increased heart rate, cardiac output, and plasma renin activity can be reduced to normal levels with propranolol, but the plasma norepinephrine concentration and blood pressure continue to remain elevated. Therefore, the enhanced plasma renin activity is believed to be a result of increased sympathetic activity and is not the primary pathogenetic factor in raising the blood pressure (Esler, Julius, Zweifler, Randall, Hardburg, Gardiner, & DeQuattro, 1977; Julius *et al.*, 1975). The obverse sequence is, however thought to account for the malignant phase of hypertension, when high plasma renin activity is found.

Nonetheless, plasma renin activity is normal in many borderline hypertensive patients and low in some (Esler, Julius, Randall, Ellis, & Kashima, 1975). Patients whose plasma renin activity is normal tend to be those with diminished stroke volume and cardiac index, normal pulse rate, but increased total peripheral resistance. Their plasma norepinephrine concentration is higher than normal but lower than in borderline hypertensive patients with high plasma renin activity. The increased peripheral resistance and blood pressure in borderline hypertensive patients with low or normal plasma renin activity is unaffected by the administration of alpha-adrenergic and beta-adrenergic blocking agents and atropine. The administration of these drugs causes a fall in blood pressure and peripheral resistance in borderline hypertensive patients with high plasma renin activity (Esler *et al.*, 1975; Esler *et al.*, 1977).

These results suggest that borderline hypertension—an harbinger of established hypertension—is a heterogeneous disturbance with perhaps three different physiologic and humoral profiles. These profiles, in turn, reflect different pathogeneses for borderline hypertension. In fact, endocrine changes in other borderline hypertensive patients are also not completely uniform. (However, these patients may not be the same ones as those who have been studied for their cardiovascular dynamics, responses to sympathetic and parasympathetic blocking agents, and plasma renin activity.) In any case, patients with borderline hypertension can be divided into those who, with reassurance and rest, experience a decline in blood pressure to below 140 mm Hg systolic, 90 diastolic, and those in whom there is no such decline (Genest, Koiw, & Kuchel, 1977). In both groups of patients there is a significant mean increase in plasma aldosterone concentration, which reverts to normal levels only in those who become normotensive. When recumbent, both groups of patients show a decreased metabolic clearance rate of aldosterone when compared to normal control subjects. Usually an upright posture considerably decreases the metabolic clearance of aldosterone, but not in patients with mild, borderline hypertension. Although other alterations in aldosterone metabolism occur (binding of the hormone to a specific plasma globulin and responses to stimulation occur in borderline hypertensive patients), the point of this discussion is that borderline patients with mild hypertension are similar in some ways and different in others.

The physiologic heterogeneity of patients with essential hypertension is also reflected in their psychological heterogeneity. Esler and his co-workers (1977) have reported on 16 males 18 to 35 years of age, belonging to the subform of borderline hypertensives, in whom high plasma renin activity and increased plasma norepinephrine levels were found. They differed psychologically from 15 borderline hypertensive males with normal plasma renin activity and from 20 males with normal blood pressure. The patients with high-renin essential hypertension differed significantly from both the normotensive patients and the hypertensive patients with normal plasma renin activity on a number of psychological measures signifying that they were controlled, guilt-ridden, submissive people with relatively high levels of unexpressed or unexpressable anger. But neither hypertensive group scored higher on scores signifying anxiety than did the control groups. The only tendency that differentiated the control group from the hypertensive patients with normal plasma renin activity is that they appeared to be more resentful, but they were as capable of expressing this resentment as were their normotensive peers.

This study documents the psychological heterogeneity of hypertensive patients; it also confirms the psychiatric description of hypertensive patients that we owe to Alexander. Nonetheless, the meaning of this important study is not clear. Julius and Esler (1975) and Esler and his co-workers (1977) have argued that the pathogenesis of high-renin borderline hypertension is neurogenic—that the high plasma renin activity is secondary to increased sympathetically mediated release of renin because the effect of propranolol is to lower plasma renin activity but not blood pressure in these patients. They have concluded that in this subform of essential hypertension, the activity of the sympathetic nervous system is increased or, alternatively, that both sympathetic nervous enhancement and diminished parasympathetic inhibition account for their findings, which are due to a disturbance in central autonomic regulation. Increased activity of the sympathetic nervous system would account for all the findings in this subform of essential hypertension.

The results of this study have major implications not only for psychosomatic theory but also for the treatment of high blood pressure by biofeedback, relaxation, or meditation rather than by drugs. In the past, the psychosomatic theory of the pathogenesis of essential hypertension was designed to explain the link between repressed or suppressed hostility and the increase in peripheral resistance (Alexander, 1950). But, as we have seen, a proportion of patients at the onset of essential hypertension have a normal peripheral resistance. On the other hand, most attempts to reduce elevations of blood pressure by psychological techniques aim at reducing increased sympathetic nervous system activity (Seer, 1979), which we have seen is a feature of only some patients with borderline hypertension. What is more, a number of physiological adjustments occur later in the course of the syndrome to overcome the increased sympathetic activity, suggesting that psychophysiological measures to reduce blood pressure must be directed to the appropriate physiological mechanism that is raising blood pressure levels.

Therefore, it follows that future research on the use of psychological techniques in the treatment of essential hypertension must be based on an awareness that subforms of the syndrome exist and that its physiology changes at different stages of its development. The minimal additional requirements in selecting patients for treatment are that the therapist should know how long the patient had been hypertensive, his or her age and sex, the criteria whereby the diagnosis was made (e.g., blood pressure level), and the history of pharmacological treatment as well as its side effects (Seer, 1979). The criteria for successful treatment should also be defined: Should a permanent reduction of blood pressure level be the sole criterion? How long should the level stay reduced? What other physiological criteria should be altered (e.g., serum or plasma norepinephrine, renin, or aldosterone levels; heart rate, cardiac output)? Should psychological treatments be combined with attempts to change the "life-styles" of patients?

Essential hypertension is not only a heterogeneous disorder but also a major risk factor in coronary heart disease and in myocardial infarction. The initiating mechanisms of myocardial infarction are also heterogeneous; it may come about through coronary artery spasm, occlusion, thrombosis, embolism, subendothelial hemorrhage, or congenital abnormalities of the coronary arteries.

In a similar vein, multiple forms of diabetes mellitus exist, and different initiating mechanisms may produce them. In some forms of diabetes mellitus, levels of circulating insulin may be normal or elevated, but the patient fails to respond to the hormone. Such a resistance to either circulating or administered insulin takes a number of forms. It may be due to a variety of antagonists to the action of the hormone or to its receptor; these antagonists consist either of antibodies to the hormone or the receptor or of still other hormones. Alternatively, the number of insulin receptors may be decreased, the receptor mechanisms may be defective, or the insulin may be genetically altered in structure due to the substitution of an amino acid for the usual one in one of the insulin chains (Tager, Given, Baldwin, Mako, Markese, Rubenstein, Olefsky, Kobayashi, Kolterman, & Poucher, 1979).

6. Social and Psychological Effects of Illness

The effects of illness on people, their families, and the social group to which they belong have been studied and written about at great length. But as I have already indicated in the introductory section of this chapter, current psychosomatic theory concerns itself with other topics. Therefore, I shall touch on the social psychology of illness only selectively and briefly; the reader is referred to the writings of Bibring and Kahana (1968), Binger (1945), Engel (1962), Karasu and Steinmuller (1978), Pasnau (1975), Strain and Grossman (1975), and von Uexküll (1979) for a detailed and extensive discussion of this complex topic.

Suffice it to say for the purpose of this chapter that illness itself constitutes a change in people's lives to which they must adapt, or be helped to adapt, should they seek help. But additional adaptive tasks are imposed on the sick person by the specific nature of the illness and its symptoms: whether the illness comes on abruptly or gradually; whether it is treatable or not; whether it carries a special stigma or not; and whether it will require hospitalization, special technical procedures, or surgery. A vital factor in the patient's successful adaptation to illness is the role and response of the caring professional person. Much has been written about the positive and negative therapeutic effects of the doctor–patient relationship and its conscious and unconscious aspects. The physician who disregards his or her role in this very powerful and important relationship does so at the patient's peril.

The successful adaptation of patients to illness is also a function of their previous ability to cope with other illnesses and with those who provided care during these periods. However, additional factors must be considered in the patient's responses to illness. For example, the illness or its symptoms may acquire a very individual meaning: the metabolic and physiological alterations caused by the illness or the drugs used to treat it may impair cerebral metabolism and function, thereby altering the patient's perception, memory, or problem-solving ability and also his or her ability to cope with the environment. Elderly people and children have fewer coping abilities and strategies than those in other stages of their lives; they require very special care in the strange environment of the hospital as well as help in adapting to illness.

Many people other than physicians are involved in the care of the chronically ill or disabled, and the blind, deaf, or dying. And economists increasingly determine how much and what kind of care should be provided and how society's resources should be distributed to care for the sick.

We know less about the factors that sustain disease than we do about its pathophysiology. Yet evidence is beginning to accrue—for example, in the case of experimental high blood pressure—that the factors inciting it differ from those that sustain it. The brain-stem and hypothalamic mechanisms that participate in the maintenance of experimental blood pressure elevations have been shown to be different (Chalmers, 1975; Ganten, Schelling, & Ganten, 1977; Weiner, 1977) from the brain mechanisms that initiate them.

In some cases of human hypertension, secondary physiological adaptations to the elevation of blood pressure include a diminution in the sensitivity of the arterial baroreceptors (Korner, West, Shaw, & Uther, 1974), an increase in peripheral resistance in response to an increase in cardiac output, structurally increased resistance to regional blood flow (Folkow & Hallbäck, 1977), and changes in cardiac performance (Frohlich, Tarazi, & Dustan, 1971).

Other changes in many systems are also found in abiding essential hypertension. To mention just two: (1) significant increases in the plasma concentration of aldosterone occur with age in essential hypertension—in contrast to a decline with age of plasma aldosterone levels in normotensive subjects (Genest *et al.,* 1977), and (2) plasma renin activity is markedly increased during the development of the malignant phase of hypertensive disease and renal failure. Complex changes also occur in renal dynamics; these are believed to be the consequence of a subform of the borderline hypertensive state, in which there is increased activity of the sympathetic nervous system (and probably diminished parasympathetic activity). Renal blood flow is reduced by reversible intrarenal vasoconstriction, and increases in circulating norepinephrine and in sympathetic drive both reduce the urinary excretion of sodium and water (Brown, Fraser, Lever, Morton, & Rubinson, 1977; Hollenberg, & Adams, 1976). But the rise in blood pressure should cause an increased excretion of sodium and water, which at first does and later does not occur. Therefore, a progressive resetting of the relationships of blood pressure to sodium and water excretion—a regulatory disturbance—is produced. Progressive renal changes ensue, accounting for the change from borderline labile hypertension to essential hypertension. In short, by a fall in renal blood flow and rein and a rise in total and renal vascular resistance, the kidney maintains the blood pressure increases that were initiated elsewhere, (Brown *et al.,* 1977).

Not only do secondary physiological (mal)adaptations occur in essential hypertension but the psychology of patients with this disease also changes during its course. Safar, Kamieniecka, Levenson, Dimitriu, and Pauleau (1978) have shown that patients in the borderline phase of essential hypertension demonstrate aggressive tendencies which are felt as dangerous and engender anxiety. Such individuals have few fantasies but a variety of psychophysiological symptoms and signs. In the later phase of sustained hypertension, these symptoms and signs vanish as anxiety disappears. The hostility is still inferable but is neither apperceived nor recognized by the patients.

Secondary metabolic alterations occur in many chronic diseases or after weight loss; they consist of a nonspecific depression of the thyroid hormone, triiodothyronine.

Patients, who have successfully been treated with antithyroid medication or thyroid surgery for Graves' disease may show persistent metabolic alterations and psychological deficits and maladaptations (Ruesch, Christiansen, Patterson, Dewees, & Jacobson, 1947).

Noncompliance to medical regimens may endanger the patient. Improper or inadequate medical care may lead him or her to eschew all further help, to resort to inexpert treatment, or to seek help from untrained people. Failure adequately to appreciate the patient's psychological responses to an illness may lead to his or her chronic invalidism; indeed, chronic symptomatology is the rule in the case of injuries sustained at work, which are compensated. Society, therefore, contributes to the maintenance of symptoms that are only indirectly related to the industrial accident or illness. On the other hand, some societies stigmatize the helpless or socially incompetent—especially the mentally ill or defective, the handicapped, and the old—providing inadequate care or insufficient funds for their education, nutrition, and housing.

These examples are selective; they do justice to only a small number of the factors that sustain disease and that may need correction before adequate treatment results can be achieved. They are mentioned only because so much of medicine is directed at correcting only the pathophysiology of disease. Medicine is dedicated to the ideal of the "cure" of this pathophysiology. In practice, however, the physician is also in a position to help patients achieve optimal functioning despite being ill, and to live with their illness; they are often able to relieve suffering, and even help patients to die with dignity. Although these more "mundane" aims are often neglected, they should be the concern of all those who are interested in the care of the ill, disabled, or dying.

8. Conclusion

The main aim of this chapter has been to survey some current psychosomatic concepts of disease. In the course of this review, it becomes apparent that many disease are complex, multifactorial in their origins, and heterogeneous in nature. For complex historical reasons, medicine has concentrated on classifying, diagnosing, studying, and treating disease after its onset and on attempting to reverse material defects (that are traditionally believed to have single causes) in organs, cells or subcellular structures. This approach has only partly been successful because it neglects both the historical (and multifactorial) antecedents of these defects and the sick person.

This chapter also attempts to point out that a comprehensive and broad approach to health and disease can and must incorporate our knowledge of the roles of social and psychological factors at every stage of illness.

If one's aim is to prevent disease, a knowledge of the many factors that predispose to a disease is essential. Furthermore, it will in the future be necessary to specify the predisposing factors of the particular subform of the disease that one is attempting to prevent. One of the main aims of this chapter is to point out that such subforms exist and that they may differ psychologically, genetically, and physiologically.

A knowledge of predisposition alone may not suffice to explain the onset of a disease. The factors that initiate disease often seem to be different than those that predispose to them (e.g., elevations of PG-I levels are neither necessary or sufficient to initiate the syndrome of peptic ulcer disease).

Different social and psychological situations, of which bereavement or separation is a common one, correlate with disease onset. Therefore, helping patients to overcome their sense of loss, grief, depression, or helplessness is an important part of the health care professional's job. It is incumbent on such a professional, however, to make certain that these feelings are related to the events in the patient's life and not to being ill, being in an ambiguous situation, or suffering pain. In addition, the knowledge of the context in which a disease began may allow the attendant to teach the patient how to cope with future loss.

The ideal of physicians is to cure disease. Like many ideologies, this one is subject to excessive and often ill-advised actions. We are far from understanding the multiple antecedents and initiating mechanisms, or the psychological and bodily adaptations of most diseases. Therefore, the possibility of cure is still remote.

The aim of health care providers is to cure whenever possible. When this is not possible, their goal is to relieve suffering, provide succor and comfort, and help patients live with their illness, the resultant disability, and the necessary treatment. These educational aims of medicine are often neglected in the heat of excessive and ill-advised therapeutic zeal. In addition, one major aim of caring for the sick is to prevent the complications of illness, even though many of these stem from the side effects of drugs, (Yet there can be little doubt that the reduction of high blood pressure greatly diminishes morbidity and mortality from its complications.)

Health providers have additional goals: they are to intervene with those factors that sustain disease and which, in turn, differ from those that predispose to and initiate it. Yet if they cannot do so, it still remains their duty to assist the seriously disabled and disadvantaged, care for the elderly, and help the dying go to their graves peacefully and gracefully.

9. References

Ackerman, S. H., & Weiner, H. Peptic ulcer disease: Some considerations for psychosomatic research. In O. W. Hill (Ed.), *Modern trends in psychosomatic medicine—3*. London: Butterworths, 1976.

Alexander, F. *Psychosomatic Medicine*. New York: Norton, 1950.

Bibring, G. L., & Kahana, R. J. *Lectures in medical psychology*. New York: International Universities Press, 1968.

Binger, C. A. L. *The doctor's job*. New York: Norton, 1945.

Brown, J. J., Fraser, R., Lever, A. F., Morton, J. J., & Rubinson, J. I. S. Mechanisms in hypertension: A personal view. In J. Genest, E. Koiw, & O. Kuchel (Eds.), *Hypertension*. New York: McGraw-Hill, 1977.

Bruhn, J. G., Chandler, B., Miller, M. C., Wolf, J., & Lynn, T. N. Social aspects of coronary heart disease in two adjacent, ethnically different communities. *American Journal of Public Health*, 1966, *56*, 1493–1506.

Caffrey, C. B. *Behavior patterns and personality characteristics as related to prevalence rates of coronary heart disease in Trappist and Benedictine monks*. (Doctoral dissertation, Catholic University of America,

Washington, D.C.). University Microfilms, 1966, No. 67-1830, pp. 45–48, coronary heart disease rates.

Chalmers, J. P. Brain amines and models of experimental hypertension. *Circulation Research*, 1975, *36*, 469–480.

Cheun, L. Y., Jubiz, W., Moore, J. G., & Frailey, J. Gastric prostaglandin-E (PGE) output during basal and stimulated acid secretion in normal subjects and patients with peptic ulcer. *Gastroenterology*, 1975, *68*, 873.

De Faire, U., & Theorell, T. Life changes and myocardial infarction. How useful are life change measurements? *Scandinavian Journal of Social Medicine*, 1976, *4*, 115–122.

De Quattro, V., & Miura, Y. Neurogenic factors in human hypertension: Mechanism or myth? *American Journal of Medicine*, 1973, *55*, 362–378.

De Waard, F. Breast cancer incidence and nutritional status with particular reference to body weight. *Cancer Research*, 1975, *35*, 3351–3356.

Dunbar, F. *Psychosomatic Diagnosis*. New York: Hoeber, 1943.

Eisenberg, L. Psychiatry and society: A sociobiological analysis. *New England Journal of Medicine*, 1977, *296*, 903–910.

Engel, G. L. *Psychological Development in Health and Disease*. Philadelphia: Saunders, 1962.

Engel, G. L. A life setting conducive to illness: The giving-up, given-up complex. *Annals of Internal Medicine*, 1968, *69*, 293–300.

Engel, G. L. The need for a new medical model: A challenge for biomedicine. *Science*, 1977, *196*, 129–136.

Esler, M. D., Julius, S., Randall, O. S., Ellis, C. N., & Kashima, T. Relation of renin status to neurogenic vascular resistance in borderline hypertension. *American Journal of Cardiology*, 1975, *36*, 708–715.

Esler, M. D., Julius, S., Zweifler, A., Randall, O., Harburg, E., Gardiner, H. & De Quattro, V. Mild high-renin hypertension. *New England Journal of Medicine*, 1977, *296*, 405–411.

Folkow, B. U. G., & Hallbäck, M. I. L. Physiopathology of spontaneous hypertension in rats. In J. Genest, E. Koiw, & O. Kuchel (Eds.), *Hypertension*. New York: McGraw-Hill, 1977.

Fries, H., & Nillius, S. J. Dieting, anorexia nervosa and amenorrhoea after oral contraceptive treatment. *Acta Psychiatrica Scandinavica*, 1973, *49*, 669–679.

Frohlich, E. D., Tarazi, R. C., & Dustan, H. P. Clinical-physiological correlation in the development of hypertensive heart disease. *Circulation*, 1971, *44*, 446–455.

Ganten, D., Schelling, P., & Ganten, U. Tissue isorenins. In J. Genest, E. Koiw, & O. Kuchel (Eds.), *Hypertension*. New York: McGraw-Hill, 1977.

Genest, J., Koiw, E., & Kuchel, O. (Eds.). *Hypertension*. New York: McGraw-Hill, 1977.

Glass, G. B. J. *Introduction to gastrointestinal physiology*. Englewood Cliffs, N.J.: Prentice-Hall, 1968.

Goldblatt, P. B., Moore, M. E., & Stunkard, A. J. Social factors in obesity. *Journal of the American Medical Association*, 1965, *192*, 1039–1044.

Greene, W. A., Jr. Psychological factors and reticuloendothelial disease. I. Preliminary observations on a group of males with lymphomas and leukemias. *Psychosomatic Medicine*, 1954, *16*, 220–230.

Grossman, M. I. Abnormalities of acid secretion in patients with duodenal ulcer. *Gastroenterology*, 1978, *75*, 524–526.

Grossman, M. I. Elevated serum pepsinogen I. A genetic marker for duodenal disease. Editorial. *New England Journal of Medicine*, 1979, *300*, 89.

Hanley, W. B. Hereditary aspects of duodenal ulceration: Serum pepsinogen level in relation to ABO blood group and salivary ABH secretor status. *British Medical Journal*, 1964, *1* (5388), 936–940.

Harburg, E., Erfurt, J. C., Hauenstein, L. S., Chape, C., Schull, W. J., & Schork, M. A. Socioecological stress, suppressed hostility, skin color, and black-white male blood pressure: Detroit. *Psychosomatic Medicine*, 1973, *35*, 276–296.

Hinkle, L. E., Jr. The effect of exposure to culture change, social change and changes in interpersonal relationships on health. In B. S. Dohrenwend & B. P. Dohrenwend (Eds.), *Stressful life events: their nature and effects*. New York: Wiley, 1974.

Hollenberg, N. K., & Adams, D. F. The renal circulation in hypertensive disease. *American Journal of Medicine*, 1976, *60*, 773–784.

Holmes, T. H. & Rahe, R. H. The social readjustment rating scale. *Journal of Psychosomatic Research*, 1967, *11*, 213–218.

Julius, S., & Esler, M. Autonomic nervous cardiovascular regulation in borderline hypertension. *American Journal of Cardiology*, 1975, *36*, 685.

Julius, S., Randall, O. S., Esler, M. D., Kashima, T., Ellis, C., & Bennet, J. Altered cardiac responsiveness and regulation in the normal cardiac output type of borderline hypertension. *Circulation Research* (6 Suppl. 1), 1975, *36*, 199–207.

Karasu, T. B., & Steinmuller, R. I. *Psychotherapeutics in medicine.* New York: Grune & Stratton, 1978.

Korner, P. I., West, M. J., Shaw, J., & Uther, J. B. "Steady state" properties of baroreceptor-heart rate reflex in essential hypertension in man. *Clinical and Experimental Pharmacology and Physiology*, 1974, *1* (1), 65–76.

Kuchel, O. Autonomic nervous system in hypertension: Clinical aspects. In J. Genest, E. Koiw, & O. Kuchel (Eds.), *Hypertension.* New York: McGraw-Hill, 1977.

Langman, M. J. S. Blood groups and alimentary disorders. *Clinical Gastroenterology*, 1973, *2*, 497–506.

Laragh, J. H., Baer, L. H., Brunner, H. R., Buhler, F. R., Sealey, J. E., & Vaughan, E. D., Jr. Aldosterone in pathogenesis and management of hypertensive vascular disease. *American Journal of Medicine*, 1972, *52*, 633–652.

Lazarus, R. S. *Psychological stress and the coping process.* New York: McGraw-Hill, 1966.

Lorimer, A. R., McFarlane, P. W., Provan, G., Duffy, T., & Lawrie, T. D. V. Blood pressure and catecholamine responses to "stress" in normotensive and hypertensive subjects. *Cardiovascular Research*, 1971, *5*, 169–173.

Louis, W. J., Doyle, A. E., Anavekar, S. N., & Chua, K. G. Sympathetic activity and essential hypertension. *Clinical Science and Molecular Medicine*, 1973, *45*, 119 (Suppl. 1).

Lundberg, U., Theorell, T., & Lind, E. Life changes and myocardial infarction: Individual differences in life change scaling. *Journal of Psychosomatic Research*, 1975, *19*, 27–32.

Marcus, D. M. The ABO and Lewis blood-group system. *New England Journal of Medicine*, 1969, *280*, 994–1006.

Marmot, M. G. *Acculturation and coronary heart disease in Japanese-Americans.* Unpublished doctoral dissertation (Epidemiology), University of California, Berkeley, 1975.

Marmot, M. G., & Syme, S. L. Acculturation and coronary heart disease in Japanese-Americans. *American Journal of Epidemiology*, 1976, *104*, 225–247.

Marty, P., & de M'Uzan, M. La "pensée opératoire." *Revue Francaire Psychoanalitique*, 1963 *27*, Supp. 1345.

Matsumoto, Y. S. Social stress and coronary heart disease in Japan. A hypothesis. *Milbank Memorial Fund Quarterly*, 1970, *48*, 9–36.

McConnell, R. B. Associations and linkage in human genetics. *American Journal of Medicine*, 1963, *34*, 692–701.

McDougall, J. The psychosoma and the psychoanalytic process. *International Review of Psychoanalysis*, 1974, *1*, 437–448.

Mirra, A. P., Cole, P., & MacMahon, B. Breast cancer in an area of high parity: São Paulo, Brazil. *Cancer Research*, 1971, *31*, 77–83.

Moos, R. H., & Solomon, G. F. Psychologic comparisons between women with rheumatoid arthritis and their nonarthritic sisters. I. Personality test and interview rating data. *Psychosomatic Medicine*, 1965, *27*, 135–149.

Moos, R. H., & Solomon, G. F. Social and personal factors in rheumatoid arthritis: Pathogenic considerations. *Clinical Medicine*, 1966, *73*, 19–26.

Nemiah, J. C., & Sifneos, P. E. Affect and fantasy in patients with psychosomatic disorders. In O. W. Hall (Ed.), *Modern trends in psychosomatic Medicine—2.* London: Butterworths, 1970.

Neuhäuser, G., Daly, R. F., Magnelli, N. C., Barreras, R. F., Donaldson, R. M., Jr., & Optiz, J. M. Essential tremor, nystagmus and duodenal ulceration. *Clinical Genetics*, 1976, *9*, 81–91.

Notkins, A. L. The causes of diabetes. *Scientific American*, 1979, *241*, 62–73.

Pasnau, R. O. (Ed.). *Consultation-liaison psychiatry.* New York: Grune & Stratton, 1975.

Rotter, J. I., & Rimoin, D. L. Peptic ulcer disease—a heterogeneous group of disorders? *Gastroenterology*, 1977, *73*, 604–607.

Rotter, J. I., Rimoin, D. L., Gursky, J. M., & Samloff, I. M. The genetics of peptic ulcer disease-segregation of serum group I pepsinogen concentrations in families with peptic ulcer disease. *Clinical Research*, 1977, *25*, 114A.

Rotter, J. I., Rimoin, D. L., Gursky, J. M., Terasaki, P. & Sturdevant, R. A. L. HLA-B5 associated with duodenal ulcer. *Gastroenterology*, 1977, *73*, 438–440.

Rotter, J. I., Sones, J. Q., Richardson, C. T., Rimoin, D. L. & Samloff, I. M. The genetics of peptic ulcer disease-segregation of serum group I pepsinogen concentrations in families with peptic ulcer disease. *Clinical Research*, 1977, *25*, 325A.

Rotter, J. I., Sones, J. Q., Samloff, I. M., Richardson, C. T., Gursky, J. M., Walsh, J. H., & Rimoin, D. L. Duodenal-ulcer disease associated with elevated serum pepsinogen I: An inherited autosomal dominant disorder. *New England Journal of Medicine*, 1979, 63–66.

Ruesch, J. The infantile personality: The core problem of psychosomatic medicine. *Psychosomatic Medicine*, 1948, *10*, 133–144.

Ruesch, J., Christiansen, C., Patterson, L. C., Dewees, S., & Jacobson, A. Psychological invalidism in thyroidectomized patients. *Psychomatic Medicine*, 1947, *9*, 77–91.

Safar, M. E., Kamieniecka, H. A., Levenson, J. A., Dimitriu, V. M., & Pauleau, N. F. Hemodynamic factors and Rorschach testing in borderline and sustained hypertension. *Psychosomatic Medicine*, 1978, *40*, 620-630.

Samloff, I. M. Immunologic studies of human group I pepsinogens. *Journal of Immunology*, 1971, *106*, 962–968. (a)

Samloff, I. M. Cellular localization of group I pepsinogens in human gastric mucosa by immunofluorescence. *Gastroenterology*, 1971, *61*, 185–188. (b)

Samloff, I. M. Radioimmunoassay of group II pepsinogens in serum. *Gastroenterology*, 1977, *72*, A-102/1125.

Samloff, I. M., & Liebman, W. M. Radioimmunoassay of group I pepsinogens in serum. *Gastroenterology*, 1974, *66*, 494–502.

Samloff, I. M., Liebman, W. M., & Panitch, M. Serum group I pepsinogens by radioimmunoassay in control subjects and patients with peptic ulcer. *Gastroenterology*, 1975, *69*, 83–90.

Schmale, A. H., Jr. Relation of separation and depression to disease: I. A report on a hospitalized medical population. *Psychosomatic Medicine*, 1958, *20*, 259–277.

Seer, P. Psychological control of essential hypertension: Review of the literature and methodological critique. *Psychological Bulletin*, 1979, *86*, 1015–1043.

Sievers, M. L. Hereditary aspects of gastric secretory function: Race and ABO blood groups in relationship to acid and pepsin production. *American Journal of Medicine*, 1959, *27*, 246–255.

Solomon, G. F., & Moos, R. J. The relationship of personality to the presence of rheumatoid factor in asymptomatic relatives of patients with rheumatoid arthritis. *Psychosomatic Medicine*, 1965, *27*, 350–360.

Strain, J., & Grossman, S. (Eds.). *Psychological care of the medically ill.* New York: Appleton Century Crofts, 1975.

Stout, C., Morrow, J., Brandt, E. N., Jr., & Wolf, S. Unusually low incidence of death from myocardial infarction. Study of an Italian-American community in Pennsylvania. *Journal of the American Medical Association*, 1964, *188*, 845–849.

Tager, H., Given, B., Baldwin, D., Mako, M., Markese, J., Rubenstein, A., Olefsky, J., Kobayashi, M., Kolterman, O., & Poucher, R. A structurally abnormal insulin causing human diabetes. *Nature* (London), 1979, *281*, 122–125.

Tarazi, R. C., Dustan, H. P., Frohlich, E. D., Gifford, R. W., Jr., & Hoffman, G. C. Plasma volume and chronic hypertension. Relationship to arterial pressure levels in different hypertensive diseases. *Archives of Internal Medicine*, 1970, *125*, 835–842.

Vaillant, G. *Adaptation to life.* Boston: Little, Brown, 1977.

Vesely, K. T., Kubickova, K. T., & Dvorakova, M. Clinical data and characteristics differentiating types of peptic ulcer. *Gut*, 1968, *9*, 57–68.

von Uexküll, T. (Ed.). *Lehrbuch der Psychosomatischen Medizin.* Munich: Urban and Schwarzenberg, 1979.

Weiner, H. *Psychobiology and human disease.* New York: Elsevier–North Holland, 1977.

Weiner, H. The illusion of simplicity: The medical model revisited. *American Journal of Psychiatry*, 1978, *135*, (Suppl.), 27–33.

Weiner, H. Psychobiological markers of disease. In C. P. Kimball (Ed.), *Psychiatric Clinics of North America*. Philadelphia: Saunders, 1979.

Weiner, H. Social and psychological factors in disease. In W. R. Grove (Ed.), *The fundamental connection between nature and nurture: A review of the evidence.* Tennessee: Lexington Books of Heath Lexington, 1981.

Weiner, H., Hofer, M. A., & Stunkard, A. J. (Eds.). *Brain, behavior and bodily disease.* New York: Raven Press, 1980.

Wynder, E. L., Escher, G. C., & Mantel, N. A. An epidemiological investigation of cancer of the endometrium. *Cancer*, 1966, *19*, 489-520.

Psychological Processes Induced by Illness, Injury, and Loss

Mardi J. Horowitz

Most serious life events involve actual or potential losses: of a loved one, of material possessions, of health, or of hopes for the future. The ideal adjustment to loss is to accept it, replace that which is lost, and go on living. Between the first pangs of recognition of loss and adaptation to circumstances as they must be, there is an important, painful interval characterized by states of both intrusion and denial.

Considering the general disparities of psychological research, a rather remarkable concordance is found in the clinical, field, and experimental studies of response to the stress of serious life events or to vicarious simulations of such events. The frequency of two broadly defined states increases after such occurrences; one is characterized by an unusual level of intrusive and emotional memories or fantasies, the other by qualities of emotional numbing and ideational avoidance or denial. These seemingly paradoxical but interrelated states have been given various names in the massive literature on stress but will here be labeled as *intrusive* and *denial states* (see Cohen, 1979; Horowitz, 1976; Horowitz, Wilner, Marmar & Krupnick, 1980; Janis, 1971; Lazarus, 1966).

MARDI J. HOROWITZ ● Department of Psychiatry and Center for the Study of Neuroses, Langley Porter Psychiatric Institute, University of California, San Francisco, California 94143. Data on which this chapter is based has been produced through research supported by an NIMH grant (MH 34337) and an NIMH Clinical Research Center Award (MH 30899-04) to Langley Porter Psychiatric Institute's Center for the Study of Neuroses, at the University of California School of Medicine, San Francisco. The Center is directed by Mardi Horowitz and codirected by Nancy Kaltreider. The information reported here is also based on the collaborative efforts of Nancy Wilner, Charles Marmar, Anthony Leong, Janice Krupnick, Daniel Weiss, Kathryn DeWitt, John Starkweather, Robert Wallerstein, and Matthew Holden.

States of intrusion and of denial or avoidance do not follow each other in a strict, unvaried pattern but rather oscillate in ways particular to each person. Nonetheless, phases have a general tendency that may be described. An initial period of outcry may occur, which is then usually followed by denial states. Intrusive states follow after this latency period and often oscillate with denial states. During this oscillation the frequency and intensity of each of these states is often reduced. When a relative baseline is reached during this period of working through, completion can be said to have occurred. The person can contemplate the events or put them out of mind at will, without frequent entry into conspicuous and intense intrusion or denial states.

A simple diagram of these phasic tendencies is found in Figure 1. As indicated above, what is called "working through" may involve many transitions between states of denial and intrusion, with gradual reduction in the intensity of these states. Completion is a restoration of the kinds of states present before the event disturbed equilibrium. Insofar as their severity is consonant with the meaning of these events to the person, such states of denial and intrusion are normal. Pathological states are those that are unusually intense and, at the same time, are maladaptive to the person. These are also shown in Figure 1. In Tables 1 and 2, the overall pattern of signs and symptoms of denial and intrusive states are organized by the same classification. These figures and tables are derived from an expanded review (Horowitz, 1976). Some ideas on the frequencies of various of these symptoms may be found in more recent publications (i.e., Horowitz, Wilner, & Alvarez, 1979; Horowitz, Wilner, Kaltreider, & Alvarez, 1980; and Horowitz, Krupnick, Kaltreider, Wilner, Leong, & Marmar, 1981).

1. Experiences during Intrusive and Denial States

As already mentioned, the qualities of experiences during these states will depend a great deal on the individual, but certain experiences and observations

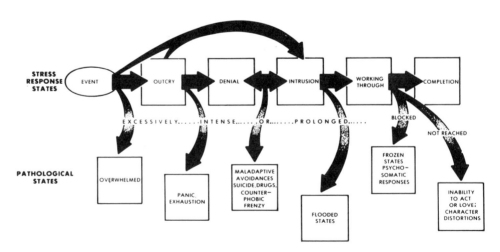

Figure 1. Phases of states following serious life events.

are common and can be contrasted. Note in Figure 1 how experiences of intrusion and denial are extremes, bracketing those of ordinary, less stressed states. This repeats the theme of in-control or adaptive states as bracketed by states that feel or appear to be under- or overcontrolled.

1.1. Perception and Attention

As summarized in Tables 1 and 2, aspects of perception and attention during denial states include varieties of daze and selected inattention. These qualities contrast with the excessive alertness and startle reactions of intrusive states. Daze and inattention include such patterns as staring blankly into meaningless space, failing to react appropriately to new stimuli, and an inner sense of clouding, graying, or loss of real vividness in perceptions of the surrounding world. There may be a quality of focusing on a diffuse background rather than on any central object. This may include lack of awareness of bodily sensations, such as absence of pain despite injury. In contrast, the excessive alertness noted during intrusive states may be reflected by constant scanning of the environment (hypervigilance) or by excessive arousal caused by relatively innocuous stimuli. The person feels and looks tensely expectant. Startle reactions range from flinching at noises or at being touched to the sudden assumption of a protective position when a stimulus reminds the person of the stressful event. A readiness to interpret a new stimulus as a repetition of the stressful life event may lead to illusions. These

Table 1. Experiences during Denial States

1. Perception and attention
   Daze
   Selective inattention
   Inability to appreciate significance of stimuli
   Sleep disturbances (e.g., too little or too much)

2. Consciousness of ideas and feelings related to the event
   Amnesia (complete or partial)
   Nonexperience

3. Conceptual attributes
   Disavowal of meanings of stimuli
   Loss of a realistic sense of appropriateness
   Constriction of associational width
   Inflexibility of organization of thought
   Fantasies to counteract reality

4. Emotional attributes
   Numbness

5. Somatic attributes
   Tension-inhibition responses of the autonomic nervous system, with felt sensations such as bowel symptoms, fatigue, headache

6. Action patterns
   Frantic overactivity
   Withdrawal

are misperceptions in which sensory perceptions of a person, object, or scene are constructed into mental images of something else. For example, a bush may be seen for a moment as an attacking person, a stranger may be misrecognized as someone who died.

During extreme forms of an intrusive state, mental images of any sensory quality (visual, auditory, olfactory, etc.) may be experienced as perceptions. In a hallucination, the person has sensations of smell, taste, touch, movement, sound, or sight which he or she take to be valid. In a pseudohallucination, the person is aware that these perceptions are not true signals of external reality, but he or she nonetheless reacts emotionally as if it were. Whether of hallucinatory or pseudohallucinatory quality, these unbidden perceptions often include felt presences, as of others in the room, even though they are dead. This is one source of various "paranormal phenomena" such as seeing or hearing "ghosts" of the deceased.

Unbidden perceptual experiences, so common in intrusive states after trauma, occur with highest intensity and frequency when the person is relaxing his or her control, as when lying down to sleep. The pseudohallucinations or hallucinations that occur at such times are called *hypnagogic phenomena*. They are frightening experiences not only because of their traumatic contents but because people associate hallucinations with madness and are afraid they are "going crazy." Actually, these hypnagogic phenomena are not serious portents of psychotic states; they are frequent after traumatic events and not uncommon even without a stressful event. Because denial states may often last for several weeks after a traumatic event, the unbidden images are often surprising. Those who have them may have been sure "it was over." In both denial and intrusive states, sleep disturbance is often present in the form of insomnia, sleeping "too much," or of experiencing nightmares or bad dreams.

Table 2. Experiences during Intrusive States

---

1. Perception and attention
   Hypervigilance, startle reactions
   Sleep and dream disturbances
2. Consciousness of ideas and feelings related to the event
   Intrusive-repetitive thoughts, emotions, and behaviors (illusions, pseudohallucinations, nightmares, ruminations, and repetitions)
3. Conceptual attributes
   Overgeneralization
   Inability to concentrate on other topics, preoccupation
   Confusion and disorganization
4. Emotional attributes
   Emotional attacks or "pangs"
5. Somatic attributes
   Sensations or symptoms of flight or flight readiness (or of exhaustion from chronic arousal) including tremor, nausea, diarrhea, sweating
6. Action patterns
   Search for lost persons or situations, compulsive repetitions

---

In the denial states, there may be complete or partial amnesia for the event or for trains of thought evoked during it. Complete amnesia for a serious event is rare, but avoidance of sectors of related ideas and feelings is common. The intrusion of images reenacting the event has already been contrasted with such avoidances. Such intrusions are accompanied by an experience of pangs of emotion.

1.2.1. Example

A young man heard that a friend of his had committed suicide. As he thought about this in various ways, one theme recurred. He regretted not having been more attentive when the friend was clearly depressed. He tried to put this out of his mind, and for a while he succeeded. Three weeks after the news of the death, he experienced anxiety states whenever he attempted to wash or lie down in bed. When he closed his eyes to wash his face, he would have a sudden visual image of the face of his dead friend. When he turned the lights off, closed his eyes, and attempted to relax, he would have a strong sense of his friend's presence in the room, standing at the foot of the bed. He began to sleep with his lights on and would not even attempt to sleep until quite late at night. A vicious cycle was created as fatigue mounted, causing the anxiety states to occur with more intensity and frequency until restful sleep became rare.

1.3. Conceptual Attributes of Intrusive and Denial States

During intrusive states, people often ruminate about the serious life event without coming any closer to resolving it. Themes related to the event overflow the immediate topic and contaminate reactions to other events and opportunities for action. This is called *overgeneralization*. It stands at an opposite pole from disavowal of the meanings of the stress event, noted during denial states. In the latter, there is often constriction rather than overextension of associations. With continued states of denial, people may carry on as if the traumatic event had not occurred or changed their lives. They maintain ordinary activities by playing a part—that is, by using automatic response patterns in a way that may appear mechanical and dehumanized to others familiar with their usual spontaneity. Temporary lapses in thought, and distortions such as minimization may be noted.

During denial states, recollection of the details or sequence of events is often inaccurate. There are areas of forgetting and disavowal of what is obvious, as well as the presence of fantasy as these states persist. For example, a person may make unrealistic plans about the future as a way of not facing the realistic implications of an amputation. In contrast, during the intrusive states, the person has difficulty in dispelling ideas once they come to mind. Even where there is a deliberate effort to think about the traumatic event, the person may find that he or she is unable to control awareness of the idea or topic, and emotions mount.

1.4. Emotional Attributes

This brings us to the extraordinary differences between the sensation of numbness during denial states and the emotional attacks or pangs that characterize the intrusive states. Numbness is not exactly the absence of a feeling but a present subjective sense of being "benumbed." That is, during this state some people feel as if they were surrounded with a kind of thickening shell, as if they are in a cocoon, especially in relation to potentially emotional and unsettling reactions to the serious life event. In contrast, the pang of emotion is an episode, wave, or "spell" of feeling. It is called a pang because it has a quality of waxing and waning. At its peak, the emotions are so intensely unpleasant as to seem unbearable, but the person comes to know that this peak will be followed by a reduction in intensity. This is what makes it possible to "live through it."

1.5. Somatic Attributes

During intrusive states there is often a fear of losing bodily control, usually related to sensations that arise from the hyperactivity of various bodily systems that are responding to the threat situation. This may include the sensation of urgency to urinate or even involuntary defecation. Although such sensations are typical of early reactions, fears of being unable to control vocalizations, arm movements, or facial expressions may endure much longer. Other common somatic responses include excessive sweating, diarrhea, tachycardia, vomiting, and rapid breathing. Denial states may also be associated with a variety of somatic changes and felt sensations such as constipation, fatigue, headache, or muscle pains. There is a great deal of clinical folk wisdom suggesting that some psychosomatic illnesses result from excessively prolonged efforts to avoid ideas and emotions instigated by a serious life event.

1.6. Action Patterns

Intrusive states sometimes contain reenactments of the serious life event. This is called *compulsive repetition*, a term referring to any behavior that repeats an aspect of the serious life event. Compulsive repetition may range from minor ticlike motions and gestures to a storylike acting out of what otherwise would be only a thought about the event. Sometimes this acting out includes such extremes as a complete reliving of the event in behavior without conscious awareness that this is what is taking place, even though it may be readily apparent to an observer. Minor repetitions such as facial expression and hand gestures related to the event are more common experiences. In the denial states, activity is also sometimes increased above usual levels as people engage in excessive sports, work, or sexual activities, in order to jam their channels of thinking and feeling and thus stifle any ideas and emotions related to the serious life event.

These various qualities found in intrusive and denial states are present most clearly after a person has been stressed by a serious life event. The same qualities may occur when the individual is stressed by internal conflicts as well as by current real losses or injuries.

2. Contents of Concern*

Here, we consider briefly the themes or constellations of ideas and emotions that are often aroused by serious life events. For a study on the numerical frequency of these concerns, see Krupnick and Horowitz (1981).

Any event is appraised and assimilated in relation to the past history and the current cognitive and emotional set of the person who experiences it. Idiosyncratic responses result. But human beings are as similar as they are different, and certain conflicts between wishes and realities seem fairly universal after stress events such as accidental injury, illness, and loss. Clinical studies reveal the themes discussed in the following paragraphs as common, albeit often unconscious, problems for the working-through process initiated by stressful life events. Such thematic contents appear as intrusive ideas, ideas that are warded off, and ideas that are deliberately contemplated.

2.1. Fear of Repetition

Any event that occurs may recur. The experience of anticipating painful stress events conflicts with the wish to avoid displeasure. People fear a real repetition and they also fear repetition in thought. A person who has had one heart attack fears another.

2.2. Shame over Helplessness or Emptiness

Fantasies of personal omnipotence express the wish for total control of one's life. One aspect of the opposite but complementary concept is the fear of helplessness.

Omnipotence, as in having an invulnerable body or being able to prevent disease breakdown in others, is unrealistic but is nonetheless a universal hope and sometimes a deeply felt personal belief. The failure to prevent a stress event such as an accident, or the breakdown that may follow an event such as an illness, are regarded as showing loss of control, and this conflicts with the wish to have power and mastery. People who have had a heart attack or back injury, for example, may apologize profusely because they cannot carry out garbage cans; they may even, inappropriately, carry them out to avoid a sense of shame for shirking their duty or becoming useless. After a fire has burned down the family house, parents may feel deflated in the eyes of their children now that the family is not as comfortable as it once was. The inability to master a stressful event may itself be regarded as a sign of personal defectiveness.

2.3. Rage at "the Source"

An important theme after stress events is anger at any symbolic figure who can, however irrationally, be considered responsible. A mother who cuts her

---

*Portions of the following text are derived from the syllabus from Psychiatry 100A, University of California, San Francisco Medical School, copyright by Mardi Horowitz, 1980.

finger while slicing meat may feel an impulse to say to a nearby child, "See what you made me do." The frequent, if not universal, phenomenon of asking, "Why did it happen?" after a stress event is associated with a need to find out who is to blame and who should be punished. Yet rage reactions commonly conflict with the person's sense of social morality. A common example is rage at a person who has fallen ill, a feeling in conflict with the recognition that it is not the victim's fault and that he or she ought to be helped, not blamed.

2.4. Guilt Feeling or Shame over Aggressive Impulses

Rage often leads to destructive fantasies directed toward anyone symbolically connected to the personal frustrations triggered by a stressful event, especially when the event itself included violent aspects. These destructive, vengeful fantasies may conflict with the person's own sense of conscience. Feelings of guilt or shame result, especially if hostility has been expressed impulsively. Negative feeling toward a person who has died, with reactive guilt or shame, is a common version of this conflict.

2.5. Fear of Aggressivity

There is another conflict between the destructive fantasies mentioned above and the wish to remain in control. A person fears being driven to act out fantasies impulsively in an out-of-control manner. For example, a soldier traumatized by repeated combat experiences often fears, on return to civilian life, that he will physically attack people who frustrate him only slightly.

2.6. Survivor Guilt

When others have been injured or killed, one is relieved to realize that one has been spared. Once again, at a level of magical thinking, there is an irrational belief that destiny chooses an allotment of victims, as if to placate the primitive gods, and that if one has eluded the Fates, it is at the expense of those inevitable victims who have not been spared. The wish to be a survivor conflicts with moral attitudes, leading to self-castigation for selfishness.

2.7. Fear of Identification or Merger with Victims

A complementary theme related to survivor guilt is the fear of not being separate from the victims. At a primitive level of thinking, people do not conceive of themselves as being discretely separate. If an event has hurt another, there is a primitive fear that it may hurt oneself. This may set in motion a train of thought—even in conflict with reality—that assumes the self as victim.

Any painful stress event includes an element of loss and conflicts with the universal wish for permanence, safety, and satisfaction. The loss may be another person, an external resource, or an aspect of the self. Naturally, some losses are more symbolic than real, but they are no less important. A person who has been laid off from work—not for personal reasons but because a plant has closed—may suffer a loss of self-esteem as a result of losing his or her work role.

2.9. Recapitulation

The common forms and contents of psychological reactions to stress have been summarized above. One should learn to look for these configurations in patients after they have experienced serious life events or after they have been given serious news about the state of their health. *It is especially important to know the signs and symptoms of the denial and intrusion phases noted above and to realize how pervasive the stage of denial may be.* The health care professional often has to repeat the information given the patient at various times and in various doses before it is completely "heard" by the patient.

Intrusive experiences, such as unwelcome fantasy images related to the stressful event, should be asked about directly, as patients often do not report such matters spontaneously. The common concerns of patients are often surprising because some of them seem irrational. Health care professionals are most often surprised by the angry response of some patients and make a common error of being personally hurt by it rather than understanding it as a stress response and maintaining rapport as the patient attempts to master the stressful situation.

3. Coping

Coping is a term that usually suggests that the person is reacting as adaptively as possible to a stress event. In the theoretical system of Kroeber (1963) and Haan (1977), coping is regarded as a more adaptive and conscious process than is a defense. Here, however, we do not make a definite distinction between coping and defense mechanisms; rather, we regard them as different perspectives or value judgments about essentially the same mental processes.

Is a process of psychological defense or a strategy of coping adaptive or maladaptive? Defensive denial can be adaptive when it prevents a person from being overwhelmed with panic; at the same time, it can be maladaptive when it tends to limit the scope of information to be used in realistic planning. To make matters more complex, the average person processes information at various levels of awareness and in relation to a variety of belief systems. For example, a person who has been hospitalized after a heart attack may be aware of the threat posed by this illness and yet be operating as if it were only a minor one. The patient's conscious level of awareness of the danger may also fluctuate.

When the chief resident comes by on ward rounds, the patient may converse in a way that indicates a full understanding of the existing situation. Yet moments later, in conversation with the nurse, the patient may insist on getting out of bed, displaying belief that the illness is not serious. Repeated conversations with the same physician may occur when the patient is in different states of mind. A conversation on Tuesday may be based on a realistic appraisal of changes in life patterns that will be necessary because of illness. A conversation on Wednesday may surprise the physician: the patient may reveal that, at some level, the implications of the illness are still being denied. The denial can be said to be adaptive in reducing fear and allowing pacing of decisions, and that may help the patient feel less troubled, but postponing awareness of what must be faced may also lead to hazardous choices of action.

Strategies for coping with or defending against threats involve choices about what topics to think about and to act on. (For some quantitative data, see also Horowitz & Wilner, 1980.) For example, one common reaction to serious news is to think intensively about it; another is to avoid thinking about it at all. By switching between thinking about it and not thinking about it, people can dose themselves with information and thereby modulate their emotional responses. For example, relatives of a patient who is undergoing serious surgery must wait in the hospital to discover the outcome of the surgical procedure. They can think about good outcomes as well as the possibility of death. Thinking about the surgery and the possibility of death will raise their fear and anxiety. By talking, reading, or thinking about other topics, they may temporarily relieve their anxiety about the threatening situation and recover emotional stability.

Another way of coping is to alter the time period that one is contemplating. For example, a person facing an unpleasant procedure—such as having an illuminated viewing tube passed down the throat into the lungs—may focus on an extremely short time interval like 2 or 3 seconds; such a person may contemplate the present moment in terms of long stretches of time, so that the length of time for the procedure pales in significance. Another common coping or defensive strategy is to switch back and forth between reality thinking and fantasy thinking. This type of oscillation between reality-oriented thought and fantasy is also common after bereavement. For example, after the death of a loved one, a person may have pleasant memories of the previous relationship or may fantasize some kind of future restoration of the lost person. Either technique may help the person to cope with intense grief. A different method of coping with the situation might be to think realistically about the many life changes that now have to take place, including alteration of day-to-day routines.

Another coping strategy involves using different modalities of thought. A person who usually thinks in words may use more visual imagery in very stressful situations. For example, a person who is in the hospital, unable to eat and being maintained only with intravenous fluids, may temporarily reduce hunger by mentally smelling or visualizing a favorite meal. The other extreme can also be present in states of stress. That is, a person who has been in an automobile accident and has seen her own or others' injured bodies may attempt to avoid all mental images and to deal with the accident verbally in order to avoid the emotions accompanying the visual recollection.

Still another common coping strategy is to change one's level of activation as in changing states of consciousness. One may become more aroused, which can be maladaptive as the person becomes hypervigilant; or one may have increased periods of sleep, lapsing into a kind of reduced activity state that seems almost like hibernation. Shifts in roles for the self and in the role relationships between oneself and others also provide opportunities for both coping and defensive behavior. When a person is placed in a hospital, lies in bed, and is attended in various ways, there is a tendency to regression. This is not necessarily maladaptive, although regression was listed as one of the mechanisms of defense. The person returns to a self-concept in which it is all right to depend on another for feeding, bathing, and toilet care; in this way, he or she does not have to feel ashamed about not being self-sufficient. Group attachments and opportunities for increased interpersonal relationships also help people to cope with stress. One advantage of having several patients in the same room is that they form bonds that help them all cope with their present situations. This advantage sometimes compensates for the disadvantages of the increased noise, disturbances, possibilities of contamination, and so forth.

People also seem to have some control over which of several possible self-images is dominant at a given moment. For example, under stress of illness, some people become more aloof, distant, and withdrawn rather than increasing their attachment to others. This may, however, be their own way of focusing energy on dealing with an internal situation. Others assume more than usual competency and behave more courageously, wisely, or altruistically than they do in their usual life circumstances.

Seeking new information is an important way of coping with a stressful event (Janis & Mann, 1977). The physician gives the patient information about topics on which he or she is an expert and the patient is not. The interpretation of this information and help in appraising its implications are important activities of the physician, who must assure patients that, as they gradually revise their goals and actions, the doctor–patient relationship will be maintained. Other members of the health team are often involved in helping the patient practice new behavior, just as a physical therapist establishes a supportive relationship with a patient learning to walk on crutches after an amputation or gradually learning to use a new prosthesis. The above are examples of common coping strategies. The achievement of humor and wisdom, the use of philosophical or religious perspectives during stressful situations, as well as the creation of new identities and capacities are some of the most impressive and unique methods of coping and personal growth in the face of crisis. (See also Moos, 1976.)

When the individual has experienced serious life events, exhibits pathological states of stress response (as illustrated in Figure 1), and has difficulty in coping within the existing social network, then treatment may be indicated. Some aspects of the therapy process are discussed below.

4. Treatment

Part of becoming a healing professional is learning to help people cope with stressful situations that cannot be immediately resolved. This ability takes time to develop and improves with experience. Difficult cases should always be referred to a mental health specialist for treatment.

4.1. Goals of Treatment for Stress Response Syndromes

We can state three general goals of therapy:

1. Despite the fact that a person may have experienced a loss of injury, an ideal goal would allow him or her to retain a sense of competence and self-worth. In doing so, the person would have to accept whatever unalterable limitations were placed on previous life plans. This should be done without loss of hope or a sense of meaning in life.
2. The person should continue progress in realistic and adaptive action. This would include maintenance of available relationships and development of new, adaptively useful ones.
3. In terms of long-range experience and behavior, an ideal goal for completion of working through reactions to a serious life event would be the use of that experience, even with its inherent loss, for some type of growth.

4.2. The Pattern of Psychological Treatment

After a serious life event, individuals usually reconsider the meanings and plans for response to that event in a manner that is systematic, step by step, and dosed. When emotional responses become excessive or threaten flooding, the person initiates control operations. Anxiety aroused by the threat of being flooded with powerful and painful emotions requires coping and defensive operations to reduce this danger. Here we will focus on some generalization about the function of such controls or such failures of control (for details, see Horowitz, 1976, 1979; Horowitz & Kaltreider, 1979, 1980).

If the mind has not been able to assimilate the sets of meanings, recollection counteracting these controls will occur. When the person cannot handle both the repetition compulsion and the defensive counters, help is sought. The therapist, after establishing a working alliance, assists the person in working through the natural responses to the event and the overall situation. In addition, efforts may be directed at modification of preexisting conflicts, developmental difficulties, and defensive styles that made the person unusually vulnerable to traumatization by this particular experience.

Therapy is dependent in part on establishing a safe relationship. Once this is done, work within therapy alters the status of the patient's controls. With a safe relationship and gradual modification of controls, the patient can then proceed to reappraise the serious life event, as well as the meaning associated with it, and make the necessary revisions of inner models of self and the world. As reappraisal and revision take place, the person is in a position to make new decisions and to engage in adaptive actions, trying out the altered models until they gradually become automatic. Overlapping with these processes is the necessity of working through reactions to the approaching loss of the therapist and the therapy.

There may be early testing by the patient both of the safety of the relationship and the therapist's ability to offer help in coping with symptoms. Most commonly, patients will seek help for intrusive symptoms. These symptoms can seem less overwhelming when the therapist provides an understanding of them and encourages the patient to work through feelings one step at a time rather than all at once. If anxiety, sleep disturbances, or depressions are profound and refractory, appropriate medications may be indicated. Patients who are more handicapped by their avoidance symptoms can be helped, through encouragement from the therapist, to recollect the stress event by way of associations while also working toward changing the attitudes that made the controls necessary.

When the person experiences relative failures of control, the activities of the therapist are geared toward helping the person regain a sense of the ability to be self-regulating. This is done through helping the patient to focus attention, by asking questions or repeating comments, and by clarifying statements. Most importantly, the process is helped by reconstructive interpretations—interpretations that help the patient to order facts in a sequence of time, to make appropriate linkages, and to separate reality from fantasy. Thus the threats of

Table 3. Priorities of Treatment

Priority	Patient's current state	Treatment goal
1	Under continuing impact of external stress event	If possible, terminate the external event or remove the patient from contact with it. If stress must continue, develop and maintain helping relationships. Help with decisions, plans, or working through of meanings.
2	Swings to intolerable levels: Ideational-emotional attacks Paralyzing denial and numbness	Reduce amplitude of swings to tolerable levels through reassurance and support or use of antianxiety medications or temporary sedatives at night. Allow person to talk repeatedly about the event or the person's reaction to it.
3	Frozen in overcontrol state of denial and numbness with or without intrusive repetitions	Help patient "dose" reexperience of event and implications; that is, help to remember for a time, put out of mind for a time, remember for a time, and so on. During periods of recollection, help patient organize as well as express experience; therapeutic relationship increases sense of safety in present so patient can allow contemplation of the event.
4	Able to experience and tolerate episodes of ideation and waves of emotion	Help patient work through associations: the conceptual, emotional, object relations, and self-image implications of the stress event. Help patient relate this stress event to prior threats, relationships, and self-concepts as well as future plans.
5	Able to work through ideas and emotions on one's own	Work through loss of therapeutic relationship. Terminate treatment.

reality may be decreased by reducing the adherence to fantasy expectations. Even when people are frightened by their own impending death, as when they have a serious and fatal illness, they can often cope with the reality of this courageously if they are helped to dissociate the real loss, real sadness, and real tragedy from imagined, fearsome consequences such as being entombed while alive, being helpless and deserted by people, and endlessly falling away from life with continued panic-stricken consciousness.

One aspect of working through a serious life event is review of the various self-images and role relationships that are associated with it. Because of the emotional pain aroused by this review, most patients will have interrupted some aspects of it. In therapy, the controls or defenses used in that interruption are set aside in a sequential manner. Most of this is done automatically by the patients themselves, once they have established a safe relationship with the therapist. When there is reluctance to do so, the therapist, using a repertoire of psycho-therapeutic interventions, may alter the defenses by interpreting them and the reasons for them, by increasing attention to warded-off material through inter-pretation and labeling, or by simply creating evocative situations into which the patient will bring the ideas and feelings that have been avoided. These oversim-plified principles of treatment are covered in more detail elsewhere (Horowitz, 1976, 1979) and are listed in Table 3 according to priorities of treatment.

4.3. Summary

Serious life events may set in motion a psychological process that manifests itself by variations in mental states. Most frequently, states of mind involve intrusive and avoidant experiences. These intrusive and avoidance or denial periods often occur in phases that typify many stress response syndromes. To these periods of strain, the person brings his or her particular personality, es-pecially as evidenced by modes of coping with and defending against the increase in stress and the implications of the specific life event. Psychotherapy is often the treatment of choice when a person develops pathological intensifications of these stress response syndromes.

5. References

Cohen, F. Personality, stress and the development of physical illness. In G. Stone, F. Cohen, & N. Adler (Eds.), *Health psychology—A handbook*. San Francisco: Jossey-Bass, 1979.

Haan, N. *Coping and defending*. New York: Academic Press, 1977.

Horowitz, M. J. *Stress response syndromes*. New York: Jason Aronson, 1976.

Horowitz, M. J. *States of mind*. New York: Plenum Press, 1979.

Horowitz, M. J., & Kaltreider, N. Brief therapy of stress response syndromes—liaison psychiatry. In *Psychiatric clinics of North America*. Philadelphia: Saunders, 1979.

Horowitz, M. J., & Kaltreider, N. Brief treatment of posttraumatic stress disorders. *New Directions for Mental Health Services*, 1980, *6*, 67–79.

Horowitz, M. J., & Wilner, N. Life events, stress, and coping. In L. Poone (Ed.), *Aging in the 1980's: Psychological issues*. Washington, D.C.: American Psychological Association, 1980.

Horowitz, M. J., Wilner, N., & Alvarez, W. Impact of event scale: A measure of subjective stress. *Psychosomatic Medicine*, 1979, *41*, 209–218.

Horowitz, M. J., Wilner, N., Marmar, C., & Krupnick, J. Pathological grief and the activation of latent self-images. *American Journal of Psychiatry*, 1980, *137*, 1157–1162.

Horowitz, M. J., Wilner, N., Kaltreider, N., & Alvarez, W. Signs and symptoms of post-traumatic stress disorders. *Archives of General Psychiatry*, 1980, *37*, 85–92.

Horowitz, M. J., Krupnick, J., Kaltreider, N., Wilner, N., Leong, A., & Marmar, C. Initial psychological response to death of a parent. *Archives of General Psychiatry*, 1981, *38*, 316–323.

Janis, I. L. *Stress and Frustration.* New York: Harcourt Brace Jovanovich, 1971.

Janis, I. L., & Mann, L. *Decision making: A psychological analysis of conflict, choice, and commitment.* New York: Free Press, 1977.

Kroeber, T. The coping functions of the ego mechanisms. In R. White (Ed.), *The study of lives.* New York: Atherton Press, 1963.

Krupnick, J., & Horowitz, M. J. Stress response syndromes: Recurrent themes. *Archives of General Psychiatry*, 1981, *38*, 428–435.

Lazarus, R. *Psychological stress and the coping process.* New York: McGraw-Hill, 1966.

Moos, R. *Coping with physical illness.* New York: Plenum Press, 1977.

The Risks and Course of
Coronary Artery Disease
A Biopsychosocial Perspective

WILLIAM H. KAPLAN AND CHASE P. KIMBALL

The focus of this chapter is on the biological, psychological, and sociocultural risk factors that impinge on the patient suffering from coronary artery disease, a condition manifested clinically by angina pectoris, myocardial infarction, or sudden death. The first section of the chapter examines precursors to the illness in the premorbid period, the time prior to the onset of signs and symptoms of coronary artery disease. Although a comprehensive review of the literature concerning the psychological and social risk factors of coronary artery disease is beyond the scope of this chapter, a wealth of research data of varying quality and sometimes contradictory results can be highlighted. For a more thorough review, one can look to articles by Jenkins (1971; 1976a,b), which study the literature through 1976.

From an economic point of view, one can appreciate the tremendous interest in identifying risk factors which, it is hoped, can be manipulated to reduce the incidence of coronary artery disease. This condition, the leading cause of death in the United States, killed 720,000 people in 1976 and represented an estimated total cost of $54 billion (Cooper & Rice, 1976). One frustration has been that established risk factors—such as hypertension, cigarette smoking, obesity, physical inactivity, diabetes mellitus, elevations of serum cholesterol and low-density lipoproteins, and a family history of coronary artery disease—fail to predict a significant number of people who develop coronary artery disease (Jenkins, 1971,

WILLIAM H. KAPLAN • Department of Psychiatry, University of Chicago, Chicago, Illinois 60637. CHASE P. KIMBALL • Division of Biological Sciences and College of the University of Chicago, Chicago, Illinois 60637.

1976a). For example, there was a large study (Keys, Aravanis, Blackburn, van Buchem, Buzina, Djordjevic, Fidanza, Karvonen, Menotti, Puddu, & Taylor, 1972a), comparing men 40 to 59 years of age in the United States and Europe who were free from coronary artery disease. At follow-up 5 years later, approximately twice as many Americans showed clear evidence of coronary artery disease as did Europeans matched for age, blood pressure, serum cholesterol, smoking habits, body weight, and level of physical activity. Although antihypertensive medication, increased physical activity, restriction of caloric intake and saturated fats, and reduction in cigarette smoking have had a salutary effect on the alarming incidence of coronary artery disease among those in the prime of life, the disease continues to afflict Americans, especially males, at a disturbing rate.

Another precursor that seems to have predictive value is the coronary-prone behavior pattern, known as Type A, typified by an individual who is highly competitive, hard-working, impatient and time-conscious, excessively driven to achieve, visibly tense, and who displays a tendency to suppress hostility. The association between personality traits and a predisposition to coronary artery disease was observed as early as 1896 by William Osler, M.D. (1896), who noted that angina was most likely to be seen in the vigorous, keen, and ambitious man "whose engine is always set at full speed ahead." As discussed by Goldband, Katkin, and Morell (1979), the Type A personality appears prone to coronary artery disease because of a hypersensitivity to stress that seems to result in an acceleration in the formation of thrombi and of atherosclerotic plaque as well as in hemodynamic changes. Nevertheless, the limitation with the "prone personality" paradigm is that it says little about the relationship between behavior and physiologic events. Much convincing research is now revealing the pathophysiologic link between personality traits, stressors, and coronary artery disease. For example, Glass (1977) has proposed the beta-adrenergic response to specific stressors as mediating between a coronary-prone behavior pattern and coronary artery disease. This chapter examines other relevant research that addresses the issue of finding a more direct measure of risk for coronary artery disease.

Social status, social mobility, status incongruity, life dissatisfactions, levels of anxiety, and neurotic traits have all been shown to have some degree of correlative value. Psychological stressors such as death in a family, loss of a job, or relocation of home may also have predictive value. The effects of these environmental stressors may be mitigated by various coping mechanisms and social supports.

Thus, one's frame of mind—that is, how the individual receives and processes stimuli from the environment—has a profound effect on the development of coronary artery disease. An environmental stimulus may elicit specific responses from the endocrine and autonomic nervous systems, responses that may stress a specific organ system which has been sensitized by predisposing genetic factors and epigenetic psychological experiences. A given stimulus may be a stressor that carries with it specific pathological implications for one individual whereas, for another, this same stimulus may cause activation of the body without untoward physiologic or psychological effects. For the latter, one may observe that the experience has coping and adaptive functions. This issue of stress versus activation is covered in detail in a recent book edited by Ursin, Baade, and Levine (1978).

Risks for the coronary patient in the illness-onset and hospital phases of the disease are influenced by personality type, the nature of defense mechanisms (such as denial), and the presence of psychopathology. The hospital course may carry additional risks in the presence of an acute-phase delirium, marked anxiety, or major depressive syndrome. The course of the illness can be exacerbated by the roles of the intensive and coronary care units, with their potential for exposing the patient to sensory deprivation and extraordinary types of sensory input that may cause considerable stress and lead to psychological complications. Sleep deprivation during the hospital phase has been shown to compromise the psychologic and physiologic adjustment of the patient who has sustained a myocardial infarction. There are iatrogenic risks to recovery stemming not only from hospital environments but also from surgery and medications. For example, psychotropic medications intended to relax and sedate a patient may have the opposite effect, resulting in agitation, confusion, and delirium.

The posthospital phase may be a period of recovery and rehabilitation or a period of nonrecovery, with deterioration or a recurrence of symptoms. One may find a seemingly paradoxical response to medical and surgical interventions in which a good physiologic outcome is documented yet the patient maintains a poor level of psychosocial functioning. What are the effective rehabilitative interventions? Can exercise, psychotherapy, and education about disease precursors reduce risk factors, improve prognosis of recovery, and militate against new cardiovascular insults?

1. Premorbid Phase: Who Is at Risk?

1.1. Mind over Body

What composite of the individual at risk for coronary artery disease can be drawn from available data regarding genetic makeup, personal habits, social and cultural biases, and personality structure? Much of the research associating a causal link between the coronary-prone personality and the development of coronary artery disease is contaminated by its retrospective nature. It raises the chicken-and-egg dilemma: that is, to what extent does coronary disease itself, perhaps even before clinical symptoms are apparent, dictate features of behavior, defensive structure, and personality? Prospective epidemiologic studies help to clarify this confusion.

Eisenberg (1979) raises the question whether health is a state of mind. Vaillant (1979) reports results from the Grant Study of Adult Development which, over a 40-year period, followed male Harvard college students identified at the outset as healthy physically and psychologically. Of the 59 men from the ages of 21 to 46 with the best mental health, only two became chronically ill or died by the age of 53. In contrast, of the 48 men with the worst mental health over a corresponding period of time, 18 suffered from chronic illness or died. Vaillant points out that the relationship between previous mental health and subsequent risk of physical disease remains statistically significant independent of the effects of alcohol, tobacco, weight, and family history of longevity.

Betz and Thomas (1979) in their 30-year follow-up study of white male medical students at Johns Hopkins suggest that temperament is a valid predictor of vulnerability to premature disease and death. The students fell into three discrete temperament categories on various psychological measures, allowing them to be defined as an Alpha Group, which was slow and solid; a Beta Group, which was rapid and facile; and a Gamma Group, which was irregular and uneven. There were significant differences in health outcomes among the three groups, with the Beta Type having acquired the fewest major physical disorders and the Gamma Type the most. For example, in one sample in which the rater of temperament remained blind to the health or disorder status of the subjects, none of the 39 Beta Type individuals had clinical evidence of coronary artery disease whereas eleven out of 60 of the Gamma Group did, with 6 dying of coronary occlusion. This sample population was drawn from the medical student classes of 1949 to 1964 and examined in 1978.

Medalie, Kahn, Neufeld, Riss, and Goldbourt (1973) followed 10,000 male Israeli government employees over a 5-year period to examine first myocardial infarctions during the study period. The study revealed the statistical significance of traditional risk factors such as obesity, smoking, elevated serum cholesterol, and high blood pressure. However, other findings point to sociocultural factors as risks. For example, the increased risk of myocardial infarction in all first-generation Israelis with a reduced incidence rate in the second generation suggests the stress of adjusting to a new type of society. Those who reported serious problems relating to superiors at work and those who felt that superiors showed little appreciation for their performance developed significantly higher rates of coronary artery disease. Subjects who reported receiving love and support from their wives had a lower incidence of myocardial infarction during the study. Finally, the researchers discovered an inverse relationship between degree of religiosity and incidence of myocardial infarction.

Berkman and Syme (1979) investigated the relationship between social and community ties and mortality in a 9-year follow-up study of 6,928 adults. They conclude that those who lack meaningful relationships were at greater risk of dying. They used four sources to assess social relatedness: marriage, contacts with close friends and relatives, church membership, and group associations. Risk of death during the study period increased 2.3 times for men and 2.8 times for women who tended toward isolation. What makes these results all the more impressive is the fact that they were valid independent of self-reported health status at the start of the survey, socioeconomic status, smoking, alcohol consumption, obesity, and physical activity.

1.2. Risks Related to Biochemistry, Personal Habits, and Family History

Stern (1979) reports that mortality from coronary artery disease declined 20.7% in the United States between 1968 and 1976. Evidence suggests that the improvement relates to changes in diet with a resulting decline in serum cholesterol, decreased cigarette smoking, better control of hypertension and possibly an increase in physical exercise. The epidemiologic evidence supporting the predictive value of genetic and biological factors plus personal habits such as diet, exercise and smoking, as they relate to risk for coronary artery disease is reviewed by Hinkle (1967); Dawber and Kannel (1962); Epstein (1971a); and Hatch, Reissel, Poon-king, Canellos, Lees, and Hagopian (1966).

Paffenbarger, Notkin, Krueger, Wolf, Thorne, LeBauer, and Williams (1966) have presented data collected on 45,000 former University of Pennsylvania and Harvard University students to assess susceptibility to chronic disease. Comparisons were made between the first 590 males known to have died from coronary artery disease and 1,180 randomly chosen classmates of equivalent age. Identified precursors to coronary artery disease included heavy cigarette smoking, higher levels of blood pressure, increased body weight, early parental death, nonparticipation in varsity sports, and a higher emotional index. Paffenbarger and Wing (1969) compared 1,146 of these students who died from coronary artery disease with 2,292 classmates. Both cigarette smoking and nonparticipation in sports increased the risk of coronary death by 50%. The authors add that since the index of physical activity was arbitrarily taken as participation in a varsity sport, the protective effect of physical activity may well have been minimized (a broader classification of athletic endeavors might have made the risk of nonparticipation more dramatic). A systolic blood pressure greater than 130 mm Hg increased the risk 40%, and increased body weight, shortness of stature, and early parental death each increased the risk of fatal coronary heart disease by 30%.

A study by Dimsdale, Hutter, Gilbert, Hackett, Block, and Catanzano (1979) compared various risk-factor combinations to predict, prior to coronary angiography, anatomical narrowing of the coronary arteries. The risk-factor orientations were: (1) clinical, including items such as history of myocardial infarction, extent of angina, and EKG abnormalities; (2) epidemiological, consisting of fasting cholesterol and triglyceride levels, blood pressure, history of diabetes, family history of coronary artery disease, and smoking; and (3) psychosomatic, including factors such as anxiety, depression, anger, denial, life stress, and Type A personality features. The clinical orientation was the best predictor, but the epidemiological model also proved useful. In contrast, the psychosomatic factors were not accurate predictors of coronary artery disease.

The Albany and Framingham studies reviewed the smoking habits of 4,120 men (Doyle, Dawber, Kannel, Heslin, & Kahn, 1962). In both groups, the men were free of coronary artery disease at the first examination. Heavy cigarette smoking raised the risk of myocardial infarction threefold by comparison with nonsmokers, pipe and cigar smokers, and former cigarette smokers. Gordon, Kannel, McGee, and Dawber (1974) conclude that the rapid drop in the incidence of coronary artery disease in men who stop smoking means that cigarettes— which increase platelet adhesiveness, raise carboxyhemoglobin, and increase myocardial irritability, all of which may contribute to myocardial infarction or sudden death—have a "reversible triggering effect."

For those who fear that the risk factors for coronary artery disease must include most of life's indulgences, one can take some relief from the study by Yano, Rhoads, and Kagan (1977), who have been following 7,705 Japanese men living in Hawaii. Their analysis of 294 new cases of coronary artery disease showed a positive association between coffee consumption and risk, but this became statistically insignificant when cigarette smoking was considered. If coffee drinkers can take some small consolation in that finding, drinkers of moderate amounts of alcohol may rejoice because there was a strong negative association between such consumption and the risk of nonfatal myocardial infarction and death from coronary artery disease. This negative association remained significant even when considering smoking and other established risk factors. This benefit from alcohol may stem from its effect on lipid metabolism. In the present cohort population, the authors found a positive correlation to high-density lipoprotein (HDL) and a negative association to low-density lipoprotein (LDL) when compared with alcohol intake. The authors have previously demonstrated that these two lipoproteins, acting independently and in opposite directions, are strongly associated with the risk of coronary artery disease (Rhoads, Gulbrandsen, & Kagan, 1976).

There is impressive physiologic and epidemiologic evidence that exercise serves a protective role with respect to coronary heart disease. Hartung, Foreyt, Mitchell, Vlasek, and Grotto (1980) report a study comparing three groups of healthy middle-aged men: namely, marathon runners, joggers, and inactive men. Differences in meat consumption did not correlate in a statistically significant manner with HDL differences in these men; the HDL for marathon runners was 65 mg per deciliter; joggers, 58 mg per deciliter; and inactive men, 43 mg per deciliter. The conclusion is that the running, not diet, accounts for the differences in HDL. The extent of running also predicted well the HDL: total cholesterol rates and had a negative correlation to total cholesterol.

Williams, Logue, Lewis, Barton, Stead, Wallace, and Pizzo (1980) studied the effects of physical conditioning on fibrinolytic activity. After a 10-week physical conditioning program, significant increases in fibrinolytic activity following venous occlusion using a blood pressure cuff were noted. The most marked rises occurred in women, people with initially low levels of stimulated fibrinolysis, and those with initially low physical activity. The authors conclude that physical exercise, by augmenting the fibrinolytic response to a thrombotic stress (simulated in the study by venous occlusion), may account in part for the reduction in risk for coronary artery disease in the physically active.

Obesity has been a variable associated with increased risk, but as Keys, Aravanis, Blackburn, van Buchem, Buzino, Djordjevic, Fidanza, Karvonen, Menotti, Puddu, and Taylor (1972b) reported in a large prospective study of men aged 40 through 59, obesity did not contribute significantly to prediction of coronary artery disease when factors of age, blood pressure, serum cholesterol, and smoking were included. Gordon, Castelli, Hjortland, Kannel, and Dawber (1977) examined the roles of diabetes, blood lipids and obesity as risk factors for women aged 49 to 82 in the Framingham Study. Women with diabetes and a low HDL cholesterol level were at increased risk for developing coronary artery disease. Both the diabetes and lipoprotein profile correlated strongly with obesity. They concluded that a low HDL with diabetes mellitus raised women's risk of acquiring coronary artery disease above that of men.

Much research has tried to tease out the relative influences of "state versus trait" characteristics, that is, the environmental and clinical picture versus innate, enduring biological characteristics as predictors of risk. For example, Medalie, Levene, Papier, Goldbourt, Dreyfuss, Oran, Neufeld, and Riss (1971), in their 5-year prospective study of 10,000 male Israeli government employees, have found a difference in genetic makeup identified by blood groups for predicting increased vulnerability. Men belonging to blood groups A1, B, A1B, or Jk^{a-} had somewhat higher incident rates for angina and myocardial infarction. The combination blood group A1BJk^{a-} seemed to sustain a strikingly higher rate of clinical coronary artery disease.

However, a consistent, all-inclusive biological marker for coronary artery disease remains elusive. Rather, the evidence seems to point to the significance of the interplay between states and traits. Epstein (1971b) notes that heredity must be a risk factor in order to explain the biological variation (Gaussian distribution) for variables such as blood pressure and cholesterol in fairly homogenous environments. Russek and Russek (1972) observe that the atherogenicity of emotional stress seems linked to diets high in animal fat. Without the dietary changes, certain racial groups—for example, Chinese, Japanese, and Koreans—seem at a relatively low risk for coronary artery disease.

Epidemiologic studies of coronary artery disease in men of Japanese ancestry residing in Japan, Hawaii, and California lend further evidence to the intermingling effects of state and trait. Mortality from coronary artery disease increases in this population from Japan to Hawaii to California (Syme, Marmot, Kagan, Kato, & Rhoads, 1975). Serum cholesterol, glucose, uric acid, and triglycerides were lower for men in Japan by comparison with Hawaii and California (Nichaman, Hamilton, Kagan, Grier, Sachs, & Syme, 1976). A comparison of the three groups for definite plus possible incidence of coronary artery disease revealed prevalence rates per 1,000 in Japan (25.4), Hawaii (34.7), and California (44.6), for a male population aged 45 to 69. This gradient is not well explained by traditional risk factors, since prevalence of hypertension in the Japan group was intermediate to that in Hawaii and California. In addition, cigarette smoking and diabetes are relatively common in Japan. Therefore, differences in diet, patterns of work, and life-style would seem to be critical variables that supersede genetic makeup and at least some of the traditional risk factors (Marmot, Syme, Kagan, Kato, Cohen, & Belsky, 1975).

The hereditary influence for risk of acquiring coronary heart disease is pronounced in a Norwegian population of men aged 20 to 49 years. Førde and Thelle (1977) found that the risk of myocardial infarction in a male before age 50 increased 12.8 times if he had a first-degree female relative with a myocardial infarction and 5.5 times if the relative was male. Thus, when environmental factors are neutralized by the homogeneity of the life experience, in contrast to the males of Japanese ancestry reported earlier, a genetic variable as a risk factor becomes more prominent.

1.3. The Risk of the Coronary-Prone Behavior Pattern

Friedman and Rosenman (1959) postulated that a particular constellation of behaviors characterized by an intense drive to achieve, a high degree of competitiveness, preoccupation with meeting deadlines, and extraordinary mental and physical alertness made one vulnerable to coronary artery disease, either in association with other risk factors or by inducing them. They defined the Type A personality as having these features and the Type B as manifesting an opposite behavior pattern. They found the Type A group to have a much higher incidence of coronary artery disease and higher serum cholesterol. Friedman, Rosenman, Straus, Wurm, and Kositchek (1968) studied at autopsy the coronary arteries of 51 men who had been enrolled in a prospective study to examine the relationship between coronary artery disease and type of behavior pattern. They concluded that those who exhibited a Type A personality in life had a sixfold increased risk of dying from coronary artery disease than subjects who were classified as Type B. Irrespective of the cause of death, the Type A personality was six times as likely to have severe atherosclerosis. To standardize assessment of this coronary-prone behavior pattern, a self-administered, machine-scored test questionnaire called the Jenkins Activity Survey (JAS) was developed. Jenkins, Zyzanski, and Rosenman (1971) reported on the success of the JAS for men in the Western Collaborative Group Study, 2,800 of whom took the test twice, in 1965 and 1966. Men who had suffered from coronary artery disease prior to taking the JAS scored significantly higher for the Type A profile than controls. Those with evidence of coronary artery disease showed a greater propensity for competitiveness, responsibility, and a hard-driving quality.

Brand, Rosenman, Sholtz, and Friedman (1976) provided further convincing evidence of the powerful tool for predicting risk that is provided by the Type A–Type B model. Again using the Western Collaborative Group Study, 257 men who at intake were between the ages of 39 and 59 were found to have developed coronary artery disease at follow up 8½ years later. Removal of the excess risk associated with Type A behavior would correspond to a 31% reduction in the incidence of coronary artery disease. The direct association between this behavior pattern and coronary artery disease gives the Type A an approximate relative risk twice that of the Type B.

Jenkins, Zyzanski, and Rosenman (1976) demonstrated the effectiveness of the Type A pattern for predicting recurrent coronary artery disease. Type A behavior, the number of cigarettes smoked, and serum cholesterol were significant discriminators between men who developed recurrent disease versus those with only a single event of coronary artery disease. The Type A pattern proved to be the strongest single predictor of coronary artery disease among the variables examined. The adaptability of the JAS for assessing progression of disease is demonstrated in a study by Krantz, Sanmarco, Selvester, and Matthews (1979), which examined patients who underwent repeat coronary angiograms within an average interval of 17 months. There was a significant positive association between the JAS Type A score and progression of coronary artery disease. Furthermore, Type B subjects were unlikely to show progression of disease.

In conclusion, the Type A model has much predictive value in identifying risk for the development of recurrence of coronary artery disease, but it does not reveal the pathophysiologic process by which it operates.

2. Biological Mediators of Coronary Artery Disease

A clearer understanding of physiologic events in the formation of atherosclerosis will assess the utility of the coronary-prone behavior pattern as a predictor of coronary artery disease and perhaps pave the way to a more precise, physiologic measure of risk.

Manuck, Craft, and Gold (1978) conducted experiments showing that Type A males had greater elevations of systolic blood pressure when introduced to a difficult cognitive task than Type B males. The cold-pressor test used by Keys, Taylor, Blackburn, Brozek, Anderson, and Simonson (1971) is a physiologic measure unconnected to the Type A behavior pattern. Blood pressure changes are measured in the subject after placing a forearm in ice water. This experiment, as a 20-year prospective study, revealed the rise in diastolic blood pressure to be a greater predictor of risk for coronary artery disease than any variable studied, including serum cholesterol, age, resting blood pressure, or smoking.

The discharge of catecholamines by the sympathetic adrenergic nervous system when the individual sustains stress sets off a cascade of events associated with coronary artery disease, including blood pressure elevation. The elevation of catecholamines raises cholesterol, lipoproteins, triglycerides, and free fatty acids. Atheromatous plaque may form in vessel walls at an augmented rate due to an increase in circulating fats. Free fatty acids may be responsible for intravascular platelet aggregation which can evolve into narrowing and occlusion of the coronary arteries (Haft & Fani, 1973; Stimmel, 1979). Psychologic stress which results in elevation of catecholamines has been shown to cause EKG abnormalities that are potentially serious, especially in the face of existing coronary artery disease (Stimmel, 1979; Froberg, Karlsson, Levi, Lidberg, & Seeman, 1970; Taggart, Carruthers, & Someiville, 1973; Lown, DeSilva, & Lensen, 1978).

3. Psychosocial Risk Factors of Coronary Artery Disease

As noted in the introduction, Jenkins does a thorough review of the relevant literature in this area up to 1976. A burgeoning of research in this field followed the development of the Social Readjustment Rating Scale by Holmes and Rahe (1967). The assumption was made that stressful life events can have a deleterious effect on one's health by triggering psychophysiologic reactions to environmental stimuli. The scheme owed a debt to the work of Adolf Meyer who, in the early part of this century, proposed the life chart; it examined the way in which biological, psychological, and sociological phenomena interacted to affect one's health and predisposition to disease. The Social Readjustment Rating Scale has shown that losses such as death of a spouse, divorce, or marital separation are the stresses consistently ranked most severe. However, many of the items on the scale carry no obvious negative connotation but simply represent life change— for example, a new home, school, or job. As the authors explain, the focus of the scale is to measure significant life changes from the existing state, without concern for psychological meaning or social desirability. Masuda and Holmes (1978) review the literature on the association between illness and accumulation of life change. They conclude that the evidence supports the notion that the greater the magnitude of life change, the greater the risk of illness. Nuckolls, Cassel, and Kaplan (1972) observed that pregnant women with high life-stress scores but a strong social support network had significantly fewer complications during the remainder of the pregnancy and delivery than pregnant women with similar stress scores but low social support scores.

Shekelle, Ostfeld, and Oglesby (1969) found a positive association between social status incongruity and incidence of coronary artery disease. Types of incongruity examined included "class of origin different from present social class," "husband's educational status less than wife's," and "husband's class of origin less than wife's." The cohort consisted of 1,472 middle-aged white males employed by the same company who were free of clinical coronary artery disease when social status was measured. Men with four or five incongruities had six times the risk of developing coronary artery disease by the time of the 5-year follow-up. This association seemed independent of other risk factors such as cholesterol, blood pressure, blood glucose, age, weight, and smoking. Lehr, Messinger, and Rosenman (1973) report a difference in the religion of one's mother and father to be a discriminant variable as a risk factor for coronary artery disease. Gillum and Paffenbarger (1978) found, in a large sample of former Harvard University students, that when intergenerational mobility involved a father of low occupational status there was increased risk of fatal coronary artery disease or myocardial infarction. In contrast, intragenerational mobility representing changes in geography or occupation was unrelated to risk of coronary heart disease. Thus, life change, depending on constitutional and psychological factors, can have a positive and adaptive effect or else become a stress with pathological implications. Caffrey (1970), who studied psychosocial factors in monks who developed myocardial infarctions as opposed to those who did not, concluded that those who became ill were more likely than their healthy peers to be from families of lower socioeconomic levels and that their parents were less likely to have attended college. This seems to again suggest that upward social mobility can be internalized as a stress that becomes a risk factor.

Finally, a study of two adjacent, ethnically different communities seemed to find the more homogenous and stable of the two to have a lower incidence of deaths from coronary artery disease. Bruhn, Chandler, Miller, Wolf, and Lynn (1966) noted, in examining patients from the two communities, that they were similar with respect to many variables. Yet the community made up exclusively of Italian Americans, who had closely knit families with much mutual support and gregariousness, seemed less vulnerable to coronary artery disease. This may point to the increased risk of coronary artery disease in the absence of a strong social network system when other significant variables are equal.

4. Psychopathology as a Risk Factor

This is a controversial subject that is viewed by Jenkins (1976a). Coronary artery disease can frequently be associated with depression and anxiety. For example, Bakker and Levenson (1967) found that patients with angina pectoris were more likely to be compulsive and conforming, tense, antagonistic, and emotionally labile than others with coronary artery disease but without angina.

Dreyfuss, Dasberg, and Assael (1969) observed that myocardial infarction during psychiatric hospitalization occurred almost exclusively in depressed patients. Thus, over a 5-year period, 29 psychiatric patients (21 men and 8 women) suffered from coronary artery disease. Of these patients, 26 were diagnosed as having a depressive disorder, compared with only about 60% of all patients in their comparable age group. The authors note that since the majority of the patients developed their myocardial infarction long after the onset of their depression, the depression is unlikely to be a reaction to the physical illness.

As Jenkins (1976a) and Friedman, Ury, Klatsky, and Siegelaub (1974) caution, symptoms such as anxiety, depression, somaticizing, sleep disturbance, and emotional drain may not be risk factors at all but rather manifestations of subclinical early signs of coronary artery disease.

5. Hospital-Phase Risk Factors

5.1. Coronary Care Unit: Risks the Technology Fails to Treat

When one develops a major coronary heart disease event such as unstable angina or a myocardial infarction, one can expect to be placed in a technologically sophisticated coronary care unit. For the patient it may be an alien, disorienting and at times terrifying environment. In the early unstable and often critical period following the myocardial infarction, the coronary care unit will increase the chance of survival and recovery, but some caveats should be noted. Stross, Willis, Reynolds, Lewis, Schatz, Bellfy, and Copp (1976) conclude that coronary care units in small community hospitals admitting less than 60 patients with myocardial infarctions yearly have an estimated mortality rate approximately twice that of hospitals admitting more than 60 per year. Also, Goldberg, Szklo, and Tonascia (1979) point out that although the in-hospital fatality rate of those admitted to coronary care units in the Baltimore Standard Metropolitan Statistical Area hospitals dropped from 27.5% in 1966–1967 to 20% in 1971, there was no significant difference in long-term prognosis between the two patient populations.

Psychological response to the illness and the environment of the coronary care unit can have untoward consequences. Cassem and Hackett (1971) found that anxiety, depression, and behavior problems were the most frequent reasons for psychiatric consultation on the coronary care unit. The time distribution for these problems differed, with anxiety being most manifest on the first two days following admission; consultations for depression peaked on days three and four; and management problems had a bimodal distribution on days two and four. Anxiety was related to fears of dying and depression followed assaults to self-esteem; management problems related to excessive denial of illness, inappropriate euphoric or sexual behavior, and hostile-dependent conflicts with staff. The authors surmise that the 4% mortality rate—three times lower than expected—may be attributable to their interventions, which included medication such as tranquilizers, confrontation, environmental manipulation, explanatory clarification, anticipation of reactions, hypnosis, and the bolstering of optimism. The authors conclude that when psychological stress is reduced, the coronary patient's risk of death or exacerbation of illness is mitigated.

Further support for the concept that a psychiatric intervention can ameliorate risks associated with psychological stress in patients with coronary artery disease comes from Gruen (1975). The study involved 70 patients with a first myocardial infarction; these were randomized into a group given psychotherapy and a control group. The psychotherapy attempted to develop a genuine interest in the patient; support the patient's positive qualities; reassure the patient that reactions such as fear, anxiety and depression were expectable reactions to their catastrophic insult; and give positive reinforcement. Significant differences between the two groups were noted. Control patients stayed longer in the coronary care unit, suffered more from congestive heart failure, and were more prone to premature ventricular contractions and supraventricular arrhythmias. Nurse and physician reports indicated that the treated group exhibited fewer signs of weakness and depression. Psychological tests found the treated group more buoyant and optimistic. Finally, an interview 4 months after discharge found the treated group less anxious and more likely to have returned to normal activity.

The defense mechanism of denial, in which the individual rejects consciously or unconsciously some part of external reality in order to cope with fear and anxiety, may have beneficial or devastating consequences depending on when and to what extent it is used. If the patient postpones treatment or does not comply with essential treatment because the existence or seriousness of the illness is denied, tragic consequences may result. On the other hand, when it does not compromise treatment and it does successfully allay anxiety, the use of denial can be a stabilizing factor that reduces risk for the coronary patient (Hackett, Cassem, & Wishnie, 1968). In a study population of 345 men who suffered a first myocardial infarction, Croog, Shapiro, and Levine (1971) found that 20% denied, 3 weeks after hospitalization, that they had had a heart attack. This group tended to minimize symptoms and complied poorly with medical advice about work, rest, and smoking. White and Liddon (1972) found that in patients who were resuscitated following a cardiac arrest, the two most prominent psychological reactions were either major denial or a transcendental redirection of their lives, as through religious conversion. The three patients in the study who used major denial made good adjustments, which supports the protective function of this defense mechanism. For example, one man described the experience of his cardiac arrest as the best feeling he ever had. He denied any knowledge of his arrest or myocardial infarction until he was informed of it just before discharge. This patient experienced no manifest anxiety, sleep disturbances, or nightmares during or after the hospitalization.

5.2. The Risk of Getting Better: Transfer from the Coronary Care Unit

On the one hand, transfer from the coronary care unit to a general ward signals stabilization of arrhythmias and sufficient improvement from the coronary insult to warrant less intrusive and vigilant care. The extraordinary foreign sensory inputs (e.g., the visual and auditory stimulation from cardiac monitors, aortic balloon pumps, ventilators, and sophisticated computer equipment) and the frequent checks and tactile stimulation from nursing staff, who always remain in view of the patient, disrupt the patient's sleep pattern and equilibrium. However, these sensory inputs, to which the patient may form a dependency, eventually become signs of security in the face of massive anxiety. Kimball (1980) reported observing one patient who, on transfer from the coronary care unit, exhibited a symbiotic, psychotic attachment to the beeping sound from his cardiac monitor; this dependency resulted in decompensation at the time of transfer. Other patients who experience the transfer as a form of rejection or lack of caring by the staff may suffer undue psychological stress from this wound to the ego.

On the assumption that adrenergic activity contributes to coronary artery disease and the initiation of arrhythmias, Klein, Kliner, Zipes, Troyer, and Wallace (1968) studied the urinary excretion of catecholamines in patients transferred from the coronary care unit to a general medical ward. The authors admit that a rise in urinary catecholamines is not attributable solely to emotional stress, since factors such as increased physical activity would elevate them. Nevertheless, there was a temporal relationship between psychological stress and a rise in the catecholamines. Their study did suggest that this increased adrenergic activity put the patient at greater risk for cardiovascular insults such as reinfarction, coronary insufficiency, and dangerous arrhythmias.

Resnekov (1977) emphasizes that the patient remains at considerable risk even after discharge from the coronary care unit. He found that of 41 fatal in-hospital cases of myocardial infarction, 43% occurred on a cardiology ward after the patient had left the coronary care unit. Arrhythmias accounted for 40% of the deaths and cardiac failure for another 54%.

5.3. The Risk of Delirium

Delirium—a reversible state of altered consciousness of varying degrees of severity—can have devastating cosequences if not properly treated. Symptoms range from brief periods of disorientation, confusion, restlessness, and bizarre behavior to frank psychotic episodes with extreme agitation, paranoid ideation, and hallucinations. It is important not to mask symptoms or delay corrective procedures by the use of major tranquilizers (antipsychotic drugs such as phenothiazines) or minor ones (e.g., benzodiazepines) before a diagnosis of the etiologic factors is made. It is prudent to assume that the symptoms are part of an acute organic brain syndrome, which must be ruled out through its extensive differential diagnosis before the altered mental state can be described as functional.

Besides the metabolic and physiologic events that can cause the delirium, there are iatrogenic and environmental culprits. Parker and Hodge (1967) suggest that sensory monotony and sleep deprivation contribute to delirious states. Medications such as lidocaine, atropine, narcotics, sedatives, tranquilizers, steroids, and propranolol have been implicated in altered states of consciousness. Gershon, Goldstein, Moss, and van Kammen (1979) discuss psychotic symptoms associated with propranolol, a frequently used antihypertensive and antiarrhythmic drug. Two other antihypertensives, reserpine and alphamethyldopa, have been implicated in depression (Goodwin, Ebert, & Bunny, 1972).

Cassem and Hackett (1978) feel that delirium is a rare problem in the coronary care unit. In contrast, Kornfeld, Heller, Frank, Edie, and Barsa (1978), in a review of the literature, conclude that the incidence of delirium after coronary artery bypass surgery is 28%. The authors found severity of illness in the recovery room and a prior history of myocardial infarction to be correlated with the incidence of delirium.

Haloperidol is the drug of choice to deal with severe agitation and psychotic symptoms. Its effects on cardiopulmonary functions are milder than those of a phenothiazine (e.g., chlorpromazine) or a benzodiazepine (Sos & Cassem, 1980). A benzodiazepine such as diazepam may have the paradoxical effect of exacerbating symptoms in the acutely agitated patient. Supportive measures—such as the reassurance of a family member; orienting materials such as clock, calendar, and radio or television; empathic responses by staff and physicians; and reduction of distracting stimuli such as bright lights and noises—can ameliorate some of the symptoms arising from disorientation, sensory deprivation, and extraordinary sensory bombardment (Cassem & Hackett, 1978).

Dimsdale (1977) states that because we are uncertain of the exact relationship between emotional arousal and sudden death, it behooves the physician to treat patients routinely, especially on a coronary care unit, for manifestations of anxiety and emotional stress. Engel (1978) proposes a model to explain the relationship between emotional arousal and sudden death. Emotional arousal and a state of uncertainty activate two biologic systems, fight–flight and conservation–withdrawal. In a healthy individual, activation of these systems may cause a vasovagal reaction (fainting) or a benign arrhythmia. However, in a patient with coronary artery disease, which may increase the risk of a conduction disturbance, lethal arrhythmias may develop.

5.4. Disturbances of Sleep in the Coronary Care Unit

The irony and risk for the patient recuperating from a major coronary insult is that sleep deprivation, a common phenomenon in the coronary care unit, has detrimental consequences for recovery; yet the longer the patient remains critically ill, the more time he or she must spend on the unit (Dlin, Rosen, Dickstein, Lyons, & Fischer, 1971). Broughton and Baron (1978) monitored the sleep of patients on an intensive care unit following a myocardial infarction. These patients, in comparison to matched controls, experienced greater wakefulness, a lower REM sleep percent, fewer REM periods, longer REM latency, more awakenings, and decreased sleep efficiency. In sum, there was a generalized disruption of the biological sleep pattern. Most nocturnal anginal attacks occurred in non-REM sleep—in contrast to angina outside this immediate postinfarction period, which generally occurs in REM sleep.

In addition, the benzodiazepines routinely prescribed on many coronary care units may disrupt REM sleep and a rebound insomnia following their discontinuance may occur (Kales, Scharf, Kales, & Soldatos, 1979).

6. Posthospital Phase

6.1. Length of Hospitalization: Is More Better?

In view of the considerable risks, both physiological and emotional, to the coronary patient during hospitalization, flexibility is required to find a reasonable balance between the alien technologic and medical security of the hospital versus the familiarity and nurturance of home. McNeer, Wagner, Ginsburg, Wallace, McCants, and Conley (1978) report on the results of patients who were free of serious complications during the first 4 days after an acute myocardial infarction and who were discharged a week after admission. Follow-up revealed no significant complications at 3 weeks postdischarge. At 6 months, there had been no deaths and the patients seemed to be making a reasonable adjustment in their lives.

In an earlier study, Hutter, Sidel, Shine, and DeSanctis (1973) report no untoward effect from discharging uncomplicated myocardial infarction patients at 2 weeks instead of the traditional 3 weeks. At the 6-month follow-up of this prospective randomized study, there was no difference between the two groups, each with 69 participants, in frequency of return to work, anxiety, depression, or physiologic changes to the heart, such as reinfarction or angina. A British study (Harpur, Conner, Hamilton, Kellett, Galbraith, Murray, & Swallow, 1971) compared patients with uncomplicated myocardial infarctions discharged from the hospital on day 15 versus day 28. These two well-matched groups manifested no significant differences with respect to mortality, complication rates, ventricular aneurysm, or return to work.

6.2. Psychological Risks during Convalescence

Wishnie, Hackett, and Cassem (1971) report a follow-up study of 24 patients, originally evaluated on the coronary care unit, who were assessed during convalescence. Many of the patients felt unprepared for the emotional travail that occurred when they got home. Unexpected and prolonged weakness, boredom, depression, anxiety, and sleep disturbances characterized the early recovery period for many of them. Eating and smoking habits resisted modification. Of 14 patients who were determined to quit smoking, 9 had failed to do so at follow-up. Likewise, 7 of 9 who wished to lose weight had failed to accomplish this goal.

Hackett and Cassem (1975) note that depression is the main psychological complication of myocardial infarction during convalescence. They point out that this depression is normal, just as is grieving after any major loss; in this case, the loss comprises assaults on self-esteem, autonomy, and health. Such a depressive reaction should be limited to a few months, but unfortunately it often becomes protracted and debilitating. The authors suggest educating the patient about the nature of the disease, since distortions that can result in needless fear and depression often exist. Anticipating some of the expectable psychological reactions for the patient before release from the hospital can be beneficial. A program of physical conditioning builds confidence and reduces distressing manifestations of passivity and weakness. Medications such as anxiolytics and antidepressants can play a useful role when judiciously prescribed.

Gundle, Reeves, Tate, Raft, and McLauren (1979) present data on the psychosocial outcome following coronary artery bypass surgery. The authors assessed 30 such patients between 1 and 2 years after surgery. Despite the apparent physiologic success of the surgery as measured by a treadmill test, only 17% of those studied returned to work, only 43% were sexually active, and only 37% were euthymic. The authors observe that those who had symptoms of angina for more than 8 months prior to surgery made the poorest adjustments. They speculate that the surgery itself reinforced the notion of their infirmity; that is, the patients may have perceived such an invasive procedure as proof that they were in a dire condition.

Self-help groups, group psychotherapy, and educational programs have been established as part of the rehabilitation phase of coronary artery disease; but whether and for whom these programs are effective in allaying anxiety, reducing morbidity, and improving prognosis remains a moot point. For example, Wallace and Wallace (1977) unexpectedly found, on the basis of the Catell IPAT Anxiety Scale that group education in and out of the hospital following myocardial infarction raised anxiety levels for patients. The authors wonder whether anxiety is raised when there is emphasis on restrictions such as smoking or diet or when there are warnings about the need for exercise and changes in life-style. Adsett and Bruhn (1968) felt that short-term group psychotherapy for postinfarct patients and wives succeeded in improving psychosocial adaptation. Ventilations of feelings and conflicts seemed to be an important characteristic of this treatment.

A low level of education may expose the convalescing coronary patient to excessive risk. Over a 3-year period, Weinblatt, Ruberman, Goldberg, Frank, Shapiro, and Chaudhary (1978) followed 1,739 males who had suffered myocardial infarction. At the start of the study, each man was placed on a cardiac monitor for 1 hour. It was discovered that men with 8 years of education or less who demonstrated premature ventricular beats in the monitoring hour had greater than three times the risk of sudden coronary death compared to others who had exhibited the same arrhythmia complex but were better educated. These differences could not be explained by risk factors for the incidence of coronary artery disease or by clinical factors affecting prognosis.

Although the reasons for the increased mortality among the less educated participants in this study are unclear, one can imagine that those with fewer resources experience greater environmental stress in the face of social deprivations. One can speculate that this psychosocial stress is responsible for increased risk of arrhythmia formation and reinfarction. This chapter has cited evidence that points to the benefits of good social support networks, which may have been lacking in this group at increased risk. In sum, the difference may stem from the individual's physiologic response to environmental stimuli—a response that may be either pathologic or adaptive.

7. Conclusion

This chapter has focused on the course and biopsychosocial risk factors of coronary heart disease, the great epidemic killer of our time. Because this disease appears to be a product of our industrialized society, we are obliged to look for ways to change our environment and life-style. It seems ironic—after the extensive, well-controlled double-blind studies and sophisticated statistical analyses—that risks relate to dietary indiscretions (too much salt and fat, too many calories), smoking, and sedentary, overly stressful life-styles. Billions of dollars have been spent on coronary care units and elaborate diagnostic and treatment modalities, including coronary artery bypass surgery; one wonders whether they may represent steps into a bottomless economic pit, introducing a technology with only limited return on investment. If the benefits of the coronary care unit are only short-term and the coronary artery bypass corrects diminished blood flow to the myocardium only to produce people who are cardiac cripples, perhaps we are reaching the saturation point of technology. Should we not look elsewhere to decrease risk and improve prognosis?

It may wound our pride to observe that we have not moved beyond Socrates' insight that states of health and disease are related to life-style (Kass, 1975). How mundane, but also how refreshing it is to read that with proper sleep, good dietary habits, exercise, and moderation in alcohol consumption we can substantially extend our life span. Such a conclusion can be drawn, as Kass notes, from the epidemiological studies on health by Belloc and Breslow (1972, 1973). It is perversely ironic that one sign of the increasing equality between the sexes is the accelerating incidence of coronary heart disease among women. As women adopt habits formerly restricted to men, specifically with regard to heavy smoking, one finds a causal relationship to the increased incidence of coronary artery disease. This has been demonstrated in a study investigating the smoking habits of women under age 50 who suffered a myocardial infarction. They had not been using oral contraceptives and other risk factors were excluded. A woman who smoked 35 or more cigarettes per day increased her risk of developing a myocardial infarction twentyfold by comparison with those who had never smoked (Stone, Shapiro, Rosenberg, Kaufman, Hartz, Rossi, Stolley, & Miettinen, 1978).

A prospective study by Haynes, Feinleib, and Kannel demonstrate a twofold increase in coronary heart disease and three times as much angina in Type A versus Type B women. Although working women under age 65 scored higher on the Type A scale than housewives of similar age, the incidence of coronary artery disease among Type A working women and Type A housewives was not significantly different. However, in a study controlled for other risk factors, suppression of hostility was found to be an independent predictor of coronary heart disease in working women but not in housewives. One wonders what effects other changes in the female life-style have on their risk of developing premature coronary artery disease, female hormones notwithstanding.

One is struck by the multiplicity of precursors and the interactive quality of risk factors that seem to have a synergistic effect. This can lead to frustrating results when one controls for traditional risk factors such as hypertension, cholesterol, cigarette smoking, and inactivity. Psychosocial risk factors are more subtle but no less pernicious. In addition, they seem more resistant to manipulation and amelioration.

What is to be done about the Type A behavior pattern, the strong predictor of coronary heart disease, both for onset and recurrence? Can modifications in the way the Type A interacts with the environment diminish the risk? Could Type A people learn to become more like their Type B colleagues? It is naive and premature to propose such a change. We simply do not understand enough about what is hazardous and what is adaptive in the Type A behavior pattern. In any case, it would probably be a Brobdingnagian task to admonish a Type A individual to behave more like a Type B, as can be inferred from the discouraging results reported by Wishnie, Hackett, and Cassem. They found that the vast majority of a follow-up sample of patients who had had myocardial infarctions did not stick to their goals of weight reduction and discontinuance of cigarettes.

In sum, we seem to be confronted with a problem that will not lend itself to simple identification or solution. The hope for a single biological marker, one blood-test result, or some inexpensive procedure that might pinpoint those at risk for coronary heart disease misunderstands the enemy, which seems to be us. If it is our life-style that condemns us, we must devise ways to change long before we are confronted with the angiogram, coronary care unit, and bypass surgery, all of which have given us a false sense of security at great expense while we continue to avoid personal responsibility.

8. References

Adsett, A., & Bruhn, J. G. Short-term group psychotherapy for post-myocardial infarction patients and their wives. *The Canadian Medical Association Journal*, 1968, *99*(12), 577–584.

Bakker, C. B., & Levenson, R. M. Determinants of angina pectoris. *Psychosomatic Medicine*, 1967, *29*(6), 621–633.

Belloc, N. B., & Breslow, L. Relationship of physical health status and health practices. *Preventive Medicine*, 1972, *1*, 409–421.

Belloc, N. B., & Breslow, L. Relationship of health practices and mortality. *Preventive Medicine*, 1973, *2*, 67–81.

Berkman, L., & Syme, S. L. Social networks, host resistance and mortality: A nine-year follow-up study of Almeda County residents. *American Journal of Epidemiology*, 1979, *109*(2), 186–204.

Betz, B., & Thomas, C. Individual temperament as a predictor of health or premature disease. *Johns Hopkins Medical Journal*, 1979, *144*, 81–89.

Brand, R., Rosenman, R. H., Sholtz, R. F., & Friedman, M. Multivariate prediction of coronary heart disease in the Western Collaborative Group Study compared to the findings of the Framingham Study. *Circulation*, 1976, *53*(2), 348–355.

Broughton, R., & Baron, R. Sleep patterns in the intensive care unit and on the ward after acute myocardial infarction. *Electroencephalography and Clinical Neurophysiology*, 1978, *45*, 348–360.

Bruhn, J. G., Chandler, B., Miller, M. C., Wolf, S., & Lynn, T. N. Social concepts of coronary heart disease in two adjacent, ethnically different communities. *American Journal of Public Health*, 1966, *56*(9), 1493–1506.

Caffrey, B. A multivariate analysis of sociopsychological factors in monks with myocardial infarctions. *American Journal of Public Health*, 1970, *69*(3), 452–458.

Cassem, N. H., & Hackett, T. P. Psychiatric consultation in a coronary care unit. *Annals of Internal Medicine*, 1971, *75*, 9–14.

Cassem, N. H., & Hackett, T. P. The setting of intensive care. In T. P. Hackett & N. H. Cassem (Eds.), *Massachusetts General Hospital Handbook of General Hospital Psychiatry*. St. Louis: Mosby, 1978.

Cooper, B. S., & Rice, D. P. The economic cost of illness revisited. *Social Security Bulletin*. Washington, D.C.: U.S. Department of Health, Education and Welfare, 1976.

Croog, S., Shapiro, D. S., & Levine, S. Denial among male heart patients. *Psychosomatic Medicine*, 1971, *33*(5), 385–397.

Dawber, T. R., & Kannel, W. B. Atherosclerosis and you: Pathogenic implications from epidemiologic observations. *Journal of the American Geriatrics Society*, 1962, *10*(10), 805–821.

Dimsdale, J. E. Emotional causes of sudden death. *American Journal of Psychiatry*, 1977, *134*(12), 1361–1366.

Dimsdale, J. E., Hutter, A. M., Gilbert, J., Hackett, T. P., Block, P. C., & Catanzano, D. M. Predicting results of coronary angiography. *American Heart Journal*, 1979, *98*(3), 281–286.

Dlin, B. M., Rosen, H., Dickstein, K., Lyons, J. W., & Fischer, K. The problems of sleep and rest in the intensive care unit. *Psychosomatics, 1971, 12*(2), 155–163.

Doyle, J. T., Dawber, T. R., Kannel, W. B., Heslin, A. S., & Kahn, H. A. Cigarette smoking and coronary heart disease: Combined experience of the Albany and Framingham Studies. *New England Journal of Medicine*, 1962, *266*, 796–801.

Dreyfuss, F., Dasberg, H., & Assael, M. F. The relationship of myocardial infarction to depressive illness. *Psychotherapy and Psychosomatics*, 1969, *17*, 73–81.

Eisenberg, L. Is health a state of mind? *New England Journal of Medicine*, 1979, *301*(23), 1282–1283. (Editorial)

Engel, G. L. Psychologic stress, vasodepressor (vasovagal) syncope, and sudden death. *Annals of Internal Medicine*, 1978, *89*, 403–412.

Epstein, F. H. Epidemiologic aspects of atherosclerosis. *Atherosclerosis*, 1971, *14*, 1–11. (a)

Epstein, F. H. International trends in coronary heart disease epidemiology. *Annals of Clinical Research*, 1971, *3*, 293–299. (b)

Førde, O. H., & Thelle, D. S. The Tramsø Heart Study: Risk factors for coronary heart disease related to the occurrence of myocardial infarction in first degree relatives. *American Journal of Epidemiology*, 1977, *105*, 192–199.

Friedman, G. D., Ury, H. K., Klatsky, A. L., & Siegelaub, A. B. A psychological questionnaire predictive of myocardial infarction. *Psychosomatic Medicine*, 1974, *36*, 327–343.

Friedman, M., & Rosenman, R. H. Association of specific overt behavior pattern with blood and cardiovascular findings. *Journal of the American Medical Association*, 1959, *169*, 96–106.

Friedman, M., Rosenman, R. H., Straus, R., Wurm, M., & Kositchek, R. *American Journal of Medicine*, 1968, *44*, 525–537.

Froberg, J., Karlsson, C. G., Levi, L., Lidberg, L., & Seeman, K. Conditions of work: Psychological and endocrine stress reactions. *Archives of Environmental Health*, 1970, *21*, 789–797.

Gershon, E. S., Goldstein, R. E., Moss, A. J., & van Kammen, D. P. Psychosis with ordinary doses of propranol. *Annals of Internal Medicine*, 1979, *90*(6), 938–939.

Gillum, R. F., & Paffenbarger, R. S. Chronic disease in former college students. *American Journal of Epidemiology*, 1978, *108*(4), 289–298.

Glass, D. C. *Behavior patterns, stress and coronary disease*. Hillsdale, N.J.: Lawrence Erlbaum, 1977.

Goldband, S., Katkin, E. S., & Morell, M. A. Personality and cardiovascular disorder. In I. G. Sarason & C. D. Spielberger (Eds.), *Stress and anxiety* (Vol. 6). Washington, D.C.: Hemisphere Publishing Corporation, 1979.

Goldberg, R., Szklo, M., & Tonascia, J. A. Time trends in prognosis of patients with myocardial infarction: A population-based study. *The Johns Hopkins Medical Journal*, 1979, *144*, 73–80.

Goodwin, F. K., Ebert, M. H., & Bunny, W. E. Mental effects of reserpine in man. In R. Shader (Ed.), *Psychiatric complications of medical drugs*. New York: Raven Press, 1972.

Gordon, T., Kannel, W. B., McGee, D., & Dawber, T. R. Death and coronary attacks in men after giving up cigarette smoking. *The Lancet*, 1974, *2*, 1345–1353.

Gordon, T., Castelli, W. P., Hjortland, M. C., Kannel, W. B., & Dawber, T. R. Diabetes, blood lipids, and the role of obesity in coronary heart disease risk for women. *Annals of Internal Medicine*, 1977, *87*, 393–397.

Gruen, W. Effects of brief psychotherapy during the hospitalization period on the recovery process in heart attacks. *Journal of Consulting and Clinical Psychology*, 1975, *43*(2), 223–232.

Gundle, M. J., Reeves, B. R., Jr., Tate, S., Raft, D., & McLauren, L. P. *Psycho-social outcome of coronary artery surgery*. Paper presented at the 132nd annual meeting of the American Psychiatric Association, Chicago, May 1979.

Hackett, T. P., & Cassem, N. H. The psychologic reactions of patients in the pre- and post-hospital phase of myocardial infarction. *Postgraduate Medicine*, 1975, *57*(5), 43–46.

Hackett, T. P., Cassem, N. H., & Wishnie, H. A. The coronary-care unit: An appraisal of its psychologic hazard. *New England Journal of Medicine*, 1968, *279*(25), 1365–1370.

Haft, J. I., & Fani, K. Intravascular platelet aggregation in the heart induced by stress. *Circulation*, 1973, *47*(2), 353–358.

Harpur, J. E., Conner, W. T., Hamilton, M., Kellett, R. J., Galbraith, H. J. B., Murray, J. J., & Swallow, J. H. Controlled trial of early mobilization and discharge from hospital in uncomplicated myocardial infarction. *The Lancet*, 1971, *2*, 1331–1334.

Hartung, G. H., Foreyt, J. P., Mitchell, R. E., Vlasek, I., & Grotto, A. M. Relation to diet to high-density-lipoprotein cholesterol in middle-aged marathon runners, joggers, and inactive men. *New England Journal of Medicine*, 1980, *302*(7), 357–361.

Hatch, F. T., Reissel, R. K., Poon-king, T. M. W., Canellos, G. P., Lees, R. S., & Hagopian, L. M. A study of coronary heart disease in young men: Characteristics and metabolic studies of the patients and comparison with age-matched healthy men. *Circulation*, May 1966, *33*, 679–703.

Haynes, S. G., Feinleib, M., & Kannel, W. B. The relationship of psychosocial factors to coronary heart disease in the Framingham Study. *American Journal of Epidemiology*, 1980, 111(1), 37–58.

Hinkle, L. E., Jr. Some social and biological correlates of coronary heart disease. *Social Science and Medicine*, 1967, *1*, 129–139.

Holmes, T., & Rahe, R. The social readjustment rating scale. *Journal of Psychosomatic Research*, 1967, *11*, 213–218.

Hutter, A. M., Jr., Sidel, V. W., Shine, K. I., & DeSanctis, R. W. *New England Journal of Medicine*, 1973, *288*, 1141–1144.

Jenkins, C. D. Psychologic and social precursors of coronary disease. *New England Journal of Medicine*, 1971, *284*, 244–255; 307–317.

Jenkins, C. D. Recent evidence supporting psychologic and social risk factors for coronary disease. *New England Journal of Medicine*, 1976, *294*(18), 987–994. (a)

Jenkins, C. D. Recent evidence supporting psychologic and social risk factors for coronary disease. *New England Journal of Medicine*, 1976, *294*(19), 1033–1038. (b)

Jenkins, C. D., Zyzanski, S. J., & Rosenman, R. H. Progress toward validation of a computer-scored test for the Type-A coronary prone behavior pattern. *Psychosomatic Medicine*, 1971, *33*(3), 193–202.

Jenkins, C. D., Zyzanski, S. J., & Rosenman, R. H. Risk of new myocardial infarction in middle-aged men with manifest coronary heart disease. *Circulation*, 1976, *53*(2), 342–347.

Kales, A., Scharf, M. B., Kales, J. D., & Soldatos, C. R. Rebound insomnia: A potential hazard following withdrawal of certain benzodiazepines. *Journal of the American Medical Association*, 1979, *241*, 1692–1695.

Kass, L. R. Regarding the end of medicine and the pursuit of health. *The Public Interest*, 1975, #40, 11–42.

Keys, A., Taylor, H. L., Blackburn, H., Brozek, J., Anderson, J. T., & Simonson, E. Mortality and coronary heart disease among men studied for 23 years. *Archives of Internal Medicine*, 1971, *128*, 201–214.

Keys, A., Aravanis, C., Blackburn, H., van Buchem, F. S. P., Buzina, R., Djordjevic, B. S., Fidanza, F., Karvonen, M. J., Menotti, A., Puddu, V., & Taylor, H. L. Probability of middle-aged men developing coronary heart disease in five years. *Circulation*, 1972, *45*, 815–828. (a)

Keys, A., Aravanis, C., Blackburn, H., van Buchem, F. S. P., Buzina, R., Djordjevic, B. S., Fidanza, F., Karvonen, J. J., Menotti, A., Puddu, V., & Taylor, H. L. Coronary heart disease: Overweight and obesity as risk factors. *Annals of Internal Medicine*, 1972, *77*, 15–27. (b)

Kimball, C. P. The experience of open-heart surgery. VI. Research and consultation-liaison psychiatry. In H. Speidel & G. Rodewald (Eds.), *Psychic and neurological dysfunctions after open-heart surgery*. Stuttgart/New York: Thieme, 1980.

Klein, R. F., Kliner, V. A., Zipes, D. P., Troyer, W. G., Jr., & Wallace, A. G. Transfer from a coronary care unit: Some adverse responses. *Archives of Internal Medicine*, 1968, *122*, 104–108.

Kornfeld, D. S., Heller, S. S., Frank, K. A., Edie, R. N., & Barsa, J. Delirium after coronary artery bypass surgery. *The Journal of Thoracic and Cardiovascular Surgery*, 1978, *76*(1), 93–96.

Krantz, D. S., Sanmarco, M. I., Selvester, R. H., & Matthews, K. A. *Psychosomatic Medicine*, 1979, *41*(6), 467–475.

Lehr, I., Messinger, H. B., & Rosenman, R. H. A sociobiological approach to the study of coronary heart disease. *Journal of Chronic Diseases*, 1973, *26*, 13–30.

Lown, B., DeSilva, R. A., & Lensen, R. Role of psychologic stress and autonomic nervous system changes in provocation of ventricular premature complexes. *American Journal of Cardiology*, 1978, *41*(6), 979–985.

Manuck, S. B., Craft, S., & Gold, K. J. Coronary-prone behavior pattern and cardiovascular response. *Psychophysiology*, 1978, *15*(5), 403–410.

Marmot, M. G., Syme, S. L., Kagan, A., Kato, H., Cohen, J. B., & Belsky, J. Epidemiological studies of coronary heart disease and stroke in Japanese men living in Japan, Hawaii, and California:

Prevalence of coronary and hypertensive heart disease and associated risk factors. *American Journal of Epidemiology*, 1975, *102*(6), 514–525.

Masuda, M., & Holmes, T. H. Life events: Perceptions and frequencies. *Psychosomatic Medicine*, 1978, *40*(3), 236–261.

McNeer, J. F., Wagner, G. S., Ginsburg, P. B., Wallace, A. G., McCants, C. B., & Conley, J. J. Hospital discharge one week after acute myocardial infarction. *New England Journal of Medicine*, 1978, *298*(5), 229–232.

Medalie, J. H., Levene, C., Papier, C., Goldbourt, U., Dreyfuss, F., Oran, D., Neufeld, H., & Riss, E. Blood groups: Myocardial infarction and angina pectoris among 10,000 adult males. *New England Journal of Medicine*, 1971, *285*, 1348–1353.

Medalie, J. H., Kahn, H. A., Neufeld, H., Riss, E., & Goldbourt, U. Five-year myocardial infarction incidence. II. Association of single variables to age and birthplace. *Journal of Chronic Diseases*, 1973, *26*, 329–349.

Nichaman, M. Z., Hamilton, H. B., Kagan, A., Grier, T., Sachs, S. T., & Syme, S. L. Epidemiological studies of coronary heart disease and stroke in Japanese men living in Japan, Hawaii, and California: Distribution of biochemical risk factors. *American Journal of Epidemiology*, 1976, *102*(5), 491–501.

Nuckolls, K. B., Cassel, J., & Kaplan, B. H. Psychosocial assets, life crisis, and the prognosis of pregnancy. *American Journal of Epidemiology*, 1972, *95*(5), 431–441.

Osler, W. Lectures on angina pectoris and allied states. *New York Medical Journal*, 1896, *64*, 177–183.

Paffenbarger, R. S., Jr., & Wing, A. L. Chronic disease in former college students. X. The effects of single and multiple characteristics on risk of fatal coronary heart disease. *American Journal of Epidemiology*, 1969, *90*(6), 527–535.

Paffenbarger, R. S., Jr., Notkin, J., Krueger, D. E., Wolf, P. A., Thorne, M. C., LeBauer, E. J., & Williams, J. L. Chronic disease in former college students. II. Methods of study and observations on mortality from coronary heart disease. *American Journal of Public Health*, 1966, *56*(6), 962–970.

Parker, D. I., & Hodge, J. R. Delirium in a coronary care unit. *Journal of the American Medical Association*, 1967, *201*(9), 132–133.

Resnekov, L. Intermediate coronary care units. *Journal of the American Medical Association*, 1977, *237*(16), 1697–1698.

Rhoads, G. G., Gulbrandsen, C. L., & Kagan, A. Serum lipoproteins and coronary heart disease in a population study of Hawaii Japanese. *New England Journal of Medicine*, 1976, *294*, 293–298.

Russek, H. I., & Russek, L. G. Etiologic factors in ischemic heart disease: The elusive role of emotional stress. *Geriatrics*, 1972, *27*, 81–86.

Shekelle, R. B., Ostfeld, A. M., & Oglesby, P. Social status and incidence of coronary heart disease. *Journal of Chronic Diseases*, 1969, *22*, 381–394.

Sos, J., & Cassem, N. H. The intravenous use of Haloperidol for acute delirium in intensive care settings. In H. Speidel & G. Rodewald (Eds.), *Psychic and neurological dysfunctions after open-heart surgery*. Stuttgart/New York: Thieme, 1980.

Stern, M. P. The recent decline in ischemic heart disease mortality. *Annals of Internal Medicine*, 1979, *91*(4), 630–640.

Stimmel, B. Anxiety, stress, and cardiovascular disease. *Cardiovascular effects of mood-altering drugs*. New York: Raven Press, 1979.

Stone, D., Shapiro, S., Rosenberg, L., Kaufman, D. W., Hartz, S. C., Rossi, A. C., Stolley, P. D., & Miettinen, O. S. The relation of cigarette smoking to myocardial infarction in young women. *New England Journal of Medicine*, 1978, *298*(23), 1273–1976.

Stross, J. K., Willis, P. W., Reynolds, E. W., Jr., Lewis, R. E., Schatz, I. J., Bellfy, L. C., & Copp, J. Effectiveness of coronary care units in small community hospitals. *Annals of Internal Medicine*, 1976, *85*, 709–713.

Syme, S. L., Marmot, M. G., Kagan, A., Kato, H., & Rhoads, G. Epidemiologic studies of coronary heart disease and stroke in Japanese men living in Japan, Hawaii, and California: Introduction. *American Journal of Epidemiology*, 1975, *102*(6), 477–480.

Taggart, P., Carruthers, M., & Someiville, W. Electrocardiogram, plasma catecholamines and lipids and their modification by oxprenolol when speaking before an audience. *The Lancet*, 1973, *2*, 341–346.

Ursin, H., Baade, E., & Levine, S. (Eds.). *Psychobiology of stress: A study of coping men*. New York: Academic Press, 1978.

Vaillant, G. E. Natural history of male psychologic health: Effects of mental health on physical health. *New England Journal of Medicine*, 1979, *301*(23), 1249–1254.

Wallace, N., & Wallace, D. C. Group education after myocardial infarction. *The Medical Journal of Australia*, August 20, 1977, 245–247.

Weinblatt, E., Ruberman, W., Goldberg, J. D., Frank, C. W., Shapiro, S., & Chaudhary, B. S. Relation of education to sudden death after myocardial infarction. *New England Journal of Medicine*, 1978, *299*(2), 60–65.

White, R. L., & Liddon, S. C. Ten survivors of cardiac arrest. *Psychiatry in Medicine*, 1972, *3*, 219–225.

Williams, R. S., Logue, E. E., Lewis, J. L., Barton, T., Stead, N. W., Wallace, A. G., & Pizzo, S. V. Physical conditioning augments the fibrinolytic response to venous occlusion in healthy adults. *New England Journal of Medicine*, 1980, *302*(18), 987–991.

Wishnie, H. A., Hackett, T. P., & Cassem, N. H. Psychological hazards of convalescence following myocardial infarction. *Journal of the American Medical Association*, 1971, *215*(8), 1292–1296.

Yano, K., Rhoads, G. G., & Kagan, A. Coffee, alcohol, and risk of coronary heart disease among Japanese men living in Hawaii. *New England Journal of Medicine*, 1977, *297*(8), 405–409.

5

Some Issues in Research on Stressful Life Events

BARBARA SNELL DOHRENWEND AND
BRUCE P. DOHRENWEND

We will start with a question: Do you believe that life stress can cause illness? If this question were included in a poll of either the general public or of concerned professionals, we would expect a nearly unanimous affirmative response; "nearly unanimous" only because if we asked a cross-section of the population whether they believed that the sun would rise tomorrow, probably someone would express doubt. At one time in human history, when belief in the rising of the sun was a matter of hope and faith, this doubt might have seemed reasonable. It no longer seems so because this daily event has long since become scientifically predictable. Can we say the same about the belief in the relation between life stress and illness? Is it firmly based on scientific evidence, or is it still a matter of faith? We will argue that at present the belief that life stress causes illness is based on faith bolstered by some scientific evidence. Given this argument, we will then describe the kind of work that seems to be needed in order to shift the balance to favor scientific evidence.

Reprinted from *The Journal of Nervous and Mental Disease*, 1978, *166*, 7–15.

BARBARA SNELL DOHRENWEND ● Division of Sociomedical Sciences, School of Public Health, Columbia University, New York, New York 10032. BRUCE P. DOHRENWEND ● Social Psychiatry Research Unit, Department of Psychiatry, Columbia University, New York, New York 10032. The work on this paper was supported in part by Grant MH-10328; by Research Scientist Award K5-MH-14663 from the National Institute of Mental Health, U.S. Public Health Service; and by the Foundations' Fund for Research in Psychiatry.

1. Evidence about the Relationship of Life Stress to Illness

The evidence currently available concerning the relation of life stress to illness falls into two general categories: the relatively indirect and incontrovertible and the more direct and largely controversial. We will review the indirect evidence first.

Part of this evidence comes from the laboratory. There, a typical procedure is to expose healthy animals to electric shock, to frigid temperature, or to some other noxious stimulus. Under specific circumstances, the animals exposed to the noxious stimuli regularly develop psychological disorders such as learned helplessness (that is, passive acceptance of avoidable punishment) or organic lesions such as stomach ulcers, or they succumb to sudden death (Seligman, 1975; Selye, 1956).

The other source of relatively strong evidence that environmental stress causes somatic and psychological disorders consists of studies of the effects of natural and other disasters. For example, when a systematic sample of the population in a rural section of Arkansas was interviewed shortly after the area was hit by a severe tornado, 90% reported "some form of acute emotional, physiological or psychosomatic after-effect" (Fritz and Marks, 1954, p. 34). Similarly, Star (1949) found that when the Neuropsychiatric Screening Adjunct was administered to men exposed to combat during World War II:

> the fear and anxiety implicit in combat brought forth the psychosomatic manifestations in so many men that these [symptom scales] served less and less to discriminate between men who were labeled psychiatric casualties and those who were not. (p. 455)

Under some combat conditions, not only elevated symptom levels but also breakdown in performance became endemic. In a study of 2,630 soldiers who had broken down during combat in the Normandy campaign in World War II, Swank estimated that the onset of combat exhaustion occurred even in previously normal soldiers when about 65% of their companions had been killed, wounded, or had otherwise become casualties (Swank, 1949, p. 501). Swank emphasized that the men in this study had been highly selected for health and ability to cope:

> They were of better than average stability and willingness by virtue of the fact that they had passed the various training tests (induction, overseas assignment, battle simulation exercises), had been selected for combat units, and had proved their mettle by remaining in combat varying lengths of time. (p. 476)

The extent to which symptomatology and disturbance of functioning produced in extreme situations in previously normal persons are transient and self-limiting is a matter of controversy (cf. Kingston & Rosser, 1974), but most observers have emphasized the transience of these reactions (cf. Dohrenwend & Dohrenwend, 1969, pp. 110–130). At the extreme of exposure to the brutalities of Nazi concentration camps, however, there is strong evidence not only that severe stress-induced psychopathology has persisted in survivors (Eitinger, 1964) but also that the survivors are more prone to suffer physical illness and early death (Eitinger, 1973).

Natural and other disasters, fortunately, are rare occurrences whose devastating effects are limited to relatively small populations. Most people live their lives without experiencing any of these extraordinary events. Yet psychopathology and somatic disturbances are far from rare in peacetime populations relatively secure from war, flood, famine, and other disasters. If stressful situations play an etiological role in these disorders, the events involved must be more ordinary, more frequent experiences in the lives of most people—things such as marriage, birth of a first child, and death of a loved one. We turn now to the more direct evidence, focused on events such as these, concerning the relation between stress experienced in the course of normal life and illness.

One conclusion firmly supported by this evidence is that the correlates of stressful life events are not limited to any particular types of disorder. On the contrary, life events have been shown to be related to many somatic disorders, including heart disease (Hinkle, 1974; Holmes & Masuda, 1974; Theorell, 1974), fractures, and childhood leukemia (Holmes & Masuda, 1974); to performance deficits among teachers and college students (Holmes & Masuda, 1974); and to psychological disorders including acute schizophrenia (Brown, 1974), depression (Hudgens, 1974; Paykel, 1974), and suicide attempts (Paykel, 1974). In addition, the range of psychological correlates extends beyond acute disorders to include elevated scores on scales that measure relatively mild symptoms of depression as well as symptoms of less specific psychological distress (Markush & Favero, 1974). Myers, Lindenthal, Pepper, and Ostrander (1972) also showed with still another measure of symptomatic distress that scores fluctuated over time and with fluctuations in the nature and number of life events experienced, and Gersten, Langner, Eisenberg, and Orzek (1974) showed that the association between various symptom measures and life events held for children. Taken all together, this evidence clearly supports the conclusion of Hinkel (1974)

> that there would probably be no aspect of human growth, development, or disease
> which would in theory be immune to the influence of the effect of a man's relation to
> his social and interpersonal environment. (p. 10)

When it comes to specifying the actual process whereby life events influence health, however, there is disagreement concerning the importance of the events themselves as against circumstances surrounding the events and vulnerabilities of the individuals experiencing them. On the one hand, Hinkle (1974) concluded from his studies of telephone company employees living in stable social situations and of political refugees whose life situations had been severely disrupted:

> that the effect of a social change, or a change in interpersonal relations, on the health
> of an individual cannot be defined solely by the nature of the change itself. The effect
> depends on the physical and psychological characteristics of the person who is exposed
> to the change and on the circumstances under which it is encountered. (p. 41)

On the other hand, Holmes's and Masuda's conclusion (1974) from their review of the extensive research on life events done with the Social Readjustment Rating Scale, a list of life events weighted according to the amount of readjustment or change that they entail (Holmes & Rahe, 1967), was that:

> The magnitude of life change was observed to be highly significantly related to time
> of disease onset. The greater the magnitude of life change (or life crisis), the greater
> the probability that the population at risk would experience disease. (p. 68)

We have, then, a body of research results which indicate that life events are associated with a wide range of disorders and distress but do not provide a clear picture of the nature and strength of this relationship. In order to clarify our understanding of how stressful life events affect health and illness, we will need to deal with methodological issues that have emerged from research to date and to tackle a major substantive problem. The methodological issues are three: definition of the populations of life events to be studied, measurement of the magnitudes of the life events, and use of a research design appropriate to the question to be answered. The substantive issue concerns factors that mediate the impact of life events. Let us examine each of these issues in turn.

2. Definition of Populations of Life Events

There are two major ways in which the definition of the population of life events can lead to confusion. The first is partly evident in the distinction between objective and subjective events made by some investigators (e.g., Thurlow, 1971).

Subjective events—for example, "sexual difficulties," "major change in number of arguments with spouse," and "major changes in sleeping habits" (Holmes & Masuda, 1974, pp. 48–49) are more likely to be manifestations of or responses to underlying pathology than causes of such pathology. Nor is the problem limited to "subjective" events, since many objective events such as "divorce" or "being fired from work" (e.g., Holmes & Masuda, 1974, pp. 48–49) are as likely to be consequences as causes of pathology. Making the correct causal inference for the latter type of events would depend on the investigator's ability to date the event in relation to the onset of somatic or psychological disorder and to learn something about whether the onset of the event was within or outside the control of the subject. The seriousness of this source of confusion in much of the research to date is suggested by Hudgens's assessment of events on the list constructed by Holmes and Rahe (1967), the most widely used list of stressful life events. By his count, 29 of the 43 events on this list "are often the symptoms or consequences of illness" (Hudgens, 1974, p. 131). As a number of authors have pointed out (Brown, 1974; Dohrenwend, 1974), this kind of bias in a sample of life events seriously limits the kinds of inferences that can be drawn from a correlation between the number or magnitude of events experienced and illness. The limitation on causal inference is especially severe in investigations of psychiatric disorders that are often of insidious onset and long duration.

Most samples of events also include major physical illness or injury, which seems appropriate, since these are negative events that often entail serious disruption of usual activities. However, it is a basic proposition of psychosomatic medicine that physical disorders are accompanied by some degree of emotional disturbance and emotional disorders by some degree of somatic disturbance. There is no instance of which we are aware in which investigations of relations between physical illness and emotional disturbance have failed to report a strong positive correlation between the two (cf. Lipowski, 1975). Moreover, as Hinkle points out with respect to different types of physical illness, "the presence of one disease may imply the presence of others and beget yet other diseases" (Hinkle, 1974, p. 39). Thus, a sample of events that includes physical illness and injury can lead to a problem of interpretation when the events are summed to provide scores for the amount of stress experienced by particular individuals. There is ambiguity about the extent to which a positive correlation indicates the impact of amount of change and hence amount of stress or, instead, the relation among physical illnesses or between physical and psychiatric symptomatology, important problems in their own right.

We propose, therefore, that there are at least three distinct populations of life events that must be sampled and kept distinct for purposes of analysis (Dohrenwend, 1974; Dohrenwend & Dohrenwend, 1974). These are (a) a population of events that is confounded with the psychiatric condition of the subject, (b) a population of events consisting of physical illnesses and injuries to the subject, and (c) a population of events whose occurrences are independent of either the subject's physical health or psychiatric condition.

As a general principle, the more a sample of events in a particular measure of stressful life events represents a summated mixture from these three event populations, the more difficult it is to assess the etiological implication of a relationship between such a measure and various types of pathology.

3. Measurement of the Magnitudes of Life Events

Turning now to the second methodological problem, measurement of the magnitude of life events, we note first that, in laboratory stress experiments with animals, there is little difficulty in defining the magnitude of the stressful event to which the subjects are exposed. The experimental animals receive shocks of greater or lesser voltage, are exposed to varying extremes of temperature, and so on. Similarly, extreme situations appear to have self-evident indications of magnitude: for example, duration of time in combat, number of wounded in the soldier's company, and so on. For the more usual life events with which we are concerned here, however, things are by no means so clear-cut. Is "marriage" more or less stressful than "divorce"? Is "birth of a first child" more or less stressful than "being laid off a job"?

Holmes and Rahe (1967) have offered an apparently simple solution to this problem in the Schedule of Recent Events and the Social Readjustment Ratings that they have secured for purposes of scoring it. They first constructed a list of events that they found were positively correlated with illness onset in a large sample of medical patients. Their method of scoring these events followed S. S. Stevens' proposal that direct estimation procedures that had been found to produce a consistent quantitative relationship between physical stimuli and perceptual responses could also be used to measure psychological dimensions related to social stimuli.

A simple form of this procedure, magnitude estimation, involves designating a modulus with an assigned value and asking judges to rate other stimuli in relation to the modulus. Holmes and Rahe designated "marriage" as the modulus, assigned it a value of 500, and obtained quantitative judgments about the amount of change or readjustment in relation to it for each of the other 42 events on their list. Life Change Unit (LCU) scores based on these ratings have been presented as a measure of the stressfulness of the rated events just as, in psychophysical experiments, ratings of sounds provide a measure of their loudness. The argument of Holmes and his colleagues is that if we weigh events in terms of their different LCU scores and pay attention to how these weights add up when a series of events occurs, the risk of illness attached to the life events will vary directly with the magnitude of the LCU scores.

Holmes in particular has emphasized the high level of consensus about the amount of change associated with each life event. He refers to correlations in the .80s and .90s between the mean ratings for each event obtained from such diverse status groups as blacks and Japanese as well as whites. His argument for the universalism of perceptions of the amount of change entailed by, and hence the stressfulness of particular life events, however, has been sharply criticized. Among others, two of Holmes's collaborators have pointed out that considerable group differences are masked by the reported correlations. Specifically, Rahe (1969) found that ratings secured in Sweden were consistently higher than Holmes's West Coast American ratings. Masuda and Holmes (1967) pointed out that certain differences in ratings of events by Japanese and American judges seem to be related to differences between the two cultures. Other researchers have also reported cultural contrasts. Miller, Bentz, Aponte, and Brogan (1974) have found sharp differences in the way their sample of rural North Carolina judges, and Holmes's and Rahe's urban West Coast sample ranked such events as "marriage" and "taking out a mortgage of greater than $10,000." In the urban sample, for example, marriage is ranked fourth by contrast with 21st in the rural sample in terms of the amount of change involved. Miller and his colleagues make a strong case that these differences are meaningful in terms of contrasts in the norms and customs of the two samples. Hough, Fairbank, and Garcia (1976) have reported differences in the judged magnitude of life events corresponding to differences in the cultural backgrounds of their college student subjects. Still other critics, such as Brown (1974), have pointed out large individual variability in the LCU ratings in Holmes's and Rahe's data.

It seems to us that there is, nevertheless, a strong argument for the general procedure developed by Holmes and his colleagues. It makes sense that some events are, objectively, of greater magnitude than others. Who would want to suggest, for example, that the "death of a pet" is inherently as large an event as "death of a spouse"? Yet, it also seems to us that much further work on the scaling procedures themselves needs to be done (cf. Hough *et al.*, 1976). Individual variability can probably be reduced by providing less ambiguous descriptions of events to be rated; for example, instead of the event "change in responsibilities at work," supply two events: "change to more responsibility" and "change to less responsibility at work." It may also be possible to simplify the rating task and thereby improve reliability of judgments by using categorization procedures rather than direct estimation of a value for each event in relation to a standard. The problem of cultural differences in judgments about the events is interesting in its own right, as Holmes is aware. As he and Masuda pointed out, the LCU ratings "offer a powerful tool for delineating quantitatively and qualitatively cross-cultural differences" (Holmes & Masuda, 1974, p. 57). If so, the procedure for dealing with such differences would be to secure ratings from members of each of the contrasting groups and compute LCU scores that are specific to each of the groups (cf. Hough *et al.*, 1976).

Moreover, it is possible to envision valuable extensions of the rating procedure. To date, the judgments have focused on the amount of change associated with the events. Yet stressful life events involve other properties that might be scaled: the desirability or undesirability of the events and—where illness, injury, or crime is involved—the seriousness or severity of the event. Some important work of this kind has already been done on physical illness of various types by Wyler, Masuda, and Holmes (1968). In general, the extension of ratings beyond the single dimension of the amount of change would probably yield improved measures of the stressfulness of life events.

4. Research Design

The third methodological issue that needs attention concerns research design. The bulk of research to date has relied on case-control studies. That is, investigators have started with a group or series of patients and compared these cases with a series of controls, usually healthy persons matched to the clinical cases on some relevant background characteristics. The results of these studies have repeatedly shown that the cases experienced more stressful life events prior to the onset of their illness than their controls did in a comparable time period. Although this finding seems to establish a relation between stressful life events and subsequent illness, it does not provide the information that we need to estimate the magnitude of the risk that disorder will follow as a consequence of experiencing stressful life events. To get this information, we need cohort studies based on samples of the population of persons who have experienced whatever life events are of interest rather than case-control studies based on samples of persons who have become ill. The implication of this shift in design is suggested by Paykel's discussion of his finding, based on case-control studies, that persons who became acutely depressed disproportionately reported that exits—events involving a departure from the subject's social field—preceded the onset of their depression; Paykel (1974) noted:

> Most of the events reported by the depressives were in the range of everyday experience rather than catastrophic, and most often are negotiated without clinical depression. (p. 139)

His best estimate, based on a number of somewhat arbitrary assumptions together with the indirect evidence available from case-control studies, was that "only a small proportion of exits, less than 10 per cent, appear to be followed by clinical depression" (p. 139).

Thus, while the results of case-control studies encourage us to think that research on stressful life events will help us to understand the etiology of a wide range of disorders, cohort studies will show us how much or how little etiological information we may gain from this research. Whether we gain much or little will depend, we believe, on how well we deal with an important substantive issue that has begun to be investigated in research on the effects of stressful life events.

5. Mediation of the Impact of Stressful Life Events

This issue concerns factors that mediate the impact of stressful life events on the individual. These factors fall into two general categories: the subjective or intrapsychic and the objective or environmental. To illustrate, in relation to heart disease, we have on the one hand the concept of vulnerability related to AB personality types (Friedman & Rosenman, 1974) and on the other hand etiological models that focus on environmental effects on the organism via, for example, diet and cigarette consumption. While diet and smoking habits have not proved easy to change, personality type is surely even less malleable. In general, if one is primarily concerned with learning how to prevent illness, the relevant question seems to be how the environment may adversely affect the individual rather than what inborn or overlearned weaknesses make some individuals more vulnerable than others to a pathogenic environment. Since we take it that the major purpose of studying stressful life events is to learn how stress-induced illness can be prevented, it appears that it is the objective or situational mediators of these events that should engage our attention.

There is, moreover, considerable evidence from both experimental studies and observations of extreme situations that situational factors are important mediators of the impact of stressful stimuli or events. Consider, for example, the evidence that exposure to electric shock can lead to learned helplessness, that is, passive acceptance of punishment. The evidence is not that the shock as such causes the learned helplessness but that, if this stressful stimulus is experienced in a situation over which the subject has no control, helplessness will be learned (Seligman, 1975). Similarly, in making deductions about the effects of combat, Swank (1949) did not conclude that a breakdown necessarily occurred once a soldier was exposed to stressful combat regardless of the circumstances, but that it occurred when combat was experienced after social supports had been severely disrupted as a result of a large number of casualties in a soldier's unit.

We propose, then, that a major substantive task for further research on stressful life events is to investigate situational factors that may mediate the impact of these events. General theoretical considerations together with findings of experimental studies and observations of extreme situations suggest at least four factors that should be included in this investigation.

By way of identifying the first factor, we note that change and adaptation are inherently related to the concept of stress, and that investigators of stressful life events assume more or less explicitly that they involve change. Yet in most studies in which subjects are asked to report their recent life events, they are not asked whether or not they had ever experienced any of the reported events before. We do not know how many times a particular event must be experienced before habituation occurs, but we can predict with confidence that, with one likely exception, repetition will bring habituation and thus reduce or eliminate the stressfulness of an event. The exception may occur when an undesirable event is repeated in fairly rapid succession, a situation that would probably lead to amplification rather than to reduction of the stressfulness of the event. Thus, one way or the other, we would predict that the impact of a life event will differ significantly depending on whether it is a novel experience or a repetition of one or more similar previous experiences.

The second situational factor that may mediate the impact of life events is suggested by Swank's observation that combat exhaustion regularly occurred in previously normal soldiers when about 65% of their companions had become casualties (Swank, 1949, p. 501). Further evidence of the protective effect of social bonds is found in a study which showed that, among women who experienced stressful life events before or during their pregnancies, those with more satisfactory marital and other social relations were less likely than those with less satisfactory relations to suffer complications in their pregnancies (Nuckolls, Cassel, & Kaplan, 1972). The fact that effects analogous to those observed in humans have been demonstrated in laboratory studies of animals suggests that social bonds provide a strong buffer against the impact of stressful situations (Cassel, 1975, p. 545).

Two other conditions that may mediate the impact of life events are suggested by recent reviews of laboratory studies of stress (Averill, 1973; Lefcourt, 1973).

The first condition is anticipation of a noxious stimulus. When a subject is able to anticipate such a stimulus, either because a warning is provided or because of the regular timing of the stimulus, the effects of the stimulus are found to be mitigated. To illustrate, one study showed that a fixed-interval noise produced less deterioration in performance on a subsequent proofreading task than did a random noise and that, in addition, this difference in regularity had a far greater impact on subsequent performance than the loudness of the noise (Glass, Singer, & Friedman, 1969).

Another generally consistent experimental finding is that when a subject controls the administration of a noxious stimulus, its effects are ameliorated. Thus, for example, when subjects were told that they could turn off a loud, random noise if it became unbearable, they performed better at a subsequent proofreading task than when they had no control over the noxious stimulus (Glass *et al.*, 1969).

Given the highly artificial settings typical of experimental studies such as these and, of ethical necessity, the rather trivial nature of the stressful experiences imposed on human subjects, the question arises as to whether these findings can be generalized to life situations. Evidence suggesting a positive answer to this question is provided by an extensive series of clinical studies by Engel (1971) and by Schmale (1972), who concluded that people who feel helpless to anticipate and control their world are particularly likely to suffer serious illness or even death when stressful events impinge on them. Experimental and clinical findings both suggest, then, that differences in the extent to which stressful life events are anticipated or their onset controlled by persons who experience them may explain some of the variability in their impact.

Thus, theoretical considerations together with experimental studies of stress and observations of extreme situations imply that reactions to stressful life events cannot be understood without taking into account the contextual factors of amount of previous experience with an event, amount of social support available, degree of anticipation, and degree of control over the occurrence of an event.

When we consider how circumstances may mediate the impact of events, it is possible, we think, to envision ways in which combinations of ordinary stressful life events would induce an approximation of the conditions involved in extreme situations such as prolonged exposure to heavy combat in wartime. Such extreme situations involve unanticipated events, such as loss of comrades, that are outside the control of the individual; they involve the individual's own physical exhaustion; and they strip him or her of the social support of comrades as the casualty rate rises. Events in civil life such as loss of loved ones, serious physical illness, or injury following on or accompanying, say, migration to a new country or community, if they occur in close proximity to each other, may resemble extreme situations. Here the events themselves would, we hypothesize, produce psychopathology in most previously normal persons in the same way that prolonged combat in a high-casualty company has proved pathogenic in wartime.

One can also envision, at the other extreme, circumstances in which the events experienced would play a relatively small part in an illness outcome by contrast with individual predispositions and other mediating factors. Events that are anticipated by most people to whom they happen and are often controlled to some extent by the performance of the individual who experiences them are the types we have in mind: a second or third divorce; a second or third time being fired from a job; causing another automobile accident as a result of reckless driving; or some combination of these—are the kinds of things we have in mind.

These are qualitative distinctions that involve major events. One can also envision distinctions along quantitative lines where, in general, the less the magnitude of the events or the combination of events, the more important the mediating factors in any illness outcome. If we are correct, future research will have to pay considerable attention to qualitative as well as quantitative distinctions among events and to the wide variety of factors that mediate their impact. It is our hope that with attention to such matters will come not only greater understanding of relationships between life events and illness but also greater precision in our ability to predict differential illness outcomes.

6. Conclusion

In conclusion, the problem as we see it is not just to establish that life events are related to health and illness, for this information alone carries a probably misleading implication of inevitability. What we need to determine is the strength of the relationship in order to assess realistically the risk of stress-induced illness. Given even a small risk of serious impairment of health, it is, further, important to specify the conditions that control that strength, so that unnecessary risk can be reduced. The issues that we have defined are central, we think, to achieving these goals.

Averill, J. R. Personal control over aversive stimuli and its relationship to stress. *Psychological Bulletin*, 1973, *80*, 286–303.

Brown, G. W. Meaning, measurement, and stress of life events. In B. S. Dohrenwend & B. P. Dohrenwend (Eds.), *Stressful life events: Their nature and effects.* New York: Wiley, 1974.

Cassel, J. Social science in epidemiology: Psychosocial processes and "stress" theoretical formulation. In E. L. Struening & M. Guttentag (Eds.), *Handbook of evaluation research* (Vol. 1). Beverly Hills: Sage Publications, 1975.

Dohrenwend, B. P. Problems in defining and sampling the relevant population of stressful life events. In B. S. Dohrenwend & B. P. Dohrenwend (Eds.), *Stressful life events: Their nature and effects.* New York: Wiley, 1974.

Dohrenwend, B. P., & Dohrenwend, B. S. *Social status and psychological disorder.* New York: Wiley, 1969.

Dohrenwend, B. S., & Dohrenwend, B. P. Overview and prospects for research on stressful life events. In B. S. Dohrenwend & B. P. Dohrenwend (Eds.), *Stressful life events: Their nature and effects.* New York: Wiley, 1974.

Eitinger, L. *Concentration camp survivors in Norway and Israel.* London: G. Allen & Unwin, 1964.

Eitinger, L. A follow-up of the Norwegian concentration camp survivors' mortality and morbidity. *Israel Annals of Psychiatry*, 1973, *11*, 199–209.

Engel, G. L. Sudden and rapid death during psychological stress, folklore or folk wisdom? *Annals of Internal Medicine*, 1971, *74*, 771–782.

Friedman, M., & Rosenman, R. H. *Type A behavior and your heart.* New York: Knopf, 1974.

Fritz, C. E., & Marks, E. S. The NORC studies of human behavior in disaster. *Journal of Social Issues*, 1954, *10*, 26–41.

Gersten, J. C., Langner, T. S., Eisenberg, J. C., & Orzek, L. Child behavior and life events: Undesirable change or change per se? In B. S. Dohrenwend & B. P. Dohrenwend (Eds.), *Stressful life events: Their nature and effects.* New York: Wiley, 1974.

Glass, D. C., Singer, J. E., & Friedman, L. N. Psychic cost of adaptation to an environmental stressor. *Journal of Personality and Social Psychology*, 1969, *12*, 200–210.

Hinkle, L. E. The effect of exposure to culture change, social change, and changes in interpersonal relationships on health. In B. S. Dohrenwend & B. P. Dohrenwend (Eds.), *Stressful life events: Their nature and effects.* New York: Wiley, 1974.

Holmes, T. H., & Masuda, M. Life change and illness susceptibility. In B. S. Dohrenwend & B. P. Dohrenwend (Eds.), *Stressful life events: Their nature and effects.* New York: Wiley, 1974.

Holmes, T. H., & Rahe, R. H. The social readjustment rating scale. *Psychosomatic Medicine*, 1967, *11*, 213–218.

Hough, R. L., Fairbank, D. T., & Garcia, A. M. Problems in the ratio measurement of life stress. *Journal of Health and Social Behavior*, 1976, *17*, 70–82.

Hudgens, R. W. Personal catastrophe and depression: A consideration of the subject with respect to medically ill adolescents, and a requiem for retrospective life-event studies. In B. S. Dohrenwend & B. P. Dohrenwend (Eds.), *Stressful life events: Their nature and effects.* New York: Wiley, 1974.

Kingston, W., & Rosser, R. Disaster: Effects on mental and physical state. *Journal of Psychosomatic Research*, 1974, *18*, 437–456.

Lefcourt, H. M. The function of the illusions of control and freedom. *American Psychologist*, 1973, *28*, 417–425.

Lipowski, Z. J. Psychiatry of somatic diseases: Epidemiology, pathogenesis, classification. *Comprehensive Psychiatry*, 1975, *16*, 105–124.

Markush, R. E., & Favero, R. V. Epidemiologic assessment of stressful life events, depressed mood, and psychophysiological symptoms—a preliminary report. In B. S. Dohrenwend & B. P. Dohrenwend (Eds.), *Stressful life events: Their nature and effects.* New York: Wiley, 1974.

Masuda, M., & Holmes, T. H. The Social Readjustment Rating Scale: A cross cultural study of Japanese and Americans. *Journal of Psychosomatic Research*, 1967, *11*, 227–237.

Miller, F. T., Bentz, W. K., Aponte, J. R., & Brogan, D. R. Perception of life crisis events. In B. S. Dohrenwend & B. P. Dohrenwend (Eds.), *Stressful life events: Their nature and effects.* New York: Wiley, 1974.

Myers, J. K., Lindenthal, J. J., Pepper, M. P., & Ostrander, D. K. Life events and mental status: A longitudinal study. *Journal of Health and Social Behavior*, 1972, *13*, 398–406.

Nuckolls, K. B., Cassel, J., & Kaplan, B. H. Psychosocial assets, life crisis and the prognosis of pregnancy. *American Journal of Epidemiology*, 1972, *95*, 431–441.

Paykel, E. S. Life stress and psychiatric disorder: Application of the clinical approach. In B. S. Dohrenwend & B. P. Dohrenwend (Eds.), *Stressful life events: Their nature and effects*. New York: Wiley, 1974.

Rahe, R. H. Multi-cultural correlations of life change scaling: America, Japan, Denmark, and Sweden. *Journal of Psychosomatic Research*, 1969, *13*, 191–195.

Schmale, A. H. Giving up as a final common pathway to changes in health. *Advances in Psychosomatic Medicine*, 1972, *8*, 20–40.

Seligman, M. E. P. *Helplessness: On depression, development and death*. San Francisco: Freeman, 1975.

Selye, H. *The stress of life* New York: MGraw-Hill, 1956.

Star, S. A. Psychoneurotic symptoms in the army. In S. A. Stouffer, L. Guttman, E. A. Suchman, P. F. Lazarsfeld, S. A. Star, & J. A. Clausen (Eds.), *Studies in social psychology in World War II. The American soldier: Combat and its aftermath*. Princeton: Princeton University Press, 1949.

Swank, R. L. Combat exhaustion. *Journal of Nervous and Mental Disease*, 1949, *109*, 475–508.

Theorell, T. Life events before and after the onset of a premature myocardial infarction. In B. S. Dohrenwend & B. P. Dohrenwend (Eds.), *Stressful life events: Their nature and effects*. New York: Wiley, 1974.

Thurlow, H. J. Illness in relation to life situation and sick-role tendency. *Journal of Psychosomatic Research*, 1971, *15*, 73–88.

Wyler, A. R., Masuda, M., & Holmes, T. H. Seriousness of illness rating scale. *Journal of Psychosomatic Research*, 1968, *11*, 363–374.

Stress, Coping, and Illness
A Transactional Perspective

JAMES C. COYNE AND KENNETH HOLROYD

Impressive gains in the control of communicable disease and the treatment of acute illness have paradoxically confronted us with the limitations of the dominant medical model. As the leading cause of death in Western countries has shifted from infectious to chronic diseases, it has become apparent that solutions to the problems of health and illness will prove far more complex than had been anticipated by scientists only a few decades ago. It is no longer possible to view illness as "a thing in itself, essentially unrelated to the patient's personality, his bodily constitution, or his mode of life" (Dubos, 1965, p. 319). Single-factor conceptions of illness derived from infectious disease are proving too linear, restrictive, and oversimplified to deal with the multifaceted nature of chronic illness (Weiner, 1977).

It is recognized that treatment and prevention must have a wider focus than the somatic parameters of health and illness. Increasingly, a person's life-style—including patterns of eating; exercise; use of alcohol, tobacco and drugs; coping with stress; and contact with environmental hazards—is being identified as the most modifiable health variable. Consistent with this, there has been a demand that the conventional biomedical model of health be expanded to a broader biopsychosocial model in which a person's psychological functioning and ongoing relationship to the environment are given added emphasis (Engel, 1977).

Psychologists have not had primary responsibility for this shifting view of medicine, but they have a great deal to contribute and are likely to have a larger and more integral role in the future health care system. Yet what is lacking is a comprehensive framework within which we can conceptualize problems of health

JAMES C. COYNE • Department of Psychology, University of California, Berkeley, California 94720. KENNETH HOLROYD • Department of Psychology, Ohio University, Athens, Ohio 45701.

and illness so that we may identify points of intervention for psychologists and other behavioral scientists.

Recent developments in stress theory and research indicate that a stress and coping perspective may be a viable possibility for such a task. In the past thirty years, the scope of the field has expanded from the study of the conditions under which skilled performance deteriorates to the determinants of morale, social functioning, and physical health. There has been a striking increase in research examining the stress and coping processes thought to influence not only the etiology and onset of disease but also the experience, course, and outcome of illness as well as the utilization of medical care and compliance with and response to treatment (Moos, 1977).

At the same time, use of the term *stress* has become somewhat problematic because of the lack of consensus as to its referents and measurement. We will begin our discussion with a brief review of conventional conceptions of stress. In our presentation we will make the case for a transactional perspective; stress is to be viewed neither as an environmental condition nor as a response but rather as a person–environment relationship in which demands tax or exceed the resources of the person (Coyne & Lazarus, 1980; Holroyd, 1979; Lazarus & Launier, 1978). A transactional viewpoint suggests distinctive issues and approaches to the role of stress in health and illness. In outlining them, we will note important convergences between our theoretical concepts and diverse intervention strategies that are developing within both the cognitive–behavioral and family therapy frameworks.

Our delineation of the field of stress, coping, and illness is broad and ambitious, including critical but poorly charted areas such as family stress theory as well as more familiar and well-researched areas such as the life-events literature. Our intent is to present an overview of central issues and problems rather than a detailed review of the literature. We hope to demonstrate the utility of a transactional perspective in identifying clinically relevant questions that need refinement and study; we shall also note the limitations of conventional conceptions of the role of stress in health and illness.

1. Stress as an Environmental Event

Stress is commonly conceptualized in environmental terms, as an event or set of circumstances presumed to elicit or require an unusual response from the person. Massive and sudden disruptive events such as tornadoes, earthquakes, or fires (Birnbaum, Caplan, & Scharff, 1976) as well as more chronic or extended circumstances such as imprisonment (Spaulding & Ford, 1976), military service (Bourne, 1969), or crowding (Freedman, 1975) have been studied within this framework.

The approach is most prominently developed in the study of the relationship between the accumulation of life events and the risk of subsequent physical illness (Holmes & Masuda, 1974). A large and active line of research, much of it employing instruments such as the Social Readjustment Rating Scale (Holmes & Rahe, 1967), has firmly established such an empirical relationship. The guiding assumption has been "that life change events, by evoking adaptive efforts by the human organism that are faulty in kind and duration, lower bodily resistance and enhance the probability of disease occurrence" (Holmes & Masuda, 1974, p. 68). It has further been assumed that stress is inherent in the accommodation required by the events and that an accumulation of life events increases the likelihood of illness regardless of whether the changes are positive or negative.

Studies of the relationship between life change and illness continue to proliferate, but it appears that earlier estimates of the magnitude of the relationship were considerably inflated. Measures of life events are often contaminated by items that directly or indirectly reflect the occurrence of illness. Over half of the items on some measures are of this nature (Hudgens, 1974). Measures of illness that have been used—such as medical self-referral—reflect variables other than the actual presence of illness (Mechanic, 1974). When these problems are taken into account, the proportion of variance in illness explained by life change is quite modest. Thus, Rabkin and Struening (1976) have concluded, "In practical terms . . . life event scores have not been shown to be predictive of the probability of future illness" (p. 1015).

Some writers have called for a moratorium on further studies employing the Social Readjustment Rating Scale (Wershaw & Reinhart, 1974). At the same time, efforts are being made to improve the predictive ability of measures of life events. Proposals have included expanding the breadth of item content and the weighing of subjective impact (Hochstim, 1970; Horowitz, Schaefer, Hiroto, Wilner, & Levin, 1977). Strategies have also been proposed for distinguishing among classes of life events that might have differential impact on health status. Thus, it has been argued that positive events (Brown, 1974; Kellam, 1946) or events that induce psychophysiological strain (Garrity, Marx, & Somes, 1977) or a sense of mastery (Mechanic, 1974) or that are unanticipated or not within the individual's control (Dohrenwend & Dohrenwend, 1974) should be distinguished from other life events.

These suggestions represent a softening of the original assumptions of the life–events approach to the study of stress. Rather than merely examining the formal properties of events, they recognize the importance of the individual's evaluations of events along various qualitative dimensions, perceptions that represent interactions between the events and the person (Redfield & Stone, 1979).

Even in the unlikely case that such innovations significantly improve on the predictive ability of measures of life events, the implications for clinical practice would remain unclear. As Mechanic (1974) has noted, the disregard in medicine for the life–change approach "stems less from its lack of plausibility than from its failure to provide the physician with a viable approach to the patient. Life situations are enormously difficult to modify even with the greatest of commitment." (p. 89). Events such as death of a spouse may be impossible to avoid, and other events such as divorce may be actively sought for reasons that are more compelling than the avoidance of an increased risk of illness.

Hinkle (1974) has suggested that major life events might owe a significant part of their impact on health to their effects on the person's everyday activities, since they will disrupt social relationships, habits, and health-related behaviors. Potentially, a person's involvement in everyday activities might prove a more suitable focus for intervention than attempting to influence the occurrence of stressful life events. Many people facing stressful life events do not become ill, and many who become ill do not report recent major stress.

DeLongis, Coyne, Dakof, Folkman, and Lazarus (in press) have compared the hassles of everyday life to major life events in terms of the strength of their relationship to physical health. Hassles have been defined as "the irritating, frustrating, distressing demands that in some degree characterize everyday transactions with the environment" (Kanner, Coyne, Schaefer, & Lazarus, 1981, p. 3). Examples of hassles include misplacing and losing things, concerns about owing money, not enough time for family, too many responsibilities and too many interruptions. In a prospective study, DeLongis *et al.* (in press) found that a person's level of hassles added significantly to the variance in health status and physical symptoms explained by life–events scores in multiple regression analyses. Hassles scores also accounted for most of the variance shared between life events and health. When the effects of life events were removed, hassles and health remained significantly correlated. Thus, the degree to which a person is hassled in everyday activities appears to have a significant impact—independent of life events—on subsequent health.

The task remains of identifying individual and situational variables mediating both the impact of life events and the accumulation of daily hassles in the absence of major life changes. Our emphasis thus shifts to the coping skills and resources of the individual and the constraints on their use. Critical reviews of the life–events literature increasingly call for the addition of these considerations, and a study of pregnancy and birth complications is cited as empirical support. Nuckolls, Cassell, and Kaplan (1972) found that 90% of the women with high life–change scores and low coping resources had one or more complications, whereas only a third of the women with equally high life–change scores but high coping resources exhibited similar complications. Thus, the influence of stressful life events on health was evident only when resources for coping with the events were not available.

It is clear that stressful life events play some role in the occurrence of illness. Yet attempts to expand on this vague generalization or to improve on the predictive ability of measures of life change inevitably require that we go beyond a conceptualization of stress in terms of the number or formal properties of life events. Of necessity we must turn our attention to the significance of events, how they impinge on a person's life, how he or she copes, and how resources and constraints come into play. We are consequently confronted with the need for a more complex conceptualization of stress, one that grants a critical role to these factors.

2. Stress as a Response

Within the biological sciences, stress is frequently equated with physiological mobilization (e.g., Cannon, 1932; Selye, 1974). For example, Selye (1956, 1976) equates stress with the general adaptation syndrome, a coordinated pattern of physiological responses that is evoked when demands are placed on the organism. Although such an approach to stress phenomena begins with the organism's mobilization instead of with a taxing event, it shares with the environmental approach an inattention to individual differences. Thus, factors that lead some individuals but not others to respond to a noxious stimulus with mobilization and some individuals but not others to remain mobilized for prolonged periods are largely ignored.

This inattention to individual differences is reflected in research methodologies that isolate stress responses from their psychological and social context. Injurious agents such as physical mutilation, bacteria, or toxins are used to mobilize the organism, while options for avoiding or combating the injurious agent are either entirely eliminated or severely restricted. These laboratory methods have allowed hormonal stress responses to be reliably elicited and have enabled investigators to document the role of adrenal medulla and adrenal cortex secretions in mobilization. However, they are unable to provide information about the determinants of these responses in individuals functioning in less restricted settings.

Even in these laboratory environments designed to minimize individual differences, stress responses appear to be powerfully influenced by psychological factors. Mason has summarized evidence indicating that the organism's appraisal of "threatening or unpleasant factors in the life situation as a whole" (1971, p. 327) is one of the most important determinants of hormonal stress responses; physical stresses may, in fact, fail to elicit these responses if the emotional distress that typically accompanies their administration is eliminated (Mason, 1968, 1971, 1975). Psychological variables can also be important determinants of the tissue damage that accompanies prolonged mobilization, for example, the stress ulcer originally identified as part of the alarm stage of the general adaptation syndrome (Weiss, 1977). We are unlikely to understand the development of stress-related illnesses outside the laboratory as long as we artificially isolate physiological stress responses from their psychosocial contexts.

The tendency to isolate physiological stress responses from their contexts is also evident in some intervention strategies within behavioral medicine. For example, biofeedback training that attempts to teach self-control of symptom-related physiological responses often proceeds as if physiological activity could be isolated from psychological processes and be modified by means of self-control strategies that are essentially context-free. This assumption has retarded the development of effective methods for facilitating the generalization of learning to extralaboratory settings, and it has limited our understanding of how biofeedback produces improvement in those instances in which it is effective.

Unfortunately, it turns out that no amount of biofeedback training in a relaxed laboratory environment will ensure the ability to control specific physiological responses in naturalistic settings. Strategies that enable effective control of responses in the laboratory may be virtually useless in more naturalistic settings (Lynn & Friedman, 1979). Not surprisingly, people are often unable to control specific physiological reactions while they engage in transactions with the environment that generate the very same responses. The realization that self-control of physiological activity acquired in the laboratory will not generalize to extralaboratory contexts without comprehensive alteration in the individual's interactions with the environment has begun to temper claims of effectiveness for biofeedback therapy (Lynn & Friedman, 1979).

In some instances—for example, with tension and migraine headaches—biofeedback has proven effective in the treatment of stress-related symptoms (Blanchard, Andrasik, Ahles, Teders, & O'Keefe, 1980). However, the tendency to ignore the psychosocial determinants of symptom-related stress responses has made investigators so ready to attribute therapeutic improvement to the learned control of physiological activity that equally plausible alternative explanations are seldom explored. In those instances where the evidence that biofeedback is strongest, symptom improvement does not appear to result from the acquired ability to control physiological responding. Well-controlled studies have found virtually no relationship between the learned control of physiological activity and symptom improvement (Kewman & Roberts, 1980; Andrasik & Holroyd, 1980). It appears more likely that biofeedback is effective in such instances because changes in coping activity that follow biofeedback training have indirect effects on symptom-related physiological activity and not because the acquired ability to regulate physiological activity enables individuals to more directly control symptom-related physiological responses (Holroyd, 1979; Holroyd & Andrasik, 1982).

3. A Transactional Conception of Stress

In the early fifties, Grinker and his associates criticized existing psychosomatic models for their detachment of the person from the environment. Grinker attempted to construct an alternative transactional model based on the assumptions "that the human organism is part of and in equilibrium with its environment, that its psychological processes assist in maintaining an internal equilibrium and that the psychological functioning of the organism is sensitive to both internal needs and external conditions" (Grinker, 1953, p. 152).

More recently, Lazarus and his colleagues (Lazarus, 1980; Coyne & Lazarus, 1980; Lazarus & Launier, 1978) have argued that psychological stress is best conceptualized in terms of person–environment transactions that tax or exceed the resources of the person. Stress is thus neither an environmental stimulus, a characteristic of the person, nor a response but a relationship between demands and the power to deal with them without unreasonable or destructive costs. Ongoing commerce between person and environment are viewed in terms of their reciprocal action, with each affecting and in turn being affected by the other. Two processes mediate the person's contribution to this relationship: *appraisal* and *coping*.

3.1. Appraisal

The Lazarus group applies the concept of appraisal to the person's continually reevaluated judgments about demands and constraints in transactions with the environment and options and resources for meeting them. A key assumption of the model is that these evaluations determine the person's stress reaction, the emotions experienced, and adaptational outcomes. The degree to which a person experiences psychological stress is determined by the evaluation of both what is at stake (primary appraisal) and what coping resources are available (secondary appraisal).

Primary appraisal takes three forms: Judgments that the transaction is (1) irrelevant to the person's well-being, (2) benign-positive, or (3) stressful. Stressful appraisals are distinguished in terms of whether they involve judgments of (a) harm-loss, (b) threat, or (c) challenge. Although all three involve some negative evaluation of one's present or future state of well-being, challenge provides the least negative or most positive one.

If primary appraisal answers the question "Am I okay or in trouble?" then *secondary appraisal* can be seen as the person's answer to "What can I do about it?" Seconary appraisal refers to the person's ongoing judgments concerning coping resources, options, and constraints. Essentially, it involves the evaluation of coping strategies with respect to their cost and probability of success. The determinants of secondary appraisal in a given stressful episode are likely to include the person's previous experiences with such situations, generalized beliefs about self and environment, and the availability of resources. The latter include the person's morale and assessment of health/energy, problem-solving skills, social support, and material resources (Folkman, Schaefer, & Lazarus, 1979).

The distinction between primary and secondary appraisal is useful mainly in the attention it draws to different sets of variables affecting cognition, coping, and adaptational outcome. The two evaluative processes are highly interrelated and are not empirically separable in many contexts. Thus a firm sense of self-efficacy (secondary appraisal) can lead one to appraise transactions as benign or irrelevant (primary appraisal), or, alternately, a sense one's coping resources are limited can lead to appraisals of threat where they would not otherwise occur.

3.2. Coping

Earlier research of the Lazarus group focused on the importance of cognitive appraisal processes both in determining stress responses and in guiding efforts to manage and control stress (cf. Lazarus, Averill, & Opton, 1970). Current work has given increased attention to the role of coping in actively shaping the stress experience.

Coping is defined as comprising efforts, both cognitive and behavioral, to manage environmental and internal demands and the conflicts among them. Two main functions of coping have been noted: the alteration of the ongoing person–environment relationship (problem-focused coping) and the control of stressful emotions or physiological arousal. Problem-oriented coping involves efforts to deal with the sources of stress, whether by changing one's own problem-maintaining behavior or by changing environmental conditions. Emotion regulation involves coping efforts aimed at reducing emotional distress and maintaining a satisfactory internal (i.e., hormonal) state for processing information and action.

Stressful transactions with the environment generally involve both coping functions. A recent study of stress and coping in middle-aged people revealed that they used both functions in 98% of the specific stressful episodes they reported in the course of a year (Folkman & Lazarus, 1980). Coping with extreme stress often involves (1) an acute phase in which efforts are most appropriately directed toward minimizing or defensively distorting the impact of the event (emotion regulation) and (2) a reorganization phase in which the harm, loss, or threat is recognized and coping efforts are focused on altering the person–environment relationship (Hamburg & Adams, 1967). However, it is also possible for the two functions to be in conflict, as when palliative (emotion-focused) coping obstructs or delays actions required to protect the person against illness (Hackett & Cassem, 1975; Pranulis, 1975; Von Kugelen, 1975).

4. Coping and Health

There are at least four pathways through which coping might influence health (see Holroyd, Appel, & Andrasik, in press). First, coping may influence health outcomes by influencing the frequency, intensity and possibly the character of the physiological stress responses the individual experiences (Holroyd, 1979; Lazarus, Cohen, Folkman, Kanner, & Schaefer, 1980). Selye (1956, 1976) has played a major role in popularizing the notion that neuroendocrine stress responses can play a significant etiological role in disease. Although it is now generally accepted that stress-related fluctuations in neuroendocrine activity can affect disease processes, we have only a limited knowledge of precisely how this occurs. On the one hand, hemodynamic control mechanisms may be disregulated in the early stages of hypertension (Kaplan, 1979) or immune mechanisms disrupted in some cases of Graves' disease and asthma (Bowers & Kelley, 1979; Morillo & Gardner, 1979; Rodgers, Dubey, & Reich, 1979). On the other hand, stress hormones may enhance the effectiveness of the immune response and act protectively against disease processes (Amkraut & Solomon, 1974). Consequently, straightforward notions about the damaging consequences of arousal (Stoyva, 1976) probably are at least overstated if not incorrect.

Second, physiological symptoms may be learned or maintained because they serve coping functions. This possibility is implicit in Miller and Dworkin's (1977) notion that genetically predisposed individuals who are unable to manage stress psychologically may learn to cope physiologically—that is, by elevating blood pressure so as to produce the sedative-like effects that accompany bororeceptor stimulation. Although these pressor responses may produce short-term reductions in stress emotions over the long run, they could be expected to contribute to the disregulation of hemodynamic control systems that occurs in essential hypertension. This possibility is also reflected in the hypothesis that illness or illness behavior serves stabilizing functions in conflicted families (Minuchin, Rosman, & Baker, 1978) or that it is maintained by secondary gains and reinforcements (Whitehead, Fedoravicius, Blackwell, & Wooley, 1979).

Third, coping may contribute to disease because it involves changes in health behaviors that expose the individual to injurious agents such as alcohol, tobacco smoke, or allergens. For example, disease processes may be initiated or aggravated when men at risk for coronary heart disease increase their smoking in response to stress (Horowitz, Hulley, Alvarez, Reynolds, Benfari, Blair, Borhani, & Simon, 1979) or when sufferers of peptic duodenal ulcer increase their consumption of alcohol in response to work stress (Weisman, 1956). When symptoms covary in a systematic manner with the occurrence of stressful events, there is a tendency to ignore the possibility that symptoms are triggered by changes in health behaviors.

Finally, the way the individual copes with the threat of acute illness (Gentry, 1975; Pranulis, 1975; Hackett & Cassem, 1975) or with the demands of chronic illness (Cohen & Lazarus, 1979; Moos & Tsu, 1977) can be an important determinant of the course of the illness and of the medical care that is received. For example, the way in which an asthmatic copes with the threat of airway obstruction can be an influential determinant of medical outcome, influencing the physician's prescriptions of steroid medication, the asthmatic's pattern of self-medication, and other health behaviors (Jones, Kinsman, Dirks, & Dahlem, 1979; Kinsman, Dirks, & Jones, Chapter 19). Therefore we must attend not only to symptoms themselves but to the individuals' efforts to regulate and control their disorders.

5. Coping Skills Treatment

To the extent that coping plays a predisposing or initiating role in illness or aggravates and maintains disease processes initiated by other factors, treatment should probably focus not only on physiological symptoms *per se* but also on coping activities that influence disease processes (Holroyd, 1979). Interventions of this sort would focus on (1) preventing stress-related illness by assisting at risk individuals to cope more effectively with stress, (2) indirectly modifying physiology by altering the way the individual copes with symptom-related stresses, and (3) managing the stressful consequences of disease and medical intervention.

Relaxation training is the simplest coping-skills-oriented intervention because it teaches clients to manage psychological and physiological stress responses by means of a simple coping strategy—relaxation. At present there is a fairly substantial body of evidence indicating that the use of relaxation as a coping skill can produce significant improvements in chronic tension and migraine headache (cf. Blanchard *et al.*, 1980) and at least moderate reductions in blood pressure in essential hypertension (cf. Agras & Jacob, 1979), and there are some promising findings with other disorders (Surwit, Williams, & Shapiro, in press). Although information about the long-term maintenance of these therapeutic gains is meager, these findings support the hypothesis that even providing individuals with simple coping responses can in some instances produce meaningful reductions in stress-related physical symptoms.

However, there are a number of reasons to believe that treatments that teach a more comprehensive set of coping skills may often be preferable to treatments that teach a single coping skill such as relaxation. First, because the complex demands of everyday life often require flexible coping skills, many stressful transactions cannot be managed by simply relaxing; alternate strategies will be required. Second, because stress responses are embedded in the individual's transactions with the environment, individuals will often find it difficult to manage arousal by relaxing while they continue to think and behave in ways that generate the very arousal they are attempting to manage (Holroyd, 1979). Finally, relaxation is likely to have only a minimal impact or even to exacerbate some stress-related symptoms. For example, relaxation can exacerbate some headaches (Bakal, Demjen, & Kaganov, 1981) and is likely to have a minimal impact on the depression that can be both a precipitant and a consequence of recurrent headaches (Holroyd & Andrasik, 1982). In asthmatics, relaxation similarly has a minimal impact on pulmonary function (Alexander, 1982), and can hardly be expected to alter the helplessness and manipulativeness that can accompany this disorder (Creer, 1979).

The development of comprehensive coping-skills-oriented treatments has, for the most part, been pioneered by cognitive behavior therapists (e.g., Beck & Emery, 1979; Goldfried, 1980; Holroyd, 1979; Holroyd et al., in press; Meichenbaum, 1977; Meichenbaum & Jeremko, in press). In addition to providing graduated practice in the use of both cognitive and behavioral coping skills, these interventions teach clients to develop cognitive strategies or plans to facilitate the assimilation of potentially threatening events and information (Meichenbaum, 1976, 1977). The coping-skills approach to stress management has been termed *stress inoculation training* (Meichenbaum, 1976), since its goal is to increase the individual's ability to resist the pathological effects of stress. Descriptions of specific treatment techniques for the management of psychological conditions such as anxiety and depression have been provided by Beck & Emery (1979) and Beck, Rush, Shaw, & Emery (1979) and for the management of somatic disorders such as recurrent tension, migraine headache, and bronchial asthma by Holroyd et al. (in press).

Coping-skills-oriented interventions are currently being employed in both the treatment and prevention of stress-related illness. They are being evaluated as preventitive interventions with individuals in high-risk occupations, for example, police officers (Novaco, 1977); with individuals undergoing stressful transitions such as divorce (Granvold & Welch, 1977), basic training (Novaco, in press), or the transition from school to work (Benner, 1974); and with individuals with characteristics that place them at risk for particular disorders, for example, Type A men (Roskies, 1980), or men who have both a family history of essential hypertension and exhibit cardiovascular reactivity in response to laboratory stress (Adams, 1981). At present this work is only in its beginning stages; more information is needed concerning useful treatment procedures and the timing of interventions. For example, with respect to the question of timing, it is likely that for some disorders interventions may have a preventative function when applied in the early stages of the disorder but have only a minimal impact once symptoms are evident (Holroyd et al., in press).

Coping-skills-oriented treatments are also being used in the management of episodically occurring symptoms. For example, chronic tension and migraine headache sufferers may be taught to recognize the sensations, thoughts, feelings, and behaviors that precede and accompany headache and then to employ coping strategies that serve to prevent headache onset or to minimize the severity of symptoms (e.g., Bakal, Demjen, & Kaganov, in press; Holroyd & Andrasik, 1978, 1982; Holroyd, Andrasik, & Westbrook, 1977). Similarly, asthma sufferers may be taught to recognize the early signs of an attack by associating subjective perceptions with objective measures of pulmonary function; they could then learn to use specific coping procedures (e.g., breathing exercises, postural drainage) to abort or terminate attacks (Creer, 1979; Clark, Feldman, Freudenberg, Millman, Wasilawski, & Valle, 1979). Preliminary work suggests that such treatments are capable of producing significant reductions in symptoms (Holroyd & Andrasik, 1982; Creer, 1981) that are, in some instances, maintained for as long as two years (Holroyd & Andrasik, in press). At this point it is important that researchers begin to compare these interventions with alternate medical interventions.

Coping-skills interventions are also being used to assist patients in managing stresses that are consequences of illness. This involves interventions that are designed to prepare patients for the stresses associated with medical interventions (Kendall, in press) as diverse as cardiac catheterization (Kendall, Williams, Pechacek, Graham, Shisslak, & Herzof, 1979), minor surgery (Langer, Janis, & Wolfer, 1975), and acute coronary care (Hackett & Cassem, 1975) as well as interventions that are designed to assist clients in managing realistic fears that accompany some disorders—for example, fears of a recurrent myocardial infarction or stroke or fears of suffocation that may plague the asthmatic.

As these research efforts proceed from small-scale demonstration studies examining the potential value of cognitive-behavioral interventions in the prevention and treatment of stress-related problems to the more systematic application and evaluation of these interventions, clinicians are likely to find themselves drawing increasingly on basic research on stress and coping. For example, cognitive behavior therapists must develop methods of assessing coping if they are to assess the changes in coping that are the goal of cognitive behavior therapy and determine how these changes in coping are related to improvements in health outcomes. Similarly, if the teaching of coping skills is not to be based solely on therapists' personal beliefs about what constitutes effective coping, we will have to gain a better understanding of the everyday stresses encountered by nonclinical populations and the multiple ways they are presumably effectively managed.

6. Transactional Conceptions of Causality

Much of the work exploring psychosocial aspects of health and illness has essentially been devoted to finding causes for given observed somatic conditions. These causes are presumed to be linearly related to their effects; that is, Condition B is occurring because psychosocial Event A is happening or previously happened. Unfortunately, adequate longitudinal studies with appropriate comparison groups are the exception, and presumed relationships are seldom examined except cross-sectionally (Weiss, 1977). Still, despite such an embarrassing simultaneity of observation, the designated "cause" and "effect" are treated as if they occurred in linear series and in the appropriate order (cf. Jackson, 1965).

Perhaps the most visible instances of such a conceptual strategy occurred in various efforts during the 1950s to relate specific personality variables causally to psychosomatic conditions. Hypotheses were formulated in terms of maternal dynamics, unconscious conflicts, physiological regression, personality types, and chronic emotional states. The hypotheses were often strongly stated in that the predisposition to and initiation of illness were viewed as entirely psychogenic. Overwhelming evidence that psychological and social factors do not determine the choice of an illness ultimately led to a repudiation of the concept of psychogenicity (Weiner, 1977). Furthermore, because the term *psychosomatic* was taken to imply an acceptance of psychogenicity, the entire field of psychosomatic medicine lost ground as a scientific discipline. The field suffered a sharp drop in popularity and credibility and seemed to be headed for the annals of medical history (Lipowski, 1977).

In general, unicausal, linear conceptions of illness are now recognized as being too restrictive and oversimplified to deal with the multifaceted nature of illness. One does not seek a sole and sufficient explanation for the occurrence of infectious disease in the presence of a microorganism; one does not even seek a sole and sufficient explanation for the occurrence of a genetic disease in the presence of abnormal genes (Hinkle, 1974). Accordingly, even in somatic conditions for which the role of psychosocial factors has been clearly established, such factors need to be conceptualized in terms of their interrelationship with a host of nonpsychosocial factors. Furthermore, since psychological events seldom occur only once but persist, overlap, and recur with maddening complexity, a circular causal model is often more appropriate than a linear one that artificially obstructs events from the intricate sequences in which they occur (Jackson, 1965).

Within a transactional perspective, firm notions of linear causality are abandoned and the existence of such reciprocal feedback loops is acknowledged. The isolation of simple temporal sequences and the designation of variables as independent and dependent, antecedent and consequent is seen merely as a provisional punctuation of the ongoing stream of social, psychological, and physiological processes—one that can be revised as needed. Rather than inquiring whether Event A is the fundamental cause of Condition B, questions are phrased in terms of "How is Event A involved in the initiation or persistence of Condition B?" (Coyne, in press).

More specific to the study of the relationship between stress phenomena and illness, it is recognized that, strictly speaking, answers to questions concerning the fundamental etiology of somatic conditions may prove irrelevant to the identification of maintaining conditions and points of intervention. For instance, even without an entire understanding the etiology of Crohn's disease or ulcerative colitis, observations that the patient's condition is exacerbated by particular types of interpersonal confrontations can lead to effective interventions (Youell & McCullough, 1975). The emphasis is on identifying problematic appraisals, coping behavior, and environment contexts associated with the persistence of a problem rather than with its "causes."

7. Stress in Its Social Context

A transactional perspective rejects conventional conceptualizations of the person and environment as substantially independent entities. Key person and environmental variables must be designated relationally. No constituents of the ongoing flow of stress and coping can be specified completely apart from the specification of other constituents (Coyne & Lazarus, 1980).

Much of the work of the Lazarus group has involved explicating the contribution of person variables in the stress and coping process. "Stress, *per se*, cannot be regarded simplistically as causal in human maladaptation because it generates such a variety of coping processes, and, in turn, is as much a product of inept coping as it is of environmental demands, or stressors" (Lazarus, 1980, p. 318). It has been emphasized that coping actively shapes the course of the ongoing person-environment relationship. Rather than a fixed entity that inevitably impinges on the person, much of the environment remains only a potential until it is actualized by coping efforts. Environmental influences may shape the constellation of coping efforts that come into play in a stressful transaction, but coping also partially determines which environmental influences will be involved and what form they will take (Coyne & Lazarus, 1980; Coyne, 1976).

The Lazarus group has given considerably less attention to environmental influences or the person-environment unit. In parallel with arguments about the manner in which the person selects and shapes critical features of the environment, it can be noted that the person's characteristic environment encourages some coping activities while constraining others. For example, although women, overall, report more emotion-focused coping than do men, this is explainable in terms of the context of stressful episodes. Women report more stressful episodes involving health issues, whereas men report more involving work. When these differences in context are controlled, sex differences in coping largely disappear (Folkman & Lazarus, 1980).

Clearly, more work needs to be done in the description of the environmental component of the person–environment relationship—in terms of the structure of demands, opportunities, resources and constraints. There has long been an interest in the social environment as a stressor (Levine & Scotch, 1970). Many of the most heavily weighed and frequent items in life–events scales are social in nature, although the theoretical implications of this have seldom been explored (Hinkle, 1974). More recently, however, there has been a growing interest in the social environment as a resource as well.

7.1. Social Support

Current interest in the social environment as a resource has centered on the social support hypothesis: namely, that social support moderates the damaging effects of stress and in other ways facilitates positive adaptational outcomes. Initial theoretical articles (Cassel, 1976; Cobb, 1976; Dean & Lin, 1977; Kaplan, Cassel, & Gore, 1977) reinterpreted studies of the effects of loss of social ties on health in light of the social support hypothesis. There are now also a number of empirical studies relating lack of support to psychopathology (Henderson, Byrne, Duncan-Jones, Adcock, Scott, & Steele, 1978; Schaefer, Coyne, & Lazarus, in press), complications of pregnancy (Nuckolls *et al.*, 1972) and all cause mortality (Berkman & Syme, 1979). Although this research appears to highlight the beneficial effects of having social support, the various studies differ greatly in how they conceptualize and measure social support and have yet to rule out alternatives to the social support hypothesis.

First, such studies generally do not distinguish between (1) the positive effects of having social support in terms of specific stress-buffering functions social support may have in stressful circumstances and (2) the absence of the deleterious effects of disconnection or losing social ties. For instance, Schaefer *et al.* (in press) noted

> Investigators who think they are studying the effects of small social networks or low perceived support may actually be studying the effects of recent separation or bereavement—very profound sources of stress whose importance goes far beyond the mere loss of potential support. The psychological distress and dislocation in everyday living caused by bereavement or separation may differ in many respects from the long-term effects of being deprived of such relationships.

Second, arguments in favor of the social support hypothesis frequently treat measures of social network size, social support, and general psychosocial assets as interchangeable. *Social network* has been defined as "the specific set of linkages among a defined set of persons" (Mitchell, 1969, p. 2) and is usually measured in terms of the number of relationships in which people are involved, perhaps weighed by their presumed intimacy. It equates the existence of relationships with the receipt of benefits from them. Social support, on the other hand, typically includes some evaluation of the supportiveness of relationships or an enumeration of the benefits received. There is likely to be an association between social network size and perceived social support, but to equate the two is to ignore differences in the demands, constraints, and conflicts, as well as the benefits that relationships provide.

A study of pregnancy complications (Nuckolls *et al.*, 1972) that we have already noted is widely cited as evidence of the stress-buffering role of support, yet it employed a composite measure of psychosocial assets rather than a simple measure of support. The Nuckolls *et al.* measure included items tapping ego strength, perception of health, extent to which the pregnancy was planned and desired, and confidence of the outcome as well as marital happiness, friendship patterns, and confidence in support from siblings, parents, and in-laws. Intended to be more than a measure of support, the Nuckolls *et al.* instrument confounds a number of psychosocial variables. Yet even with more refined measures of support, we cannot be sure that we are simply assessing the availability of social resources in an environment and we cannot rule out alternative interpretations of the relationship between support and health.

The social support hypothesis is already leading to numerous clinical and community intervention programs designed to increase the availability of social support to people under stress or otherwise at risk. The hope is that added social support will increase their coping capabilities, reduce their need for professional help, limit periods of disability, and strengthen positive health-related behaviors. Yet the effectiveness of such programs may be limited by narrow conceptions of social support and how it can be established and utilized. For instance, if a target person lacks requisite social skills or a receptivity to others, merely linking him to a supportive environment is not likely to succeed. Heller (1979) has suggested that we need to better understand the process of social support in terms of:

1. The relationship between the individual and supportive others
2. The behavior of supportive companions and the context of support
3. Personality, demographic characteristics, and role behavior that influence the receptivity to support
4. The skills necessary to access and maintain supportive relationships
5. Environmental structures that are conducive to the establishment and maintenance of support systems (p. 367)

The growing social support literature provides an important balance to previous treatments of the social environment as a stressor. Yet it has tended to perpetuate a simplistic distinction between person and environment in that social support is often conceptualized as an environmental condition to be linked to the person rather than a characteristic of the person–environment unit mediated by what the person does and how receptive he or she is to the efforts of others. Furthermore, notions of the social environment as a source of stress or, alternatively, as a buffer against stress do not begin to exhaust the richness of the person's involvement with the environment and its impact on health. Such notions are not a substitute for knowledge of how members of the social environment affect appraisals, decisions, and coping in specific health-relevant contexts such as efforts to change one's life-style, adhere to treatment, or interpret ambiguous bodily symptoms. Adjustments required to preserve health or cope with chronic illness tend to affect not only the individual but also those with whom he or she is intimately involved. Our conceptualizations and our interventions generally ignore such features of the ecology of individual health and illness, but we cannot afford to continue to do so.

This is particularly true for the person's involvement with the family. If an extraterrestrial being were able to examine the current literature concerning stress, coping, and illness, it would get little sense that families are the important source of both stress (Croog, 1970) and support (Lasch, 1977) that they are. Neither would it comprehend the extent to which the family is the context and determinant of so many critical health-related decisions and behaviors.

7.2. The Family

The majority of Americans live in some conjugal unit (Maddox, 1975), and it would seem that a description of psychosocial factors related to health and illness would be incomplete without reference to home life. Yet a perusal of the index of a recent 700-page volume on health psychology (Stone, Cohen, & Adler, 1979) reveals only *one* entry under *family*, and this is in reference to use of a family assessment instrument as a teaching aid. A variety of data can be cited as evidence of our need to widen our lens and take a fuller look at the individual in the context of the family.

Families develop their own levels of health and illness, and these levels tend to persist over time. Thus, members of some families have a consistently high incidence of diverse illnesses, while members of other families have a low incidence (Downes, 1949; Dingle, Badger, & Gordon, 1964; Pratt, 1976). There are also patterns of illness within families that cannot be explained readily in terms of biological vulnerabilities. For example, Cobb, Kasl, French, and Norstelo (1969) replicated previous findings of an association between wives with rheumatoid arthritis and husbands with peptic ulcers and produced additional data suggesting a mediator's role for the manner in which hostility is handled in such marriages. Also, in families of people with hypertension, members of the household who are not related to the patient are more likely to suffer from hypertension than is the general population (Chazan & Winkelstein, 1964).

The treatment of chronic illness is definitely a home-care situation in that only 4% of those who report restrictions of activities are a result of chronic disease or impairment live in institutions; the vast majority live mainly at home (American Hospital Association, 1971). In many chronic conditions, patients receive less than a total of one day per year in direct contact with doctors and nurses. The rest of medical care is provided by self, family, and friends (Pratt, 1976).

Families represent more than collectivities of individuals. There are patterned regularities in transactions among individual family members, and between the family and the larger community, that may have important implications for their health and well-being. Family theorists have sometimes underestimated the large areas of autonomy in the lives of family members and their ability to transcend the limits of the family's influence. Nonetheless, they have alerted us to the need to observe how involvement in a family regulates and constrains or facilitates the coping of the individuals.

Stress theory and research with the family as the unit of analysis are not as developed as the corresponding study of the individual in isolation (Hanson & Johnson, 1979). Until recently, the focus has been on the family as a *reactor* to stress and on the way in which resources are managed in the face of it. Yet there is now a shift in progress to considerations of the family's active coping strategies and transactions with the community that affect the vulnerability of family members (McCubbin, 1979). Efforts are being made to delineate the nature of response patterns, the processes of successful and unsuccessful adaptation, and factors associated with differential responses of the family to stress. There is still a predominance of clinical descriptive studies, and a great deal of conceptual clarification is required if we are to progress to systematic, well-controlled studies (Coyne & DeLongis, 1981).

The task of relating family stress, coping, and adaptation to that of its individual members is complex. It may often be that characteristic features of a family that ensure its orderly functioning may maintain or exacerbate the unsuccessful adaptation of a given member.

The role of stressful family circumstances in somatic conditions is underscored by repeated findings that separation of severely ill asthmatic children from their families resulted in the improvement of about half of all cases studied (Weiner, 1977). Two studies have demonstrated that the improvement is not likely to be due to the children's removal from specific allergens to which they are exposed at home (Lamont, 1963; Long, Lamont, Whipple, Bardler, Blum, Boum, Burgin, & Jessner, 1958). These studies found that no new asthma attacks occurred when dust collected from the children's homes was sprayed into their rooms.

Anorexia nervosa is perhaps the syndrome that is most successful in drawing attention to the role of family transactions in somatic conditions. Historically, it was among the syndromes most responsible for convincing the medical profession that there may be a psychological background for some physiological conditions (Weiss & English, 1957), and it may again be facilitating a paradigmatic shift, this time from the individual in isolation to the transactional system in which the individual functions.

The work of Minuchin and his colleagues (Minuchin, 1974; Minuchin, Rosman, & Baker, 1978) is playing a critical role in this shift. Anorexia is a condition in which potentially fatal self-starvation takes place, with death ensuing in perhaps 10% to 15% of all cases. Traditional medical, psychodynamic, and behavioral approaches to the problem have not met with outstanding success, yet Minuchin's group reports 86% showing full medical recovery and an additional 4% showing a fair degree of improvement (Minuchin *et al.*, 1978). A number of reviewers have indicated that these results are better than those reported for any other method (Aponte & Van Deusen, 1981; Goldstein, 1979; Gurman & Kniskern, 1981). Minuchin's group have also extended their approach with considerable success to the families of asthmatics, diabetics, and patients suffering from psychogenic abdominal pain.

On the basis of a variety of data—including observations of structured family tasks, free-fatty-acid responses of patients to family transactions, and treatment outcome—the group has developed a clinical model of characteristics they consider specific to psychosomatic families. It is argued that the patient's symptoms contribute in important ways to the maintenance of the family's functioning. The families are characterized as rigid, lacking in conflict resolution, hypersensitive to the distress of individual family members, and enmeshed—that is, family members are overinvolved in each other's difficulties. The illness of the child takes on a critical role in the family's avoidance of conflict and strengthens members' overinvolvement and hypersensitivity to each other's distress. When typical transactional patterns become threatened from within or outside the family, the child's symptoms may become intensified in a way that legitimizes and strengthens the structure of the family.

It should be made clear that no argument is made that the family transactions cause the psychosomatic problems occurring in a given family member. Instead, it is assumed that the illness and patterns of functioning coevolve. Although in some families, symptoms may foster the development of problematic family organization, particularly when the symptoms are highly visible or life-threatening, it may also be the case that the role the patient has in the family is stressful and exacerbates his or her condition. The key issue is not what caused the illness but rather the dynamic interplay of family and individual factors that mutually maintain each other.

Weakland (1974) has coined the term *family somatics* to indicate the family's involvement in health and illness. He argues that it is important to describe concretely how both illness and the maintenance of health pose problems for a given individual and other members of the family, how they cope, and how, in turn, these coping efforts feedback and affect the conditions to which they are directed. In such a perspective,

The idea of disease as an entity which is limited to one person, and can be transmitted from one individual to another, fades into the background, and disease becomes an integral part of the continuous process of living. The family is the unit of illness because it is the unit of living.(Richardson, 1945, p. 76)

The same is, of course, true for positive health.

7.3. Family Interventions

During the past thirty years the field of family therapy has grown with astounding rapidity. There are numerous distinct approaches grounded in systems and communications theory and sharing a rejection of the assumption that the individual can be considered apart from the social context. The individual influences the social context and is in turn influenced by it in a constantly recurring sequence of transactions. As a context, the family is seen as a rule-governed system; members behave among themselves in an organized, repetitive fashion, and the pattern that develops constrains the behavior of the family.

An important distinction in the field is that between structural (Minuchin *et al.*, 1978) and strategic approaches (Coyne & Segal, in preparation; Watzlawick, Weakland, & Fisch, 1974). Structural approaches are aimed at basic changes in the social organization of the family in the direction of it becoming more clearly defined as well as more elaborated, flexible, and cohesive (Aponte & Van Deusen, 1981). The structural family therapist views problematic behavior as sustained by the structure of the family system and seeks to solve the problem by changing the underlying systemic structure.

In contrast, strategic therapists are more pointedly problem-focused. Attention is directed to how ineffective coping maintains the problems, rather than to the problem itself (Watzlawick, Weakland, & Fisch, 1974). Thus, a stroke victim's depression and failure to exercise his remaining capabilities is conceptualized in the context of his family's oversolicitous and overprotective behavior. Interventions are aimed at interdicting the family's response, so that the stroke victim can discover his own resourcefulness. In an actual such case, the family was treated in the absence of the demoralized patient (Watzlawick & Coyne, 1980). Similarly, in a pilot program, spouses of difficult-to-manage coronary patients were treated in an effort to modify the patients' behavior indirectly (Hoebel, 1977).

Unfortunately, the family therapy literature is dominated more by provocative case examples and clinical speculations than by controlled research. Pinsof (1981) has lamented, "The family therapy field is characterized by a plethora of theories about the nature and relative effectiveness of different techniques and by a dearth of research testing these clinical theories" (p. 699). Yet there are clear signs of a change. Whereas a review in the early 1970s could report only 13 outcome studies (Wells, Dilkes, & Trivelli, 1972), a more recent survey found over 200 reports involving almost 5,000 families (Gurman & Kniskern, 1978).

It appears that family interventions are indeed effective (Gurman & Kniskern, 1978). Furthermore, family therapy is the most empirically supported of any psychotherapeutic intervention for childhood psychosomatic conditions (Gurman & Kniskern, 1981). Clearly, more work needs to be done; it is premature to draw any but the most tentative of conclusions. We know comparatively little about the effects of family functioning on health or the effectiveness of family therapy as an intervention in health-related problems. However, that more research is not currently available reflects yet another unfortunate result of the assumption that we can ignore the social context of health and illness. Remedying this situation ought to rank high among our priorities.

8. Concluding Remarks

The fields of health psychology and behavioral medicine are emerging accompanied by considerable excitement and enthusiasm but also occasionally by extravagant promises and unrealistic expectations. Thus it is asserted that "over 99 percent of us are born healthy and suffer premature death and disability only as a result of personal misbehavior and environmental conditions" (Knowles, 1977, p. 1104). In the same passage, we are told further that we could drastically reduce human misery and improve the quality of life if only

> no one smoked cigarettes or consumed alcohol and everyone exercised regularly, maintained optimal weight on a low fat, low refined carbohydrate, high fiber content diet, reduced stress by simplifying their lives, obtained adequate rest and recreation ... drank fluoridated water, followed the doctor's orders for medication and self-care once disease was detected, used available health resources. (p. 1104)

Yet the practical details of implementing such profound changes in our lifestyles—aside from troubling questions as to their desirability—remain unclear. Certainly, the unremarkable success of efforts to convince people to stop smoking, fasten their seat belts, floss their teeth, and, when necessary, take medication to control hypertension should encourage considerable modesty in our promises. Moreover, we simply do not know that the changes in behavior that we are advocating—for example, changes in eating habits that are designed to reduce cholesterol levels—will, in fact, promote health without unwanted side effects (Herbert & Mann, 1980). There is a danger that overoptimism and ambitious programs undertaken without an adequate scientific base will lead to disillusionment and a discrediting of the field such that the development of genuinely effective interventions will be retarded (Miller, 1979).

We believe that the transactional stress and coping framework that we have sketched in this chapter provides a useful basis for phrasing questions about the role of psychosocial factors in health and illness. The emphasis on the person–environment unit seems to give it a distinct advantage over perspectives that view the person or environment in isolation. We noted, for instance, the potential usefulness of this framework in understanding the mechanisms underlying the effectiveness of biofeedback therapy and the limitations of biofeedback treatments.

There are other ways in which a transactional perspective can assist us in identifying our prospects and limitations. Namely, it can allow us to explore health-related transactions in their context in a way that will enable us to identify the compatibility of health as a value with other considerations. For instance,

Hinkle (1974) gives the example of a man who has disagreements with his wife. The man suppresses his anger in a way that maintains a shaky marriage even though he is aware that this activates his ulcer. Hinkle (1974) argues that although this coping may be ineffective and inappropriate from the point of view of physical health, it is consistent with the apparently compelling goal of preserving the marriage.

When issues of health and health-related activities are considered in their social context, conflicts with other values become apparent. Utopian conceptions of health—and therefore of the goals of health psychology—seldom take this into account. For instance, the World Health Organization has defined health as "a state of complete physical, mental, and social well-being and not merely the absence of disease or infirmity." Given the awareness that comes with a transactional perspective, however, Dubos's (1961) definition of health seems much more workable as a goal for health psychology. He defines health as "a modus vivendi enabling imperfect men to achieve a rewarding and not too painful existence while they cope with an imperfect world."

9. References

Adams, N. *Relaxation and self-control interventions to lower physiological responsiveness to stress in college students at risk for hypertension.* Unpublished doctoral dissertation. Ohio University, 1981.

Agras, S., & Jacob, R. Hypertension. In O. Pomerleau & J. P. Brady (Eds.), *Behavioral medicine: Theory and practice.* Baltimore: Williams & Wilkins, 1979.

Alexander, A. B. The treatment of psychosomatic disorders: Bronchial asthma in children. In A. B. Lahey & A. E. Kazdin (Eds.), *Advances in clinical child psychology.* (Vol. 3). New York: Plenum Press, 1980.

Alexander, A. B. Asthma. In S. N. Haynes & L. Gannon (Eds.), *Psychosomatic disorders: A psychophysiological approach to etiology and treatment.* New York: Gardner, 1982.

American Hospital Association. *Report of a Conference on care of chronically ill adults,* Chicago, 1971.

Amkraut, A., & Solomon, G. F. From the symbolic stimulus to pathophysiologic response: Immune mechanisms. *International Journal of Psychiatry in Medicine,* 1974, 5, 541–563.

Andrasik, F., & Holroyd, K. A test of specific and non-specific affects in the biofeedback treatment of tension headache. *Journal of Consulting and Clinical Psychology,* 1980, 48, 575–586.

Aponte, H. J., & Van Deusen, J. M. Structural family therapy. In A. S. Gurman & D. P. Kniskern (Eds.), *Handbook of family therapy.* New York: Bruner-Mazel, 1981.

Bakal, D., Demjen, S., & Kaganov, J. A. Cognitive behavioral treatment of chronic headache. *Headache,* 1981, 21, 81–86.

Beck, A. T., & Emery, G. *Cognitive therapy of anxiety and phobic disorders.* Philadelphia: Center for Cognitive Therapy, 1979.

Beck, R. T., Rush, R. J., Shaw, B. F., & Emery, G. *Cognitive therapy of depression.* New York: Guilford Press, 1979.

Benner, P. Reality testing a reality shock program. In M. Kramer (Ed.), *Reality shock: Why nurses leave nursing.* St. Louis: Mosby, 1974.

Berkman, L. F., & Syme, S. L. Social networks, host resistance, and mortality: A nine-year follow-up study of Alameda County residents. *American Journal of Epidemiology,* 1979, 109, 186–204.

Birnbaum, F., Caplan, J., & Scharff, T. Crisis intervention after a natural disaster. In R. H. Moos (Ed.), *Human adaptation, coping with life crises,* Lexington, Mass.: Heath, 1976.

Blanchard, E. B., Andrasik, F., Ahles, T. A., Teders, S. J., & O'Keefe, D. Migraine and tension headache: A meta-analytic review. *Behavior Therapy,* 1980, 11, 613–631.

Bourne, P. G. (Ed.). *The psychology and physiology of stress.* New York: Academic Press, 1969.

Bowers, K. S., & Kelly, P. Stress, disease, psychotherapy, and hypnosis. *Journal of Abnormal Psychology,* 1979, 88, 498–505.

Brown, G. W. Meaning, measurement, and stress of life events. In B. S. Dohrenwend & B. P. Dohrenwend (Eds.), *Stressful life events.* New York: Wiley, 1974.

Cannon, W. B. *The wisdom of the body.* New York: Norton, 1932.

Cassel, J. The contribution of the social environment to host resistance. *American Journal of Epidemiology,* 1976, *104,* 107–123.

Chazan, J. A., & Winkelstein, W. Household aggravation of hypertension. *Journal of Chronic Disease,* 1964, *17,* 9–16.

Clark, N. M., Feldman, C. H., Freudenberg, N., Millman, E. J., Wasilawski, Y., & Valle, I. *Developing education for asthmatic children through study of self-management behavior.* Paper presented at the meeting of the American Public Health Association. New York, November 1979.

Cobb, S. Social support as a moderator of life stress. *Psychosomatic Medicine,* 1976, *38,* 300–314.

Cobb, S., Kasl, S. V., French, J. R., & Norstelo, G. Intrafamilial transmission of rheumatoid arthritis: VII. Why do wives with rheumatoid arthritis have husbands with peptic ulcers? *Journal of Chronic Disease,* 1969, *22,* 279–294.

Cohen, F., & Lazarus, R. S. Coping with the stresses of illness. In G. C. Stone, F. Cohen, & N. E. Adler (Eds.), *Health psychology: A Handbook.* San Francisco: Jossey-Bass, 1979.

Coyne, J. C. Depression and the response of others. *Journal of Abnormal Psychology,* 1976, *85,* 186–193.

Coyne, J. C. A critique of cognitions as causal entities with particular reference to depression. *Cognitive therapy and research,* in press.

Coyne, J. C., & DeLongis, A. M. Review of *Marital interaction: Empirical investigations* by J. Gottman. *Family Process,* 1981, *20,* 370–371.

Coyne, J. C., & Lazarus, R. S. Cognitive style, stress perception, and coping. In I. L. Kutash & L. B. Schlesinger (Eds.), *Handbook on stress and anxiety: Contemporary knowledge, theory, and treatment.* San Francisco: Jossey-Bass, 1980.

Coyne, J. C., & Segal, L. A brief strategic interactional approach to psychotherapy. In J. C. Archin & D. J. Kiesler (Eds.), *Handbook of Interpersonal Psychotherapy.* New York: Plenum Press. Book in preparation.

Creer, T. L. *Asthma therapy: A behavioral health care system for respiratory disorders.* New York: Springer, 1979.

Croog, S. H. The family as a source of stress. In S. Levine & N. A. Scotch (Eds.), *Social Stress.* Chicago: Aldine, 1970.

Dean, A., & Lin, N. The stress-buffering role of social support. *Journal of Nervous and Mental Disease,* 1977, *169,* 403–417.

DeLongis, A., Coyne, J. C., Dakof, G., Folkman, S., & Lazarus, R. S. Relationship of daily hassles, uplifts and major life events to health status. *Health Psychology,* in press.

Dingle, J. H., Badger, G. F., & Gordon, W. S. *Illness in the home.* Cleveland: The Press of Western Reserve University, 1964.

Dohrenwend, B. S., & Dohrenwend, B. P. (Eds.). *Stressful life events: Their nature and effects.* New York: Wiley, 1974.

Downes, J. *Social environment factors in illness.* Milbank Memorial Fund Background of Social Medicine, New York: 1949.

Dubos, R. *Mirage of health.* Garden City, New York: Doubleday (Anchor Books), 1961.

Dubos, R. *Man adapting.* New Haven: Yale University Press, 1965.

Engel, G. L. The need for a new medical model: A challenge for biomedicine. *Science,* 1977, *196,* 129–136.

Folkman, S., & Lazarus, R. S. An analysis of coping in a middle-aged community sample. *Journal of Health and Social Behavior,* 1980, *21,* 219–239.

Folkman, S., Schaefer, C., & Lazarus, R. S. Cognitive processes as mediators of stress and coping. In V. Hamilton & D. M. Warburton (Eds.), *Human stress and cognition: An information-processing approach.* New York: Wiley, 1979.

Freedman, J. *Crowding and behavior.* New York: Viking, 1975.

Garrity, T. F., Marx, M. B., & Somes, G. W. The relationship of recent life change to seriousness of later illness. *Journal of Psychosomatic Research,* 1977, *22,* 7–12.

Gentry, W. D. Preadmission behavior. In W. D. Gentry & R. B. Williams, Jr. (Eds.), *Psychological aspects of myocardial infarction and coronary care.* St. Louis: Mosby, 1975.

Goldfried, M. R. Psychotherapy of coping skills training. In M. J. Mahoney (Ed.), *Psychotherapy process: Current issues and future directions.* New York: Plenum Press, 1980.

Goldstein, H. S. Psychosomatic families: A model in need of testing. *Contemporary Psychology*, 1979, *24*, 523–525.

Granvold, D. K., & Welch, G. J. Intervention for postdivorce adjustment problems: The treatment seminar. *Journal of Divorce*, 1977, *1*, 81–92.

Grinker, R. R. *Psychosomatic concepts.* New York: Norton, 1953.

Gurman, A. J., & Kniskern, D. P. Research on marital and family therapy: progress, perspective, and prospect. In S. Garfield & A. Bergin (Eds.), *Handbook of psychotherapy and behavior change* (2nd ed.). New York: Wiley, 1978.

Gurman, A. J., & Kniskern, D. P. Family therapy outcome research: Knowns and unknowns. In A. J. Gurman & D. P. Kniskern (Eds.), *Handbook of family therapy.* New York: Bruner-Mazel, 1981.

Hackett, T. P., & Cassem, N. H. Psychological intervention in myocardial infarction. In W. D. Gentry & R. B. Williams, Jr. (Eds.). *Psychological aspects of myocardial infarction and coronary care.* St. Louis: Mosby, 1975.

Hamburg, D. A., & Adams, J. E. A perspective on coping behavior: Seeking and utilizing information in major transitions. *Archives of General Psychiatry*, 1967, *17*, 277–284.

Hanson, D. A., & Johnson, V. A. Rethinking family stress theory: Definitional aspects. In W. R. Burr, R. Hill, F. I. Nye, & I. L. Reiss (Eds.), *Contemporary theories about the family.* New York: Free Press, 1979.

Heller, K. The effects of social support: Prevention and treatment implications. In A. P. Goldstein & F. P. Kanfer (Eds.), *Maximizing treatment gains: Transfer enhancement in psychotherapy.* New York: Academic Press, 1979.

Henderson, S. K., Byrne, D. G., Duncan-Jones, P., Adcock, S., Scott, R., & Steele, G. P. Social bonds in the epidemiology of neurosis: A preliminary communication. *British Journal of Psychiatry*, 1978, *132*, 463–466.

Herbert, P. N., & Mann, G. V. *The diet/heart debate.* Paper presented at the Second Annual Meeting of the Society of Behavioral Medicine. New York, November 1980.

Hinkle, L. E. The effects of exposure to culture change, social change and changes in interpersonal relationships to health. In B. S. Dohrenwend & B. P. Dohrenwend (Eds.), *Stressful life events.* New York: Wiley, 1974.

Hochstim, J. R. Health and ways of living. In I. J. Kessler & M. L. Levin (Eds.), *The community as an epidemiological laboratory.* Baltimore: Johns Hopkins Press, 1970.

Hoebel, F. C. Coronary artery disease and family interaction: A study of risk modification. In P. Watzlawick & J. H. Weakland (Eds.), *The interactional view.* New York: Norton, 1977.

Holmes, T. H., & Rahe, R. H. The social readjustment rating scale. *Journal of Psychosomatic Research*, 1967, *11*, 213–218.

Holmes, T. H., & Masuda, M. Life change and illness susceptibility. In B. S. Dohrenwend & B. P. Dohrenwend (Eds.), *Stressful life events: Their nature and effects.* New York: Wiley, 1974.

Holroyd, K. Stress, coping, and the treatment of stress related illness. In J. R. McNamara (Ed.), *Behavioral approaches in medicine: Application and analysis.* New York: Plenum Press, 1979.

Holroyd, K., & Andrasik, F. A cognitive behavioral approach to the treatment of recurrent headache. In P. Kendall (Ed.), *Advances in cognitive behavior therapy.* New York: Academic Press, 1982.

Holroyd, K., & Andrasik, F. Do the effects of cognitive therapy endure?: A two year follow-up of tension headache sufferers treated with cognitive therapy or biofeedback. *Cognitive Therapy and Research*, in press.

Holroyd, K., Andrasik, F., & Westbrook, T. Cognitive control of tension headache. *Cognitive Therapy and Research*, 1977, *1*, 121–133.

Holroyd, K., Appel, M., & Andrasik, F. A cognitive behavioral approach to psychophysiological disorders. In D. Meichenbaum & M. Jeremko (Eds.), *Stress management and prevention: A cognitive behavioral approach.* New York: Plenum Press, in press.

Horowitz, M., Schaefer, C., Hiroto, D., Wilner, N., & Levin, B. Life events questionnaires for measuring presumptive stress. *Psychosomatic Medicine*, 1977, *6*, 413–431.

Horowitz, M. J., Hulley, S., Alvarez, W., Reynolds, A. M., Benfari, R., Blair, S., Borhani, N., & Simon, N. Life events, risk factors, and coronary disease. *Psychosomatics*, 1979, *20*, 586–592.

Hudgens, R. W. Personal catastrophe and depression: A consideration of the subject with respect to mentally ill adolescents, and a requiem for retrospective life-event studies. In B. S. Dohrenwend & B. P. Dohrenwend (Eds.), *Stressful life events.* New York: Wiley, 1974.

Jackson, D. D. The study of the family. *Family Process*, 1965, *4*, 1–20.

Jones, N. F., Kinsman, R. A., Dirks, J. F., & Dahlem, N. W. Psychological contributions to chronicity in asthma: Patient response styles influencing medical treatment and its outcome. *Medical Care,* 1979, *17,* 1103–1118.

Kanner, A. D., Coyne, J. C., Schaefer, C., & Lazarus, R. S. Comparison of two modes of stress measurement: Daily hassles and uplifts versus major life events. *Journal of Behavioral Medicine,* 1981, *4,* 1–39.

Kaplan, B. H., Cassel, J. C., & Gore, S. Social support and health. *Medical Care,* 1977, *15*(5), 47–58.

Kaplan, N. M. The Goldblatt Memorial Lecture, Part II: The role of the kidney in hypertension. *Hypertension,* 1979, *1,* 456–461.

Kellam, S. C. Stressful life events and illness: A research area in need of conceptual development. In B. S. Dohrenwend & B. P. Dohrenwend (Eds.), *Stressful life events: Their nature and effects.* New York: Wiley, 1974.

Kendall, P. C. Preparation for surgery. In D. Meichenbaum & M. Jeremko (Eds.), *Stress prevention and management: A cognitive behavioral approach.* New York: Plenum Press, in press.

Kendall, P. C., Williams, L., Pechacek, T. F., Graham, L. E., Shisslak, G., & Herzof, N. Cognitive-behavioral and patient education interventions in cardiac catheterization procedures: The Palo Alto Medical Psychology Project. *Journal of Consulting and Clinical Psychology,* 1979, *47,* 49–58.

Kewman, D., & Roberts, A. H. Skin temperature biofeedback and migraine headaches. *Biofeedback and Self-Regulation,* 1980, *5,* 327–345.

Knowles, J. H. *Science,* 1977, *198,* 1103–1104. (Editorial)

Lamont, J. H. Which children outgrow asthma and which do not? In H. I. Schneer (Ed.), *The asthmatic child.* New York: Hoeber, 1963.

Langer, E. J., Janis, I. L., & Wolfer, J. A. Reduction in psychological stress in surgical patients. *Journal of Experimental Social Psychology,* 1975, *11,* 155–165.

Lasch, C. *Haven in a heartless world: The family besieged.* New York: Basic Books, 1977.

Lazarus, R. S. The stress and coping paradigm. In L. A. Bond & J. C. Rosen (Eds.), *Competence and coping during adulthood.* Hanover, N.H.: University Press of New England, 1980.

Lazarus, R. S., Averill, J. R., & Opton, E. W., Jr. Toward a cognitive theory of emotions. In M. Arnold (Ed.), *Feelings and emotions.* New York: Academic Press, 1970.

Lazarus, R. S., & Launier, R. Stress-related transactions between person and environment. In L. A. Pervin & M. Lewis (Eds.), *Perspectives in Interactional Psychology.* New York: Plenum Press, 1978.

Lazarus, R. S., Cohen, J. B., Folkman, S., Kanner, A., & Schaefer, C. Psychological stress and adaptation: Some unresolved issues. In H. Selye (Ed.), *Selye's guide to stress research.* (Vol. 1). New York: Van Nostrand Reinhold, 1980.

Levine, S., & Scotch, N. A. *Social Stress.* Chicago: Aldine, 1970.

Lipowski, Z. J. Psychosomatic medicine in the seventies: An overview. *American Journal of Psychiatry,* 1977, *134,* 233–244.

Long, R. T., Lamont, J. H., Whipple, B., Bardler, L., Blum, L., Blum, G., Burgin, L., & Jessner, L. A psychosomatic study of allergic and emotional factors in children with asthma. *American Journal of Psychiatry,* 1958, *114,* 890–899.

Lynn, S., & Friedman, R. R. Transfer and evaluation in biofeedback treatment. In A. P. Goldstein & F. Kanfer (Eds.), *Maximizing treatment gains: Transfer enhancement in psychotherapy.* New York: Academic Press, 1979.

McCubbin, H. I. Integrating coping behavior in family stress theory. *Journal of Marriage and the Family,* 1979, *41,* 237–244.

Maddox, G. L. Families as context and resource in chronic illness. In S. Sherwood (Ed.), *Long-term care: A handbook for researchers, planners and providers.* New York: Spectrum, 1975.

Mason, J. W. Organization of psychoendocrine mechanisms. *Psychosomatic Medicine,* 1968, *80,* 565–608.

Mason, J. W. A re-evaluation of the concept of "nonspecificity" in stress theory. *Journal of Psychiatric Research,* 1971, *8,* 323–333.

Mason, J. W. Clinical psychophysiology. In M. F. Reiser (Ed.), *American handbook of psychiatry.* (Vol. 4). New York: Basic Books, 1975.

Mechanic, D. Discussion of research programs on relations between stressful life events and episodes of physical illness. In B. S. Dohrenwend & B. P. Dohrenwend (Eds.), *Stressful life events: Their nature and effects.* New York: Wiley, 1974.

Meichenbaum, D. A self-instructional approach to stress management: A proposal for stress-inoculation training. In C. Spielberger & I. Sarason (Eds.), *Stress and anxiety in modern life.* New York: Halsted Press, 1976.

Meichenbaum, D. *Cognitive-behavior modification.* New York: Plenum Press, 1977.

Meichenbaum, D., & Jeremko, M. *Stress prevention and management: A cognitive behavioral approach.* New York: Plenum Press, in press.

Miller, N. E. Behavioral medicine: New opportunities but serious dangers. *Behavioral Medicine Update,* 1979, *1,* 5.

Miller, N. E., & Dworkin, B. R. Critical issues in therapeutic applications of biofeedback. In G. E. Schwartz & J. Beatty (Eds.), *Biofeedback.* New York: Academic Press, 1977.

Minuchin, S. *Families and family therapy.* Cambridge: Harvard University Press, 1974.

Minuchin, S., Rosman, B. L., & Baker, L. *Psychosomatic families.* Cambridge: Harvard University Press, 1978.

Mitchell, J. C. (Ed.). *Social networks in urban situations.* Manchester, England: Manchester University Press, 1969.

Moos, R. H. (Ed.). *Coping with physical illness.* New York: Plenum Press, 1977.

Moos, R. H., & Tsu, V. D. The crisis of physical illness: An overview. In R. H. Moos (Ed.), *Coping with physical illness.* New York: Plenum Press, 1977.

Morillo, E., & Gardner, L. Bereavement as an antecedent factor in thyrotoxicosis of childhood: Four case studies with survey of possible metabolic pathways. *Psychosomatic Medicine,* 1979, *41,* 545–555.

Novaco, R. W. A stress inoculation approach to anger management in the training of law enforcement officers. *American Journal of Community Psychology,* 1977, *5,* 327–346.

Novaco, R. W. Military recruits and policemen. In D. Meichenbaum & M. Jeremko (Eds.), *Stress prevention and management: A cognitive behavioral approach.* New York: Plenum Press, in press.

Nuckolls, C. G., Cassel, J., & Kaplan, B. H. Psychosocial assets, life crises, and the prognosis of pregnancy. *American Journal of Epidemiology,* 1972, *95,* 431–441.

Pinsoff, W. M. Family therapy process research. In A. C. Gurman & D. P. Kniskern (Eds.), *Handbook of Family Therapy.* New York: Bruner-Mazel, 1981.

Pranulis, M. Coping with acute myocardial infarction. In W. D. Gentry & R. B. Williams, Jr. (Eds.), *Psychological aspects of myocardial infarction and coronary care.* St. Louis: Mosby, 1975.

Pratt, L. *Family structure and effective health behavior.* Boston: Houghton Mifflin, 1976.

Rabkin, J. G., & Struening, E. L. Life events, stress, and illness. *Science,* 1976, *194,* 1013–1020.

Redfield, J., & Stone, A. Individual viewpoints of stressful life events. *Journal of Consulting Psychology,* 1979, *47,* 147–154.

Richardson, H. B. *Patients have families.* New York: Commonwealth Fund, 1945.

Rodgers, M., Dubey, D., & Reich, P. The influence of the psyche and the brain on immunity and disease susceptibility: A critical review. *Psychosomatic Medicine,* 1979, *41,* 147–164.

Roskies, E. Considerations in developing a treatment program for the coronary-prone (Type A) behavior pattern. In P. O. Davidson & S. M. Davidson (Eds.), *Behavioral medicine: Changing health lifestyles.* New York: Brunner/Mazel, 1980.

Roskies, E. A cognitive behavioral approach to modifying the coronary prone behavior pattern. In D. Meichenbaum & M. Jeremko (Eds.), *Stress prevention and management: A cognitive behavioral approach.* New York: Plenum Press, in press.

Schaefer, C., Coyne, J. C., & Lazarus, R. S. The health-related functions of social support. *Journal of Behavioral Medicine,* in press.

Selye, H. *The stress of life.* New York: McGraw-Hill, 1956.

Selye, H. *Stress without distress.* Philadelphia: Lippincott, 1974.

Selye, H. *The stress of life* (Rev. ed.). New York: McGraw-Hill, 1976.

Spaulding, R. C., & Ford, C. V. The *Pueblo* incident: Psychological reactions to the stresses of imprisonment and repatriation. In R. H. Moos (Ed.), *Human adaptation: Coping with life crises.* Lexington, Mass.: Heath, 1976.

Stone, G., Cohen, F., & Adler, N. (Eds.). *Health psychology: A Handbook.* San Francisco: Jossey-Bass, 1979.

Stoyva, J. Self-regulation and the stress-related disorders: A perspective on biofeedback. In D. Mostofsky (Ed.), *Behavior control and modification of physiological activity.* Englewood Cliffs, N.J.: Prentice-Hall, 1976.

Surwit, R. S., Williams, R. B., & Shapiro, D. *Behavioral approaches to cardiovascular diseases.* New York: Plenum Press. Book in preparation.

Von Kugelen, E. *Psychological determinants of the delay in decision to seek aid in cases of myocardial infarction.* Unpublished doctoral dissertation. University of California, Berkeley, 1975.

Watzlawick, P., & Coyne, J. C. Depression following stroke: Brief, problem-focused family treatment. *Family Process*, 1980, *19*, 13–18.

Watzlawick, P., Weakland, J. W., & Fisch, R. *Change: Principles of problem formation and problem resolution*. New York: Norton, 1974.

Weakland, J. W. Family somatics—a neglected edge. *Family Process*, 1974, *16*, 263–272.

Weiner, H. *Psychobiology and human disease*. New York: Elsevier, 1977.

Weisman, A. A study of the psychodynamics of duodenal ulcer excerbations with special reference to treatment and the problem of specificity. *Psychosomatic Medicine*, 1956, *18*, 2–42.

Weiss, E., & English, O. S. *Psychosomatic medicine*. Philadelphia: Saunders, 1957.

Weiss, J. M. Ulcers. In J. D. Maser & M. E. P. Seligman (Eds.), *Psychopathology: Experimental models*. San Francisco: Freeman, 1977.

Wells, R. A., Dilkes, T., & Trivelli, N. The results of family therapy: A critical review of the literature. *Family Process*, 1972, *7*, 189–207.

Wershaw, H. J., & Reinhart, G. Life change and hospitalization—a heretical view. *Journal of Psychosomatic Research*, 1974, *18*, 393–401.

Whitehead, W. E., Fedoravicius, A. S., Blackwell, B., & Wooley, S. A behavioral conceptualization of psychosomatic illness: Psychosomatic symptoms as learned responses. In J. P. McNamara (Ed.), *Behavioral approaches to medicine: Application and analysis*. New York: Plenum Press, 1979.

Youell, K. J., & McCullough, J. P. Behavioral treatment of mucous colitis. *Journal of Consulting and Clinical Psychology*, 1975, *43*, 740–745.

Coping with Acute Health Crises

Rudolf H. Moos

How can the process and determinants of coping with acute health crises be described? What are the major adaptive tasks seriously ill patients encounter and what types of coping skills do they use? How does the patient adapt to the existential crisis created by learning that he or she has a life-threatening illness? What stressors are encountered by health care professionals and how can they facilitate effective coping and adaptation by patients and their families? I deal with these questions here by presenting a conceptual framework of physical illness as a life crisis and describing how patients and staff cope with the stress of illness and of treatment.

1. Crisis Theory as a General Perspective

Crisis theory is concerned with how people cope with major life crises and transitions. Historically "crisis theory" has been influenced by four major intellectual developments: evolution and its implications for communal and individual adaptation, fulfillment or growth theories of human motivation, a life-cycle approach to human development, and interest in coping behavior under extreme

Part of the material in this chapter is adapted from R. Moos (Ed.), *Coping with Physical Illness*, New York, Plenum Press, 1977.

RUDOLF H. MOOS ● Social Ecology Laboratory, Department of Psychiatry and the Behavioral Sciences, Stanford University and the Veterans Administration Medical Center, Palo Alto, California 94305. Preparation of this chapter was supported by NIMH Grant 28177 and Veterans Administration Health Services Research and Development Funds.

stresses such as natural disasters (Moos & Tsu, 1976). Crisis theory has provided a conceptual framework for preventive mental health care and for the handling of severe physical illness or injury. The fundamental ideas were developed by Lindemann (1944), who described the process of grief and mourning and the role community caretakers could play in helping bereaved family members cope with the loss of their loved ones. Combined with Erikson's (1963) formulation of "developmental crises" at transition points in the life cycle, these ideas paved the way for Caplan's (1964) formulation of crisis theory.

In general, crisis theory deals with the impact of disruptions on established patterns of personal and social identity. Similar to people's need for physiological homeostasis is their need for a sense of social and psychological equilibrium. When people encounter something that upsets their characteristic pattern of behavior and life-style, they employ habitual problem-solving mechanisms until a balance is restored. A situation so novel or so major that the usual, habitual responses are inadequate to deal with it constitutes a crisis and leads to a state of disorganization often accompanied by heightened fear, guilt, or other unpleasant feelings which contribute further to the disorganization.

A crisis is by definition self-limited, since a person cannot remain in an extreme state of disequilibrium. Within a few days or weeks, some resolution, even though temporary, must be found and some equilibrium reestablished. The new balance achieved may represent a healthy adaptation that promotes personal growth and maturation or a maladaptive response that signifies psychological deterioration and decline. A crisis experience may thus be seen as a transitional period, a turning point, which has important implications for an individual's long-term adaptation and ability to meet future crises.

The crisis of physical illness is an unusually potent stressor that may extend over a long period of time and lead to permanent changes among patients and their family members. The potency of the crisis stems from the typically sudden and unexpected onset and the pervasive threat to the essence of an individual's life and adaptation. A person may face hospitalization and separation from family and friends, overwhelming feelings of pain and helplessness, permanent changes in appearance or in bodily function, the loss of key roles, and an uncertain unpredictable future involving the prospect of an untimely death. Furthermore, patients often achieve a state of tentative equilibrium in the course of an illness only to have it shattered by a complex set of new issues and circumstances. Such stages of the illness process as the perception and evaluation of symptoms, the decision to seek medical help, the assessment and diagnosis of the illness, hospitalization and attendant treatment, and convalescence and rehabilitation each involve unique adaptive tasks and the need to use new coping skills.

As Haan (1979) points out, these problems are compounded by specific features of health crises that make it difficult for an individual to select appropriate coping strategies to assimilate and accommodate to the sudden turn of events. For instance, health crises usually cannot be anticipated, their meaning for the individual is ambiguous, clear information is lacking, and it is often necessary to make definitive decisions quickly. A high potential for maladaptive coping is created by the sudden, life-threatening anxiety coupled with the fact that little or nothing can be done to change the crisis itself. Family members, who also may be uncertain about what to do, may react in ways that encourage maladaptive responses on the part of the illness-stricken individual. In addition, a person typically has only limited prior experience in handling serious illness and thus cannot rely on previously successful coping responses.

Patients often regard their disease as the source of major discontinuity in their lives and report permanent changes in their adaptation, self-concept, and perception of the future (Croog & Levine, 1977; Mages & Mendelsohn, 1979). Some of the problems accompanying an acute health crisis are illustrated by Benjamin's (1978) description of eight families in which a child was stricken with a sudden, life-threatening illness. Even though all children made good medical recoveries, family adjustment problems were marked, including incomplete mourning, feelings of loss of control, and fantasies of death and return on the part of the children and parents. The most pervasive long-term difficulty was the sense of helplessness experienced by the afflicted children and their parents. The sudden onset and progression of illness accompanied by an equally quick recovery left parents unable to trust their judgment or capacity to evaluate situations affecting their children. Patients may recover medically from the acute phase of an illness, but such problems as enhanced vulnerability, serious depression, rejection of essential treatment regimens, unnecessary loss of function in family and work roles, and significant suicide potential often remain (Croog & Levine, 1977; Holland, 1977).

On the other hand, most patients do cope adequately with the aftermath of a crisis. Long-term survivors of serious illness can attain levels of psychological and social functioning that are similar to those of their "normal" counterparts in the community (Craig, Comstock, & Geiser, 1974). Furthermore, some people report enhanced personal growth and integration after experiencing an illness (White & Liddon, 1972). In a study of survivors of serious illness, Smith (1979) noted greater concern for and sense of community with others, a change in focus of energy from the constant pressure of work to family relationships, more realism and acceptance of life, and heightened awareness of religious and humanitarian values. The conceptual framework presented next outlines the factors that influence how adaptively an individual will cope with an acute health crisis.

2. A Conceptual Framework

As we have seen, an acute episode of a serious physical illness or injury can be understood as a life crisis or transition; a cognitive appraisal of its significance leads to the formulation of basic adaptive tasks to which various coping skills can be applied. The individual's cognitive appraisal, definition of the adaptive tasks involved, and selection and effectiveness of relevant coping skills are influenced by three sets of factors: sociodemographic and personal characteristics, aspects of the illness such as its timing and stage, and features of the physical and sociocultural environment. These factors together affect the resolution of the initial phase of the crisis, and this resolution, in turn, may result in changes in all three sets of factors and thereby influence the ultimate outcome (see Figure 1).

2.1. Sociodemographic and Personal Factors

Demographic and personal characteristics include age, gender, socioeconomic status, intelligence, cognitive and emotional development, ego strength and self-esteem, philosophical or religious beliefs, and previous illness and coping experiences. These factors influence the meaning that a new illness episode carries for an individual and affect the psychological and intellectual resources available to meet the crisis (see Figure 1). For instance, men may be particularly threatened by the decreases in ambition, vigor, and physical prowess that often result from serious illnesses because, by comparison with women, they are more confident in the stability of their physical abilities and bodily functioning. The enforced dependency and passivity associated with illness is especially likely to interfere with the independent, assertive roles usually occupied by men (Mages & Mendelsohn, 1979).

With respect to socioeconomic factors, Hackett and Cassem (1976) have described variations in the reactions of blue-collar and white-collar patients to a heart attack. Specifically, blue-collar patients displayed more regressive behavior, knew less about the equipment in the coronary care unit (CCU) and found it more frightening, blamed their hearts for artifacts caused by the monitoring equipment, were uninformed about the process of cardiac repair, avoided asking questions about the future, resisted taking needed tranquilizing medication, and were less able to establish adequate communication with their doctors.

The timing of an illness in the life cycle is particularly important. A child invalided by rheumatic heart disease has different concerns than an elderly patient incapacitated by a heart ailment. Some adolescents have a difficult time coping with physical illness, since it imposes an additional stress at a time when the tasks of gaining independence from parents and establishing personal identity and a stable body image already create complex challenges. Although greater maturity and more extensive coping experience may provide middle-aged persons with greater resources on which to draw, serious illness threatens the disruption of established roles and the fulfillment of cherished life goals (see Chapter 20 for examples of personality factors and their relationship to coping and health outcomes).

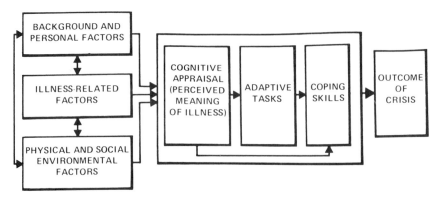

Figure 1. A conceptual model for understanding the crisis of physical illness.

Illness-related factors include the type and location of symptoms, whether painful, disfiguring, disabling, or in a body region vested with special importance like the heart or reproductive organs. Such factors are a major component in defining the exact nature of the tasks patients and others face and, consequently, their adaptive responses. Different organs and functions may have a psychological significance that has little to do with biological factors related to survival. For instance, an injury to the face or amputation of a breast can have greater psychological impact on a woman than severe hypertension directly threatening her life.

The parents of a leukemic child in remission may halt the process of anticipatory mourning that was begun when the diagnosis was first announced, only to have to resume their preparation when the child relapses. Localized cancer, like any other threat, can be dealt with by seeking information and help; but once the cancer is widespread, the individual is presented with more diverse problems and tends to use different coping skills. Patients who formerly spoke openly about their medical situation and treatment may prefer to remain silent because they are afraid of provoking guilt or rejection among their friends and relatives. In advanced stages of cancer, patients often turn their feelings inward and withdraw from intimate communication so as to avoid confronting the grave significance of their deteriorating condition (Abrams, 1974).

Some health crises (and treatments designed to alleviate them) are so overwhelming that they present essentially unresolvable problems for all but the hardiest patients. Although there is a 5-year survival rate of 38%, patients treated for cancer by the "aggressive" therapy of total pelvic exenteration (TPE) face just such extreme stress. TPE consists of the removal of the rectum, distal sigmoid colon, urinary bladder, and all pelvic reproductive organs as well as the entire pelvic floor with accompanying pelvic peritoneum, levator muscles, and perineum. Fisher (1979) found that all six of the women she interviewed who had undergone this procedure had major unresolved psychosexual problems, felt they lacked femininity, verbalized stress about their appearance, and communicated a constant sense of worry, frustration, and personal inadequacy. The termination of sexual function due to obliteration of the vagina and the extensive alteration of excretory functions by creation of a fecal colostomy and urinary ileostomy present a set of adaptive tasks with which few if any patients can cope successfully.

2.3. Physical and Social-Environmental Factors

Features of the physical and social environment affect the adaptive tasks patients and their families must face and the choice and outcome of the coping skills they utilize. The aesthetic quality of the surroundings, the amount of personal space available, and the degree of sensory stimulation may influence a person's cognitive functioning, mood, and general morale (Moos, 1976). For instance, the use of prosthetic and orientational aids such as color patterns, color coding, informational signs, textural markers, and handrails can ease an impaired patient's adaptive tasks and facilitate the recovery process.

The human environment includes the relationships of patients and their families, features of work settings, social supports in the wider community, and sociocultural norms and expectations. The course of an illness tends to be more stormy and recovery slower than expected when it occurs in the context of serious interpersonal conflict or of recent bereavement. Conversely, family support is positively related to morale and maintenance of social functioning among seriously ill patients. Families of myocardial infarction patients whose wives acknowledged more sources of network support and who used sources other than their families of origin tended to experience more favorable outcomes (Finlayson, 1976).

The characteristics of a patient's work setting can be especially important in affecting the course of recovery. The psychologist C. Scott Moss (1972) graphically described how the intellectual environment of the psychology department at the University of Illinois hampered his recovery from aphasia following a stroke. Moss was confronted with a fundamental difference between his cognitive–dynamic framework and the values of his departmental colleagues, most of whom were oriented toward learning theory and behavior modification. Moss felt that he was faced with an unusually difficult predicament when he sustained a stroke within weeks of entering such an intellectually adverse environment. Martha Weinman Lear (1980) recounts how her husband gave up a lucrative private medical practice to fulfill his lifelong dream of pursuing a research career in a university-affiliated medical school. He sustained a serious heart attack soon after the change and found that the problems in the university situation (such as lack of guaranteed salary support, cramped office space, minimal research funds, and the competitive pressures and relative lack of freedom) sharply exacerbated his general burden of stress.

2.4. Mediating Factors: Appraisal and Activation

The role of cognitive appraisal has been heavily emphasized, most notably by Lazarus (1981), who uses it as a central construct in his formulation of the coping process (see Chapter 13). Lazarus argues that one cannot usually relate an "objective" illness-related variable directly to a "dependent" outcome variable. The individual's cognitive appraisal—that is, how the potential stressor is perceived—is usually (though not always) a critical mediating factor. Both the environmental system (for instance, through air pollution or carcinogens) and the personal system (through genetic or constitutional predisposition) can affect health outcomes directly; that is, their effects are not necessarily mediated through cognitive appraisal. However, cognitive appraisal is an important mediating factor in the majority of problems addressed by health care professionals.

Activation or arousal usually occurs when the environment is appraised as necessitating a response. This stimulates efforts at adaptation and coping which are directed toward the perceived adaptive tasks. The nature of these tasks is affected by the meaning of the illness (for instance, if the illness is perceived as life-threatening, the patient may feel it necessary to make a will), by other personal factors (a heart attack patient who has already retired does not need to face the task of returning to work), and by environmental factors (such as the adaptive tasks encountered if a patient with a spinal cord injury lives in an environment that is not barrier-free).

Resulting efforts at adaptation and coping may affect the outcome of the crisis; for example, being able to request reassurance and support may allow family members to participate in a home hemodialysis program. Such efforts may also affect environmental factors (the patient with an injured spinal cord may move to a barrier-free environment) and personal factors (a person may seek and obtain information that changes her attitudes and expectations), which, in turn, influence the resolution of the crisis.

2.5. Major Adaptive Tasks

The major tasks of adapting to acute health crises can be divided into seven categories. Three of these tasks are primarily illness-related while the other four are more general and are relevant to all types of life crises (see Table 1).

The first set of tasks involves dealing with the discomfort, incapacitation, and other symptoms of the illness or injury, including such distressing problems as pain, weakness, dizziness, incontinence, paralysis, loss of control, the feeling of suffocation, permanent disfigurement, and the like. Patients must also learn to recognize the signs of impending medical crises and, more generally, to control their symptoms whenever possible. For instance, a person with a heart disorder must learn to regulate his or her diet and daily exercise, while a diabetic person must be able to prevent potential crises (caused either by sugar shortage or insulin shock) as well as to recognize the signs of an oncoming crisis (Strauss, 1975).

A second and closely related set of tasks entails the management of the stresses of special treatment procedures and of various aspects of the hospital or institutional environment. The increasing sophistication of medical technology has created a host of new problems for patients. Surgical procedures like mastectomy and colostomy, debridement as a treatment for burns, radiotherapy and chemotherapy with their concomitant side effects, the necessity of wearing a cumbersome brace for certain orthopedic disorders, long-term hemodialysis and organ transplantation—all these represent therapeutic measures that create adaptive tasks for patients.

Table 1. Major Sets of Adaptive Tasks

Illness-Related Tasks
1. Dealing with pain, incapacitation, and other symptoms
2. Dealing with the hospital environment and special treatment procedures
3. Developing and maintaining adequate relationships with health care staff
General Tasks
4. Preserving a reasonable emotional balance
5. Preserving a satisfactory self-image and maintaining a sense of competence and mastery
6. Preserving relationships with family and friends
7. Preparing for an uncertain future

This set of tasks includes deciding whether or not to comply with the recommended treatment. Estimates indicate that up to 50% of patients do not receive the full benefit of treatment regimens due to their failure to adhere to the details of the treatment procedure. Factors involved in their decisions include the nature and stage of the illness, the complexity and degree of behavioral change required, the evidence that the regimen works either to control symptoms or the disease itself, the extent to which distressing side effects appear, the degree of discomfort and interference with daily activities, the influence and stability of family and friends, and the degree of supervision and feedback provided by physicians and other health care staff (Sackett & Haynes, 1976).

The third set of tasks consists of developing and maintaining adequate relationships with medical and other health care staff. Consider the questions patients may ask themselves: Can I express my anger at the doctor for not coming to see me? How can I ask for additional medication for pain when I need it? How can I deal with the disagreement among different physicians about my treatment? How can I handle the condescension and pity I sense in the nurses who care for me? How do I let my doctor know how I wish to be treated if I am incapacitated and near death? The frequent turnover and change in personnel, particularly among staff who come into direct contact with patients, makes this an unusually complex set of tasks (see Lear, 1980, for a description of how difficult such tasks can be even for a physician-patient who is familiar with hospital settings).

The fourth category of tasks involves preserving a reasonable emotional balance by managing upsetting feelings aroused by the illness. Many negative emotions are associated with medical crises, such as the sense of failure and self-blame at giving birth to a deformed child, the anxiety and apprehension of not knowing the outcome of an illness, the sense of alienation and isolation and the feelings of inadequacy and resentment in the face of difficult demands. An important aspect of this task is for the patient to maintain some hope even when its scope is sharply limited by circumstances.

The fifth set of tasks consists of preserving a satisfactory self-image and maintaining a sense of competence and mastery. Changes in physical functioning or appearance such as permanent weakness or scarring must be incorporated into a revised self-image. This "identity crisis" can necessitate a change in personal values and life-style, as, for example, when permanently disfigured burn victims and their families learn to play down the importance of physical attractiveness. Patients who must rely on mechanical devices like cardiac pacemakers or hemodialysis to sustain their lives must come to terms with a "half human–half machine" body image.

Defining the limits of independence and readjusting goals and expectations in light of changes brought by the illness are other tasks that belong in this category. The need to depend on others for physical care and emotional support can be highly stressful. It is important to find a personally and socially satisfactory balance between accepting help and taking an active and responsible part in determining the direction and activities of one's life. Resuming independent status after a long period of enforced passivity can also be difficult, as, for example, when a successful organ-transplant patient is suddenly no longer an invalid. This conflict is further complicated for children by the normal developmental drive to gradually increase independence and self-direction, which may be seriously hampered by illness-imposed dependence and parental protectiveness.

The sixth set of tasks includes those of preserving relationships with family and friends. The physical separation and sense of alienation occasioned by hospitalization and being labeled as a "patient" or as a "dying person" often disrupt normal relationships with friends and relatives. Serious illness can make it difficult to keep lines of communication open and to accept comfort and support at the very time when these are most essential. Close relationships with other people can help patients gather the data necessary to make informed decisions about their medical care, find emotional support for their decision, obtain reassurance with respect to the many threats they face, and allow significant others time to prepare for the tasks they themselves will encounter (Kaplan & Grandstaff, 1979).

The seventh set of tasks involves preparing for an uncertain future in which significant losses are threatened. The loss of sight, speech, hearing, a limb or breast by surgery, or life itself all must be acknowledged and mourned. Ironically, new medical procedures that raise hope for patients with previously incurable illnesses may make this task more difficult. Patients must prepare for permanent loss of function while maintaining hope that restoration of function may be possible. When death seems likely, patients and family members must engage in anticipatory mourning and initiate the grieving process while maintaining hope that new treatment procedures may prove beneficial.

These seven groups of tasks are generally encountered with every illness, but their relative importance varies depending on the nature of the disease, the personality of the individual involved, and the unique set of environmental circumstances. For the person suddenly rendered blind, the physical discomfort may be minor while the difficulty of restoring social relations can be overwhelming. A bone cancer patient, on the other hand, must usually deal with severe pain. A woman who has had a mastectomy may find that accepting her new self-image is her most significant task. Someone who is physically active, like a professional athlete or a construction worker, probably will experience more difficulty adjusting to a wheelchair than a person with a more sedentary occupation.

These tasks can be as difficult for family members and friends as for patients themselves. Family members must help patients control their symptoms, try to prevent new medical crises, assist in carrying out special treatment procedures, and develop adequate relationships with health care professionals. They must maintain a sense of inner mastery of their divergent emotions, try to preserve a satisfactory self-image (helping the patient as much as possible but not feeling overwhelmed by guilt when they cannot do everything they are asked), handle the task of maintaining family integrity and their relationship with the patient, and simultaneously prepare for an uncertain future. Active participation in health care procedures can help family and friends recognize and cope with these common tasks. For example, parents may feel less helpless and experience increased self-esteem when they are able to participate in the care of their child, even when such participation includes deciding that the prospects of their child's survival are hopeless and respirator support should be withdrawn (Benfield, Leib, & Vollman, 1978).

2.6. Major Types of Coping Skills

Any response to a health crisis may serve an adaptive function. An overview is offered here of seven types of coping skills commonly employed to deal with the adaptive tasks just described (see Table 2). These skills may be used individually, consecutively, or—more likely—in various combinations. Specific coping techniques are not inherently adaptive or maladaptive. Skills that are appropriate in one situation may not be so in another. Skills that may be beneficial given moderate or temporary use may be harmful if relied on exclusively. The word *skill* underscores the positive aspects of coping and depicts coping as an ability that can be taught (like any other skill) and used flexibly as the situation demands.

The first category covers an array of skills based on denying or minimizing the seriousness of a crisis. These may be directed at the illness itself, as when a myocardial infarct patient maintains "it was just severe indigestion." Or, after the diagnosis is accepted, they may be directed at the significance of an illness, as, for example, when the parents of a fatally ill child still go from doctor to doctor looking for an alternate diagnosis. They may also be directed at the potential consequences of an illness, such as the initial denial and bland affect that is often seen in those who have had a stroke (Moss, 1972). A related skill is the ability to isolate or dissociate one's emotions when dealing with a distressing situation. This occurs when the parents of a hemophiliac child react quickly and calmly to a bleeding episode rather than showing their terror or dismay, or when patients discuss their symptoms with "clinical detachment." These skills often are described as "defensive mechanisms" because they are self-protective responses to stress. This term does not convey their constructive value; they may temporarily rescue the individual from being overwhelmed or provide the time needed to garner other personal coping resources.

The second set of coping skills consists of seeking relevant information about the illness and alternative treatment procedures and their probable outcome. Parents of leukemic children seek information about the degree of their responsibility for the illness (initially blaming themselves, for example, for not having paid more attention to the early nonspecific manifestations of the disease), about hospital procedures (questioning ward physicians and nurses and scrutinizing newspaper and magazine articles), and about ways of coming to terms with their expected loss. Learning about the causes of birth defects can mitigate a sense of guilt or failure felt by the mother of a deformed baby. People who are feeling helpless may find that adequate information can relieve anxiety caused by uncertainty or misconceptions and restore a sense of control.

Table 2. Major Types of Coping Skills

1. To deny or minimize the seriousness of the crisis
2. To seek information about the illness, treatment procedures, and probable outcomes
3. To learn specific illness-related procedures such as giving oneself insulin injections or running a home dialysis machine
4. To maintain regular routines and set concrete, limited goals
5. To manage one's self-presentation and be able to request needed reassurance and support
6. To prepare oneself mentally and rehearse potential alternative outcomes
7. To find a general purpose or pattern of meaning in the course of events

The third set of coping skills involves active, problem-focused efforts to learn specific illness-related procedures, such as feeding and caring for a premature baby, running a home dialysis machine, or giving oneself insulin injections. These accomplishments can provide much-needed confirmation of personal ability and effectiveness at a time when opportunities for independent and meaningful action are scarce. Patients take pride in being able to care for themselves; relatives find relief in being able to offer concrete help. This set of skills includes learning how to control symptoms by such techniques as sitting in certain kinds of chairs (for sufferers of back pain), planning changes in daily regimens to minimize the appearance and/or effects of potentially painful symptoms (as when a person who has had a heart attack chooses a level route for walking), and physically reorganizing or redesigning a home to accommodate decreased mobility (when crutches or wheelchairs are used).

The fourth set of coping skills entails maintaining regular routines, insofar as possible, and setting concrete, limited goals such as walking again or attending a special event (such as a wedding or graduation). This often gives patients something to look forward to and offers them a realistic chance of achieving a goal they consider meaningful. The strategy of "progressive desensitization," whereby patients with severe disfigurements gradually "expose" themselves to others and dull their own sensitivity to others' reactions, also falls within this category. This set of skills includes the ability to break seemingly overwhelming problems into small, potentially manageable bits.

The fifth set of coping skills involves managing one's self-presentation and being able to request reassurance and emotional support from family, friends, and health care staff. Patients and others who keep their feelings bottled up or who withdraw from social interaction cut themselves off from help of this type. Emotional support can be an important source of strength in facing difficult times, but individuals must deal with the tension between seeking support and wanting to avoid passive-dependent roles. One means of seeking support is to join such special groups as national self-help organizations (e.g., Mended Hearts for open-heart-surgery patients and Reach for Recovery for mastectomy patients) or smaller ad hoc groups for patients or relatives (such as spouses of hemodialysis patients). These groups may provide types of support that are less available from alternate sources—for example, information about the impact of treatment procedures.

Rehearsing alternative outcomes comprises the sixth set of coping skills. This category includes mental preparation (anticipation and mental rehearsal) and the discussion of potential alternative outcomes with family and friends. It is often used in combination with information seeking, as patients try to prepare themselves to handle expected difficulties by thinking through the steps involved and by acquainting themselves with the demands that might be made on them. This technique is commonly used to allay anxiety, as, for example, when unfamiliar medical procedures are scheduled. Reminding oneself of previous successes in handling difficult problems in order to ease one's fears and bolster one's confidence fits into this category. On a broader scale, it also encompasses the anticipatory mourning process in which an expected death or other loss is acknowledged beforehand.

When life's happenings seem capricious and uncontrollable, as with the sudden onset of an acute health crisis, it is often easier to manage if one can find a general purpose or pattern of meaning in the course of events. Efforts in this direction constitute a seventh type of coping skill. Belief in a divine purpose or in the general beneficence of a divine spirit may serve as a consolation or as encouragement to do one's best to deal with unavoidable difficulties. White and Liddon (1972) reported that 5 of 10 cardiac arrest patients they studied experienced a "transcendental redirection" of their lives as a result of their illness, and, in that sense, viewed their heart attacks as having been of positive value. Cowie (1976) described a process whereby patients engage in reconstructive coping work to "normalize" and attempt to make their heart attacks intelligible, something that was not really unexpected but rather was building up slowly as the "obvious outcome" of a particular life-style. Putting an experience into a long-term perspective (with or without religious orientation) often makes individual events more manageable.

Having provided a general conceptual framework, I shall now illustrate the relevance of the framework to the crisis of illness and of treatment by focusing on how patients cope with cancer and with unusual hospital environments.

3. The Crisis of Illness: Coping with Cancer

Cancer is a particularly frightening set of illnesses because its cause is unknown, its treatment can involve great discomfort or even incapacitation, and its cure is uncertain. Although improved treatment of neoplastic processes has increased the survival rates of patients with such cancers as Hodgkin's disease (Stages 1 and 2), acute lymphocytic leukemia, and osteogenic sarcoma, there is often considerable physical and emotional cost involved (Holland, 1977). The increase in dependency brought about by the loss of the work role, the financial burden on the family, and the necessity of relying on other people for personal physical care is very disturbing. The sense of total reliance on the doctor is often accompanied by the fear of displeasing him or her, a fear that makes many patients become passive, uncomplaining, and overly cooperative (Abrams, 1974).

To improve the understanding of the typical problems patients experience, Weisman (1979a) has described four general psychosocial phases that are related to the stage, treatment, and progression of cancer: (1) existential plight, (2) accommodation and mitigation, (3) recurrence and relapse, and (4) deterioration and decline (see Weisman, 1979b, for a slightly different description). Weisman believes that there are characteristic changes throughout the four stages in patients' primary concerns, goals, attitudes, time perspectives, coping patterns, and quality of life.

For instance, in the phase of existential plight, which covers about a hundred days during the period of the initial evaluation and primary treatment, patients are most concerned about their mortality, show an optimistic attitude, hope for a cure, and tend to develop an open time perspective. They initially use denial and then tend to switch to active problem-solving and coping strategies. The degree of vulnerability and distress experienced by five groups of cancer patients during this phase was influenced by illness-related, personal, and contextual factors. Although the number of systemic symptoms (such as weight loss, fatigue, and insomnia) was the best index of vulnerability and distress, the type and stage of cancer were also important illness-related factors. Patients with colon cancer and malignant melanoma showed peak vulnerability immediately after surgery, whereas patients with breast cancer and Hodgkin's disease experienced the most distress about 2 months after the initiation of radiation or chemotherapy treatment. As would be expected, patients with advanced lung cancer showed both the most severe distress and increasing levels of vulnerability and mood disturbance (Weisman & Worden, 1976–77; Weisman, 1979b).

Personal factors related to distress include low socioeconomic status; multiproblem family of origin; living alone due to separation, divorce, or widowhood; pessimism and regrets about the past; and a history of alcohol abuse, psychiatric treatment, or suicidal ideation. Patients who lacked ego strength showed more somatic concerns, higher mood disturbance, more current psychosocial problems, and stronger feelings of annihilation and alienation, even after statistically controlling for the effects of socioeconomic status and cancer site (Worden & Sobel, 1978). Relevant social factors related to distress include marital problems, infrequent church attendance, and lack of anticipated support from physicians and relatives.

The second phase, accommodation and mitigation, begins when a patient is able to return to a regular routine. Here the patient aims at surveillance of the disease, has a generally optimistic attitude and open time perspective, uses both denial and active coping skills, suffers from variable impairment, and may experience drastic alterations in quality of life (such as changes in family and sexual role functions). Weisman points out that patients often feel neither sick nor well during convalescence and that those who return to work must adapt to reduced energy, morale, and a diminished capacity for rapid decision making.

The third phase, recurrence and relapse, constitutes a secondary existential plight, especially if the cancer reappears long after the end of the initial treatment. The patient is now concerned about controlling the progression of the disease and obtaining a reprieve, has a guarded attitude and a restricted time perspective, and experiences increased functional impairment and a declining quality of life. Finally, in the phase of deterioration and decline, many of the initially pressing problems recede as acceptance of the inevitable outcome provides a sense of distance that reduces distress. In general, worries about returning to work or chronic family problems become less important when patients can no longer do anything to resolve them. Weisman concludes that psychosocial issues are most likely to arise during transitions in the course of the illness, for instance, during the emotional impact of diagnosis, early convalescence, episodes of relapse or recurrence, and the time of progressive decline and deterioration.

The treatment received by the patient may itself be conceptualized in terms of a series of discrete phases. For example, some recent work has described the process of bone marrow transplantation (which may be used as a treatment for acute lymphoblastic leukemia) and patients' and family members' reactions to this process (Patenaude, Szymanski, & Rappeport, 1979). Brown and Kelly (1976) divide the process into eight stages, which include the decision to accept treatment and the anticipation of it (Stage 1), the initial admission evaluation and care planning or "preparation" (Stage 2), and the process of immunosuppression and entry into isolation (Stage 3). Patients are hopeful during Stage 1 and usually feel a mixture of hope and fear in Stage 2. Although Stage 3 is the "point of no return"—since, unlike kidney transplantation, there is no equivalent to dialysis on which to depend once the procedure has begun—the patient's reaction is one of calm resignation. The transplant itself comprises Stage 4, while in Stages 5 and 6 the patient must "take one day at a time" and wait to see whether the graft takes or is rejected, a process that becomes increasingly difficult as the days in isolation mount. Concern with issues of daily living is heightened during the preparation for discharge and posthospital phases (Stages 7 and 8). Each of the stages present the patient and family (and health care staff) with new adaptive tasks for which different coping skills may be most facilitative of positive treatment outcome.

Several investigators have described the coping skills that patients use to deal with these varied problems (Moos, 1977; Weisman, 1979a,b). One relatively common emotionally protective device is for the person to deny that there is any real cause for distress by ignoring symptoms or explaining them as the result of some other, less threatening illness. Such denial may have disastrous results, since, for example, potential breast cancer patients must promptly acknowledge the existence of a lump, evaluate its potential risk, and initiate procedures for medical diagnosis if they are to maximize their chances for recovery (Kaplan & Grandstaff, 1979). After the diagnosis, many people are disturbed by the question "Why me?" They may blame their own past wrongdoings, their heredity, the doctor, or the hospital staff and thus find a target for their pent up anger.

Fear of the unknown is a major component of the general anxiety patients experience. One of the most basic ways in which people allay this fear is to seek out information about their situation and about what to expect (Ryan & Ryan, 1979). Klagsbrun (1971) describes a librarian who, on learning that she had cervical cancer, went through recent medical journals reading about her illness, the survival statistics, and preferred treatment procedures. Anticipation of the probable future course of the disease and mental rehearsal for it is another way of dealing with anxiety. After learning of his tongue cancer, John Bennett spent some time imagining what lay ahead of him, examining it, becoming accustomed to it, and reassuring himself that he would be able to manage it (Bennett & Sagov, 1973). Some people are reassured by reminding themselves of past difficulties with which they have coped successfully. Others may displace their anxiety onto someone else, worrying about the other person's problems rather than their own.

In complementary work focused on family members, Futterman and Hoffman (1973) have described the coping processes used by parents of children with leukemia. Parents tend to use "search and rescue operations" in the diagnostic phase (obtaining information and trying to provide the best possible care for their child) and "preservation and reversal" operations in the remission phase (participating in health care procedures but doubting the accuracy of the diagnosis of leukemia).

Other predominant coping skills include adhering to familiar work routines and continuing the usual patterns of family interaction, reaching out for emotional support from other family members and friends, and controlling the expression of feelings and the timing of grieving (by erecting a protective facade of common acceptance to conceal anguish). Anticipatory mourning, which is most prominent in the relapse and decline phases, includes the processes of acknowledgement and a narrowing of hope, grieving, reconciliation, and memorialization of the child (through pictures and shared memories). Finally, there is detachment, whereby parents gradually withdraw emotional investment from the child, reorganize the family, and reaffirm the value of their own lives.

There is very little empirical information relating the use of different coping skills to outcome criteria such as mood disturbance, perceived vulnerability, compliance with treatment regimens, and longevity. Weisman and his colleagues (Weisman & Worden, 1976–77; Weisman, 1979b) found that, during the existential phase, less disturbed patients were likely to use coping skills of sharing concern and talking with others (mutuality), confronting the problem by taking firm action, accepting the situation but redefining it by finding something favorable, and seeking direction and complying with treatment procedures. More disturbed patients, on the other hand, were likely to use such strategies as withdrawal and disengagement from others, externalization or projection of blame, attempts to forget the situation (suppression), tension reduction through excessive use of alcohol or drugs, and passive acceptance or submission to "inevitable" fate.

Some preliminary findings suggest that specific personal factors in conjunction with the use of certain coping skills may facilitate survival. Patients who are pessimistic, apathetic, and discouraged die earlier than expected, whereas those who communicate their needs openly and are able to receive supportive care from physicians and relatives tend to live longer than expected (Weisman & Worden, 1975). In a study of patients with metastatic breast cancer, Derogatis, Abeloff, and Melisaratos (1979) corroborated these results by noting that women who were able to be open in expressing negative emotions (including anger) and psychological distress survived longer than women whose coping styles involved suppression or denial of affect.

There is also growing evidence that many long-term survivors of cancer adapt to their life situations relatively well. In a study of the psychological effects of mastectomy, Polivy (1977) concluded that a process of denial used immediately after the operation allowed a woman to integrate her new body slowly into her self-image so that the ultimate decline in self-image was not so severe. Craig, Comstock, and Geiser (1974) noted that the quality of physical and psychosocial functioning was remarkably similar among long-term survivors of breast cancer and matched community controls. For instance, physical disabilities were reported by 19% of the cases and 16% of the controls; the slight excess of disability among the cases was related to surgical treatment. There was no evidence of increased psychosocial disability among the cases. These results offer the hope that some successfully treated cancer patients can achieve "normal" physical and psychological adjustment.

4. The Crisis of Treatment: Unusual Hospital Environments

Hospital environments are designed to facilitate the delivery of special medical care and to promote healing. But because of the unfamiliar equipment and procedures, many patients are as upset and frightened by their hospital experience as they are reassured by the medical resources made available to them. Such mandatory requirements as the need to obtain "informed consent" can exacerbate stress by forcing patients to confront the risk inherent in diagnostic and treatment procedures. For instance, prior to the process of bone marrow transplantation, the patient and donor must sign an explicit consent form that outlines in frightening detail the entire procedure and potential risks involved (for an example, see Brown & Kelly, 1976). Cohen and Lazarus (1979) describe the risks of an arteriogram and note that knowledge of these risks may deter patients from accepting such potentially lifesaving diagnostic procedures. Submitting to the medical technology of ablative chemotherapy in a laminar airflow room represents a complete surrender to modern medicine in exchange for a promise of potential survival. There is an almost total loss of control for both patient and family and a significant risk of depression as those involved experience the dramatic limitations the situation imposes on them.

Coronary care units and other intensive care facilities have received attention recently because of the unexpected difficulties patients experience in these specialized environments. The setting is a significant factor in the occurrence of postcardiotomy delirium and disorientation and may contribute to high anxiety levels among myocardial infarction (MI) patients. Hackett and Cassem (1975) have described the responses of such patients to hospitalization and the initial stress of being left alone and of having a priest administer the last rites. A patient may also witness a fellow patient suffer a cardiac arrest, which is a stressful event often followed by increased requests for tranquilizers and pain medication. Unlike other critically ill people, those who have just had an MI are alert, aware of their surroundings, and communicative. They usually begin to feel better soon after their attack, so their stay in the CCU allows them time to think about the prospect of greater dependence and other changes in their life-styles, the damage to their hearts, and the reality of death. Although many find the array of monitoring equipment reassuring, it is also evidence of the danger their lives are in.

The stressors involved in hospitalization led Norman Cousins (1979) to develop the conviction that "a hospital is no place for a person who is seriously ill," whereupon he proceeded to move into a hotel room that afforded peace and quiet and cost only about one-third as much as his hospital room. Cousins noted that such factors as "the surprising lack of respect for basic sanitation, the rapidity with which staphylococci and other pathogenic organisms can run through an entire hospital, the extensive and sometimes pernicious use of x-ray equipment" (p. 29), make the task of adapting to the hospital exceedingly difficult for a patient. Cousins believes that there is a circular paradox to intensive care units, because patients are provided with "better electronic aids than ever before for dealing with emergencies that are often intensified because they communicate a sense of imminent disaster" (p. 133). Most patients cannot cope with the task of dealing with the hospital environment by abandoning it; but as patients become better informed about medical procedures, they will wish to participate as partners in the management of their illness and increasingly may reject the advice of physicians and other health care staff.

The importance of the social environment of medical wards is illustrated by Klagsbrun (1970), who conducted a project designed to alter the social milieu of a cancer research unit. The poor morale of the ward was manifested by patients' frequent complaints of being used as guinea pigs by "uncaring doctors" and "unavailable nurses" and the high turnover rate among nurses. After instituting supportive group discussions for nurses, Klagsbrun tried to enable the patients to see themselves as functioning, productive people rather than "walking dead." Patients were encouraged to take over such aspects of their physical care as making their beds and filling their water pitchers. To counteract the tendency toward withdrawal and isolation, a small dining room was set up so patients could eat communally. An active group of patients took over a variety of ward duties and began to organize social activities. The whole atmosphere on the unit changed, with an increase in self-esteem, mastery, and involvement for patients and a sharp decline in nursing staff turnover (see Hoffman & Futterman, 1971, for an example of an intervention project designed to help patients and their families cope with the stressful aspects of a pediatric oncology clinic).

Kornfeld (1972) has noted the value of intervention measures such as a preoperative visit by the anesthesiologist to prepare the patient psychologically by answering questions, describing what to expect in the recovery room, and offering general reassurance. Lindheim, Glaser, and Coffin (1972) provide specific design guidelines for changing hospital environments to meet the needs of children and young adults as well as of family members and health care staff. It is important for adolescents, for instance, to develop a sense of identity, a goal that can be fostered by (1) providing a variety of room accommodations; (2) surrounding each bed with a space large enough to accommodate medical equipment and personal possessions; (3) identifying a clearly defined territory in which each teenager can keep possessions and thereby personalize the environment; (4) developing screens or dividers that have olfactory, acoustic and visual screening properties; and (5) placing each patient's bed next to a window and in a corner of the room.

Adolescents also need to develop independence and responsibility (by being allowed some personal control over the environment), to maintain a positive body image and learn appropriate health care procedures (by providing private and aesthetically pleasing bathrooms and laundry facilities), to maintain peer-group relationships (which can be fostered by having a snack bar and kitchenette adjacent to a dayroom and including a telephone jack by each hospital bed), to develop their cognitive and intellectual abilities (by having a hospital schoolroom, for instance), and to participate in informal interaction (by providing a quiet room with soft, comfortable floors and a low light level). The implementation of such design guidelines should help to improve hospital settings and reduce their stressful impact.

5. The Therapeutic Role of Staff

Crisis theory asserts that the individual is more receptive to outside influence at a time of disequilibrium. This greater accessibility offers health care professionals and others who deal with patients an unusual opportunity to exert a constructive influence. Failure to cope in a realistic and timely manner with tasks presented in the initial phases of an illness can result in a permanent pattern of impaired adjustment. This potential for disruptive psychological "side effects" renders the early detection of unsuccessful coping reactions as important as the early diagnosis of the disease itself (Geist, 1979; Kaplan & Grandstaff, 1979).

In order to give real assistance, care givers must know the usual responses to a given illness situation, including the sequence of phases in emotional processes like mourning and the inevitability and value of the expression of negative emotions such as anger or sadness. Staff should understand the time dimension involved, for instance, in grieving for a loss. It entails a progression from an initial reaction of numbness or disbelief to a growing awareness of pain, sorrow—and often anger and a preoccupation with the lost object—and gradually to a reorganization in which the loss is accepted and equilibrium restored. When staff encounter a woman who has just lost a breast, a disfigured burn victim, or a patient who is terminally ill, they should not mistake numbness for stoicism or label depression or anger as pathological responses. In practical terms, it means that staff who must announce an impending loss should be prepared to repeat their explanations after the initial shock has subsided, for very little may be taken in at the first hearing.

Staff members should also know the major tasks and typical coping strategies so that they can recognize and respond to the adaptive efforts which their patients make. One of the most important ways in which health care staff can help is to give information: to respond to patients' questions, clarify misconceptions, prepare patients or family members by advising them of events or emotions that are likely to occur, and identify other sources of available assistance like self-help groups and relevant community agencies. Mastectomy patients, for instance, should be told that they may have crying spells, trouble sleeping, and numbness in their arms after surgery. Then, if these occur, they need not fear that they are having an emotional breakdown, or, as one woman did, that a nerve was mistakenly cut (Harrell, 1972).

Health care staff need to understand that patients who use minimization or avoidance coping strategies may not be able to handle threatening information, and, furthermore, that there is a limit to the degree of candor even the most vigilant patients desire. In describing his hospitalization at the National Institutes of Health (NIH), Stuart Alsop (1973) points out that the NIH policy that staff should be completely candid with patients made it more difficult for him to preserve a reasonable emotional balance and maintain hope. The experience led him to conclude that a patient should be told the truth and nothing but the truth—but not the whole truth: "My rule would be: never tell a victim of terminal cancer the whole truth—tell him that he *may* die, even that he will *probably* die, but do not tell him that he *will* die" (p. 84).

Another way in which health care staff can assist patients and family members is by developing mutual support or therapy groups. Such groups can provide a support system within the hospital, help patients and family adjust to the diagnosis and treatment, serve as an information and referral source, and enable group members to share the problems and solutions of living with a life-threatening illness. Spiegel and Yalom (1978) describe specific aspects of group situations that can be especially helpful to individuals with metastatic carcinoma and other serious illnesses. Among these aspects are (1) the sense of shared problems and experiences, which can diminish feelings of isolation and alienation; (2) the experience of helping oneself by helping others; (3) the development of hope by seeing other people with similar problems move past these problems; and (4) identification with group members who have overcome specific problems and modeling of the successful behavior. Involvement in therapy groups can help patients "demystify" death, reduce their fear of the dying process, lower their mood disturbance, and lead them to use fewer maladaptive coping responses to manage stress (Spiegel, Bloom, & Yalom, 1980; see also Ferlic, Goldman, & Kennedy, 1979).

To be of maximum help to patients, health care professionals need to understand their own reactions to acute health crises. They need to know that they too face certain tasks, go through specific phases in reaction to patients, and employ certain coping skills. An awareness of this process can help staff to deal with the stress inherent in the nature of their work and to keep negative feelings about a particular patient or situation from affecting the quality of care they provide. Cartwright (1979) has noted that the psychological strain associated with assuming responsibility for others' lives, the affective climate surrounding disease, and the contradictory and unrealizable aspects of the roles that healers are currently expected to play are among the more important factors implicated in staff distress. She points out that over 5 million people are employed in the health sector; that many health professionals suffer from such serious problems as coronary heart disease, suicidal tendencies, drug abuse, psychiatric illness, and marital difficulties; and that the problems of providers can seriously interfere with the care of patients (for example, see Hay & Oken, 1972, for a discussion of the stresses involved in intensive care unit nursing).

The importance of dealing openly with these issues is underscored by descriptions of how unresolved staff anger can affect the quality of health care. For instance, Geist (1977) found that uncooperative patients might be subjected to subtly cruel treatments channeled through the details of nurses' daily work: painfully administered injections, forcing a patient to wait for medications, and delays in answering call lights. More direct forms of "punishment" that were justified by medical rationale included administration of placebos (to avoid potentially harmful medications); isolation of patients in a treatment room (so as not to disturb other patients); secretly adding weights to a patient's traction (so she would not feel the pain). A more "sadistic" example is when "the staff mouth words without sounds in the room of a patient who is obsessively concerned about deafness" (Geist, 1977, p. 438). Geist believes that one reason for such reactions is that although staff are taught not to express anger at patients, their daily work stimulates anger and other emotional reactions without providing channels for appropriate expression of these emotions.

Some attempts have been made to help staff deal with these problems by developing teaching-oriented seminar programs for physicians (Artiss & Levine, 1973) and ward-based consultation programs to create more positive social environments on medical units (Geist, 1977; Klagsbrun, 1970). In this connection, Koran and Moos (1980) obtained systematic information about the actual and preferred work environments of staff on three medical units in a general hospital. They used the Work Environment Scale (WES), which assesses staff members' perceptions of their work setting on 10 dimensions that fall into three basic domains: the relationship domain (involvement, peer cohesion, and supervisor support), the personal growth or goal orientation domain (autonomy, task orientation, and work pressure), and the system maintenance and system change domain (clarity, control, innovation, and physical comfort). After the assessment, the staff in each unit was provided with feedback on the WES results and on the discrepancies between their actual and preferred work milieus. Target areas for change were identified, and Koran and his colleagues worked with unit staff to formulate and implement changes. Staff in each of the three units felt that the actual work setting improved on one or more dimensions after the intervention period—as shown, for example, by increases in task orientation and staff autonomy and decreases in work pressure. The results indicate that a consultation program can help make the environments of health care work more satisfactory for employees (see Moos, 1979, for a discussion of this type of change process).

In his penetrating analysis of the "Gregor effect," Preston (1979) issues a warning to those who would intervene to make health care staff more humanitarian, pointing to the complexity of the issues with which they must contend. Kafka's *Metamorphosis* describes how the man Gregor Samsa, transformed overnight into a giant beetle, is insidiously and eventually rejected by his family. This rejection or "Gregor effect" occurs because human beings are dominated by a drive for self-orientation, must defend themselves against the implications of human ambiguity, and thus are driven to reject "ambiguous people" (that is, seriously ill and dying persons). According to Preston, hospitals are heroic systems of denial that specialize in enforced equanimity in the face of manifest mortality. He believes that the typical ways in which health care staff try to develop humanitarian competence will not help them to tolerate human ambiguity and may even hamper their current adjustment. For example, the development of a sociopsychological orientation may make a "science out of humanitarianism," trivialize humanitarian motives, and merely make tender loving care "more conscious." Another approach is to ease the time–task pressures on nurses; but, as the author points out, nurses generally do not use their free time to intensify their contact with more "ambiguous" patients. Preston concludes that health care staff must deal with these feelings and moderate their influence on patient care.

Professional care givers have a special responsibility to help those whose lives have been disrupted by illness. Sensitivity to the psychological effects of their routine actions may lead to alterations of behavior or procedure, with positive consequences for patients and their families. For instance, Golden and Davis's (1974) practical suggestions for the physician who must inform new parents that their child is defective reflect this kind of awareness: the mother should be told with her husband or other close friend present, not alone; the doctor should hold the infant while giving the news (giving a clear message that the child is still human and lovable); the clinical findings should be demonstrated directly on the baby; the physician should stress the similarity of the child to normal children; questions should be encouraged, and all the information should be reviewed again the next day. It is impossible to enumerate behavioral cues of this type for each illness, but with a general understanding of coping tasks and skills, as well as of their own reactions to patients, involved health professionals should be able to minimize the negative impact of the illness experience and support healthy coping.

ACKNOWLEDGMENTS

Andy Billings, Ruth Lederman, and Roger Mitchell provided valuable assistance in the review of recent literature and of an earlier draft of the manuscript.

6. References

Abrams, R. *Not alone with cancer*. Springfield, Ill.: Charles C Thomas, 1974.

Alsop, S. *Stay of execution: A sort of memoir*. Philadelphia: Lippincott, 1973.

Artiss, K., & Levine, A. Doctor-patient relations in severe illness: A seminar for oncology fellows. *New England Journal of Medicine*, 1973, *288*, 1210–1214.

Benfield, D., Leib, S., & Vollman, J. Grief responses of parents to neonatal death and parent participation in deciding care. *Pediatrics*, 1978, *62*, 171–177.

Benjamin, P. Psychological problems following recovery from acute life-threatening illness. *American Journal of Orthopsychiatry*, 1978, *48*, 284–290.

Bennett, J., & Sagov, S. An experience of cancer. *Harpers*, 1973, *274*, pp. 94, 97–98, 100, 102.

Brown, H., & Kelly, M. Stages of bone marrow transplantation: A psychiatric perspective. *Psychosomatic Medicine*, 1976, *38*, 439–446.

Caplan, G. *Principles of preventive psychiatry*. New York: Basic Books, 1964.

Cartwright, L. Sources and effects of stress in health careers. In G. Stone, F. Cohen, & N. Adler (Eds.), *Health psychology: A handbook*. San Francisco: Jossey-Bass, 1979.

Cohen, F. & Lazarus, R. Coping with the stresses of illness. In G. Stone, F. Cohen, & N. Adler (Eds.), *Health psychology: A handbook*. San Francisco: Jossey-Bass, 1979.

Cousins, N. *Anatomy of an illness as perceived by the patient*. New York: Norton, 1979.

Cowie, B. The cardiac patient's perception of his heart attack. *Social Science and Medicine*, 1976, *10*, 87–96.

Craig, T., Comstock, G., & Geiser, P. The quality of survival in breast cancer: A case-control comparison. *Cancer*, 1974, *33*, 1451–1457.

Croog, S., & Levine, S. *The heart patient recovers*. New York: Human Sciences Press, 1977.

Derogatis, L., Abeloff, M., & Melisaratos, N. Psychological coping mechanisms and survival time in metastatic breast cancer. *Journal of the American Medical Association*, 1979, *242*, 1504–1508.

Erikson, E. *Childhood and society* (2nd ed.). New York: Norton, 1963.

Ferlic, M., Goldman, A., & Kennedy, B. Group counseling in adult patients with advanced cancer. *Cancer*, 1979, *43*, 760–766.

Finlayson, A. Social networks as coping resources: Lay help and consultation patterns used by women in husbands' post-infarction career. *Social Science and Medicine*, 1976, *10*, 97–103.

Fisher, S. Psychosexual adjustment following total pelvic exenteration. *Cancer Nursing*, 1979, *2*, 219–225.

Futterman, E., & Hoffman, I. Crisis and adaptation in the families of fatally ill children. In E. J. Anthony & C. Koupernik (Eds.), *The child and his family: The impact of disease and death*. New York: Wiley, 1973.

Geist, R. Consultation on a pediatric surgical ward: Creating an empathic climate. *American Journal of Orthopsychiatry*, 1977, *47*, 432–444.

Geist, R. Onset of chronic illness in children and adolescents: Psychotherapeutic and consultative intervention. *American Journal of Orthopsychiatry*, 1979, *49*, 4–23.

Golden, D., & Davis, J. Counseling parents after the birth of an infant with Down's syndrome. *Children Today*, 3, 1974.

Haan, N. Psychosocial meanings of unfavorable medical forecasts. In G. Stone, F. Cohen, & N. Adler (Eds.), *Health psychology: A handbook*. San Francisco: Jossey-Bass, 1979.

Hackett, T., & Cassem, N. Psychological management of the myocardial infarction patient. *Journal of Human Stress*, 1975, *1*, 25–38.

Hackett, T., & Cassem, N. White collar and blue collar responses to heart attack. *Journal of Psychosomatic Research*, 1976, *20*, 85–95.

Harrell, H. To lose a breast. *American Journal of Nursing*, 1972, *72*, 676–677.

Hay, D., & Oken, D. The psychological stresses of intensive care unit nursing. *Psychosomatic Medicine*, 1972, *34*, 109–118.

Hoffman, I., & Futterman, E. Coping with waiting: Psychiatric intervention and study in the waiting room of a pediatric oncology clinic. *Comprehensive Psychiatry*, 1971, *12*, 67–81.

Holland, J. Psychological aspects of oncology. *Medical Clinics of North America*, 1977, *61*, 737–748.

Kaplan, D., & Grandstaff, N. A problem-solving approach to terminal illness for the family and physician. In C. A. Garfield (Ed.), *Stress and survival: The emotional realities of life-threatening illness*. St. Louis: Mosby, 1979.

Klagsbrun, S. Cancer, emotions and nurses. *American Journal of Psychiatry*, 1970, *126*, 1237–1244.

Klagsbrun, S. Communications in the treatment of cancer. *American Journal of Nursing*, 1971, *71*, 944–948.

Koran, L., & Moos, R. *Changing stressful work environments in medical settings*. Unpublished manuscript, Department of Psychiatry and Behavioral Sciences, Stanford University, 1980.

Kornfeld, D. The hospital environment: Its impact on the patient. *Advances in Psychosomatic Medicine*, 1972, *8*, 252–270.

Lazarus, R. The stress and coping paradigm. In C. Eisdorfer, D. Cohen, A. Kleinman & P. Maxim (Eds.), *Theoretical bases for psychopathology*. New York: Spectrum, 1981.

Lear, M. W. *Heartsounds*. New York: Simon & Schuster, 1980.

Lindemann, E. Symptomatology and management of acute grief. *American Journal of Psychiatry*, 1944, *101*, 1–11.

Lindheim, R., Glaser, H., & Coffin, C. *Changing hospital environments for children*. Cambridge, Harvard University Press, 1972.

Mages, N., & Mendelsohn, G. Effects of cancer on patients' lives: A personalological approach. In G. Stone, F. Cohen, & N. Adler (Eds.), *Health psychology: A handbook*. San Francisco: Jossey-Bass, 1979.

Moos, R. *The human context: Environmental determinants of behavior*. New York: Wiley, 1976.

Moos, R. (Ed.), *Coping with physical illness*. New York: Plenum Press, 1977.

Moos, R. Improving social settings by social climate measurement and feedback. In R. Munoz, L. Snowden, & J. Kelly (Eds.), *Social and psychological research in community settings*. San Francisco: Jossey-Bass, 1979.

Moos, R., & Tsu, V. Human competence and coping. In R. Moos (Ed.), *Human adaptation: Coping with life crises*. Lexington, Mass.: Heath, 1976.

Moss, C. S. *Recovery with aphasia: The aftermath of my stroke*. Urbana, Ill.: University of Illinois Press, 1972.

Patenaude, A., Szymanski, L., & Rappeport, J. Psychological costs of bone marrow transplantation in children. *American Journal of Orthopsychiatry*, 1979, *49*, 409–422.

Polivy, J. Psychological effects of mastectomy on a woman's feminine self-concept. *Journal of Nervous and Mental Disease*, 1977, *164*, 77–87.

Preston, R. P. *The dilemmas of care: Social and nursing adaptions to the deformed, the disabled, and the aged*. New York: Elsevier, 1979.

Ryan, C., & Ryan, K. M. *A private battle*. New York: Simon & Schuster, 1979.

Sackett, D., & Haynes, B. (Eds.). *Compliance with therapeutic regimens*. Baltimore: Johns Hopkins University Press, 1976.

Smith, D. Survivors of serious illness. *American Journal of Nursing*, 1979, *79*, 441–446.

Spiegel, D., Bloom, J., & Yalom, I. *Group support for metastatic cancer patients: A randomized prospective outcome study*. Unpublished manuscript, Department of Psychiatry and Behavioral Sciences, Stanford University, 1980.

Spiegel, D., & Yalom, I. A support group for dying patients. *International Journal of Group Psychotherapy*, 1978, *28*, 233–245.

Strauss, A. *Chronic illness and the quality of life*. St. Louis: Mosby, 1975.

Weisman, A. A model for psychosocial phasing in cancer. *General Hospital Psychiatry*, 1979, *1*, 187–195. (a)

Weisman, A. *Coping with cancer*. New York: McGraw-Hill, 1979. (b)

Weisman, A., & Worden, J. Psychosocial analysis of cancer deaths. *Omega*, 1975, *6*, 61–75.

Weisman, A., & Worden, J. The existential plight in cancer: Significance of the first 100 days. *International Journal of Psychiatry in Medicine*, 1976–77, *7*, 1–15.

White, R., & Liddon, S. Ten survivors of cardiac arrest. *Psychiatry and Medicine*, 1972, *3*, 219–225.

Worden, J. W., & Sobel, H. Ego-strength and psychosocial adaptation to cancer. *Psychosomatic Medicine*, 1978, *40*, 585–592.

Adaptation to Chronic Illness and Disability

Franklin C. Shontz

Although the procedure is unusual, this chapter begins by finding fault with its own title. The practice is justified because it suggests a new way of thinking about an important matter. The phrase "adaptation to chronic illness and disability" seems harmless enough and is consistent with common usage, but it could be taken to imply that the topic of this chapter is how people alter themselves to accommodate to impersonal physical conditions. Psychologically, that implication leaves much to be desired.

Like most diseases and impairments, chronic illnesses and disabilities are typically treated in theory as if their natural residence were "out there" somewhere, beyond the boundary of the personal body image (Fisher & Cleveland, 1968). When not "out there," where they supposedly belong, but within a human being, they are treated as alien and dangerous influences that have invaded those who "have" or "are afflicted by" them. At best, they are thought of as passive impediments to normal living, which must be overcome or bypassed. At worst, they are feared as attacking enemies that must be fought off and repelled, like pirates boarding a peaceful ship. From a psychological point of view, this conception of illnesses and disabilities is not the only one possible, nor is it necessarily the most useful.

The expression "adaptation to chronic illness and disability" may also suggest that this chapter adopts what Dembo (1969, 1970) calls an *outsider's* rather than an *insider's* perspective. It may imply that, for people who have chronic illnesses or disabilities, the primary problem of life is to come to terms with physical limitations. However, many people whom society classifies among the chronically

FRANKLIN C. SHONTZ ● Department of Psychology, University of Kansas, Lawrence, Kansas 66045.

ill, disabled, or handicapped do not regard themselves as such. This group is not limited to those who blatantly deny the realities of obviously atypical physiques; in any case, that population is probably far smaller than outsiders find it easy to admit. It contains mainly people who are never seen by professional helpers or are seen so briefly and take care of themselves so well that physicians or therapists quickly forget them. These people organize the personal structures of their lives so successfully that they fail to understand how anyone can regard them as being limited, deprived, or in need of special help. In fact, many in this group vigorously resent any outsider's tactless insistence that they are inferior to the slightest degree.

In extreme cases, such people may have adopted, *in toto*, Meyerson's third strategy of adjustment, in which an individual stays within those regions' of behavior and experience that are ordinarily accessible only to people without disabilities (Meyerson, 1963). (The other two strategies are either to live entirely within the regions associated with disability or to try to live in both sets of regions at once.) In any case, people who reject the status of being ill or disabled demonstrate how important it is to understand that chronic illness and disability are, in the final analysis, deviations from social norms at least as much as they are states of the body. This idea is not new, though it is not yet influential among those engaged in professional care or rehabilitation (Shontz, 1980).

1. A Paradox

An apparent paradox often arises when psychological adaptation, to any state of affairs that cannot be changed, is successfully completed. The paradox is generated by the fact that, from the perspective of the person with the condition, the illness, disability, impediment, or impairment that causes the problem exists only while the person is not adapted to it. Once adaptation is successfully completed, the handicap no longer exists because it no longer interferes with effective behavior. It is no more disruptive to the person's life than any other bodily state or condition. Nevertheless, particularly when a deviant or atypical somatic state is visibly evident, society will continue to regard and treat the person as a handicapped individual.

The successfully adjusted person has not adapted *to* chronic illness or disability because the person no longer *has* a chronic illness or disability. From the insider's point of view, these terms are applied only to conditions that interfere with the conduct of the affairs of daily life. In adaptation, the interference disappears, though the physical condition (e.g., less than average visual acuity, restriction of movement of the joints, etc.) may still exist.

The problem is most troublesome when pejorative terms are applied to well-adjusted individuals with atypical physiques. Someone who uses leg braces or crutches but manages to travel with little difficulty may reject the labels *crippled* or *handicapped*, even if giving them up means becoming ineligible for charitable monetary help. Yet such a person cannot be accused of denying the physical condition or its implications, for it is obvious to all concerned that the condition makes walking more than usually difficult.

The difficulty stems from the fact that terms like *chronic illness, disability, handicap,* and *impairment* are defined normatively and from the viewpoint of outsiders—people who do not have these conditions. An insider, who has such a condition, accepts these terms as valid only when he or she feels incompetent, inadequate, inferior, or unsuccessful. When the insider reaches the point of feeling adequate, competent, and complete, he or she no longer feels that terms like *ill, disabled,* or *handicapped* are accurate. They emphasize difference from statistical normality (usually in unfavorable directions), but the person no longer feels different and does not wish to be labeled as such.

The outsider reacts only to the apparently deviant or atypical condition, and usually only to what Wright calls its succumbing aspects (Wright, 1960, 1967, 1974). The successful insider reacts to a total life situation in which the physical state, which bothers everyone else, plays a slight or even insignificant role. The true insider cannot understand how others can call someone ill, disabled, or handicapped who is living a life that is perfectly satisfactory and complete.

1.2. Adaptation to What?

In summary, people who are identified by society as having chronic illnesses or disabilities do not adapt to these conditions. Like everyone else, they adapt to the full array of possibilities and limitations that are afforded by the complete panorama of their biological states and their social and physical environments. Also like everyone else, they may do so with greater or less success. When they are unsuccessful, their maladjustment is not specifically caused by failure to adapt to their bodily conditions any more than the fact that I did not become a track star was caused by my inability to accept the limitations of my physique. Just as I am comfortable with life without being a track star, someone else may be comfortable with life in a wheelchair. The issue for psychology is not how those people who are generally considered to be chronically ill or disabled adapt to their bodies or how closely they meet normative standards; instead, the question is how they come to satisfactory and satisfying terms with the same world in which everyone lives.

2. Implications

The foregoing discussion is more than an exercise in semantic nit-picking. The implications of a shift in perspective from outsider to insider are not trivial. For example, if taken to an extreme, the insider's view could be used to justify a demand for the rejection of all studies and psychological tests that purport to assess the adjustment of patients or clients to their conditions. Some tests that might have to be discarded, for instance, would be Bell's (1967) scale of adjustment of the physically disabled and Linkowski's (1971) scale to measure acceptance of disability; instruments like these tend to treat the problem of adjustment as if disability itself were the only thing the person had to contend with.

The insider's perspective could also require the discontinuance of research on attitudes toward people with handicaps or disabilities. Such research sustains the idea that these people differ in some essential way from everyone else, although in fact they are deviant only because social judgment makes them so. It is not profitable merely to prove again and again that social attitudes of rejection are expressed toward a group that consists of people whom society rejected in the first place. The insider argues that research money should be spent to support not studies that make deviants seem different but rather those that will reveal how to reduce perceptions of deviance and difference where none are justified.

The new perspective could also require changing many scientific and professional procedures. For instance, in research it would mean studying the process of adjustment as it is experienced by the person who must do the adjusting—rather than as it looks to someone who observes it from the outside, in the role of professional, therapist, counselor, or experimenter. In treatment settings, it could mean granting people with troublesome physical conditions more authority in determining the content, direction, and goals of their own care.

At present, almost nothing systematic is known about the natural history of adaptation of people who are identified as having chronic illnesses or disabilities. Spontaneously produced first-person and biographical accounts are helpful and may serve as sources of research hypotheses, or they may provide data sources for preliminary analyses. See, for example, my own use (Shontz, 1973) of the first-person accounts in Henrich and Kriegel (1961). However, such materials are unauthoritative, not because they are false or inaccurate but because they are incomplete and imprecise due to the lack of advanced planning for their preparation and the failure to use objective data-collection methods in addition to impressionistic information.

2.1. An Example

Even otherwise well-conceived and executed research could often be improved if investigators would recognize when they are adopting the outsider's position and consider how the insider's viewpoint might enrich the design, execution, and interpretation of their projects. A case in point is a study reported by Bulman and Wortman (1977), which examined some reactions of 29 adult patients with spinal cord injuries. The following comments show that even a good project can one-sidedly adopt the outsider's point of view and that research can be enriched by paying proper attention to the viewpoints of insiders.

The first question that an insider's point of view stimulates about this research is whether it is proper to describe the state of a person who has been through an accident as one of victimization. Regardless of how the term *victim* is used in technical or theoretical writing in social psychology (i.e., as in the work of Lerner, 1971, and Lerner & Simmons, 1966), the common-language meaning of the word *victimization* implies being cheated, duped, tricked, or sacrificed. Consequently, it suggests something about a patient's state or reaction that may not be true.

The report of Bulman and Wortman's research assumes that their subjects either are victimized, according to some absolute standard of victimization, or that they feel victimized, in response to their own perceptions of their conditions. Although this assumption may be correct, some data from the study itself indicate that, with respect to personal feelings, it is not so in every case. For example, one "victimized person" is reported as saying: "I see the accident as the best thing that could have happened."

To an outsider, who assumes that this person has been cheated, duped, tricked, or assaulted, the idea that an accident resulting in a spinal cord injury and paralysis could be a good thing is unrealistic. At best, the belief that it is must be regarded as a coping or defensive strategy on the part of the victim; it may even be irrational. In the report of this research, this response is presented as an example of "reevaluation of the victimization as positive." The classification conveys the outsider's belief that the true (or realistic) value of the condition is negative and that to perceive positive features in it presupposes the occurrence of a reevaluation (and possible distortion of the real situation) by the victim. Even if the assumption that accidents are always negative forces in the lives of those who have them is correct, the outsider is typically prone to stop analyzing responses once the negative impact has been diminished and to remain relatively blind to the positive benefits that may accrue to the person subsequently.

In this instance, the patient in question finished his statement by saying " 'cause I was forced to decide my faith, whereas there would have been the possibility that I would have lived and never made a decision—been lost the rest of my life. . . . Then I was saying to myself, 'You fool, you know, you're alive.' If you get into life, then . . . the function of the human body isn't that necessary" (p. 359).

Why do investigators not accept statements like these as accurate descriptions of patients' psychological conditions or beliefs? Apparently, the possibility does not easily occur to outsiders that, if the person's whole life situation were taken into account, the insider may be the more accurate of the two.

In the report of this research, the outsider's approach is made apparent in several additional ways. For one thing, the study is rationalized in the introduction by associating it with several social-psychological hypotheses relating to attribution theory. The hypotheses are described in terms of the differential predictions they yield about how people should react to their own victimization. The study is justified in part as an attempt to decide, by studying real-life situations, which hypotheses the data support. Preference for research problems that are drawn from impersonal theory rather than direct human need is characteristic of the outsiders' approach.

It is also typical of the scientific outsider to be concerned mainly with "prediction and control," and a major purpose of the research was "to determine the best predictors of successful coping" (p. 353). A research purpose more suitable to insiders might be to determine the best ways to relieve suffering or help people deal more effectively with misfortune and live fuller, happier lives.

To be fair, an investigator, as a human being, may actually have such a purpose in mind, but it would probably be unacceptable to say so in a technical report.

In this research, *coping* was defined and rated only by nurses and social workers, not by patients. Using this procedure, good coping naturally turned out to mean such things as "accepting the reality of their injury," having "a positive attitude toward physical therapy," being "motivated to work toward improvement of their physical abilities," and reflecting "a desire to be as physically independent as possible" (p. 355). These are classical outsiders' goals; they are what professionals want for their patients, though not necessarily what patients want for themselves. Whether the patients studied would agree with or be able to supplement these criteria of good coping with criteria of their own is not mentioned. Neither is the possibility entertained that there may be individual patients for whom some of these goals are either meaningless or counterproductive of good psychological adjustment.

The report cites a somewhat low though statistically significant correlation ($r = .346$) between nurses' and social workers' ratings of patients' coping, but it describes no effort to obtain patients' ratings of themselves as a check on the opinions of the professional staff. Had that been done, interrater agreement would probably have been lower.

In the discussion of results, the report asserts that clear evidence had been found "for a correlation between the attributions of blame made by the victims and their ability to cope with victimization." Apparently, self-blame is adaptive while blaming others is not. This conclusion is untempered by recognition that the results are valid only (1) if a patient actually places blame in one place or another and (2) if adequacy of coping is defined from the perspective of outsiders on treatment teams.

A great deal of interesting speculative discussion is presented in the report regarding additional ways in which patients interpret their conditions and react to them. However, none of these speculations was tested by seeking out the opinions of patients, who should know more about their probable validity than anyone else. Obviously, this procedure would not be conclusive, but it might help eliminate obviously incorrect interpretations, suggest a few that might not have been thought of otherwise, or sharpen up questions and procedures for future studies.

From an insider's point of view, the most valuable part of this research is its discussion and presentation of examples of patients' responses to the question "Why me?" By pointing out that all patients examined had asked themselves and had answered that question, the study reveals an important, perhaps nearly universal response to misfortune. By categorizing patients' answers, the report gives some insight into the process of adjustment that follows. Certainly, more research on this topic would be valuable.

This methodological analysis shows that improvement in knowledge, gained from research and clinical practice, requires investigators and therapists to be more careful about considering and including the contributions of patients or clients. A more formal look at the general distinction between the viewpoints of outsiders and insiders shows why this is so. The discussion that follows derives from Dembo's (1970) original analysis but elaborates upon it in ways that may be unique.

3.1. Introduction

Detailed examination of the distinction between insiders' and outsiders' points of view serves two important purposes. First, it points out the primary reason why so little knowledge gained from research in psychology is directly applicable in clinical and rehabilitation practice. As a corollary, it suggests some directions for inquiry that may produce more useful knowledge in the future.

Second, the illustrations and examples that are used to explain how the two viewpoints differ provide a survey of what is known or believed about how people with chronic illnesses or disabilities adapt to the conditions under which they, as well as the rest of us, must live.

The distinctions in the following discussion do not constitute a scientific social-psychological theory about differences between the attitudes and behaviors of professional people and clients and should not be treated as such. Such differences may be empirically examined (Leviton, 1971, 1973), but Dembo's distinction is metatheoretical. It does not distinguish between psychological states but between philosophical positions. It makes no assumption that all scientists and professional care givers endorse or adopt all characteristics of the outsider's viewpoint all the time. Nor does it imply that sufferers are incapable of understanding, appreciating, or adopting an outsider's point of view. Indeed, as therapeutic practices are currently carried out, patients must adopt an outsider's view if they wish to be regarded as cooperative and helpful. Furthermore, many professional people are capable of appreciating the points of view of those whom they serve. The distinction between outsider and insider is a true dialectic (Buss, 1979; Rychlak, 1968, 1977); as such, its polarities can be separately described. However, it is a resolvable dialectic and becomes a source of difficulty only when satisfactory resolution is not sought.

3.2. Research Implications

Because the distinction between insider and outsider is not a theory, it would be inappropriate to attempt to "test its validity" by predicting group differences in viewpoints between staff and patients. However, it would be appropriate for an enterprising psychometrician to develop an instrument to assess the degree to which individuals—whether patients, staff, or investigators—adopt one philosophical stance to the exclusion of the other. Using such an instrument, hypotheses might be tested about how people with extreme scores (whether staff, patient, or scientist) act in or respond to situations that involve the experience or treatment of, or research on, chronic illness and disability.

In developing this instrument, the test constructor should avoid the temptation to force respondents to make ratings along a scale of agreement and disagreement. This procedure could incorrectly imply that the best resolution of the dialectic is compromise, or a middle-of-the-road position. Allowance must be made for the possibility that a respondent may have performed a successful synthesis of the two points of view and realized that one perspective can be appropriate in one situation (e.g., during surgery), the other can be appropriate under other circumstances (e.g., talking with the client's family about future plans), and an intermediate position can be appropriate at still other times (e.g., when transmitting technical information to the patient). Developing such an instrument may be difficult, but it is not beyond the range of current technology.

4. Scope and Limitations

Broadly speaking, the insider–outsider distinction applies to any situation in which a set of life experiences is accessible to some people but not others. For example, in the entertainment business, performers and producers are insiders; most members of audiences are outsiders.

This discussion concerns only one form of insider-outsider distinction, that in which the insider regards himself or herself as having experienced misfortune (i.e., as a sufferer) due to a loss or lack (such as might ensue from chronic illness or disability) of some personally important behavioral possibilities. Not all disabilities or chronic illnesses produce misfortune. There are instances (though they may not be common) in which these conditions either do not affect the person greatly or actually enrich, rather than limit, personal or psychological growth—for example, by alleviating guilt over sins of the past or by serving as a challenge to be met by aggressive coping action.

The implications of this discussion probably spread well beyond the confines of losses due to states of the body. Losses of many kinds (death of a loved person, dismissal from a job, etc.) can produce suffering that is just as intense as that which stems from losses due to illness or disability. Delineation of all possibilities goes beyond the scope of this analysis. However, as the discussion proceeds, the reader should consider how to extend the ideas presented here into other areas of human experience.

The following discussion is limited in that the only outsider groups taken into account are treatment personnel and research scientists. People with chronic illnesses and disabilities encounter other types of outsiders as well, such as potential employers, people without chronic illnesses or disabilities, or even others with some other form of chronic illness or disability. The same contrasts may not apply in relations with all such groups, and analyses of other forms of insider-outsider relations may prove profitable in the search for broader, more inclusive principles of comparison.

5. Differences in Problem Definition

One of the main differences between the two viewpoints is their conception of what constitutes an adequate problem for service or research. From the perspective of an insider (one who seeks service), a problem exists when personal suffering cannot be alleviated by one's own efforts; the assistance of others must therefore be solicited. From the perspective of a service provider (an outsider), someone else's problem becomes genuine (i.e., service provision becomes legitimate) when official gatekeepers (physicians, social workers, police, etc.) have agreed that the candidate deviates from social norms in a defined way and to a sufficient degree.

From the perspective of a scientific investigator (another outsider), acceptable problems for research derive from impersonal, abstract theoretical systems, not from the sufferings of individuals. Insiders who are subjected to research on such problems may feel that they are being treated as guinea pigs because they are asked to serve as subjects for the good of "mankind" or science in the abstract—not for any benefit or relief they may experience personally.

5.1. Possible Resolutions

Differences in the conception of what constitutes a problem in service delivery often tend to be managed by attempting to convince those who seek care (but whom gatekeepers leave outside the pale) that they are being unreasonable or selfish. Negative social pressures are sometimes used against such persons. They are called malingerers, hypochondriacs, or other unflattering names or are shuffled off to the least desirable facilities or given the least possible attention. This is a rather one-sided solution, and it is possible because only gatekeepers have the power to determine who gets help. The need for greater participation by insiders in gatekeeping activities is obvious.

The way to improve research is also obvious. It is to include insiders in the investigative process wherever possible. One way to do this is to treat such persons not as subjects but as equal participants in the research enterprise or as consultants who are experts regarding their own conditions and experiences. This alternative may feel uncomfortable to some scientists because it removes experimenters from the pedestal of assumed superiority they have traditionally occupied. However, it has the advantage of placing scientists in a better position to select for investigation problems that are not only theoretically relevant but also likely to have beneficial effects on the people being studied.

6. Perceptions of Locus of Problems

Outsiders' and insiders' viewpoints differ not only in what they identify as problems but also in where they believe problems are located. Professional care giving regards problems as stemming from deficiencies or weaknesses within sufferers—as a form of helplessness or incompetence to deal with the vicissitudes of life. In cases of chronic illness and disability, professional care givers find it easy to see the patient's physical condition as all-important, as pervading and weakening the entire life structure of the individual. Thus, the care giver is tempted to take over all responsibilities and make all decisions for the sufferer until the "victim's" strength has been restored.

A sufferer may indeed feel helpless, but from the insider's standpoint, the problem is confined to the specific condition that brought the helplessness about; generalized incompetence is not the issue. Thus, sufferers want relief only from the specific condition that seems to be bringing about discomfort. They do not want the rest of their lives to be altered or interfered with.

In research, the outsider insists that the problem has nothing to do with individuals. It arises from and resides within a theory or set of hypotheses. These describe in abstract terms processes that take place in all human beings. The proper place to study them is in the controlled environment of the laboratory—not the clinic or rehabilitation center—and the applications of findings to individuals, particularly to relieve suffering, is not a matter of science but of art (Holt, 1962).

Nothing could interest the person who is suffering less than whether some scientist gains objective, impersonal confirmation of an abstract theory. Sufferers' problems are immediate and personal. A given individual might participate in clinical trials of a new drug on the chance that it may provide relief. Still, such a person is not likely to care why or how the drug works as long as it is not dangerous (i.e., does not increase suffering).

6.1. Possible Resolution

In service delivery, resolution of this difference in viewpoint clearly calls for professionals to be more willing to give up demands for control over the lives of the people they are trying to help. By the same token, it calls for greater efforts to prepare clients and patients to make their own decisions and take more responsibility for their own care. More specifically, psychologists who assess and evaluate people with chronic illnesses and disabilities should be prepared to assume new roles. Except in very unusual circumstances, they should stop being "diagnosticians" and "therapists" who identify, label, and treat psychopathology. For example, they should stop relying routinely on tests like the Minnesota Multiphasic Personality Inventory, that are designed only to detect psychiatric disturbances. Instead, they must use, or develop if necessary, measuring instruments that will yield information that clients themselves will find helpful. One such instrument, the Millon Behavioral Health Inventory (MBHI), was developed specifically for use with medical patients and addresses issues of interpersonal style and psychosocial stressors believed to contribute significantly to the precipitation or exacerbation of physical illness (Millon, Green, & Meagher, 1979). Practitioners must come to realize that many problems attributed to poor adjustment on the part of the patient actually stem from failures of impersonal environments to take each client's special needs into account. As one who should be able to appreciate both the outsider's and the insider's points of view, the psychologist will probably more often be in the position of serving as advocate for the latter than as servant of the former.

In research, a good deal of ingenuity may be called for to resolve this difference. It may be necessary for scientists, who wish to study real human problems, to adopt a new attitude toward theory and hypothesis testing. For example, they may find it necessary to reverse the usual logic of experimental method. Instead of thinking of case studies as being merely exploratory and of large-scale research as the "real" test of hypotheses, they might learn to consider large-scale studies to be merely exploratory and carefully controlled case-studies to be the ultimate test of the validity of a theory—that is, by determining whether it really holds for individuals or is true only for group averages (cf. Spotts & Shontz, 1980, pp. 27–30, 477–479).

Something else the scientist might do is select for testing theories that promise, if true, to benefit individuals in significant ways. An example of such a theory is Fink's (1967) model of stages of reaction to crisis. This model was derived from clinical experience and proposes that the individual who experiences crisis of any kind, including chronic illness or disability, first undergoes shock, next defensive retreat (denial), and then a series of reencounters with the critical circumstances until final adjustment is achieved, possibly at a higher level of psychological maturity than that which preceded the critical event. The model does not propose that everyone experiences the stages in exactly the same way or at specified times following the onset of the crisis. In fact, it is quite likely that the stages are manifested somewhat differently in each individual and that different aspects of life are affected by the stages at different rates.

Clearly, a theory like this cannot be evaluated in large-scale studies that use rating scales as measuring instruments and statistical averages as measures. Its value must be assessed in individuals, who are examined one at a time over long periods, using assessment techniques appropriately selected or designed for each person. This type of research treats the individual studied as the final authority on what is happening. It openly professes to try to help, in ways the person finds acceptable, in exchange for the privilege of examining what both experimenter and patient hope will be a successful course of adaptation.

7. Attitudes toward Subjectivity

Another area of difference stems from the tendency of the outsider to be distrustful and suspicious of subjectivity. Distrust need not arise from the belief that patients are deliberate liars. It may stem from the opinion that most people are simply not good or well-trained observers of their own states and conditions.

In a service delivery system, distrust of insiders' reports is partly responsible for the establishment of complex bureaucratic procedures designed not only to ensure that patient data are accurate but also to detect malingering and to prevent undeserving or "merely lazy" people from receiving benefits. One long-range effect of introducing such precautions may be to reduce the number who receive help by eliminating those whose claims are inadequate. However, another effect is to motivate those who feel they are being unjustly deprived of assistance to devise newer and cleverer ways to beat the system. A vicious circle may be established in which service providers and service recipients become opponents rather than partners in the therapeutic or rehabilitative enterprise.

Suspiciousness of verbal report shows clearly in the study and diagnosis of experiences like pain, where outsiders are often tempted to presume—without supporting evidence—that the insider either will not or cannot provide reliable and valid information about subjective experience (Fordyce, Fowler, Lehmann,

DeLateur, Sand, & Trieschmann, 1973; Lasagna, 1960; Sternbach, 1968). Distrust of verbal reports is evident in the general acceptance by American experimental psychology of the antimentalistic philosophy that underlies the doctrine of behaviorism, first proposed in 1913 by John Watson and not seriously challenged, except in details, since that time.

7.1. Possible Resolution

The problem of suspiciousness of patient reports can probably never be resolved completely in the service delivery system. There will always be those who pretend to have conditions they do not have in order to gain the social approval they need in order to acquire economic benefits from welfare and rehabilitation programs. To be fair, it must be said that gatekeepers probably incline to err on the side of leniency rather than harshness. Most complaints about misuse of helping services seem to come from people who are outside the delivery system and not exposed to the plights of sufferers. They often base their objections on the philosophy that those who can pay deserve the best care while only the sickest and most helpless deserve to get assistance free, and they should get only what is absolutely needed and socially justified.

Yet, lenience on the part of gatekeepers is not a fully satisfactory answer to the problem of suspiciousness, for in an atmosphere of distrust, lenience may be taken for softness and exploitability. It can encourage additional attempts on the part of sufferers to take unfair advantage of the system. Because attitudes that determine who "deserves" care and who does not are deeply ingrained in the social structure, this may be a problem for which the only possible solution is a large-scale program of attitude change on both sides.

With respect to research, the solution to the problem is at hand, though not much used. Throughout the history of psychology, there have always been a few—like William Stern, Gordon Allport, Carl Rogers, Robert White, and Kurt Goldstein—who have spoken out for the careful study of individuals as unique entities. Most of these investigators have not been behaviorists; a few, like Rogers, were avowed phenomenologists. Others, like Goldstein, advocated studying all aspects of the whole person, including physique, behavior, and subjective experience. The approaches of these investigators usually involve collecting data under conditions that make lying unnecessary on the part of the person being studied. Another possible solution to the problem of deceit on the part of either insider or outsider would be to discover the conditions that cause any person to engage in deceit (deception must be as lawful as all other behavior) and to provide service or perform research only in circumstances where such conditions do not operate.

8. Values

Service professionals and research scientists are typically taught to take pride in their "objectivity," which usually means their ability to make rational and unemotional decisions about what is best or right in any situation within their area of expertise. For present purposes, it is necessary to overlook the confusion that is produced by assuming that objectivity is incompatible with emotional responses and value judgments, for an analysis of the concept of objectivity can become immensely complex (see, for example, Earle, 1968). It is enough to point out that, in most treatment settings, therapists and practitioners are restricted to highly specialized roles and are taught to draw diagnostic conclusions in a uniform manner—that is, to administer care only on prescription and only in professionally approved ways. As outsiders with respect to patients, their personal need is to be judged competent by the standards of their professions, not necessarily by those of the people whom they serve. Of course, professional care givers do apply values, but the values are those of their professions rather than their patients. Thus, for instance, a therapist who identifies with the outsider's point of view may have difficulty understanding how patients can resist or refuse treatments that are painful or uncomfortable when it is obvious (to the therapist) that the treatment is necessary in order to control or cure the patient's disease. Such therapists may also have difficulty appreciating how important the struggle to maintain hope can be to a person who is suffering. For therapists are guided by their knowledge of the most probable outcome of the patient's condition, while sufferers prefer to hope for that which may be only remotely possible from an "objective" point of view (Dembo, 1970).

Science is famous for admiring objectivity, and in research objectivity is assumed to imply, in part, freedom from value judgments. Again, however, the issue is not whether scientists make value judgments, for they make them all the time. Their insistence on achieving a type of objectivity which is actually unattainable is itself a value judgment—that is, an ideal rather than an actuality. Furthermore, in cases of doubt, individual scientists' preferences for their own theories, as distinct from those of their opponents, are always based on values. The very existence of disagreement between scientists shows that facts alone are not the determining factors in scientists' behavior; if they were, disagreement would not occur.

As has been shown, scientists tend to devalue clients as sources of "objective" data. The extreme to which denigration of patients' reports can be taken is illustrated by the following remark. It was cited in an article that was making the case for disregarding verbal reports in assessing pain: "The investigator who would study pain is at the mercy of the patient, upon whose ability and willingness to communicate he is dependent" (Lasagna, 1960, quoted in Fordyce, Fowler, Lehmann, DeLateur, Sand, & Trieschmann, 1973, p. 399).

From the point of view of a person experiencing pain, this statement, which ostensibly places the investigator "at the mercy of" the sufferer, is utter nonsense. Nothing is more certain to one who adopts the point of view of sufferers than that it is the sufferer who is at the mercy of the helper and that the sufferer is the only valid source of data about his or her own internal psychological states.

8.1. Possible Resolution

One solution to the problem of differences between the values of outsiders and insiders is to provide greater representation for patients or clients in the planning and execution of treatment. When this cannot be accomplished by direct patient participation or comanagement (Wright, 1960), it might be achieved through the assignment of a staff member—who genuinely likes a client and is given time to get to know the client well—to act as the patient's advocate or liaison agent. Another solution might be to provide staff with preprofessional and in-service training that will sensitize them to clients' subjective experiences and life situations. Although value clashes can probably never be avoided completely, mutual respect and appreciation can go a long way toward minimizing their deleterious effects.

Several specific solutions to the problems of including client values in research have already been suggested. In general, these problems can be solved by including clients' viewpoints in the entire research enterprise and by treating their views and opinions with greater respect and acceptance than is implied by the label *verbal reports*.

9. Temporal Perspective

Service personnel and scientists tend to adopt a longer time perspective than do sufferers. Professionals think in terms of the entire course of a client's treatment or rehabilitation and, in cases involving life-threatening illnesses, to the extreme of a client's death. Furthermore, each professional sees each client as only a brief episode in the course of the professional's entire career. Scientists extend their time frame even further, for their ultimate goal is to discover truths or laws that are timeless and absolute. A devoted scientist will tolerate years, perhaps an entire lifetime, of waiting if there is a chance that at the end a single eternal truth will be closer to discovery.

Not so in the sufferer's frame of reference. There, problems demand immediate solutions and moments may seem an eternity. The person who lies in pain for hours in the emergency room of a modern hospital gains no relief from being told (if anyone takes the trouble to do so) that a few hours' wait for care will do no harm. The person who lives in a wheelchair gains relatively little immediate consolation from knowing that the diligent application of political pressure may produce a barrier–free environment in 20 years.

Much of the consumerist reaction and "anti-guinea-pigism" that began in the 1960s (Brieland, 1970) among people with chronic illnesses and disabilities can probably be attributed to rebellion against the enforcement of outsiders' long-term values and an assertion of the demand that insiders' perspectives, especially with regard to the need for immediate results, be given more serious attention.

9.1. Possible Resolution

Both professionals and scientists would gain from direct participation in patients' or clients' experiences. Some of this might be accomplished through role-playing exercises, some by having professionals spend periods of actual living in the institution for several days under the same conditions as patients.

As client self-help groups grow in influence, they may provide valuable input that will help outsiders view treatment and research plans and goals from an insider's perspective as well as their own.

Some of the need is clearly political and economic. People with special requirements to accommodate themselves to atypical physiques must become politically active and exert direct pressures on social and governmental institutions.

10. Units of Measurement and Conceptualization

The viewpoint of treatment professionals and research scientists tends to break experiences down into smaller and more precise units than does that of sufferers. A specific plan of therapy or rehabilitation consists of a detailed set of particularized procedures and objectives. Each is designed to supplement the others, and each has its place in the scheme of things. Nowhere is this more obvious than in surgery. All the patient may think of is getting a troublesome appendix removed. But the surgeon must consider every step of the procedure, from the beginning of preoperative preparation to the end of postoperative recovery.

The insistence on precision in scientific research is too well known to require further comment.

This breaking down or analysis of experience is not inconsistent with the longer temporal perspective of the professional's or scientific outsider's points of view. Both are committed to the philosophy that only by taking pains to make sure that every detail is perfect and every measurement precise can the long-range goals of good patient care or the increase of scientific knowledge be achieved.

The insider's frame of reference is fundamentally different because the sufferer is less interested in facts than implications. As Herzlich (1973) observed, for most people illness is not a state of the body but a condition of inability to function normally. However much physical damage a person incurs, one is not really sick, as an insider, until one really understands that one can no longer participate in life in accustomed ways (Shontz, 1975). It follows that a person's reaction to self-diagnosis depends primarily on what the illness means for the conduct of daily affairs and only secondarily on what the illness or disability is in terms of scientific data or professional diagnosis.

10.1. Possible Resolution

Many treatment personnel attempt to anticipate patients' or clients' concerns and to provide information they think will be helpful ("You'll be up and around again in no time, Mr. Jones," or "Don't worry about it, Mrs. Smith, all patients with strokes go through periods like this"). Such efforts are only partially successful if the information is offered impersonally or without real understanding of the patient's individual feelings and situation.

Following the first shock of recognition that something is radically wrong, a common first reaction to severely disabling or life-threatening conditions is to refuse to acknowledge all the limitations the new physical state is likely to impose. People having this reaction do not want to get well soon but to be well now. They care not about how the average patient reacts or how others have reacted but about how they are reacting themselves. They want to be reassured that their condition will not affect the important relationships that constitute the core of their personal structures. Only after some time does it become possible for a person whose life has been drastically altered to come to terms with that fact and appreciate the outsider's position, which may be needed as a basis for building cooperative relations with treatment personnel.

Both scientists and professional care givers must learn to recognize that differences in units of measurement and conceptualization are fundamental causes of what are often described as "failures of communication." These differences are not merely semantic but pervade the entire structure of perception and interpretation of the social environment. All human beings become sufferers at one time or another in their lives, but not all sufferers are trained in the helping professions or science. Therefore, the burden of adaptation in this instance lies more with the outsiders than on the insiders (Dembo, 1964, 1970).

11. Decision Making

It should come as no surprise to find that the outsider's perspective facilitates different decisions than does the insider's perspective. One cause of difference is the outsider's tendency to rationalize decisions in terms of outcome probabilities. According to this line of reasoning, treatment should be administered only if it stands a good chance of working and, if facilities are scarce, only to those who are most likely to benefit from it.

Another cause of difference is the outsider's insistence on uniformity of care, especially in long-term treatment or rehabilitation facilities. The professional standpoint requires that, to avoid favoritism, patients with the same physical conditions be given the same course and quality of treatment regardless of personal considerations. A currently troublesome case in point is the ethic surrounding the provision of elaborate and expensive medical care to people with terminal illnesses who may not wish to continue living but are offered little choice. A more specific example is afforded by the fact that, despite the discovery that many people on chemotherapy for cancer feel that marijuana relieves the nausea that commonly accompanies this treatment and despite the fact that many patients desire to use the substance for that purpose only, the drug is not commonly supplied for this use at present. Along similar lines, many physicians are often reluctant to prescribe morphine for relief of pain until a patient is virtually in the agony of death. Under such circumstances, sufferers might prefer to make exceptions to rigid rules of treatment and care. To them, relief may be more important than whether one breaks the law by using a generally accepted though illegal substance or whether one acquires an addiction to opiates.

The traditional indifference of science to the personal lives of experimental subjects is well known. Scientific truth is impersonal and decisions about experiments are ideally made only in terms of whether a procedure will yield a clear-cut test of a hypothesis. Naturally, people who suffer do not like to think of themselves as objects to be manipulated by aloof scientific investigators. A sufferer may submit to experimentation, but usually only in the hope that the experimental treatment will provide relief that is otherwise unattainable—not because of any shared enthusiasm for precision, objectivity, and the search for general laws.

From an outsider's perspective, a sufferer's decisions may seem unrealistic, even irrational. Often, a sufferer throws over the rule of probability and exchanges it for hope in the merely possible, however unlikely that may be. People with chronic illnesses and disabilities are more sensitive than professionals and scientists to the fact that predictions and decisions made by outsiders are often wrong. Patients recover who were told they were about to die. Employers consistently refuse to hire fully capable persons with apparent handicaps, even though people with handicaps know they can perform the work. People with chronic illnesses and disabilities who have adapted successfully to life are therefore much more likely to be willing to take a chance, to try the "unreasonable." They resent the withholding of opportunities on the ground that too much risk is involved or that their presence may offend the sensibilities of others who may feel uncomfortable in the company of those with atypical physiques.

11.1. Possible Resolution

Only successful client or patient comanagement in the treatment process can resolve the decision-making issue. Insiders must participate as individuals, either through self assertion or through someone else who advocates their cause. They should also participate as groups either through representation in important institutional decision-making bodies or as pressure groups of individuals who band together to promote their own common welfare. The issue of comanagement has been discussed in detail by Wright (1960) whose writings are recommended to both insiders and outsiders.

12. General Reconciliation of the Two Viewpoints

Some authorities have called for resolving the differences between insiders and outsiders by requiring professionals and scientists to take into account more fully the opinions and suggestions of people with chronic illnesses and disabilities (Dembo 1969; 1970). As indicated above, Wright has suggested that clients be brought into treatment planning and evaluation conferences as equal partners in the rehabilitation enterprise. Suggestions like these hold promise. Optimism seems further justified as one views a gradual increase in accessibility of public buildings, increases in the number of self-help groups among people with chronic illnesses and disabilities, the "mainstreaming" of children with disabilities into public school systems, and recent increases in the number of adults with disabling conditions who occupy positions of authority and decision-making responsibility (Wright, 1973). These developments should be encouraged, for there is no question but that greater participation in society at large will provide needed opportunities for people with chronic illnesses or disabilities to make the insider's point of view more effective in the formulation of general social policies and the design of scientific projects.

However, optimism must be tempered by appropriate caution. The point bears repeating that it does not follow that someone will take the viewpoint of the insider simply because that person has an illness or a disability. The insider–outsider distinction is only probabilistically related to physical, social, or professional status. Not all professionals or scientists adopt an outsider's position all the time. Neither do all clients adopt the insider's viewpoint consistently. Indeed, empirical data might show relatively little overt disagreement between patients and staff when both are asked to express their opinions on specific relevant issues (Leviton, 1973).

The distinction between insider and outsider penetrates to fundamental philosophical differences. How these are manifested in the stands taken on specific issues by any given individual is more important than whether that person is or is not professionaly or scientifically trained or has or has not been identified by society as having a chronic illness or disability. Client participation in treatment planning contributes nothing if the client unthinkingly adopts the viewpoint of those who provide care. A professional would make poor treatment plans, and a scientist would design poor research, if they abandoned the viewpoints of their disciplines altogether and always took the sufferer's word as law.

Without doubt, the number of problems aroused by adjusting to the world when one has a chronic illness or physical disability can be diminished by taking steps to ensure that the viewpoint of insiders is heard and taken seriously. However, it will be vital to make sure that those who are chosen to expound and espouse that viewpoint truly adopt it themselves. As suggested previously, this may require developing suitable psychological assessment techniques. Perhaps the very process of developing such techniques will provide the first example of true cooperation between the outsiders, who perform the technical tasks, and the insiders, whose participation assures that the resulting instrument is valid.

13. A Final Question

Throughout this very general discussion, one question has not been specifically raised, though both the question and its answer have been implied. Phrased in the same inaccurate language as the title of this chapter, the question is: How does one know when a person has adjusted successfully to a chronic illness or disability? Phrased somewhat less objectionably, the question is: How does one know when a person with a chronic illness or disability is well adjusted?

A general answer is that the signs of good psychological adjustment are no different for people with chronic illnesses and disabilities than for anyone else. This answer implies that there is no special psychology of persons with these conditions, and the implication is correct, though it is not entirely complete.

A more specific and useful answer is that a person with a chronic illness or disability has satisfactorily come to terms with his or her physical condition to the extent that the problem of contending with it ceases to be the dominant element in that person's total psychological structure (or "life space").

Note that this statement does not emphasize the physical condition *per se* but the problem of contending with it. A person who denies a personal physical illness or disability may reach a stage at which the physical condition as such no longer seems central to the life space. However, in denial, the problem of contending with the condition remains a dominant force nonetheless, for it is the search for a solution to the problem of contending with the condition that brings about denial in the first place and that maintains denial once it has been established.

This answer generates a paradox for rehabilitation, for it suggests that the process of treatment, which is intended to foster good adjustment to illness or disability, may actually foster poor psychological adjustment by forcing patients to pay constant attention to the limitations their physical conditions impose. In some instances and under some circumstances, such may be the case. It is especially likely to be so when a patient's tendency to minimize or deny his or her condition is counteracted by staff insistence that the patient face up to the restrictions imposed by illness or disability. For the most part, however, people with chronic illnesses and disabilities possess sufficient integrative and anticipative resources to absorb the stress of rehabilitative care and to benefit from it provided that they can see themselves making progress and that they have sufficient hope in the future to justify the effort it takes to learn new ways of adapting.

The answer may not apply so clearly to people who suffer terminal conditions. However, a case can be made that even they benefit psychologically when they see in their forthcoming demise something other than a biological death and find hope in the prospects of a life hereafter or satisfaction in the thought that their lives were full and complete and that they live on in the hearts and memories of others.

14. References

Bell, A. H. Measure for adjustment of the physically disabled. *Psychological Reports*, 1967, *21*, 773–778.

Brieland, D. Rehabilitation psychologists: Roles and functions. In W. S. Neff (Ed.), *Rehabilitation psychology*. Washington, D.C.: American Psychological Association, 1970.

Bulman, R. J., & Wortman, C. B. Attributions of blame and coping in the "real world": Severe accident victims react to their lot. *Journal of Personality and Social Psychology*, 1977, *35*, 351–363.

Buss, A. R. *A dialectical psychology*. New York: Wiley, 1979.

Dembo, T. Sensitivity of one person to another. In R. L. Noland (Ed.), *Counseling parents of the mentally retarded: A sourcebook*. Springfield, Ill.: Charles C Thomas, 1970. Reprinted from *Rehabilitation Literature*, 1964, *25*, 231–235.

Dembo, T. Rehabilitation psychology and its immediate future: A problem of utilization of psychological knowledge. *Rehabilitation Psychology (Psychological Aspects of Disability)*, 1969, *16*, 63–72.

Dembo, T. The utilization of psychological knowledge in rehabilitation. *Welfare in Review*, 1970, *8*(4), 1–7.

Earle, W. *Objectivity, an essay in phenomenological ontology.* Chicago: Quadrangle Books, 1968.

Fink, S. L. Crisis and motivation: A theoretical model. *Archives of Physical Medicine and Rehabilitation,* 1967, *48,* 592–597.

Fisher, S., & Cleveland, S. E. *Body image and personality* (2nd ed.). New York: Dover, 1968.

Fordyce, W. E., Fowler, R. S., Jr., Lehmann, J. F., DeLateur, B. J., Sand, P. L., & Trieschmann, R. B. Operant conditioning in the treatment of chronic pain. *Archives of Physical Medicine and Rehabilitation,* 1973, *54,* 399–408.

Henrich, E., & Kriegel, L. *Experiments in survival.* New York: Association for the Aid of Crippled Children, 1961.

Herzlich, C. *Health and illness.* New York: Academic Press, 1973.

Holt, R. R. Individuality and generalization in the psychology of personality. *Journal of Personality,* 1962, *30,* 377–402.

Lasagna, L. Clinical measurement of pain. *Annals of the New York Academy of Sciences,* 1960, *86,* 28–37.

Lerner, M. J. Observer's evaluation of a victim: Justice, guilt, and veridical perception. *Journal of Personality and Social Psychology,* 1971, *20,* 127–135.

Lerner, M. J., & Simmons, C. H. Observer's reaction to the "innocent victim": Comparison or rejection? *Journal of Personality and Social Psychology,* 1966, *4,* 203–210.

Leviton, G. L. Professional-client relations in a rehabilitation hospital setting. In W. S. Neff (Ed.), *Rehabilitation psychology.* Washington, D.C.: American Psychological Association, 1971.

Leviton, G. L. Professional and client viewpoints on rehabilitation issues. *Rehabilitation Psychology,* 1973, *20,* 1–80.

Linkowski, D. C. A scale to measure acceptance of disability. *Rehabilitation Counseling Bulletin,* 1971, *4,* 236–244.

Meyerson, L. A psychology of impaired hearing. In W. M. Cruickshand (Ed.), *Psychology of exceptional children and youth* (2nd ed.). Englewood Cliffs, N.J.: Prentice-Hall, 1963.

Millon, T., Green, C., & Meagher, R. The MBHI: A new inventory for the psychodiagnostician in medical settings. *Professional Psychology,* 1979, *10,* 529–539.

Rychlak, J. F. *A philosophy of science for personality theory.* Boston: Houghton Mifflin, 1968.

Rychlak, J. F. *The psychology of rigorous humanism.* New York: Wiley, 1977.

Shontz, F. C. Severe chronic illness. In J. F. Garrett & E. S. Levine (Eds.), *Rehabilitation practices with the physically disabled.* New York: Columbia University Press, 1973.

Shontz, F. C. *The psychological aspects of physical illness and disability.* New York: Macmillan, 1975.

Shontz, F. C. Theories about the adjustment to having a disability. In W. M. Cruickshank (Ed.), *Psychology of exceptional children and youth* (4th ed.). Englewood Cliffs, N.J.: Prentice-Hall, 1980.

Spotts, J. V., & Shontz, F. C. *Cocaine users: A representative case approach.* New York: The Free Press, 1980.

Sternbach, R. A. *Pain, a psychophysiological analysis.* New York: Academic Press, 1968.

Wright, B. A. *Physical disability—a psychological approach.* New York: Harper & Row, 1960.

Wright, B. A. Issues in overcoming emotional barriers to adjustment in the handicapped. *Rehabilitation Counseling Bulletin,* 1967, *11,* 53–59.

Wright, B. A. Changes in attitudes toward people with handicaps. *Rehabilitation Literature,* 1973, *34,* 354–357, 368.

Wright, B. A. An analysis of attitudes—dynamics and effects. *New Outlook for the Blind,* 1974, *67,* 108–118.

The Clinical Settings of
Health Psychology

II

The Psychologist as Health Care Clinician

ALVIN G. BURSTEIN AND SANDRA LOUCKS

1. Historical Review

1.1. Ideological Issues

Clearly, the health care field is turf dominated by the physician, and working in that field means involvement with physicians. As we will explore below, physician–psychologist contact in the health care field has been characterized—especially of late—by some friction. Accommodating to and constructively dealing with interprofessional role strain will be facilitated by knowing something of the history of medical/psychological involvement and something about the contemporary forces at work at that interface.

Membership in any profession involves adherence to a set of relatively unexamined beliefs—subscription to the ideology of that profession (Burstein, Barnes, & Quesada, 1976). As religious wars have taught us, ideological conflicts are more often characterized by casualties than conversions. Nevertheless, these ideological differences do generate friction, often misattributed to other sources, and the constructive resolution of those difficulties will be facilitated by an understanding and exploration of their ideological origins. We will examine a series of five modal ideological positions as they relate to health care and to mental and physical suffering: (1) the disease model, (2) the medical model, (3) the psychobiological model, (4) the holistic model, and (5) the psychological model.

ALVIN G. BURSTEIN • Department of Psychiatry, University of Texas Health Science Center at San Antonio, San Antonio, Texas 78284.   SANDRA LOUCKS • Department of Psychology and Center for Personal and Educational Development, Trinity University, San Antonio, Texas 78212.

1.1.1. The Disease Model

This model is sometimes called the *illness model* and is sometimes confused with the *medical model*. Nevertheless, they are considered separately because the latter is basically a political or organizational view while the former deals with the nature of humanity as viewed by patients and doctors.

The meaning of the disease model is best understood as an expression of the historical evolution of the social role of medicine. In a panoramic view, medicine (and surgery) began with limited functions: treating fevers and inflammations, repairing fractures and lacerations. As the scientific basis of medicine grew, impressive successes were achieved in applying biological knowledge to problematic conditions—notably, using thyroid extract to treat cretinism, insulin for diabetes, and anesthetics, antibiotics, and haemodialysis in various other situations. These successes helped to foster a reductionist view of disease, that is, the view that biological factors are the most real or most effective, and an orientation toward declaring war on disease processes which are—like political enemies—to be extirpated or destroyed. Germs were the enemy.

Medicine's victories led to an increasingly expansionist view of the profession's functions. What had previously been defined as moral failings (e.g., excessive drinking) became diseases; physicians have in latter days even undertaken to resolve gender dissatisfaction! This expansionism was given further impetus by the optimism and beneficent temper of the post-World War II era. The ultimate expansion of what a physician might be thought responsible for is found in the implications of the World Health Organization's view that *health* is a sense of complete physical, mental, and social well-being as well as in the fusion of political and psychiatric missions in the community mental health center movement of the sixties.

Although the high tide of optimism has receded noticeably, the disease model—with its loose implication that painful or undesirable human states are the results of alien and external forces best defeated by biological agents—remains current. It is this view that makes tranquilizing drugs the most commonly prescribed medicines (anxiety being seen as a disease to be vanquished rather than part of a potential growth process) and regards death as an enemy the physician must seek endlessly to vanquish.

1.1.2. The Medical Model

This organizational model has two basic elements. The first component is a commitment to the generic nature of medical training and licensure; the second is a related view that any health-related activity or treatment performed by a physician is performed more competently or effectively than when the same act is carried out by nonphysicians. Nowhere has this view been more vigorously pressed than in connection with the controversies surrounding health insurance coverage for psychotherapy provided by nonmedical psychotherapists. Insurance companies are state-regulated (except in the District of Columbia) and numerous states have enacted laws or regulations providing that policies covering psychotherapy must reimburse for appropriate psychotherapy charges made by any licensed professional. Physician-controlled insurance companies have particularly resisted this pressure, asserting that psychotherapy performed by physicians is intrinsically different from and better than that provided by others.

Some state legislatures, insurance boards, and federal agencies are concerned by the lack of data to support such a view and are sensitive to the generally favorable effects of price competition on costs. Arguments parallel to those made relative to the psychotherapy controversy have also been made with regard to the practice of other nonphysician health care providers, for example nurse–anaesthetists, nurse–practitioners, and midwives.

The core of the medical model is that health services are best performed or controlled by physicians. The justification is that physicians are very highly trained and broadly experienced and thus best equipped to control the health team. The counterarguments point out that physicians lack managerial training; that they are raised in a solo-practice culture that stresses autonomy, not accountability and cooperation; that the political and fiscal benefits (to the physician) of control are the primary issue; and that the notion of health has expanded to the point that a health team would have to include the whole community (with the physician, of course, as leader).

The other element in the medical model is that, although physicians and nonphysicians are nonfungible, physicians are said to be entirely fungible. States license physicians only generically, and any licensed physician is deemed by law qualified to perform any medical treatment. This commitment to the totally generic nature of physician practice and education deters physicians from recognizing the limits of their competence, commits undergraduate medical education to a lockstep no-option format that ignores the realities of physician specialization at the level of practice, and defers the possibility of exploring an alternative model in which varieties of medical practitioners are specifically and efficiently trained to provide a clearly defined range of activities—a development foreshadowed by emergency medical service technicians, midwives, optometrists, audiologists, and so on.

1.1.3. The Psychobiological Model

However disease and the practice of medicine are defined, the control of pain is a core element. Biologically reductionist views of medicine and disease were therefore confronted with a crucial paradox by the studies of Beecher. From the reductionist point of view, pain is the subjective experiential aspect of tissue damage; however, Beecher's (1946) finding that badly wounded soldiers at Anzio experienced surprisingly little pain, as well as Merskey's (1974) results, indicate that the lack of relationship between the degree of reported pain and the degree of biopathology constituted a serious challenge. This challenge was intensified by the more recent successes in using psychological, learning-theory-based approaches to the management of pain: a Pavlovian approach (psychoprophylaxis) to the pain of childbirth (Vellay, 1960) and a Skinnerian, operant-conditioning approach to intractable pain (Fordyce, 1973). To the list of such challenges might also be added the successful psychoeducational treatments for such "reflexive" problems as anorgasmia and premature orgasm (Masters &

Johnson, 1970) and some recent applications of hypnosis to the treatment of asthma (Barbour, Zeltzer, Kalmowitz, Kniker, Rao, Littlefield, & Fisher, 1979) and hemophilia (Dubin & Shapiro, 1974; Levine & Zeltzer, 1980).

A response to these paradoxes is to abandon the disease model in its reductionist form in favor of a psychobiological model or, more elaborately, a psychosocial–biological model. This model views the human organism as the summation of a series of increasingly complex processes—a system that can effectively be entered at a number of points or levels.

This model has a good deal of appeal but some problems as well. One problem is confusion about whether the complexity of an organism implies that the professional must deal simultaneously with all variables, as Erikson (1963) seems to imply in his references to triple-entry bookkeeping. If one were to endorse this view fully, the training of a practitioner might become a practically impossible task. In addition, this view, together with a commitment to the disease model, would argue for the most expansive possible definition of the purview of medicine. Finally, it is possible to use a psychobiological label for a point of view that in effect argues that psychological events are only the subjective aspect of biological events. In this way one would become, as it were, a cryptoreductionist.

1.1.4. The Holistic Model

Recent years have seen an outbreak of references to the terms *holistic health* and *holistic medicine*. These phrases resonate vaguely with distant but fondly remembered adjurations to treat the whole person. At the same time, they have a contemporary, humanistic, mildly countercultural ring. Holistic medicine and health seem like good things, but the referent is unclear.

Among the unsettling vagaries of the adjective *holistic* is an apparent uncertainty about how to spell it. It is variously rendered "holistic," "wholistic," and, more recently "(w)holistic." If this orthographic diffusion has a meaning, it would seem to lie in a simultaneous reference to the philosophical doctrine of holism or emergent qualities; to the psychobiological principle, enunciated by Adolf Meyer, that the human being can only be studied as a whole person in action; and to systems theory. Whatever the allusive referents of the term, however, holistic medicine reminds us that the whole is more than the sum of its parts. A human being cannot be adequately described by a simple summation of physiological systems. Medical interventions must be seen not as linear causes triggering singular results but as diffuse probes generating myriad ripples in numerous linked compartments. That holistic medicine reminds us of these complexities is valuable; however, the term seems to have additional, if uncertain, meaning.

Consider next the phrase *holistic health*. Does this mean health achieved by special, presumably holistic means, or health of the whole mind–body system? The former makes little sense, because a healthy state is a healthy state. We do not distinguish weight reduction achieved by dieting from that achieved by exercise; nor do we distinguish between the absence of cavities achieved by dental prophylaxis from that achieved by avoiding sweets. Health is health.

The second meaning, health of the whole system, makes little sense either.

If systems and subsystems genuinely interact, as the doctrine of holism suggests, then no subsystem can be healthy if other related systems are not. All the parts and the whole are healthy, or they are not. Health is health and the qualifier *holistic* is a better example of alliteration's artful aid to rhetoric than it is a way of adding meaning.

Despite the frequency with which the term *holistic medicine* is now appearing, explicit definitions are rare. Understanding and evaluation are matters not only of tracking allusions but also sifting implications. One loose implication of the holistic approach to health and medicine would seem to be a bias toward inducing general attitudinal change rather than utilizing pharmacologic treatments. For example, it is more holistic to teach a hypertensive patient values that will encourage diet and exercise than it is to prescribe diuretics.

An even looser implication of holism is a bias toward self-control and personal rather than professional responsibility. Good nutrition and control of one's own mind are important ingredients in the holistic formulary.

A third implication is the primacy of the mental. Especially with the advent of biofeedback treatment for many ills ranging from migraine to borborygmi (Birk, 1973), the mind is seen as the system that interacts with and correlates all other human systems. Hence, the holistic interest in yoga, meditation, and the like.

Three implications, all attractive, of the holistic approach to medicine are, then, (1) a recognition of human complexity and diversity, (2) an emphasis on the importance of mental events and personal value systems, and (3) a recognition of the desirability of responsibility for oneself. These may be taken as the hallmarks of the holistic movement in health care.

Holistic medicine is *à la mode:* the new medicine. Doctors used to treat infections, reduce inflammations, and set fractures, but we are all beyond that hoary old disease model. Today's doctors deal with many nondiseases. Anxiety is not a disease, but the most commonly prescribed medicine in America is a minor tranquilizer. For that matter, pregnancy is hardly a disease, but the termination of pregnancy by delivering a baby or inducing an abortion is usually regarded as a medical prerogative. Being ugly is surely not a disease, but many health insurance programs reimburse for cosmetic surgery. These examples reflect an expansionist view of medicine. Perhaps holistic medicine is a reflection of this wider stance. Clearly, persuading people to live healthy lives is better than pushing pills or resorting to surgery. *Holistic medicine* still has a pretty good ring.

But there are some problems. Preventing fractures means legislating crash helmets and seat belts. Preventing cavities means legislating fluoridation. Preventing lead poisoning means legislating paint components. Preventing lung cancer may mean legislating cigarette taxes or air quality controls. Any or all of these laws may be desirable, but medicine does not involve training in political pragmatics, and the exchange of health for freedom is properly a political, not a medical process. Persuading Americans to jog, shun cholesterol, and avoid tobacco is probably at least as desirable as teaching them thrift and honesty (Ben Franklin made dietary recommendations in addition to giving budgetary advice), but those worthwhile hortatory efforts are not peculiarly medical or psychotherapeutic.

The mentalistic bias, too, poses some difficulties. Phenomena like hypnosis, behavioral treatment of sexual dysfunction, and biofeedback control of "autonomic" functions are dramatic reminders that the mind–body system can be entered at either end. As reminders, they are valuable correctives to the biological reductionism that has dominated medicine. We need to be reminded that placebo effects are not unreal—that the mind does affect the body. However, there is no advantage in replacing biological reductionism with mentalistic reductionism. In fact, if we had to choose between Christian science and a biomechanistic model, the latter would be preferable in most situations. As a scientific matter, however, psychology and medicine can and should avoid both oversimplifications.

Finally, we may be prone to confuse humaneness with humanism and flexibility with personal idiosyncracy. It is clearly desirable for practitioners to be tactful, to see their patients on time, and to avoid exploiting those who depend on them. They need not be poets or musicians. It may be desirable for physicians to abandon the posture of the austere, socially and emotionally inaccessible specialist; it is not necessary for them to wear beads, smoke marijuana, or hold deluded or quackish beliefs. If holistic medicine has something of value and clear legitimacy to offer beyond the importance of a practitioner's being careful and considerate, I confess to not seeing what it is.

1.1.5. The Psychological Model

In distinction to reductionism, the doctrine of emergent qualities assumes that natural phenomena can usefully be studied at various levels of complexity and that these levels are not mutually reducible. From this point of view, psychology implies the scientific study of behavior on a fairly molar organismic level of individual human beings as they interact with each other. It is a study carried out at a "higher" level than that of separate physiological systems and a "lower" one than that group behavior. It is at this level that the concepts of consciousness and mind emerge and are most useful. An emergent qualities assumption does not imply that the various levels of complexity in natural phenomena are unrelated—that, for example, mind is independent of brain—but that the levels are not totally reducible to one another. By a "scientific" study, two things are implied. The first is an empirical base, meaning that the study is founded on veridical observation. The second has to do with an epistemological commitment to develop, at any specified level of complexity, a comprehensive theory—one that spans the full range of human behavior. Psychology must account for behavior and subjective experience, for altruism and competitiveness, for creativity and stereotypy. Scientific psychologists may differ as to their strategy for building a comprehensive theory—whether by accretion of microtheories or by inductive leaps—but they should feel the pressure of an imperative towards that goal.

Knowledge, Francis Bacon tells us, is power; the potential power of the psychological model lies in its fit with social enterprises of moment that revolve in a central way around the actions of the individual: education, medicine, business, and so on. The psychologist as a health care clinician seeks to bring to bear on the social enterprise of healing a theory of individual human function that is basically continuous with and enriched by psychology's engagement with theory building and all its applications.

1.2. Traditional and More Recent Hospital Roles for Psychologists

Although interest in behavioral science applications to the health care system has become highly conspicuous in the last few years, "medical psychologists" have a much larger history. Medical school departments of psychiatry have, since the end of World War II, played host to psychologists and psychology sections. Many of the most eminent of these have had a strong research orientation, but others have included significant input into the undergraduate and postgraduate (i.e., psychiatry residency) training of physicians, the development of parallel training programs for psychologists, and patient care activities.

Psychologists in psychiatric settings have occurred in three modes: the prestigious academic unit, often with a major research orientation; the "have-not" state hospital that finds it difficult to recruit adequate numbers of competent psychiatrists and turns to more readily available psychologists to meet service needs; and the Veterans Administration system, which has met a post-World War II explosion of service needs with a highly developed network of medically related psychological services now represented in psychology services parallel to other clinical medical services—medicine, surgery, psychiatry, and so on. In all three modes, however, there is an expectation that psychologists will be skilled in the administration and interpretation of psychological tests—including projective tests—and knowledgeable about psychotherapy, both insight-oriented and supportive.

Neurology departments or services have also played host to psychologists, especially as administrators of the neuropsychological battery of tests used to help diagnose a problem and/or characterize the type of lesion suspected. The Halstead Reitan battery is currently the best known of these instruments, but other approaches, such as the Nebraska Luria, are beginning to emerge.

A third hospital context in which psychologists are familiar is that of rehabilitation services. Here once again the psychologist's expertise in measuring residual abilities and interests comes to the fore. Those settings also top the reality-oriented and cathartic counseling that is integral in helping patients to deal with their altered circumstances. Rehabilitative centers often make heavy use of bachelor's and master's level personnel—such as speech therapists, occupational therapists, and so on—who may seek consultative relationships with the psychologists.

In addition to the well-established roles played by psychologists in departments of psychiatry, neurology, and physical medicine, newer functions are crystallizing in other departments or services. Patients with intractable pain are likely to be referred to comprehensive pain clinics, which draw on a range of techniques including psychological approaches such as hypnosis, operant pain management, and biofeedback.

Obstetrics and gynecology services may ask psychologists to select patients who are appropriate for LaMaze-Vellay training (to minimize the use of narcotics at delivery) or to help assess the motivation of patients seeking sex-change surgery. Dialysis and organ-transplant teams have similar requests to make of psychologists, as do surgeons who undertake heroic approaches to obesity (with intestinal bypass and gastric stapling procedures) or who may wish to assess the rehabilitation potential of patients for whom extensive orthopedic repairs are being considered.

Nowhere are the psychologist's contributions greater than in the primary-care health services of pediatrics, internal medicine, and family practice. The number of psychologists with faculty positions in these academic departments and clinical services has increased sharply in the last 5 years. The psychologist's role in pediatrics is multifaceted because the needs are so great. Developmental assessment, research, and teaching; brief intervention strategies for common childhood disorders and crises, such as divorce; behavior or disciplinary problems; learning problems; encopresis and enuresis; and the teaching of interviewing and counseling skills to residents are all obvious and important areas of contribution in pediatrics. In internal medicine, typical areas of concern are those of patient compliance with treatment regimens, communication with patients, pain reduction, and problems of aging. Family practice unites the more adult-related medical concerns and those of children, focusing more on the family unit and its total cultural context. The psychologist's roles include the provision of direct service; intervention with patients by referral; consultation (seeing patients and family members together and separately from the physician for expert opinion as to the physician's questions); teaching; training residents, medical students, and faculty in certain types of psychological diagnosis and intervention; evaluation; assessing the effectiveness of the psychological interventions and researcher; and promoting the systematic and thoughtful improvement of intervention techniques.

Finally, the psychologist as health care clinician often functions in private practice within a loose partnership with physicians. In some cases, the psychologist is part of a group practice accepting referral from the physician members of the group. Due to some disparity in income, this model is limited in acceptance. More frequently, the health care psychologist will locate with a group of physicians but will be financially independent, accepting referrals and consultations. Finally, a frequently encountered model is that of the health care psychologist who can see patients on his own turf but more frequently travels to the physician's offices to run patient groups, see individual patients, and work as a member of several private-practice health care teams while maintaining an independent base.

In many of these newer settings, the physician is recognizing the complex nature of human motivation and seeking the help of behavioral scientists in assessing and focusing institutional components in ways that contribute to the work of repair and healing. The psychologist is presented with an opportunity to extend his or her understanding of human behavior into areas which are highly consequential and in which the outcomes are often unambiguously clear. Nowhere is the Boulder model of the psychologist as scientist–practitioner more appropriate.

2.1. Problems in the Health Care System

What might be loosely described as our society's health care system has been less a planned affair than a concatenation of accidents. Indeed, the very term *private practice* connotes professional activity conducted between individuals unrelated to institutions and social forces. Certainly medical care has been seen as a cottage industry in which practitioners "did their own thing" with patients who chose to see them; there was also a general assumption that health care costs were subject to free-market constraints and were controlled effectively on the basis of supply and demand.

The situation has always been more complex than that, but these innocent beliefs have been especially sharply challenged by the frightening escalation of health care costs. The proportion of the gross national product spent on health care has risen from 5% in 1960 to nearly 10% today. Because we are talking about proportions, not dollar figures, this change does not reflect the effect of inflation but rather a real increase in costs. Economists and physicians have expressed concern about this trend (McClure, 1976; Fisher, 1980), because competing needs for our resources—such as education, defense, welfare, and capital expansion—are being constrained and because the trend does not seem to respond to efforts to contain it.

Many serious critics see our health care system as in crisis. Illich (1976) and Carlson (1975) challenge it on philosophical grounds; McClure (1976) and Fisher (1980) do so on structural, economic grounds.

There is a building consensus that escalating health care costs and delivery problems are due to a series of related tendencies: attenuation of the individual's responsibility for his or her own well-being, a focus on cure rather than prevention, pursuit of high technology, and a bifurcation between the utilization of health services and payment for them. The operation of these factors requires the health care system to, in McClure's striking metaphor, behave like a vacuum cleaner that will suck up every dollar made available to it.

This analysis indicates that our health delivery problems will not be solved by universal health insurance, either private or governmental. Rather, such a development might well exacerbate our difficulties by further separating consumption of health services from payment for health services, accelerating the escalation of costs, and moving closer to a potential collapse of our economic system. It is more plausible that the problems require a rigid governmental limit (perhaps by region) on health care expenditures (especially for inpatients), strict prioritization of health care activities, and substantial copayment by the consumer at the point of use for health care.

These problems and prospective solutions raise questions about the health system goals reflexively endorsed by many psychologists. Universal health insurance covering all outpatient psychotherapy services does not seem feasible and indeed might be disastrous. It might be more appropriate on grounds of both social policy and professional self-interest to argue for substantial copayments for psychotherapy and all other elective nonemergency outpatient services.

Second, there is a real question whether it will be desirable, in the long run, for psychologists to seek financial parity with physicians. Physicians' fees do not appear to follow the law of supply and demand and have increased much more rapidly than the general inflation rate in recent years. It appears that physicians' fees may increase not because of an increase in the value of services given but because of market constraints, such as monopolistic decisions to increase prices independent of demand. Some of the legal conflict with psychiatry described below is based on the assumption that competition between professions will tend to lower fees. In such a climate, public policy and professional self-interest might suggest that psychology should—like the Japanese auto makers—keep quality up and prices down. Moderated expectations about their income might put psychologists also in a position to work with low-income clients by virtue of their willingness to work on salary or to extend low cost or free services to clients with minimal financial resources (Burstein, 1979).

2.2. Credentialing and Intraprofessional Strains

Even though universal health care insurance does not appear to be likely, health insurance covering psychotherapy has had a significant impact on professional psychology. Health care has increasingly been paid for by third parties—Medicare for recipients of social security, Medicaid for indigents, insurance companies for the employed. Coverage for outpatient psychotherapy has been minimal, however, except for two federal policies: Civilian Health and Medical Program for the Uniformed Services (CHAMPUS), which pays for dependents of military personnel, and federal Blue Cross–Blue Shield, which pays for federal employees. Encouraged by these examples, many psychologists have begun to anticipate, however unrealistically, that health insurance will shortly provide third-party reimbursement for all psychotherapy.

Requests for reimbursement for psychotherapy provided by psychologists raise a question as to whether all psychologists are qualified to provide such services. Clearly they are not, but psychology licensing laws in the various states identify psychologists generically rather than distinguishing applied psychologists from academic psychologists. One response to this problem was the emergence of the *National Register of Health Service Providers in Psychology* (1980). This register is helpful, but it has the limitation of relying heavily on state licensure and self-identification of providers. A second response has been a move by the various state boards to identify health providers. Both these attempts must deal with several pressures, all generated by the possibly illusory prospect of third-party payment.

One such pressure comes from individuals with doctoral degrees in fields other than psychology but related to it—such as communication or education—who wish to be identified and licensed as psychologists. A second is from psychologists who wish to be eligible for third-party payments (but with training in skills different from but related to diagnosis and therapy, such as vocational assessment and counseling). Finally, there are counterpressures from psychologists who offer indirect services, such as consultation, to programs and institutions, but not direct services to individuals. Some of these psychologists have objections to a requirement that they hold a license.

In the face of these pressures, the American Psychological Association (APA) and other groups have been trying to identify the curricular and training elements that are crucial in becoming a psychologists in a generic sense and those that are required for adequate functioning as a direct service provider. Agreement on these points does not currently exist and will not develop without some friction among the constituencies involved.

2.3. Legal Conflict with Psychiatry

As psychologists have begun to compete for health care dollars and as the impending health care crisis has become more apparent, tension between psychologists and psychiatrists has substantially increased. In sharp contrast to the "hail fellow well met" days of the 1950s and 1960s, when a generalist mental health team, like the comic strip superheroes, was going to solve the world's ills or at least mental ills, the community mental health movement has collapsed. This plus the realization that our resources are not limitless but actually rather tightly stretched has led to an increasingly sharp sense of competition between applied psychology and psychiatry. This competition has been played out on three major fronts: hospital privileges, eligibility for third-party reimbursement, and federal training funds.

Psychologists have long been active on psychiatric inpatient units and, more recently, in nonpsychiatric hospital departments. It is rare, however, for their function to be explicitly recognized in and sanctioned by hospital bylaws. Hospitals, to compete for physicians, staff, and patients, seek and value accreditation by the Joint Council on Accreditation of Hospitals (JCAH). The APA has sought representation on JCAH in order to influence hospital regulations and bylaws more explicitly to recognize the role and function of psychologists in hospitals. When it did not receive a positive response, the APA complained to the Federal Trade Commission, which has initiated an investigation to determine whether, among other things, failure to accord hospital-staff privileges to psychologists constitutes a restraint of trade.

In addition to the FTC action, the state of Virginia has seen a trio of lawsuits dealing with the issue of third-party reimbursement to psychologists for providing mental health services. The first, by the state psychological association against Blue Cross–Blue Shield, alleges that there has been a conspiracy by the insurance company to avoid reimbursing psychologists. That case was won on appeal but may be appealed further. The second, brought by the state against Blue Cross–Blue Shield, contended that the insurance companies were in violation of a state law requiring those that provided mental health coverage to reimburse psychologists as well as psychiatrists. That case was won but is pending appeal. The third is a class-action suit on behalf of policyholders alleging that they have been deprived by the insurance company of a choice to seek services from a psychologist. This suit has been heard but no decision has been rendered; any decision is likely to be appealed.

The third front is on the level of attempting to secure federal training funds. Here both psychiatry and psychology have fared poorly in recent years, as the federal government has struggled with runaway inflation and attempted—unsuccessfully—to trim back the federal budget. A recent development in the struggle for federal support for training was the reversal of a Veteran's Administration decision to move almost $1 million in training money from psychology to medicine. Although that move was deferred for the current year, funding for future years is far from secure.

3. The Pragmatics of Practice

The delivery of health care services, *ipso facto*, involves practitioners in the complexities and functions of the health care system that were described above. In addition, it involves them in a number of other quasi-legal issues: licensure, insurance, and hospital privileges.

Psychology licensing laws have been passed in all 50 states and the District of Columbia. Typically, these laws require that in order to offer psychological services to the public, one has to have a doctoral degree in psychology and one or two years of supervised experience. Since the original passage of these bills, many states have enacted "sunset" legislation requiring that all state agencies and boards be expired at the end of a stated period—usually 5 years—unless their renewal is specifically provided for after a review of their function. Unfortunately, sunset review has led to the dissolution of psychology licensing laws in three states, largely, it would appear, on the grounds of legislative impatience with squabbling between psychologists with doctoral degrees and people holding master's degrees in psychology who would like to be licensed for independent practice. Legislators, too, have heard complaints from doctoral-level psychologists who want to be involved in consultative and program–development activities without being licensed and from academic psychologists who see as an invasion of academic freedom the licensing boards' interest in establishing requirements for training in the various specialty areas of psychology.

Still, the majority of states still have licensing laws, and the psychologist who wishes to practice as a health service provider will be required to have a doctoral degree in psychology plus two years of supervised experience, one of which may be predoctoral.

Having obtained a license, the practicing psychologist will be eligible for professional liability insurance. This insurance is available at various levels of coverage, ranging from $100,000 to $1 million. The policies generally indemnify the psychologist against damages claimed as a result of hie or her professional activities. Some caution must be exercised in choosing a carrier, because at least one very popular carrier excludes coverage—and will not provide a legal defense for—the psychologist who is accused of sexual misconduct with a patient. Because one of the chief advantages of such insurance is the provision of legal counsel, excluding a class of complaints is a serious shortcoming. In addition, since the quality of the legal support offered by the company is not a function of the level of coverage and because very high levels of coverage may attract suits, it might be advisable for the psychologist to obtain the lowest possible level of coverage under a policy that does not exclude a class of complaints from coverage.

Many practicing psychologists employ assistants or technicians who work under their supervision. Unless technicians are specifically named in the policy, they may *not* be covered under the psychologist's professional liability policy even though the psychologist is covered for work done by the technicians. Where a technician is employed, the psychologist is responsible for being sure that they are adequately supervised and that all concerned parties know who the responsible psychologist is.

In a hospital context, responsibility for the quality of professional services usually lies with the chief of staff or medical director and appropriate committees of professional staff. As mentioned above, unfortunately, it is rare for psychologists to be regular voting members of the hospital staff organization or to sit on staff committees. It is important for psychologists working in such settings to press for regular staff status and to be specifically authorized to provide specific services within the hospital context by means of a document specifying their staff privileges. The list of possible staff privileges should be sufficiently detailed to recognize the varying areas of competence possessed by varying psychologists. For example, various modes of assessment and intervention should be specified in considerable detail. There should also be provision for periodic review of each individual's privileges to take account of the acquisition of new skills or the erosion of old ones.

4. The Future Yield

Predictions about the varieties of psychological practice in the years ahead are risky. No doubt a significant number of health care clinicians will continue to be committed to the classical forms of psychotherapy and psychodiagnosis for individuals feeling mental distress. In addition, the involvement of psychologists in the medical treatment of physically ill patients may well increase. Counseling dying patients and their families is an important means of preventing psychological scarring in the survivors as well as, perhaps, in avoiding the physical illnesses that survivors are all too prone to contract shortly after a major loss (Lynch, 1977). In addition, short-term education *cum* affect-exploration groups of the sort that Kurt Lewin used in order to alter appetite preferences have proved effective in inducing patients to alter their life-styles constructively so as to adapt to chronic disease (Rahe, O'Neil, Hagan, & Rausam, 1975). Outside the hospital context, psychologists may become involved in preventive or creative programs implemented by private industry to induce healthier life-styles in their executives or other employees, thus reducing illness days and increasing productivity. Programs dealing with alcoholism, smoking, and stress management are already represented in such contexts.

In addition to providing direct health care services, psychologists can play an increasingly significant role in educating other health professionals. Behavioral science training for physicians and nurses is grossly deficient, consisting in most cases of a thin stew of Kraepelinian psychopathology flavored with indigestible lumps of trivialized psychosexual theory. Many medical students have heard the story of Monica (Engle, Reisman, & Segal, 1956), who spent most of her second year of life hospitalized with a condition that required her to be fed through a tube opening directly into her stomach, enabling the physician to use her situation to explore the factors leading to the production of hydrochloric acid in her stomach. One of the astonishing findings was that the amount of acid produced by the injection of histamine—presumably a fairly direct precursor of gastric acid production—was dramatically different as a function of which nurse gave the injection. How many medical students have the benefit of so convincing a demonstration of the importance of nonrational and unconscious elements in motivation or of an analysis of the factors leading to compliance?

An improvement in the behavioral science teaching of health professionals will require the psychologist to familiarize himself with illness and health cares and to develop empirically based theories dealing with the issues of concern to doctors, nurses, and patients. This will mean the involvement of the psychologist in the delivery of health-related services but, one hopes, without obscuring his or her primary function: the production of empirically based theories of behavior and personhood, including those relevant to health and illness.

5. Implications for Training

The views outlined above have implications for the training of psychologists in the health care field. The first is that their training must cultivate the roots of psychology, must include knowledge of the contemporary scientific core of psychology, and—equally important—must provide a knowledge of the history of the important ideas in psychology.

A second implication is that research training must continue to be crucial. Psychologists can play a unique role in developing empirically based theories relevant to health and illness and in elaborating new techniques and applications based on those theories. Kübler-Ross's (1969) views about the steps of dying are a very weak theory. They are unoriginal, having been earlier applied to the adjustment to traumatic blindness by Cholden (1958) and others, and are largely descriptive rather than explanatory. However, the impact of these views in modifying the treatment of dying patients, including the development of the hospice as an institution, are evidence of the power of theory to modify practice. Her ideas had consequences.

A third training implication is that, because health care psychologists must be practitioners if their ideas are to be relevant, internship training will continue to be vital. For these psychologists, internship training will have some special functions: demystifying the health delivery system and illness, forging interprofessional links and inducing familiarity with the phenomenology of other health practitioners, and encouraging a special sense of respect for the rights of people who are frightened, in pain, and therefore vulnerable and easily exploited. Finally, the internship should provide an opportunity for the psychologist to explore the activity of psychotherapy, not because psychotherapy is the treatment of choice for physical ills but because the psychologist has the responsibility for knowing about people, what motivates them, and how they think as well as the subtleties of transference and countertransference. No laboratory can duplicate the opportunities provided by careful, sensitive, and empathic exploration of another person's world to obtain such knowledge.

6. References

Barbour, J., Zeltzer, L., Kalmowitz, J., Kniker, W., Rao, K., Littlefield, L., & Fisher, J. Self-hypnosis as an adjunctive treatment in adolescent asthmatics. *Clinical Research*, 1979, *27*(5), 82. (Abstract)

Beecher, H. K. Pain in men wounded in battle. *Annals of Surgery*, 1946, *123*, 96–105.

Birk, L. (Ed.). *Biofeedback: Behavioral medicine*. New York: Grune & Stratton, 1973.

Burstein, A. G. Socialized psychotherapy. *Psychotherapy, Theory Research, and Practice*, 1979, *16*, 428–431.

Burstein, A. G., Barnes, R. H., & Quesada, G. M. Training clinical psychologists in medical settings. *Professional Psychology*, 1976, *7*, 396–402.

Carlson, R. J. *The end of medicine*. New York: Wiley, 1975.

Cholden, L. S. *A psychiatrist works with blindness*. New York: American Foundation for the Blind, 1958.

Dubin, L. L., & Shapiro, S. S. Use of hypnosis to facilitate dental extraction and hemostasis in a classic hemophiliac with a high antibody titer to factor VIII. *American Journal of Clinical Hypnosis*, 1974, *17*, 79–83.

Engel, G. L., Reichsman, F., & Segal, H. A study of an infant with a gastric fistula. *Psychosomatic Medicine*, 1956, *6*, 374–398.

Erikson, E. H. *Childhood and society*. New York: Norton, 1963.

Fisher, G. R. *The hospital that ate Chicago*. New York: Saunders, 1980.

Fordyce, W. An operant conditioning method for managing chronic pain. *Postgraduate Medicine*, 1973, *53*, 123–128.

Illich, I. *Medical nemesis*. New York: Pantheon, 1976.

Kübler-Ross, E. *On death and dying*. New York: Macmillan, 1969.

Levine, P., & Zeltzer, L. K. *Management of pain for hemophiliacs*. New York: National Hemophilic Foundation, 1980.

Lynch, J. J. *The broken heart*. New York: Basic Books, 1977.

Masters, H., & Johnson, E. *Human sexual inadequacy*. Boston: Little, Brown, 1970.

McClure, W. T. The medicine delivery system under national health insurance: Four models. *Journal of Health, Politics, & Law*, 1976, *6*, 22–68.

Merskey, H. Psychological aspects of pain relief. In M. Swerdlow (Ed.), *Relief of intractable pain*. New York: Exerpta Medica, 1974.

National Register of Health Service Providers in Psychology. Washington, D.C.: Council for the National Register of Health Service Providers in Psychology, 1980.

Rahe, R. H., O'Neil, T., Hagan, A., & Rausam, A. J. Brief group therapy following myocardial infarction. *International Journal of Psychiatry in Medicine*, 1975, *6*, 349–358.

Vellay, P. *Childbirth without pain*. New York: Dutton, 1960.

Pediatric Psychology
Health Care Psychology for Children

MICHAEL C. ROBERTS, JAMES E. MADDUX,
SANDY K. WURTELE, AND LOGAN WRIGHT

1. Introduction

1.1. Rationale of Pediatric Psychology

Pediatric psychology combines aspects of several disciplines in the delivery of health care to children and their families. This field came into existence primarily to fill an observed need: pediatric physicians are confronted with a large number of problems that require a comprehensive medical–psychological treatment approach. For example, in a study of pediatric practices, only 12% of all patients presented problems that were considered purely physical; 36% had problems that were considered to be psychological; and the remaining 52% had problems that were both physical and psychological in nature (Duff, Rowe, & Anderson, 1973). As a result of such demands in their actual practice, pediatricians are becoming cognizant of the emotional and psychological aspects of the problems they are called on to treat. Concomitantly, psychologists are discovering the varied types of psychopathology related to organic illnesses as well as the utility of behavioral interventions for some medical disorders.

Comprehensive health care in pediatrics is returning to the notion of responding to the "whole patient" instead of focusing on the separate physical components. Thus, services in children's health care settings now include psy-

MICHAEL C. ROBERTS and SANDY K. WURTELE • Department of Psychology, University of Alabama, University, Alabama 35486. JAMES E. MADDUX • Department of Psychology, Texas Tech University, Lubbock, Texas 79409. LOGAN WRIGHT • Institute of Health Psychology for Children, Oklahoma City, Oklahoma 73019.

chological, social, and educational professions in addition to the usual medical specialties. As evidenced by this volume, medical and psychological professionals are asserting that mental and physical health cannot be achieved independently. The treatment of individuals is best approached from medical *and* behavioral perspectives. Although there has been an increasing interest in health care psychology for patients of all ages, the liaison of psychology with pediatrics typically has been longer and stronger than with other medical specialties (Schneider, 1978; Wright, 1979a,b).

The specialty of health care clinical psychology for children, or pediatric psychology, developed as practitioners found they could not meet the challenge of critical problems in childhood from within the frameworks of traditional pediatrics or traditional child psychology. As noted by the Duff *et al.* (1973) study and others, the types of problems presenting in pediatric practices involve a significant number of psychological, developmental, behavioral, educational, and child-management issues. According to one study, 37% of all "well-child" visits to pediatrician involved support and counseling around issues of child rearing and behavioral management (McClelland, Staples, Weisberg, & Berger, 1973). An additional 19% of parents' questions to pediatricians concerned academic performance. Thus, over half the questions asked of pediatricians during routine office visits are concerned with nonmedical matters. Unfortunately, the practicing pediatrician usually has had inadequate training to manage these types of problems competently, he or she may have little personal proclivity to treat them, and he or she needs more time to focus on medical problems (Roberts & Wright, 1982).

Traditional psychological approaches to treating children have also been inadequate. According to the Bureau of Education of the Handicapped, 87% of children considered emotionally disturbed are not receiving treatment (White, Day, Freeman, Hartman, & Messenger, 1973). Furthermore, those children who are seen by mental health professionals have often gone through a shaping process by referral to numerous agencies (Walker, 1979a).

It is with these two phenomena as a background that pediatric psychology developed: pediatricians have the need for psychological services and psychologists have the goal to provide more accessible services. A profitable collaboration has been the result. A new breed of psychologist has emerged; one who specializes in the growth, development, and problems of children; practices in a primary health care setting; and collaborates with pediatricians and medical personnel.

1.2. Characteristics of Pediatric Psychology

As an entity distinct from traditional psychology, pediatric psychology has developed a unique constellation of characteristics. These include (1) a health care setting for clinical practice; (2) a medically based referral mechanism and source of patients; (3) an emphasis in clinical practice involving an appreciation of the developmental process; (4) a model of consultation to physicians and parents and, at times, the provision of direct treatment of child patients; and (5) a practical orientation to treatment techniques that are demonstrably effective, time-efficient, and economical. Because pediatric psychologists practice in a health care rather than a psychiatric setting, they encounter patient problems that vary widely from those encountered by a traditional clinical child psychologist. Although patients with the traditional problems of neuroses, psychoses, and character disorders are encountered in a children's medical setting, other disorders frequently seen in this field are relatively rare in other settings. Pediatric psychological problems that are commonly presented include psychological–behavioral concomitants of physical illness, handicap, or medical procedures (such as sequelae to meningitis, adjustment to diabetes, and presurgical operation anxiety). Additionally, a wide range of presenting problems includes medical–psychological disorders for which effective psychological interventions are available (e.g., psychogenic pain, seizure disorders, encopresis). Table 1 presents a selected list of presenting problems in pediatric psychology settings. A comprehensive examination of the background literature and treatment interventions for 114 entities is made in the *Encyclopedia of Pediatric Psychology* by Wright, Schaefer, and Solomons (1979).

Table 1. A List of Selected Pediatric Psychological Problems

1. Cardiology—Congenital Heart Defects
   A. Parents (infantilizing and other possible psychogenic tendencies)
   B. Cardiac-involved child (emotional and intellectual concomitants of heart disease)
2. Dentistry
   A. Thumbsucking, tongue thrust, swallowing, bruxism
   B. Dental phobia
   C. Malocclusions
   D. Toothbrushing and braces
3. Dermatology
   A. Albinism
   B. Acne vulgaris
   C. Dermatitis, eczema, psoriasis, and hives
   D. Trichotillomania
4. Endocrinology
   A. Precocious puberty
   B. Sexual ambiguity
   C. Failure to thrive or psychosocial dwarfism
   D. Hypothyroidism, cretinism, and other thyroid problems
5. Gastroenterology
   A. Anorexia
   B. Ulcers
   C. Encopresis
   D. Consummatory responses
   E. Pica
   F. Lead poisoning (emotional and intellectual sequelae)
   G. Psychogenic vomiting
   H. Ulcers and gastrointestinal spasms
6. Hematology
   A. Hemophilia
   B. The leukemic child and parents
7. Medical Hospitalization
8. Infectious Diseases
   A. Meningitis
   B. Rocky Mountain Spotted Fever

(continued)

Table 1 (continued)

9. Metabolism
   A. Juvenile diabetes
   B. Pickwickian syndrome
   C. Obesity
10. Neonatology
    A. Abortion
    B. APGAR ratings (developmental correlates)
    C. Early stimulation research
    D. Prematurity and low birth weight
    E. Illegitimacy (behavioral correlates)
    F. Intrauterine environmental influences on subsequent development
    G. Sudden unexplained infant death
11. Neurology
    A. Seizures
    B. Sleep disturbances
    C. Hydrocephalus
    D. Cerebral palsy
    E. Familial dysautonomia
    F. Subdural hematoma and other forms of intracranial pressure
    G. Multiple sclerosis
    H. Spinal cord injuries
12. Orthopedics (Arthritis)
13. Otorhinolaryngology
    A. Cleft palate and lip
    B. Tracheotomy addiction
    C. Elective mutism
    D. Stuttering
14. Psychiatry
    A. Battered child
    B. Programs for aiding parents of chronically ill children
    C. Self-mutilation
    D. Suicide
    E. Psychogenic pain
15. Respiratory Diseases
    A. Asthma
    B. Cystic fibrosis
16. Surgery
    A. Effective pre- and postoperative psychological care
    B. Burns and disfigurement
17. Urology
    A. Enuresis
    B. Kidney transplants

1.3. Overview of Chapter

Our purpose in this chapter is to examine pediatric psychology by attempting a definition of the field, elucidating the reasons for its development, outlining a brief history, describing the content areas, and noting the numerous opportunities for expanding and solidifying it through research. Pediatric psychology may be defined in a number of ways—by the goals of the profession, by its unique characteristics of problems and settings, by the roles and functions fabricated by participant observers who developed the concept, and by the clinical and research activities of the psychologist. We will provide an overview of these various definitions.

2. Definitions and Conceptualizations of Pediatric Psychology

2.1. Underlying Philosophy

The objective of most child professionals is to assist children along their passage into adulthood by facilitating developmental, physical, mental, and social growth. Both the concept and practice of pediatric psychology developed in response to a need for a multidisciplinary effort in the care of children. A fundamental tenet has been that psychological services should be focused where the majority of problems are first presented, that is, in medical settings and not in psychiatric facilities or mental health centers, which are away from the site of initial presentation.

Physicians typically serve as front-line health care professionals. Salk (1969) stated that "the pediatrician sees more human beings than any other professional during the most crucial stages of early development ... he is the first to be brought face to face with more developmental, learning, and emotional problems and has the greatest potential influence on child care practices" (p. 2).

2.2. Definitional Characteristics

In a seminal paper proposing a role model for pediatric psychology, Wright (1967) stated that "a pediatric psychologist is any psychologist who finds himself dealing primarily with children in a medical setting which is nonpsychiatric in nature" (p. 323). Wright also asserted that "the pediatric psychologist is a person who is trained in both child development and in the child clinical area" (p. 323). Later, Salk (1974) defined the pediatric psychologist as a "scientist–clinician who serves as a consultant ... on matters concerning mental health needs as they arise in pediatric practice" (p. 112). In a similar setting-oriented definition, the *Journal of Pediatric Psychology* (1980) has defined its content area as "the interests and concerns of psychologists who work in interdisciplinary settings such as children's hospitals, developmental clinics, and pediatric or medical group practices" (Masthead). Tuma (1975) placed the pediatric psychologist as a subspecialist within clinical child psychology. She stated that a pediatric psychologist is "a clinical child psychologist ... with training and expertise in evaluating and treating a special kind of child population found in the pediatric setting" (p. 12). More recently Walker (1979a), described the area as having less orientation to traditional child psychology, but as "a specialty within medical psychology dealing with children and their behavioral–developmental problems" (p. 227).

These statements contain a number of common characteristics that can be enumerated as definitions of pediatric psychology.

1. Pediatric psychology is closely allied with clinical child psychology. The American Psychological Association recognizes the Society of Pediatric Psychology as affiliated within the specialty Section of Clinical Child Psychology under the larger Division of Clinical Psychology.

2. Pediatric psychology is a field within medical or health care psychology. As such, pediatric psychology is concerned with physical health and illness and the relationship between psychological factors and physical health, illness, and disease. Health is seen as a global concept with less importance placed on physical–mental distinctions (Schofield, 1975).

3. The pediatric psychologist typically works in a medical or a primary health care setting. These locations may include hospitals, clinics, pediatric practices, developmental centers, and health maintenance organizations. This medical setting is basically nonpsychiatric. The implications of this include the following characteristics: (a) the psychologist is at the point of initial patient presentation rather than at the end of a series of referrals; (b) presenting problems are seen in their earlier stages of development, usually before they become moderately or seriously debilitating; (c) problems include a higher proportion of medically related disorders; (d) diagnostic evaluations and therapeutic interventions are primarily psychologically formulated rather than oriented to psychiatric modalities; and (e) the pediatric psychologist sees more patients and spends less contact time with each one.

4. The pediatric psychologist may serve in multiple roles. One may, at different times and often at the same time, function as consultant, diagnostician, therapist, researcher, information resource, and innovator.

2.3. Psychological Aspects

In the health care setting, the major contribution of pediatrics is its concern with the physical well-being or medical maintenance of the child patient. Psychology contributes to the understanding of psychologically related etiology and concomitants of disorders and in behavioral interventions for their remediation. The psychological contribution derives from its basis in empiricism and training of research-oriented behavioral scientists. The scientist–practitioner model of clinical psychology adds both unique content and approach to children's problems. Any practical intervention should be empirically grounded, ideally in a well-controlled investigation or at least through careful observation of clinical procedures. To meet this need, the pediatric psychologist is trained in psychological research as well as clinical procedures.

The pediatric psychologist considers psychological problems within the context of the developmental process. Thus, a knowledge of child development as well as life-span change is fundamental. Since working with children necessitates working with parents, the psychologist also needs the ability to understand and work with adults. Although the psychologist need not possess a medical degree or have extensive medical training, he or she does need an understanding of children's medical problems and their behavioral–psychological concomitants. To this end, Schofield (1969) urged that the medical psychologist should have "a particular sophistication in physical illness [and be] equipped to research and consult with regard to the psychological concomitants of physical disease" (p. 574). Additionally, since the psychology practice takes place in another discipline's setting, the pediatric psychologist needs to be able to work effectively with pediatricians and allied staff. Diplomacy, communication, and social skills are often needed in order to implement psychological projects.

2.4. Conceptualizations of Roles and Functions

Authorities in the area have offered varying definitions of the roles and functions of a pediatric psychologist. Wright (1967) proposed a model including roles of a consultant to physicians and parents and as a scientist–practitioner. Smith, Rome, and Friedheim (1967) saw the pediatric psychologist primarily as a specialist–consultant. Salk (1974) differentiated the function of a pediatric psychologist as a consultant from that of being a technician. The latter role involves the extensive use of time-consuming psychological testing. The consultative role involves discussion between psychologist and pediatrician in regards to case management. Nixon (1975) provides a systems approach to pediatric consultation. In his outline of a graduate training program in pediatric psychology, Routh (1969) gave more emphasis to diagnostic testing than to a therapeutic role. Finally, Stabler and Murray (1974) have noted that there is a lack of consensus as to what roles and functions a pediatric psychologist should pursue. In the final analysis, a composite model of child diagnostician, parent counselor, resource person and consultant is most likely to emerge. The differences in these various models appear to lie in the degree of emphasis on the various roles—some including more involvement in traditional psychological services and others requiring innovative and unique activity.

The legitimate functions of the pediatric psychologist are determined both by the proclivity of the individual psychologist and the service demands of a particular institution. Most psychologists in a pediatric setting are broadly prepared and flexible enough to function in a multitude of ways. This ability likely results from the training and experiences common to most pediatric psychologists. Although few graduate programs offer training specifically in pediatric psychology, most professionals acquire knowledge of and facility in basic psychological principles through traditional doctoral programs in clinical psychology. This background prepares the psychologist to adapt old methods to new situations and to apply research skills in order to establish a basis for practice.

In summary, pediatric psychologists function within a pediatric setting, provide consultative service to pediatricians, deal with problems early in their development because of early screening by medical personnel, emphasize psychological concomitants to physical problems more than traditional psychiatric problems, and work with parents and children in brief therapeutic interventions.

3.1. Historical Milestones

Pediatric psychology as it is practiced today represents the confluence of several interrelated developments: clinical psychology in general and clinical child psychology in particular; pediatric medicine; and, more recently, health care psychology. Despite an early start, pediatrician–psychologist liaisons did not develop rapidly (Routh, 1975). Through the years, numerous calls have been made for the greater involvement of psychologists in the medical treatment of children. Anderson (1930), in an address to the 81st Annual Meeting of the American Medical Association, suggested a collaboration between pediatrics and child psychology. He suggested that two areas in which child psychologists were well equipped to make special contributions to pediatrics included intelligence testing and consultation to parents regarding child-rearing practices.

The impetus for collaborative efforts occurred later, when Kagan (1965), a psychologist, announced a "new marriage" between psychology and pediatrics. Kagan envisioned that this collaboration would give pediatricians the opportunity to gain sophistication in the theory of personality dynamics and in research inquiry. He suggested numerous problems of childhood that could benefit from this collaboration and emphasized prevention, early detection, and treatment. Two years later, Wright (1967) coined the term *pediatric psychology* and offered a role model for the functions of a psychologist in a pediatric setting. Wright called for (1) the delineation of a group identity for pediatric psychologists through a formal organization (within the American Psychological Association) and the distribution of a newsletter, (2) more specific training of future practitioners, and (3) the construction of a new body of knowledge through applied research. Each of these requirements for the development of the profession can be examined for progress.

3.2. Society of Pediatric Psychology

In the first area, that of the emerging identity of pediatric psychology, the development has been dramatic. In 1967, a Committee on Pediatric Psychology was appointed by the American Psychological Association. The Society of Pediatric Psychology was founded in 1968, with the publication of the *Pediatric Psychology* newsletter following in 1969 (Wright, 1969). In 1976, this newsletter became the *Journal of Pediatric Psychology* (see Routh, 1975, for more details), an event that clearly established the field as a truly scientific and professional enterprise. Business meetings and symposia are now annually sponsored by the Society at the American Psychological Association conventions. Regional psychological conventions often list topical programs in pediatric psychology (e.g., the Southeastern Psychological Association). The Society's membership roll now lists over five hundred psychologists as well as nonpsychologist members (e.g., social workers, physicians, and nurses) in a variety of countries. Additionally, pediatric psychology interest groups are being formed within the more recently organized Society of Behavioral Medicine and the Division of Health Psychology (division 38 of the American Psychological Association).

199

PEDIATRIC
PSYCHOLOGY

3.3. Training

Training in pediatric psychology has also undergone a substantial expansion. Specialized training in this area was nonexistent until recently. Before, the skills and procedures needed by pediatric psychologists were often acquired through experience in the settings in which the psychologists found themselves. Although there are identified training programs in clinical child psychology (Roberts, 1982), pediatric psychology training has not been as formal. Increasingly, however, university graduate departments are adding specialized practicums in pediatric psychology. Ottinger and Roberts (1980) have described such a practicum at Purdue University, and Drotar (1978) has provided a description of a similar program affiliated with Case Western Reserve University.

The largest component of pediatric psychology training is represented by internship programs in medical settings. In 1977, 63 of 153 facilities surveyed offered some training in pediatric psychology (Tuma, 1977). Programs are offered for predoctoral and postdoctoral students desiring didactic and practical experience in pediatric psychology for one or two years (e.g., University of Oklahoma Health Sciences Center, University of North Carolina Medical Center, University of Maryland Medical Center, Duke University Medical Center). Examples of such training are outlined by Kenny and Bauer (1975) and Drotar (1975a).

3.4. Accumulation of Knowledge through Research

Regarding the third point from Wright's (1967) paper—the accumulation of a body of knowledge—substantial progress has also been made. The rapid accumulation of information has resulted in several volumes summarizing research and clinical practice, for example, the *Encyclopedia of Pediatric Psychology* (Wright *et al.*, 1979), the two-volume *Psychological Management of Pediatric Problems* (Magrab, 1978), and *The Practice of Pediatric Psychology* (Tuma, 1982). Additionally, individual chapters note progress in this area (e.g., Christophersen & Rapoff, 1980; Walker, 1979a). The *Journal of Pediatric Psychology* and the *Journal of Clinical Child Psychology* also track the research in pediatric psychology. Other psychological and medical journals are publishing articles related to the field (most notably, *Journal of Consulting and Clinical Psychology*, and *Pediatrics*).

4.1. Types of Interventions

We have identified seven general types of interventions undertaken by the pediatric psychologist. In this section, we will examine each in turn before illustrating the actual functioning of the practicing psychologist. Finally, we will present several models of consultation that serve as guidelines for determining the daily activities of psychologists in health care settings.

4.1.1. Quasi-Medical Intervention

Health care psychologists become involved in more organic or quasi-medical forms of intervention and are likely to employ techniques that require the "laying on of hands" and/or medication that chemically alters the organism's functioning. Nonprescription treatments in which psychologists can become involved with include muscle–practice regimens and dietary and/or exercise prescriptions. Some techniques that entail the "laying on of hands" include filing the fingernails to treat onychophagia, or morbid nail biting, or temporarily closing off the tracheotomy tubes of patients with tracheotomy addiction. Other methods of intervention directly affecting the body include aversive conditioning and biofeedback methods. Finally, there are the chemical "prescriptions" (which, of course, do not require a prescription), such as the use of suppositories and enemas in the treatment of encopresis (Wright, 1975).

4.1.2. Behavioral Intervention

With medical–psychological problems, a particular symptom may be threatening either to the development of the child or to life itself and thus must be brought under control as rapidly and efficiently as possible. For this, behavior therapies are generally superior to their alternatives. Behavior therapy techniques have emerged as the treatment of choice for a variety of disorders, including enuresis, obesity, anorexia nervosa, refusal of oral medication, psychogenic vomiting, and many other problems. These types of interventions will be elaborated in later sections of this chapter.

4.1.3. Self-Help Organizations

A number of self-help organizations or peer-support techniques have also proved worthwhile with many medical–psychological disorders. These include Parents Anonymous activities and nurturant mothering for battering parents, the use of parents of previous victims of sudden infant death syndrome as counselors to parents of new victims, and the activities of local chapter members from the Foundation to Combat Huntington's Disease to teach when, where, and how to inform children and potential spouses about the degree of risk associated with Huntington's chorea.

Another phenomenon that characterizes the treatment process in the area of health care psychology for children has been a greater reliance on rearranging the patient's environment. For instance, some children with chronic diseases exhibit delays in personality and emotional development as well as cognitive and intellectual development. These delays seem related to a tendency on the part of parents to infantilize such children and make them "vulnerable children." The treatment of choice is manipulation of the environment through the psychologist's contact with the parents, so that the home or hospital becomes more stimulating and accelerating for psychological growth.

4.1.5. Mass Media Methods

Use of the mass media is another unique feature of primary mental health care. This has been accomplished through television programs, regular monthly magazine columns, and even the use of cassette tapes. Topics presented through mass media may include general child management information, aspects of normal child development, or specific problems of concern. This method has also been successfully employed in behavioral medicine (e.g., with pica and lead poisoning, de la Burde & Reames, 1973). Mass media campaigns centering on a specific problem may involve posters, newspapers, television, and radio to inform parents and children about the particular problem and what can be done.

4.1.6. Developmental Intervention

Child psychology has typically been concerned with personality and emotional development, and intervention has correspondingly been aimed at affect, personality traits, or behavioral symptoms. Health care psychology, however, has added the area of early stimulation or developmental intervention. For example, manuals for directing parents in developmental acceleration and stimulation have been prepared. Pediatric psychologists become involved in the evaluation stage when a child has been identified as being "at risk." Psychological interventions can take several forms depending on the problems, which include: (1) prenatal problems, (2) low birth weight or shortened gestation, (3) birth defects, (4) illness during infancy, (5) rearing in a deprived environment, (6) institutionalized living, and (7) sensory-motor impairment (Wright *et al.*, 1979).

4.1.7. Compliance Techniques

With certain problems, compulsive adherence to the medical treatment regimens accounts for the largest percentage of variance in therapeutic gain. But with many treatments involving medication, diet, and so forth, compliance is a rare exception rather than the rule. Behavioral practitioners have thus developed compliance or adherence regimens that are superimposed on treatment regimens. The variety of compliance methods is increasing and now includes (1) educating the patient or parent regarding the rationale for the treatment regimen, (2) altering the regimen to fit the patient's daily routine, and (3) using shaping techniques to approximate adherence. We will discuss this problem and the psychological techniques for dealing with it in more detail in sections 5.2.3. and 6.1.

4.2. Examples of Pediatric Psychological Functioning

Walker (1979a) has detailed the procedures used in day-to-day functioning of the pediatric psychology service at Oklahoma Children's Memorial Hospital. Additional descriptions of procedures used in other institutions may be found in Rie (1969), Salk (1970), Fischer and Engeln (1972), and Drotar (1976). Two general characteristics of such practice will become evident. First, the pediatric psychologist functions in a multidisciplinary setting and serves as a member of a team to treat the child as a whole—*not* fragmented into separate considerations of physical, familial, emotional, or mental components. Second, the psychologists function within a hospital or clinic setting that provides primary health care, usually in the department of pediatrics, rather than physically and often conceptually in the department of psychiatry. In order to illustrate the various combinations of approaches taken by the pediatric psychologist, a description of problems encountered and procedures employed in a pediatric setting will be provided in the following sections.

4.2.1. Tracheotomy Addiction

The treatment of tracheotomy addiction exemplifies pediatric psychological procedures. This disorder occurs when a young patient with a tracheotomy develops a dependency on a tube for breathing such that when normal air passageways are again opened, he or she still cannot breath. If the cannula (tube) is removed or occluded, the child will manifest progressively more labored breathing, become cyanotic, and eventually lose consciousness and die. Several referrals to psychologists from otorhinolaryngology services have been made for this problem over the years, as the attending physicians have become frustrated in their own unsuccessful attempts to decannulate and as word of successful psychological remediation has spread. In one hospital setting, a behavior modification program was devised to shape tracheotomy-addicted children toward normal breathing by offering social reinforcement when breathing occurred through the mouth or nose and not offering reinforcement when breathing occurred through the cannula. This program has been shown to overcome the addiction problem in about three weeks as a rule (Wright, Nunnery, Eichel, & Scott, 1968). The treatment of choice prior to this procedure was "time"; that is, just letting the child grow and develop and seeing whether the cannula could be given up.

This type of case exemplifies a basic treatment approach of pediatric psychology. The referral for consultation comes from attending physicians in a pediatric hospital for a medical problem requiring a psychological treatment. The intervention does not involve lengthy therapy and can be carried out under the psychologist's direction of medical and nursing personnel. Furthermore, these kinds of cases do not present themselves to a psychiatric agency but are unique to medical settings. This situation exemplifies a major reason why pediatric psychology has developed so rapidly. A physician has patients with problems but does not have the psychological expertise to make an application. Many problems can be handled by getting medicine and psychology together.

4.2.2. Encopresis

A more common problem encountered by a pediatric psychologist is encopresis, or fecal soiling. Thousands of children exhibit this difficulty; estimates are that between 80% and 99% of the cases have a psychogenic basis. Multiple etiologies have been identified and interpretations have been made from behavioral as well as psychoanalytic frameworks. Whatever the etiology, however, a behavioral treatment has been found most effective. A cost-efficient and experimentally validated treatment program was developed by the pediatric psychologist who was called on to treat large numbers of these patients (Wright, 1973a, 1975; Wright & Walker, 1976, 1977). Here again, the initial medical diagnosis and referral are made by the pediatrician. The pediatric psychologist then typically meets once with the affected child and the parents to outline recommended procedures on an outpatient basis. Weekly telephone contact is then maintained to monitor compliance and suggest changes as needed. The procedure itself is relatively simple. It involves the primary use of rewards and the selective use of punishment and cathartics for defecation. This program has been found effective in almost 100% of cases, with only about 2 hours of therapist–patient contact time. Additional successful treatment procedures for encopresis also involve primarily behavioral techniques (e.g., Christophersen & Rainey, 1976; Doleys, McWhorter, Williams, & Gentry, 1977).

4.2.3. Failure to Thrive

Another clinical example illustrates how the pediatric psychologist works with other professionals as a treatment team member to make effective interventions. Roberts and Horner (1979) demonstrated the collaboration of psychologists, pediatric nurse practitioners, physicians, social workers, and occupational therapists in the treatment of failure to thrive (see also Drotar, 1975b). A 9-month-old infant was diagnosed as being below the third percentile in weight and height, with no underlying physical causes producing the lack of growth. The pediatric psychologist assessed the developmental status of the child and made input to the treatment team regarding interventions for stimulating psychological growth and enhancing food intake. Other interventions included home evaluation and improvement by social workers, physical exercises by an occupational therapist, maternal instruction by a pediatric nurse practitioner, and continued medical monitoring by the physician. The mother of the infant was treated with cognitive–behavioral techniques for her depression. Significant therapeutic changes in the child were documented by charting of physical growth and the Bayley Scales of Infant Development.

4.2.4. Examples of Outpatient Intervention

Other examples of intervention have been described in *outpatient* settings as well. LaGreca and Ottinger (1979) reported a case of a child with cerebral palsy for whom psychological intervention was made to increase participation in muscle-stretching exercises, while the medical aspects were checked by the conferring pediatrician. Roberts and Ottinger (1979) described outpatient therapy for an adolescent with encopresis and numerous other problems. Interventions were made through social, assertion, and academic study skills training as well as medically for the encopresis. On referral from a dermatologist, Litt (1980) treated as an outpatient a 5-year-old mentally retarded boy for trichotillomania. The boy's hair-pulling was precipitated by anxiety resulting from misinterpretations of traumatic events and family disruption. Therapy consisted of maternal counseling and clarification for the child. Varni (1980) presented a behavioral management program for a 4½-year-old hemophiliac child who exhibited inappropriate behavior at home and school. These case examples typify the basic approach employed by a pediatric psychologist.

4.3. Models of Consultation

In addition to providing direct service to patients, the pediatric psychologist also contributes to their welfare through consultative services. The psychologist consults not only to parents, pediatricians, and medical staff but also to school systems for learning problems and behavior management; to state and county social welfare departments regarding optimal placement and child-abuse investigations; to the juvenile court system for child-custody questions, rehabilitation efforts, and others. Thus, the pediatric psychologist must be comprehensive and flexible with regard to other areas of child care. A number of conceptual models of pediatric consultation have been advanced (Burns & Cromer, 1978; Drotar, 1978; Stabler, 1979). Roberts and Wright (1982) present three adaptive models describing liaison relationships with pediatricians to provide pediatric psychological services. The three basic models are: (1) the independent functions model, (2) the indirect psychological consultation model, and (3) the collaborative team model.

4.3.1. Independent Functions Model

Following this pattern, the psychologist acts as a specialist who independently undertakes diagnoses and/or treatment of a patient referred by the pediatrician. Except for exchanges of information before and after the referral of a patient, the pediatrician and psychologist work noncollaboratively. This consultation model is likely the most prevalent type of relationship between the two professions because it follows a traditional pattern of independent practice with referrals to each other. In this model, the pediatrician makes a referral and continues to see a patient for medical treatment. The psychologist concurrently sees the patient or family and does what is needed in the psychological realm. This model may be applied, for example, to the medical and behavioral management of juvenile diabetes (Lowe & Lutzker, 1979).

Under this model, the pediatrician retains major responsibility for the care and management of the patient while the psychologist provides indirect services through the physician. The psychologist usually has little or no contact with the patient but obtains information from the pediatrician. This model involves greater collaboration than the first and is more common in the medical center than in private practice. The psychologist's services can be made either through on-the-spot consultation, telephone contact, or didactic presentation of information in seminars, conferences, and continuing education programs. This consultation model is exemplified by the types of indirect psychological interventions recommended by Christophersen and Rapoff (1980), wherein the pediatrician and clinical staff can institute standardized procedures for treating encopresis and enuresis under the supervision of the pediatric psychologist.

4.3.3. Collaborative Team Model

The third major model is one of true collaboration as the pediatrician and psychologist jointly manage patient care and share responsibility for treatment decisions. The team approach of collaboration epitomizes the interdisciplinary ideal and joint decision making. Treatment teams may include social workers, medical doctors, psychologists, clergy, audiologists and speech pathologists, educational experts, and others. This conjoint approach allows for the unique contributions of various disciplines. Team collaborations have been described, for example, for hospital departments, including oncology–hematology (Koocher, Sourkes, & Keane, 1979; Lewis, 1978), renal dialysis (Berger, 1978; Brewer, 1978; Magrab, 1975), surgery (Geist, 1977), and neonatal intensive care (Magrab & Davitt, 1975).

4.4. Characteristics of Practice Procedures

These descriptions of clinical practice demonstrate the applications of the various roles and functions of a pediatric psychologist. Several other considerations are important for understanding the various procedures and quasi-theoretical approaches utilized by practitioners in this area.

4.4.1. Pragmatism

One major characteristic that has permeated the field's development has been an emphasis on pragmatism and empiricism (Rie, 1969; Walker, 1979a). To this end, pediatric psychology includes activities in both the areas of clinical work and research. Additionally, this pragmatic philosophy holds that if a procedure works, the pediatric psychologist will probably use it. Intellectual and developmental evaluations performed by pediatric psychologists tend to be less speculative regarding intrapsychic dynamics or personality characteristics; they, along with the recommendations, are more likely to be pragmatic and to the point. As a result, intervention strategies are more likely to be implemented by the physicians and parents and are, therefore, more likely to be successful (cf. Rie, 1969).

4.4.2. Time-Limited Psychotherapy

In terms of therapy contacts, psychiatrists and some clinical psychologists have been able to gear their activities to lengthy and repeated visits with patients. Pediatric medical practice, however, typically involves fewer and briefer contacts. For example, pediatric office visits average 13 minutes (Bergman, Dassel, & Wedgwood, 1966; DeLozier & Gagnon, 1975) and the pediatrician may see twenty, thirty, or even fifty patients a day (Wright, 1979a,b). For these reasons, pediatric psychologists have sought to make use of techniques that are more economical and more effective, particularly with the amount of professional time invested. Some of these techniques are indirect forms of treatment that involve assisting parents who, in turn, assist their children. This type of indirect intervention may include a limited number of individual sessions with parents, during which principles of behavior management that they can employ in dealing with their own children are outlined. One particularly efficacious technique has been bibliotherapy. Parents are given reading materials on child behavioral management (e.g., Wright, 1978b) and told to return for further consultation if they need additional assistance. This type of service provision has been found effective in combination with parenting skills training groups (Wright, 1976). Telephone contacts with parents sometimes also prove sufficient (Mesibov, Schroeder, & Wesson, 1977; Schroeder, 1979; Schroeder, Goolsby, & Stangler, 1975).

4.4.3. Traditional Psychotherapy

For those cases in which extended individual psychotherapy appears to be needed, most are referred to more traditional clinical child psychologists outside the pediatric psychology service. However, pediatric psychologists do engage in a limited amount of psychotherapy in a traditional framework. A number of disorders have proved to be most amenable to supportive-relationship psychotherapy. These include the problems of (1) death and dying, (2) abortion, (3) suicide, (4) precocious and delayed puberty, and (5) gynecomastia.

4.4.4. Use of Behavioral Techniques

Because the pediatric setting demands pragmatic treatment procedures (Harper, 1975; Walker, 1979b), behavior modification has proven particularly effective. This type of technique has been successfully applied to such pediatric problems as enuresis and encopresis (Doleys, 1980a,b; Walker, 1978); seizures (Wright, 1973b); habitual vomiting (Wright & Thalassinos, 1973); consumption responses involving the refusal of medicine, fluids, or solid food (Wright, 1971; Wright, Woodcock, & Scott, 1969); renal dialysis compliance (Magrab & Papadopoulou, 1977); tongue thrusting in spastic cerebral palsy (Thompson, Iwata, & Poynter, 1979); and many other problems.

The types of procedures and problems previously noted do not exhaust those to be found in the universe of pediatric psychology. Although standardized procedures can often be repeatedly applied (e.g., in the treatment of childhood encopresis using the Wright method), many cases have never before been treated successfully and therefore usually require a unique intervention or combination of interventions (e.g., in the treatment of adolescent encopresis as reported by Roberts & Ottinger, 1979). Indeed, the pediatric psychologist continually faces new situations requiring innovation or the modification of standardized techniques. The psychologist must often extend the application of scientific technology and knowledge to new problems (e.g., in the application of the "Premack principle" or the use of behavior analysis). Serendipity, careful observation, and reasoning also play major roles in this endeavor.

5. A Survey of Research: Selected Topics

5.1. Range of Research Activity

Despite its youth, pediatric psychology has generated considerable literature. The field has moved from reports of interventions that have been based mainly on intuition to more research projects employing scientific rigor. Because unique problems are continually encountered and novel treatment procedures developed, case study reports remain an important part of the literature. Publications cover the commonplace (at least for those settings) as well as cases of unique pathology. The former are represented by studies on the prevalence and treatment of hyperactivity (Routh, 1978) and adjustment to cystic fibrosis or asthma (Bronheim, 1978); whereas the unique is evidenced in such problems as fear of hand shrinking (Waye, 1979) and foot fetishism (Shaw & Walker, 1979).

The medical setting generates a high frequency of referrals for psychological concomitants of disease. A major concern is often the child's adjustment to disease or physical injury and/or the treatment procedures (see Magrab & Calcagno, 1978). A related issue is acceptance of and adjustment to the child's condition by the family. Both acute and chronic medical conditions impose stress on children and families, and this may result in adverse personality and behavioral changes. The child's adjustment to a disease will affect how he or she accepts treatment, adheres to medical regimens, and develops in a psychologically healthy manner.

5.2. Chronic Conditions

Chronic disease conditions often involve repeated medical interventions and may require changes in life-styles. A considerable amount of psychological research on chronic conditions has focused on the emotional and cognitive functioning of the patient, the reactions of individual family members, and styles of family interaction (Friedrich, 1977; Lavigne & Ryan, 1979; Travis, 1976). Recent investigations involving patients with cystic fibrosis and diabetes exemplify research into the psychological and behavioral effects of chronic disease.

5.2.1. Cystic Fibrosis

Cystic fibrosis is a genetically determined disease characterized by the formation of fibrous tissue within a vital organ (typically the lungs, kidneys, or intestine). The disease usually manifests itself in infancy and causes death in early childhood or adolescence (Bronheim, 1978; Wright *et al.*, 1979). The chronicity of the condition results in repeated hospitalizations for the patient, tremendous financial burdens for the family, and stressful relationships among family members. Research regarding psychological damage to the patient and family has been equivocal. Although earlier studies revealed evidence of psychological distress (Lawler, Nakielny, & Wright, 1966; Tropauer, Franz, & Dilgard, 1970), recent research has found generally little evidence for serious negative psychological and emotional effects on the patient (Gayton & Friedman, 1973; Gayton, Friedman, Tavormina, & Tucker, 1977; Tavormina, Kastner, Slater, & Watt, 1976). Research with the families of these patients has found that the parents may defend against unpleasant emotional reactions by filling their lives with activity (Leiken & Hassakis, 1973). Additional personality assessment research has indicated that 32% of fathers and 22% of mothers obtained scores suggestive of emotional disturbance (Gayton *et al.*, 1977). The authors of this study suggested that "the effect of cystic fibrosis on family interaction occurs primarily in forms of decreased family satisfaction and family adjustment" (Gayton *et al.*, 1977, p. 892). Other research has found the families of well-adjusted patients to be more creative problem solvers and more flexible in their problem-solving approaches than were families of maladjusted children (Kucia, Drotar, Doershuk, Stern, Boat, & Matthews, 1979; Odom, Seeman, & Newbrough, 1971).

Psychological research on cystic fibrosis has been more concerned with description than treatment. In addition, the focus has been largely on negative psychological concomitants. To expand our knowledge of this chronic disorder, several authors (Gayton *et al.*, 1977; Kucia *et al.*, 1979; Pless & Pinkerton, 1975) have advocated a broader research focus that examines: (1) possible positive personality growth resulting from a chronic and handicapping illness, (2) the strength and resilience of the children and their families, (3) family-oriented interventions based on studies of interaction patterns, and (4) the cause–effect relationship between the patient's adjustment and family interaction. Although descriptive studies are a necessary first step, increasing emphasis needs to be placed on using this knowledge in designing effective interventions (e.g., Drotar, 1978). This conclusion applies not only to cystic fibrosis but also to a wide range of childhood medical problems.

5.2.2. Juvenile Diabetes

Another chronic condition that has been the subject of descriptive research is juvenile diabetes. Diabetes is a genetically determined condition that is characterized by excess blood glucose (hyperglycemia) and sugar in the urine (glycosuria). Management of the disease usually requires attention to diet, exercise, self-administration of insulin, and self-obtained urinalysis. Psychological adjustment to the chronic state is important for the management of the disease (Garner & Thompson, 1978; Wright *et al.*, 1979). Research has found that no characteristic personality profile holds for *all* diabetics (Koch & Molnar, 1974). Most diabetic children do not perceive themselves as different from other children (Partridge, Garner, Thompson, & Cherry, 1972). Contrary to stereotype, severe psychopathology is not more prevalent in diabetics, although they are somewhat more alienated and rebellious than normal children (Sayed & Leaverton, 1974; Tavormina *et al.*, 1976) and show slightly more social maladjustment as a group (Delbridge, 1975).

Psychological acceptance of and adjustment to diabetes by the family is related to management of the disease (Grey, Genel, & Tamborlane, 1980). Emotionally maladjusted families tend to manage the child's disease poorly, whereas accepting parents tend to manage well (Delbridge, 1975). Knowledge of the disease and its control has been positively related to careful control by parents and children by some researchers (Delbridge, 1975; Etzwiler & Robb, 1972), although not by others (Garner & Thompson, 1975; Partridge *et al.*, 1972).

5.2.3. Compliance in Chronic Conditions

Nonadherence or noncompliance with medical regimens in the treatment of chronic diseases is a major research consideration. A patient's adherence to medical recommendations is requisite for successful treatment. Obviously, "no treatment can help if it is not applied" (Dunbar & Stunkard, 1977, p. 391). Compliance is a critical issue, particularly for chronic conditions requiring continual intervention. With the diabetic patient, for example, Lowe and Lutzker (1979) reported using a point system to enhance compliance. Other chronic states have also received attention. LaGreca and Ottinger (1979) employed a self-monitoring procedure to increase the muscle-stretching exercises of a child with cerebral palsy. Magrab and Papadopoulou (1977) designed a diet program for children on hemodialysis based on a token system of reinforcement. Similarly, using tokens redeemable for prizes has been successful in training asthmatic children to use their inhalation equipment accurately (Renne & Creer, 1976). Improved adjustment to the disease or handicap also helps to improve the management and the psychological state of the child (Johnson, 1979). For example, therapy groups have been employed with renal dialysis patients (Magrab, 1975), and muscular dystrophy patients (Bayrakal, 1975). Drotar (1975c) used traditional psychotherapy with a maladapted boy following renal transplantation.

Psychological research on chronic diseases has produced descriptive studies of the personalities and behavior of afflicted children and their families; it has also validated treatment interventions used for regimen compliance and in aiding adjustment. Additional studies of both types may be found for such chronic medical problems as hemophilia (Agle, 1975; Salk, Hilgartner, & Granich, 1972; Varni, 1980), leukemia (Fife, 1978; Kalnins, Churchill, & Terry, 1980; Katz, Kellerman, & Siegel, 1980; Koocher & Sallan, 1978; Spinetta, 1977), congenital heart disease (LaGreca, 1980), phenylketonuria (Katz, 1978), and epilepsy or seizure disorders (Livingston, 1977; Willis & Thomas, 1978).

5.3. Acute Conditions

Research efforts have also concentrated on short-term medical conditions. This research explores the effects of the disorder and its medical treatment as well as ways to manage psychological concomitants. Pediatric disorders of immediate medical concern that have been treated effectively physically often have long-lasting psychological effects. Research has investigated the psychological sequelae to several medical entities and ways of alleviating the stress associated with hospitalization and surgery.

5.3.1. Sequelae to Acute Conditions

In a study of sequelae of meningitis, Wright and Jimmerson (1971) found that the primary deficits in patients who had had this illness occurred in the areas of perceptual–motor skills and abstract thinking ability. Other studies have examined sequelae to burns (Wright & Fulwiler, 1974), lead poisoning (Wright & Fulwiler, 1972), encephalitis (Rie, Hilty, & Cranblitt, 1973), and Rocky Mountain spotted fever (Wright, 1972).

5.3.2. Enuresis and Encopresis

Other acute conditions have also received attention in the literature through evaluations of psychological interventions to treat the medical problem. Encopresis, as noted earlier, is one such problem (e.g., Wright & Walker, 1977). Enuresis, a related problem frequently presented to pediatricians, has also been relieved through psychological techniques (Doleys, 1977, 1980b; Walker, 1978). Christophersen and Rapoff (1980) note that the procedures developed by Azrin and Foxx (1974) are the only true empirically validated interventions in pediatric psychology. Other research reports describe the characteristics of children and the various modes of treating enuresis (Butler, 1976; Ciminero & Doleys, 1976; Doleys & Ciminero, 1976; Schaefer, 1979).

5.3.3. Hospitalization

Hospitalization for whatever reason is an event of major psychological importance. Along with the physical disorder itself, this stressful experience often leads to emotional maladjustment (Vernon, Foley, Sipowicz, & Schulman, 1965). Prevention of adverse psychological sequelae has received much attention (Altshuler, 1974; Roberts, 1979; Siegel, 1976). In a survey of pediatric hospitals, Peterson and Ridley-Johnson (1980) found that 70% offer prehospital preparation of various types to parents and patients. Empirical research has demonstrated the effectiveness of anxiety-reducing preparation, including preadmission home visits by a nurse (Ferguson, 1979), puppet play (Cassell & Paul, 1967), information, emotional support, anticipation to develop coping strategies (Visintainer & Wolfer, 1975; Wolfer & Visintainer, 1975, 1979), and filmed modeling (Melamed & Siegel, 1975; Melamed, Meyer, Gee, & Soule, 1976).

Additional research has investigated hospital preparation combining peer modeling and anxiety-coping skills (Peterson, 1978; Peterson, Hartmann, & Gelfand, 1980) and modeling to decrease general fears of medical settings for children who are not facing immediate hospital admission (Roberts, Wurtele, Boone, Ginther, & Elkins, 1981). Psychological principles are also invoked for special medical treatments (e.g., plastic surgery; Gluck, 1977).

This section has briefly examined some of the research on the psychological aspects of acute medical conditions. The area of acute problems has not received the research or clinical attention that the more chronic disorders have, perhaps reflecting the relative importance placed on the latter by medical personnel (Rachman & Phillips, 1980).

5.4. Developmental Disorders

5.4.1. Range of Research

Pediatric psychologists have produced a wealth of information regarding a number of pediatric problems usually categorized as developmental disorders. These disabilities are conditions in which the normal processes of physical, emotional, and intellectual growth are delayed. For example, research has investigated the effects of prematurity (Goldberg, 1974), Down's syndrome (Katz, 1978), autism (Mesibov & Shea, 1980), rumination and feeding problems (Sajwaj, Libet, & Agras, 1974), various handicaps (Perlman & Routh, 1980), and also infants generally described as "at risk" for later problems (Aylward & Kenny, 1979; Field, Dempsey, & Shuman, 1979; Maisto & German, 1979). Sudden infant death has a severe emotional impact on families (Salk, 1971), and psychological processes have been implicated in its cause (Lipsitt, 1979; Lipsitt, Sturner, & Burke, 1979).

5.4.2. Failure to Thrive

The medical–psychological disorder of failure to thrive (FTT) involves the lack of normal physical growth without known physical causes. FTT infants fall at or below the third percentile on growth charts. The condition affects approximately 3% of the general pediatric population and 5% of pediatric hospital admissions (Elmer, Gregg, & Ellison, 1969; Lipsitt, 1979; Rosen, 1977). Though FTT is often diagnosed and treated as a medical/physical disorder, several psychosocial conceptualizations have been proposed. These are often subsumed under the labels of social, environmental, or maternal deprivation (Yarrow, 1961), though the term *maternal deprivation* has been criticized as inadequate (Rutter, 1972a,b). An alternative model (Roberts & Horner, 1979; Roberts & Maddux, 1980) views FTT as the consequence of the interaction of three types of influences: (1) psychological–emotional factors, (2) educational factors, and (3) environmental factors. One advantage to this type of view is that it allows for a diversity of intervention techniques (e.g., Drotar, 1975b; Roberts & Horner, 1979), and discourages reliance on strictly medical treatment. Lipsitt (1979) has suggested a developmental–process approach to understanding FTT (and other disorders of infancy such as sudden infant death syndrome). This approach suggests that FTT may be the result of a learning insufficiency (Ramey, Hieger, & Klisz, 1972), particularly a failure on the part of the infant to produce adaptive reciprocating behaviors under conditions of threat—a response pattern that may be likened to learned helplessness (Lipsitt, 1979).

5.4.3. Hyperactivity

Hyperactivity is a frequently diagnosed childhood behavior disorder (Schnackenberg, 1977) with the prevalence rate in the general population estimated at 5% (Sroufe & Stewart, 1973). Clinical descriptions of hyperactivity include severe overactivity, short attention span, hyperexcitability, marked distractibility to extraneous stimuli, impulsiveness, and inability to delay gratification (Arnold, 1973; Ross & Ross, 1976; Stewart & Olds, 1973). The variety of the symptoms suggests that, rather than a unitary syndrome, hyperactivity is a disorder composed of heterogeneous symptom constellations. Concomitantly, a lack of consensus exists regarding causation (Schierlberl, 1979; Wright et al., 1979). Explanations of hyperactive symptomatology include such physiological parameters as central nervous system damage (Shekim, Dekirmenjian, & Chapel, 1979), the genetic transmission of hyperactivity (Cantwell, 1972; Willerman, 1973), artificial lighting (Hartley, 1974), allergies to food additives and colorings (Feingold, 1975), and chronically low arousal levels (Satterfield & Cantwell, 1974). Ross and Ross (1976) posit other physiological factors that may be related to hyperactivity: lead poisoning, maternal smoking and drinking, and radiation stress. O'Leary and O'Leary (1977) suggest that a child's increased activity level may have been operantly reinforced.

Interventions based on physical models are the most frequent treatments with hyperactive children. The "Feingold diet" (Feingold, 1975) attributes hyperactive behavior to "natural salicylates" found in synthetic flavors and colors. Much debate and some experimentation has followed this theory, with results being found both for and against it (Conners, Goyette, Southwick, Lees, & Andrulonis, 1976; Rose, 1978; Sieben, 1977; Spring & Sandoval, 1976; Weiss, Williams, Margen, Abrams, Caan, Citron, Cox, McKibben, Ogar, & Schultz, 1980).

Pharmacological intervention is a major treatment mode for hyperactivity. While psychostimulants (e.g., dextroamphetamine and methylphenidate) have been shown to be effective in short-term management (Sroufe, 1975), concerns about such side effects as insomnia, loss of appetite, and reduction in the rate of weight gain (Roche, Lipman, Overall, & Hung, 1979; Safer & Allen, 1976), have led to an increased interest in the use of behavior therapy, alone or in conjunction with drug therapy (Gittleman-Klein, Klein, Abikoff, Katz, Gloisten, & Kates, 1976; O'Leary & Pelham, 1978; Pelham, 1976; Pelham, Schnedler, Bologna, & Contreras, 1980; Shafto & Sulzbacher, 1977). Concomitantly, recent research suggests that drug interventions, regardless of their effectiveness in reducing the hyperactive symptomotalogy, are of little importance in helping the hyperactive child in academic, emotional, or societal adjustment (Milich & Loney, 1979; O'Leary, 1980; Rie & Rie, 1977). Such findings suggest that, in combination with physiological parameters, consideration of family and environmental variables may facilitate successful early intervention and treatment of hyperactive children. Related to hyperactivity, the problem of learning disabilities is another area of research into developmental disorders. Researchers have considered such factors as classroom behaviors (Bryan, 1979), diagnosis (Kaslow & Abrams, 1979; Raskin & Bloom, 1979), motor and other skills, attention (Koenigsberg, 1973), and various interventions (Cellucci & Cellucci, 1979; Guerney, 1979; LaGreca & Mesibov, 1979).

5.5. Terminal Illness and Death

The critically ill or dying child requires special services that are typically difficult to provide in most medical settings (Wright *et al.*, 1979). Koocher (1977) has pointed out that the needs of these children and their families cannot be fully anticipated and are often inadequately addressed. He has also stated that the proper and effective source of assistance and support is the pediatric treatment unit, not the outside community. Although a variety of intervention approaches with the critically ill and dying child have been attempted (Drotar, 1977; Gogan, O'Malley, & Foster, 1977; Sourkes, 1977; Spinetta, 1977), much of the literature is descriptive and anecdotal rather than empirically based. A notable exception is the work of Katz, Kellerman, and Siegel (1980) on conditioned anxiety in child cancer patients undergoing medical treatment. For example, it has been found that younger children exhibit greater anxiety than older children and that there is a developmental trend toward behavioral withdrawal and increased muscle tension (Katz *et al.*, 1980). Other efforts have included studies of the child's understanding of his or her illness, what children want to know about their illness (Kalnins, 1977), and the awareness and coping of terminally ill children (Bluebond-Langer, 1974). Special issues of the *Journal of Clinical Child Psychology* (Williams, 1974) and the *Journal of Pediatric Psychology* (Koocher, 1977) have been devoted to issues and research on terminally ill children and contain descriptions of several approaches to intervention.

6. Research: The Future of Pediatric Psychology

Despite the considerable amount of research described in the last section, the problem of establishing an empirical basis for pediatric psychology remains large. We affirm the original position articulated by Wright (1967) that the pediatric psychologist should function as scientist–clinician and strive to move pediatric psychology beyond the intuitive stage to the empirical. In this way, a better understanding of the relationships between health care and psychological conditions can be fostered, more effective intervention and prevention systems developed, and more adequate services provided to children and their families. Only through substantive research efforts can practitioners achieve the major goal of health management—to help the child enter adulthood at an optimal state of development. All the problems reviewed in the previous section remain in need of psychological research. In the present section, we outline a few topics in need of further empirical investigation.

6.1. Compliance to Medical Regimens

As noted previously, the problem of patient compliance to the health regimen is a crucial issue facing practitioners and researchers. In order to maximize children's chances of recovery from illness and to optimize the maintenance of good health, the problem of noncompliance must be addressed further. This might appear to be less a problem with children than with adults, because children are seemingly under the control and management of their parents or adult caregivers. However, every pediatric clinic and hospital undoubtedly has an unwritten list of patients who are notoriously noncompliant and require frustratingly frequent medical intervention. Information is needed on the possible factors influencing medical conformance. Such aspects as etiology, developmental level, adjustment or acceptance, and personality/behavioral factors need to be investigated in terms of how they affect the management of the medical condition (Roberts & Wurtele, 1980).

Researchers in this area need to develop a conceptual approach with which to investigate an individual's health actions—for example, how various components of the Health Belief Model (Rosenstock, 1966) are associated with both the child's and the parents' acceptance of health-related advice (e.g., Gochman, 1971; Weisenberg, Kegeles, & Lund, 1980). Additionally, researchers should focus attention on investigating children's perceptions of medical and psychological disorders (Dollinger, Thelen, & Walsh, 1980; Marsden & Kalter, 1976; Roberts, Beidleman, & Wurtele, 1981; Simeonsson, Buckley, & Monson, 1979). This type of investigation should increase understanding of how children view themselves and others while also facilitating the development of intervention strategies to which children will comply.

Pediatric psychologists serve a vital role in advocating, conceptualizing, and coordinating compliance-enhancing programs. To facilitate the selection of the most efficacious design, further experimental work is needed to evaluate techniques employed to maintain and improve compliance. Possible strategies include (1) using patient contracts, (2) encouraging patient self-monitoring of adherence, (3) tailoring the prescribed health regimen to the patient's habits and life situations, (4) manipulating the antecedents and consequences of compliant behavior, and (5) encouraging parental participation in the compliance program. Compliance-enhancing strategies ought to be an integral part of clinical management to ensure maximum opportunity for pediatric patients to benefit from recommended health programs. Roberts and Wurtele (1980) attempted to study child patients who were identified as being noncompliant. The study found that 82% were also noncompliant with the study by refusing to participate. The investigators pose the question of whether there is a noncompliant personality that refuses to cooperate with any request regardless of its nature or the situation in which it was made. Second, these authors ask whether noncompliance is a way for the patient to regain the control that is lost because of the disease's restrictions. These questions remain to be researched.

Another major research problem confronting pediatricians and parents is the child who complains of somatic problems (e.g., headaches, stomachaches) that have no physical basis (Friedman, 1972). Through behavior analysis, this baffling problem often can be found to be the result of operant reinforcement or "secondary gains." For example, the child may be receiving considerable medical attention and parental concern and/or may be being excused from school or household duties (e.g., Miller & Kratochwill, 1979; Wasserman, 1978). However, operant processes are not always present, and other psychological factors may be playing a role (e.g., stress related to family disruption; Stabler, 1979). More information is needed to improve understanding of this frequent pediatric problem so that effective screening and treatment approaches can be developed.

6.3. Prevention

Traditional mental health practice, like traditional medical practice, has focused primarily on the treatment and remediation of presenting problems rather than on methods of preventing these conditions. More recently, however, both the physical and mental health professions have been placing greater emphasis on crisis prevention in addition to intervention. Health care psychologists are probably more keenly aware of the value of prevention than are psychologists in more traditional settings. Pediatric psychologists have been concerned with prevention since the inception of the field. Attention to prevention makes particularly good sense for the pediatrician and pediatric psychologist, since childhood is the logical point at which to begin the prevention of later-life difficulties (Stachnik, 1980). Christophersen and Barnard (1978) also have cited prevention as one of the four basic areas with which pediatricians (and thus pediatric psychologists) should be concerned. Peterson, Hartmann, and Gelfand (1980) have argued that the prevention of new cases is the most effective way to resolve the existing imbalance between public health needs and inadequate service delivery. The pediatric psychologist is concerned with two major areas of prevention: (1) the prevention of psychopathology and (2) the prevention of medical and physical disorders.

6.3.1. Prevention of Psychopathology

Psychologists are becoming increasingly skillful at identifying children who are at risk for the development of later psychopathology (Blau, 1977, 1979; Garmezy, 1974; Kendall, 1972; Paykel, 1972; Zubin & Spring, 1977). Logically, early identification of children at risk is the first step toward the prevention of later disturbance. The pediatrician's office is an ideal setting for early identification and prevention of behavioral and psychological problems. Anticipatory guidance may be provided in this setting by preparing the parents for upcoming developmental changes and possible behavioral problems. Parents may be given simple, routine procedures to reduce common child-management problems and prevent the development of more serious problems (Brazelton, 1975; Christophersen & Barnard, 1978; Roberts & Wright, 1982). Rather than just asking whether a child is exhibiting behavioral problems, Christophersen and Barnard (1978) have suggested that a physician ask the parent to describe a typical day at home, being alert for behavioral patterns that may be indicative of more serious future problems. Peterson *et al.* (1980) describe a number of teacher and parent training programs that emphasize the prevention of behavioral problems. These authors also outline the steps required in designing and implementing a prevention program.

6.3.2. Prevention of Medical and Physical Disorders

Psychologists have numerous opportunities to assist in the prevention of medical disorders. Although some investigations have considered this topic, research has not adequately addressed the potential for pediatric psychology in decreasing medical fears in a general population of children (Roberts *et al.*, 1980), in enhancing inoculation against pediatric diseases (Peterson, 1980), in promoting the use of car safety restraints for children (Christophersen, 1977), in preventing bathtub drownings (Pearn, Brown, Wong, & Bart, 1979), in poison control (Wright & Buck, 1979), in decreasing adolescent smoking (McAlister, Perry, & Maccoby, 1979), in improving the safety of infants' sleeping conditions (Smialek, Smialek, & Spitz, 1977), and in school screening for psychological problems (Durlak & Mannarino, 1977).

Most of the serious health problems facing Americans today are related to life-style and chronic behavior patterns, not to infectious disease; thus they fall within the province of psychology (Stachnik, 1980). In addition, because children are in the process of developing stable life-styles (Stachnik, 1980), the pediatrician and pediatric psychologist can be especially influential in the prevention of medical disorders related to life-style. Prevention of behavioral and emotional problems associated with medical treatment is another important area of focus, as discussed in relation to hospitalization preparation.

6.4. Protocols and Standardized Procedures

One recent development has been the use of protocols, checklists, and questionnaires to aid the psychologist and pediatrician in both screening and referral and in implementing standardized treatment procedures (Roberts & Wright, 1982). The first type of protocol is used to differentially diagnose and identify problems. Psychologists have prepared medical–psychological screening protocols for such problems as encopresis, anorexia nervosa, psychosomatic problems, sequelae to diseases, and so on (Wright, 1978a). These screening protocols need to be empirically validated; to accomplish this, large-scale research efforts are needed. Wright and Buck (1979), for example, have proposed nationwide participation in validating a checklist on repeated accidental poisoning.

The second type of protocol can be used for the standardized treatment of common pediatric problems following a differential diagnosis. Treatment protocols have been developed for bedtime problems and temper tantrums (Rainey & Christophersen, 1976), use of car-safety restraint seats (Christophersen, 1977), behavior in supermarkets (Barnard, Christophersen, & Wolf, 1977), and encopresis (Wright, 1980). Other disorders for which protocols would be useful include juvenile diabetes compliance, psychogenic pain, school refusal, obesity, impulsivity, and eating disorders. The use of protocols and standardized procedures has the advantages of maximizing cost-efficiency, minimizing staff time, providing needed services, and allowing a focus on more complicated psychological cases (Roberts & Wright, 1982). However, these protocols for screening and treatment need, above all, to be tested through the application of the research ability of pediatric psychologists.

Christophersen and Rapoff (1980) call, in general, for the experimental validation of all treatment procedures employed by pediatric psychologists. These authors assert that too many interventions are made without proved efficacy or feasibility. Throughout this chapter, we have endorsed this position. We consider experimental and quasi-experimental studies to be of utmost importance in establishing the empirical underpinnings of this field of practice and research. The progress which has been made since Wright's (1967) position paper appeared can still be for naught unless the approaches have demonstrated worth. With such validation, the utility and importance of pediatric psychology in the provision of health care services will be firmly established.

6.5. Additional Areas of Research

There are many additional topics in pediatric psychology that are in need of research and application; these occur in the general areas of psychological concomitants of disease entities, psychological interventions, and professional activities. It would be a difficult task to enumerate them all. Table 1, the list of content areas in pediatric psychology, can serve as a starting place for investigation. In addition, a perusal of recent child-related journals, particularly in the discussion sections of the articles, will reveal some very specific and important ideas for research. That there is much to be done in the clinical as well as the research realms makes this discipline exciting. It is the challenge of the pediatric psychologist to be innovative, creative, and adaptive and by so doing to make this profession a live, vibrant, and growing phenomenon.

7. Concluding Comments

Many functions and facets of pediatric psychology have been outlined in this chapter. The role of the pediatric psychologist expands as other disciplines take note of joint concerns and potential relationships that will enhance the services provided to children and youth. Research and practice will continue to expand the parameters of the field. Pediatric psychology will also benefit from the increased interest in health care psychology. The acceptance of psychologists in health care settings will be a critical issue. We are finding that the psychologist–consultant is accepted as a peer much as any other specialist might be (Drotar, 1974; McCrory, 1969; Stabler & Murray, 1974). This acceptance, of course, is contingent upon the provision of competent services. And the growth of these services is accomplished because psychology is meeting previously unmet needs. As long as psychologists in pediatrics and other health care areas are competent and are providing worthwhile services, we can expect their role to expand. The psychologist can take an active part in shaping the future of the specialty. We endorse the position of Tefft and Simeonsson (1979) that psychology should participate in the creation of health care settings. Pediatric psychology can secure a permanent place in the provision of health care services through competent application fostered by a commitment to scientific research and empirical validation of clinical services.

8. References

Agle, D. Psychological factors in hemophilia—the concept of self-care. *Annals of the New York Academy of Science*, 1975, *240*, 221–225.

Altshuler, A. *Books that help children deal with a hospital experience.* Washington, D.C., U.S. Government Printing Office, DHEW Publication No. (HSA) 74-5402, 1974.

Anderson, J. E. Pediatrics and child psychology. *Journal of the American Medical Association*, 1930, *95*, 1015–1018.

Arnold, L. E. Is this label necessary? *Journal of School Health*, 1973, *23*, 510–514.

Aylward, G. P., & Kenny, T. J. Developmental follow-up: Inherent problems and a conceptual model. *Journal of Pediatric Psychology*, 1979, *4*(4), 331–343.

Azrin, N. H., & Foxx, R. M. *Toilet training in less than a day.* New York: Simon & Schuster, 1974.

Barnard, J. D., Christophersen, E. R., & Wolf, M. M. Teaching children appropriate shopping behavior through parent training in the supermarket setting. *Journal of Applied Behavior Analysis*, 1977, *10*, 49–59.

Bayrakal, S. A group experience with chronically disabled adolescents. *American Journal of Psychiatry*, 1975, *132*, 1291–1299.

Berger, M. The role of the clinical child psychologist in an endstage renal disease program. *Journal of Clinical Child Psychology*, 1978, *7*, 17–18.

Bergman, A. B., Dassel, S. W., & Wedgwood, R. J. Time-motion study of practicing pediatricians. *Pediatrics*, 1966, *38*, 254–263.

Blau, T. H. Torque and schizophrenic vulnerability. *American Psychologist*, 1977, *32*, 997–1005.

Blau, T. H. Diagnosis of disturbed children. *American Psychologist*, 1979, *34*, 969–972.

Bluebond-Langner, M. I know, do you? A study of awareness, communication and coping in terminally ill children. In B. Schoenberg, A. C. Carr, A. H. Kutscher, D. Peretz, & I. Goldberg (Eds.), *Anticipatory grief.* New York: Columbia University Press, 1974.

Brazelton, T. B. Anticipatory guidance. In S. B. Friedman (Ed.), *The pediatric clinics of North America.* Philadelphia: Saunders, 1975.

Brewer, D. The role of the psychologist in a dialysis and transplantation unit. *Journal of Clinical Child Psychology*, 1978, *7*, 71–72.

Bronheim, S. P. Pulmonary disorders: Asthma and cystic fibrosis. In P. R. Magrab (Ed.), *Psychological management of pediatric problems* (Vol. I). Baltimore: University Park Press, 1978.

Bryan, T. Learning disabled children's classroom behaviors and teacher-child interactions. *Journal of Pediatric Psychology*, 1979, *4*, 233–246.

Burns, B. J., & Cromer, W. W. The evolving role of the psychologist in primary health care practitioner training for mental health services. *Journal of Clinical Child Psychology*, 1978, *7*, 8–12.

Butler, J. F. The toilet training success of parents after reading "Toilet training in less than a day." *Behavior Therapy*, 1976, *7*, 185–191.

Cantwell, D. Psychiatric illness in the families of hyperactive children. *Archives of General Psychiatry*, 1972, *27*, 414–417.

Cassell, S., & Paul, M. A. The role of puppet therapy on the emotional responses of children hospitalized for cardiac catheterization. *Journal of Pediatrics*, 1967, *71*, 233–239.

Cellucci, P. M. C., & Cellucci, A. J. An evaluation of a community sponsored summer program for learning disabled children. *Journal of Clinical Child Psychology*, 1979, *8*, 216–218.

Christophersen, E. R. *Little people: Guidelines for common sense child rearing*. Lawrence, Kan.: H. & H. Enterprises, 1977.

Christophersen, E. R., & Barnard, J. D. Management of behavior problems: A perspective for pediatricians. *Clinical Pediatrics*, 1978, *17*, 122–124.

Christophersen, E. R., & Rainey, S. K. Management of encopresis through a pediatric outpatient clinic. *Journal of Pediatric Psychology*, 1976, *1*, 38–41.

Christophersen, E. R., & Rapoff, M. A. Pediatric psychology: An appraisal. In B. Lahey & A. Kazdin (Eds.), *Advances in Clinical Child Psychology* (Vol. 3). New York: Plenum Press, 1980.

Ciminero, A. R., & Doleys, D. M. Childhood enuresis: Considerations in assessment. *Journal of Pediatric Psychology*, 1976, *1*, 17–20.

Conners, C. K., Goyette, C. H., Southwick, D. A., Lees, J. M., & Andrulonis, P. A. Food additives and hyperkinesis: A controlled double-blind experiment. *Pediatrics*, 1976, *58*, 154–166.

de la Burde, B., & Reames, B. Prevention of pica, the major cause of lead poisoning in children. *American Journal of Public Health*, 1973, *63*, 737–743.

Delbridge, L. Educational and psychological factors in the management of diabetes in childhood. *The Medical Journal of Australia*, 1975, *2*, 737–739.

DeLozier, J. E., & Gagnon, R. O. *The national ambulatory medical care survey: 1973 Summary United States, May 1973–April 1974*. Vital and Health Statistics, Series 13, Data from the National Health Survey, No. 21. U.S. Department of Health, Education, and Welfare, Publication No. (HRA) 76-1772, 1975.

Doleys, D. M. Behavioral treatments for nocturnal enuresis in children: A review of the recent literature. *Psychological Bulletin*, 1977, *84*, 30–54.

Doleys, D. Encopresis. In J. M. Ferguson & C. B. Taylor (Eds.), *The comprehensive handbook of behavioral medicine* (Vol. 2). Jamaica, N.Y.: SP Medical & Scientific Books, 1980. (a)

Doleys, D. Enuresis. In J. M. Ferguson & C. B. Taylor (Eds.), *The comprehensive handbook of behavioral medicine* (Vol. 1). Jamaica, N.Y.: SP Medical & Scientific Books, 1980. (b)

Doleys, D. M., & Ciminero, A. R. Childhood enuresis: Considerations in treatment. *Journal of Pediatric Psychology*, 1976, *1*, 21–23.

Doleys, D. M., McWhorter, A. Q., Williams, S. C., & Gentry, W. R. Encopresis: Its treatment and relation to nocturnal enuresis. *Behavior Therapy*, 1977, *8*, 77–82.

Dollinger, S. J., Thelen, M. H., & Walsh, M. L. Children's conceptions of psychological problems. *Journal of Clinical Child Psychology*, 1980, *9*, 191–194.

Drotar, D. The role of the pediatric psychologist in the training of pediatricians. *Clinical Psychologist*, 1974, *27*, 20–21.

Drotar, D. Clinical psychology training in the pediatric hospital. *Journal of Clinical Child Psychology*, 1975, *4*, 46–49. (a)

Drotar, D. Mental health intervention in infancy: A case report on "failure to thrive." *Journal of Clinical Child Psychology*, 1975, *4*, 18–20. (b)

Drotar, D. The treatment of a severe anxiety reaction in an adolescent boy following renal transplantation. *Journal of the American Academy of Child Psychiatry*, 1975, *14*, 451–462. (c)

Drotar, D. Psychological consultation in a pediatric hospital. *Professional Psychology*, 1976, *7*, 77–83.

Drotar, D. Family oriented intervention with the dying adolescent. *Journal of Pediatric Psychology*, 1977, *2*, 68–71.

Drotar, D. Training psychologists to consult with pediatricians: Problems and prospects. *Journal of Clinical Child Psychology*, 1978, *7*, 57–60.

Duff, R. S., Rowe, D. S., & Anderson, F. P. Patient care and student learning in a pediatric clinic. *Pediatrics*, 1973, *50*, 839–846.

Dunbar, J., & Stunkard, A. J. Adherence to diet and drug regimen. In R. Levey, B. Rifkind, B. Dennis, & N. Ernst (Eds.), *Nutrition, lipids, and coronary heart disease*. New York: Raven Press, 1977.

Durlak, J. A., & Mannarino, A. P. The Social Skills Development Program: Description of a school-based preventive mental health program for high-risk children. *Journal of Clinical Child Psychology*, 1977, *6*, 48–52.

Elmer, E., Gregg, G. S., & Ellison, P. Late results of the "failure to thrive" syndrome. *Clinical Pediatrics*, 1969, *8*, 584–589.

Etzwiler, D. D., & Robb, J. R. Evaluation of programmed education among juvenile diabetics and their families. *Diabetes*, 1972, *21*, 967–971.

Feingold, B. *Why your child is hyperactive*. New York: Random House, 1975.

Ferguson, B. Preparing young children for hospitalization: A comparison of two methods. *Pediatrics*, 1979, *64*, 656–664.

Field, T., Dempsey, J., & Shuman, H. H. Bayley behavioral ratings of normal and high-risk infants: Their relationship to Bayley Mental Scales. *Journal of Pediatric Psychology*, 1979, *4*, 277–283.

Fife, B. L. Reducing parental overprotection of the leukemic child. *Social Science and Medicine*, 1978, *12*, 117–122.

Fischer, H. L., & Engeln, R. G. How goes the marriage? *Professional Psychology*, 1972, *3*, 73–79.

Friedman, R. Some characteristics of children with "psychogenic" pain. *Clinical Pediatrics*, 1972, *11*, 331–333.

Friedrich, W. N. Ameliorating the psychological impact of chronic physical disease on the child and family. *Journal of Pediatric Psychology*, 1977, *2*, 26–31.

Garmezy, N. Children at risk: The search for the antecedents of schizophrenia. *Schizophrenia Bulletin*, 1974, *9*, 55–125.

Garner, A. M., & Thompson, C. W. Psychological factors in the management of juvenile diabetes. *Journal of Clinical Child Psychology*, 1975, *4*, 43–45.

Garner, A. M., & Thompson, C. W. Juvenile diabetes. In P. R. Magrab (Ed.), *Psychological management of pediatric problems* (Vol. 1). Baltimore: University Park Press, 1978.

Gayton, W. F., & Friedman, S. B. Psychosociological aspects of cystic fibrosis: A review of the literature. *American Journal of Diseases of Children*, 1973, *126*, 856–859.

Gayton, W. F., Friedman, S. B., Tavormina, J. F., & Tucker, F. Children with cystic fibrosis: I. Psychological test findings of patients, siblings, and parents. *Pediatrics*, 1977, *59*, 888–894.

Geist, R. A. Consultation on a pediatric surgical ward: Creating an empathic climate. *American Journal of Orthopsychiatry*, 1977, *47*, 432–444.

Gittleman-Klein, R., Klein, D. F., Abikoff, H., Katz, S., Gloisten, A. C., & Kates, W. Relative efficacy of methylphenidate and behavior modification in hyperkinetic children: An interim report. *Journal of Abnormal Child Psychology*, 1976, *4*, 361–379.

Gochman, D. S. Some correlates of children's health beliefs and potential health behavior. *Journal of Health and Social Behavior*, 1971, *12*, 148–154.

Gogan, J. L., O'Malley, J. E., & Foster, D. J. Treating the pediatric cancer patient: A review. *Journal of Pediatric Psychology*, 1977, *2*, 42–48.

Goldberg, R. T. Adjustment of children with invisible and visible handicaps: Congenital heart disease and facial burns. *Journal of Counseling Psychology*, 1974, *21*, 428–432.

Gluck, M. R. Psychological intervention with pre-school age plastic surgery patients and their families. *Journal of Pediatric Psychology*, 1977, *2*, 23–25.

Grey, M. J., Genel, M., & Tamborlane, W. V. Psychosocial adjustment of latency-aged diabetics: Determinants and relationship to control. *Pediatrics*, 1980, *65*(1), 69–73.

Guerney, L. F. Play therapy with learning disabled children. *Journal of Clinical Child Psychology*, 1979, *8*, 242–244.

Harper, R. G. Behavior modification in pediatric practice. *Clinical Pediatrics*, 1975, *14*, 962–967.

Hartley, E. R. Radiation that's good for you. *Science Digest*, 1974, *76*, 39–45.

Johnson, M. R. Mental health interventions with medically ill children: A review of the literature: 1970–1977. *Journal of Pediatric Psychology*, 1979, *4*, 147–164.

Journal of Pediatric Psychology, 1980, *5*(1), masthead.

Kagan, J. The new marriage: Pediatrics and psychology. *American Journal of Diseases of Childhood*, 1965, *110*, 272–278.

Kalnins, I. V. The dying child: A new perspective. *Journal of Pediatric Psychology*, 1977, *2*, 39–41.

Kalnins, I. V., Churchill, M. P., & Terry, G. E. Concurrent stresses in families with a leukemic child. *Journal of Pediatric Psychology*, 1980, *5*, 81–92.

Kaslow, F. W., & Abrams, J. C. Differential diagnosis and treatment of the learning disabled child and his/her family. *Journal of Pediatric Psychology*, 1979, *4*, 253–264.

Katz, K. S. Inherited disorders: Down's syndrome and phenylketonuria. In P. R. Magrab (Ed.), *Psychological management of pediatric problems* (Vol. 1). Baltimore: University Park Press, 1978.

Katz, E. R., Kellerman, J., & Siegel, S. E. Behavioral distress in children with cancer undergoing medical procedures: Developmental considerations. *Journal of Consulting and Clinical Psychology*, 1980, *48*, 356–365.

Kendall, R. E. The classification of depressions: A review of contemporary confusion. *British Journal of Psychiatry*, 1972, *121*, 183–196.

Kenny, J. J., & Bauer, R. Training the pediatric psychologist: A look at an internship program. *Journal of Clinical Child Psychology*, 1975, *4*, 50–52.

Koch, M. F., & Molnar, G. D. Psychiatric aspects of patients with unstable diabetes mellitus. *Psychosomatic Medicine*, 1974, *36*, 57–68.

Koenigsberg, R. S. An evaluation of visual versus sensorimotor methods for improving orientation discrimination for letter reversal by preschool children. *Child Development*, 1973, *44*, 764–769.

Koocher, G. P. (Ed.). Special issue on death and the child. *Journal of Pediatric Psychology*, 1977, *2*(2), entire issue.

Koocher, G. P., & Sallan, S. E. Pediatric oncology. In P. R. Magrab (Ed.), *Psychological management of pediatric problems* (Vol. 1). Baltimore: University Park Press, 1978.

Koocher, G. P., Sourkes, B. M., & Keane, W. M. Pediatric oncology consultations: A generalizable model for medical settings. *Professional Psychology*, 1979, *10*, 467–474.

Kucia, C., Drotar, D., Doershuk, C. F., Stern, R. C., Boat, T. F., & Matthews, L. Home observation of family interaction and childhood adjustment to cystic fibrosis. *Journal of Pediatric Psychology*, 1979, *4*, 189–195.

LaGreca, A. M. Psychosocial management of children with congenital heart disease and their families. In M. C. Roberts (Chair), *Psychological intervention in the pediatric setting*. Symposium presented at the meeting of the Southeastern Psychological Association, Washington, D.C., March 1980.

LaGreca, A. M., & Mesibov, G. B. Social skills intervention with learning disabled children: Selecting skills and implementing training. *Journal of Clinical Child Psychology*, 1979, *8*, 234–241.

LaGreca, A. M., & Ottinger, D. R. Self-monitoring and relaxation training in the treatment of medically ordered exercises in a 12-year-old female. *Journal of Pediatric Psychology*, 1979, *4*, 49–54.

Lavigne, J. V., & Ryan, M. Psychologic adjustment of siblings of children with chronic illness. *Pediatrics*, 1979, *63*, 616–627.

Lawler, R. H., Nakielny, W., & Wright, N. A. Psychological implications of cystic fibrosis. *Canadian Medical Association Journal*, 1966, *94*, 1043–1046.

Leiken, S. J., & Hassakis, P. Psychological study of parents of children with cystic fibrosis. In E. J. Anthony & C. Koupernik (Eds.), *The child in his family: The impact of disease and death*. New York: Wiley, 1973.

Lewis, S. Considerations in setting up psychological consultation to a pediatric hematology–oncology team. *Journal of Clinical Child Psychology*, 1978, *7*, 21–22.

Lipsett, L. P. Critical conditions in infancy: A psychological perspective. *American Psychologist*, 1979, *34*, 973–980.

Lipsett, L. P., Sturner, W. Q., & Burke, P. Perinatal indicators and subsequent crib death. *Infant Behavior and Development*, 1979, *2*, 325–328.

Litt, C. J. Trichotillomania in childhood: A case of successful short-term treatment. *Journal of Pediatric Psychology*, 1980, *5*, 37–42.

Livingston, S. Psychosocial aspects of epilepsy. *Journal of Clinical Child Psychology*, 1977, *6*, 6–12.

Lowe, K., & Lutzker, J. R. Increasing compliance to a medical regimen with a juvenile diabetic. *Behavior Therapy*, 1979, *10*, 57–64.

Magrab, P. R. Psychological management and renal dialysis. *Journal of Clinical Child Psychology*, 1975, *4*, 38–40.

Magrab, P. R. (Ed.). *Psychological management of pediatric problems*. Baltimore: University Park Press, 1978, 2 vols.

Magrab, P. R., & Calcagno, P. C. Psychological impact of chronic pediatric conditions. In P. R. Magrab (Ed.), *Psychological management of pediatric problems* (Vol. 1). Baltimore: University Park Press, 1978.

Magrab, P. R., & Davitt, M. K. The pediatric psychologist and the developmental follow-up of intensive care nursery infants. *Journal of Clinical Child Psychology*, 1975, *4*, 16–18.

Magrab, P. R., & Papadopoulou, Z. L. The effect of a token economy on dietary compliance for children on hemodialysis. *Journal of Applied Behavior Analysis*, 1977, *10*, 573–578.

Maisto, A. A., & German, M. L. Variables related to progress in a parent infant training program for high-risk infants. *Journal of Pediatric Psychology*, 1979, 409–419.

Marsden, G., & Kalter, N. Children's understanding of their emotionally disturbed peers: I. The concept of emotional disturbance. *Psychiatry*, 1976, *39*, 227–238.

McAlister, A. L., Perry, L., & Maccoby, N. Adolescent smoking: Onset and prevention. *Pediatrics*, 1979, *63*, 650–658.

McClelland, C. Q., Staples, W. P., Weisberg, I., & Berger, M. E. The practitioners' role in behavioral pediatrics. *Journal of Pediatrics*, 1973, *82*, 325–331.

McCrory, W. W. A pediatrician views the role of the pediatric psychologist. *Pediatric Psychology*, 1969, *1*, 4–5.

Melamed, B. G., Meyer, R., Gee, L., & Soule, L. The influence of time and type of preparation on children's adjustment to hospitalization. *Journal of Pediatric Psychology*, 1976, *1*, 31–37.

Melamed, B. G., & Siegel, L. J. Reduction of anxiety in children facing surgery by modeling. *Journal of Consulting and Clinical Psychology*, 1975, *43*, 511–521.

Mesibov, G. B., Schroeder, C. S., & Wesson, L. Parental concerns about their children. *Journal of Pediatric Psychology*, 1977, *2*, 13–17.

Mesibov, G. B., & Shea, V. Social and interpersonal problems of autistic adolescents and adults. In M. C. Roberts (Chair), *Psychological intervention in the pediatric settings*. Symposium presented at the meeting of the Southeastern Psychological Association, Washington, D.C., March 1980.

Milich, R., & Loney, J. The role of hyperactive and aggressive symptomatology in predicting adolescent outcome among hyperactive children. *Journal of Pediatric Psychology*, 1979, *4*, 93–112.

Miller, A. J., & Kratochwill, T. R. Reduction of frequent stomachache complaints by time out. *Behavior Therapy*, 1979, *10*, 211–218.

Nixon, G. Systems approach to pediatric consultation. *Journal of Clinical Child Psychology*, 1975, *4*, 33–35.

Odom, L., Seeman, J., & Newbrough, J. R. A study of family communication patterns and personality integration in children. *Child Psychiatry and Human Development*, 1971, *1*, 275–285.

O'Leary, K. D. Pills or skills for hyperactive children. *Journal of Applied Behavior Analysis*, 1980, *13*, 191–204.

O'Leary, K. D., & O'Leary, S. G. *Classroom management: The successful use of behavior modification* (2nd ed.). Elmsford, N.Y.: Pergamon Press, 1977.

O'Leary, S. G., & Pelham, W. E. Behavioral therapy and withdrawal of stimulant medication with hyperactive children. *Pediatrics*, 1978, *61*, 211–217.

Ottinger, D. R., & Roberts, M. C. A university-based predoctoral practicum in pediatric psychology. *Professional Psychology*, 1980, *11*, 707–713.

Partridge, J. W., Garner, A. M., Thompson, C. W., & Cherry, T. Attitudes of adolescents toward their diabetes. *American Journal of Diseases of Children*, 1972, *124*, 226–229.

Paykel, C. S. Correlates of a depressive typology. *Archives of General Psychiatry*, 1972, *27*, 203–209.

Pearn, J. H., Brown, J., Wong, R., & Bart, R. Bathtub drownings: Report of seven cases. *Pediatrics*, 1979, *64*, 68–70.

Pelham, W. E. Behavioral treatment of hyperkinesis. *American Journal of Diseases of Children*, 1976, *130*, 565.

Pelham, W. E., Schnedler, R. W., Bologna, N. C., & Contreras, J. A. Behavioral and stimulant treatment of hyperactive children: A therapy study with methylphenidate probes in a within-subject design. *Journal of Applied Behavior Analysis*, 1980, *13*(2), 221–236.

Perlman, J. L., & Routh, D. K. Stigmatizing effects of a child's wheelchair in successive and simultaneous interactions. *Journal of Pediatric Psychology*, 1980, *5*, 43–55.

Peterson, L. *The use of a self-control procedure to minimize pain and anxiety in hospitalized children*. Unpublished doctoral dissertation, University of Utah, 1978.

Peterson, L. *Increasing immunization levels in high-risk preschoolers*. Paper presented at the convention of the Midwestern Psychological Association, St. Louis, May 1980.

Peterson, L., Hartmann, D. P., & Gelfand, D. M. Prevention of child behavior disorders: A lifestyle change for child psychologists. In P. O. Davidson & S. M. Davidson (Eds.), *Behavioral medicine: Changing health lifestyles*. New York: Brunner/Mazel, 1980.

Peterson, L., & Ridley-Johnson, R. Pediatric hospital responses to survey on prehospital preparation for children. *Journal of Pediatric Psychology*, 1980, *5*, 1–7.

Pless, I. B., & Pinkerton, P. *Chronic childhood disorder: Promoting patterns of adjustment*. Chicago: Year Book Publishers, 1975.

Rachman, S. J., & Phillips, C. *Psychology and behavioral medicine*. Cambridge: Cambridge University Press, 1980.

Rainey, S. K., & Christophersen, E. R. Behavioral pediatrics: The role of the nurse clinician. *Comprehensive Issues in Pediatric Nursing*, 1976, *1*(4), 19–28.

Ramey, C. T., Hieger, L., & Klisz, D. Synchronous reinforcement of vocal responses in failure-to-thrive infants. *Child Development*, 1972, *43*, 1449–1455.

Raskin, L. M., & Bloom, A. S. Kinetic family drawings by children with learning disabilities. *Journal of Pediatric Psychology*, 1979, *4*, 247–251.

Renne, C. M., & Creer, T. L. Training children with asthma to use inhalation therapy equipment. *Journal of Applied Behavior Analysis*, 1976, *9*, 1–11.

Rie, H. D. Pediatrics and changing practices in clinical child psychology: *I. Issues concerning the expansion of psychology within pediatric settings*. Symposium presented at the 77th Annual Convention of the American Psychological Association, Washington, D.C., September 1969.

Rie, H. E., Hilty, M. D., & Cranblitt, H. G. Intelligence an- coordination following California encephalitis. *American Journal of the Disabled*, 1973, *125*, 824–827.

Rie, E. D., & Rie, H. E. Recall, retention, and Ritalin. *Journal of Consulting and Clinical Psychology*, 1977, *45*, 967–972.

Roberts, M. C. Psychological preparation for pediatric hospitalization and surgery. In M. C. Roberts (Chair), *Pediatric psychology: Theory and intervention for psychological–medical problems with children*. Symposium presented at the meeting of the Midwestern Psychological Association, Chicago, May 1979.

Roberts, M. C. Clinical child programs: What and where are they? *Journal of Clinical Child Psychology*, 1982, *11*, 13–21.

Roberts, M. C., Beidleman, W. B., & Wurtele, S. K. Children's perception of medical and psychological disorders in their peers. *Journal of Clinical Child Psychology*, 1981, *10*, 76–78.

Roberts, M. C., & Horner, M. M. A comprehensive intervention for failure-to-thrive. *Journal of Clinical Child Psychology*, 1979, *8*, 10–14.

Roberts, M. C., & Maddux, J. E. *A psychosocial conceptualization of failure-to-thrive*. Manuscript submitted for publication, 1980.

Roberts, M. C., & Ottinger, D. R. A case study: Encopretic adolescent with multiple problems. *Journal of Clinical Child Psychology*, 1979, *8*, 15–17.

Roberts, M. C., & Wright, L. Role of the pediatric psychologist as consultant to pediatricians. In J. Tuma (Ed.), *The practice of pediatric psychology*. New York: Wiley, 1982.

Roberts, M. C., & Wurtele, S. K. On the noncompliant research subject in a study of medical noncompliance. *Social Science and Medicine*, 1980, *14A*, 171.

Roberts, M. C., Wurtele, S. K., Boone, R. R., Ginther, L. J., & Elkins, P. D. Reduction of medical fears by use of modeling: A preventive application in a general population of children. *Journal of Pediatric Psychology*, 1981, *6*, 293–300.

Roche, A. F., Lipman, R. S., Overall, J. E., & Hung, W. The effects of stimulant medication on the growth of hyperkinetic children. *Pediatrics*, 1979, *63*, 847–850.

Rose, T. L. The functional relationship between artificial food colors and hyperactivity. *Journal of Applied Behavior Analysis*, 1978, *11*, 439–446.

Rosen, G. Reversible growth and developmental retardation in the first year of life. *Clinical Proceedings, Children's Hospital National Medical Center*, 1977, *33*, 193–205.

Rosenstock, I. M. Why people use health services. *Milbank Memorial Fund Quarterly*, 1966, *44*, 94–127.

Ross, D. M., & Ross, S. A. *Hyperactivity: Research, theory and action*. New York: Wiley, 1976.

Routh, D. K. Graduate training in pediatric psychology: The Iowa program. *Pediatric Psychology*, 1969, *1*, 4–5.

Routh, D. K. The short history of pediatric psychology. *Journal of Clinical Child Psychology*, 1975, *4*, 6–8.

Routh, D. K. Hyperactivity. In P. R. Magrab (Ed.), *Psychological management of pediatric problems* (Vol. 1). Baltimore: University Park Press, 1978.

Rutter, M. *Maternal deprivation reassessed*. Penguin Books, Harmondsworth, England: 1972. (a)

Rutter, M. Maternal deprivation reconsidered. *Journal of Psychosomatic Research*, 1972, *16*, 241–250. (b)

Safer, D. S., & Allen, D. P. *Hyperactive children: Diagnosis and management*. Baltimore: University Park Press, 1976.

Sajwaj, T., Libet, J., & Agras, S. Lemon juice therapy: The control of life threatening ruminations in a six-month-old infant. *Journal of Applied Behavior Analysis*, 1974, *7*, 557–563.

Salk, L. The purposes and functions of the psychologist in a pediatric setting. Paper presented in *Issues concerning the expansion of psychology within pediatric settings*. Symposium presented at the 77th Annual Convention of the American Psychological Association, Washington, D.C., September 1969.

Salk, L. Psychologist in a pediatric setting. *Professional Psychology*, 1970, *1*, 395–396.

Salk, L. Sudden infant death: Impact on family and physician. *Clinical Pediatrics*, 1971, *10*, 248–249.

Salk, L. Psychologist and pediatrician: A mental health team in the prevention and early diagnosis of mental disorders. In G. J. Williams & S. Gordon (Eds.), *Clinical child psychology: Current practices and future perspectives*. New York: Behavioral Publications, 1974.

Salk, L., Hilgartner, M., & Granich, B. The psycho-social impact of hemophilia on the patient and his family. *Social Science and Medicine*, 1972, *6*, 491–505.

Satterfield, J. H., & Cantwell, D. P. CNS function and response to methylphenidate in hyperactive children. *Psychopharmacology Bulletin*, 1974, *10*, 36–37.

Sayed, A. J., & Leaverton, D. R. Kinetic family drawings of children with diabetes. *Child Psychiatry and Human Development*, 1974, *5*, 40–50.

Schaefer, C. E. *Childhood encopresis and enuresis: Causes and therapy*. New York: Van Nostrand Reinhold, 1979.

Schierberl, J. P. Physiological models of hyperactivity: An integrative review of the literature. *Journal of Clinical Child Psychology*, 1979, *8*, 163–172.

Schnackenberg, B. C. Minimal brain dysfunction syndrome in children. *The Psychiatric Forum*, 1977, *7*, 26–32.

Schneider, S. F. Psychology and general health: Prospects and pitfalls. *Journal of Clinical Child Psychology*, 1978, *7*, 5–8.

Schofield, W. The role of psychology in the delivery of health services. *American Psychologist*, 1969, *24*, 565–584.

Schofield, W. The psychologist as a health care professional. *Intellect Magazine*, 1975, *203*, 255–258.

Schroeder, C. S. Psychologist in a private pediatric practice. *Journal of Pediatric Psychology*, 1979, *4*, 5–18.

Schroeder, C. S., Goolsby, E., & Stangler, S. Preventive services in a private pediatric practice. *Journal of Clinical Child Psychology*, 1975, *4*, 32–33.

Shafto, F., & Sulzbacher, S. Comparing treatment tactics with a hyperactive preschool child: Stimulant medication and programmed teacher intervention. *Journal of Applied Behavior Analysis*, 1977, *10*, 13–20.

Shaw, W. J., & Walker, C. E. Use of relaxation in the short-term treatment of fetishistic behavior: An exploratory case study. *Journal of Pediatric Psychology*, 1979, *4*, 403–407.

Shekim, W. O., Dekirmenjian, H., & Chapel, J. L. Urinary MHPG excretion in minimal brain dysfunction and its modification by d-amphetamine. *American Journal of Psychiatry*, 1979, *136*, 667–671.

Sieben, R. L. Controversial medical treatments of learning disabilities. *Academic Therapy*, 1977, *13*, 133–147.

Siegel, L. J. Preparation of children for hospitalization: A selected review of the research literature. *Journal of Pediatric Psychology*, 1976, *1*, 26–30.

Simeonsson, R. J., Buckley, L., & Monson, L. Conceptions of illness causality in hospitalized children. *Journal of Pediatric Psychology*, 1979, *4*, 77–84.

Smialek, J. E., Smialek, P. Z., & Spitz, W. U. Accidental bed deaths in infants due to unsafe sleeping situations. *Clinical Pediatrics*, 1977, *16*, 1031–1036.

Smith, E. E., Rome, L. P., & Friedheim, D. K. The clinical psychologist in the pediatric office. *The Journal of Pediatrics*, 1967, *71*, 48–51.

Sourkes, B. Facilitating family coping with childhood cancer. *Journal of Pediatric Psychology*, 1977, *2*, 65–67.

Spinetta, J. J. Adjustment in children with cancer. *Journal of Pediatric Psychology*, 1977, *2*, 49–51.

Spring, C., & Sandoval, J. Food additives and hyperkinesis: A critical evaluation of the evidence. *Journal of Learning Disabilities*, 1976, *9*, 560–569.

Sroufe, L. A. Drug treatment of children with behavior problems. In F. Horowitz (Ed.), *Review of child development research* (Vol. 4). Chicago: University of Chicago Press, 1975.

Sroufe, L. A., & Stewart, M. A. Treating problem children with stimulant drugs. *New England Journal of Medicine*, 1973, *289*, 407–413.

Stabler, B. Emerging models of psychologist–pediatrician liaison. *Journal of Pediatric Psychology*, 1979, *4*, 307–313.

Stabler, B., & Murray, J. P. Pediatricians' perceptions of pediatric psychology. *The Clinical Psychologist*, 1974, *27*, 13–15.

Stachnik, T. J. Priorities for psychology in medical education and health care delivery. *American Psychologist*, 1980, *35*, 8–15.

Stewart, M. A., & Olds, S. *Raising a hyperactive child.* New York: Harper & Row, 1973.

Tavormina, J. B., Kastner, L. S., Slater, P. M., & Watt, S. L. Chronically ill children: A psychologically and emotionally deviant population? *Journal of Abnormal Child Psychology*, 1976, *4*, 99–110.

Tefft, B. M., & Simeonsson, R. J. Psychology and the creation of health care settings. *Professional Psychology*, 1979, *10*, 558–570.

Thompson, G. A., Iwata, B. A., & Poynter, H. Operant control of pathological tongue thrust in spastic cerebral palsy. *Journal of Applied Behavior Analysis*, 1979, *12*, 325–333.

Travis, G. *Chronic illness in children: Its impact on child and family.* Stanford, Calif.: Stanford University Press, 1976.

Tropauer, A., Franz, M. N., & Dilgard, V. W. Psychological aspects of the care of children with cystic fibrosis. *American Journal of Diseases of Children*, 1970, *119*, 424–432.

Tuma, J. Pediatric psychologist . . .? Do you mean clinical *child* psychologist? *Journal of Clinical Child Psychology*, 1975, *4*, 9–12.

Tuma, J. M. Practicum, internship, and postdoctoral training in pediatric psychology: A survey. *Journal of Pediatric Psychology*, 1977, *2*, 9–12.

Tuma, J. (Ed.). *The practice of pediatric psychology.* New York: Wiley, 1982.

Varni, J. W. Behavior therapy in the management of home and school behavior problems with a 4½-year-old hemophiliac child. *Journal of Pediatric Psychology*, 1980, *5*, 17–23.

Vernon, D. T. A., Foley, J. M., Sipowicz, R. R., & Schulman, J. L. *The psychological responses of children to hospitalization and illness.* Springfield, Ill.: Charles C Thomas, 1965.

Visintainer, M. A., & Wolfer, J. A. Psychological preparation for surgical pediatric patients. The effect on children's and parent's stress responses and adjustment. *Pediatrics*, 1975, *56*, 187–202.

Walker, C. E. Enuresis and encopresis. In P. Magrab (Ed.), *Psychological management of pediatric problems.* Baltimore: University Park Press, 1978.

Walker, C. E. Behavioral intervention in a pediatric setting. In J. R. MacNamara (Ed.), *Behavioral approaches to medicine: Application and analysis.* New York: Plenum Press, 1979. (a)

Walker, C. E. Behavior therapy for medical/psychological problems. In L. Wright, A. B. Schaefer, & G. Solomons (Eds.), *Encyclopedia of pediatric psychology.* Baltimore: University Park Press, 1979. (b)

Wasserman, T. H. The elimination of complaints of stomach cramps in a 12-year-old child by covert positive reinforcement. *The Behavior Therapist*, 1978, *1*, 13–14.

Waye, M. F. Behavioral treatment of a child displaying comic-book mediated fear of hand shrinking: A case study. *Journal of Pediatric Psychology*, 1979, *4*, 43–47.

Weisenberg, M., Kegeles, S. P., & Lund, A. K. Children's health beliefs and acceptance of a dental preventive activity. *Journal of Health and Social Behavior*, 1980, *21*, 59–74.

Weiss, B., Williams, J. H., Margen, S., Abrams, B., Caan, B., Citron, L. J., Cox, C., McKibben, J., Ogar, D., & Schultz, S. Behavioral responses to artificial food colors. *Science*, 1980, *207*, 1487–1489.

White, S. H., Day, M. C., Freeman, P. K., Hartman, S. A., & Messenger, K. P. Federal programs for young children: Review and recommendations. *Recommendations for federal program planning* (Vol. 3). Department of Health, Education, and Welfare, 1973.

Willerman, L. Activity level and hyperactivity in twins. *Child Development*, 1973, *44*, 288–293.

Williams, G. J. (Ed.). Special issue on death and children. *Journal of Clinical Child Psychology*, 1974, *3*(2), entire issue.

Willis, D. J., & Thomas, E. D. Seizure disorders. In P. R. Magrab (Ed.), *Psychological management of pediatric problems* (Vol. 2). Baltimore: University Park Press, 1978.

Wolfer, J. A., & Visintainer, M. A. Pediatric surgical patients' and parents' stress responses and adjustment. *Nursing Research*, 1975, *24*, 244–255.

Wolfer, J. A., & Visintainer, M. A. Prehospital psychological preparation for tonsillectomy patients: Effects on children's and parents' adjustment. *Pediatrics*, 1979, *64*, 646–655.

Wright, L. The pediatric psychologist: A role model. *American Psychologist*, 1967, *22*, 323–325.

Wright, L. Pediatric psychology: Prospect and retrospect. *Pediatric Psychology*, 1969, *1*(1), 1–3.

Wright, L. Conditioning of consummatory responses in young children. *Journal of Clinical Psychology*, 1971, *27*, 416–419.

Wright, L. Intellectual sequelae of Rocky Mountain spotted fever. *Journal of Abnormal Psychology*, 1972, *80*, 315–316.

Wright, L. Handling the encopretic child. *Professional Psychology*, 1973, *4*, 137–144. (a)

Wright, L. Aversive conditioning of self-induced seizures. *Behavior Therapy*, 1973, *4*, 712–713. (b)

Wright, L. Outcome of a standardized program for treating psychogenic encopresis. *Professional Psychology*, 1975, *6*, 453–456.

Wright, L. Indirect treatment of children through principles oriented parent consultation. *Journal of Consulting and Clinical Psychology*, 1976, *44*, 148.

Wright, L. Assessing the psychosomatic status of children. *Journal of Clinical Child Psychology*, 1978, *7*, 94–112. (a)

Wright, L. *Parent power: A guide to responsible child rearing*. New York: Psychological Dimensions, Inc., 1978. (b)

Wright, L. A comprehensive program for mental health and behavioral medicine in a large children's hospital. *Professional Psychology*, 1979, *10*, 458–466. (a)

Wright, L. Health care psychology: Prospects for the well-being of children. *American Psychologist*, 1979, *34*, 1001–1006. (b)

Wright, L. The standardization of compliance procedures, or the mass production of ugly ducklings. *American Psychologist*, 1980, *35*, 119–122.

Wright, L., & Buck, P. An instrument for identifying potential repeaters among accidental poisoning victims. *Professional Psychology*, 1979, *10*, 649–650.

Wright, L., & Fulwiler, R. Sequelae of lead poisoning in children. *Oklahoma State Medical Association Journal*, 1972, *65*, 372–375.

Wright, L., & Fulwiler, R. Emotional sequelae of burns: Effects on children and their mothers. *Pediatric Research*, 1974, *8*, 931–934.

Wright, L., & Jimmerson, S. Intellectual sequelae of *Hemophilus influenzae* meningitis. *Journal of Abnormal Psychology*, 1971, *77*, 181–183.

Wright, L., Nunnery, A., Eichel, B., & Scott, R. Application of conditioning principles to problems of tracheotomy addiction in children. *Journal of Consulting and Clinical Psychology*, 1968, *32*, 603–606.

Wright, L., Schaefer, A. B., & Solomons, G. *Encyclopedia of pediatric psychology*. Baltimore: University Park Press, 1979.

Wright, L., & Thalassinos, P. A. Success with electroshock in habitual vomiting: Report of two cases in young children. *Clinical Pediatrics*, 1973, *12*, 594–597.

Wright, L., & Walker, C. E. Behavioral treatment of encopresis. *Journal of Pediatric Psychology*, 1976, *1*, 35–37.

Wright, L., & Walker, C. E. Treating the encopretic child. *Clinical Pediatrics*, 1977, *16*, 1042–1045.

Wright, L., Woodcock, J. M., & Scott, R. Conditioning children when refusal of oral medication is life threatening. *Pediatrics*, 1969, *44*, 969–972.

Yarrow, L. J. Maternal deprivation: Toward an empirical and conceptual re-evaluation. *Psychological Bulletin*, 1961, *58*, 459–490.

Zubin, J., & Spring, B. Vulnerability—A new view of schizophrenia. *Journal of Abnormal Psychology*, 1977, *86*, 103–126.

The Psychologist as Geriatric Clinician

JEFFREY R. SOLOMON, MARTIN V. FALETTI,
AND STEVEN S. YUNIK

Geriatric psychology is such that its practitioners must often call upon their professional resources and skills rather than relying on the simple application of generic principles.

The interface between the body systems and the environment as it exists in senescence requires one to look at the older person in a special light. Most significantly, later life is marked by a number of progressive losses. For example, health, vocation, financial security, status, beauty, friendship, and even—eventually—life itself are all at risk for older people.

Abnormal development occurs when the elderly individual is unable to cope successfully with the large number of losses that he or she is apt to experience in the course of a life time. The symptoms that the elderly individual exhibits in the face of these stresses are likely to represent exacerbations of long-standing or well-established patterns of behavior.

This chapter will provide an introduction to the many and diverse physical and psychosocial changes that may affect the functioning of the older adult. It will consider the implications of these changes for assessment, clinical practice, and research.

JEFFREY R. SOLOMON ● Altro Health and Rehabilitation Services, New York, New York 10017.   MARTIN V. FALETTI ● Miami Jewish Home and Hospital for the Aged, Miami, Florida 33137.   STEVEN S. YUNIK ● Douglas Gardens Community Mental Health Center of Miami Beach, Miami Beach, Florida 33139.

1. Developmental Features of Later Life

Probably the most pervasive and difficult problem we face in seeking to understand human development from a life-span perspective is the separation of major life events from chronological age and a time/date referent. Being a particular age at the time of a study has several combined effects that are distinct from and yet related to chronological age; this complicates efforts to understand the effects of age on behavior patterns or characteristics. For example, three subjects of a 1980 study were aged 70, 80, and 90; they were born in 1910, 1900, and 1890 respectively. If we found that these three subjects differed in attitude with respect to some social and political feature of society, the origins of the difference may have less to do with chronological age than with life experience. Reaching adolescence during a war or raising a family during a major depression may have effects separate and distinct from chronological age. Differences in health and susceptibility to disease may stem from age differences or, perhaps, be due to very different levels of prenatal care and medical knowledge between any two birth years.

Although the reader may find a fine explication of the nuances of the problem both for theory building and research design in Schaie and Schaie (1977), for the present it suffices to say that chronological age is not as simple a variable in behavioral research as might be expected. Being older or younger also carries with it concurrent but perhaps highly varied differences in individual physical and experiential characteristics. Diet, social habits, major social and political events, and other factors all change with time, as does age. Thus, we must be cautious when we attribute observed differences to the effects of aging when other factors that are simply associated with age may be at work.

1.1. Health Changes

This chapter cannot provide more than a brief overview of the health-related physical changes that affect psychological and psychosocial functioning, it is imperative that the geriatric practitioner be aware of the full range of common diagnoses observed in the older patient.

Physical functioning and health decline in old age. Although aging does not affect the entire organism uniformly, we observe negative changes in nine body systems (musculoskeletal, cardiovascular, respiratory, nervous and special senses, gastrointestinal, urinary, integumentary, reproductive, and endocrine). Whether we look at the thinning of muscular fibers, loss of muscle tone in the bladder, or decreased basal metabolic rate, we discover a decline in the older person's vital functions. It is of special importance to the psychologist to recognize that all five senses suffer loss in even *normal* aging; thereby skewing perception. For the most part, these conditions are more like chronic, debilitating illnesses, as opposed to acute episodes as seen earlier in life.

People over 65 are hospitalized at a rate greater than 2½ times that for younger people. Further, the United States Department of Health and Human Services indicates that the average length of stay for the over-65 population is almost twice as long as that for younger people. Polliak and Shavitt (1977) reported that the number of admission days was 1,117 per thousand people over age 65 as compared with 570 days per thousand for those under 65. For the typical noninstitutionalized elderly person, the average number of restricted activity days is 38 per year. Thirteen of these days were spent in bed. Approximately two-thirds of these days of restricted activity are accounted for by chronic conditions and one-third by acute illness or injury (Kalish, 1977).

1.2. Psychological Changes

1.2.1. Intelligence

Studies on developmental aspects of intelligence suggest that contrary to initial beliefs, there is no simple relationship between intelligence and aging. Findings suggest that some intellectual abilities do not decline with age, while other abilities decline at different rates. In general, verbal abilities tend to be maintained while psychomotor speed and problem solving tend to decline. Bellak (1976) reports that studies using the Wechsler Adult Intelligence Scale (WAIS) indicated the elderly do best on information, vocabulary, and comprehension sub-tests; less well on arithmetic and picture completion subtests; and worst on tests of object assembly, block design, and picture arrangement.

1.2.2. Memory

The question of how the aging process affects an individual's memory is a complex one. Abilities may vary in the various components of memory, that is registration, storage, and retrieval of information. Bellak (1976) reports that elderly individuals may remember better when information is personally meaningful, offered in small amounts, and presented in a way that is easy to code for storage.

Since memory problems are a frequent complaint of elderly clients who are depressed, discriminating between memory problems that are organic versus functional in nature cannot be easily done. This seriously complicates the task of establishing developmental norms for memory in the elderly.

1.3. Social Changes

Social losses among the elderly are a major concern. Almost 10 million widowed women live in the United States; there are only one-fourth as many widowed men. Widowed elders lose the psychosocial role of being a spouse and are much more likely to experience isolation and loneliness (Brink 1976). People who experience isolation and loneliness are documented as being at high risk for mental illness (Kraus, Spasoff, Beattie, Holden, Lawson, Rodenburg, & Woodcock, 1976), it is therefore not surprising that mental health problems and level of dysfunction among older adults are substantiated by an extremely high rate of suicide. The elderly represent 11% of the population and over 25% of all recorded suicides in the United States. (President's Task Panel, 1978).

The economics of old age continues the litany of problems resulting in the biopsychosocial crises experienced by the elderly. The elderly poor live on relatively fixed incomes, and inflation has drastically limited even this modest purchasing power. High costs of health care (which are often unanticipated because of the misconception that Medicare is a universal health insurance) further jeopardize the precarious microeconomy of old age. At present, Medicare pays only 30% of the health care costs of the elderly (*Miami Herald*, 1980). Lack of mobility, limited public transportation, poor intergenerational relationships, criminal victimization or fear thereof, loss of status due to retirement, societal agism, and prejudice result in synergistic blend of conditions that lead to a high rate of psychopathology and need for services among the old.

1.4. Personality Changes

Traditionally, psychologists have focused their attention on understanding the individual in childhood and adolescence. Individuals are seen as evolving through a series of phases as they move from infancy, during which they are extremely dependent on others for survival, to adulthood, when they are able to survive independently. Adult development from early adulthood to midlife to later life has been a largely neglected area of study. Recently, however, increasing attention has been given to this end of the life span. Here, too, a developmental approach is being utilized. Thus, as during the formative childhood and adolescent years, the adult is viewed as passing through various life phases. During these phases, the individual's perspective on life and death, personal accomplishments, and interpersonal relationships are ever evolving.

Elderly individuals have a unique perspective on the life cycle, because only they can glimpse a life span in its entirety. It is the task of the elderly individual to make sense of existence—enumerating success, accepting failures, resolving unresolved conflicts, and accepting those problems that must remain unresolved. Before this work can be finished, the elderly individual must face and accept the inevitability of death. Acceptance of death as part of the life cycle is often important to the elderly individual seeking to put life events in proper perspective.

The many changes that occur with human aging are, as we have briefly illustrated, such that we must revise many assumptions that are often made about them. For example, we cannot assume, as we may often do with younger people, that the individual's sensory capacities (required by many of our assessment and indeed treatment approaches or styles) are fully intact. Nor can we assume that an excessive focus on bodily complaints or illnesses among the elderly is, *per se*, inappropriate or cause for concern. This is not to say that we should move like automatons to the converse assumptions. Rather, the many changes faced by the elderly quite often call for a team approach to dealing with their problems. Mental health problems may be one of many issues confronting the client and hence the health care team.

Indeed, mental health conditions may be inextricably tied to other physical or social problems in the client's life. Although this can be the case with any client, we emphasize it here because human development makes this multiple problem profile a more frequent reality among older adults. The psychologist as geriatric clinician requires a broad awareness and understanding of the role of other body systems as well as needs for care and support in order to be able to effectively address and integrate mental health treatment into the overall care plan for the older client.

2. Testing and Assessment

Psychological assessment occupies a salient role in clinical training programs because of its importance to clinical practice. For those who would provide therapeutic interventions, there is obviously a need to establish the psychological disorders or problems that are present (diagnosis), as well as the potential sources of such difficulties (etiology). In this broad sense, the business of assessment for the psychologist as geriatric clinician is not fundamentally different from psychological assessment as it has been developed with middle-aged adult populations. The often cited and long-standing neglect of older adults by mental health professionals has been reversed in recent years; it is now recognized that treatment of mental health problems in the aged is both appropriate (e.g., Verwoerdt, 1976) and attended by a reasonable likelihood of success (Butler & Lewis, 1973). However, there is also enough experience to suggest that assessment with older persons cannot and should not be considered in terms of a simple, direct application of established techniques and practices. There appear to be significant differences, both conceptually and methodologically, in assessment practice with older adults relative to our more in-depth experience with midlife adults. In this section, we will try to use the brief space allotted to outline these major sources of difference in terms of issues concerned with goals and objectives of clinical assessment and methods and approaches to the conduct of assessment.

2.1. Goals in Clinical Assessment with Older Adults

The goals of assessment in clinical settings can be viewed as threefold: diagnosis, etiology, and progress. Diagnosis attempts to distinguish pathological or disordered psychological functioning from what might be called normal or normative for aging persons. *Etiology* concerns identification of intrapsychic and situational (extrapsychic) sources of disorders for the purpose not only of accurate diagnosis but also of contemplating entry points for therapeutic interventions. Finally, reassessment or evaluation of older adult clients seeks to ascertain *progress* or outcomes of various treatment plans or programs. The realization of these goals in the context of work with older adults requires a broader scope of assessment activity and a wider perspective on behavior than those that are usual in clinical assessment.

Although it is often difficult to separate assessment issues in diagnosis from those in etiology (because of the latter's relevance to determinations made in pursuit of the former), we shall do so only to clarify the implications of two major conceptual problems that attend our application of psychological assessment practice to the older adult. The first of these problems concerns the need to focus on multiple dimensions of functioning (e.g., Spencer & Dorr, 1975; Hendricks & Hendricks, 1977) in developing a clinical picture of the older person and specifying the sources of problems as a vehicle for initiating remedial interventions. This we consider more related to the business of etiology than of diagnostic practice. While presenting problems that may in fact be clearly psychological, the sources of these problems are, with older adults, likely to encompass life events and physical problems rather than personality disorders *per se*. The second problem concerns the use of norms or criteria by which we differentiate pathological behavior and functioning from that which can be attributed to "normal" aging. This is considered to be more within the realm of diagnosis, since the rendering of such norms and criteria implies that we have in fact decided that particular patterns of behavior evidence "disorder" in the older person's functioning and hence the need for intervention. Since there is much in the aging process that, if found in a younger person, would be considered "disordered" or "problematic", there is a very real question concerning the relevance of existing diagnostic norms to older persons and how the appropriate norms, when needed, might be developed.

2.1.1. Etiology: Functional Impairments and Mental Health

The term *functional assessment*, now widely used in the field of aging, seems to have become an established feature with the advent of multidimensional assessment techniques as represented in the five-dimensional approach of Pfeiffer (1975). This protocol provides for assessment of physical and mental health, social engagement and supports, economic resources levels, and the ability to carry out basic activities of daily living. Although the specific instrumentation developed for this approach has been criticized within the field as to length and item content, it is striking to observe the extent to which the *conceptual* approach has been widely accepted.

The spectrum of human functioning implicit in a multidimensional approach suggests what is newly called behavioral medicine or a biopsychosocial perspective on human behavior. There is probably no other population where this view of behavior is more appropriate or more needed. (Kart, Metress, & Metress, 1978). As we have seen, the older person's behavior patterns can reflect more varied and multiple problem sources ranging from physical changes or disabilities (Saxon & Etten, 1978) to the cumulative effects of a range of stresses (Eisdorfer & Wilkie, 1977). Further, performance on various assessment scales can be significantly affected by sensory or neurological defects.

The psychologist as geriatric clinician must thus contend with far more potential sources of "true", as well as performance, variance than has been the case with adults in the middle years—a group which, until recently, has formed most of the basis for our current views of behavior and methods whereby to assess behavior (Schaie & Schaie, 1977). The need for a broader and more integrative clinical picture of the client must be kept in mind in assessment activity with older people (Brink, 1979). We do not suggest here that a multifunctional battery of assessments should be the goal of assessment with older adults. To the contrary, as Schaie and Schaie (1977) have observed; "In modern clinical assessment, we do not give a test battery and then try to figure out what the results mean. Rather, the assessment goals are first defined and expressed in the form of hypotheses about the client's behavior" (p. 692). We wish to suggest here that exclusive attention to psychogenic etiology as a basis for behavioral disorders is not likely to provide the clinician with a complete or even a realistic understanding of an older person's mental health problems. Further, it will fail to recognize the relevance and resources of the physician, social worker, home-care specialist, and other professionals who can provide care and support to older people in other problem areas and thus affect mental health treatment and client progress.

2.1.2. Diagnostics: A Problem of Criteria

There is probably no other single issue more central to assessment with older adults than that of criteria by which to differentiate behavior disorders from the range of possible adaptive choices that older people must often make to cope with the physical and social realities of human aging. There is a critical need to establish levels or ranges of functioning that might be termed "normative" for aging persons. This is complicated by the range and variety of systems changes associated with aging and the fact that older persons, in addition to being faced with potentially larger aggregate of situational stresses, may also bring less reserve capacity for adaption to a given situation (Lowenthal & Chiriboga, 1973). The norms and standards for adaptive functioning used with adults in midlife and reflected in much of our assessment practice are based upon assumptions about life situations and adaptive capacities that have little relevance to the adult in late life.

The diagnosis of a disorder implies something that is considered to be problematic for the person and uncharacteristic of the way in which others function. Because the older person is confronting a different set of demands for adaption and a different set of resources to use in service of adaption, it is necessary to characterize what is normal or normative for older adults versus what is normal or normative for all people at any stage of the developmental cycle. For example, the most frequently found diagnoses in studies of clinical practice with older adults are organic brain syndromes, depression, and related affective disorders. The first represents a disorder that is presumably relevant mostly to older adults because of the implied gradual deficits occurring as a result of physical changes in the brain. Although neurological deficits are found in the young, these are considered to be different; at least they are given different classifications in terms of established diagnostic practice. Depression and affective disorders, however, may be manifested by anyone at any age. Although it is likely that severe depression may indicate different processes in older persons, the criteria for establishing the existence of the disorder are reasonably applicable to all adults.

The problem in clinical assessment is the development of diagnostic perspectives that realistically describe disordered patterns of behavior in terms applicable to older adults, particularly as regards etiology and hence intervention strategies. Because older adults, like any other age group, vary on any dimension of functioning or behavior one might choose, they are not a homogenous group that can be readily contrasted with younger people to provide the clinician with clear-cut criteria for what is "normative" in older people.

Further, the lack of any clear consensus on personality changes in the aging does not at present suggest that an understanding of behavioral problems in older people requires extensive assessment for personality dynamics. Given existing experience in the major trends for presenting problems and a judious application of Occam's razor, it appears clear that aging in this society carries with it increased stress and demands for new adaptive patterns as well as an often decreased inventory of physical, psychological, and social resources to marshal in service of such adaptions. Thus, clinical assessment must properly focus on scales that delineate the patterns in adaptive or nonadaptive behavior from the standpoint of functioning—that is, the ability to make and implement adaptive behaviors appropriate to the person's life situation. It remains for the emergent focus on life-span developmental theory to provide us with models of adaptive development and behavior that will serve as the basis for diagnostic practice over the life span.

2.1.3. Progress: Assessing Change over Time

It follows from the above that assessment focusing on dimensions of personality changes over time may be less informative than assessment focused on changes in the older person's ability to adapt and function that can arise from therapeutic interventions. An illustrative example here may be found in depressive disorders following death of a spouse. Although interventions may, in fact, improve and support the older adult's motivation and ability to function with reasonable effectiveness in a particular environment following bereavement, it may be expected that some depressive symptoms may be manifested by the older adult. In our own assessment experience, a focus on behavior and social functioning has proved valuable in determining the extent to which intervention programs and approaches have supported the continued independence and adaptive functioning of clients in their community settings.

2.2. Instrumenting Assessment

Major conceptual problems discussed above continue to inhere in assessment with older persons and are especially relevant when existing psychological assessment instruments are considered. First, the problem of norms carries over into the development and use of data on various tests and their relevance to diagnostic practice with older adults. This is particularly the case in the area of intelligence and personality assessment. Most normative data for these instruments were developed in a context oriented toward nondevelopmental, pathology. Standardizing populations did not typically include older people, nor were norms adjusted for older age groups. Given the systems changes that are often associated with advanced age and the increased incidence of life stress, it is likely that existing norms may not be applicable. There are two schools of thought regarding the resolution of this problem. One holds simply that we need to develop normative data on older adults populations for the spectrum of instruments we now have available. A second approach, emerging in the form of life-span developmental psychology, suggests that, as with cross-cultural issues, there is a need to reconceptualize what we want to assess and the patterns of behavior important to adaptive versus pathological functioning. The latter view is supported by evidence for differences in motivation and in criteria for "success" at any point along the developmental continuum. It can be suggested that modifications in norms for scores cannot, in the absence of structural changes in the instruments themselves, correct for different manifestations of social desirability, presenting "good," or "bad," or other variables related to the assessment situation in which older adults differ from younger.

Second, and directly related to the problem of performance variance, sensory and neural deficits can present serious difficulties for current techniques that assume fairly intact capabilities in both areas as a condition of responding. Although this problem area in assessment is a familiar one for those in mental retardation, existing techniques have not shown the sensitivity to subtle changes in capability or deficit that are often encountered with older adults. Since many current techniques emphasize client self-report or actual client completion of forms, there are difficulties in ensuring that clients can, in fact, meet the baseline response assumptions with which instruments were developed. In most mental health settings serving older adults, interviews serve as the basic mode for all assessment activities even when portions provide for client completion of forms. This provides an active entry point to check assumptions about the adult's response capabilities. This is important because of the tendency of many older adults to mask sensory deficits in order to avoid the possiblity of being judged too impaired to be allowed to continue living independently. A number of authors have addressed problems in communications (e.g., Oyer & Oyer, 1976) with the older adult, and the capacity to deal with these problems become invaluable for those who would do assessment with older people.

2.3. Psychological Assessment

Clearly, the increased role of life events as situational stressors implies, as experience confirms, the greater frequency of depression and other affective disorders as the major psychological problem area confronting the geriatric clinician. Because of this, it seems more useful to focus on symptom scales in assessment than on in-depth personality assessments. Although the use of multiaxial inventories (e.g., MCMI, MMPI, 16PF,) is likely to yield both types of information, it is not likely that such extensive procedures can be viable in many clinic settings serving older adults. In the sense that one may be forced to choose which information to obtain (as we have had to do), symptom scales and inventories (e.g., the Beck Depression Inventory; Beck & Beck, 1972) that are brief and focus on affective disorders are more viable and informative with older adult populations.

Because of the role neural and sensory deficits in assessment performance, procedures must provide for a reliable indication of the extent to which basic impairments are present and the implications of this impairment for both other assessments as well as response to treatment. Coupled with this, it is our view that changes in psychological functioning (e.g., changes in assessed levels of depressive symptoms) should be only part of the total profile. Although social functioning is admittedly difficult to assess except by self-reports, we have found it possible to gauge this to some degree. This is valuable first because it can indicate areas of life where stressors may exist and second because many treatment or supportive interventions should, in the process of addressing psychological functioning, have some effect on the older person's ability to function. Given that our objective should be the extension and enhancement of the older person's independent and adaptive functioning in community settings, assessment procedures should provide for including this in both the presenting clinical profile and in termination or outcome assessment profiles.

3. Therapy and Clinical Practice

3.1. Efficacy

Articles on psychotherapy and the elderly invariably begin with a note on the historic neglect of service provided to the elderly by mental health professionals except perhaps for custodial care (Rechtschaffen, 1959; Small, 1979; Butler & Lewis, 1973). Psychologists have not been immune to this criticism and Gottesman (1977), for one, points out that clinical service is the most notable area within the broader field of gerontology in which contributions by psychology are lacking.

In attemtping to account for this neglect of clinical services for the elderly, one must consider the pessimism that psychotherapists have traditionally felt toward the efficacy of psychological treatment for the elderly—a pessimism that does not appear to have strong scientific grounds.

It is true that Freud was somewhat skeptical about the successful application of pyschoanalytic techniques to the elderly. In fact, Freud even questioned the utility of psychoanalysis for individuals approaching their fifties. He argued that older people were too rigid to be educated and that the accumulation of psychic material over the years would prolong therapy indefinitely. Hollender (1952) has argued a third point: "Perhaps the best explanation for the fact that analysis is not a procedure for people in their fifties and over is that there is not enough to hope for in the near future to provide the motivation needed to endure the tensions mobilized by the analysis" (p. 342).

Whether these arguments are valid or not is open to dispute. As early as 1919, Abraham (1978) reported anecdotal evidence for the successful treatment of older individuals (with psychoanalysis). Rechtschaffen (1959) chronicles the adaptations made by various clinicians in applying psychoanalytic practices to the elderly.

It may, in fact, be true that traditional psychoanalysis is not the treatment of choice for the elderly. That is not the argument here. The point here is that one must be careful not to equate traditional psychoanalysis with psychotherapy. Even if Frued's hypothesis concerning the efficacy of psychoanalysis for the elderly is correct, there are a host of other schools of psychotherapy, therapeutic modalities, and techniques of intervention that may be effective modes for effecting behavior change. The fact is, there is little sound basis in theory for excluding the elderly from psychotherapy.

The scientific literature also provides little support for the exclusion of the elderly from psychotherapy. Levy, Dirogatis, Gallagher, and Gate (1980) point out that well-executed outcome studies of psychotherapy and the elderly are sparse and studies of the differential effectiveness of two or more modalities are nonexistent. Ironically, they attribute the impoverished state of the literature to the fact that, due to referral and treatment selection biases, few elderly people are available for systematic process and outcome studies. Traditionally the elderly have simply not been treated in the community on an outpatient basis. Much of the support found for successful treatment of the elderly in outpatient psychotherapy, therefore, rests on anecdotal evidence.

A review of a series of studies by Garfield (1978) suggested that there was no relationship between age and successful outcome in psychotherapy. Levy *et al.* (1980), in reviewing the literature, conclude that at least some older adults can benefit from psychotherapy at least for short-term gain. This conclusion may be a modest one, but it does not appear to be any less modest than that which can be drawn from any other age segment of the population. It appears, then, that most of the pessimism of mental health professionals concerning the effectiveness of psychotherapy for the elderly is based less on science than on emotion.

Butler and Lewis (1973) suggest that biases and the misconceptions of mental health professions have created a professional agism, which has systematically excluded the elderly from psychotherapeutic services. They state:

> Countertransference in the classic sense occurs when mental health personnel find themselves perceiving and reacting to older persons in ways that are inappropriate and reminiscent of previous patterns of relating to parents, siblings, and other key childhood figures . . . . Agism takes this a step further. Staff members not only have to deal with leftover feelings from their personal pasts . . . they must also be aware of a multitude of negative cultural attitudes toward the elderly which pervade social institutions as well as individual psyches.(p. 142)

Butler's (1975) perception concerning the existence of professional agism may apply more to the past than the present. At least it does not appear to be as widespread a phenomenon today as it once was. The literature reflects a gradual break down of myths and misconceptions regarding the elderly and a growing awareness of their real capabilities. Concomitant with this is an increasing awareness of the possibilities that psychotherapy holds for the elderly. If articles on psychotherapy and the elderly begin with a note on the historic neglect and pessimism about treating the elderly, these articles go on to sound a more optimistic note for the future.

3.2. Technique

A special section on psychotherapy for the elderly client implies that treatment of the elderly is somehow different from the treatment of adults in other phases of the life span. Although it is true that important revisions in the treatment of the elderly must be made (Busse & Pfeiffer, 1977), it is also important for the clinician to remember that the elderly client, being a responsible adult, can be treated with many of the same methods of psychotherapy as other adults.

Thus the elderly can be treated by all schools of psychotherapy, from behavioral to gestalt to psychodynamic. Further, all therapeutic modalities are appropriate to them—including individual, group, couples, and family therapy—as are a variety of goals, from crises intervention to supportive therapy to personality reconstruction.

Despite the fact that psychotherapy for the elderly client parallels psychotherapy for adults of other ages in many essential ways, some generalizations can be made about the differences between treatment for the elderly and that for other age groups. Two notes of caution are in order: (1) these statements are not applicable to all elderly individuals, they merely indicate trends, and (2) these statements cannot necessarily be applied exclusively to treatment of the elderly. For example, in the discussion of elderly client's attitudes toward treatment that follows, the attitudes indicated are not universally held by all elderly clients; in turn, they *are* representative of the attitudes of at least a small segment of a population that is not elderly.

Differences in psychotherapy for the elderly can roughly be divided into two categories. First, there are those differences that appear to be cohort-related. These differences emanate from the specific history of the current generation of elderly and do not appear to be age-related. Future generations of elderly may not require these different approaches to treatment. Second, there are those differences in treatment that do appear to be age-related. These differences stem from the unique physical, social, and psychological changes that confront the elderly. These treatment differences can be expected to apply to future generations of elderly.

3.2.1. Cohort-Related Differences

When doing psychotherapy with the elderly, one must keep in mind that a majority of them were born before Freud published his initial papers on psychoanalysis. The attitudes that these elderly have toward the treatment of emotional-behavioral problems are quite different from those held by the generation born after World War II and raised during the keyday of the human potential movement.

These attitudes held by the elderly have implications for (1) whether the elderly come for psychotherapy, (2) the kinds of problems they present, (3) the kind of help they expect to receive, and (4) the kind of help they eventually will accept.

For the present generation of elderly, the idea of seeking help for an emotional/behavioral problem is generally a foreign one. To them, it is natural to seek medical attention when one is physically ill. For help with spirtual problems, one might turn to a respected member of the family or a religious leader in the community for counseling. Among members of that generation, individuals who had serious psychological problems were cared for by families or put into long-term facilities to seek psychological services, then, was equated with being crazy.

As a result, the elderly associate a great stigma with seeking psychological help. Many come for treatment only on the recommendation of a physician or family members and are often in need of assurance that their need for psychological services does not mean they are crazy. Perhaps the foremost task of the clinical psychologist is outreach in the community to raise the consciousness of the elderly concerning the value of psychotherapy in an overall attempt to destigmatize the seeking of psychological services.

Elderly individuals will often present somatic concerns in their initial complaints; this is partly due to the fact they feel it is more acceptable to present physical problems than it is to present emotional ones. The elderly are often unaware of what psychotherapy is and may expect to be given medication for whatever problems they are experiencing. They may not be aware of nor perceive the value of "talking therapies," and they tend not to be psychologically minded.

The elderly most often come to treatment in the face of one or more major losses (either real or symbolic); the goal of therapy then becomes to help the individual regain his or her premorbid level of adjustment. The elderly individual rarely comes to therapy for "personal growth," and personality reconstruction is unlikely to be accepted as a goal of therapy. Action-oriented, time-limited, problem-solving therapies seem more acceptable to the elderly than long-term, introspective, insight-oriented treatments.

3.2.2. Age-Related Differences

The *parameters of psychotherapy* sometimes need to be modified in working with the elderly client. Weinberg (1957) suggests that therapy may be done over a shorter period of time with increased frequency of sessions. A number of other modifications are suggested (Rechtschaffen, 1959; Ronch & Maizler, 1977). These include greater activity on the part of the therapist, since the aging adult may not be able to assume as much responsibility for the conduct of the session as younger patients do. Therapy might better be gradually tapered off rather than abruptly terminated, since the kind of relationship that is built up may not be available in the patient's milieu. Thus it may be necessary to see the patient on an intermittent basis with longer intervals between sessions rather than concluding treatment suddenly.

It is important to be conscious of the physical decrements of aging. Consequently, the facial cues or intonational variations that therapists use with younger and unimpaired patients may well be inappropriate. The awareness of hearing impairments creates difficulty, as, for example, in attempting to deliver reassuring messages at a volume loud enough to be heard by the hard of hearing. This is especially important in group psychotherapy, where the multidirectional nature of verbal communications can complicate the participation of a hearing-impaired patient. The use of microphones and speakers in group settings with the elderly, although somewhat cumbersome and intrusive, often helps the psychotherapist to make sure that the group effort will be maximized.

An extremely important consideration for the geriatric psychotherapist is the application of his or her knowledge of common physical illnesses among the elderly to specific patients. These chronic, debilitating diseases interfere with the communication process and may mask the etiology of particular modes of communication or behavior modifications (Maizler & Solomon, 1976). Often the elderly person's expressions, comprehension, and intuition suffer commensurately with the degree of physical impairment. Reduced physical strength may necessitate the shortening of the usual length of group sessions. The elderly often show a decrease in attention span or duration of response. Therefore, the therapist must plan sessions very carefully, since there is often less time to achieve goals.

The *content of psychotherapy* is, of course, geared to the developmental issues associated with aging. In this vein, Ronch and Maizler (1977) point out:

> Unlike the child, adolescent or younger adult, our treatment of the older adult is aided by neither biology (as in the developmental progression in children) or society. We cannot hope that the aged will outgrow the problem, receive increased familial or educational support, or find satisfaction in different vocational choices, living arrangements, peer group changes, or life style adjustments. Unfortunately, but realistically, most of our elderly will not likely experience any radical biosocial changes of a progressive or enhancing nature. Rather, the elderly will continue to experience decrements in biological and, to some extent, psychological functioning as they age. Our direction and perspective in individual psychotherapy must therefore be adjusted to meet the needs of these patients. (p. 277)

A younger aged group of about 55 to 65 are in a transition phase from the middle years to the later years. These individuals often have regrets about moving on in years, concerns about what their later years will bring, and in some instances have already begun to experience some of the losses that will be the hallmark of the later years. An older age group, although more accepting of having grown old than this younger group, enter therapy in the face of the many losses associated with growing older. These individuals must often deal with the loss of their social role, the death of their spouse or child, and the decline of their physical and cognitive abilities. Elderly individuals often come to therapy for help in coping with their own impending death. Reminiscence becomes a critical part of treatment of the elderly as individuals attempt to put their lives in perspective, acknowledging their successes and accepting their failures in terms of both individual accomplishments and interpersonal relationships.

The goal of the clinician is to help the individual who is moving into old age to accept the aging process and to choose an adaptive life pattern for this stage of life. With the older elderly client, the clinician must support the individual in the face of some of the major losses that occur in these years and attempt and help him or her come to some resolution concerning approaching death while also supporting the search for meaning in what remains of life.

Another important issue that is often neglected in working with the elderly is the heightened resurgence of dependency conflicts, with increased manifestations of ambivalence and anger toward the providers of dependency gratification and the correlated fear of abandonment (Ronch & Maizler, 1977). Goldfarb (1969) argues that independence will never be achieved in the elderly and that psychotherapy should instead aim at making the person less dependent. He defines progress in therapy as the therapist's acceptance of the role of surrogate parent and the patient's adjustment to this relationship, thus allowing the patient to grow more independent only within its context.

Transference and countertransference patterns are also different in therapy with the elderly. Hiatt (1971) noted the complexity of transference phenomena among the elderly; this is due in part to the great age differences between client and therapist and also to the many and various roles played by important people in the elderly patient's life. Small (1979) outlines four typical transferences reactions: (1) parental transference, whereby the client attaches omnipotence to the therapist and becomes extremely dependent; (2) a peer or sibling transference, whereby the therapist is taken on as a colleague of the client; (3) a child transference, whereby the therapist is seen as a needing child; (4) an erotic and sexual transference.

Because the therapist is often younger, the older client often claims that the therapist lacks insight, not knowing what it is like to be old. This attitude should be subjected to vigorous examination. Lines of communications may be opened when the therapist points out that the feelings generated by chronic illnesses are not age-specific, that professional training overcomes some of the years of difference, and to categorize him or her as a younger person may represent the same stereotypical thinking that characterizes generalizations about the elderly.

With regard to countertransference reactions, Stern, Smith, and Frank (1953) have spoken of the therapist's reaction to the perceived helplessness of the elderly client, which often creates feelings of anxiety or hostility in the therapist. Meerloo (1955) has discussed the difficulty therapists have in dealing with the sexual feelings and sexual problems of the elderly. He suggests that the therapist's own conflicts over sexuality may lead him or her to the unrealistic notion that the elderly should be beyond sin and sex.

Grotjahn (1955) has discussed the countertransference implications of the reversed transference constellation, that is, the tendency of the older person to perceive the therapist as his or her child. He states: "The good son-therapist should not feel guilty for being younger. If necessary he may develop an almost paternal attitude. He must be secure enough to withstand the onslaught of the older patient's hostility and [the patient's] attempt to make the younger man feel guilty and defensive for being young" (p. 423).

Finally, *psychotherapy with the elderly client*, more so than with any other age group, must be coordinated with many different physical and mental health services. The elderly often take medication for physical problems, and the clinician must be aware of possible negative interactions between this medication and the psychotropic medication. The psychologist must work closely with a competent psychiatrist who is knowledgeable in working with the elderly.

The elderly client is also likely to be in need of some social service, and the psychologist must be prepared to refer the client to appropriate community agencies. Here the clinician must gauge the abilities of his elderly client and have him or her do as much of the legwork as possible.

4. Research

Recent years have seen a manifold increase in the amount of research devoted to characterizing psychological functioning in older adults. The broad array of research directions and accumulated findings is best illustrated by a brief review of chapter topics in Birren and Schaie's (1977) handbook on the psychology of aging. Although many address more traditional areas of psychological inquiry—such as perception, sensory processes, learning, and personality—other suggest newer and more integrative areas of concern such as "environment" and "stress," which are used as rubrics for considering a variety of interrelated physical, psychological, and social processes. This more integrative perspective has been a feature of much thinking about human aging (e.g., Kart, Metress, & Metress, 1978), but broader attention is now being given to such approaches within psychological training—for example, the behavioral medicine programs focusing on a biopsychosocial perspective on behavior. There is, perhaps, no other developmental stage where this approach to behavior is more appropriate or more needed. To the psychologist as geriatric clinician, the older person presents an aggregate of changes in physical capabilities (Saxon & Etten, 1978), social and interpersonal roles (Butler & Lewis, 1973), and psychological orientations toward the self and the surrounding environment (Glenwick & Whitbourne, 1978). The etiology and implications of these changes as revealed in research are of central concern to the psychologist in the role of geriatric clinician. The brevity of this discussion forbids any attempt at an exhaustive review of findings relevant to psychological functioning of the older adult. Rather, it seems more productive here to focus on some structural aspects of research on aging that are important to the professional's own ongoing review of new findings.

We seek here to give the psychologist assuming the role of geriatric clinician some exposure to the current state of the art in terms of approaches to research on aging and other research problems and directions likely to yield results with clinical relevance.

Specifically, we would like to first consider designs for research on aging and, in particular, perspectives on the utility of findings from longitudinal, cross-sectional, and single-sample designs. We will also attempt to highlight aspects of the field-research approach most often found in aging research and contrast them with the laboratory focus that has more widely characterized research in social and personality psychology. Second, we will offer some discussion of emerging areas of integrative research to illustrate what the literature on aging is likely to contain in the future. We will focus here on mental function, stress, and correlates of "risk" in older persons as well as on person–environment research in aging as examples of some of the areas where major issues need resolution and in which research directions now being explored are likely to develop findings relevant to clinical work with other adults.

4.1. Designs in Aging Research

Although distinctions between cross-sectional and longitudinal research designs are a major feature of current training for developmental psychologists, their respective applications to behavioral issues in aging have features not often encountered in work with children and adolescents. The basic distinction remains between longitudinal designs that follow a sample (or samples) of people over time versus cross-sectional approaches that select samples of people of differing age ranges to reflect different time spans. Although not always formally structured as a "cross-sectional" design, a research design stratifying age as a factor may generally be viewed in this context. Cross-sectional research designs provide an approach to examining differences among samples of different ages or age ranges in single-point assessment. Such approaches, however, leave unclear whether obtained effects are *age effects* relating to the aging process or to "being older," *cohort effects* relating to when one was born (which is *per se* covaried with age), or *period effects* relating to being a particular age at (1) the point when the study is done or (2) a particular time in the life cycle (e.g., draft age in time of war). The three do not represent similar sources of variation even though these effects are concurrent. More often, they are confounded with their individual effects, which are separable only in well-designed longitudinal studies. For the research community concerned with the development and extension of basic knowledge about the aging process and its impact on behavior, the longitudinal study with cross-sectioned birth cohorts is a preferred approach to achieving the most reliable and valid estimates of the effects on behavior and psychological functioning due to aging as a process versus other factors covarying with age.

However, we would suggest that other designs have great potential utility for the psychologist as geriatric clinician. The basic issue involves the extent to which one seeks results that describe a "true" effect of aging as a process or whether one seeks more simply to describe "older people" as that population now exists. For example, if we consider sample subjects 60 years of age and older in studies conducted between 1970 and 1980, our results concern people born between 1910 and 1920. In terms of generalizing results from these birth cohorts to future elderly cohorts, the question can be raised with respect to the *source* of the observed differences; are the differences associated with that particular age *per se* or with the unique character of the particular time periods through which one has lived. Although the concern is valid, it may not be of pressing concern to the clinician seeking to utilize research findings in service of greater awareness or skills in dealing with problems of older adults. The psychologist in the role of geriatric clinician should consider the subjective utilities involved in either reviewing or accomplishing research. In many cases, the most informative research might be that which simply but reliably relates physical, psychological, or social factors to behavior patterns in groups of older adults. Major clinical interest is likely to focus on patterns of behavior associated with types of events, physiological conditions, drug therapies, or other characteristrics found with greater frequency in older adult populations. These informational agendas can be well served by study designs of a nonlongitudinal type. The major caveat in considering the implications of the various approaches is that the researcher must know the extent of information available from a study design as well as the information likely to be lacking or confounded in the design when it is used in a particular setting for aging research.

Within clinical settings focusing on the mental health needs of older persons, the practitioner confronts several issues that can be addressed by extant reports and published findings from other populations of older people. Behavioral patterns or corrolaries of behavioral patterns identified in the literature can be used to develop a better sense of the normative with respect to older people and thus perhaps improve one's grounds for diagnosing pathological or problem behavior. In considering published research on assessment, intervention strategies, or outcome assessment, the best yardstick to use in judging the utility of the research is not the extent to which designs are of the preferred longitudinal type but rather the extent to which the findings are relevant with respect to personal or presenting problem characteristics of the population with which one is involved. One fortunate feature of much behavioral research on aging is the often extensive listing of sociodemographic characteristics of study populations. These can be extremely useful in deciding the extent to which particular findings have implications for the populations involved in one's own work. For example, many reviews of assessment tools and scales (e.g., Salzman, Kochansky, Shader, & Cronin, 1972; Salzman, Shader, Kochansky, & Cronin, 1972) provide information on the types of populations with which instruments were standardized or used. Much of the work usually referred to as being in the area of "social gerontology" presents sample information in terms of gender, age strata, physical health, and social characteristics. The extensive demographic characterization practiced in sociological work and, to some extent, in "community psychology," has been carried forward in much of the literature on aging because of the early involvement of these disciplines in aging. Also, research on aging requires samples of "real people" rather than undergraduate psychology students, who have long comprised the populations used by social psychologists. Therefore, it has been necessary to pay increased attention to the role of sample characteristics in results. In reviewing research or contemplating their own investigations, the psychologists must consider the structure of samples and their role in the study's design to a much greater degree than has been our usual practice.

4.2. Issue Areas in Aging Research

4.2.1. Mental Function

The nature and etiology of changes in mental functioning with aging probably represent the most compelling area for the application of the "behavioral medicine" type of approach now becoming current in psychological training. As has been alluded to elsewhere, it is an issue that requires amplification of knowledge in physiology, particularly neurophysiology, as well as in behavioral psychology. The major task before us is an accurate differentiation of neural deficits and their etiology from more psychogenic changes in the ability to process and recall information.

Research seeking to understand and specify the dynamics and effects of the aging process on mental functioning should be a major concern of the psychologist assuming the role of geriatric clinician. The notion of senility has attended our views of human aging for some time. The major behavioral features related to this condition include loss of short-term memory, confusion about present or recent past events, and a general loss of mental acuity in the sense of being oriented to persons, places, and times. Although many professionals had taken more cautious views, the dominant picture *was* one of senility as being inevitably and irreversably associated with aging because the major etiology was thought to be damage to or loss of neural tissue in the central nervous system and hence a corresponding effect on behavior. Advances in recent years have begun to suggest that the relationship between age-related changes in the brain and observable behavioral changes is far more complex. Since assumptions about mental abilities (i.e., memory, problem solving, intelligence) play a central role in mental health assessment and intervention, it is incumbent on the geriatric clinician to be familiar with the issues and problems surrounding mental function in aging and to be aware of new knowledge that can sharpen diagnostic techniques and offer better specification of etiology.

Brocklehurst and Handley (1976) provide an introduction to the problem in a text for medical students by considering mental confusion as a description of mental function and not a diagnosis. This is both accurate and important. Although such states may arise from chronic brain syndrome also known as senile dementia (an organic condition associated with changes in neural function and composition) or from other diseases ranging from cerebral hypoxia (insufficient oxygenation of the brain), they can also be traced to nutritional deficiencies or severe depression. The salient distinction here is that mental confusion or loss function as manifested in behavior may be viewed as being symptomatic or functional (e.g., severe depression) and thus can be ameliorated via potential interventions. It is the former (e.g., organic brain syndromes) that are more likely to result in a protracted, steady decline in mental ability. Clearly, the decision as to the source of mental confusion or seeming loss of basic function has fundamental implications for any course of intervention or treatment. Although techniques such as the Mental Status Questionaire have been utilized to develop some indication of the severity of the problem, we must accept the fact that, at best, our tools for identification and characterization of underlying causes is behavioral while many of the supposed sources (e.g., neuronal changes, formation of lesions) are physiological. Further, stress, depression, and other psychogenic causes can and do underlie behavior patterns present with many of the correlates of dementia of the type understood to be chronic. For those seeking greater sophistication, the recent work by Nandy (1978) and selected chapters on neural functioning in Birren and Schaie (1977) and Brocklehurst and Handley (1976) are commended to the reader.

The major and most needed thrusts of current research focus primarily on characterizing what appear to be a variety of distinct types of neurophysiological conditions, all of which are associated with overt clinical evidence of loss of mental function and confusional states. But there remains evidence for the role of depression, stress, nutrition, and other potentially reversible conditions in the population of similar symptom constellations. The characterization of conditions is the first step toward improved differential diagnostics, more accurate characterization of patient conditions, and more effective medical and psychological approaches to treatment.

4.2.2. Life Stress and Risk in Aging

There is increasing evidence that life events associated more with aging for current groups of older persons have much to do with the mental health problems and behavior disorders so widely associated with being older in this society. Perhaps two of the most relevant aspects of the concept of stress as related to clinical work with older adults are the notion of cumulative stress effects and the related notion of life events which, through major stress loadings, appear to "age" the individual in the behavioral sense. Although stress remains a rather difficult construct to employ, there is a growing consensus that it involves not only psychological reactions such as tension and anxiety but also physiological reactions in the form of endocrine secretions and other neural responses (Eisdorfer & Wilkie, 1977). There has been a steadily emerging interest in behavioral and psychosocial factors related to health problems since Rosenman, Friedman, Straus, Wurm, Kositchek, Han, and Werthessen (1964) began to associate stress and anxiety with a higher incidence of cardiovascular disease. The Holmes and Rahe (1967) Social Readjustment Rating Scale embodies a checklist of life events that are indexed in terms of their potential for providing anxiety and stress. This is clearly an area with relevance to aging. Although views of normative aging as being a process of progressive social disengagement (e.g., Cummings & Henry, 1961) have not been supported by recent findings, there is a recognition that aging brings with it a greater likelihood and frequency of events that can raise anxiety through demands for adaptive responses (e.g., loss of spouse or significant others through death, loss of valued work roles, loss of economic status and resources).

The concept of stress remains elusive because of the wide range of individual differences in responses to "stressful" life events, and recent evidence suggests that the dynamics of stress adaption in aging may play a major role in the onset of or susceptibility to physical and mental health problems experienced by many older people. Lowenthal and Chiriboga (1973) suggested a view of adaptation in terms of demands versus resources for adaptation, with disparities in the two being associated with stress. Clearly, much evidence indicates that aging does present this situation more frequently than is the case for other age spans in the life cycle. It remains a major task for research to elaborate more fully models that can relate adaptive demand and response capabilities to the levels of stress experienced by older adults. Given the evidence supporting the negative effects of long-term stress, it is clear that "better" as well as longer aging can be facilitated by such findings.

4.2.3. Person–Environment Research

There has been strong interest in environment and aging over the past decade. The work of Lawton (1980) has recently extended into a more transactional view of relationships between environment on the one hand and the person on the other. In some senses, the conceptual approach here is reminiscent of that described previously for stress. Many problems in aging, such as impairments in the activities of daily living and social interaction, seem to be effectively modeled in terms of the relationships between demands or opportunities present in an environment or situation and the ability of the person to respond or adapt to these demands or opportunities. In activities of daily living, many of which are instrumental behaviors (e.g., shopping, cooking, dressing), there is a growing recognition that the structure of physical environments can affect the extent to which older people with given levels of physical capabilities can successfully "transact with these environments to accomplish daily tasks." Similar approaches have also been taken toward social environments and the older person's responses to them.

Major theories currently describing person–environment relations with special attention to older persons and their characteristics include congruence models (Kahana, 1980) and the adaptive range of Lawton and Nahemow (1973). These approaches to people and their environments have particular relevance to life-span views of human behavior and adaptation. They seek to activate the dynamics underlying behavioral responses (impairment, life satisfaction, utilization of social or physical environments) by viewing behavior as the result of the functional interrelation between environmental characteristics demanding or inhibiting behavior and the person's capabilities to utilize or adapt to these contingencies. What is most encouraging about these approaches is the potential they suggest for understanding and modifying environmental characteristics in ways that can produce optimal environments stimulating to the older person, thus avoiding excessive dependencies, yet that do not over-stimulate and thus stress the adaptive capabilities of older persons.

5. Concluding Statement

The field of psychological care for the aging is evolving and gaining sophistication at a relatively rapid pace. Thus, we must emphasize that the field as a whole, including that part which is most relevant to the psychologist as geriatric clinician, is more diverse and complex than we have been able to review. The "principles" of aging have a dynamic quality that the psychologist is unlikely to find in other, more established areas of work. It is an immensely fertile ground for the psychologist utilizing the perspective of behavioral medicine. For the psychologist, the effects of the physical, psychological, and social dimensions of aging are unsurpassed in their ability to challenge and reward.

6. References

Abraham, K. The Applicability of psychoanalytic treatment to patients at an advanced age. In S. Steury & M.L. Blank (Eds.), *Readings in Psychotherapy with Older People*. National Institute of Mental Health, DHEW Publication No. (ADM) 78–409, 1978. (Originally published, 1919.)

Beck, A. T., & Beck, R. W. Screening depressed patients in family practice: A rapid technique. *Postgraduate Medicine*, 1972, 52 81–85.

Bellak, L. Psychological aspects of normal aging. In L. Bellak & B.D. Tokso (Eds.), *Geriatric Psychiatry*. New York: Grune & Stratton, 1976.

Birren, J. E., & Schaie, K. W. *Handbook of the psychology of aging*. New York: Van Nostrand Reinhold, 1977.

Brink, T. L. Geriatric Psychotherapy. In E. Busse & E. Pfeiffer (Eds.), *Behavior and adaptation in later life* (2nd ed.). Boston: Little, Brown, 1977.

Brocklehurst, J. C., & Hanley, T. *Geriatric Medicine for Students*. Edinburgh, Scotland: Churchill Livingstone, 1976.

Busse, E. and Pfeiffer, E. Functional psychiatric disorders in old age. In E. Busse & E. Pfeiffer (Eds.), *Behavior and adaptation in later life*. (2nd ed.). Boston: Little, Brown, 1977.

Butler, R. *Why survive: Growing old in America*. New York: Harper & Row, 1975.

Butler, R., & Lewis, M. *Aging and mental health: Positive psychosocial approaches*. St. Louis: Mosby, 1973.

Cummings, E., & Henry, W. *Growing old: The process of disengagement*. New York: Basic Books, 1961.

Eisdorfer, C., & Wilkie, F. Stress, disease, aging and behavior. In J. E. Birren & K. W. Schaie (Eds.), *Handbook of the psychology of aging.* New York: Van Nostrand Reinhold, 1977.

Garfield, S. L. Research on client variables in psychotherapy. In S. L. Garfield & A. E. Bergin (Eds.), *Handbook of psychotherapy and behavior change.* New York: Wiley, 1978.

Glenwick, D. S. & Whitbourne, S. K. Beyond despair and disengagement: A transactional model of personality development and later life. *International Journal of Aging and Human Development,* 1978, *6,* 261–267.

Goldfarb, A. *The psychodynamics of depending and the search for aid in the dependencies of old people.* Ann Arbor, Mich.: Institute of Gerontology, University of Michigan, 1969.

Gottesman, L. E. Clinical psychology and aging: A role model. In D. Gentry (Ed.), *Geropsychology: A model of training and clinical service.* Cambridge, Mass.: Ballinger, 1977.

Green I., Fedewa B. E., Deardorff, H. L., Johnston, C. A., & Jackson W. M. *Housing for the elderly: The development and design process.* New York: Van Nostrand Reinhold, 1975.

Grotjahn, M. Analytic psychotherapy with the elderly. *Psychoanalytic Review.* 1955, *42,* 419–427.

Hendricks, J. & Hendricks, C. D. *Aging in mass society: Myths and realities.* Cambridge, Mass.: Winthrop, 1977.

Hiatt, H. Dynamic psychotherapy with the aging patient. *American Journal of Psychotherapy,* 1971, *25* (4), 591–600.

Hollender, M. H. Individualizing the aged. *Social Casework,* 1952, *33,* 337–342.

Holmes, T. H., & Rahe, R. H. The Social Readjustment Rating Scale. *Journal of Psychosomatic Research.* 1967, *2,* 213–218.

Kahana, E. A congruence model of person–environment interaction. In M. P. Lawton, P. G. Windley, & T. O. Byerts (Eds.), *Aging and the environment directions and perspectives.* New York: Garland STPM Press, 1980.

Kalish, R. A., *The later years: Social implications of gerontology.* Belmont, Calif.: Brooks/Cole, 1977.

Kart, C. S., Metress, E. S., & Metress, J. F. *Health and aging: Biological and social perspectives.* Menlo Park, Calif.: Addison-Wesley, 1978.

Kraus, A. S., Spasoff, R. A., Beattie, E. J., Holden, D. E. W., Lawson, J. S., Rodenburg, M., & Woodcock, G. M. Elderly applicants to long term care institutions: II. The application process; Placement and care needs. *Journal of the American Geriatrics Society,* 1976, *24* (8), 364–467.

Lawton, M. P. *Environment and Aging.* Belmont, Calif: Brooks/Cole, 1980.

Lawton, M. P., & Nahemow, L. Ecology and the aging process. In C. Eisdorfer & M. P. Lawton (Eds.), *Psychology of adult development and aging.* Washington, D.C.: American Psychological Association, 1973.

Levy, S. M., Dirogatis, L. R., Gallagher, D., & Gate, M. Intervention with older adults and the evaluation of outcome. In Poon, L. W. (Ed.) *Aging in the 1980s: Psychological Issues.* Washington, D.C.: American Psychological Association, 1980.

Lowenthal, M. F., & Chiriboga D. Social stress and adaptation: Toward a life-course perspective. In C. Eisdorfer & M. P. Lawton (Eds.) *The psychology of adult development and aging.* Washington, D.C.: American Psychological Association. 1973.

Maizler, J., & Solomon, J. "Therapeutic group process with the institutional elderly. *Journal of the American Geriatrics Society,* 1976, *24* (12), 542–546.

Meerloo, J. A. Transference and resistance in geriatric psychotherapy. *Psychoanalytic Review,* 1955, *42,* 72–82. Miami Herald. *Medicare share of costs decreases.* October 4, 1980.

Nandy, K. (Ed.). *Senile dementia: A biomedical approach.* New York: Elsevier/North Holland Biomedical Press, 1978.

Oyer, H. J., & Oyer, E. J. (Eds). *Aging and communication.* Baltimore: University Park Press, 1976.

Pfeiffer, E. (Ed.). *Multidimensional functional assessment: The OARS methodology.* Durham, N.C.: Center for the Study of Aging and Human Development, 1975.

Polliak, M. R., & Shavitt, N. Utilization of hospital in-patient services by the elderly. *Journal of The American Geriatric Society,* 1977, *25* (8), 364–367.

Rechtschaffen, A. Psychotherapy with geriatric patients: A review of the literature. *Journal of Gerontology,* 1959, *14,* 73.

Ronch, J. & Maizler, J. Individual psychotherapy with the intitutionalized aged. *American Journal of Orthopsychiatry,* 1977, *47* (2), 275–283.

Rosenman, R. H. M., Friedman, R., Straus, M., Wurm, R., Kositchek, W., Han, W. & Werthessen, N. T. A predictive study of coronary heart diseases: The Western Collaborative Group Study. *Journal of the American Medical Association.* 1964, *189,* 15–22.

Salzman, C., Kochansky, G. E., Shader, R. T., & Cronin, D. M. Rating scales for psychotropic drug research with geriatric patients: II. Mood ratings. *Journal of the American Geriatrics Society,* 1972, *20,* 215–221.

Salzman, C., Shader, R. T., Kochansky, G. E., & Cronin D. M. Rating scales for psychotropic drug research with geratric patients: I. Behavior ratings. *Journal of the American Geriatrics Society,* 1972, *20,* 209–214.

Saxon, S., & Etten, M. *Physical change and aging: A guide for the helping professions.* New York: Tiresias Press, 1978.

Schaie, K. W., & Schaie, J. P., Clinical assessment aging. In J. E. Birren & K. W. Schaie (Eds.), *Handbook of the psychology of aging.* New York: Van Nostrand Reinhold, 1977.

Small, L. *The briefer psychotherapies.* New York: Brunner/Mazel, 1979.

Spencer, M. G., & Dorr, C. J. *Understanding aging: A multidisciplinary approach,* New York: Appleton Century Crofts, 1975.

Stern, K., Smith, J., & Frank, M. Mechanisms of transference and counter-transference in psychotherapeutic and social work with the aged. *Journal of Gerontology,* 1953, *8,* 328–332.

Task Panel Reports. Submitted to the President's Commission on Mental Health. Vol. III, appendix. U.S. Government Printing Office, Washington D.C., 1978.

Verwoerdt, A. *Clinical geropsychiatry.* Baltimore: Williams & Wilkins, 1976.

Weinberg, J. Psychotherapy of the aged. In J. Masserman & J. Moreno (Eds.), *Progress in Psychotherapy.* New York: Grune & Stratton, 1957.

Collaborative Efforts in Liaison Psychiatry

JAMES J. STRAIN

There is compelling evidence that psychological, social, and cultural—as well as biological—factors are involved to varying degrees in the initiation, course, and outcome of pathophysiological processes. Lipowski (1975) for example, has proposed an ecological viewpoint which states that "the study of every disease must include the person, his body, and his human and nonhuman environments as essential components of the total system" (p. 6). Reiser's (1975) biopsychosocial field theory of disease emphasizes the interaction and interrelationship of all systems—physical, mental, psychological, environmental, and so on. Finally, Engel (1977) has vigorously urged the adoption of a biomedicopsychosocial model of disease that would be applicable to psychological as well as physiological dysfunction and would recognize that complex interactions between the individual and his or her total environment are major determinants of health and disease. For example, such life stresses as bereavement, crowding, and so on are now considered to play a critical role in the onset and exacerbation of certain forms of physiological dysfunction. It follows, then, that psychological care is coordinate with medical care. In fact, 50 to 70 of all medical patients seen by primary-care physicians present with a primary psychological problem or manifest psychological dysfunction secondary to their physical illness (Lipowski, 1967).

The contemporary teaching hospital provides an ideal setting for treatment of the total patient. Internists, psychiatrists, and psychologists all espouse the principle that if treatment is to be effective, the patient must be viewed as a whole person. But to subscribe to this orientation cannot, in itself, ensure ade-

JAMES J. STRAIN ● Mount Sinai School of Medicine, 1 Gustave L. Levy Place, New York, New York 10029.

quate psychological care for medical patients. Humanism must be bolstered by a psychological and physiological understanding of illness behavior and of normal individual reactions to the stress of illness and hospitalization. Techniques that will facilitate the assimilation and application of this knowledge are also needed.

My purpose in this chapter is to define the ways in which this goal might be achieved and, in particular, to describe the ways in which collaboration between the psychiatry and psychology can foster holistic medical care. In short, my thesis is that enormous opportunities for collaboration between these disciplines exist in every sector of medicine—clinical, teaching, and research. My emphasis here will be on the specific collaborative opportunities presented by the "alliance" model of liaison psychiatry (Strain & Spikes, 1977).

1. The Precepts of Liaison Psychiatry

Teaching programs in psychological medicine can, I believe, be conceptualized in terms of the autonomous model, the integrated model, the alliance model, and the team model. In the autonomous model, devised by George Engel at the University of Rochester, the teacher of psychological medicine must be a nonpsychiatric physician. In fact, Engel contends that liaison psychiatry programs in which the psychiatrist serves as teacher and role model are doomed to fail (1980). More specifically, in Engel's approach the psychiatrist is used as a "primary messenger" the faculty and their fellows are "secondary messengers," and the medical practitioner is conceived of as a "tertiary messenger." If medical practitioners are adequately trained, they can diagnose, manage, and treat mental health issues or refer patients to the psychiatrist if necessary. The point Engel makes is that the medical practitioner, because of personal resistances, is not inclined to learn from the psychiatrist.

The dual trained model, devised by Shemo, Withersty, Spradlin, and Waldman (1980) at the University of West Virginia, postulates an integrated training approach in which the person acting as role model and teacher is qualified in both psychiatry and medicine. Thus the success of this program depends on whether its "protagonist" is sufficiently sophisticated and respected in each specialty to serve as teacher.

The alliance model, as conceptualized by Strain, has as its goal the formation of teaching alliances between psychiatrist and nonpsychiatrist (Strain & Grossman, 1975). This pedagogic duo then become the teachers and role models. As time goes on the nonpsychiatric physician is able to assume increased responsibility for the teaching of psychological issues, while the psychiatrist, to an increasing degree, assumes the role of resource person.

The team approach advocated in family practice programs is used by Stevens at the University of Alabama and by Bufford in social medicine programs at the Albert Einstein College of Medicine. It employs a psychiatrist as a member of the teaching faculty who functions as an equal member of an interdisciplinary team.

Finally, another group of workers feel that some aspects of psychological medicine can be taught by nonphysicians: Kagan at Michigan State has developed an immediate-feedback method to enhance sensitivity and cognitive awareness in primary-care physicians about patients and themselves.

The alliance model of liaison psychiatry, which provides the frame of reference for this chapter, evolved from the alliance teaching model. Thus it attempts to transmit psychological knowledge in a systematic manner and is an ideal mode for the dissemination of biopsychosocial data among physicians and health care workers. As noted above, the liaison psychiatrist who subscribes to this model seeks to enhance knowledge, skills, and attitudes toward psychological care among the nonpsychiatric staff, seeking to foster their ability to function with greater autonomy in the psychological sector. This model of liaison psychiatry is also unique in that it draws heavily upon the team approach for clinical care, teaching, and research. As a result, because of its structure and methodology, we believe it is a more powerful pedagogic tool than psychiatric consultation. Unlike psychiatric consultation, liaison psychiatry focuses on process rather than outcome.

The detailed discussion of the precepts of the alliance model of liaison psychiatry presented below is intended to highlight potential areas of collaboration between the psychologist and psychiatrist. These precepts include:

1. The practice of primary, secondary, and tertiary prevention
2. The fostering of diagnostic accuracy (with particular emphasis on case detection)
3. Clarification of the status of the caretaker
4. Provision of ongoing education to the nonpsychiatric staff to promote autonomy
5. The development of core biopsychosocial knowledge
6. Promotion of structural changes in the medical setting

2. The Practice of Primary, Secondary, and Tertiary Prevention

Liaison psychiatry enhances the quality of psychological care for the medically ill by using Caplan's model of prevention (1961)—that is, by anticipating and preventing the development of psychological symptoms (primary prevention); by treating such symptoms after they have developed (secondary prevention); and by rehabilitating patients who have manifested such symptoms, in order to prevent their recurrence (tertiary prevention).

Within the framework of liaison psychiatry, these prevention schemas are concerned with the predisposing, initiating, and sustaining factors that interdigitate in the biological, psychological, and social sectors of illness. Coronary heart disease can be used as an example of the application of this thesis.

The physiological factors that are thought to predispose to coronary heart disease (e.g., smoking, high serum lipids, diet, excessive body weight, the presence of other illnesses such as diabetes and hypertension, inadequate regular exercise, and genetic endowment) have been discussed at length in the literature. As a result of the combined efforts of several investigators (e.g., Friedman &

Rosenman, 1950; Jenkins, 1971; Jenkins, Rosenman, & Zyzanski, 1974), certain predisposing psychological factors—such as psychological stress; a particular personality type (Type A) described as driving, competitive, time-conscious, and the like; and socioeconomic phenomena—have been implicated as well. Admittedly, the precise nature of the interrelationship between these psychological variables and the physiological risk factors mentioned above is not yet fully understood. Nor has it been determined which combination of these variables is most pernicious in terms of the predisposition to this illness. Nevertheless, to the degree that these risk factors are known to exist, the physician is in an ideal position to counsel the vulnerable patient and thereby reduce their potential impact. More importantly, interdisciplinary collaboration in this area has resulted in the identification not only of the risk factors but also the methods for screening individuals at risk and developing modes of altering behavior (e.g., smoking, eating, lack of exercise, etc.).

The goals of secondary prevention are to reduce the factors in all three sectors that initiate the actual outbreak of coronary heart disease, to deal with the stress of illness, and to attend to the symptoms (e.g., anxiety, depression, exaggerated character traits, etc.) that frequently appear at this stage and may impede recovery. Jenkins, Zyzanski, and Rosenman (1978) have suggested that an important first step in the study of these symptoms is the categorizations of four kinds of coronary heart disease: (1) myocardial infarction, (2) silent myocardial infarction, (3) angina, and (4) sudden death. Specifically, Jenkins and his colleagues suggest that angina patients may be more reactive to their environment and more irritable, whereas acute myocardial infarction patients may be more time-conscious and competitive on the job, though not in their interpersonal interactions. From these observations, biological mechanisms that provide strategies for further collaborative research have been hypothesized.

Finally, liaison psychiatry attempts to alter the psychological sustaining factors in coronary heart disease (e.g., those psychological conflicts that result in disturbances of mood as well as in depression, anxiety, inhibitions, phobias regarding return to work and sex despite physiological competence to do so, etc.). With regard to the coronary patient, clearly, productive areas for collaboration between the liaison psychiatrist and psychologist include efforts to distinguish illness behavior from illness; to identify stresses that predispose, initiate, and sustain illness in the individual; and to understand the coping strategies employed either to prevent illness, manage illness, or lessen the chance of its recurrence.

3. The Fostering of Diagnostic Accuracy

Case detection in the medical setting is a major skill of the liaison psychiatrist; it can be further refined by collaboration with the psychologist. The organic brain syndromes, which are among the psychological disorders most frequently encountered and most frequently undetected in the contemporary teaching hospital (Lipowski, 1967; Wells, 1978) provide an excellent example of this aspect of the alliance model of liaison psychiatry and of the benefits to be derived from interdisciplinary collaboration.

Engel (1967) has estimated that 10% to 15% of all patients hospitalized on acute medical and surgical services manifest an acute organic brain syndrome (delirium) of varying severity. Delirium is present in every patient who is approaching or recovering from coma, who is terminal, who is recovering from general anesthesia, or who is drugged to the point of confusion. It is present in most patients with severe anemia, fever, peripheral circulatory collapse, cardiac arrest, congestive heart failure, respiratory failure, pulmonary insufficiency, hepatic or renal insufficiency, acidosis or alkalosis, electrolyte imbalance, or infection. It is also present in those suffering from the effects of many different drugs and from the effects on the central nervous system of almost every disease that produces a disturbance in physiological homeostasis. Yet, because of the problem their detection presents, the organic brain syndromes are also among the psychological disorders which are the most undertreated. It is generally recognized that the internist is not always able to diagnose an organic brain syndrome. But the psychiatrist and the psychologist may also have some difficulty in detecting the presence of this dysfunction. In part, these diagnostic difficulties stem from the characteristics of this patient population.

Some patients manage to conceal their mental defects, so that these problems are only apparent on direct, specific examination. The internist may not regard apathy, sleepiness, weakness, or excessive fatigue as indicative of the possible presence of an organic syndrome. And obviously, if these symptoms are not regarded as significant and no further attempt to examine the patient is made, the physician is not likely to delve deeper or request a psychiatric consultation to establish a definitive diagnosis.

Other patients with organic brain syndromes manifest such deranged behavior that it is frightening to the internist and psychiatrist alike. These patients are profoundly disturbed, showing diffuse anxiety, agitation, and bizarre mental and motor behavior. Internists do not hesitate to request psychiatric consultation in such cases, but their aim is to press for the patient's transfer to the psychiatric service.

A third group of organic patients manifest, to varying degrees, the psychological and behavioral disturbances that characterize patients in the first two categories. If the patient is confused, disoriented, forgetful—and elderly—the internist may, without further attempts at diagnosis, automatically ascribe his or her behavior to the presence of degenerative brain disease and initiate plans for the patient's disposition. If, on the other hand, the patient is young, the internist may interpret the behavioral disturbance as evidence of a functional disorder.

Clinical neuropsychological approaches to diagnosis of the organic brain syndromes are categorized as (1) "fixed battery," involving the administration of a comprehensive, invariant series of tests, and (2) "branching or adjustive," calling for selection of tests according to the reason for referral, background data, and findings obtained during an interview which may suggest the presence of specific deficits and gauge the patient's ability to cooperate (Levin, 1981).

Until recently, the contemporary teaching hospital's primary diagnostic tool in the organic brain syndromes was the conventional Mental Status Examination (Figure 1), which, it is generally recognized, may not be sufficiently sensitive to its task. As is well known, several workers have now identified defects in the standard mental status examination. For example, Talland (1965) found that even patients with severe Korsakoff's psychosis performed adequately on the part of the examination designed to test memory by requiring the patient to repeat a series of digits forward (digit span). Tests that take these possibilities into account are now available. Others have been constructed that allow for quantifiable and reproducible results and which consider the issues of age and demographic background (Mattis, 1979). Schwartz (1981) has developed a delayed recall and interposed task that has significantly enhanced the discriminatory diagnostic power of the routine digit-span test. Other workers have also tried to develop more sensitive measures. As most psychologists know, concretization of thought is one of the most frequent results of brain damage or cortical

---

MENTAL STATUS EXAMINATION

General Information

1. Level of consciousness: alert, lethargic, stuporous, stable, fluctuating
2. Cooperation: good, fair, poor
3. Reliability of information provided
4. Motor status: posture
5. Affect: appropriate–inappropriate, euphoric–depressed, liabile–flat
6. Language: expression, comprehension, coherence, voice quality (pitch, intensity, rate of speech, etc.), relevance, productivity, deviations
7. Patterns of thought: depressive, obsessive, paranoid, hypochondriacal; evidence of presence of illusions, hallucinations, delusions

Specific Information

1. Orientation (time, place, person)
2. Insight (e.g., Why are you in the hospital? What is the matter with you? Who am I?)
3. Remote memory (storage, retrieval)
    (a) Previously learned material (e.g., days of the week, months of the year, patient's birthday and place of birth)
    (b) Naming visual stimuli (e.g., colors, objects, shapes)
    (c) General fund of information (e.g., Who is the president of the United States, the governor of the state, the mayor of the city?)
4. Recent memory (registration, storage and retrieval)
    (a) General information (e.g., How did you get to the hospital? What did you eat for breakfast?)
    (b) Immediate recall (e.g., Digit span: The patient is given a series of numbers by the examiner and asked to repeat them forward and backward.)
    (c) Delayed racall (e.g., Three items are read to the patient, who is asked to repeat them 5 minutes later.)
5. Calculation (e.g., The patient is asked to do simple arithmetic problems, such as serial sevens.)
6. Abstract thinking
    (a) Similarities (e.g., How are a pear and an apple alike?)
    (b) Differences (e.g., What is the difference between a lie and a mistake?)
    (c) Proverb interpretation (e.g., What does "A bird in the hand is worth two in the bush" mean?)
7. Judgment (e.g., What would you do if you found a stamped, addressed envelope in the street?)
8. Other frequently given tasks
    (a) Writing
    (b) Spatial organization (match design, map drawing, etc.)
    (c) Drawing (e.g., figure copying; patient is asked to draw a clock, a daisy, etc.)
    (d) Body image (e.g., Patient is asked to draw a person; identification of body parts.)

Figure 1. Mental Status Examination.

dysfunction. Mattis (1981) strongly recommends the use of categorization tasks to detect the presence of concretetization, such as those included in the (WAIS) Similarities Substest. He feels that these tasks, which are relatively insensitive to disturbance due to psychogenic factors, may be the most valid measures of concrete thinking. To the WAIS Similarities Subtest question, "How are a dog and a lion alike?" the brain-damaged patient will characteristically respond: "They are not alike. A dog is a dog, and a lion is a lion. One is tame and the other is wild. They are not the same at all." Further discrimination can be achieved by way of the Mattis Dementia Rating Scale (1979). Here the patient is asked to name three things in a specific category, for example, what people eat. Most patients with organic brain syndromes can offer three items, such as "hamburgers, frankfurters, and baked beans." But they are unable to give the name of the category to which these items belong. Mattis infers from such a response that the patient's deductive reasoning is relatively intact, but inductive reasoning (abstraction) is no longer available.

Again, at times the mental status examination may not be sufficiently sensitive for differential diagnosis. On the one hand, depression, anxiety, catastrophic reactions, and so on are frequently encountered in the brain-damaged patient. On the other hand, short-term memory can be seriously disrupted in an organically intact patient by anxiety, depression, intrusive ideation, and idiosyncratic associational thinking. Thus the task of differentiating between a functional disorder and an organic brain syndrome may pose an insoluble diagnostic dilemma.

In the final analysis, judgment of the value of any mental status examination must be based on practical considerations, that is, on whether it can be applied in the medical setting by the staff in place. For example, a pilot attempt to construct such a diagnostic technique resulted in the Cognitive Capacity Screening Examination (CCSE), Figure 2, recently developed through the combined efforts of psychiatry and psychology by Jacobs, Bernhard, Delgado, and Strain (1977).

This brief 30-item mental status questionnaire, which can be routinely administered to all medical patients on admission, is also designed to correct some of the deficiences of the standard mental status examination and thereby facilitate the prompt diagnosis of a diffuse organic brain syndrome (i.e., delirium). For example, questions requiring the performance of an interposed task were formulated. (The patient is told to remember four digits, to count to ten out loud, and then to repeat the four digits.) This task can be used in much the same way an exercise test (e.g. the two-step Masters test) is used to uncover previously unrecognized cardiac dysfunction.

Because of the exigencies of the medical setting, the authors felt it was essential to limit the amount of time required for administration of the test to approximately 5 minutes. The test form includes instructions for its use and scoring. Further and most important, in an attempt to help the nonpsychiatric physician focus on the physiological basis of the organic brain syndrome, the form directs the administrator, in the event of a low score, to assume the presence of organic (rather than functional) pathology and to review the patient's vital physiological data.

The psychiatrist and the psychologist need to make the caretakers aware that although a low score on this questionnaire does not of itself substantiate a diagnosis of organic brain syndrome, it does identify patients with diminished cognitive capacity. It must be emphasized that this deficit may arise, in turn, from one or a combination of factors: an organic brain syndrome, mental retardation, a low level of intelligence, minimal education, cultural deprivation, impaired English-language comprehension, poor hearing, and so on. In practice,

Cognitive Capacity Screening Examination

Examiner _____ Date _____

Instructions: Check items answered correctly. Write incorrect or unusual answers in space provided. If necessary, urge patient once to complete task.

Introduction to patient: "I would like to ask you a few questions. Some you will find very easy and others may be very hard. Just do your best."

Addressograph Plate

1) What day of the week is this? _____
2) What month? _____
3) What day of month? _____
4) What year? _____
5) What place is this? _____
6) Repeat the numbers 8 7 2. _____
7) Say them backwards. _____
8) Repeat these numbers 6 3 7 1. _____
9) Listen to these numbers 6 9 4. Count 1 through 10 out loud, then repeat 6 9 4. (Help if needed. Then use numbers 5 7 3.) _____
10) Listen to these numbers 8 1 4 3. Count 1 through 10 out loud, then repeat 8 1 4 3. _____
11) Beginning with Sunday, say the days of the week backwards. _____
12) 9 + 3 is _____
13) Add 6 (to the previous answer or "to 12"). _____
14) Take away 5 ("from 18"). _____
Repeat these words after me and remember them, I will ask for them later: HAT, CAR, TREE, TWENTY-SIX.
15) The opposite of fast is slow. The opposite of up is _____

16) The opposite of large is _____
17) The opposite of hard is _____
18) An orange and a banana are both fruits. Red and blue are both _____
19) A penny and a dime are both _____
20) What were those words I asked you to remember? (HAT) _____
21) (CAR) _____
22) (TREE) _____
23) (TWENTY-SIX) _____
24) Take away 7 from 100, then take away 7 from what is left and keep going: 100 − 7 is _____
25) Minus 7 _____
26) Minus 7 (write down answers; check correct subtraction of 7) _____
27) Minus 7 _____
28) Minus 7 _____
29) Minus 7 _____
30) Minus 7 _____

TOTAL CORRECT (maximum score = 30) _____

Patient's occupation (previous, if not employed) _____ _____ _____ Education _____ Age _____

Estimated intelligence (based on education, occupation, and history, not on test score):

Below average, Average, Above average _____

Patient was: Cooperative _____ Uncooperative _____ Depressed _____ Lethargic _____ Other _____

Medical diagnosis: _____

IF PATIENT'S SCORE IS LESS THAN 20, THE EXISTENCE OF DIMINISHED COGNITIVE CAPACITY IS PRESENT. THEREFORE, AN ORGANIC MENTAL SYNDROME SHOULD BE SUSPECTED AND THE FOLLOWING INFORMATION OBTAINED.

Temp. _____   BUN _____   Endocrine dysfunction? _____

B.P. _____   Glu _____ T_3, T_4, Ca, P,   etc.

Hct _____ Po_2 _____   History of previous psychiatric difficulty _____

Na _____ Pco_2 _____   Drugs: _____

K _____   Steroids? L-Dopa? Amphetamines? Tranquilizers? Digitalis?

Cl _____

CO_2 _____   Focal neurological signs: _____

EEG _____   DIAGNOSIS: _____

ECG _____

Figure 2. Cognitive Capacity Screening Examination.

the caretaker will find that with this device it is relatively easy to differentiate those patients who score low on the questionnaire because of diffuse organic dysfunction from those who score low as a result of defective hearing, cultural deprivation, and so forth. In any case, the prompt identification of cognitive deficits whatever their source is critical to good patient care. If a patient does not know how to add or subtract as a result of limited intelligence or poor education, he or she may not be able to take medication alone without danger. Most nonpsychiatric physicians assume that patients have these skills, and few patients will readily acknowledge their absence. Partially deaf or amnesic patients will frequently nod their heads in agreement rather than admit to themselves or their doctor that their hearing or memory is failing.

This screening device has the further advantage that it appears to be relatively immune to contamination by disturbances of mood—that is, anxiety and/ or depression. On the other hand, the caretakers must also be made aware of its limitations. As mentioned above, it does not identify an organic brain syndrome *per se,* nor does it identify focal lesions (e.g., epilepsy, abscess, tumors, etc.). For example, in a recent study, when cognitive deficits detected by the CCSE were compared to those elicited through the standard neurological history and physical on patients admitted to a neurological service (Kaufman, Wineberger, Strain, & Jacobs, 1979) we found that the CCSE had correctly identified 73% of those patients who had demonstrable cognitive deficits on neurological evaluation. It did not, however, identify all the cases of dementia or limited intellectual deficit. Specifically, it did not identify some patients with cognitive deficits associated with major cerebral pathology. The significant incidence (15%) of false-negative results in this follow-up study stemmed in part from the arbitrary distinction made originally between cognitive deficits caused by focal lesions and those caused by diffuse cerebral dysfunction. Focal lesions in certain areas produce aphasia, constructional apraxia, or other discrete intellectual deficits. Destruction of cerebral tissue in any area may create intellectual impairment in proportion to the volume of tissue damaged. Therefore, large or critically situated focal lesions can lead to diffuse dysfunction (e.g., hydrocephalus, massive edema, and seizures, which are associated with either dementia or delirium). It is our impression that false-negative results also occurred because the CCSE did not include tests of language, judgment, or fund of knowledge (which are routine parts of the neurological screening device) and because its results were based on an arbitrary, fixed "cutoff" score. Correction of these defects would increase the high yield (73%) of this device.*

Reliable and valid screening devices for the two other most frequently encountered psychological entitities in the medical setting—the presence of significant depression and/or anxiety— also need to be developed. Collaborative efforts to detect depression have been made and are described below. However, methods for routine psychological screening of the medically ill which can be easily applied by nonpsychiatric caretakers are not yet available.

The benefits of collaboration between the psychiatrist and psychologist may,

---

*Folstein, Folstein, and McHugh (1975) have constructed a "Mini-Mental-State" examination, a practical method for grading the cognitive state of patients for clinicians. But, like the CCSE, it does not necessarily identify focal lesions. In addition, Folstein (1981) has developed a tachistoscopic approach to assessing delirium which correlates with the Mini-Mental-State examination.

of course, extend beyond the detection of specific psychological disorders to include fostering diagnostic (and prognostic) accuracy in the psychological sector in general and differentiating between somatic and psychological disorders in particular.

That problems in diagnosis (misdiagnosis, diagnostic ambiguity, and lack of diagnosis) currently abound in the medical setting is well known. Obviously, these problems are compounded when physical diseases find expression in psychological symptoms, or vice versa. This phenomenon has been observed by Leeman (1975) in the busy emergency room of a general hospital. In this setting, the tendency of physicians, on the sole basis of their initial impressions of the patient's manifest symptomatology, to regard patients as either having physiological or functional disease has often led to inaccurate diagnosis and improper treatment.

It is an interesting paradox that often, under the pressure to make a diagnosis and to make one quickly, the physician is overzealous in making use of a psychological diagnosis. For example, carbon monoxide intoxication may present with psychiatric symptoms; as a result, the underlying physiological dysfunction may be overlooked. The symptoms of insulinoma often lead to its diagnosis as a neurological or psychiatric disorder. Cancer of the pancreas frequently presents as depression; anxiety can be a symptom of hyperthyroidism; paranoia can be a symptom of a brain tumor. Neurological disorders such as psychomotor dysfunction and petit mal or grand mal epilepsy frequently present with signs and symptoms that are usually associated with psychological disorders.

Or the physician may resort to a psychological diagnosis simply because of his or her inability to arrive at a definitive physical diagnosis. The stresses the physician experiences in this situation may be equal to those experienced by the patient. Although, on an intellectual level, physicians accept their limitations in this regard, their feeling of being in control and professional self-esteem may both be threatened when a diagnosis remains elusive. It is at this point that the problem is most likely to be solved through a premature diagnosis, by over or underdiagnosis, or by the formulation of a psychological rather than a physical diagnosis (and vice versa).

Through their joint efforts, the liaison psychiatrist and the psychologist can help the physician to resolve this dilemma by assuring accuracy of psychological diagnosis, by delineating more clearly the points at which psychic and somatic factors may interdigitate, and hopefully, by the process of elimination, facilitate more specific identification of the patient's medical (or psychological problems) and the associated prognosis.

4. Clarification of the Status of the Caretaker

We have made the point that the alliance model of liaison psychiatry incorporates the proposition that responsibility for the psychological care of the medically ill hospitalized patient cannot be relegated solely to the psychiatrist—or the psychologist. Rather, optimal psychological care of the patient is a consequence of the joint efforts of those with whom he or she comes into daily contact—the doctor, nurses, important family members—and the psychological climate of the ward in which the patient has been placed. It follows, then, that the crucial functions of the liaison psychiatrist currently include the measurement and assessment of the degree of stress the patient evokes in medical caretakers and family; their capacity to adapt to the patient and to his or her illness (and to the interventions of psychological caretakers); and, above all, their capacity for psychological "work." The two aspects of the process selected for discussion below demonstrate the complexities of this task; they also permit the inference that evaluation of the myriad variables that can influence the patient's illness behavior can provide a potentially fruitful area for collaboration between the psychologist and psychiatrist.

4.1. Evaluating the Doctor

In general, the liaison psychiatrist tries to find the best way to help internists use their capacity for empathy and convince them of the value of what he or she can do to foster the patient's psychological well-being. However, the psychiatrist must also recognize the need to respect and work with the internist's limitations.

At times, these "limitations" must be identified with greater specificity. It may be necessary, for example, to further assess the internist's ability to think in psychological terms. But at other times it is important to establish whether the stress evoked by a particular patient is undermining the internist's capacity to adapt to that patient and his or her illness.

> When the psychiatrist saw the doctor who had initiated a request for consultation for a depressed patient, it immediately became apparent that it was the doctor who was despondent. Although Dr. N. realized they would prolong the patient's life, she was afraid to administer "poisons" (immunosuppressant drugs) to her young, healthy-looking patient, who, in fact, was dying from leukemia.

Dr. N. had not been consciously aware of how upset she was, or of the source of her anxiety and despondency, before she discussed the situation with the liaison psychiatrist with whom she had daily contact on the ward. However, she was aware of the fact that her consequent inability to talk with the patient had increased his concern and anxiety. After she had expressed her feelings about her patient, she recognized that she could not continue to function as his doctor. Dr. N. was clearly overwhelmed by her patient.

On the other hand, a tendency automatically to discount the internist's capacity to deal with a patient's psychological needs may prove equally unfortunate.

> Mr. M., an Englishman in his 50's, suffered from chronic leukemia that was fairly asymptomatic, except for one acute episode, marked by weakness, which had required his hospitalization. The patient, who had spent most of his life at sea, had little capacity to relate to others—even his wife—on an intimate level. He had defended against closeness and passive longings by cultivating the image of a *bon vivant*, and even after the onset of his illness continued to maintain that facade. His underlying melancholy, associated with his fears of weakness and death, became manifest during the brief exacerbation of his illness.
>
> Mr. M.'s physician, a sensitive oncologist, dealt with him on a man-to-man basis

and made no attempt to make him aware of his feelings. However, the psychiatrist who had seen him while he was despondent during his hospitalization recommended the the internist probe the patient's defenses, that Mr. M.'s underlying depression should be explored. Although the physician was reluctant to follow the psychiatrist's advice, such an attempt was made—and produced only increased defensiveness in the patient, a further diminishing of his self-esteem, and some agitation.

In making his recommendations, the psychiatrist had used a therapeutic formula that fails to take into account the individual's psychological makeup. In contrast, the internist had a "feel" for his patient. Once this became apparent, the liaison psychiatrist and the internist agreed that the defenses the patient had erected against his responses to his illness should be respected and strengthened until they could no longer withstand the reality of his physical symptoms.

In a third case the psychiatrist was able to evaluate accurately the seemingly paradoxical ability of a young, inexperienced intern to fulfill the psychological needs of a patient who was a senior attending at the hospital.

> Dr. S. had a fever of undetermined origin and a probable occult neoplasm. While awaiting the results of diagnostic tests, the patient became increasingly anxious. His private physician, who was a close friend, was understandably distressed about his condition, to the extent that he could not discuss the situation with Dr. S., or, in fact, talk with him at all.
>
> When Dr. S. was subsequently presented at medical rounds, he expressed his fear and his intense desire to talk to someone. The psychiatrist felt that Dr. S. would form an immediate relationship with anyone who would listen. Consequently, when a young intern expressed an interest in Dr. S., and wondered whether he could help an older patient, and a physician at that, the psychiatrist encouraged him to try. The patient's psychological status improved significantly as a result.

It is the exquisite tailoring of the assessment not only to the needs of the patient but also to the needs and capacities of the doctor that is the hallmark of the liaison methodology.

As noted earlier, the psychiatrist's evaluation of the doctor necessarily includes an assessment of his or her response to the psychological caretakers on the ward. However, the psychiatrist must also evaluate the doctor's attitude toward the psychological interventions of the nonphysician staff. For example, inasmuch as they are in daily contact with the patient, the nurses' ability to fulfill psychological needs may be a crucial determinant of his or her mental and emotional well-being. It is important, therefore, that the psychiatrist evaluate the nurse's psychological skills. At the same time, the doctor's stance in this regard must be evaluated in order to ascertain the degree to which the nurse is expected to utilize psychological skills. Obviously, when the nurse is permitted to give full rein to these, he or she can enhance the psychiatrist's understanding of the patient and become an important therapeutic ally.

Finally, perhaps the doctor's capacity for empathy and psychological-mindedness as well as his or her ability to assimilate the principles of psychological medicine emerge most clearly when they are considered in the context of the psychological and medical climate of the patient's ward. As "leader" of the ward, it is the doctor's philosophy of patient care that, to varying degrees, will determine the psychologically relevant characteristics of that ward.

> Patients remain on the vascular surgery ward for one to six months. During this period, they proceed through soaks, grafts, sympathectomies, femoral bypasses, meta-

tarsal, below-knee amputations, with no assurance that further surgery will not be necessary before healing is secured. The patients have little opportunity to obtain information about their condition from the surgical staff. They become increasingly angry as they wait, and since the surgeons aren't there, their anger is directed at the nurses and the "establishment." Unfortunately, although the nurses want to help, usually they are not "expected" (or able) to deal with the stresses that evoke this anger.

Fortunately, the vascular surgery ward is not typical. But each ward presents its own set of problems. For this reason it is essential for the psychological teacher and caretaker to get a "sense" of the ward with regard to its patient population and the attitudes and functions of its nursing and house staff, which, in turn, will reflect its leadership and its philosophy of patient care. These variables—the ward culture—will influence the psychiatrist's evaluation of the doctor, and, of course, of the patient's psychological problem; this will then lead to appropriate therapeutic recommendations.

4.2. Evaluating the Family

The expanded involvement of the liaison psychiatrist with the patient carriers with it an obligation to query the family's perceptions of the patient. The psychiatrist may be able to assess the severity of the patient's psychological problem on the basis of the family's description of the patient's personality and behavior prior to the onset of illness; on the other hand, these data may be misleading. To resolve this dilemma, the psychiatrist must evaluate the quality of the patient's intrafamiliar environment. Minuchin (1974) contends that family interactional patterns as well as intrapsychic phenomena may trigger the onset and/or hamper the subsidence of psychophysiological processes—that illness may disrupt family organization or serve as a homeostatic mechanism that regulates family interactions. In any event, the psychiatrist's evaluation of the patient's intrapsychic functioning in the contet of the family system will enhance diagnosis and management of that patient.

5. The Provision of Ongoing Education to the Nonpsychiatric Staff to Promote Autonomy

The liaison psychiatrist has an opportunity to teach the nonpsychiatric staff at morning rounds, weekly nurses' conferences, combined ward–staff meetings, staff-run patient groups, and grand rounds presentations. In addition, the liaison psychiatrist is asked to evaluate specific patients in the presence of the house staff and nurses, so that in time they will become more skillful in eliciting, interpreting, and applying psychosocial data. In fact, these ongoing medical activities offer an excellent opportunity for collaborative joint teaching by all mental health care professionals.

Liaison psychiatry also seeks to develop other methods that can provide a suitable setting for the dissemination of psychological skills, attitudes, and knowledge. An example of one such vehicle in which psychologists can play an effective collaborative role is ombudsman rounds, described below (Strain, 1978; Strain & Hamerman, 1978).

The ombudsman program was initially established in response to the request by the house staff for additional help and support in resolving intrastaff disputes and clinical problems and to ensure continuing communication among the house staff, nursing staff, social workers, and the psychiatrist on the medical wards. Thus, at present, the medical attending physicians, permanently assigned to manage the day-to-day life of a particular ward, who serve as ombudsmen, are asked to perform a dual function for which there are no specific guidelines or formal training; this function is radically different from their accustomed role as ward attendants. They are required to co-chair (with the liaison psychiatrist) a discussion of the interrelationship between psychosocial and physical factors in the patient on the one hand and of the existence of resistance and conflicts surrounding psychological care for the medical patient that may be inherent in certain staff attitudes on the other. Finally, the ombudsmen also need to develop a close working relationship with the liaison psychiatrist with whom they continually interact before, during, and after the conferences. For, ideally, they will, in time, provide most of the psychosocial explanations themselves, with the liaison psychiatrist acting as a resource person.

Ombudsman rounds consist of two distinct phases—the pre-ombudsman meeting and the ombudsman rounds *per se*.

5.1. The Pre-Ombudsman Meeting

At present, the ombudsman, head nurse, liaison psychiatrist, chief medical resident, and social worker meet a day or two prior to the weekly ombudsman rounds to review the ward routine and functioning during the previous week; to evaluate interstaff relationships (e.g., house staff–nursing, social service–house staff, etc.); and to discuss the optimal use of the forthcoming rounds.

In accordance with the basic thrust of the ombudsman program, the participants in the pre-ombudsman meeting identify and select for presentation a series of medically ill patients who highlight universal psychosocial–medical issues and/or currently present urgent management problems, such as noncompliance, character trait disturbances (excessive passivity or activity), organic brain syndromes, depression, hypochondriasis, family reactions to medical illness, the appropriate use of psychotropic medication, and so forth. An informed consent is then obtained from the patient selected to join the ward staff at ombudsman rounds to discuss his or her reactions to illness and hospitalization. (In the case of the private patient, it is not enough to obtain the patient's consent to be interviewed; the private attending physician's permission must also be secured, and he or she is invited to attend and participate in the rounds.)

5.2. The Ombudsman Rounds

Once a week, an hour of regularly scheduled medical attending rounds is devoted to ombudsman rounds. The personnel at this meeting currently include the ombudsman, house staff and medical students, liaison psychiatrist, social worker, ward charge nurse and staff, ward monthly attending physician, ward secretary and unit manager, patient representatives (when they are involved with the patient), and representatives of the hospital administration.

5.2.1. Preinterview Discussion

Once the group has assembled, the ombudsman and/or liaison psychiatrist announces the name of the patient (who is not yet present), states the focus of the presentation, and invites comments from the staff regarding their perception of the patient, difficulties his or her care presents, and their impression of the patient's reaction to illness and hospitalization. The interviewer is selected from among the members of the ward staff (e.g., ombudsman, house staff, social worker, nurse, or psychiatrist). The group makes suggestions to the interviewer with regard to areas they would like explored.

5.2.2. The Interview

The patient is brought in, introduced to the group, and seated next to the interviewer. A typical greeting might be: "You remember we spoke to you about coming to this meeting, and the staff is very grateful to you for coming. We would like to ask you a few questions." At the end of the interview, the patient is asked if he or she would mind if some questions were asked from other staff members or if he or she has questions for the staff. The ombudsman and the liaison psychiatrist attempt to correct the patient's misconceptions as well as answer his or her questions if they can. When the interview is concluded, the patient is thanked and escorted out.

5.2.3. Postinterview Discussion

The ombudsman or liaison psychiatrist begins the discussion by asking the group what their responses to the patient were. Once these have been elicited, the psychiatrist and ombudsman attempt to formulate a psychosocial–medical understanding of the patient's behavior and to synthesize a treatment plan that encompasses all aspects of this—psychological, social, and medical. Through such understanding, they attempt to help the patient adapt to illness and, at the same time, to help the staff adapt to the patient.

5.2.4. Postmeeting Follow-up

One of the members of the group (a nurse, social worker, or resident) visits the patient shortly after the interview to learn of the patient's reactions and to deal with any problems or questions that may have emerged. Ideally, at the postmeeting follow-up the staff member attempts to assess ongoing patient behavior, further correct misconceptions, and provide psychosocial support in areas where the need for such support has become obvious from the rounds or follow-up. The accumulation of psychosocial data throughout the patient's hospital stay permits confirmation of the accuracy of the original psychosocial–medical formulations, and, when indicated, further refinement of the therapeutic intervention.

It is difficult to convey the actual tone and conduct of the ombudsman rounds by a single abbreviated clinical example. The following case is respresentative of the problems that might arise during these rounds. In this case, the relationship between the patient's behavior and her medical illness emerged with particular clarity, and the treatment protocol was influenced by the staff's enhanced understanding of the patient's psychosocial problems.

> Mrs. L, a 23-year-old asthmatic Puerto Rican woman, had been hospitalized for medical supervision while she was being withdrawn from steriods. Mrs. L.'s husband had abandoned her and their 4-year-old daughter; and her parents, with whom she had virtually no contact, live in Puerto Rico.
>
> The resident, Dr. F., had requested that Mrs. L. be interviewed because she continued to demand prednisone although "she could get along without it," and because she refused all attempts to persuade her to participate in a withdrawal program. According to Dr. F., this patient equated pills with attention, and used her illness and medication to control both her environment and him. Dr. S., another resident on the ward, questioned the effectiveness of Dr. F.'s approach to the patient. He agreed that Mrs. L.'s behavior was inappropriate and difficult, but he also felt that getting angry or arguing with her was not the answer. Dr. S. felt this patient needed to be referred to a psychiatrist.
>
> When Mrs. L. was introduced at the rounds, she was asked directly by the interviewer why she couldn't "get off" her medication. To the surprise of both Dr. F. and Dr. S., the patient replied that she wanted to because the pills were making her "old and ugly," but that she was afraid she would die if she stopped taking steroids. The questioning then took on a more personal quality. Following Dr., S.'s earlier suggestion that Mrs. L. needed psychotherapy, the patient was asked about her social and emotional life, whether there was anyone she could depend on or turn to, and how she felt about herself. In her answers to these questions, Mrs. L. emerged as a lonely, frightened, isolated individual, who felt rejected, but unconsciously invited rejection—by her parents, whose letters she would not answer; by her neighbors, whose invitations she would not return; and by her doctor, whose suggestions she would not listen to. Mrs. L. seemed determined not to allow herself to be "manipulated," even in the service of parental support, friendship, or recovery.

After the interview was concluded, there was a greater expression of empathy for Mrs. L. (at least in contrast to the irritation verbalized in the preinterview discussion). Dr. S., who had indicated his sensitivity to Mrs. L.'s distress, continued to maintain that he did not have the "skills to deal with a patient like this." Two crucial guidelines for Mrs. L's management emerged, however. First, the patient obviously needed to be helped to correct her misconseption that she would die unless she was given prednisone on a long-term basis. Second, it seemed equally apparent that Mrs. L. might benefit from a constant relationship with a physician who could provide the reassurance—over a period of time—that she required to be able to comply with a withdrawal program. Such a relationship would alleviate her feelings that she was alone and helpless and would reduce her dependence on prednisone, the only thing she felt she could depend on to keep her going.

The conference also allowed a more precise understanding of Mrs. L.'s reactions. Dr. F. and Dr. S. both expressed surprise at how they had misread Mrs. L.'s behavior. Dr. F. said, "I pegged her wrong; I thought she was just being difficult. She's really frightened, confused, and very alone—another side of her came through I hadn't seen." More importantly, the view of Mrs. L. that emerged at the ombudsman rounds led Dr. F. to take a different approach to his "uncooperative, manipulative" patient. Furthermore, the house staff realized that this patient's psychosocial problems, which had appeared to Dr. S. to be "deep" and insoluble initially, might actually require only minimal psychotherapeutic intervention as part of the ward treatment plan—an intervention that could be provided within the context of a continuing doctor–patient relationship.

Given the limitations inherent in the acute medical ward setting for such teaching, it is our conviction that ombudsman rounds serve an important function, even if they only heighten the staff's awareness of those psychosocial factors that predispose, initiate, and perpetuate disease as well as of the psychosocial reactions that are typically evoked by illness and hospitalization. The staff's interaction during and after the patient interview creats a climate of interest in these factors. The liaison psychiatrist provides a synthesis of the psychosocial data that facilitates an interpretation of the patient's behavior.

The ombudsman rounds also provides a forum for discussion of the feelings that arise within the house staff regarding such personal and professional issues as deciding whether a patient should be resuscitated in the event of a cardiac arrest, how the disoriented elderly can best be cared for, whether the use of heroic measures is indicated in terminal disease, how to deal with the noncompliant patient, and how to cope with the inability to arrive at a diagnosis. These issues have the greatest clinical relevance but are seldom confronted in the course of traditional medical training. Such issues do not lend themselves to formal didactic presentation; they are too far-reaching, and, as opposed to didactic material, do not fit into a theoretical framework and cannot be taught by routine methods. In short, ombudsman rounds create a setting in which anxieties, conflicts, and stresses in patients—as well as in their doctors and nurses—can be examined, where the approach to medical care is enhanced by moving beyond physiological content to an awareness of the psychological needs of the patient as well as the doctor and other medical caretakers.

The benefits inherent in the ombudsman rounds can be heightened by the psychologist who can actively participate in them, conduct them, and most important, perhaps, accurately evaluate their impact on staff attitudes toward psychological issues in the medically ill. More specifically, because of his or her unique skills in methods of evaluation, the psychologist can determine how effective learning is in group situations such as ombudsman rounds. These findings, in turn, will provide scientific data, justification, and guidelines for future program development, for possible changes in the organization and structure of the ward, for methods to facilitate routine follow-up and reinforcement of topics and cases discussed at rounds, and for ways to enhance communication. A definitive evaluation study may counter the view held by some that ombudsman rounds are potentially damaging to patients and the belief that the patient (or the staff) may be hopelessly overwhelmed by the intense feelings elicited in this setting. Evidence of shifts in staff attitudes, enhanced intrastaff communication, improved skills in interviewing, acquisition of salient knowledge (e.g., the kinds of depressive phenomena routinely seen in the medically ill, the use and abuse of psychopharmacological agents in this patient population, etc.), would enable us to move beyond impressionistic assessments of the value of psychosocial teaching in the acute-care medical setting. If valid studies of the effectiveness of various psychological teaching vehicles, such as ombudsman rounds, can be constructed, then psychosocial–medical interviewing, evaluation, diagnosis, and the management of the medically ill under the tutelage of a medical attending physician—on medicine's time, with the liaison psychiatrist or psychologist serving as a resource behavioral scientist—may become routine procedures in the contemporary teaching hospital.

6. The Development of Core Biopsychosocial Knowledge

The liaison psychiatrist seeks to transmit to the nonpsychiatric staff a theoretical substrate enabling them to organize their thinking in regard to pychosocial considerations. These teaching efforts will be greatly enhanced by collaborative efforts to abstract a workable scheme for the application of data on human behavior, psychobiological correlations, treatment modalities, and so on that have relevance for an understanding of problems commonly seen in the medically ill (e.g., organicity, depression, the problem of pain, psychopharmacological treatment, hypochondriasis, etc.). For example, one such study currently under way at the Mount Sinai School of Medicine, by Rifkin, Strain, and Endicott (1980) is designed to provide the first randomized, controlled double-blind investigation of the diagnosis and effects of the psychopharmacological treatment of depression in the medically ill.

As is well known, the incidence of depression in medically ill hospitalized patients ranges from 13% to 40), depending on the stringency of the criteria of depression and the accuracy of the diagnosis (Schwab, Bialow, Brown, & Holzer, 1980; Taintor, Gise, Spikes, & Strain, 1979). Yet, despite this high incidence, standardized diagnostic criteria (for example, the *Research and Diagnostic Criteria*) have not been applied (Spitzer, Endicott, & Robins, 1978). Nor has the value of antidepressant medication in these patients been systematically studied. Although its use is widespread, it is often applied to the wrong diagnostic groups or given in too low a dosage or, for far too short a period of time.

Depression in the medically ill is often overlooked or discounted because it is considered a result of the stress evoked by physical illness. Concomitantly, it is commonly assumed that depression that is "understandable" (e.g., as a response to the fear and discomfort of organic illness) is not responsive to drug treatment. However, in depression not associated with organic illness, research findings have shown that the presence or absence of a clear precipitating event is not necessarily a prediction of drug responsiveness, whereas clinical symptoms are (Klein, 1974). Specifically, "endogenous" depression, which is responsive to antidepressant drugs, is characterized by persistent anhedonia, loss of interest, persistent sad mood, sleep disturbance, guilt, retardation or agitation, fatigability, and suicidal ideation. Other depressive syndromes that present a different clinical picture are less responsive to antidepressant medication, especially the tricyclics. Another problem in dealing with depressive phenomena in the medically ill is the fact that many of the signs and symptoms that would support the diagnosis of depression also occur with medical illness. For example, the following criteria are needed to render a *DSM-III* diagnosis of a major depressive disorder (which would be an indication for antidepressant medication; *DSM-III*, 1980):

A. Dysphoric mood or loss of interest or pleasure in all or almost all usual activities and pastimes. The dysphoric mood is characterized by symptoms such as the following: depressed, sad, blue, hopeless, low, down in the dumps, and irritable. The mood disturbance must be prominent and relatively persistent, but not necessarily the most dominant symptom, and does not include momentary shifts from one dysphoric mood to another dysphoric mood, e.g., anxiety to depression to anger, such as are seen in states of acute psychotic turmoil. (For children under six, dysphoric mood may have to be inferred from a persistently sad facial expression.)

B. At least four of the following symptoms have each been present nearly every day for a period of at least two weeks (in children under six, at least three of the first four):

    (1) poor appetite or significant weight loss (when not dieting) or increased appetite or significant weight gain (in children under six consider failure to make expected weight gains),

    (2) insomnia or hypersomnia,

    (3) psychomotor agitation or retardation (but not merely subjective feelings of restlessness or being slowed down) (in children under six, hypoactivity),

    (4) loss of interest or pleasure in usual activities, or decrease in sexual drive not limited to a period when delusional or hallucinating (in children under six, signs of apathy),

    (5) loss of energy; fatigue,

    (6) feelings of worthlessness, self-reproach, or excessive or inappropriate guilt (either may be delusional),

    (7) complaints or evidence of diminished ability to think or concentrate, such as slowed thinking, or indecisiveness not associated with marked loosening of associations or incoherence,

    (8) recurrent thoughts of death, suicidal ideation, wishes to be dead, or suicide attempt.

Dysphoric mood, poor appetite, sleep disturbance, changes in gastric intestinal motility, decreased libido, anhedonia, and so on may all accompany medical illness and be relatively persistent, which is necessary for the diagnosis of a major depressive disorder. To overcome this contingency in the study, we elected to observe patients for at least 2 weeks after discharge from the hospital for an acute medical illness and reevaluate the presence of vegetative signs and mood disturbance.

In this psychologist–psychiatrist collaborative study our attention is focused on patients with depression who are most likely to be drug-responsive and who meet the criteria of Major Depressive Disorder, Endogenous subtype, as set forth in the *Research Diagnostic Criteria* of Spitzer *et al.* (1978). Other depressed patients who are not participating in the study are being seen for a follow-up interview to obtain naturalistic data on the course of their depression and their response to nondrug treatment (if any is provided). A final aim of the study is to enhance our understanding of the role of precipitants of depression in this group.

Psychiatrists are, of course, aware of the necessary components of depression. In this instance, however, it was the psychologist who devised scales that elevated this investigation to a higher scientific level. Every effort was made to design a comprehensive study. Thus, we utilized the Clinical Global Impressions

(Guy, 1976a), Schedule for Affective Disorders and Schizophrenia Change Version (SADS-C; Spitzer & Endicott, 1978), Dosage Record and Treatment Emergent Symptom scale (DOTES; Guy, 1976b; Raskin *et al.*; 1979), and Symptom of Disease State (SODS; Rifkin *et al.*, 1980).

In addition to the study of depression currently under way, we have developed a systematic method for accumulating a data base and for psychiatric consultations and modes of processing these data (Gise, Strain, Taintor, & Endicott, in press). More specifically, we are attempting to provide a data base for needs assessment, learner appraisal, systems analysis, and a measure of the impact of liaison teaching on the consultation referral process. Briefly, this form incorporates data referring to *DSM-III* criteria; significant biological data (e.g, abnormal EEG, blood chemistries, and CAT scan); and social data (e.g., family constellation, recent stress, social class, etc.).

Thus, the form focuses the trainees' attention on categories of data essential to performing a consultation:

1. Consultee data, e.g., who referred patient
2. Demographic data
3. Psychosocial issues, e.g., history of recent stress
4. Psychotropic medicine in current use before consultant arrives
5. A structured mental status
6. *DSM-III*, five-axis diagnosis
7. Recommendations:
   (a) Treatment by unit staff
   (b) Treatment by consultation staff
   (c) Psychiatric treatment recommended
   (d) Administrative action

The form also makes provision for a termination section that organizes essential follow-up data:

1. Physical findings
2. Diagnostic tests
3. Social network
4. Medical medications (dosage and reaction)
5. Consultee data:
   (a) Primary consultee
   (b) Patient prepared for consult
   (c) Psychosocial information available before consultation
   (d) Psychosocial information recorded in chart
6. Consultant data:
   (a) Consult terminated by
   (b) Time required for consultation,
   (c) Number of follow/up visits
7. Systems data:
   (a) Number of changes in primary physician
   (b) Number of unit changes
   (c) Satisfaction with consultation
   (d) Social service note present
   (e) Unit conflict present

8. Repeat *DSM-III* five-axial diagnosis
9. Repeat assessment of recommendations to determine:
   (a) Suggested and done
   (b) Suggested and not done
   (c) Not suggested—done
   (d) Suggested—results uncertain

Of the myriad advantages of this form, I would emphasize two aspects that have far-reaching significance for our teaching efforts. First, the form elicits the consultee's stated reason and the consultant's assessment of the reason for the consultation, thus permitting identification of gaps in the consultee's knowledge. Second, the form permits identification of those psychological syndromes that occur most frequently in the medically ill at our hospital. It is now known that 75% of the consultation patients studied over a 1-year period fell into three diagnostic categories: (1) depressive reactions, (2) organic brain syndromes, and (3) adjustment reactions and personality difficulties. Clearly, if one has only limited teaching access to medical staff (e.g., house staff, monthly rotations) then it is essential to focus on these issues. With a weekly psychosocial teaching conference, it should be possible to teach recognition and referral skills for these three entities.

The findings generated by the studies described above and the numerous collaborative studies undertaken in the past, as well as those which are ongoing and contemplated, will add to the core knowledge on which the biopsychosocial model must rest.

7. Promotion of Structural Changes in the Medical Setting

Liaison psychiatry strives to effect structural changes in various departments throughout the hospital—changes that will endure beyond the tenure of a given individual. For example, after it became apparent at one teaching hospital that psychological factors were responsible for the failure to maintain patients in the "life island" (the complete isolation technique) for immunosuppressant therapy of leukemia and aplastic anemia, psychiatric clearance became mandatory for all life island candidates. Similarly, psychiatric clearance is now mandatory for all drug overdose patients before they are discharged from the intensive care unit. The next logical step would be to make psychiatric clearance mandatory for other high-risk patients—for example, candidates for open-heart surgery, where the mortality rate is known to be higher among depressed patients; patients who present diagnostic problems, and where some doubt exists about the need for surgery; and patients who have repeated hospital admissions, apparently as a consequence of self-abuse through neglect. Psychiatric clearance in such cases should not depend on the whim of a patient, a physician, or a department. Rather, psychological assessment of these patient groups—and others yet to be identified—should be regarded as an intrinsic part of patient evaluation and management in the contemporary teaching hospital. The point is that structural changes should become part of hospital routine and not be instituted at random. As a result of these structural changes, psychological issues will be "in the air" and will become an intrinsic part not only of ward life and thinking but of the overall operation of the hospital. As mentioned earlier, if a brief mental screening device for medical patients were incorporated into every admission work-up, the physician would be forced to think about the possibility of organicity. Furthermore, high standards of patient care would be assured if, when the screening device reflected a certain minimal rating score suggesting the possibility of organicity, the admitting physician would automatically request a psychiatric consultation (similar to the hematology consult that follows any hematocrit value below 30% in some hospitals). In addition, the use of techniques to assess mood disturbances (anxiety, depression) and maladaptive coping in the medically ill and to counteract the inappropriate use of psychotropic drugs should be made part of hospital procedure. For example, all candidates for antidepressant medication should be screened by a mental health professional.

Structural changes in patient care systems may be brought about by the efforts of the liaison psychiatrist and the psychologist, who in combination make a judgment as to what to do, where to do it, and with whom. For example, some services and wards do best with consultations; the attendings and house staff on these services are simply not interested in or capable of fulfilling the psychological needs of their patients. When a service *is* responsive to the concept of the team approach, a "contract" with that service is written to change the "guest in the house" status normally afforded the consultant to that of a bona fide member of the team.* The contract includes this provisional clause: "I will show you how to provide psychological care for the patient if you will agree ultimately to try to take over this function yourself." The contract must be explicit as to the responsibilities of both the recipient–host service and the liaison psychiatrist; it should enumerate the overall goals and objectives of the program (Greenhill, 1977). These may vary according to the models described below.

For one, in the *milieu model,* emphasis is placed upon the group aspects of patient care, group process, staff reactions and interactions, interpersonal theory, and creating a therapeutic environment on the ward.

The second alternative, the *critical care* model, provides for the assignment of mental health personnel to critical care units rather than to clinical departments. The goal is patient care with the psychiatrist as a participating member of the unit team; thus the psychiatrist often becomes the unnamed leader. Teaching combines behavioral approaches, biological psychiatry, and psychoanalytic theoretical models. The Einstein Hospital and the Massachusetts General Hospital utilize this model, which was developed in this decade as a result of changes within clinical medicine.

The *biological* psychiatric model is a more exacting example of the critical care model, with strict emphasis upon neuroscience and psychopharmacology. Here the psychiatrist stands on his or her security as a peer scientist, providing psychological care through recommendation, management with psychotropic drugs, and assignment of patients to diagnosis-centered treatment units (i.e., dysphoria clinic, pain center, psychopharmacology clinic, hypochondriasis clinic, and affective states center). This model has been partly tested at Montefiore Hospital and is in early process at Columbia.

*This concept was developed by Dr. Walter Gadlin, group psychologist, Montefiore Hospital and Medical Center (Gadlin, 1981).

The *integral model* is emerging as a result of social pressure upon medicine; it relies more upon hospital governance than upon triage by physicians. The aforementioned models of liaison programs depend in the main upon consulation with patients and staff and upon working relationships with physicians. This model is based, in addition, upon the inclusion of psychological care as an integral component of patient care and provides for the availability of the psychiatrist to function openly at the point of administrative and clinical need. It is developing at the Mount Sinai Hospital, the Einstein Hospital, and at Montefiore Hospital as part of the changing concept of the liaison program.

8. Commentary

In this chapter I have attempted to outline and illustrate the precepts of liaison psychiatry. I have also attempted to show that the placement of liaison psychiatry within the medical setting offers exciting and potentially productive collaborative opportunities with psychology on several levels: research, training, and patient care.

The relationship between the disciplines of psychology and medicine has, of course, existed for centuries. However, it began to coalesce only in the past decade under the rubrics of behavioral medicine and behavioral health (Matarazzo, 1980). During this period, major steps have been taken to initiate programs designed to foster collaboration between psychologists and nonpsychiatric physicians in the medical setting: doctoral and postdoctoral research training programs related to Health Psychology and supported by the National Heart, Lung, and Blood Institute have been established at nine schools of medicine in such areas as central nervous system control over circulation, cardiovascular disease prevention, and nutritional–behavioral cardiovascular disease prevention (Matarazzo, 1980). Furthermore, with the establishment 2 years ago of Division 38 (health psychology) within the American Psychological Association, psychologists have participated to an increased degree in almost every facet of general health care. Yet despite these activities, the relationship between psychology and medicine has never been codified. Liaison psychiatry has followed a similar course of development except that major advances have been made in the codification of working arrangements and agreements between medicine and psychiatry in the clinical setting. Nevertheless, as medicine is currently practiced, liaison psychiatry (and psychology) are still regarded as "soft" disciplines, despite the unfolding neuroscientific data they both have to offer.

It seems apparent that the psychologist who wants to work at the interface of medicine and psychology must move beyond the traditional and more comfortable role of consultant. If, in short, he or she wants to adapt to the liaison mode, the psychologist must be prepared to cope with resistance, hostility, frustration, avoidance, and so on from the nonpsychiatric staff. And, by the same token, the liaison psychiatrist who wishes to persevere in the liaison mode without regressing to the more comfortable role of consultant must wage a continuing effort to cope with the forces that work against collaboration.

The relationship between liaison psychiatry and psychology requires further codification as well. Many psychiatric liaison services now routinely incorporate psychologists as members of the faculty, and some services have been led by psychologists (e.g., at the University of South Dakota). But the role of the psychologist in administration, teaching, and clinical services (psychotherapy, biofeedback, groups, etc.) and research has not been described with sufficient specificity. One can speculate, however, as to the areas in which future collaborative research will be done. Behavioral studies that affect patient performance in primary, secondary, and tertiary prevention are essential, since the outcome of much of medical intervention will depend upon behavioral alteration to secure compliance, adaptation, and rehabilitation. In addition, in the future, postdoctoral training psychology might include the evaluation of liaison psychiatry—that is, the evaluation of the effectiveness of training by patient outcome (e.g., the use of hospital, laboratory tests, return to home, or work, adaptation to illness, etc.). To illustrate, Levitin and Kornfeld (1981) and the liaison group at Columbia Presbyterian Hospital have conducted a preliminary study comparing two groups of approximately 25 orthopedic patients over the age of 65 who have fractured hips. Psychiatric counseling and liaison services were available to the test group but not the control group. Patients in the test group left the hospital an average of 12 days earlier than the control patients and were twice as likely to return home rather than go to a nursing home or other intermediate-care facility. There were substantial savings in medical costs as well. Estimates of the control group's extra medical costs were based on the daily cost per patient for extra days spent in the hospital plus the expenses of the higher percentage of the control group that left the hospital for an institution rather than home or family. Thus an investment of $10,000 for the psychiatrist's services for the test group saved approximately $200,000 in costs.

The overriding goal in the liaison setting, whether the patient suffers from acute illness or chronic disease, is the development of an appropriate biopsychosocial diagnosis, formulation, and treatment plan. These are essential to promote maximal adaptation to the disease state. It is hoped that this chapter has demonstrated that this goal can be achieved most expeditiously through the joint efforts of psychiatrists and psychologists.

9. References

Caplan, G. *Principles of preventive psychiatry.* New York: Basic Books, 1961.
Diagnostic and statistical manual of psychiatric disorders (3rd ed.). Washington, D.C., American Psychiatric Association, 1980.
Engel, G. L. Delirium. In A. M. Freedman & H. Kaplan (Eds.), *The comprehensive textbook of psychiatry.* Baltimore: Williams & Wilkins, 1967.
Engel, G. L. The need for a new medical model: A challenge for biomedicine. *Science,* 1977, *196,* 129.
Engel, G. L. *The status of consultation/liaison psychiatry.* Paper presented at the American Psychosomatic Society Annual Meeting, New York, March 1980.
Folstein, M. F. Personal communication, 1981.
Folstein, M. F., Folstein, S. E., & McHugh, P. R. "Mini-mental-state": A practical method for grading the cognitive state of patients for the clinician. *Journal of Psychological Research,* 1975, *12,* 189–198.

Friedman, M. & Rosenman, R. H. Association of specific overt behavior patterns with blood and cardiovascular findings. *Journal of the American Medical Association*, 1950, *169*, 1286–1296.

Gadlin, W. The contract in the liaison setting. Personal communication, 1981.

Gise, L., Strain, J., Taintor, Z., & Endicott, J. Revision of the computerized consultation form. (In press.)

Greenhill, M. H. The Development of liaison programs. In G. Usdin (Ed.), *Psychiatric medicine*. New York: Brunner/Mazel, 1977.

Guy, W. *Clinical Global Impressions. ECDEU assessment manual for psychopharmacology*. (Rev. ed.). Washington, D.C., U.S. Department of Health, Education, and Welfare, 1976. (a)

Guy, W. *Dosage Record and Treatment Emergent Symptom Scale. ECDEU assessment manual for psychopharmacology*. (Rev. ed.) Washington, D.C., U.S. Department of Health, Education, and Welfare, 1976. (b)

Jacobs, J., Bernhard, R., Delgado, A., & Strain, J. J. Screening for organic mental syndromes in the medically ill. *Annals of Internal Medicine*, 1977, *86*, 40.

Jenkins, C. D. Psychological and social precursors of coronary disease. *New England Journal of Medicine*, 1971, *284*, 244–255.

Jenkins, C. D., Rosenman, R. H., & Zyzanski, S. J. Prediction of clinical coronary heart disease by a test for the coronary-prone behavior pattern. *New England Journal of Medicine*, 1974, *290*, 1271–1275.

Jenkins, C. D., Zyzanski, S. J., & Rosenman, R. H. Coronary-prone behavior: One pattern or several? *Psychosomatic Medicine*, 1978, *40*, 25.

Kaufman, D., Wineberger, M., Strain, J., & Jacobs, J. The Cognitive Capacity Screening Examination: A reappraisal. *General Hospital Psychiatry*, 1979, *1*(3), 247–255.

Klein, D. F. Endogenomorphic depression. A conceptual and terminological revision. *Archives of General Psychiatry*, 1974, *31*, 447.

Leeman, C. P. Diagnostic errors in emergency room medicine: Physical illness in patients labelled "psychiatric" and vice versa. *Journal of Psychiatric Medicine*, 1975, *6*, 533.

Levin, H. S. Clinical neuropsychological testing. I: Description of test background. Personal communication, 1981.

Levitin, S. J. & Kornfeld, D. Clinical and cost benefits of liaison psychiatry. *American Journal of Psychiatry*, 1981, *138*, 790–794.

Lipowski, Z. J. Review of consultation psychiatry and psychosomatic medicine. II. Clinical aspects. *Psychosomatic Medicine*, 1967, *29*(3), 201–224.

Lipowski, Z. J. Physcial illness, the patient and his environment: Psychosocial foundations of medicine. In M. Reiser (Ed.), *American handbook of psychiatry*, (Vol. 4). New York: Basic Books, 1975.

Matarazzo, J. D. Behavioral health and behavioral medicine: Frontiers for a new health psychology. *American Psychologist*, 1980, *35*, 807–817.

Mattis, S. The mental status examination for organic mental syndrome in the elderly patient. In L. Bellak & T. B. Karasu (Eds.), *The concise handbook of geriatric psychiatry*. New York: Grune & Stratton, 1979.

Mattis, S. Personal communication, 1981.

Minuchin, S. *Families and family therapy*. Cambridge: Harvard University Press, 1974.

Raskin, A.. Schukterbrandt, J. G., & Reatig, H. Differential response to chlorpromazine, imipramine and placebo. *Archives of General Psychiatry*, 1970, *23*, 164–173.

Reiser, M. F. Changing theoretical concepts in psychosomatic medicine. In M. Reiser (Ed.), *American Handbook of Psychiatry* (Vol. 4). New York: Basic Books, 1975.

Rifkin, A., Strain, J., & Endicott, J. Personal communication, 1980.

Schwab, J. J., Bialow, M., Brown, J., & Holzer, C. E. Diagnosing depression in medical inpatients. *Annals of Internal Medicine*, 1967, *67*, 695.

Schwartz, F. Personal communication, 1981.

Shemo, J. P. D., Withersty, D., Sprodlin, W. W., & Waldman, R. H. Psychiatry as an internal medicine subspecialty: An educational model. *Journal of Medical Education*, 1980, *55*, 354–361.

Spitzer, R., & Endicott, J. *Schedule the affective disorders and schizophrenia—change version*(3rd ed.). New York State Department of Mental Hygiene, New York State Psychiatric Institute, Biometrics Research, 1978.

Spitzer, R., Endicott, J., & Robins, E. Research diagnostic criteria. *Archives of General Psychiatry*, 1978, *35*, 773–782.

Strain, J. The application of psychological concepts in the hospital–inpatient setting. *Psychological interventions in medical practice.* New York: Appleton Century Crofts, 1978.

Strain, J. J. & Grossman, S. *Psychological care of the medically ill: A primer in liaison psychiatry.* New York: Appleton Century Crofts, 1975.

Strain, J. J., & Hamerman, D. Ombudsman (medical–psychiatric) rounds. An approach to meeting patient–staff needs. *Annals of Internal Medicine,* 1978, *88,* 550.

Strain, J. J., & Spikes, J. *Teaching models of liaison psychiatry.* Paper presented at the American Psychiatric Association Annual Meeting, Toronto, May 1977.

Taintor, Z., Gise, L., Spikes, J., & Strain, J. Recording psychiatric consultations. *General Hospital Psychiatry,* 1979, *1,* 122.

Talland, G. A. *Deranged memory: A psychonomic study of the amnesic syndrome.* New York: Academic Press, 1965.

Wells, C. E. Chronic brain disease: An overview. *American Journal of Psychiatry,* 1978, *1,* 135.

The Psychologist as Social Systems Consultant

Rebecca M. Warner

1. Introduction

1.1. Definition of System

In the discussion that follows, *social system* refers to a set of two or more people who are linked by social relationships or who are engaged in social interaction with each other. This definition is a special case of a more general definition of a system. Miller (1978) defined a system as "a set of interacting units with relationships among them." Thus defined, the idea of a system is sufficiently general that it encompasses such diverse entities as a cell, an organ, an organism, or a social group. A basic premise of general systems theory is that there are essential similarities among all systems. (For instance, all systems engage in boundary maintenance and exchange information with their environments.) Another fundamental idea is that "the whole is greater than the sum of its parts." Systems theory, like Gestalt psychological theories, emphasizes the importance of studying relationships among parts. Since each entity is involved in relationships with its environment, no entity (whether it is a cell or a person) can be adequately understood without taking its environment into account.

By using the term *system* this discussion intentionally invokes the historical context of general systems theory, as developed by von Bertalanffy (1968) and elaborated by Miller (1978), Schwartz (1979), and others who study living sys-

REBECCA M. WARNER • Department of Psychology, University of New Hampshire, Durham, New Hampshire 03824.

tems. No attempt will be made here to give comprehensive terminology to describe systems, since this is provided by the authors just cited. This discussion has two purposes: first, to identify ways in which social relationships can be rigorously studied and, second, to suggest the practical implications of a systems perspective for health care consultants.

1.2. General Systems Theory

The best current illustration of general systems theory is Miller's (1978) theoretical outline of living systems. An essential feature of his theory is that living systems are hierarchical. Lower-level systems (such as cells) are the components of higher-level systems (such as organs), and higher-level systems are the environment within which lower-level systems exist. This embedding of small systems within larger systems implies that there may be interdependence among levels. Events that affect the whole organism will affect the tissues and cells, and events that occur at a tissue or cell level may affect the whole organism. Miller listed many specific hypotheses about this cross-level linkage.

Critics charge that systems theories are full of circular definitions, untestable hypotheses, and vague generalizations (e.g., Maher, 1979). Although these criticisms have sometimes been warranted, these weaknesses are not necessarily inherent in all systems approaches. Systems theory can generate hypotheses that are empirically verifiable and have nontrivial implications for research and applications.

A specific example that illustrates a nontrivial systems approach is a study by Jaffe, Stern, and Peery (1973). They collected time-series data on the "gaze dialogue" between mothers and infants. At each $\frac{1}{3}$-second interval, they recorded whether each person was looking toward or away from the other. Statistical analysis of this gaze dialogue revealed that, even at the age of 3 weeks, an infant responds differentially to the mother's behavior; the probability that the infant will gaze at the mother when the mother is gazing at the infant is significantly higher than the probability that the infant will gaze at the mother when the mother is looking away. The authors' analysis demonstrates a specific instance of mutual contingency among the activities of system members; they have shown that the infant's gaze behavior is subject to social influence at a very early age. As additional information about other parent–infant behaviors is collected, we can evaluate the extent to which the parent affects the infant's behavior and vice versa. New observational methods and statistical analyses make it possible for us to describe social systems in specific terms. Using a similar coding procedure (parent active, parent inactive, infant active, infant inactive), Bakeman and Brown (1977) have shown that there are significant differences in the amount and patterning of activity in dyads that include male versus female infants and first-born versus later-born children.

Any research that focuses on social relationships or social interactions can conceivably be called a "systems approach." This discussion will not attempt to review all existing systems approaches to social interaction. Instead, it identifies four key concepts for the analysis of social systems and explores their possible implications for health care consultants.

Social systems can be dyads (e.g., parent–infant, husband–wife, practitioner–patient), small groups (e.g., family, friendship clique, health care team), organizations (e.g., school, hospital, business), or large systems (e.g., the U.S. economy, a city, a state). All the systems just named have been studied in relation to illness and health care. This discussion will deal primarily with smaller-scale systems, since it is generally easier to design and implement interventions in small systems than in large ones (Taylor, 1978).

In addition to differences in the size of the social systems, there are also differences in system duration. Some systems, such as families, exist for a long time: other systems may endure only briefly. Although longer-lasting systems may have greater influence on their members, many briefly formed systems may be important in the health care process. For instance, a single doctor–patient interview can be analyzed as a social system. Each of the key concepts outlined in section 2 can be applied (e.g., What are the roles of the participants, how are the behaviors of doctor and patient contingent, and how open or closed is the doctor–patient system to inputs from outsiders such as relatives of the patient?). The key concepts outlined in this chapter are primarily applicable to small-scale social systems, but they apply equally well to either short- or long-lasting social systems.

To illustrate how small-scale social systems are relevant to health care, consider four stages that might be included in a typical patient career (cf. Suchman, 1965): (1) health maintenance behaviors, (2) help-seeking behavior, (3) contact with the health care system, and (4) patient adjustment to illness and/or recovery. At each point, the patient's attitudes, behaviors, and emotional adjustment are affected by the patient's social system memberships. Conversely, key social systems to which the patient belongs may be affected by the patient's illness. Examples of these effects are discussed briefly. These examples illustrate situations in which knowledge of social systems might be useful in treating the patient.

1.3.1. Health Maintenance Behaviors

It is generally believed that effective prevention of major physical disorders such as cardiovascular disease requires that individuals adopt life-styles that are conducive to health. This includes no smoking, appropriate diet, moderate exercise, adequate sleep, and so forth (Knowles, 1977). Each of these life-style components is subject to social influence. Evans, Rozelle, Mittlemark, Hansen, Bane, and Havis (1978) note that adolescent smoking is affected by peer pressure and parental nagging. Evans has demonstrated that an effective means of reducing smoking is to teach teenagers the social coping skills they need to deal effectively with peer-pressure tactics.

This social systems approach can be contrasted with the Health Belief Model (Becker, 1974), which has dominated this area. The Health Belief Model is derived from value expectancy theories, which assume that an individual's decisions are based on a cost–benefit analysis of alternatives. For instance, the individual weighs the pleasures of smoking against the risk of lung cancer, along with other considerations. The decision to smoke or not to smoke depends on the perceived seriousness of risk, the subjective probability of developing cancer, and so forth. This theory implies that the most effective way to persuade people not to smoke is by exposing them to threatening messages to the effect that lung cancer is a likely outcome of smoking and that cancer is serious and costly. Evans points out that such threats are not very persuasive to high school students, because the negative consequences of smoking occur in the distant future. A social systems approach to smoking reduction, which focuses on the social pressures to smoke and negative social reactions to smoking, may be far more effective for some people than the "threat" approach that is derived from the Health Belief Model. These approaches are not mutually exclusive and could be used in combination.

Other health habits, such as diet and exercise, are equally subject to social influence. Overeating may be encouraged by an ethnic or cultural group or by a family. Any intervention that focuses exclusively on the individual patient and fails to change the social systems that originally led to the eating problem may be ineffective.

Thus far, the negative contribution of social system membership to health maintenance has been emphasized. There are also social systems that encourage good health habits. One example is the Mormons, who discourage use of tobacco and alcohol and have an unusually low incidence of cardiovascular diseases (Fuchs, 1974).

Since social systems are so influential in health maintenance behavior, intervention strategies must take this influence into account. In some instances, individuals may need to learn coping skills so that they can resist social pressure. In other instances, it may be helpful to enlist the support of the individual's social systems to change health habits.

1.3.2. Help-Seeking Behavior

Once an individual notices symptoms, there are many courses of action available: ignoring the symptoms; self-medication; consultation with family and friends (Freidson's "lay referral network," 1961); contacting a health care practitioner such as a faith healer, chiropracter, or physician; or going to the hospital emergency room. The choice among these alternatives depends on many factors, including the nature of the symptoms (if symptoms are painful or interfere with the person's normal activities, the person is more likely to seek help; Mechanic, 1978). There are individual personality characteristics that may affect the individual's readiness to seek help. Social system memberships are another important factor in help-seeking behavior, for several reasons. First of all, social system membership may affect access to resources (time, money, transportation), and access to resources is a major determinant of utilization of physician and hospital services (Mechanic, 1978). Members of large families with a low per capita income may therefore have lower rates of utilization unless the availability of state and federal subsidies offsets this disadvantage. In fact, although the poor now have higher rates of physician utilization than the middle-income groups, there is reason to suspect that they are still receiving fewer services than they need (Aday & Eichhorn, 1972).

An individual's role within social systems may affect help-seeking behavior. Consider the well-documented sex difference in health care utilization (Gove & Hughes, 1979). It has been suggested that the male sex role discourages reporting of symptoms and seeking of help, since these are admissions of weakness. Furthermore, wives who do not have outside employment may have fewer obligations and therefore may more easily utilize health services than people who have full-time jobs. The responsibilities of the mother role may make many women more health-conscious. It has not been resolved whether the sex differences in health care utilization are due to differences in actual incidence of illness or whether they reflect sex differences in illness behaviors (Cohen, 1979). Nor do we know whether sex differences in incidence of illness are due to biological or social factors. However, many authors currently favor the interpretation that differences in the social obligations and roles of men and women are the reason for the sex difference in health care utilization (Nathanson, 1975).

Certain patterns of utilization become established and are then transmitted by families to their children as accepted methods of dealing with illness. For instance, many ethnic minorities in the city of Miami consult folk healers for certain disorders that they identify as specific to their own cultural group (such as the Cuban *susto;* Scott, 1974); they take other health problems to physicians. Any attempt to change this pattern of utilization must take into account the social system memberships of individual patients.

Some people frequently consult physicians when they have no clinically detectable physical disorder; physicians refer to these as the "worried well" (or, less kindly, as "crocks"; Mechanic, 1978). They are often seeking emotional support, reassurance, or legitimacy for the "sick role" to free them from unwanted responsibilities (Parsons, 1951). Psychological counseling can reduce this type of inappropriate utilization by people who are seeking social support (Rosen & Wiens, 1979). Essentially, many people turn to the medical care system for social support that they have not been able to obtain from their families, friends, or other social relationships. A lack of social ties or poor quality of social ties may thus be a determinant of (inappropriate) health care utilization.

Thus, information about the social systems that an individual belongs to may be useful in assessing whether he or she will seek help in dealing with symptoms and also whether that individual will seek medical attention in the absence of physical illness.

1.3.3. Patient Adjustment

Patient adjustment means many things depending on the nature of the disorder. For minor, acute, self-limiting disorders (such as upper-respiratory or gastrointestinal complaints) there are rarely any problems with emotional adjustment. However, some individuals may need help in coping with short-term medical crises (such as surgery). Some disorders (such as myocardial infarction) require a gradual period of rehabilitation, during which the patient gradually resumes normal activities. Many patients need assistance during this period of rehabilitation. Some patients are too eager to return to normal activities and strain themselves, whereas others remain too fearful and never regain as much of their functional capacity as they could. Some disorders involve chronic disability or dependence (such as dialysis), so that the patient's life must be rearranged to take this permanent disability into account. Finally, patients who have terminal diseases (such as certain types of cancer) need to prepare themselves emotionally for death. In each of these cases, however, it is not only the individual patient whose emotional well-being is affected. Medical crises also affect the patient's family, friends, and social obligations.

Two major needs exist: first of all, patients who do not have adequate social support to help them cope emotionally with the medical problem may need to be provided with new social supports. Even if the individual had good social relationships prior to illness, many patients find that their disease isolates or stigmatizes them and that healthy people do not fully empathize with their problems. Wortman and Dunkel-Schetter (1979) note that dying patients feel particularly isolated. Groups of patients who are experiencing the same medical problems can provide each other with emotional support, information about what to expect, and advice (Pavlou, Johnson, Davis, & Lefebvre, 1979, describe such social support groups for multiple sclerosis patients). Social support can be extremely useful in assisting patients with emotional adjustment during rehabilitation or during terminal illness. In such instances, individual counseling can still be used to teach specific coping skills.

The second major problem is minimizing the disruptive impact of illness on the family. Serious illness can limit the ability of the patient to carry out his or her former responsibilities in the family (such as earning income, housekeeping, child care, etc.). In addition, it can affect the patient's intellectual and emotional condition: the patient may change substantially. The family needs to adjust to a redistribution of responsibilities and may also need to adjust to a member whose personality has been altered by illness. Although the patient generally receives help and attention from outsiders, such as the physician, other family members may feel that they have no help in dealing with the problems posed by the illness or disability. For example, kidney dialysis is now becoming much more common. The families of dialysis patients have to adjust to the diet and liquid intake restrictions of the patient, and they must usually live close enough to a dialysis clinic that the patient can go there several times a week for several hours per day. This puts strain on the family, and there are frequently problems of emotional and sexual adjustment between dialysis patients and their spouses. Counseling for the spouse and other family members, as well as for the patient, may be necessary if the entire family is to cope effectively with the medical problem.

1.3.4. Summary

The examples in the previous sections illustrate how frequently social system problems are encountered in the medical care system. It is not an exhaustive list, but it shows that at every point in the patient career, the patient's memberships in social systems such as family and friendship groups influence the patient's behavior and emotions. Knowledge of how social systems work therefore has many potential applications in the health care process. Later sections focus on four key concepts in systems theory that are particularly amenable to systematic research and particularly useful for designing interventions.

2. Basic Issues in Social System Theory

2.1. Introduction

In order to translate general systems theory into specific, testable hypotheses, it is necessary to examine the idea of social relationship more closely. How can a concept as fuzzy as *social relationship* be studied empirically? Four key concepts about relationships in social systems are described below.

2.2. Social Ties

The first key concept is *social tie*. Social tie can refer to any relationship (acquaintance, legal obligation, blood kinship, etc.) between persons. By merely examining the presence and absence of ties or the frequency of ties within some set of persons, we can describe the social network and identify social system boundaries (White & Breiger, 1975). A social system can be defined as a set of people who share a larger number of ties (or more intimate ties) with each other than they share with outsiders (cf. Miller, 1978). There are statistical techniques (block models) that make it possible to sift through information about the presence and absence of friendship ties and to identify friendship cliques that involve many ties among the clique members and few ties between clique members and outsiders.

A social system is defined as closed if there are no ties between group members and outsiders. Obviously, there are very few true closed systems. Systems do differ in their degree of openness or permeability. Some systems have many ties with outsiders while others have fewer ties.

Mere frequency counts of an individual's social ties can be very informative (although obviously information about the intimacy, duration, and other qualities of the social ties is also useful). An individual with few or no social ties is an isolate. An individual with a large number of social ties may be popular, but a large number of social contacts might be a sign that the individual lives in a crowded environment. Furthermore, examination of social ties reveals whether the individual belongs to any unusually closed systems. Examples of closed systems would include a family that has very few social ties with outsiders or a cultural minority group that has few interactions with outsiders.

Isolation can be quantitatively assessed by looking at presence or absence of social ties (or at frequency of communications). The individual's access to social support depends not only on the number of ties but also on the quality of those ties (duration, intimacy, and so forth). Isolation and social support are important to both physical and mental health (Haggard, 1973).

2.3. Social Roles

When we focus on a specific social tie such as marriage, we need terms to describe the effects that the tie has on the behavior of the individuals involved. The concept of social role is useful. Unfortunately, the term *role* is used to mean many different things. The definition used here is taken from Deutsch and Krauss (1965): role consists of a set of shared expectations about the behavior of a person who occupies a certain social position (such as husband) toward persons who occupy other social positions (such as wife). Mechanic (1978) similarly designates *role* as a collection of task skills, attitudes, and behaviors that are associated with particular social positions (such as husband, physician, patient). Obviously, since these definitions involve values and expectations, most assessments of roles are necessarily based either on self-report by social system participants or on reports of observers who interpret the social interactions in terms of intentions of the actors. It is difficult to translate the role concept into objective, quantitatively measurable variables. In spite of this difficulty, the role concept is retained here because it captures certain aspects of social systems that it is difficult to describe in other terms.

Social roles describe an individual's position within a social system since they prescribe the way that individual is supposed to behave toward others. Many roles come in complementary pairs such as husband–wife, parent–child, doctor–patient, teacher–student, and so forth. There is considerable diversity in the way that individuals enact the same role. For instance, it is generally accepted that the parent's responsibility toward the child include providing the child with food, shelter, and other necessities; yet parents differ greatly in many aspects of parenting, such as styles of discipline. The expectations associated with particular roles such as "parent" differ cross-culturally and may change over time.

A corollary of social role is the idea of social power. Some roles have built into them certain power prerogatives over others (the parent–child roles are a good example). Generally, power is associated with control over resources (such as time, money, or other social reinforcements). Control of resources is a useful variable, since it is easier to assess than other aspects of role.

2.4. Cross-Level Linkage among Systems

The general systems theory notion that living systems are hierarchically organized can be applied to social systems. This raises two types of questions. First, individual persons are the components of social systems, and each individual person is made up of complex physiological systems. Since physiological systems are embedded in social systems, it follows logically that physiological and social processes may be interdependent. Changes in the social environment can affect physiological processes, and changes in the physiological substrate may affect social systems. Over long periods of time, it is possible that a social environment can produce cumulative damage to physiological systems. As a first step toward mapping out the interdependence between physiological and social systems, however, it may be more useful to focus on the immediate and short-term effect that the social environment has on physiological processes, since it is much easier to study these short-term effects in well-controlled laboratory settings. Recent advances in biomedical instrumentation have made it feasible to monitor physiological processes during naturally occurring social stress situations and social interactions.

Ultimately, knowledge of the interrelationship between physiological and social systems will be necessary if we are to formulate intelligent theories that specify how social stress leads to "diseases of adaptation" (Selye, 1976).

Another possible area of cross-level linkage occurs because many small-scale social systems (such as friendship cliques or families) operate within the context of larger social systems such as schools, neighborhoods, cities, cultural groups, and so forth. Events in small-scale social systems (such as patient–practioner dyad) may well be affected by events in larger systems (such as hospitals). However, the issues involving linkages among larger and smaller social systems will not be explored here.

2.5. Mutual Contingency

It is obvious that the activities of those who belong to a social system are mutually contingent. For instance, speakers in conversations take turns speaking and listening, married couples may reciprocate positive and negative remarks when they discuss disagreements, and people tend to reciprocate attraction (i.e., they like people who like them and dislike people who dislike them). Only recently have researchers begun to study these types of mutual contingency in detail by collecting detailed observational data and doing statistical analyses, including time-series analysis (Gottman, 1979a). For example, Duncan and Fiske (1978) have collected extensive data on conversational turn taking; Gottman (1979b) has analyzed marital interaction, and Kenny and Nasby (1980) have shown that reciprocity of attraction does occur. Mutual contingency of actions has also been extensively studied for parent–infant dyads; the work of Jaffe, Stern, and Peery (1973), cited earlier, is particularly noteworthy, since it illustrates a way to test whether or not the infant's behavior is statistically dependent upon the parent's behavior over time.

Each of these research projects has yielded interesting details, but the most general conclusion is that the behavior in social systems is not randomly sequenced. Each member's behavior is contingent on the behavior of other members, and the nature of that contingency can be precisely specified using simple statistical models such as Markov chains and time-series analysis. An obvious implication of this mutual contingency is that an intervention that changes the behavior of one member of the system will also indirectly affect that of the other members.

There are many questions about mutual contingency in social systems that can be answered using methods similar to those of Gottman (1979b); Jaffe, Stern, and Peery (1973); and others cited above. These include the following: Are there asymmetries in the mutual contingency, such that member A's behavior is more dependent on member B's behavior than B's behavior is on A's? Gottman (1979a) has suggested statistical methods for detecting this asymmetry, and he suggests that this asymmetry implies that A dominates B in some ways. If A dominates

B then probably an intervention that changes A's behavior will ultimately have a greater impact on the system than an intervention that changes B's behavior.

Another question that could be asked is whether the degree to which a system member's behavior is affected by other system members depends systematically on factors such as the members' ages or the length of membership.

The examples cited here described mutual contingency for very limited sets of behaviors (such as on–off patterns of speech and gaze). Mutual contingency can be assessed for any behavior that can yield time-series data (repeated measurements at regular time intervals).

2.6. Summary of Key Concepts

The four key concepts listed here specify researchable aspects of social relationships. Each of these concepts has useful applications to health care. These four concepts do not exhaust the possibilities, but they provide a framework for the discussion that follows.

2.7. Patient Assessment

Clearly, any clinical assessment of an individual patient needs to include information about that individual's social system participation. Leigh and Reiser (1980) have proposed a specific outline for patient assessment that they call the Patient Evaluation Grid (PEG). Their recommendations about patient assessment are explicitly based on a systems theory perspective. This outline includes three dimensions—biological, psychological, and environmental. The biological dimension of patient assessment includes self-reported symptoms, vital signs, observations by the physician, and laboratory test results. The psychological dimension involves assessment of the patient's intellectual and emotional functioning. The environmental dimension includes information on the social support available to the patient.

Briefly, this section outlines the types of information that might be included in psychological and environmental assessment. The patient's current, recent, and background status on each of these three dimensions should be included.

There has been considerable interest in developing psychological assessment techniques tailored specifically to medical problems. Instruments already in use include the Social Readjustment Rating Scale, the Jenkins Activity Schedule, and the Millon Behavioral Health Inventory (Millon, Green, & Meagher, 1979). These instruments include items that have to do with the patient's social relationships, bereavement, and so forth (along with items that are oriented more to the individual). Actually, psychological assessment of the individual is not completely separable from assessment of the social environment. However, the primary focus of the instruments just named is on the emotional adjustment of the individual patient.

Instruments that assess the characteristics of social systems have begun to emerge (e.g., the Ward Atmosphere Scale, Moos, 1974; the Family Environment Scale, Waters, 1976). Kiritz and Moos (1974) have suggested basic dimensions that should be included in the assessment of social systems, such as social support, cohesion, control, work pressure, and so forth. These investigators review evidence that social support has positive effects on physical well-being, such as reducing time required for recovery from illness; whereas work pressure has negative effects, such as increased likelihood of disease. Some of the instruments developed for research on social systems might possibly be useful for clinical assessment of the environments that patients must live or work in.

Leigh and Reiser (1980) suggest that the minimum information needed by the physician about the patient's social environment includes who accompanied the patient, whether the patient lives alone or with others, marital status, and effects of the patient's illness on his or her family and employers. These "significant others" may be sources of information, social support, or consent. Mere enumeration of the number of the relationships of patients is useful, but in some cases an assessment of the quality of these relationships might also be needed. This is an area where new assessment techniques might be helpful (for example, as a means of evaluating whether a family is a source of stress or social support to the patient).

3. Applications of the Systems Approach to Health Care

3.1. Social Ties and Health

3.1.1. Isolation as Risk Factor

An individual who has few or no social ties is a social isolate. There are many demographic variables that provide a rough index of isolation. For example, marital status is often used as a category in epidemiological research. Lynch (1979) has reviewed data from various sources indicating that married people have a lower incidence of many types of disease than the single, widowed, or divorced. Based on correlational data, it is difficult to know whether isolation *per se* is a risk factor or whether isolation is associated with other behaviors—such as irregular routines and poor diet—that might account for the differential morbidity. It is also conceivable that persons with poor health are less likely to marry, which could also partially account for the difference in life expectancy between married and unmarried people. However, Lynch (1979) argues that isolation in and of itself is probably a risk factor for cardiovascular disorders and other diseases. He admits that unhappily married people are likely to find the marriage tie less beneficial to health than those who are happily married; however, the *lack* of social ties is clearly correlated with morbidity and mortality.

3.1.2. Crowding and Health

If a lack of social ties can be detrimental, it is also possible that living in an environment that forces people to deal with large numbers of social contacts might also be detrimental to health. Too many ties could also be a health risk factor. Extensive research has been done on the short-term and long-term effects of crowding. Crowding can be defined in many different ways—for instance, in terms of the number of people that each individual interacts with, in terms of the amount of physical space available per person, or in terms of the subjective psychological feeling of being crowded. Results of crowding research are mixed. Some studies correlate crowding to crime rates as well as mental and physical illness. Insel and Moos (1974) suggested that "input overload," the pressure of having to deal with too many sensory inputs, is responsible for these problems. Freedman (1976) has argued that many of the apparent detrimental effects of crowding are actually due to poverty. He argued that crowding tends to intensify emotional and physiological responses and is not necessarily harmful in itself. However, he reviewed several studies suggesting that crowding may affect physiological well-being; for example, rats that had to interact with large numbers of other animals developed enlarged adrenal glands. Additional research is needed to clarify the relationship between crowding and disease.

There may well be individual differences in tolerance for isolation and crowding, and the number of social ties that is considered optimal by one person or one culture may not be acceptable to other people or cultures. A key consideration in patient assessment may be whether the individual is satisfied with the number and quality of his or her social ties.

3.1.3. Social Boundaries and Contact with Health Care System

The number of social ties an individual has may affect his or her health status. Furthermore, membership in a social system that has very few ties with outsiders, such as an isolated ethnic minority group, may pose problems for the individual. A patient who does not share the language, culture, or values of the formal medical system may have difficulty getting access to medical services or communicating with the physician. Scott (1974) has described typical incidents of failure to communicate because of cultural boundaries. For instance, a basic premise of Haitian folk medicine is that disease is caused by problems with the blood; the blood is too sweet, too thin, too cold, and so forth. If the medical practitioner shows no interest in their blood-related symptoms, Haitians are likely to feel that they have not received appropriate diagnosis or treatment; therefore they do not comply with instructions or supplement the treatment with folk remedies.

Medical anthropologists point out the need for intermediaries who can act as go-betweens in the doctor–patient interaction when cross-cultural differences make communication difficult (Foster & Anderson, 1978). This need is particularly great in areas such as contraception, where patient adherence to instructions is essential for effectiveness and where there are many folk beliefs that run counter to professional medical advice.

3.2. Doctor and Patient Roles

3.2.1. Overview

The traditional model of the doctor–patient relationship was that the patient was the passive recipient of actions by the physician (drugs, surgery, etc.; Szasz & Hollander, 1956). The physician exercised power over the patient and controlled the decisions. During the past decade, this has begun to change. Consumers have become more militant in general, and the idea of the patient as consumer of medical services has emerged. The question of who controls resources (such as time, money, treatment access) is important. Several of the more influential theories of patient role are reviewed briefly here.

3.2.2. "Sick Role"

Parsons (1951) was one of the first sociologists to analyze the medical system in terms of roles. A patient who believes that he or she is sick goes to the physician seeking legitimacy for the claim to the sick role. Adoption of the sick role means that the patient is freed from normal social obligations but assumes special obligations to try to get well and to cooperate with health care professionals. Illness is a form of deviance from social norms because it supplies a means of escape from responsibilities and duties. A social system as a whole cannot afford to have too many members in the sick role. Therefore, access to the sick role is limited by authorities, who may require proof of disability.

The sick role probably applies better to self-limiting minor illnesses than to chronic disabilities or medical crises. Although it has recently been criticized, the sick role formulation has had great influence on research in medical sociology (Twaddle, 1969).

3.2.3. Deviant Role and Stigma

Since illness can be defined in terms of deviance from norms, it is useful to note that deviance is labeled in two different ways. Mechanic (1978) notes that deviance for which an individual is not held responsible is labeled "sickness" (e.g., cancer, cardiovascular disease). Deviance for which an individual *is* held responsible is labeled "badness" (e.g., homicide, robbery). There has long been a trend to reclassify many forms of deviance from "badness," which should be handled by the penal and justice systems, to "sickness," which falls under the purview of the medical system (Fox, 1977). For instance, alcoholism, drug addiction, hyperactivity, and obesity are now generally regarded as medical problems. The effect of the relabeling is that many forms of once-punished deviant behavior are now medically treated. Szasz (1960) and others note that this expanded power for the medical system has its sinister side.

Partly because of the shadowy boundary between "sickness" and "badness," there is a strong tendency to blame medical patients for their problems. Janis and Rodin (1979) have described many ways in which attributional biases affect social reactions to medical patients. Specifically, there is a tendency to blame the victim for his or her own misfortunes. The patients also tend to blame themselves inappropriately for having caused their own illnesses.

Goffman's (1963) discussion of stigma is applicable. Any visible sign of deviance (such as physical handicap, disfigurement, physical characteristics of a socially devalued ethnic or racial group) is called a stigma. Stigma tend to elicit negative reactions such as horror, revulsion, or curiosity. Many diseases are accompanied by symptoms such as muscular deterioration, skin discoloration, or other visible signs. Thus, many medical patients confront the problems of stigma. Unfortunately, many people have stereotyped expectations about the behavior and abilities of handicapped persons (for instance, they assume that the blind are also deaf), and it can be difficult for the diseased or handicapped person to overcome these stereotyped expectations. Sontag (1978) notes that particular diseases such as cancer may be particularly stigmatizing. Because of this, medical patients may often find that they are forced into an unaccustomed role and that other people react to them in unnatural ways. Coping with stigma may be a major problem for people with disfiguring disease.

3.2.4. Active Patient Orientation

Recent developments in patient-role theory have focused on the theme of control rather than deviance. This shift in emphasis may be partly due to the changes in the types of disorders that physicians deal with. Chronic disorders (particularly hypertension and other cardiovascular disorders) now comprise a far greater share of the cases than they did 20 years ago, while acute communicable diseases such as tuberculosis, smallpox, and poliomyelitis have greatly declined in frequency. Chronic disorders tend to require much more patient cooperation for effective treatment than acute disorders, since drugs and surgery alone are not sufficient. Changes in life-style (smoking, diet, etc.) are also required for effective management of hypertension and reduction of risk of myocardial infarction. Patient compliance with instructions to change these life-style components is generally quite poor (Sackett & Haynes, 1976). The traditional models of the doctor–patient relationship involved an active physician and a passive patient (Szasz & Hollander, 1956), but recently the idea of a more active role for the patient has begun to gain acceptance. The idea is that the patients should participate in decisions about treatment and accept responsibility for themselves.

Research has been done to see whether offering a more active role to patients enhances treatment effectiveness. Schulman (1979) measured active patient orientation (including supportive attitudes of health professionals, patient input into the decision process) and found that active patient orientation in a hypertension clinic correlated positively with control of blood pressure.

3.2.5. "Good Patient"/"Bad Patient" Roles

Taylor (1979) notes that hospitals are total institutions (according to Goffman's 1961 definition) and that they tend to be dehumanizing, depersonalizing environments. Patients can cope with this hospital environment by assuming the "good patient" role (helpless, calm, accepting). This helplessness can be accompanied by depression, and it may be an obstacle to recovery. Hospital staff prefer the "good patients" because they are easy to work with. Alternatively, they can become "bad patients" (suspicious, demanding, angry) who engage in continual efforts to obtain information and attention. Taylor argues that the "good patient" role encouraged by hospital staff may be detrimental to the patient's emotional and physical welfare.

3.2.6. Patient as Consumer

Mechanic (1978) has noted how unusual the medical marketplace is. Demand for medical services is almost entirely under the control of physicians.

Patients tend to accept whatever services they are told that they need, generally without comparison shopping for price or quality of services available. In part, this noncritical behavior by consumers of medical services was based on faith in the physician's judgment. Recently, however, some patients have begun to raise questions about overmedication, unnecessary surgery, and overbilling. Systematic research has begun to determine what factors are decisive in termination of the doctor–patient relationship. Kasteler, Kane, Olsen, and Thetford (1976) found that "doctor shopping" is becoming more prevalent. Lack of confidence in the doctor's competence and unwillingness of doctors to spend time talking were major reasons given for changing physicians. Hayes-Bautista (1976) similarly found that changes in practitioner competence were a major cause of termination of the doctor–patient relationship.

3.2.7. Summary

These various roles—"sick role," "good patient," patient as consumer, and so forth—each highlight different aspects of the social expectations about appropriate behavior for the sick person. Although not explicitly considered here, the changes in the patient role imply changes in ways that other people are expected to behave toward patients, particularly changes in the physician role over time. During the 1950s and 1960s, illness was viewed primarily in terms of deviance from social norms. Medicine, therefore, was viewed as an agent of social control. During the 1970s and 1980s, there has been more concern about who controls the decisions and resources. Allocation of resources is a problem now being intensively studied.

3.3. Interface between Social and Physiological Processes

3.3.1. Environmental Impact on Physiological Responses

There is an extensive literature dealing with the impact of social environments on physiological responses. Kiritz and Moos (1974) noted that a socially supportive environment appears to be beneficial to physical health, whereas a stressful environment may be conducive to the development of illness. In general, we have more reliable information about the short-term effects of social situations, since these can be studied in controlled laboratory settings. There are correlational data linking chronic exposure to social stress to the development of physical disorders, such as cardiovascular diseases (Lynch, 1979).

Most of the existing studies share a limitation that the physiological response is measured only once or a few times. Because of this, intraindividual response variability due to fatigue, habituation, periodic physiological rhythms, and other sources of intraindividual response variability (Fiske & Rice, 1955) are not taken into account. Time-series data consisting of frequent and regular measurements of physiological variables yield not only information about baseline intraindividual response variability in the absence of treatment but may also provide essential information about the manner in which social stress disrupts normal physiological processes. Specifically, there is evidence that desynchronization among physiological rhythms can be detrimental to cognitive, emotional, and behavioral functioning. A supportive social environment may facilitate synchronization of physiological rhythms, while social stress may cause desynchronization. This desynchronization may be one of the key mechanisms through which the social environment has an effect on physical health.

Subsequent sections develop the idea that desynchrony among physiological and behavioral rhythms may lead to illness. This is not the only aspect of the interface between social and physiological processes that deserves study, but it is a promising new area in which a rigorous systems approach can be productive.

3.3.2. Periodic Rhythms in Physiology and Behavior

Periodic rhythms are cycles that repeat at regular time intervals. Physiological processes tend to be periodically organized, with cycles of various lengths such as .1 second (alpha waves in EEG), 90 minutes (occurrence of REM sleep episodes), 24 hours (cycle in body temperature), 28 days (female menstrual cycle), and so on (Luce, 1970). These cycles are not merely due to periodic changes in the environment (such as the 24-hour light–dark cycle) but represent rhythms that persist even under conditions of constant light and temperature (Bunning, 1973). Originally biological rhythms were viewed as a mere curiosity, but now some theorists regard these periodicities as crucial mechanisms for maintaining a dynamic equilibrium in living systems (Goodwin, 1970). Organisms need to coordinate many physiological processes to function (e.g., DNA replication must be timed to coordinate with cell division; Goodwin, 1970). Therefore, synchrony (temporal coordination) among physiological processes is important to the well-being of the organism. If this internal temporal order breaks down, the organism suffers physiological penalities, even death (Pittendrigh, 1975).

Virtually all physiological processes show periodic rhythms (Yates, 1974), although the cycle lengths are not always especially regular. Some overt activities in social systems also tend to be periodic, particularly those that have to do with communication. Kimberly (1970) found that attempts to initiate social contact showed a 3- to 6-minute cycle; Warner (1979) has also found 3- to 6-minute cycles in amount of talk in conversations. Maxim, Bowden, and Sackett (1976) reported a 45-minute cycle in aggressive behavior in rhesus monkeys. Although these are isolated examples, they are consistent with theories arguing that social interactions tend to be periodic (Chapple, 1970; Iberall & McCulloch, 1969). Many of the periodicities in social behavior are tied to the clock, the calendar, and institutional routines (Young & Ziman, 1971). Others may possibly be related to internal physiological rhythms. Chapple (1970) hypothesized that many internal physiological processes that are periodically organized (i.e., rhythms in body temperature, periodic fluctuations in adrenocortical hormones, etc.) may affect the individual's readiness to initiate social activity. Therefore, periodicities in social activity may reflect internal physiological rhythms. Although there is some evidence for Chapple's conjecture, it is not a widely accepted idea at this time.

3.3.3. Detrimental Effects of Desynchrony

Coordination among internal physiological processes is essential to the physical well-being of the organism; however, coordination between internal physiological processes and the overt activities of the organism is also important. For example, body temperature and other physiological variables are elevated during the day, when the individual is more active (Bunning, 1973). An example of a situation that causes these physiological rhythms to get out of phase with the person's wake–sleep cycle is "jet lag."

Rather little data have been collected on the normal relationship between physiological rhythms and cycles in social activity (such as turn taking in conversational speech). However, there are some studies suggesting that desynchrony among internal physiological rhythms, or desynchrony between a physiological rhythm and an overt activity rhythm, is detrimental. Porges, Bohrer, Cheung, Drasgow, McCabe, and Keren (1980) reported that desynchrony between heart rate and respiration is correlated with hyperactivity; they suggested that this breakdown of internal order among physiological processes interfered with cognitive processing. Lund (1974) found that the synchrony between body temperature and the wake–sleep cycle broke down more easily in neurotic subjects than normal subjects. Wehr, Wirz-Justice, Goodwin, Duncan, and Gillin (1979) demonstrated that a shift in the time of going to bed was an effective treatment for depression; they inferred that perhaps depression is partly caused by desynchrony between the patient's wake–sleep cycle and internal physiological rhythms. Interference with the internal synchrony of an animal's physiological rhythms can cause the death of the organism (Pittendrigh, 1975). However, the effects of desynchrony on physical health in humans have been little studied. Riemann (1975) notes the existence of many diseases affecting humans that exhibit periodic recurrence of physical symptoms. Therefore there is some reason to suspect that physiological rhythms are related to resistance to infection and other aspects of the disease process.

These studies suggest that desynchrony can be detrimental to the individual's psychological and physical well-being.

3.3.4. Social Interaction as Synchronizer

During daily social interactions, people frequently coordinate their activities: they take turns speaking and listening, they walk together, they coordinate meals and sleep schedules, and so forth. Biologists have primarily studied the light–dark cycle as a synchronizer of physiological rhythms. However, for humans, social cues are probably more important as synchronizers (Aschoff, Fatranska & Giedke, 1971; Bunning, 1973). Aschoff, Fatranska, and Giedke (1971) have shown that sharing the same activity schedule for meals, work, rest, and so forth was sufficient to produce synchrony among the body temperature cycles of a group of men. McClintock (1971) reported the synchronization of menstrual cycles among college women. Wade, Ellis, and Bohrer (1973) found synchronized cycles in heart rates of play groups of children. A general hypothesis was suggested by Chapple (1970): he stated that a social system, like a physiological system, requires the coordination of activities of its members. Since the physiological processes are embedded in the social system, the physiological processes within each individual are affected by the overt social activities among group members.

3.3.5. Conflicting Demands

The ideal situation (from a systems theory perspective) would be one in which the members of the social system coordinate their activities with each other and each member's social activities are coordinated with that member's internal physiological processes. However, the external environment and the internal physiological processes may often impose conflicting constraints on the individual's activity. For instance, social norms require that individuals take turns speaking and listening during conversations. However, since speech is work done by the respiratory system, the individual's readiness to initiate and maintain speech may depend upon rhythmically organized respiratory variables such as ventilation and blood gas CO_2 levels (Lenneberg, 1967; Warner, 1979). An individual who engages in a lower or higher level of activity than he or she is comfortable with is subject to stress (according to a definition of stress given by Scott & Howard, 1970). An individual who cannot maintain synchrony in either the external social environment or the internal physiological environment may suffer short-term and long-term damage, as suggested in an earlier section.

3.3.6. Summary

This section has suggested that the interface between social and physiological systems can be studied in terms of a dynamic framework (changing over time) rather than a static one. Desynchronization among physiological rhythms or between physiological and social rhythms may be implicated in the development of physical and psychological disorders. Several specific hypotheses are suggested for further study. For example, one reason why social isolation is detrimental to physical health may be that social isolates have relatively few opportunities to synchronize physiological processes with social cues. Opportunities for social synchrony may be essential to health. Thus, one of the benefits provided by socially supportive environments may be the opportunity to synchronize. Perhaps, as Iberall and McCulloch (1969) suggested, all organisms "seek to entrain."

Along similar lines, perhaps one reason why crowding is detrimental is that it places too many conflicting social demands on the physiological system. It is interesting to note that Wade *et al.* (1973) found much more clearly synchronized rhythms in heart rate in dyads than in groups of children. This suggests that it may be much easier to synchronize physiological rhythms to a single partner than to several partners.

The Type A coronary-prone personality is noted for a hostile and abrupt manner and a sense of time urgency. These people may be relatively inflexible in their social and/or physiological rhythms; this may be why Type A's often find themselves in social conflict situations.

Recent advances in biomedical instrumentation and in statistical analysis of relationships between time series (Gottman, 1979a; Porges *et al.*, 1980) make it possible to study the relationship between physiological and social rhythms rigorously. There are many other aspects of the interface between social and physiological systems that are deserving of study. The purpose of this section was to discuss a promising new line of research that is derived from a systems perspective. This suggests some mechanisms (certainly not the only mechanisms) through which social situations might produce detrimental effects on physiological processes.

3.4. Doctor–Patient Communication

The doctor–patient dyad is the social system most directly involved in diagnosis and treatment. In an earlier section, the role perspective was used to analyse this system. However, it is also possible to describe the interaction process that occurs within the doctor–patient dyad to see how the behaviors of doctor and patient are mutually contingent.

A simplified analysis of communication divides it into two parts: message content and message style. Content consists of what is said, or the information conveyed. Style involves how the message is presented; it includes voice tone, gestures, speech rate, and other paralinguistic or nonverbal cues to the emotion of the speaker.

3.4.1. Message Content in Doctor–Patient Interview

Data on message content can be obtained by direct observation of the doctor–patient interview; by examination of a video or audiotape recording of the interaction; by examining the patient's records; or by questioning each participant afterwards. Data can be summarized by listing questions most frequently asked (either by the patient or by the physician) or advice and instructions most frequently given by the physician.

To organize data on message content, it is helpful to have coding categories that can be used to classify each statement. An example of such a system is the Interaction Process Analysis system (Bales, 1970). Bales assumes that there are three underlying dimensions of social behavior: (1) positive versus negative affect, (2) dominant versus submissive behavior, and (3) task-oriented versus non-task-oriented behavior (non-task-oriented behaviors involve distraction or disruption from the task to be accomplished). Bales set up 12 categories to be used for classification of communications within small groups: these included *gives opinion, gives information, seeks information, releases tension, shows agreement, shows disagreement*, and so on. Each communication is coded as an instance of one of these 12 categories. Each behavior is related to one or more of the three dimensions—for instance, *shows disagreement* would clearly be an indication of negative affect; *gives opinion* would be an indication of dominance. The frequency of each of the 12 types of behavior can thus be used to score each participant on the three dimensions. A physician who gives advice and instructions in a friendly, agreeable way would be scored as positive and dominant. By their very nature, many of these categories are complementary: *asks for information* tends to elicit *gives information*.

Korsch and Negrete (1972) have applied the Bales coding system to 800 pediatric clinic interviews between mothers and doctors. Although their results do not provide a definitive description of doctor–patient interviews in general, they do illustrate issues frequently encountered in this research area. Averaged across interviews, the most frequent behavior for both mothers and doctors was *gives information*. The category *shows tension* accounted for 10% of all the mother behaviors. The complementary category *releases tension*, which refers to joking or reassurance, accounted for only about 2% of doctor behaviors.

This suggests that mothers frequently voiced worries that doctors did not respond to. In later interviews by the researchers, the most common reasons that mothers gave for dissatisfaction with the physician contact were that they received no clear diagnosis, that they received no prognosis, or (the most common complaint) that the doctor did not seem interested in their worries about the child. It was found that mothers who were dissatisfied with the clinic visit were less compliant with medical instructions than mothers who were satisfied. Several authors suggest that outcomes such as patient satisfaction, compliance with therapeutic regimens, and time required for recovery may be related to the quality of communication between physician and patient (see review by DiMatteo & Taranta, 1979).

The most commonly cited problem in doctor–patient communication is that patients and physicians enter the situation with different expectations about the type of social interaction (and sometimes also different theories of illness and treatment). In particular, physicians put a higher priority on the "curing" functions of medicine (drugs, surgery, and other treatment technologies). Patients are often more concerned with the "caring" functions of medicine (sympathy, emotional support, and hope; Field, 1971). Field and others have argued that neither the "curing" nor the "caring" aspect of medicine is sufficient treatment for illness. Faith in the physician can make a patient react more favorably to drug therapy. Placebo effects dramatically demonstrate how influential the patient's beliefs are in determining response to treatment.

DiMatteo and Taranta (1979) note that it is not enough to recommend that health care practitioners cultivate a "bedside manner." Systematic research is needed to identify the components of communication that are involved in the establishment of good rapport between physician and patient and to determine whether these skills are teachable.

3.4.2. Message Style in Doctor–Patient Communication

Message style is determined by tone of voice, gestures, facial expressions, and other nonverbal and paralinguistic cues that communicate emotions. Effective communication by a physician requires that he or she be able to decode the emotional message of the patient's gestures, expressions, and tone of voice. It is also necessary for the physician to be able to encode emotions appropriately so that concern and sympathy are communicated to the patient by appropriate nonverbal behaviors. These nonverbal cues to emotion may affect patient behavior. For instance, Milmoe, Rosenthal, Blane, Chafetz, and Wolf (1967) found that physicians whose tone of voice was rated as "anxious" were more successful in getting alcoholics to seek further treatment.

DiMatteo and Taranta (1979) have shown that patient satisfaction with medical care is correlated with the physician's skills at encoding and decoding nonverbal cues to emotion. They suggested that these skills might be teachable. The most widely implemented training program in communication skills for physicians at present is based on techniques from counseling psychology (Kagan, 1979).

297

THE PSYCHOLOGIST
AS SOCIAL SYSTEMS
CONSULTANT

4. Discussion

Typically, medical treatments are designed with an individual patient in mind. However, they will also indirectly affect other members of the social systems to which the patient belongs. Removing a parent to a hospital for long-term treatment will affect the children; disfiguring surgery may distress the patient's spouse; and so forth. One useful contribution of a social systems consultant could be to assist physicians in identifying these effects on the patient's social systems and, where possible, to anticipate and prevent them. A systems approach advises caution when planning interventions in complex systems, since it is difficult to anticipate all the consequences of an intervention.

In some situations, it may be more effective to direct the intervention at a member of the patient's social systems rather than directly at the patient. For instance, Wright (1979) suggested that it may be more effective for a therapist to work with a parent than to work directly with the disturbed child. Working directly with the child, the therapist can only provide a different environment for a few hours a week. By teaching new skills to the parent, it may be possible to change the child's environment for all the hours spent at home. Research to unravel the details of contingency between parent and child behaviors can provide specific guidelines for such indirect interventions.

Psychologists may make a valuable contribution by teaching interviewing and communication skills to physicians; these communication skills clearly influence patient satisfaction, and they may facilitate other specifically medical components of the treatment process (Kagan, 1979).

Social systems consultants may act as intermediaries in settling disputes or clarifying misunderstandings between health professionls and patients. These misunderstandings can arise from cultural differences, different expectations about medical care, the patient's or health care practitioner's lack of communication skills, and so forth. Sank and Shapiro (1979) mention this role as one of many roles that psychologists can fill in Health Maintenance Organizations.

Psychologists can be helpful in preventive medicine and public health. They can contribute to program design and to the evaluation of health care programs either on small or large scales. The Stanford Heart Disease Prevention Program (Meyer, Nash, McAlister, Maccoby, & Farquhar, 1980) exemplifies a large-scale intervention; Evans, Rozelle, Mittelmark, Hansen, Bane, and Havis (1978) exemplifies a small-scale intervention. The social systems perspective can be combined with cognitive and behavior modification approaches to develop effective interventions to change health habits.

Another role for a social systems consultant would involve providing assistance to patients who lack social support. Group therapy for patients who share the same medical problem has become more common (Pavlou et al., 1979).

The value of the social systems perspective is that it directs attention to the effects that medical care and physical health have on social relationships and also to the effects that social relationships have on the effectiveness of medical treatment and the maintenance of physical health.

5. References

Aday, L., & Eichhorn, R. The utilization of health services: Indices and correlates (Pub. No. HSM 73-3003). Rockville, Maryland: U. S. Department of Health, Education, and Welfare, 1972.

Aschoff, J., Fatranska, M., & Giedke, H. Human circadian rhythms in continuous darkness: Entrainment by social cues. *Science*, 1971, *171*, 213–215.

Bakeman, R., & Brown, J. Behavioral dialogues: An approach to the study of mother–infant interaction. *Child Development*, 1977, *48*, 195–203.

Bales, R. F. *Personality and interpersonal behavior*. New York: Holt, Rinehart & Winston, 1970.

Becker, M. H. (Ed.). The Health Belief Model and personal health behavior. *Health Education Monographs*, 1974, *2* (Whole no. 4).

Bunning, E. *The physiological clock* (3rd Ed.). London: English Universities Press, 1973.

Chapple, E. D. *Culture and biological man*. New York: Holt, 1970.

Cohen, F. Personality, stress and the development of physical illness. In G. C. Stone, F. Cohen, & N. E. Adler (Eds.), *Health psychology*. San Francisco: Jossey-Bass, 1979.

Deutsch, M. & Krauss, R. M. *Theories in social psychology*. New York: Basic Books, 1965.

DiMatteo, M. R. The social psychological analysis of physician–patient rapport: Toward a science of the art of medicine. *Journal of Social Issues*, 1979, *35*, 12–33.

DiMatteo, M. R., & Taranta, A. Nonverbal communication and physician patient rapport: An empirical study. *Professional Psychology*, 1979, *10*, 540-547.

Duncan, S., & Fiske, D. *Face-to-face social interaction: Research, methods and theory*. New York: Wiley, 1977.

Evans, R. I., Rozelle, R. M., Mittelmark, M. B., Hansen, W. B., Bane, A. L., & Havis, Jr. Deterring the onset of smoking in children: Knowledge of immediate physiological effects and coping with peer pressure, media pressure and parent modeling. *Journal of Applied Social Psychology*, 1978, *8*, 126–135.

Field, M. G. The health care system of industrial society: The disappearance of the general practitioner and some implications. In E. Mendelsohn, J. P. Swazey, & I. Taviss (Eds.), *Human aspects of biomedical innovation*. Cambridge, Mass.: Harvard University Press, 1971.

Fiske, D., & Rice, L. Intra-individual response variability, *Psychological Bulletin*, 1955, *52*, 217–250.

Foster, G. M., & Anderson, B. G. *Medical anthropology*. New York: Wiley, 1978.

Fox, R. C. The medicalization and demedicalization of American society. In J. H. Knowles, (Ed.), *Doing better and feeling worse*. New York: Norton, 1977.

Freedman, J. *Crowding and behavior*. New York: Freeman, 1976.

Freidson, E. *Patients' views of medical practice*. New York: Russell Sage Foundation, 1961.

Fuchs, V. R. *Who shall live? Health economics and social choice*. New York: Basic Books, 1974.

Goffman, E. *Stigma*. Englewood Cliffs, N.J.: Prentice-Hall, 1963.

Goffman, E. *Asylums*. New York: Doubleday, 1961.

Goodwin, B. Biological stability. In C. H. Waddington (Ed.), *Toward a theoretical biology* (Vol. 3). Chicago: Aldine, 1970.

Gottman, J. M. Detecting cyclicity in social interaction. Psychological Bulletin, 1979a, *86*, 338–348.

Gottman, J. M. *Marital interaction: Experimental investigations*. New York Academic Press, 1979b.

Gove, W. R., & Hughes, M. Possible causes of the apparent sex differences in physical health: An empirical investigation. *American Sociological Review*, 1979, *44*, 126–146.

Haggard, E. A. Some effects of geographic and social isolation in natural settings. In J. E. Rasmussen (Ed.), *Man in isolation and confinement*. Chicago: Aldine, 1973.

Hayes-Bautista, D. E. Termination of the patient–practitioner relationship: Divorce, patient style. *Journal of Health and Social Behavior*, 1976, *17*, 12–21.

Iberall, A. S., & McCulloch, W. S. The organizing principle of complex living systems. *Journal of Basic Engineering*, 1969, *91*, 290–294.

Insel, P. M., & Moos, R. H. The social environment. In P. M. Insel & R. H. Moos (Eds.), *Health and the social environment*. Lexington, Mass.: D. C. Heath, 1974.

Jaffe, J., Stern, A. N., & Peery, J. C. "Conversational" coupling of gaze behavior in prelinguistic human development. *Journal of Psycholinguistic Research*, 1973, *2*, 321–328.

Janis, I. L., & Rodin, J. Attribution, control and decision making: social psychology and health care. In G. C. Stone, F. Cohen, & N. E. Adler (Eds.), *Health psychology*. San Francisco: Jossey-Bass, 1979.

Kagan, N. Counseling psychology, interpersonal skills, and health care. In G. C. Stone, F. Cohen, & N. E. Adler (Eds.), *Health psychology*. San Francisco: Jossey-Bass, 1979.

Kasteler, J., Kane, R., Olsen, D. M., & Thetford, C. Issues underlying prevalence of "doctor-shopping" behavior. *Journal of Health and Social Behavior*, 1976, *17*, 328–339.

Kenny, D. A., & Nasby, W. Splitting the reciprocity correlation. *Journal of Personality and Social Psychology*, 1980, *38*, 249–256.

Kimberly, R. P. Rhythmic patterns in human interaction. *Nature*, 1970, *228*, 88–90.

Kiritz, S., & Moos, R. H. Physiological effects of the social environment. *Psychosomatic Medicine*, 1974, *36*, 96–114.

Knowles, J. H. The responsibility of the individual. In J. H. Knowles, (Ed.), *Doing better and feeling worse*. New York: Norton, 1977.

Korsch, B. M., & Negrete, V. F. Doctor–patient communication. *Scientific American*, 1972, *227*, 67–74.

Leigh, H., & Reiser, M. F. *The patient: Biological, psychological, and social dimensions of medical practice*. New York: Plenum Press, 1980.

Lenneberg, E. *Biological foundations of language*. New York: Wiley, 1967.

Luce, G. *Biological rhythms in human and animal physiology*. New York: Dover, 1970.

Lund, R. Personality factors and desynchronization of circadian rhythms. *Psychosomatic Medicine*, 1974, *36*, 224–228.

Lynch, J. J. *The broken heart: The medical consequences of loneliness*. New York: Basic Books, 1979.

Maher, B. Theory in the grand manner: Review of J. G. Miller, Living Systems. *Contemporary Psychology*, 1979, *24*, 451–453.

Maxim, P. E., Bowden, D. M., & Sackett, G. P. Ultradian rhythms of solitary and social behavior in rhesus monkeys. *Physiology and Behavior*, 1976, *17*, 337–344.

McClintock, M. K. Menstrual synchrony and suppresion. *Nature*, 1971, *229*, 244–245.

Mechanic, D. *Medical sociology* (2nd. Ed.). New York: Free Press, 1978.

Meyer, A., Nash, J. D., McAlister, A. L., Maccoby, N., & Farquhar, J. W. Skills training in a cardiovascular health education campaign. *Journal of Consulting and Clinical Psychology*, 1980, *48*, 129–142.

Miller, J. G. *The living systems*. New York: McGraw Hill, 1978.

Millon, T., Green, C. J., & Meagher, R. The MBHI: A new inventory for the psychodiagnostician in medical settings. *Professional Psychology*, 1979, *10*, 529–539.

Milmoe, S., Rosenthal, R., Blane, H., Chafetz, M. E., & Wolf, I. The doctor's voice: Postdictor of successful referral of alcoholic patients. *Journal of Abnormal Psychology*, 1967, *72*, 78–84.

Moos, R. H. *Evaluating treatment environments: A social ecological approach*. New York: Wiley, 1974.

Nathanson, C. A. Illness and the feminine role: a theoretical review. *Social Science and Medicine*, 1975, *9*, 57–62.

Parsons, T. *The social system*. New York: Free Press, 1951.

Pavlou, M., Johnson, P., Davis, F. A., & Lefebvre, K. A program of psychologic service delivery in a multiple sclerosis center. *Professional Psychology*, 1979, *10*, 503–510.

Pittendrigh, C. S. *Circadian oscillations and organization in nervous systems*. Cambridge: M.I.T. Press, 1975.

Porges, S. W., Bohrer, R. E., Cheung, M. N., Drasgow, F., McCabe, P. M., & Keren, G. New time-series statistic for detecting rhythmic co-occurrence in the frequency domain: The weighted coherence and its application to psychophysiological research. *Psychological Bulletin*, 1980, *88*, 580–587.

Riemann, H. A. Rhythms and periodicity in health and disease. *Annals of Clinical and Laboratory Science*, 1975, *5*, 417–420.

Rosen, J. C., & Wiens, A. N. Changes in medical problems and use of medical services following psychological intervention. *American Psychologist*, 1979, *34*, 420–431.

Sackett, D. L., & Haynes, R. B. *Compliance with therapeutic regimens*. Baltimore: Johns Hopkins University Press, 1976.

Sank, L. I. & Shapiro, J. R. Case examples of the broadened role of psychology in Health Maintenance Organizations. *Professional Psychology*, 1979, *10*, 402–508.

Schulman, B. A. Active patient orientation and outcomes in hypertensive treatment. *Medical Care*, 1979, *17*, 267–280.

Schwartz, G. The brain as a health care system. In G. C. Stone, F. Cohen, & N. E. Adler (Eds.), *Health psychology*. San Francisco: Jossey-Bass, 1979.

Scott, C. S. Health and healing practices among five ethnic groups in Miami, Florida. *Public Health Reports*, 1974, *89*, 524–532.

Scott, R., & Howard, A. Models of stress. In S. Levine & N. Scotch (Eds.), *Social stress*. Chicago: Aldine, 1970.

Selye, H. *The stress of life*. (Rev. Ed.) New York: McGraw Hill, 1976.

Sontag, S. Illness as metaphor. *New York Review of Books*, January 26, 1978; February 9, 1978; February 23, 1978.

Suchman, E. A. Stages of illness and medical care. *Journal of Health and Human Behavior*, 1965, *6*, 114–128.

Szasz, T. S. The myth of mental illness. *American Psychologist*, 1960, *15*, 113–118.

Szasz, T. S. & Hollander, M. H. A contribution to the philosophy of medicine: The basic models of the doctor–patient relationship. *Archives of Internal Medicine*, 1956, *97*, 585–592.

Taylor, S. A developing role for social psychology in medicine and medical practice. *Personality and Social Psychology Bulletin*, 1978, *4*, 515–523.

Taylor, S. Hospital patient behavior: Helplessness, reactance, or control? *Journal of Social Issues*, 1979, *35*, 156–194.

Twaddle, A. C. Health decisions and sick role variations: An exploration. *Journal of Health and Social Behavior*, 1969, *10*, 105–115.

von Bertalanffy, L. *General Systems Theory*. New York: Braziller, 1968.

Wade, M. G., Ellis, M. J., & Bohrer, R. E. Biorhythms in the acitivty of children during free play. *Journal of the Experimental Analysis of Behavior*, 1973, *20*, 155–162.

Warner, R. M. Periodic rhythms in conversational speech. *Language and Speech*, 1979, *22*, 381–396.

Waters, J. *Using the family environment scale as an instructional aid for studying the family*. Unpublished manuscript, Social Science Division, Gordon Junior College, Barnesville, Georgia, 1976.

Wehr, T. A., Wirz-Justice, A., Goodwin, F. K., Duncan, W., & Gillin, J. C. Phase advance of the circadian sleep-wake cycle as an antidepressant. *Science*, 1979, *206*, 710–713.

White, H. C., & Breiger, R. L. Pattern across networks. *Society*, 1975, *12*, 68–73.

Wortman, C. B., & Dunkel-Schetter, C. Interpersonal relationships and cancer: A theoretical analysis. *Journal of Social Issues*, 1979, *35*, 120–155.

Wright, L. A comprehensive program for mental health and behavioral medicine in a large children's hospital. *Professional Psychology*, 1979, *10*, 458-466.

Yates, F. E. Modeling periodicities in reproductive, adrenocortical, and metabolic systems. In M. Ferin, F. Halberg, R. N. Richart, & R. L. Van de Wiele (Eds.). *Biorhythms and human reproduction*. New York: Wiley, 1974.

Young, M., & Ziman, J. Cycles in social behavior. *Nature*, 1971, *229*, 91–95.

Behavioral Cardiology with Emphasis on the Family Heart Study
Fertile Ground for Psychological and Biomedical Research

JOSEPH D. MATARAZZO, WILLIAM E. CONNOR, STEVEN G. FEY, TIMOTHY P. CARMODY, DIANE K. PIERCE, CHERYL S. BRISCHETTO, LAURENCE H. BAKER, SONJA L. CONNOR, AND GARY SEXTON

1. Introduction

The relationships between medicine and psychology may be traced to antiquity; more specifically, references to the exquisite relationship between mind and

JOSEPH D. MATARAZZO • Department of Medical Psychology, Oregon Health Sciences University, Portland, Oregon 97201. WILLIAM E. CONNOR • Department of Medicine, Oregon Health Sciences University, Portland, Oregon 97201. STEVEN G. FEY • Department of Rehabilitation Medicine, University of Washington, Seattle, Washington 98105. TIMOTHY P. CARMODY • Department of Medical Psychology, Oregon Health Sciences University, Portland, Oregon 97201. DIANE K. PIERCE • Department of Medical Psychology, Oregon Health Sciences University, Portland, Oregon 97201. CHERYL S. BRISCHETTO • Department of Medical Psychology, Oregon Health Sciences University, Portland, Oregon 97201. LAURENCE H. BAKER • Department of Psychology, University of Connecticut, Newington, Connecticut 06111. SONJA L. CONNOR • Department of Medicine, Oregon Health Sciences University, Portland, Oregon 97201. GARY SEXTON • Department of Medicine, Oregon Health Sciences University, Portland, Oregon 97201. The studies described in this chapter were supported in part by National Heart, Lung, and Blood Institute Grants HL20910, HL07332, HL24233, and HL07295.

body, including one's health and one's behavior, will be found in humankind's earliest writings, dating back to 5000 B.C. It is, however, an interesting historical fact that in the mountains of early volumes and in the scores of new volumes written in recent times by such leaders in modern psychosomatic medicine as Sigmund Freud, Flanders Dunbar, Franz Alexander, and others, up to the middle of the 20th century the major evidence for the existence of psychosomatic relationships was anecdotal. That is, this past and very recent evidence consists primarily of interesting case histories and such isolated physiologic demonstrations as those of the effect of emotions on gastric function described by Beaumont (1833) in the 19th century and elicited in the subject Tom described by Wolf and Wolff (1947) in the middle of the 20th century.

That emotional and attitudinal states influenced physiological functioning and, if chronic, could irrevocably injure such systems as the cardiovascular, gastrointestinal, and others was a truism accepted for thousands of years as well as in the recent past by all but a few skeptics in medicine and psychology. Yet, even by the years 1950–1970, robust empirical demonstrations of such mind–body disease states that could begin to meet the usual canons of science were little in evidence. Writers of textbooks in medicine, psychiatry, psychology, cardiology, and other fields were in almost monotonous agreement that behavior influenced physiology. To use the field of cardiology as an example, essential hypertension was believed to be a chronic physiologic dysfunction in which one's behavior, especially attitudes relating to repressed anger, was a critical etiologic component. However, no robust research evidence to support this belief was or is available even today. Numerous other examples of research that has failed to validate widely accepted behavioral–biological relationships could be cited.

Fortunately, during the 1960s, this barren state of affairs began to change. For example, Friedman and Rosenman (1974) first reported in the early 1960s that a chronic behavioral pattern, Type A behavior, *doubled* the individual's risk of coronary heart disease. Subsequent research in numerous other laboratories confirmed this interesting relationship between behavior and cardiovascular functioning (Glass, 1977; Jenkins, 1978; Jenkins, Zyzanski, & Rosenman, 1979). Still other relationships between physiology and behavior have been demonstrated during the past two decades (e.g., smoking and lung and cardiovascular disease; life stress and a variety of medical disabilities, etc.).

These recent breakthroughs and others that space precludes describing provided the impetus for a wealth of developments which culminated in the emergence of two new scientific, educational, and applied disciplines. Some of the leaders in these fields believe that their work will help to articulate the relationships between the behavioral sciences and the biomedical sciences more efficiently. These new disciplines are the fields of *behavioral medicine* and *behavioral health*.

Although it is admittedly much too soon to chronicle objectively the myriad influences which culminated in the development of these two fields, Matarazzo (1980) recently provided a short history of them from his perspective as a participant in a number of the national conferences relating to them, as chairperson for 3 years of the NIH Behavioral Medicine Study Section, and as the 1978 charter president of the newly formed Division of Health Psychology of the American Psychological Association.

In his 1980 paper, Matarazzo reproduced the following definition, which mounting evidence suggests most workers in the field currently accept as a working definition:

> Behavioral Medicine is the interdisciplinary field concerned with the development and integration of behavioral and biomedical science knowledge and techniques relevant to health and illness and the application of this knowledge and these techniques to prevention, diagnosis, treatment and rehabilitation. (Schwartz & Weiss, 1978a,b, p. 7)

Although acknowledging that this definition of behavioral medicine no doubt will be improved upon as this field matures, Matarazzo wrote that, while it was an important beginning definition, it did not emphasize enough the two-pronged elements of each person's responsibility for the maintenance of one's own health and the critical importance of one's own behavior in the prevention of poor health. Accordingly, he offered the following additional definition in the hope that it would articulate and channel and thus help accelerate the numerous developments which currently are under way in our country:

> Behavioral Health is an interdisciplinary field dedicated to promoting a philosophy of health that stresses *individual responsibility* in the application of behavioral and biomedical science knowledge and techniques to the *maintenance* of health and the *prevention* of illness and dysfunction by a variety of self-initiated individual or shared activities. (Matarazzo, 1980, p. 813)

It was within the context of the above briefly identified national developments that a research program in behavioral cardiology, to be described below, was inaugurated by faculty in the Departments of Medicine and Medical Psychology at the University of Oregon School of Medicine in 1977.

1.1. Behavioral Cardiology

As is well known, cardiovascular diseases, specifically myocardial infarction, stroke, and related hypertension, are foremost among health problems in the United States and other highly industrialized nations. The monetary cost of heart disease to the nation exceeds $26 billion annually. More than 31 million (1974 figures) people in this country are afflicted with some form of these diseases, which account for over a million deaths per year, or 54% of deaths from all causes (American Heart Association, 1974; Kannel & Gordon, 1971; Moriyama, Krueger, & Stamler, 1971; Stamler, 1974). Hypercholesterolemia (specifically, plasma cholesterol levels greater than 220 mg/dl) and hypertension (arterial blood pressures greater than 140/90 mm Hg) are considered to be major contributors in the pathogenesis of coronary heart disease (American Heart Association, 1970; Cassell, 1971; Chiang, Perlan, & Epstein, 1969; Stamler, 1974).

Laboratory and epidemiological research have shown that dietary, environmental, and behavioral factors are paramount in the development and maintenance of hyperlipidemia (Connor & Connor, 1972; Doyle, 1966; Katz & Stamler, 1953). An elevated plasma cholesterol level is associated with excessive intake of dietary cholesterol and saturated fats (Connor & Connor, 1972; McGill & Mott, 1976). Hypertension is related to excessive sodium intake and caloric intake or obesity (Dahl, 1972; Reisin, Abel, Modan, Silverberg, Eliahou, & Modan,

1978). Obesity results from a self-generating spiral of excessive caloric intake and decreased physical activity. Cigarette smoking has been associated with more severe and extensive atherosclerosis of the aorta and coronary arteries than is found among nonsmokers (Stamler, 1968; U.S. Department of Health, Education and Welfare, 1979). Additionally, highly stressed individuals, particularly those temperamentally inclined to a hard-driving life style (Type A behavior pattern), are found to have a higher incidence of coronary disease (Glass, 1977; Jenkins, 1978).

Thus, current evidence indicates that the development of coronary disease is in part strongly related to various behaviors (e.g., eating, exercise, and smoking) and the complex psychological, attitudinal and social determinants of these behaviors (Carmody, Fey, Pierce, Connor, & Matarazzo, 1982). An increasing number of experts in the field of cardiovascular disease agree that behavioral changes resulting in a diet low in cholesterol, saturated fat, and sodium; weight loss; abstinence from tobacco; and reduced stress are all desirable to prevent coronary artery disease. These medical professionals believe that a number of "unhealthy behaviors and attitudes"—such as a high-fat, high-calorie diet and cigarette smoking—may well lead to the development of heart disease, and that behavioral attitude change should begin in young children and healthy adults to prevent such cardiovascular dysfunction. Thus, the best treatment for hypertension, hyperlipidemia, obesity, and smoking is the early development and maintenance of a behavioral style and habits that prevent the occurrence of these effects. (Carmody *et al.*, 1982; Connor & Connor, 1972; 1977). With cigarette smoking, for example, given its resistance to change once started (Hunt & Matarazzo, 1973; Lichtenstein & Danaher, 1976) the best treatment is to deter it before it ever begins (Evans, Rozelle, Mittlemark, Hansen, Bane, & Havis, 1978; Smith, 1970).

This brief review of a few of the developments during the past decade suggests that a partnership between the disciplines of cardiology and psychology is underway; its continuance appears heuristically desirable. Thus, assigning a name to this interdisciplinary relationship may help add still others to the many isolated examples of such research collaboration between members of these two disciplines. To facilitate such cross-fertilization in other research and clinical settings and to encourage others to contribute to a definition that will eventually gain broad acceptance, we propose the following as a beginning definition of behavioral cardiology, a field which we consider to be a subdiscipline of behavioral medicine and behavioral health.

> *Behavioral Cardiology* is the interdisciplinary field concerned with the development and integration of behavioral and biomedical science knowledge and techniques relevant to *cardiovascular health and illness and related conditions* and the application of this knowledge and these techniques to prevention, diagnosis, treatment, and rehabilitation.

Behavioral cardiology involves a focus on the study of how people (both individuals and groups) develop behavior, attitudes, and life-styles that prevent or are associated with coronary heart disease and cardiovascular dysfunction as well as what to do about them before and after they are manifested. The preventive aspect of this definition arises from the assumption that prevention is the most effective route toward the reduction of coronary heart disease in this country. More important, however, such an initial definition and subsequent development of a recognized subspecialty will help the process of bringing together the many psychologists and other behavioral researchers with cardiologists and biomedical specialists who today are attacking the problem of coronary heart disease in isolated efforts that are not well coordinated. For example, people working separately today in the weight loss, smoking cessation, nutritional, attitude change, and stress reduction fields might be brought together more effectively under the discipline of behavioral cardiology and thus have their expertise applied directly to the coronary heart disease problem in a more concentrated, systematic, and programmatic effort. What we are here proposing, then, is a more visible interdisciplinary effort in behavioral cardiology that would grow and develop in the same manner as the more general behavioral medicine field with, as warranted, appropriate recognition from national scientific societies and an increased base of research and training-grant support from federal and nonfederal agencies and institutions.

2. The Evolution of Behavioral Cardiology at the University of Oregon School of Medicine

Behavioral scientist and cardiologist teams have been working together quite effectively in a number of medical centers throughout our country during the past decade (e.g., The Massachusetts General Hospital and the Duke University Medical Center). It is upon this base of experience that a more visible discipline of behavioral cardiology may be built. As our contribution toward this end, in the rest of this chapter we will describe the development of a behavioral cardiology activity at the School of Medicine of the University of Oregon Health Sciences Center. Behavioral cardiology at this Health Sciences Center began with the fortuitous joining of research interests in 1976 of William E. Connor, a physician whose research field was lipid metabolism–nutrition, and Joseph D. Matarazzo, a psychologist whose research area was health psychology. Based on their earlier research at the University of Iowa, Connor's research group (made up of physicians, nutritionists, nurses, and biochemists) proposed in this new setting to study a sample of free-living Americans and attempt to modify their typical American diet (which is high in cholesterol, fat, and sodium) to one of an "alternative diet" that gradually reduces these dietary constituents in the hope of slowing the atherosclerotic process (Connor, Connor, Fry, & Warner, 1976; Connor & Connor, 1977). A population of family-based groups was identified as the most suitable research sample. The method of dietary modification decided on by the newly assembled medical and behavioral team included the use of intensive dietary instruction, including behavioral modification techniques that stressed group support and cohesiveness. Inasmuch as Matarazzo and his colleagues in medical psychology had the expertise to contribute the behavioral component to this family-based community intervention study, the necessary scientific, clinical, and related support resources from medical psychology and cardiology were brought to bear on a joint research problem. The approach combined the latest information on nutrition and heart disease within a psychological–behavioral framework which was designed to maximally utilize individuals and families, groups, and community support toward the goal of affecting cardiovascular and related biological endpoints through a significant change in individual and family eating behavior. The research design stemming from these ideas was approved for funding in 1977 by the National Heart, Lung, and Blood Institute; thus the joint Cardiology–Nutrition–Medical Psychology Family Heart Study was born.

2.1. The Family Heart Study: Recruitment and Baseline

Basic to the conception of the Family Heart Study was the selection of subjects. The design of the study called for a cross section of urban American families of all age ranges who were living, working, and, most importantly, shopping and eating together. Clearly, the prospective participants would have to volunteer, but the desire was to avoid the inherent problem with "volunteerism," where only those already sympathetic to the study's aims would come forward to join. The solution involved hiring a research marketing firm and selecting families at random throughout a representative neighborhood in the Portland, Oregon, metropolitan area, visiting each in their homes and inviting those that were interested to join the 5-year study. The families were selected from the Hollywood district in northeast Portland because this neighborhood met several criteria: (1) a large enough pool of families, (2) a relatively high degree of stability (single-family residences with low turnover from moving), (3) a cross section of Portland's socioeconomic levels, and (4) a relatively concise geographical district which utilized the same churches, schools, stores, and, most importantly, a YMCA in whose rented quarters the study came to be based. A "random cluster" statistical selection procedure was employed where certain blocks of homes were selected to increase the chances of drawing families who were neighbors and thus possibly knew each other. Qualified homes in the selection grids were identified by the research marketing firm and visited by their trained interviewers, who administered a 30-minute demographic and health survey. A qualified residence consisted of a home with two or more people between the ages of 6 and 65 who shopped and ate together. Although the majority of the people surveyed were husband–wife families with or without children, same- or opposite-sex roommates and single parents were accepted as long as these individuals also shopped and ate together.

After the family residences were identified by sampling methodology, a 30-minute Home Health Survey constructed by our research group was administered by the professional interviewers in each home to the person in the family responsible for the food preparation. It consisted of basic demographic questions about all family members as well as questions about their food shopping and eating patterns, individual health, and special dietary habits and patterns. The survey also included a knowledge questionnaire about nutrition and heart disease, the cholesterol content of selected foods, and health attitude questions drawn from the health-belief-model literature (Becker & Maiman, 1975; Kasl,

1974; Kirscht, 1974) and from the Health Locus-of-control literature which address personality-based expectancies about health and illness and resultant health behavior (Wallston, Wallston, Kaplan, & Maides, 1976).

At the completion of the home survey interviews, the same families were contacted by telephone by a medical psychologist and invited to come to the local YMCA for an information meeting to learn more about the project. The families were telephoned as many times as necessary until they either attended a recruitment meeting, missed three meetings in a row, or refused and wished no further contacts. Families without telephones and those who had declined to give their phone numbers to the home interviewers were extended the same invitation by letter. The recruitment meetings at the neighborhood YMCA were described as informational only, with no pressure or obligation to join. In order to facilitate attendance, the recruitment meetings were held in the evenings, and anywhere from 1 to 20 families attended. At the meeting, the families were given an overall description of the project, a review of the evidence linking nutrition and heart disease, a brief description of the alternative diet, and a review of the time commitments involved in the project. The tone of the presentation reflected the philosophy that families who joined would be presented with the scientific data related to heart disease and nutrition, advised about the alternative diet and its use, and, if they wished to participate, supported in its gradual adoption over a period of 5 years. It was emphasized that no one would be forced to eat certain foods or be "put on a diet"; rather, we would be evaluating their family's response (successful or not successful) to a gradual life-style nutritional dietary change over a long period of time. Thus, skeptics were encouraged to join and every effort was made to be positive and to encourage all points of view.

Families were invited to join as families. Some families did join at the end of that first YMCA meeting, and some went home to discuss the project and joined or refused to join at a later time. Some families decided outright (by telephone or at the first YMCA meeting) not to join the study. Most of the families who did not refuse the telephone invitation outright and came to the recruitment meeting joined the study. It appeared that most of these families had made the decision to join the study before attending the first meeting. Since the outcome of the recruitment effort was critical to the success of the project, every effort was made to follow those who failed to join or did not join immediately and to answer their concerns and assist them in deciding whether the project would be good for their families.

The recruitment effort, then, brought in volunteer families (joiners) made up of people who were genuinely interested in finding out more about heart disease and nutrition, those that were curious enough about the program to make a commitment to join, and a smaller group of skeptics who were willing to join despite beliefs in the opposite direction. In many cases, several of these joining characteristics and points of view were present in one family, and those family members with less enthusiasm were encouraged to join by those members who had greater interest. Thus, the selection process recruited a greater mixture of people, life-styles, and points of view than probably would have been gleaned by a straight "volunteer" study. The characteristics of these joiners and nonjoiners will be discussed in detail in a later portion of this chapter.

The joining families began their formal participation in the study with an extensive *baseline examination* during which their biomedical, nutritional, and psychological characteristics were assessed in three 1½-hour clinical data recording sessions spread over a month. The biomedical assessment consisted of three separate determinations (to ensure measurement reliability) of plasma cholesterol, triglyceride, and lipoprotein fractions along with measurements of height, weight, blood pressure, apical heart rate, and triceps skinfold thickness. (Blood was not drawn from children under age 6.) *Nutritional* data were collected from each member of the family 12 years and older. This information included a 24-hour dietary recall, an assessment of individual eating and food preparation habits at home (Diet-Habit Survey), and an evaluation of each family's restaurant visits, shopping habits, and typical cookbooks and recipes used in the home. The *psychological* evaluation consisted of two components. The first was an individual interview with each family member aged 16 and older. It focused on self-reported psychological stress, health habits (including smoking, alcohol, coffee, drug and exercise habits) and a personal, family, and, for the young children, pediatric health history. The second component involved an individually administered battery of psychological assessment tests consisting of the Cornell Medical Index (Brodman, Erdmann, Lorge, & Wolff, 1949), the Hopkins Symptom Checklist (Derogatis, 1977), the Test of Attentional and Interpersonal Style (Nideffer, 1976), the Life Experiences Survey (Sarason & Johnson, 1976), and a nutrition attitude questionnaire specifically designed for this study.

The purpose of this extensive biomedical, nutritional, and psychological baseline examination was fourfold: (1) to determine for each adult and child in the study a reliable physiological starting point so as to be able to evaluate subsequent changes (5 years later) in plasma cholesterol levels, blood pressure, and weight that might result from dietary change; (2) to identify at baseline potential dietary problem areas in order to assist the investigators in their preparation of nutrition educational material that would serve as the *content* of the 5-year educational treatment phase; (3) to identify components of eating habits that could be modified through intervention; and (4) to develop a baseline psychosocial profile that, 5 years hence, could retrospectively characterize those individuals and families who successfully changed their diets in contrast to those whose diet and resulting physiological indices were not altered.

2.2. The Family Heart Study: Intervention Phase

Completion of the baseline examination initiated the beginning of the 5-year intervention phase of the project. This first phase involved education about voluntary adherence to the alternative diet in a gradual three-phased approach (Connor & Connor, 1972, 1977; Connor, Connor, Fry, & Warner, 1976).

Table 1 presents an overview of the alternative diet compared to today's more "typical" American diet. Basically, the alternative diet gradually reduces cholesterol intake from the usual American level of 500 mg per day to a total of only 100 mg per day (for example, initially by reducing the total number of egg yolks eaten per week). Additionally, dietary fat is decreased from an expected baseline mean of 40% of total calories to 20% of total calories at the end of 5 years. Most of the fat reduction is in the saturated or "hard" fats. It is recognized that even well-motivated people will not make such changes rapidly; hence the alternative diet is designed to be applied in a three-phased approach, with the maximal changes taking place in the late years.

Phase I of the 5-year program calls for avoidance of foods extremely high in cholesterol and saturated fat such as egg yolks, butter, lard, and organ meats. Adequate substitutes include soft margarine, vegetable oils, skim milk, and egg whites. Phase II calls for a reduction of meat consumption from the American average of up to 15 oz. per day to 6 to 8 oz. per day and a reduction of high-fat cheese. Meat as the center of the meal is deemphasized and meatless sandwiches are introduced. Phase III calls for the further reduction of meat consumption to 3 to 4 oz. per day and the exclusive and minimized use of low-cholesterol cheese. The diet in Phase III consists mainly of cereals, legumes, fruits, and vegetables, with meat used as a "condiment" much as in the dishes served in many Chinese–American restaurants.

It was recognized by our research group that abruptly switching to this type of diet would be difficult for most Americans, who have developed their present eating habits and preferences over a long period of time. Consequently the intervention program was designed to ease the way toward behavioral change by removing the barriers and reinforcing adherence over the long run rather than promoting rapid change, which typically results in relapse. The first decision by our behavioral cardiology team was to use the inherent psychological support available in families and groups to help promote and maintain change. The adult members of our families were grouped together into small discussion meetings

Table 1. Present American Diet and the Alternative Diet[a]

	American diet	Alternative diet
Cholesterol (mg/day)	500	100
Fat (% total calories)	40	20
Saturated fat (% calories)	15	5
Monounsaturated fat (% calories)	16	8
Polyunsaturated fat (% calories)	6	7
P:S value[b]	0.4	1.3
Iodine number	63	99
Vegetable fat (% fat)	38	75
Animal fat (% fat)	62	25
Protein (% total calories)	15	15
Vegetable protein (% protein)	32	56
Animal protein (% protein)	68	44
Carbohydrate (% total calories)	45	65
Starch (% calories)	22	40
Sucrose; added to food (% calories)	15	10
Fructose, glucose, sucrose, lactose, maltose; naturally present in foods (% calories)	8	15
Crude fiber (g)	2–3	12–15
Sodium (mEq)	200–300	50–75
Potassium (mEq)	30–70	120–150

[a]Adapted from Connor and Connor (1977).
[b]Ratio of polyunsaturated fat to saturated fat.

of 10 to 12 families; these met once each month in the evenings with a research team consisting of a medical psychologist and a dietitian. In addition to presenting dietary information at each monthly meeting, the psychologist–dietitian group-leader teams encouraged active discussion by the participants and utilized the developing group dynamics to foster cohesiveness and identification with the project. The basic approach adopted for this group intervention was patterned after Kurt Lewin's Iowa model in which he utilized a nondirective group process with American homemakers to facilitate an increase in consumption of underutilized, traditionally unpalatable organ meats during the Second World War (Lewin, 1958).

An attempt is made by our Family Heart Study group leaders to develop group cohesiveness and a commitment to the project, especially to the behavior change necessary in the participating families. At each meeting the two leaders work closely together to provide a group atmosphere in which participants will feel comfortable about disclosing personal experiences concerning their own or their family's dietary change, in confronting barriers to change, and in sharing ideas used for solving problems that arise in changing family eating patterns. Resistance to such dietary change is accepted and even labeled as normal by the leaders and by the group itself. Group cohesiveness as well as development of an identification with the study are being facilitated by several additional features. These include the *Family Heart Newsletter,* which is mailed monthly to each family and contains a photograph and a short personal sketch of a member of the Family Heart Study research staff, new recipes families may try, and a short factual item on a topic dealing with the cardiovascular system. Additionally, the small individual groups of 10 to 12 families that meet monthly are encouraged to develop social friendships outside the monthly meetings and, as natural, to share recipes and alternative diet experiences, visit in each other's homes, and so on. Finally, at the request of several of the small groups, a picnic was held at the end of the second summer to which all 233 of our Family Heart Study families and the project research staff and their families were invited.

Only small dietary changes were encouraged in the first year and individual experimentation and successive approximation were strongly reinforced. In the second and succeeding years, larger changes are being suggested, with continued support for rehearsal, practice, and success with new foods. Lack of change is still defined as nonfailure by all concerned. In addition to group discussion, the technique of behavioral modeling of new food uses is used to demonstrate, by the introduction of new recipes and cooking techniques— at each monthly group meeting—the use of new (alternative) foods that could be used by individual families. Additionally, staff members always prepare samples of recommended alternative diet foods for the monthly meeting and serve these to the subjects for taste-testing to encourage their use within the participating families.

In order to assess potential changes from baseline, all the subjects in the groups return to the YMCA-based research clinic every 4 months for repeat clinical measurements. These periodic measurements serve several purposes: (1) to evaluate individual and family progress (if any) toward the study's physiologically focused endpoints (lower plasma lipids and blood pressure); (2) to evaluate the efficacy of the ongoing dietary education and modeling intervention approach and to make changes if necessary: (3) to provide private feedback to each participant about his or her physiological values, so that each person might better monitor his or her own eating patterns; and (4) to provide the necessary time for the clinical research staff to develop and maintain a personal relationship with each participant. (We are currently ending the *third* year and these return clinics will continue to provide these data points for the full 5 years of the study).

2.3. The Family Heart Study: Control Groups

It is known that biological changes occur in individuals and in communities even without planned intervention. Messages from the media alone may and do result in behavioral and biological changes. Thus, in order to more clearly evaluate the effect of our experimental treatment approach, the Family Heart Study design includes *three* control groups which will serve to monitor any "population drift" of plasma cholesterol and blood pressure in the Portland area over the same 5-year period of study. That is, it very well might be true that cholesterol levels may drop in our community over time due only to the repeated discussion in the media of the nutrition–heart disease problem and a general change in the American diet. Thus the need arose for three control groups rather than one. Control Group I consists of a random sample of families taken from another district in Portland (Sellwood), using a sampling and home-visit recruitment technique identical to the one used in the Hollywood sample. These families were examined by an abbreviated baseline procedure to determine plasma lipids and lipoproteins as well as blood pressure values; without any intervention, they are to be reexamined two additional times over the 5-year study period. They will be given neither nutritional information nor the group process experience, but each person *will* be offered the results of his or her own physiological findings and given an explanation of such results at a group meeting. Inasmuch as even this minimal contact may have some effect, two additional control groups were included. Control Groups II and III consist of spot samples of 85 families taken from other Portland districts in the same manner, with a one-time-only assessment of lipids, blood pressure, and other physiological measures as well as smoking and other life-style characteristics for each spot sample during the same 5-year period.

Inasmuch as the Family Heart Study has only been under way for 3 years and some of the families are still only in Phase I, the remainder of this chapter presents analyses of the baseline data collected and *analyzed to date*. The first section consists of the results of the recruitment effort; that is, the characteristics of those families who joined the study and those who refused. The next section focuses on the *baseline health attitudes* of those families that joined the study and the relationship of such attitudes to cardiovascular risk. The final results report the baseline tobacco-smoking patterns of the participants and the concurrent behavioral, psychological, and physiological differences between smokers, ex-smokers, and nonsmokers. Other baseline data are currently being analyzed but are not yet ready for presentation. Before conducting the analyses to be reported below, we were aware that our participants consisted of a random sample of essentially *normal* Americans and that, thus, any findings accruing from our analyses of potential interrelationships between and among our baseline psychosocial and biologic variables might be attenuated by the statistical artifact of a moderate or severe restriction of the range in many of our variables.

3. Recruitment Studies

The survey by the research marketing firm was carried out from May 1978 to June 1979 with a goal of enrolling 20 to 25 families per month in the study. By use of a standard sampling approach, 936 families were identified from a total Hollywood area base population of 3,579 families. These 936 families were contacted at home by an interviewer; 501 were interviewed and judged eligible for potential recruitment into the study by the criteria described earlier (e.g., two or more adults who ate together regularly, and so on). From this pool of 501 eligible families, the three medical psychologists and other staff were able to recruit 233 families (46.5%); with 268 (53.5%) refusing to join. In this joiner group of 233 families, there were 742 individuals, of whom 474 were adults. As described earlier, one of the medical psychologists telephoned each of these 501 families until the family either joined, refused, or agreed to join but failed to show up three times in succession at the meeting to which its members were assigned.

Since the majority (76%) of the 233 families who joined did so following the first telephone call and the first scheduled informational meeting, this suggests that the idea of the Family Heart Study both had a strong appeal to them and that they had easily reached consensus within the family to join. The remaining percentage (24%) of the eventual 233 joiner families took longer to join (some up to 10 months), citing such problems as busy family schedules, reluctance on the part of one or more family members to join, or temporary obstacles such as illness, remodeling, or an impending family move to another neighborhood. In addition, a majority (55%) of the eligible 268 nonjoining families refused within the first month. The rest (45%) took anywhere from 2 to 12 months to decline the invitation to join. They gave a number of reasons for being unable to reach a decision, including busy family schedules or reluctance to join on the part of one or several family members.

3.1. Joiners versus Nonjoiners

Several demographic characteristics of the joiners and nonjoiners are presented in Table 2. The occupational classifications of the main family breadwinner (usually a husband) were available for 499 of the 501 surveyed households. These data show that the joining families were more likely to represent the professional (59% vs. 41%) and managerial (62% vs. 38%) classifications; whereas the nonjoiners were more likely to be classified as clerical–sales workers (71% vs. 29%), skilled (63% vs. 37%) and semi-skilled and unskilled (59% vs. 41%) laborers, and persons unemployed outside the household (78% vs. 22%). The study population was predominately white, with few minorities. (The nonwhite population of Portalnd is only 5.6% according to 1970 U.S. Census data, and 2.9% in the larger metropolitan tri-county area according to 1977 figures.)

The family constellation figures in the middle of Table 2 show a slightly greater tendency for the joiners to be represented by families with primarily young children (53%) compared to the nonjoiners (47%), who were likely to have no children 18 years of age or less (56% vs. 44%) or mostly children in the teenage years (61% vs. 39%). Viewed from another perspective, as shown at the bottom of Table 2 (reading down among joiners), intact couples with children at home showed a slightly greater tendency to join than couples without children at home (52% vs. 46%); whereas (reading across) single parents fell more often in the refusal category (74% vs. 26%).

Thus, demographically, the model participant in our study was the white middle-class family either without children or with younger children in the home. Blue-collar families, single parents, and families with teenage children were more likely to refuse to join the study. One common thread underlying this joining behavior appears to be the issue of time commitment; that is, the single parent and families with teenagers tended to perceive the Family Heart Study as too-time consuming in view of their already overloaded schedules. Evidence from the telephone calls supports this hypothesis, as a large percentage (65%) of the

Table 2. *Occupational Classification, Family Constellation, and Family Status of Joiners and Nonjoiners at Baseline*

Occupation of breadwinner	Number of breadwinners	Joiners, percentage	Nonjoiners, percentage
Professional, technical	135	59	41
Managerial, self–employed	103	62	38
Clerical, sales	76	29	71
Skilled labor	99	37	63
Semi- and unskilled labor	59	41	59
Not employed outside the home[a]	27	22	78
Total	499	47	53

Family constellation	Number of families	Joiners, percentage	Nonjoiners, percentage
Majority of children 12 years old or less	211	53	47
Majority of children 13–18 years old	93	39	61
Half of children 12 years or less, other half of children 13–18	19	47	53
No child 18 years old or less	177	44	56
Total	500	47	53

Family status	Number of families	Joiners, percentage	Nonjoiners, percentage
Single parents	43	26	74
Couples with children at home	283	52	48
Couples without children at home	138	46	54
Other[b]	36	36	64
Total	500	47	53

[a]Includes homemakers, students, the disabled, the retired, the unemployed, and civic volunteers.
[b]Includes same-sex roommates, single parents, and couples with adult offspring living at home as well as miscellaneous and unknown relationships.

nonjoiners gave "too busy" as their primary reason for refusal. Furthermore, family stress played a role in the reluctance of many single parents to join the study, inasmuch as many of these people were recently divorced or in the process of divorce. The low joining rate in the blue/collar ranks speaks for the difficulties in reaching this segment of the population in order to engage them in preventive or epidemiological effort.

3.2. Health Survey Results

Results from the test questions in the initial Health Survey, designed by us and administered by a trained interviewer during the home visit, are presented in Table 3. First, regarding family food habits and patterns, the 233 families who joined and the 268 families who did not showed little difference in the frequency of lunches and other meals eaten by a family member out of the home (10.63 vs. 10.55 per week), and the frequency of dinners eaten together as a family. Similarly, there was little difference between joiners and nonjoiners in terms of the use of convenience foods by the cook and experimentation with new recipes. On the battery of questions designed to test knowledge of risk factors for coronary heart disease and the cholesterol content of selected foods, the joiners showed a slight tendency to be more accurate in their knowledge of heart disease (76.1% vs. 72.2%, p of .01). No significant difference was found with regard to knowledge about the cholesterol content of foods.

Thus, with regard to food knowledge and habits, the joiners proved to be just sightly more knowledgeable about heart disease than did the nonjoiners, suggesting an interest in the topic that was perhaps reflected in their decision to join a heart disease prevention project.

Table 3. Family Food Patterns and Knowledge of CHD of Joiners and Nonjoiners

Family food patterns	Joiners (n = 233)			Nonjoiners (n = 268)	
	Mean	SD		Mean	SD
Meals eaten out/week	10.63	9.28		10.55	9.28
Convenience foods/week	0.66	1.08		0.85	1.46
Try new recipes/month	3.25	3.57		2.82	3.85

Frequency of eating dinner as a family	Number of families	Joiners, percentage	Nonjoiners, percentage
Almost always	331	47	53
4 or 5 times a week	80	50	50
1 to 3 times a week	64	44	56
Almost never	23	30	70
Total	498	47	53

Knowledge battery	Joiners, percentage correct	Nonjoiners, percentage correct	p value
Coronary heart disease	76.1	72.2	.01
Cholesterol content of food	60.9	58.6	

Table 4 represents the questions dealing with health beliefs and attitudes administered by the research marketing firm. First, concerning the Health Belief Model's conception of coronary health–illness attitudes relating to perceived susceptibility, severity, benefits, and barriers (Becker & Maiman, 1975), the joiners and nonjoiners showed no differences in perceived susceptibility to (10.58 vs. 10.73) and severity of (9.37 vs. 9.32) coronary heart disease or the perceived barriers to changing their coronary risk behavior (11.22 vs. 11.05). As would be reasonable, the joiners showed a slight tendency (p of .05) to see greater benefits accruing from heart disease prevention approaches (3.80 vs. 4.07). On the Health Locus of Control Scale (Wallston, Wallston, Kaplan, & Maides, 1976) administered by the research marketing firm, the joiners scored significantly higher (p of .01) in the direction of believing that the status of their individual health was under the influence of an *internal* locus of control than did the nonjoiners (34.50 vs. 32.79), although the mean difference between the groups was quite small. This finding appeared to support the idea of "internals" being more health conscious. It might have been that those with an internal locus of control were more likely to join because they saw the 5-year Family Heart Study as providing the kind of structure and framework they needed to change their own health behavior.

The lower half of Table 4 presents the types of environmental cues that the respondents identified as influential to their health behavior. As shown in Table 4, there were no differences between joiners and nonjoiners in the self-reported influence from the electronic media, physicians, or friends, but there was a slight difference (2.67 vs. 2.40, p of .05) in the influence from reading about heart disease, with the joiners having read more on the subject. Interestingly, on a rating scale from 1 to 4, both joiners and nonjoiners reported the greatest influence on their behavior from the written and electronic media, next greatest from discussions with friends, and the least from discussion with their physicians. The more powerful influence of reading about heart disease for the joiners compared to nonjoiners might relate to their higher occupational and educational (socioeconomic) backgrounds.

Table 4. Health Attitudes of Joiners and Nonjoiners

Health belief scale[a]	Mean scale scores		
	Joiners	Nonjoiners	p value
Susceptibility	10.58	10.73	
Severity	9.37	9.32	
Benefits	3.80	4.07	.05
Barriers	11.22	11.05	
Health locus of control	34.50	32.79	.01
Cues for action			
Reading about CHD	2.67	2.40	.05
Advice from physician	1.48	1.47	
Discussion with friends	2.09	2.01	
Electronic media	2.74	2.66	

[a]The lower the individual's score on each of these four scales, the more that individual perceives the relevance of that scale item for him or her.

3.3. Recruitment Phase: Summary of Results

Summarizing the recruitment survey thus far, the following conclusions are supported by our data:

1. It is possible to recruit participants for a nutritionally based heart disease prevention program from a random sample of urban, free-living Americans. The majority of the recruited participants appear to have been positively disposed to the project's goals and readily made up their minds to join. A large portion of the nonjoiners had trouble making their decisions and required a considerable amount of the experimenters' time in repeated calls and appointments.

2. Occupational level and related aspects of socioeconomic status (SES) appear to be an important factor in the recruitment process, with the skilled and unskilled blue-collar classes joining at a less frequent rate. This SES division in all probability accounts for some of the other differences between joiners and nonjoiners in that higher-SES families might be more flexible in their eating patterns and read more about heart disease.

3. Families with members who are undergoing life stress or who perceive themselves as having too many time commitments appear to have been more likely to choose not to participate in the study. Our intervention population is also underrepresented by families with a single parent or with teenage children.

4. There appear to be no clinically significant attitudinal differences between the joiners and nonjoiners in the areas of health beliefs and locus of control as these are assessed by currently available techniques. Joiners showed a statistically but not clinically significant trend toward internality; that is, they are individuals who describe their health as largely determined by factors they potentially have control over.

This recruitment experience adds to the growing illness prevention literature; it also suggests the desirability of further public health research aimed specifically at designing techniques required to stimulate the health-promoting interests of the population of Americans represented in the subsample we missed (nonjoiners). The prevalence of coronary disease in all socioeconomic segments of this society demands multiple strategies in dietary change trials in order to involve the families who decided not to participate. Although the Family Heart Study employed a field-trial approach, the need for controlled studies in this area is obvious. For example, future studies could specifically examine the barriers to joining a preventive health program such as this and develop alternative programs that might overcome these barriers. Electronic and other educational media as used by the Stanford Heart Disease Prevention (Farquhar, Maccoby, & Wood, 1977; Meyer, Nash, McAlister, Maccoby, & Farquhar, 1980) and the Baylor group (Foreyt, Scott, Mitchell, & Gotto, 1979) might appeal to busy or stressed families. Also, incorporating the prevention program into already existing activities such as school, church, or work settings—in contrast to a monthly evening meeting in their own neighborhood—might also be more effective. There are, however, many methodological problems in these just-cited studies; they have been described by Kasl (1980), Leventhal, Safer, Cleary, and Gutman (1980) and rebutted, in turn, by Meyer, Maccoby, and Farquhar (1980).

The Health Locus of Control (HLC) Scale (Wallston *et al.*, 1976) administered during the home interview was included in an attempt to apply the "locus of control" personality trait to the area of health-related behaviors. More recently, the Multidimensional Health Locus of Control (MHLC) Scales were developed to measure a more complex array of health dimensions; specifically: (1) the belief that health is determined by one's own behavior, that is, an orientation suggesting an *internal* locus of control; (2) a reliance on *powerful others* (e.g., health professionals) for one's own health maintenance; and (3) the belief that one's health or lack of it is largely due to *chance* (Wallston, Wallston, & DeVellis, 1978). Our Alternative Diet Family Heart Study Clinic provided an excellent testing ground for examination of such questions, inasmuch as many psychological and physiological measures were gathered concurrently on the same individual. The Multidimensional Health Locus of Control Scale—Form A (MHLC) was included in this battery instead of the Health Locus of Control Scale used earlier by other investigators; it was administered by the medical psychologists to all family members aged 16 or older.

In order to reduce the problem of statistically significant but unreliable findings from our study, the present results from the MHLC are based on two *randomly selected* subsamples from the Family Heart Study participants: one a *test sample* and the other a *cross-validation sample*. The test sample was a random subsample of the first 299 members of the 474 adult participants and consisted of 180 adults (91 males and 89 females), with a mean age of 37.9 (range 20 to 70 years). The validation sample consisted of the remaining 119 additional adults (61 males, 58 females), with a mean age of 35.4 (range 22 to 69 years). The biomedical measures studied included height, weight, blood pressure, plasma cholesterol, and plasma triglyceride. In addition to the MHLC—Form A, the psychological assessment measures included the Hopkins Symptom Checklist (SCL-90; Derogatis, 1977) and the Cornell Medical Index (CMI) (Brodman, Erdmann, Lorge, & Wolff, 1949). The baseline information pertaining to exercise and smoking habits was also evaluated in the test and cross-validation samples.

Locus of control data from the MHLC were correlated with the psychological and biomedical variables and these correlations are shown in Table 5. These correlations were computed on the total number of subjects in Sample 1 and also in Sample 2. In currently ongoing analyses, these computations are being run separately for males and for females on the chance that potential sex differences are being masked in the findings shown in Table 5 and in many of the other tables reported in this chapter. The MHLC inventory assesses whether the individual believes his or her health status is a function of "chance" (CHLC), due to the actions of "powerful others" (PHLC), or a product of one's own "internal" beliefs and behaviors (IHLC). Table 5 reveals that an "internal" locus of control orientation was negatively correlated in the same individuals with the "chance" subscale ($-.23$ and $-.23$, p of .01 and .05, respectively due to the smaller number of subjects in the cross-validation sample); whereas the external determinants, "powerful others" and "chance," were positively correlated with each other (.29 and .31 both p of .01). Neither the plasma cholesterol nor the body mass index (wt/ht^2 × 10,000) were significantly correlated with any of the health locus of control dimensions. The Cornell Medical Index (total medical symptoms) was significantly correlated (.41 and .38, both p of .01) with the Hopkins Global Severity Index (GSI), which is a measure of acute psychological distress, in only one sample with plasma cholesterol (p of .01). Finally, the physiological measures of coronary risk were highly related to each other, with both plasma cholesterol and body mass values being significantly correlated with age (.41 and .23 respectively, both p of .01). However, the replication of these figures in the validation sample upheld only the plasma cholesterol–age correlation. Inasmuch as the psychological measures did not correlate with age (Table 5), neither they nor the physiological measures were age-adjusted for the analyses shown in Table 5. (This contrasts with the analyses in Tables 12 and 13.) We were surprised by the lack of correlation between the MHLC measures and the biomedical measures and decided to pursue our analyses further by using extreme groups on one variable in an attempt to reveal even weak relationships that may exist.

Table 5. Correlation Matrix for Health Locus of Control and Biomedical Measures

		Internal (IHLC)	Powerful others (PHLC)	Chance (CHLC)	Cornell (Total)	Hopkins (GSI)	Plasma cholesterol	Body-mass index	Age
Internal	I[a]		.01	−.23[d]	.14	.06	−.07	−.02	−.01
(IHLC)	II[b]		−.12	−.23[c]	−.07	.01	.08	−.06	−.10
Powerful others	I			.29[d]	.01	−.07	.10	.09	.19[c]
(PHLC)	II			.31[d]	.24[c]	.21[c]	.17	.08	.03
Chance	I				.05	.01	.13	.07	.12
(CHLC)	II				.03	.06	−.01	−.01	.14
Cornell Medical Index	I					.41[d]	.11	.14	.33[d]
(Total Sx.)	II					.38[d]	.27[d]	.14	.31[d]
Hopkins Symptom	I						.08	−.02	.15
Checklist GSI	II						−.04	.07	.15
Plasma	I							.34[d]	.41[d]
cholesterol	II							.04	.34[d]
Body mass	I								.23[d]
index	II								.14

[a]Correlations for test Sample I.
[b]Correlations for cross-validation Sample II.
[c]p of .05.
[d]p of .01.

In a further attempt to study the potential relationships between selected behavioral and biomedical characteristics of the same individual, we next created subsets of the 474 study participants. Table 6 divides sub-groups of the subjects in both samples into high- and low-risk groups based on each individual's own level of plasma cholesterol. The highest and lowest 12th percentile groups for plasma cholesterol level (namely, individuals at either end of the plasma cholesterol distribution curve) were compared on their responses to the measures of MHLC, the Cornell Medical Index, the Hopkins Symptom Checklist, and physiological measures. As shown in Table 6, the high-cholesterol group was significantly older (p of .01) than the low-cholesterol group in the test sample and scored higher (p of .01) on the *chance* subscale of the MHLC. However, on replication in the cross-validation sample, the age differences were again present (p of .01) but no "chance" score difference was found. The high-cholesterol group also appeared to be higher in the test sample on each of the four other potential biomedical risk factors (plasma triglyceride, body-mass index, and blood pressure, all with a p of .01); however, only the statistically significant (p of .01) plasma triglyceride difference was replicated in the cross-validation sample. Interestingly, there were no consistent and cross-validated differences between the low-cholesterol and high-cholesterol groups on the Hopkins, Cornell, or MHLC measures.

4.2. Health Attitudes and Obesity

The subjects in both samples were next grouped according to the body-mass index into the highest and lowest groups. In order to have a large enough

Table 6. Mean Scores on Psychological and Biomedical Measures for High and Low Plasma Cholesterol Groups

	Sample I			Sample II		
Measures	High plasma cholesterol	Low plasma cholesterol	p value	High plasma cholesterol	Low plasma cholesterol	p value
Total subgroup (n)	20	20		26	26	
Males (n), females (n)	12,8	9,11		11,15	10,16	
Age	46.15	30.80	.01	39.69	31.85	.01
Internal HLC	26.75	28.35		28.77	28.77	
Powerful others HLC	15.35	14.35		15.19	13.92	
Chance HLC	15.40	10.55	.01	14.12	14.50	
Cornell (total)	14.85	14.20		23.38	14.15	.05
Hopkins (GSI)	53.10	51.05		50.73	52.19	
Plasma						
triglycerides (mg/dl)	166.50	63.40	.01	130.96	76.92	.01
Body-mass index (wt/ht² × 10,000)	27.22	23.07	.01	24.08	24.01	
Systolic BP (mm Hg)	122.65	109.25	.01	109.27	109.69	
Diastolic BP (mm Hg)	79.00	69.10	.01	72.96	67.46	

number of individuals in each extreme group, the top and bottom 14th percentiles on weight and height were selected in contrast to the 12th percentiles. The results (not shown here in tabular form) showed *no* differences between these groups in the Multidimensional Health Locus of Control subscales, the Cornell Medical Index, or Hopkins Symptom Checklist scores. Again, the people with the greatest body-mass index values were found, as expected, to be older and to have a higher profile of cardiovascular risk when compared on the other physiological measures.

4.3. Internal Locus of Control and Biomedical Status

The subjects in both the test and the cross-validation samples were then again divided according to their degree of internality on the MHLC; specifically, the highest and lowest 14th percentile groups on the IHLC subscale were next compared on all these same measures. Although not shown here in tabular form, subjects with higher internal scores had lower scores (p of .01) on the "chance" subscale. Using these extreme groups on IHLC, there were again *no* differences on the Cornell Medical Index, the Hopkins Symptom Checklist, or on the physiological measures except for blood pressure, with the low "internals" having higher blood pressures (p of .05). However, this latter result was not cross-validated in the second sample. Thus, even procedures using only extreme groups on each of these various psychological and biomedical variables failed to provide relationships among them other than the statistically significant correlations shown in Table 5 for the entire range of individuals on these same measures.

4.4. Health Attitudes of Smokers and Nonsmokers

The individuals in the test and the cross-validation samples were next grouped by smoking status (smoker, ex-smoker, never smoked), and these groups were compared in terms of their answers to the MHLC measures of health locus of control. To provide sufficient numbers in these three smoking groups, the data from the 474 subjects from the test and validation subsamples were combined into a single test sample, without a cross-validation group. No consistent differences were found among the three smoking classification groups on any of the three MHLC subscales (IHLC, PHLC, and CHLC). This finding is surprising inasmuch as smokers conceivably are less internal in locus of control as judged by their demonstrated (and thus presumed) greater susceptibility to tobacco advertisements, role modeling, and peer and other pressures to begin and to maintain smoking.

4.5. Health Attitudes and Leisure Activity

Finally, in a further look at the data from the test and cross-validation samples, self-reported leisure activity and physical exercise were compared for the high- and low-internal MHLC groups. Subjects were asked at baseline to estimate their own amount of sedentary activity and television watching in terms of average number of hours per day. Amounts of light, moderate, and heavy physical exercise were reported by the subjects in terms of minutes per week and then converted into kilocalories expended per week. The results are presented in Table 7. In Sample I, high-internal subjects reported significantly more *heavy* exercise per week than did low-internal subjects (2,264 vs. 624 kilocalories, p of .05). This finding was replicated in the cross-validation sample (1,529 vs. 253 kilocalories, p of .05). Although the amount of moderate physical exercise reported by high-internal subjects was almost double the amount for low internals in the first sample (1,502 vs. 872), this difference was reversed in the second sample and did not reach statistical significance in either. No other significant differences were found between high- and low-internal subjects in leisure activity or exercise in either sample.

4.6. Health Attitudes: Implications of Our Findings

These preliminary results from our study on the relationships between biomedical and behavioral characteristics have several important implications. First, the MHLC scale itself as developed by Wallston *et al.* (1978) appears to show a high level of consistency among the three subscales as indicated in the correlation matrix shown in Table 5 and described above. The internal and external dimensions show a negative relationship, with the higher "internals" showing a lower belief in chance. Thus, people who reported that their own actions were important in determining their health were less likely to be fatalistic regarding the role of chance events. In addition, the external subscales ("powerful other" and "chance") were found to be significantly positively correlated (p of .01), suggesting that externality as a health constant encompasses both chance events and the power of health care professionals. However, even when we studied only individuals at the extremes, these locus of control dispositions did not distinguish between people at high and low risk for coronary disease as measured by plasma cholesterol, blood pressure, and body-mass index (see Table 6). Thus, if it can be assumed that these risk factors are partially due to lifetime behavioral patterns (consumption of excessive dietary cholesterol and saturated fat, calories, and cigarettes), the results from this initial study suggest that these health locus of control variables do *not* appear to relate to the biomedical risk endpoints associated with the initiation and maintenance of these unhealthy behaviors. Clearly, considerable more research is needed before we conclude

Table 7. Leisure Activity and Physical Exercise for High and Low Internals

Measures	Sample I			Sample II		
	High internals	Low internals	p value	High internals	Low internals	p value
Number (*n*)	21	26		21	19	
Television (hr/day)	1.5	1.6		1.3	1.7	
Sedentary (hr/day)	3.5	3.4		2.9	4.3	
Light exercise (kcal/wk)	974	938		977	750	
Moderate exercise (kcal/wk)	1502	872		793	818	
Heavy exercise (kcal/wk)	2264	624	.05	1529	253	.05

from these findings either that there is no such relationship or that it is not possible to validly measure the attitudes that accompany the unhealthy behaviors (smoking, overeating) known to influence later physiological endpoints.

Factors contributing to a lack of consistency in the previous research findings regarding studies of health locus of control (Strickland, 1978) include a lack of standard or consistent self-report measures of locus of control, theoretical confusion as to the meaning of this psychological construct, and a lack of appreciation for the complexity of the relationship between health locus of control and specific health behaviors. In this regard, Wallston and Wallston (1978) have emphasized the need to explore the interaction between health locus of control and other factors contributing to health-related behavior, such as motivation, social support, previous behavior, attitudes and values about health care, and demographic variables.

The use of biomedical endpoints in the present study represented an attempt to examine some of these critical factors. The present findings are that the only consistent behavioral or biomedical difference between MHLC high- and low-internal subjects was in the amount of heavy physical exercise they reported. Specifically, the presumed lifelong personality– attitude characteristic of internal locus of control was found to be associated with a greater amount of self-reported heavy exercise. But how is it that internal locus of control would be related to heavy exercise but not to body-mass index, cigarette smoking, or other leisure activity? Again, the complex and incompletely understood characteristics of this attitude–behavior relationship must be considered. It might be hypothesized, for example, that in the case of an addictive behavior such as cigarette smoking, internal locus of control is much less of an influence on behavior than it is in the area of heavy physical exercise. Further work is planned to test this hypothesis. Moreover, although this was cross-validated, it was puzzling to find that internal locus of control related only to heavy exercise and not to other forms of leisure and physical activity. Additional studies are needed to explain this finding. For example, from the results shown in Table 7, it would seem reasonable to suggest that locus of control is not a determining factor for milder forms of exercise but has more influence on presumably more exhausting heavy physical exercise such as jogging or calisthenics, which involve considerable time and effort. However, the question "why" begs to be asked. (We thus see our initial results as only preliminary findings.)

The measurements of physiological risk for heart disease show the expected clustering, with plasma cholesterol and blood pressure being positively related to age and weight (Table 5). The psychological stress measures (Cornell Medical Index and Hopkins Symptom Checklist) show relationships to each other (Table 5) but, surprisingly, do not appear to be associated with differing levels of physiological risk (Table 6).

In summary, this series of studies of some potential interrelationships between behavioral and biomedical variables show that each of the measures of locus of control, physiological risk, and psychological stress has strong internal relationships but none that are related with statistical significance to each other. Thus the findings do not allow the development of hypotheses that begin to explain the complex psychological concomitants of coronary risk. We are exploring restriction in the range of some of our measures as a possible reason for this absence of significant relationships.

The 474 adult subjects in the Family Heart Study were divided into three groups according to their smoking status. *Smokers* included all those subjects currently smoking tobacco in some form (cigarette, pipe, or cigar). The smokers were further divided by the number of cigarettes smoked per day; with *lighter smokers* smoking less than 3/4 of a pack per day, *pack smokers* smoking from 3/4 to 1 1/4 packs per day, and *heavier smokers* smoking more than 25 cigarettes per day. Non-cigarette-smoking pipe and cigar smokers were included in the *light smokers* category. Ex-smokers were those who had smoked in the past but currently used no tobacco at all. *Nonsmokers* were those who never used tobacco products except perhaps for brief experimentation. As in the health locus of control studies, the smoking studies were done on a randomly selected test group from the 474 adult subjects and cross-validated on the remaining sample. However, the subjects were treated as a single group for the analyses in Tables 8 and 9 because there were too few subjects in a number of the cells.

The demographic and smoking pattern data are presented in Tables 8 and 9. As shown in the last column of Table 8, 47.9%, or almost half of our total population of 474 adults, were nonsmokers (never smoked in any form). Nonsmoking males constituted 41.5% of our total of 229 males, whereas females who had never smoked constituted 53.9% of all the females in our study sample of 245 females. Adding the 25.1% of our total sample who were ex-smokers to the 47.9% nonsmokers reveals that a total of 73.0% of our population were not using tobacco at the time they entered the study. The figures for the current smokers show a higher proportion of male smokers (33.2%) than female smokers (21.2%), with a total sample average of 27% smokers. Additional analyses revealed that the smokers were significantly older than the nonsmokers (38.2 vs. 34.4 years, p of .01). Although not shown in tabular form, there were significantly more people in the 26 to 35 age range among the smokers, with the largest portion of the smoking population being 26 years of age or older. Not surprisingly, given the slightly high SES characteristics of our joiners (see Table 2), data on income and educational level showed no difference among the three smoking classification groups (this is shown in Table 8).

Table 9 presents the cigarette usage of smokers and shows that the males and females differed little in the mean number of cigarettes per day. The ma-

Table 8. Smoking Status of Family Heart Participants

	Total	Smokers		Ex-smokers		Nonsmokers	
	n	n	Percent	n	Percent	n	Percent
Males	229	76[a]	33.2	58	25.3	95	41.5
Females	245	52	21.2	61	24.9	132	53.9
Total	474	128	27.0	119	25.1	227	47.9
Mean age		38.2		36.6		34.4	
Mean years of education		14.91		14.81		15.35	
Mean income		$24,226		$22,647		$22,312	

[a]The 76 current male smokers included 61 who smoked cigarettes only and 15 pipe and/or cigar smokers (some of whom also smoked cigarettes). Additional tables in this chapter show the characteristics of these smokers in one or another combination of such smoking status and are so labeled.

jority reported smoking a pack or less per day. Although not shown in Table 9, cigarette consumption increased with age and duration of the smoking habit. The majority of male and female smokers reported that they have smoked for 10 years or more. For the ex-smokers, males reported having previously smoked significantly more cigarettes per day (p of .01). Males also tend to smoke longer before quitting (5 years or longer) than did females (less than 5 years). Most of the male and female ex-smokers reported successful abstinence for periods greater than 5 years.

In sum, as nonsmokers or ex-smokers, the majority (73%) of the Family Heart Study participants did not use tobacco when they joined the study, with almost half (47.9%) reporting that they had never smoked at all. The smokers as a group smoked about a pack a day, with the amount increasing with age and duration of the habit. The quitters (ex-smokers) showed similar one-pack-per-day consumption levels, with males reporting a heavier cigarette-smoking record than females. The male ex-smokers tended to have smoked longer than the females before quitting, but both groups reported relatively long periods of abstinence since their last cigarette.

5.1. Smokers' Use of Coffee, Alcohol, and Other Drugs

Table 10 shows the coffee, alcohol, and drug patterns of our total population of 474 study participants sorted in the three smoking categories. One-way analyses of variance of the coffee patterns indicated that smokers in Sample I drink more coffee than do ex-smokers or nonsmokers (4.44 vs. 3.16 vs. 1.97, p of .001). This finding was cross-validated in Sample II (p of .001). On the other hand, ex-smokers appeared to use *more* decaffeinated coffee than either smokers or nonsmokers (p of .05). However, the latter finding was not statistically affirmed in the cross-validation sample. Although not shown in Table 10, there were no group differences in tea consumption. However, the smokers in Sample I reported more frequent use of marijuana than either the ex-smokers or nonsmokers (p of .05); although this finding was more true of the ex-smokers and also fell short of statistical significance in the cross-validation sample. Thus, with regard to this class of habits, heavier coffee use and marijuana smoking seem to be more prevalent among the cigarette smokers. The ex-smokers and nonsmokers, on the other hand, appear to gravitate toward less coffee drinking, ex-smokers make greater use of decaffeinated coffee, and fewer nonsmokers use marijuana in any form. There were no cross-validated statistically significant differences between smoking status and use of aspirin or prescribed drugs.

Table 9. Smoking Patterns of Current Cigarette Smokers

				Mean number of cigarettes/day						
	n	Mean	Range	1–9	10–19	(pack)	21–29	30–39	(2 packs)	41+
Males	61	21.2	1–60	11	11	18	2	11	4	4
Females	52	18.3	1–80	12	11	20	0	4	4	1
Total	113	20.02	1–80	23	22	38	2	15	8	5

Table 10. Coffee, Alcohol, and Drug Consumption of Cigarette, Pipe, and Cigar Smokers, Ex-smokers, and Nonsmokers

Measure	Sample I (n = 235)				Sample II (n = 239)			
	Smokers	Ex-smokers	Nonsmokers	p value	Smokers	Ex-smokers	Nonsmokers	p value
Number (n)	59	61	115		69	58	112	
Coffee (mean no. cups/day)	4.44	3.16	1.97	.001	4.88	2.81	2.20	.001
Decaffeinated coffee (mean no. cups/day)	.35	.90	.11	.05	.64	.86	.43	
Total coffee consumption (mean no. cups/day)	4.79	4.06	2.08	.001	5.52	3.67	2.63	.001
Alcohol user (percentage)	81.9	72.7	55.6	.01	67.6	75.8	58.8	.12
Alcohol problems (percentage)	10.2	1.7	0	.005	10.1	1.7	2.7	.05
Aspirin (percentage)	44.0	50.8	40.0		43.5	50.0	44.6	.05
Marijuana (percentage)	23.7	13.1	9.6	.05	11.6	17.6	9.8	
Prescribed drugs (percentage)	16.9	37.7	37.4	.025	43.5	39.7	32.1	

The alcohol consumption patterns by smoking status are also presented in Table 10. These analyses also were performed on the test sample ($n = 235$) and then repeated on the cross-validation sample ($n = 239$). Chi-square analyses of these data, which are shown in Table 10, indicate that a significantly larger portion of both smokers and ex-smokers consume alcohol as compared to non-smokers (p of .01 and .12 in the first and cross-validation samples, respectively). The smokers also reported a higher percentage of alcohol problems (treatment for alcoholism and driving while intoxicated) than either ex-smokers or non-smokers (p of .005 and .05). Whereas there were no differences among the groups in beer and wine consumption (not shown in Table 10), the smokers reported consuming larger amounts of hard liquor than the nonsmokers.

5.2. Psychological Characteristics and Smoking Status

The psychological data from the Hopkins Symptom Checklist and the Cornell Medical Index were compared for smokers, ex-smokers, and nonsmokers. Although not reported here in tabular form, analyses of variance showed that the smokers were more anxious than the ex-smokers on the Hopkins Anxiety Scale but, surprisingly, this finding did not hold up on cross-validation in the second sample.

As shown in Table 11, female smokers reported significantly more medical symptoms on the Cornell Medical Index (20.79 vs. 15.79 vs. 14.48, p of .005) and more total symptoms (27.35 vs. 20.56 vs. 19.15, p of .005) than did female ex-smokers and nonsmokers. This difference in self-reported medical symptom-atology was not found among males. Also, among the females, heavier cigarette smokers reported more medical symptoms than pack-a-day and lighter smokers (28.44 vs. 24.60 vs. 14.48, p of .005); again, this difference was not found among males. Heavier female smokers also checked more total symptoms (the sum of medical and psychiatric symptoms) on the 195-item Cornell Medical Index (37.22 vs. 31.25 vs. 20.09, p of .025). A similar finding did not emerge among males.

5.3. Biomedical Characteristics and Smoking Status

Table 12 presents the physiological findings for the smoking groups sorted by sex. Smoking status was correlated with weight and age. Therefore, after means and standard deviations were obtained using the raw scores only, all the biomedical data were statistically adjusted for both age and weight before being analyzed. The data in Table 12 include the adjusted values.

With regard to the lipid data, analyses of variance were done only on these adjusted values. This revealed significant differences in plasma triglycerides, with the smokers having higher values than both ex-smokers and nonsmokers among both males (137 vs. 101 vs. 98, p of .001) and females (100 vs. 83 vs. 81, p of .05). The total plasma cholesterol showed significant differences among males (203 vs. 186 vs. 192, p of .05) but not among females. The very low density lipoproteins (VLDL) cholesterol also showed group differences, with the smokers having higher VLDL cholesterol levels than ex-smokers and nonsmokers among

Table 11. Cornell Medical Index and Cigarette, Pipe, and Cigar Smoking Status

Measure	Males (n=229)				Females (n=236)			
	Smokers (n=76)	Ex-smokers (n=58)	Nonsmokers (n=95)	p value[a]	Smokers (n=52)	Ex-smokers (n=56)	Nonsmokers (n=128)	p value
Cornell (medical sx.)	10.74	11.69	9.68		20.79	15.79	14.48	.005
Cornell (psych. sx.)	2.62	1.69	2.13		6.56	4.77	4.67	.10
Cornell (total sx.)	13.36	13.38	11.81		27.35	20.56	19.15	.005

Measure	Male smokers (n=76)				Female smokers (n=52)			
	Heavier (> 1¼ pk) n=21	Pack (¾-1¼ pk) n=18	Lighter[b] (< ¾ pk) n=37	p value	Heavier (> 1¼ pk) n=9	Pack (¾-1¼ pk) n=20	Lighter (< ¾ pk) n=23	p value
Cornell (medical sx.)	13.09	9.56	9.97		28.44	24.60	14.48	.005
Cornell (psych. sx.)	2.86	2.00	3.11		8.78	6.65	5.61	.005
Cornell (total sx.)	15.95	11.56	13.08		37.22	31.25	20.09	.025

[a] p values for one-way analysis of variance.
[b] "Lighter smokers" for males includes 15 light-cigar or pipe smokers

Table 12. Biomedical Characteristics according to Smoking Status

Measure	Males				Females			
	Smokers	Ex-smokers	Nonsmokers	p value[a]	Smokers	Ex-smokers	Nonsmokers	p value[a]
Number (n)	76	58	95		52	56	128	
Plasma Lipids and Lipoproteins								
Cholesterol (mg/dl)	203	186	192	.05	195	189	190	.10
HDL cholesterol (mg/dl)	46	50	48	.10	59	64	63	
LDL cholesterol (mg/dl)	150	137	140		123	113	112	.10
VLDL cholesterol (mg/dl)	26	20	20	.005	20	17	17	.10
Triglyceride (mg/dl)	137	101	98	.001	100	83	81	.05
Blood pressure								
Systolic (mm Hg)	116	117	116		107	109	109	
Diastolic (mm Hg)	74	76	75		69	69	71	
Apical heart rate (beats/min)	73	70	69	.005	75	75	75	
Anthropometric								
Height (cm)	176	176	181	.005	164	165	164	.025
Weight[b] (kg)	77.1	78.9	79.2		58.1	65.9	65.1	
Body-mass index (wt/ht^2 × 10,000)[b]	25.0	25.1	24.3	.005	23.6	23.1	23.5	
Triceps skinfold thickness (mm)	15.3	14.8	14.7	.05	24.6	24.8	25.0	
Midarm circumference (cm)	31.8	31.2	31.4		28.6	28.6	28.5	

[a] One-way analysis of variance.
[b] These scores are age-adjusted only; all others in this table are both age- and weight-adjusted.

Note: The findings in this and our other tables are based on a first look at our Family Heart Study data and have not been crosschecked. Those firm data will be published at a later date. Also, the 76 male smokers above include 15 pipe smokers plus 61 cigarette smokers. These two sub-samples are now being analyzed separately.

the males (26 vs. 20 vs. 20, p of .005). There was a trend in the same direction among the females (p of .10).

In general, as shown in Table 12, many more significant physiological differences between smokers and nonsmokers were found among males than among females, with male smokers being at greater health risk on these various biomedical measures than male nonsmokers.

Table 13 presents physiological data for the smokers only, broken down into heavier, pack, and lighter smokers. Again, analyses were performed on weight- and age-adjusted values. Significant differences were found among heavier, pack, and lighter smokers for total plasma cholesterol (221 vs. 198 vs. 180, p of .025) and LDL cholesterol (155 vs. 125 vs. 109, p of .005) among females and for HDL cholesterol (39 vs. 38 vs. 44, p of .025) among males. There was a similar finding for apical heart rate among both males (77 vs. 69 vs. 70, p of .005) and females (79 vs. 78 vs. 71, p of .025).

In general, plasma triglyceride levels and VLDL cholesterol appeared to increase with heavier cigarette consumption. The HDL cholesterol values showed the opposite effect, with heavier smokers evidencing the lower values. Resting apical heart rate also showed significant differences, with the faster heart rates appearing in the heavier smokers. There were no significant blood pressure differences in the analyses of the amount of smoking.

5.4. Leisure Exercise and Smoking Status

As shown in Table 14, no significant differences were found among smokers, ex-smokers, and nonsmokers in terms of time spent viewing TV, reading, doing hobbies, or in total sedentary time in Sample I. A trend toward a significant difference was found in Sample I among groups in moderate and heavy exercise, with ex-smokers and smokers reporting more moderate exercise than nonsmokers (190 vs. 157 vs. 91 minutes per week, p of .10). Ex-smokers and nonsmokers reported more heavy exercise than smokers (115 vs. 108 vs. 43 minutes per week, p of .10). This trend in heavy exercise also was found in the cross-validation sample. Specifically, in the second sample, ex-smokers and nonsmokers reported more heavy exercise than smokers (94 vs. 99 vs. 30 minutes per week, p of .05). In terms of total exercise, ex-smokers in Sample I were found to report significantly more total exercise than smokers and nonsmokers (582 vs. 518 vs. 410 minutes per week, p of .05). However, this finding was not replicated in the cross-validation sample.*

A separate analysis of the 128 smokers only (heavier, pack, and lighter smokers' groups), shown in Table 15, revealed significant differences among groups for hours of TV watching per day (p of .005) and total sedentary time (p of .025). The pack-per-day middle smokers showed the highest values of each of these activities; the heavier smokers ran a close second. Interestingly, heavier smokers also reported doing the most moderate exercise in terms of minutes per week (274 vs. 99 vs. 47 minutes, p of .025).

---

*The reader should note that due to a missing subject or two in one or another of the three exercise measures, the means for total exercise in Table 14 vary by a few minutes from the means that would be obtained by summing into a single total the means for light, moderate, and heavy exercise making up this total. The same holds true in Table 15 for the mean for total exercise for the pack smokers.

Table 13. Biomedical Characteristics according to Type of Smoker

Measure	Males				Females			
	Heavier (> 1¼ pk/day)	Pack (¾–1¼ pk/day)	Lighter[a] (< ¾ pk/day)	p value[b]	Heavier (> 1¼ pk/day)	Pack (¾–1¼ pk/day)	Lighter (< ¾ pk/day)	p value[b]
Number (n)	21	18	52		9	20	23	
Plasma lipids and lipoproteins								
Cholesterol (mg/dl)	212	217	215		221	198	180	.025
HDL cholesterol (mg/dl)	39	38	44	.025	49	56	59	.005
LDL cholesterol (mg/dl)	144	146	154		155	125	109	
VLDL cholesterol (mg/dl)	28	32	23		22	21	18	
Triglyceride (mg/dl)	158	160	116	.10	117	106	86	
Blood Pressure								
Systolic (mm Hg)	119	119	119		113	105	106	
Diastolic (mm Hg)	77	79	76		70	69	69	
Apical heart rate (beats/min)	77	69	70	.005	79	78	71	.025
Anthropometric								
Height (cm)	174	176	177		160	164	167	
Weight[c] (kg)	76.1	76.1	78.2		56.3	54.4	62.1	
Body mass index[c] (wt/ht² × 10,000)	24.7	24.4	24.2		24.5	23.6	23.1	
Triceps skinfold thickness (mm)	17.4	16.2	16.0		23.8	24.4	24.2	
Midarm circumference (cm)	31.9	31.1	31.3		28.5	28.7	28.6	

[a] Male "lighter" smokers include 15 light-cigar or pipe smokers.
[b] One-way analysis of variance.
[c] These scores are age adjusted only, all others in this table are both age- and weight-adjusted.

Table 14. Exercise Patterns of Cigarette, Pipe, Cigar Smokers, Ex-smokers, and Nonsmokers

Measures	Sample I (n = 235)				Sample II (n = 239)			
	Smokers (n = 59)	Ex-smokers (n = 61)	Nonsmokers (n = 115)	p value[a]	Smokers (n = 69)	Ex-smokers (n = 58)	Nonsmokers (n = 112)	p value
TV (hr/day)	2.1	1.5	1.8		2.2	1.9	1.4	.01
Reading (hr/day)	1.7	1.4	1.5		1.3	1.6	1.4	
Hobbies (hr/day)	1.1	1.0	0.7		0.7	0.5	0.7	
Total sedentary time (hr/day)	4.9	3.9	3.9		4.2	3.8	3.5	
Light exercise (min/wk)	313	274	232		351	244	212	.05
Moderate exercise (min/wk)	157	190	91	.10	97	148	125	
Heavy exercise (min/wk)	43	115	108	.10	30	94	99	.05
Total exercise (min/wk)	518	582	410	.05	478	485	439	.05

[a] p values for one-way analysis of variance.

5.5. Cigarette Smoking: Implications of Our Findings

The analyses in Tables 10 to 15 provide a fresh look at the question of the relationship between heart disease and smoking and have several important implications. First, comparing the Family Heart Study population with the data provided in the 1979 U. S. Surgeon General's Report, it appears that our Family Heart Study population with 33.2% male and 21.2% female current smokers, contains a smaller percentage of female smokers than the general population (about 33% male and 29% female smokers). However, when it is considered that the Family Heart Study population is more like the skilled, managerial, and professional segments of American society, the smoking statuses represented in our population are quite likely representative of their counterparts in the American population. Second, our results taken as a whole suggest that smokers are both less healthy as assessed by the various plasma lipid measurements and less healthy with regard to other habits of overconsumption (inasmuch as they were found to drink more alcohol, caffeinated coffee, have a higher rate of alcoholism, and engage in more sedentary habits except moderate exercise). It is also apparent that the magnitudes of these biomedical and behavioral risk factors tend to increase (correlate) as the amount of smoking is increased. Thus, the heaviest smokers tended to have the poorest plasma lipid profile (higher cholesterol, triglyceride, VLDL cholesterol, apical heart rate, and lower HDL cholesterol) and the poorest health-habit profile (use of more caffeine and alcohol and less exercise). The smokers thus appear to be at higher risk for coronary disease not only because they smoke but also because they engage in a cluster of other less healthy habits and have a more dangerous array of plasma lipid concentrations. These undesirable lipid values might result in part from eating habits that lead to the overconsumption of high-cholesterol, high-fat foods (Kurt, Perrin, & Bronte-Stewart, 1961; Thomas & Cohen, 1960), and also in part (for HDL cholesterol) because of smoking itself.

The present data are generally consistent with studies finding higher LDL cholesterol and lower HDL cholesterol levels among smokers across race and sex (Garrison, Kannel, Feinleib, Castelli, McNemara, & Padgett, 1978; Heyden, Heiss, Manegold, Tyroler, Hames, Bartel, & Cooper, 1979). In addition, our results suggest that the number of cigarettes smoked made a difference, with

Table 15. Leisure Activity and Smoking Status

	Heavier	Pack	Lighter[a]	p value[b]
Number (n)	30	38	60	
TV (hr/day)	2.7	2.7	1.6	.005
Reading (hr/day)	1.7	1.5	1.4	
Hobbies (hr/day)	0.9	1.2	0.6	
Total sedentary time (hr/day)	5.2	5.5	3.6	.025
Light exercise (min/wk)	274	246	418	
Moderate exercise (min/wk)	274	47	99	.025
Heavy exercise (min/wk)	5	45	47	
Total exercise (min/wk)	553	339	564	

[a]"Lighter smokers" include 15 light-cigar or pipe smokers.
[b]p values for one-way analysis of variance.

the lipid profile becoming more pathological as the amount of smoking increased

The present findings are also consistent with those studies focusing on coffee and alcohol consumption among smokers, ex-smokers, and nonsmokers. We found that compared to smokers, ex-smokers drank less regular (caffeinated) coffee. Gilbert (1979) and Kozlowski (1976) found a similar pheonmena in their studies; Kozlowski suggested that the habitual connection between coffee and tobacco is strong, and that giving up both substances raises the ex-smoker's chances of remaining abstinent. Our smoking and alcohol findings are consistent with those of Craig and Pearl (1977), who in general population surveys found a significant correlation between smoking and drinking habits; and with those of Moody (1974), who reported an association between heavy smoking and problem drinking.

An interesting result in the present data was our failure to find that smokers have higher levels of anxiety and neuroticism than nonsmokers. Other studies in this area have suggested differences between smokers and nonsmokers in anxiety levels, extraversion, antisocial tendencies, locus of control, and impulsiveness and neuroticism (Eysenck, 1965; Matarazzo & Saslow, 1960; McCrae, Costa, & Bosse, 1978; Smith, 1970). However, although such differences often reached statistical significance, the magnitudes of the differences reported have been so small as to be of little practical significance (Matarazzo & Saslow, 1960, pp. 508–510).

6. Conclusion

This chapter outlines data collected by a research team consisting of cardiologists, nutritionists, and medical psychologists at the School of Medicine of the University of Oregon Health Sciences Center which is now conducting a family-focused intervention trial. This effort is representative of other interdisciplinary research teams that are helping to give visibility to the emerging field of behavioral cardiology. A search for interrelationships among biomedical and psychological variables of the types reported here has considerable potential in the prevention of coronary disease. Nevertheless, in concluding this chapter, it is important to emphasize a point that was suggested earlier but not elaborated. Specifically, the findings presented in the majority of tables in this chapter, although heuristically interesting in their own right, do not pertain to the major hypotheses that guided the design and execution of our ongoing Family Heart Study. That hypothesis is that a behavioral intervention consisting of a composite of an educational and a group process component might lower in some cases and, in other, retard the normal cardiovascular changes that are expected to take place over 5 years in the members of a randomly selected population of free-living and seemingly normal Americans. Examination throughout this chapter of the tables of means of numerous physiological measures in our participants will reveal that these individuals, with a small percentage of expected exceptions were, at baseline, fully in the statistically normal (but not clinically optimal) range. Our research design involves study of these individuals over a 5-year period in order to ascertain whether, relative to our three control groups, the members of the intervention group are relatively less at risk 5 years from baseline. If they are, this will constitute preliminary evidence for the guiding hypothesis of the Family Heart Study that *behavioral intervention can influence selected biologic endpoints related to cardiovascular functioning.* The many analyses reported in the present chapter (namely, our search for intervariable relationships at baseline) were thus a fortuitous by-product of this main hypothesis and not a test of the main hypothesis itself. Had we chosen to include a clinical subsample and thus had a larger number of individuals in our study with *abnormal* biomedical measures (thus eliminating what in our present data may be an artifact of the methodological problems associated with a restriction in range), it is conceivable that we would have found even more statistically significant associations among our baseline psychological and biomedical measures than those shown in our tables. That we did not find many associations between the various psychological and biomedical variables, although we studied these only in a cross section of essentially normal American adults, should nevertheless in itself be of interest to behavioral cardiology research teams in other centers. These essentially negative findings may also be of interest to investigators in the areas of personality assessment and in social psychology research who, increasingly, are being attracted to health psychology as a potentially fertile area for testing a number of hypotheses generated over the past several decades.

Finally, although the findings discussed in this chapter constitute only an *initial* report, they represent for us a rich example of the types of important behavioral–biomedical problems now available for study by teams of psychologists and physicians interested in behavioral cardiology. For psychologists from each of the subfields of psychology who, like us, have been looking for a stimulus to broaden their role as health scientists in research and service, the field of coronary disease prevention provides that stimulus. Applied and experimental psychologists, health educators, nutritionists, nurses, and other health care professionals who wish to study ways to reduce cardiovascular risk will find receptive colleagues among the growing numbers of physicians who are turning to a broadened biopsychosocial model of illness, treatment, and prevention. Matarazzo (1982) recently suggested that interested psychologists from *all* subdisciplines of psychology are needed to help map some of the important landmarks in this beckoning and relatively unexplored frontier, *the health behavior of individuals.* In no other area is this challenge greater than in the area of cardiovascular risk reduction—one of the foundations of today's behavioral cardiology.

7. References

American Heart Association: Report of Inter-society Commission for Heart Diseases: Primary prevention of atherosclerotic disease. Atherosclerosis and Epidemiology Study Groups, *Circulation,* 1970, *42,* 1–55.

American Heart Association: Report of Inter-society Commission for Heart Diseases. *Circulation,* 1974, *42,* 1–56.

Beaumont, W. *Experiments and observations on gastric juice and the physiology of digestion.* Plattsburgh, N.Y.: F. P. Allen, 1833.

Becker, M. H., Maiman, L. A. Sociobehavioral determinants of compliance with health and medical care recommendations. *Medical Care,* 1975, *13,* 10–24.

Brodman, K., Erdmann, A. J., Lorge, I., & Wolff, H. G. The Cornell Medical Index: An adjunct to medical interview. *Journal of American Medical Association*, 1949, *140*, 530–534.

Carmody, T. P., Fey, S. G., Pierce, D. K., Connor, W. E., & Matarazzo, J. D. Behavioral treatment of hyperlipidemia: Techniques, results, and future directions. *Journal of Behavioral Medicine*, 1982, in press.

Cassel, J. Summary of major findings of the Evans County cardiovascular studies. *Archives of Internal Medicine*, 1971, *128*, 887–889.

Chiang, B. N., Perlan, L. V., & Epstein, F. H. Overweight and hypertension. *Circulation*, 1969, *39*, 403–421.

Connor, W. E., & Connor, S. L. The key role of nutritional factors in the prevention of coronary heart disease. *Preventive Medicine*, 1972, *1*, 49–83.

Connor, W. E., & Connor, S. L. Dietary treatment of hyperlipidemia. In B. Rifkind & R. Levy (Eds.), *Hyperlipidemia: Diagnosis and therapy*. New York: Grune & Stratton, 1977.

Connor, W. E., Connor, S. L., Fry, M. P., & Warner, S. *The alternative diet book*. Iowa City, Iowa: University of Iowa Press, 1976.

Craig, T. J., & Pearl, A. The association of smoking and drinking habits in a community sample. *Journal of Studies on Alcohol*, 1977, *7*, 1434–1439.

Dahl, L. K. Salt and hypertension. *American Journal of Clinical Nutrition*, 1972, *25*, 231–242.

Derogatis, L. R. *SCL-90-R Manual-1*. Baltimore: Johns Hopkins University Press, 1977.

Doyle, J. T. Etiology of coronary disease: Risk factors in influencing coronary disease. *Modern Concepts of Cardiovascular Disease*, 1966, *35*, 81–86.

Evans, R., Rozelle, R., Mittlemark, M., Hansen, W., Bane, A., & Havis, J. Deterring the onset of smoking in children: Knowledge of immediate physiological effects and coping with peer pressure, and parent modeling. *Journal of Applied Social Psychology*, 1978, *8*, 126–135.

Eysenck, H. J. *Smoking, health and personality*. New York: Basic Books, 1965.

Farquhar, J. W., Maccoby, W., & Wood, P. D. Community education for cardiovascular health. *Lancet*, 1977, *1*, 1192–1195.

Foreyt, J. P., Scott, L. W., Mitchell, R. E., & Gotto, A. M. Plasma lipid changes in the normal population following behavioral treatment. *Journal of Consulting and Clinical Psychology*, 1979, *47*, 440–452.

Friedman, M., & Rosenman, R. H. *Type A behavior and your heart*. New York: Knopf, 1974.

Garrison, R. J., Kannel, W. B., Feinleib, M., Castelli, W. P., McNemara, P. M., & Padgett, S. J. Cigarette smoking and HDL cholesterol. *Atherosclerosis*, 1978, *30*, 17–25.

Gilbert, R. M. Coffee, tea and cigarette use. *Canadian Medical Association Journal*, 1979, *120*, 522–523.

Glass, D. C. *Behavior patterns, stress, and coronary disease*. Hillsdale, N.J.: Lawrence Erlbaum, 1977.

Heyden, S., Heiss, G., Manegold, C., Tyroler, H., Hames, C., Bartel, A., & Cooper, G. The combined effect of smoking and coffee drinking on LDL and HDL cholesterol. *Circulation*, 1979, *1*, 22–25.

Hunt, W. A., & Matarazzo, J. D. Three years later: Recent developments in the experimental modification of smoking behavior. *Journal of Abnormal Psychology*, 1973, *81*, 107–114.

Jenkins, C. D. Behavioral risk factors in coronary artery disease. *Annual Review of Medicine*, 1978, *29*, 543–562.

Jenkins, C. D., Zyzanski, S. J., & Rosenman, R. H. *Manual for the Jenkins Activity Survey*. New York: Psychological Corporation, 1979.

Kannel, W. B., & Gordon, T. The Framingham study: An epidemiological investigation of cardiovascular disease. *Public Health Reports*, Sections 1–23, 1971.

Kasl, S. V. The health belief model and chronic illness behavior. *Health Education Monographs*, 1974, *2*, 433–454.

Kasl, S. V. Cardiovascular risk reduction in a community setting: Some comments. *Journal of Consulting and Clinical Psychology*, 1980, *48*, 143–149.

Katz, L. N., & Stamler, J. *Experimental atherosclerosis*. Springfield, Ill.: Charles C Thomas, 1953.

Kirscht, J. Research related to the modification of health beliefs. *Health Education Monographs*, 1974, *2*, 455–469.

Kozlowski, L. J. Effects of caffeine consumption on nicotine consumption. *Psychopharmacology*, 1976, *47*, 165–168.

Kurt, L. H., Perrin, M. J., & Bronte-Stewart, B. Smoking and food preferences. *British Medical Journal*, 1961, *1*, 384–388.

Leventhal, H., Safer, M. A., Cleary, P. D., & Gutmann, M. Cardiovascular risk modification by community-based programs for life-style change: Comments on the Stanford Study. *Journal of Consulting and Clinical Psychology*, 1980, *48*, 150–158.

Lewin, K. Group decision and social change. In N. Maccoby, T.M. Newcomb, & E.L. Hartley (Eds.), *Readings in Social Psychology* (3rd ed.). New York: Holt, Rinehart & Winston, 1958.

Lichtenstein, E., & Danaher, B. Modification of smoking behavior: A critical analysis of theory, research and practice. In M. Hersen, R. Eisler, & P. Miller (Eds.), *Progress in behavior modification*. New York: Academic Press, 1976.

Matarazzo, J. D. Behavioral health and behavioral medicine: Frontiers for a new health psychology. *American Psychologist*, 1980, *35*, 807–817.

Matarazzo, J. D. Behavioral health's challenge to academic, scientific and professional psychology. *American Psychologist*, 1982, *37*, 1–14.

Matarazzo, J. D., & Saslow, F. Psychological and related characteristics of smokers and nonsmokers. *Psychological Bulletin*, 1960, *57*, 493–513.

McCrae, R. R., Costa, P. T., & Bossé, R. Anxiety, extraversion and smoking. *British Journal of Clinical Psychology*, 1978, *17*, 269–273.

Mc Gill, H. C., & Mott, G. E. Diet and coronary heart disease. In D. Hagsted (Ed.), *Present Knowledge in Nutrition*. Washington, D.C.: Nutrition Foundation, Inc., 1976.

Meyer, A. J., Maccoby, N., & Farquhar, J. W. Reply to Kasl and Leventhal *et al. Journal of Consulting and Clinical Psychology*, 1980, *48*, 159–163.

Meyer, A. J., Nash, J. D., McAlister, A. L., Maccoby, N., & Farquhar, J. W. Skills training in a cardiovascular health education campaign. *Journal of Consulting and Clinical Psychology*, 1980, *48*, 129–142.

Moody, P. M. Drinking and smoking behavior in hospitalized medical patients. *Journal of Studies on Alcohol*, 1974, *9*, 1316–1319.

Moriyama, I. M., Krueger, D. E., & Stamler, J. *Cardiovascular Diseases in the United States*. Cambridge: Harvard University Press, 1971.

Nideffer, R. M. Test of attentional and interpersonal style. *Journal of Personality and Social Psychology*, 1976, *11*, 232–241.

Reisin, E., Abel, R., Modan, M., Silverberg, D. S., Eliahou, H. E., & Modan, M. Effect of weight loss without salt restriction in the reduction of blood pressure in overweight hypertensive patients. *New England Journal of Medicine*, 1978, *288*, 1–6.

Sarason, I. G., & Johnson, J. H. *The life experiences survey: Preliminary findings*. (SCL-LS-001). Arlington, Va.: Office of Naval Research, Organizational Effectiveness Research Program, May 1976. (Contract No. N00014-75-C-0905, NR 170-804.)

Schwartz, G. E., & Weiss, S. M. Yale Conference on Behavioral Medicine: A proposed definition and statement of goals. *Journal of Behavioral Medicine*, 1978, *1*, 3–12. (a)

Schwartz, G. E., & Weiss, S. M. Behavioral Medicine revisited: An amended definition. *Journal of Behavioral Medicine*, 1978, *1*, 249–251. (b)

Smith, G. M. Personality and smoking: A review of empirical literature. In W. A. Hunt (Ed.), *Learning mechanisms in smoking*. Chicago: Aldine Press, 1970.

Stamler, J. Cigarette smoking and atherosclerotic coronary heart disease. *Bulletin of the New York Academy of Medicine*, 1968, *44*, 1476–1494.

Stamler, J. Hypertension and coronary risk: Implication of current knowledge. *ACTA Cardiology Supplement*, 1974, *20*, 119–157.

Strickland, B. R. Internal-external expectancies and health-related behaviors. *Journal of Consulting and Clinical Psychology*, 1978, *46*, 1191–1211.

Thomas, C. B., & Cohen, B. H. Comparison of Smokers and Nonsmokers. *Bulletin of the Johns Hopkins Hospital*, 1960, *106*, 205–214.

U.S. Department of Health, Education and Welfare, *Smoking and health: A report of the surgeon general*. DHEW Publication No. (PHS) 79-5066, 1979.

Wallston, B. S., & Wallston, K. A. Locus of control and health: A review of the literature. *Health Education Monographs*, 1978, *6*, 107–116.

Wallston, K. A., Wallston, B. S., & DeVellis, R. Development of the Multidimensional Health Locus of Control (MHLC) scales. *Health Education Monographs*, 1978, *6*, 160–170.

Wallston, B. S., Wallston, K. A., Kaplan, G. D., & Maides, S. A. Development and validation of the Health Locus of Control (HLC) scale. *Journal of Consulting and Clinical Psychology*, 1976, *44*, 580–585.

Wolf, S., & Wolff, H. G. *Human Gastric Function*. New York: Oxford University Press, 1947.

III

The Clinical Functions of the Health Psychologist

15

Psychological Assessment in Medical Settings

CATHERINE J. GREEN

The majority of physicians who note emotional problems among their patients act on an idiosyncratic set of beliefs regarding optimal psychological assessments and interventions. Most will rely heavily on their personal experience with psychologists and psychiatrists rather than on a particular theoretical orientation. Most commonly, the physicians' attitudes toward psychological services largely derive from their frustrations and limitations in managing difficult patients. This stems in part from the fact that the traditional medical disease model, which developed along with the great advances of medicine in the past half-century, no longer appears fully effective or relevant in managing many problems now seen in medical practice. Physicians have turned to psychology out of frustration, hoping that it will offer a successful method for maximizing their treatment effectiveness, largely through improved patient compliance.

The movement toward more psychologically oriented medical care reflects an increased focus on the interrelationship of mind and body, a concept that has moved in and out of favor throughout the development of modern medicine. The literature in this field shows little integration as yet. Researchers and clinicians posit a variety of salient issues, addressing only those they consider of import and leading to a literature replete with studies that lack shared conceptual frameworks. Some of these differences are the natural consequence of differing professional responsibilities and settings. Regardless of these differences, however, and they are not insignificant, a major factor is how the relationship between mind and body is conceived and the consequent effects of this conception. Thus, William Osler (1971, p. 14) stated "It is more important to know what kind of

CATHERINE J. GREEN • Department of Psychology, University of Miami, Coral Gables, Florida 33124.

man has a disease than to know what kind of disease a man has." Elaborating this view, Osler described psychosomatic medicine as that part of medicine concerned with an appraisal of the interaction of both emotional and the physical disease mechanisms involved in the individual patient. Osler's conception seems as apt today as when it was first formulated. Assessment in clinical health psychology, to follow Osler's guidance, should be designed to appraise the role of emotional factors in that interaction within specific individuals.

1. Psychological Analysis in Medical Settings

In traditional medicine the goal of clinical diagnosis is the identification of the ongoing disease process and the formulation of a plan to deal with the disease. When psychosocial factors are added to the medical symptomatology, the patient cannot be seen simply as a vessel, so to speak, who carries a group of predictable or constant symptoms available for evaluation. Rather, the psychosocial events and the patient's premorbid personality covary to create a changing constellation. Under these circumstances clinical analysis must not only systematically evaluate these varied elements but also elucidate their interrelationships and dynamic flow. Current behaviors and attitudes must be interpreted in conjunction with the physical basis of the presenting problem. The premorbid background of the problem must be delineated in an effort to clarify the historical context or pattern of the syndrome. Moreover, personality and environmental circumstances must be appraised to optimize therapeutic recommendations. Ultimately, the goal of psychological assessment is the development of a preventive or remedial plan.

As in other settings, problems occur when this assessment relies solely on the evaluative skills and impressions of the clinician involved. Clinicians often see what they anticipate. It is unlikely that the data obtained will be at variance with these expectancies. Moreover, questions likely to elicit unanticipated information are rarely asked. It is in this regard that objective psychological assessment is so important; these tools serve to standardize clinical evaluations and ensure comprehensive coverage. Moreover, it seeks to appraise the patient's present status within the context of the past and within his or her larger social environment, including both current physical and psychosocial stressors. Although clinicians evaluate patients caught at one point of time, they seek to trace the sequence of events preceding and leading to that point. This knowledge permits the formulation of a remedial plan that is based on an understanding of the interface between the patient's illness and the resources available to manage the problem successfully.

2. Assessment Trends in Medical Settings

Medicine has a traditional belief in the necessity of clinical diagnosis and the importance of systematic patient assessment. This stance should make the physician receptive to psychodiagnostic testing. Psychologists are likewise comfortable in turning to their traditional diagnostic testing role.

Initially, psychologists employed traditional psychometric instruments, that is, those that had proven of value in mental health or psychiatric settings. Although these instruments could answer specific questions regarding problems of psychopathology, they did not illuminate questions posed in requests for nonpsychiatric psychological services. New instruments designed to assess the general medical patient developed very slowly. Unfortunately, many of these efforts were carried out by clinicians unfamiliar with psychometric theory. Consequently, these new tests were often poorly grounded in theory and gave minimal evidence of validity or reliability. Emerging to meet urgent needs, these instruments were often distributed before they could be judged adequate according to satisfactory psychometric or empirical criteria.

Serious practitioners are now looking at the emerging body of literature regarding assessment of medical patients and evaluating the utility and scientific grounding of the instruments employed. The following sections of this chapter will serve as a guide to the evaluation and use of selected objective and self-report instruments. These tools have been chosen because of the ease with which they can be employed in medical settings. Although the list is by no means exhaustive, it does encompass a variety of approaches, theoretical stances, and issues found significant for medical patients. Although other psychological tests—behavioral and projective tools such as the Rorschach—are occasionally utilized with medical patients, the expense they involve (e.g., in personnel time) limits their clinical utility.

The instruments selected will be evaluated in terms of general psychological test criteria and their relevance to medical–psychological issues specifically. If an instrument fails to meet general psychometric considerations, its value as a medical diagnostic instrument is already seriously compromised.

2.1. General Criteria for Test Evaluation

The first criterion for evaluating a psychometric instrument is whether it addresses a characteristic relevant to a target population. Tests are usually developed with a specific population in mind and are constructed on a sample drawn from this population.

These instruments should be tailored to gauge some specific trait or behavior through the parsimonious use of questions. The information utilized to draw conclusions concerning the characteristic in question must be readily obtainable. An important consideration in this regard, particularly in medical settings, is simplicity of administration and economy of time. Brevity, clarity, and minimal intrusiveness will maximize patient compliance and minimize fatigue.

2.1.1. Construction of the Instrument

Although different methods have been employed in the development of the following tests, the same criteria of test construction must be applied. Published APA standards (1974) will serve as the guide for this evaluation.

Reliability addresses the issue of replication of a given score. Unless a test can produce consistent results, it would be unwise to put credence in them. Different gauges of reliability can be utilized; each contributes to the value of an instrument. These include reliability over time as determined by test–retest results, reliability among various forms of the instrument, and evidence of internal consistency. Without reliability, it would be impossible for the test to have validity, although the presence of reliability in no way guarantees the validity of the test.

Validity also has a number of definitions and gauges. Construct validity, for example, refers to the theory undergirding the development of the test and the extent to which the test provides evidence in support of the theory. Content validity refers to whether the domain of characteristics to be included is, in fact, covered by the test, or if the sample drawn from the domain is balanced in its representation. Empirical validity addresses the relationship between the scores obtained on the test and some predictive or concurrent criterion.

2.1.2. The Test Manual and User Instructions

Even the best-constructed test would be subject to serious errors of interpretation and utilization without an adequate manual to instruct the user in the applications and limitations of the instrument. The manual should assist the reader in making correct interpretations by noting what data must necessarily be taken into account. The nature of the population for whom the test is appropriate must be clearly stated, along with the purposes for which the evaluation is appropriate. Methods of administration and information on norms and standardization must also be included. On the basis of the manual's information concerning construction, reliability, and validity, the reader should be able to draw conclusions regarding the quality of the test.

2.2. Criteria for Assessing Tests Used with Medical Populations

Further evaluation criteria must be applied to those instruments which are utilized in medical settings. First, are the behaviors, traits, and attitudes addressed relevant to the patient's problem? In other words, does the test aid in treatment planning? Unless the instrument provides the clinician with reasonable and tangible treatment recommendations, it has little utility. Another major criterion relates to the predictive value of the instrument. Thus, one must ask whether it can answer the following questions: What is the likelihood of illness occurring in a patient who is otherwise asymptomatic? What is the likely course or reaction to treatment of an ongoing disease process?

In the following sections we will seek to evaluate these criteria for the instruments selected. First, a description of the test and what it seeks to measure will be given. Administration and scoring information will be followed by an evaluation of construction and postconstruction empirical data. The instrument will next be evaluated in terms of its use and relevance with medical populations. Finally, some current research applications will be presented for each instrument.

Symptoms checklists, developed out of the clinician's needs for a rapid yet accurate survey of symptomatology, are seen as attractive tools owing to their ease of administration and simplicity of interpretation. The Cornell Medical Index and the Symptom Check List-90 represent the most widely used of these in medical settings.

3.1. Cornell Medical Index (CMI)

The CMI, a 195-item true–false inventory (Brodman, Erdman, & Wolff, 1949), was developed to collect a large body of pertinent medical and psychological data with minimal expenditure of the physician's time. It was designed not as a replacement but as an adjunct to the medical examination. As a traditional medical review, it is most useful for physicians who seek to practice comprehensive medicine (e.g., 57 of the 195 items address moods, feelings, and habits). Written in informal language, it is meant to be used with a wide range of adult populations for whom medical information is required.

3.1.1. Administration, Scoring, and Development of Norms

3.1.1a. Administration. The test is self-administered. Printed directions given at the top of the form instruct the patient to circle *yes* or *no* after each question. The inventory takes the average patient 15 to 30 minutes to complete.

3.1.1b. Scoring. Scores are calculated as the sum of endorsements in each of several separate "organ system" sections; they are also totaled for the entire inventory. According to the manual, a "diagnostic sheet" should be used to compile results. Physicians must utilize their clinical judgment to make assessments regarding problem severity. Rather simplistic guidelines are given for converting scores into their psychological meaning. No information is given as to the logic or rationale of these guidelines, and their value has frequently been discounted (Leavitt, 1972).

3.1.1c. Norms. A number of patient samples were used to collect normative information for the CMI. These norms included hospital employees, health populations, hospital patients, and psychiatric patients. No information is given concerning differences among these groups across several pertinent criteria. Norms give data on total endorsements only; a rough percentile rank can be gauged without a breakdown into defined comparison groups. It would be unwise to utilize these norms until further descriptive and comparative information is available.

3.1.1d. Interpretation. The CMI is meant to serve as a cue to physicians who wish to select patients for further testing and evaluation in selected problem areas. No guidelines are given as to the interpretation of symptoms: such interpretations depend entirely on the physician's prior knowledge and clinical experience. One exception are guidelines regarding psychological difficulties; however, these are so general and sophomoric as to be unusable.

3.1.2. Construction

Although the instrument's manual alludes to the development of the original item pool, no details are given as to the manner in which these were derived. It is stated that a number of forms of each question were tested in a variety of local settings to optimize wording. Without further details, it is difficult to address any of a wide variety of construction procedures.

3.1.3. Postconstruction Empirical Evaluation

After the final items were selected, the instrument was administered to 179 consecutive outpatients to determine its efficacy in identifying item responses as compared to more traditional history-taking procedures. The CMI was found to be more inclusive than a typical nonstructured interview. A study was also done evaluating the accuracy with which organ systems were identified as problematic by comparing the results against hospital histories. The majority of systems were picked up by the CMI; however, no statistical analyses were provided in support of these conclusions. In addition, no efforts appear to have been made to evaluate the validity of the instrument or to assess its efficacy in tapping the full domain of presenting problems. Although apparently effective as a face-valid symptom checklist for medical problems, it is an extremely poor quantitative gauge of psychological adjustment; other, more brief instruments will serve equally well in achieving the quality of psychological information provided by the CMI (Gunderson & Arthur, 1969).

3.1.4. Applications of Medical Criteria

As just noted, the main role of the CMI is that of a medical diagnostic tool; it is minimally suitable for discriminating data of a psychological nature. Psychiatric patients do obtain higher scores than general medical patients, and physical and psychological symptoms do correlate on the CMI about .60 (Stout, Wright, & Bruhn, 1969; Weiss, 1969).

3.1.5. Current Research

The CMI has often been used as one component of a test battery, serving as an index of general symptomatology. Some studies address symptom problems in specific patient populations (Bruhn, Chandler, Lynn, & Wolf, 1966: Pilowsky & Bond, 1969; Weiss, 1969). Others look to this instrument as an evaluative tool (Stout, Wright, & Bruhn, 1969). Some efforts have been made to refine its utility as a mental health screen, with but minimal success (Gunderson & Arthur, 1969; Seymour, 1976).

3.2. Symptom Check List—90 (SCL-90)

This 90-item self-report symptom inventory was based on the Hopkins Symptom Checklist (HSCL) and was designed to reflect psychological symptom patterns of psychiatric patients; Derogatis, its most recent developer, suggests its utility for medical patients, as well (1977). Each item is rated on a 5-point scale of distress from "not at all" to "extremely." These responses are then interpreted along nine primary symptom dimensions: somatization, obsessive–compulsive, interpersonal sensitivity, depression, anxiety, hostility, phobic anxiety, paranoid ideation, psychoticism. In addition, three global indices of distress are calculated: Global Severity Index, Positive Symptom Distress Index, Positive Symptom Total. The SCL-90 is intended as a measure of current psychiatric symptom states, not as a measure of personality. It is designed to be interpreted on three levels. The first level is the global, and the Global Severity Index (GSI) is employed as the gauge. The primary symptom dimensions address the patient's level of psychopathology. Individual items are used to relate to the presence or absence of specific symptoms.

3.2.1. Administration, Scoring, and Development of Norms

3.2.1a. Administration. Instructions are simple and written on the test form. There is a note that asks the patient to record how much discomfort a particular problem has caused during the last *x* numbers of days. Most patients take 15 to 30 minutes to complete the task.

3.2.1b. Scoring. Scoring requires either templates or transferring the 90 item scores from the test paper to a profile sheet, where weighted scores are summed to arrive at distress scores for each of the nine symptom dimensions. The Global Severity Index, Positive Symptom Total, and Symptom Distress Index are also calculated. Raw scores are transformed into T-scores utilizing nonpsychiatric patient norms.

3.2.1c. Norms. The nonpsychiatric normative group (females, $n = 480$; males, $n = 493$) was a stratified random sample drawn from one county in a mid-Atlantic state. No determination of their status as medical patients was made.

3.2.1d. Interpretation. Brief descriptions of the clinical significance of each scale and the global indices are provided. The GSI is considered an indicator of overall distress while the nine primary symptom dimensions provide a profile of the patient's status in psychopathological terms. Discrete symptoms may also be noted. Small-sample profiles are provided as guides.

3.2.2. Construction

The SCL-90 was constructed to serve as a checklist of psychiatric symptomatology. It was developed through a combination of clinical/rational and empirical/analytic procedures. The original item pool was drawn from the Hopkins Symptom Checklist (Derogatis, Lipman, Rickels, Vhlenhuth, & Corey, 1974a,b) which, in turn, can be traced back to the CMI item pool (Wider, 1948). Core items of the HSCL were retained, some were dropped, and 45 new items were added to create four new symptom dimensions. The distress continuum was expanded to a 5-point scale. The method of developing these new items is in no way detailed in the manual, nor is the method for the initial reduction of the HSCL given. In developing the instrument, Derogatis states that he chose to look only at those constructs that lent themselves to the self-report mode. Relying on factor analysis to establish construct validity, he arrived at internal consistency measures of .77 to .90 for scales. Although this high measure of internal consistency may indicate a true homogeneity of scale dimensions, closer examination suggests that it may simply be the product of items which appear to restate the same concept in slightly different words. One week test–retest reliability ranges from .78 to .90.

In an effort to evaluate the empirical validity of the instrument, the concurrence of physician and patient reported levels of psychological distress have been compared; the exact figures are not cited in the manual, although the study is mentioned (Derogatis, Abeloff, & McBeth, 1977). Concurrent validity studies have proved somewhat disappointing. Of course, scales with the same name may not measure the same construct; thus, if the correlation of two similarly named scales proves to be low, it may be a function of tapping different constructs. MMPI correlations with similarly labeled scales were in the .50 to .60 range. The full matrix of MMPI correlations is not presented; thus, the Wiggins Depression Content Scale rather than the original MMPI Depression Scale was recorded. Such presentations leave the reviewer with the feeling that the unreported scores were less than impressive.

3.2.3. Applications of Medical Criteria

The SCL-90 includes both medical and psychiatric symptoms but is geared primarily to the level and nature of psychopathology present. Although a brief cataloging of psychiatric distress is of value, the majority of nonpsychiatric medical patients will vary along such a narrow band of differences that the results will be of minimal value. Furthermore, the information obtained from the SCL-90 is unlikely to contribute to treatment planning among general medical patients. Although profile scores are presented to discriminate among various medical and psychiatric groups, there is little evidence that these profiles represent anything other than the mean scores obtained for selected patient groups. Even if these profiles are representative of particular clinical populations, it is psychometrically and diagnostically simplistic to assume that a single profile would represent all group members; most often, such profiles merely average several very discrete patient subgroups. Turning to other criteria, the SCL-90 does not attempt to gauge prognosis or probable occurrence of later illness: rather, it calculates the presence of current feelings and behaviors. Its major utility in patient management is in relation to psychiatric complications. The problems of utilizing a test developed for psychiatric patients in a nonpsychiatric setting is a serious one. Even a well-designed psychiatric instrument will provide information that is either irrelevant or distorted when applied to a medical population. Problems arise because of the unsuitability of norms, the questionable relevance of clinical signs, and the consequent inapplicability of interpretations. In brief, a standard interpretation of results obtained with a medical sample on a diagnostic test that was developed and designed to assess a psychiatric population runs hard against every major principle of sound test use.

3.2.4. Current Research

Research studies have sought to determine the test's utility and validation (Derogatis, Yevzeroff, & Wittelsberger, 1975; Derogatis, Rickels, & Rock, 1976).

Profile determinations for a variety of disease entities have been established and evaluated (Abeloff & Derogatis, 1977; Craig & Abeloff, 1974; Wise & Fernandez, 1977). The SCL-90 has also been used as a tool to evaluate psychiatric symptomatology in partners seeking treatment for sexual dysfunction (Derogatis, Meyer, & Gallant, 1977). Comparisons of patient and physician evaluation of psychiatric symptoms have also been carried out (Derogatis *et al.*, 1977).

347

PSYCHOLOGICAL
ASSESSMENT IN
MEDICAL SETTINGS

4. Single-Trait Instruments

A number of instruments have been developed to evaluate individuals along a single trait or dimension rather than a fuller domain of traits or behaviors. The instruments chosen to represent this group are the Internal–External Scale, the Beck Depression Inventory and the State–Trait Anxiety Inventory.

4.1. Internal-External Scale (I-E Scale)

The effects of reward or reinforcement on behavior depends to some measure on whether or not the individual perceives a causal relationship between his or her own behavior and the reward. The I-E Scale was developed to measure the degree to which an individual feels that reinforcement is or is not contingent upon his or her own action.

Brought to its final form by Rotter, Liverant, and Crowne (1961), the I-E Scale is composed of 29 items in which the respondent selects which of two statements is more strongly believed. Twenty-three of the items refer directly to the subject's "externality"; six serve as filler in an effort to disguise the intent of the instrument somewhat. The authors see this as an instrument suitable to measure group differences; it is not meant to be used for individual or clinical prediction. No specific population was targeted and items are applicable to many life settings. No manual has been written for the I-E Scale and users must rely on the 1966 monograph for information on construction and utilization of the instrument.

4.1.1. Administration, Scoring, and Development of Norms

4.1.1a. Administration. Self-report instructions for the I-E Scale are printed at the top of the questionnaire and are geared to an upper high school reading level. Subjects are told to select which of a pair of statements is more strongly believed. The testee is admonished to select the one that seems to be more true rather than the one he or she thinks *should* be chosen or wishes to be true. The 29 items are usually completed in 15 to 20 minutes.

4.1.1b. Scoring. Scoring is accomplished by totaling the number of "external" responses. One appendix provides a frequency distribution for male and female samples of university undergraduates; no statement is made regarding the generalizability of this distribution or its applicability to other samples or populations.

4.1.1c. Norms. Means and standard deviations are reported for a number of samples; full distributions are not described and no attempt is made to present a set of norms. Users are encouraged to create their own local norms.

4.1.1d. Interpretation. Simply stated, the higher the score, the more reinforcement is seen to be the product of luck, chance, or under the control of others.

4.1.2. Construction

The I-E Scale evolved through a number of developmental stages. The first instrument developed by Phares (1957) was composed of 26 items selected *a priori* with 13 stated as external attitudes and 13 as internal. Following this, James (1957) developed a test employing Phares's most successful items, building the total to 26 by adding several filler items as well. Subsequently, researchers sought to broaden the test by developing a series of subscales. A 100-item scale was analyzed and reduced back to 60 items. Control for social desirability bias was considered and a forced-choice format was instituted. Item analyses showed that the subscales failed to generate separate predictions. A series of further construction steps sought to reduce the instrument's social desirability and to improve its internal consistency. The final 29-item scale is composed of 23 real and 6 filler items.

At no point does it appear that considerations of empirical validity entered into the construction of the instrument. Subsequent to the construction shape, it was found that the correlation between interviewer ratings of externality and the I-E Scale score were in the .60 range. Having gone through a sequence of construction steps, the I-E is internally consistent and reliable. There is some question, however, as to what the instrument is really measuring and whether, in fact, it adequately covers the domain specified. The absence of normative data is a serious problem, forcing users of the instrument to make their own judgments as to the meaning of given scores. These concerns appear more serious in light of the research literature, since many studies find that the instrument fails to predict expected behaviors consistent with the measured construct (Lambley & Silbowitz, 1973; Marston, 1969).

4.1.3. Postconstruction Empirical Evaluation

Internal consistency (KR_{20}) ranges from .69 to .73, while test–retest reliability at 1 to 2 months ranges from .49 to .83. Significant efforts had been made to reduce the relationship between the I-E Scale and social desirability. This appears to have been accomplished. In one study the correlation between the I-E Scale and Taylor Manifest Anxiety Scale was .24; in another, the correlation was .00 (Efran, 1963). Nonquestionnaire "projectives" correlated modestly with the I-E Scale scores (Adams-Webber, 1963), and Cardi (1962) found a significant correlation between a semistructured interview measure of locus of control and the I-E Scale.

4.1.4. Criteria for Utilization with Medical Patients

The I-E Scale evaluates a single concept, externality. Although this construct is an appealing one, the instrument makes no effort or claim to tap any of the vast number of other variables that relate to health behaviors. In spite of this, it might serve well in treatment planning for the individual patient if it truly measured what it intends to measure. However, the general weakness of the instrument and its value as a group measure only effectively eliminate it as a tool for medical evaluation or for prediction.

Other researchers, in an attempt to overcome the weakness of the I-E Scale, have developed scales specific to the assessment of locus of control among medical patients. The most widely used of these is the Health Locus of Control (Wallston, Wallston, Kaplan, & Maides, 1976). This brief, face-valid instrument, although more focused, has not been proved to be superior to simple interview determinations of externality.

4.1.5. Current Research

Regardless of its limitations, the I-E Scale has been the only instrument available to researchers interested in the issue of locus of control and its relationship to the management of illness. Consequently, a significant body of literature has developed. The following studies of locus of control with medical patients do not all employ the I-E Scale but were based on Rotter's construct (Rotter, 1966).

Some studies have related the subjects' reactions to specific life events (Auerbach, Kendall, Cuttler, & Leavitt, 1976; Cromwell, Butterfield, Brayfield, & Curry, 1977). Others have dealt with adaptation to chronic illness (Dinardo, 1972; Goldstein, 1976; Rosenbaum & Rez, 1977; Wendland, 1973). Particular interest has been directed towards smoking and obesity (Bellack, Rozensky, & Schwartz, 1974; Coan, 1973: Danaher, 1977; Mlott & Mlott, 1975). The I-E Scale has also been utilized in studies of biofeedback training (Berggren, Ohman, & Fredrichson, 1977). The results of these studies have often proved disappointing, with many researchers unable to reproduce earlier findings or uncovering unexpected differences at variance with theoretical predictions (Barrios, Barrios, & Topping, 1977; Bellack, Rozensky, & Schwartz, 1974; Danaher, 1977). One must draw the conclusion that the instrument has not lived up to the hopes of its users, who often wish that it might exceed the expectations of its developers. Further development of the original instrument does not appear to be forthcoming, and little effort has been made to rectify recently noted shortcomings. The absence of further development data places continued use of the instrument in medical settings in serious question.

4.2. Beck Depression Inventory

The Beck Depression Inventory (Beck, 1972) is an instrument that seeks to approximate clinical judgments of depression intensity. Efforts were made also to clearly differentiate depressed from nondepressed psychiatric patients. The inventory is composed of 21 multiple-choice items reflecting specific behavioral signs of depression which are weighted in severity from 0 to 3.

Depression was defined by Beck (1972) as an abnormal state of the organism manifested by signs and symptoms such as low subjective mood, pessimistic and nihilistic attitudes, loss of spontaneity and specific vegetative signs. This construct could be identified in many diverse types of patients who differ vastly in terms of other characteristics, such as degree of conceptual disorganization, presence of anxiety, prognosis. (p. 201)

It should be noted that the inventory was designed for research purposes and was conceived as appropriate for discriminating levels of depression only in psychiatric populations.

4.2.1. Administration, Scoring, and Development of Norms

4.2.1a. Administration. Originally designed to be administered by a trained interviewer who read each statement and asked the patient to select the statement that fit best, the instrument is now often presented as a self-administered inventory. No information is given regarding the possible impact upon norms and scores of this modification to a self-administered format.

4.2.1b. Scoring. The total score is obtained by adding the weighted values for each response endorsed by the patient. No attempt is made to transform raw scores. Scores of 0–9 are considered normal, the 10–15 range is seen as representing mild depression, 16–19 represents mild to moderate severity, 20–29 is judged as moderate to severe, and 30–63 represents severe depression.

4.2.1c. Norms. Two patient samples were utilized in the development of the inventory. Both groups of patients were drawn from routine admissions to the psychiatric outpatient department of a university hospital and to the psychiatric outpatient department and psychiatric inpatient service of a metropolitan hospital. Patients were usually seen the day of their first visit or at a later appointment within a few days. The majority of patients were white, of lower socioeconomic class, and ranged in age from 15 to 44. Patients were excluded if they had organic brain damage or mental deficiency. The major diagnostic categories represented included psychotic disorder (41%), psychoneurotic disorder (43%), and personality disorder (16%).

4.2.2. Construction

The test developer sought to develop explicit rather than inferred behavioral criteria for evaluating depression. To accomplish this, items were selected from the literature and clinical experience. Each subcategory describes a specific behavioral manifestation of depression and consists of a graded series of self-evaluative statements. The items were chosen on the basis of their relationship to overt behavioral manifestations of depression and do not reflect a particular theory regarding etiology or viewpoint concerning the psychological processes underlying depression.

4.2.3. Postconstruction Empirical Evaluation

Two methods for evaluating the internal consistency of the instrument were used. Two hundred cases were analyzed, with the score for each category compared to the total score on the Depression Inventory. It was found that all categories showed a significant relationship to the total inventory score. In a later study, the subcategories also correlated positively with the total score (range .31 to .68). Split-half reliability results in a coefficient of .86.

Test–retest was not employed in the traditional manner because of the assumption that change would be occurring and that this would significantly alter the interpretation of results. Indirect methods were utilized to assess change scores over time: in general, total depression tended to parallel clinical changes.

Concurrent validity was addressed by comparing scores with clinical assessment of levels of depression (correlations between test scores and clinical judgments averaged .66). It is of some note that prediction of clinical change was accurate in 85% of the cases. At the same time, it was seen that the instrument was capable of discriminating between anxiety and depression, correlating .59 with clinical ratings of depression and only .14 with clinical ratings of anxiety.

4.2.4. Applications of Medical Criteria

The total depression score seeks only to address level of severity among psychiatric patients, having been developed expressly for this purpose. It can serve a function with medical patients in this regard if clinical levels of depression are suspected, and it may help to direct the health team to psychotherapeutic or pharmacologic intervention.

4.2.5. Current Research

Although not widely available, the Beck Depression Inventory is being utilized in a number of settings. As yet, however, few published reports of its use have appeared. It has been utilized to study heroin addicts (Shaw, Steer, Beck, & Schut, 1979) as well as medical patients, such as asthmatics (Teuramaa, 1979) and patients with amyotrophic lateral sclerosis (Houpt, Gould, & Norris, 1977). It has also been used to study the relationship between life events and depression (Head, 1979).

4.3. State–Trait Anxiety Inventory (STAI)

This inventory was originally developed as a research instrument for investigating anxiety in normal adults (Spielberger, Gorsuch, & Lushene, 1970). It is composed of two questionnaires of similar format, one asking the subjects to indicate how they feel *right now*, and the other how the individual *generally* feels. The subject choices are either "almost never," "sometimes," "often," or "almost always." This instrument was specifically developed to evaluate feelings of tension, nervousness, worry, and apprehension. It was posited by the test developers that it could serve either as a clinical tool for evaluating anxiety proneness or, in the case of state scores, the evaluation of level of anxiety or anxiety change.

4.3.1. Administration, Scoring, and Development of Norms

4.3.1a. Administration. The STAI was designed to be self-administered and may be given individually or in groups: complete instructions are printed on the test form. College students generally require less than 15 minutes to complete both questionnaires, while disturbed or less educated individuals often take 30 minutes or more.

4.3.1b. Scoring. Subjects respond to each STAI item by rating themselves on a four-point scale. The scoring weights for items relate to anxiety: 4 is a high-anxiety response and 1 a low-anxiety response. These figures are then converted to T scores or percentiles. Templates and machine scoring are available.

4.3.1c. Norms. Normative data are available for large samples of college and high school students. The sample of general medical patients is both small ($n = 161$) and all male. Given the difference between male and female responses on this inventory with high school and college samples, it would be unwise to view the medical sample as an adequate comparison group.

4.3.1d. Interpretation. Interpretation is straightforward; higher scores on A-Trait indicate higher levels of anxiety proneness. High A-State scores are conceptualized as transitory or characterized by subjective or consciously perceived feelings of apprehension.

4.3.2. Construction

The STAI was originally developed as a research instrument to be used for investigating anxiety in normal adults. The major problem is that the respondent must have a clear understanding of the difference between the state and the trait instructions. The instrument was developed from the item pool of the IPAT Anxiety Scale, the Taylor Manifest Anxiety Scale, and the Welsh Anxiety Scale. Items that correlated with all three full scales were then rewritten to reflect both trait and state anxiety. The 177 items meeting the criterion were then given to advanced undergraduate psychology students to critique with regard to clarity and content; this reduced the item number to 124. A new sample of students were then given the inventory and asked to rate items on how well they generally described the individual. They were then asked to complete the instrument for state. Items were retained if the item-remainder correlations with both A-Trait and A-State instructions were .35 or higher; not more than 20% of the subjects stated "doesn't apply." The 66 remaining items were administered in both trait and state situations. Forty-four items survived this evaluation, and these were cross-validated on a large sample of students asked to reply under A-State, relaxation, and examination conditions. This brought the inventory to 32 items. Further item-validation procedures reduced the form to 23 items. Form A of the STAI represented 20 of these 23. It was at this point that the developers turned to the idea of separate but parallel state–trait questionnaires. Form B, a later version, utilized the 20 best A-Trait items to compose two questionnaires, A-State and A-Trait, each with its own set of instructions. The final construction stage involved the addition of the 20 next-best items to each questionnaire. Six A-Trait and seven A-State items were replaced, leading to the STAI (Form X). despite the extensive revisions and refinements, it is questionable whether the final result was the best possible product of a sequential construction methodology. The test authors' own dissatisfaction with these approaches indicates that they shared similar concerns. Although a variety of student groups were utilized in various stages of construction, the normative samples are extremely narrow in scope, including very few noncollege or nonclinical populations.

As would be expected, test–retest reliability for state was low, .20 to .40, regardless of time elapsed. Trait anxiety test–retest was higher at about .80; KR_{20}s ranged from .83 to .92. Not surprisingly, the A-Trait corresponds highly with the IPAT Anxiety Scale (.75) and the Taylor Manifest Anxiety Scale (.80) from which its items were drawn, while correlating less strongly with the Affect Adjective Checklist (.57). A-State, as would be expected, varies considerably across conditions. Content validity and empirical validity of the instrument are two critical issues. At no point was the score obtained on these inventories compared to any nontest evaluation of anxiety, although item selection sometimes employed hypothetical stress situations. In fact, the STAI was built solely on the belief that the initial item pool covered the full domain of anxiety and that further selection on the basis of internal consistency would not distort this circumstance. The bridge from construct to instrument to the "real world" was therefore never satisfactorily bridged.

4.3.4. Criteria for Utilization with Medical Patients

This instrument seeks to address the issue of anxiety only. It is possible to see how both state and trait anxiety can contribute to an ongoing disease process or complicate its management. Since it is not certain, however, whether the full domain of anxiety has been tapped and since norms for medical patients are inadequate, the results obtained with the STAI would have little meaning beyond the fact that patients within a given sample can be ranged along a continuum.

4.3.5. Current Research

Several studies have been reported in the literature utilizing this measure to compare specific types of patients (Chapman & Cox, 1977; Garron & Leavitt, 1979; Whitehead, Blackwell, Desilva, & Robinson, 1977). Other studies have looked at such diverse issues as pregnancy complications (Edwards, 1969), the relation of life events to the experience of pain (Leavitt, Garron, & Bieliauskas, 1979), and treatment-seeking behavior (Magarey, Todd, & Blizard, 1977). In spite of its serious limitations, this instrument is often utilized because of its ready availability, its brevity, and the ease of administration and scoring. Numbers without validity, however, are only numbers; although comforting, they may have little substantial bearing on either clinical or research problems.

5. Life-Style Inventories

A recent element in evaluating medical patients involves the impact of life-styles and recent life events upon physical health. Among the instruments employed in this task are the Jenkins Activity Survey and the Life Experiences Survey.

5.1. Jenkins Activity Survey (JAS)

The Jenkins Activity Survey (Form C), developed by Jenkins, Zyzanski, and Rosenman (1979), is the latest version of a 52-item self-report questionnaire designed to measure the Type A behavior pattern. This pattern is characterized by extreme competitiveness, striving for achievement, aggressiveness, self-imposed responsibility, impatience, haste, restlessness, feelings of being challenged and under the press of time. The behavior pattern is not conceived as a personality trait or a standard reaction to a challenging situation but rather as the reaction of a predisposed person to a challenging situation. A large body of research has been built around the significance of this pattern in the development and persistence of coronary heart disease (CHD). The test developers recommend that the instrument be used primarily for research into group differences. Given the multifactorial pathogenesis of CHD, they state that the test should not be used by itself to predict individual risk. The instrument proposes to tap three factors within Type A: speed and impatience, job involvement, and hard-driving competition.

5.1.1. Administration, Scoring, and Development of Norms

5.1.1a. Administration. The JAS is easily administered to individuals and groups and is suitable for use with currently or recently employed adults who can read at the eighth-grade level or better. The majority of subjects complete the instrument in 15 to 20 minutes.

5.1.1b. Scoring. Each response is assigned numerical points based on an optimal scaling weight for that response. The sum of the points for all items constitutes the raw score. Hand-scoring templates are available, but machine scoring is encouraged.

5.1.1c. Norms. Normative data are based on a 2,588-male sample drawn exclusively from individuals in middle- and upper-echelon jobs. Scores were normalized with the mean set at zero and each standard deviation equal to 10 points. Scores on the plus side indicate Type A behavior; minus scores signify a Type B inclination. Percentile rankings are also provided. One serious flaw in this area of evaluation is the total absence of female subjects in both the development and normative stages of test construction. This compounds the narrowness of the socioeconomic group employed for building norms.

5.1.1d. Interpretation. JAS scores and the factors they comprise are briefly described in the manual and are conceived as contributing independently to the total Type A behavior pattern.

5.1.2. Construction

The JAS was constructed over an 8-year period; four earlier editions were developed. Previous to this instrument, Rosenman, Friedman, Straus, Wurm, Kositchek, Hahn, and Werthessen (1964) designed a structured interview protocol to assess the Type A behavior pattern. Items for the JAS were derived from this interview as well as from Jenkins's observations of interview behavior and the theory of Type A behavior. This early form of the instrument was administered to 120 males who had also been rated on the structured interview.

Because they were found to correlate with these ratings, 40 items were kept, and 21 new questions were devised and added to comprise the 1965 edition. No information on the basis for these new questions or the specific purpose for adding them is given in the manual. This form was then taken by a sample of 2,951 males. Discriminant function analysis was employed to select items that might best differentiate between independently assessed Type A and Type B groups. Only 73% valid identifications were made on the 19 best items, a disappointing finding at best. In the following year a new sample of 844 men were tested on a second edition in which several new items were deleted and added. At this time 26 items produced optimal discrimination. Not all of the 19 items from the previous year's analysis entered this form. This time only 71% valid identifications were made with the construction sample. Factor analysis of the second form produced three derived factors: S, or speed and impatience; J, or job involvement; and H, or hard-driving and competitive. A 64-item third edition of the instrument utilized earlier test forms as criterion measures. Discriminant functions sought to reduce the total item pools to subsets based on their presumed predictive accuracy and brevity. No cross-validation steps were taken after the item list had been reduced. Efforts to remove sex biases resulted in Form B; Form C consists of the most discriminatory 52 items from Form B. A major flaw in the entire development sequence was the use of discriminant function as the prime tool of scale construction. Each successive form of the test was changed substantially in terms of specific item content. Without adequate data on cross validation, items were dropped, while others, retained on the basis of discriminant utility, had to be dropped later when new samples were employed. Discriminant function always separates construction sample groups; these discriminations may not hold up on further cross-validational work. At no point in the construction sequence did the test developers submit their items to empirical validation, choosing to rely first on the validity of the structured interview and later on the validity of earlier forms of the JAS.

5.1.3. Postconstruction Empirical Evaluation

Test–retest reliabilities at 4- to 6-month intervals ran from .65 to .82 on the four factors, with internal consistency ranging from .73 to .85.

Turning to validity, the construct underlying the test has some intuitive logic as well as empirical support. Initially developed to maximize its correlation with the structured interview, the JAS attempts to adhere closely to its major features. As development progressed, however, particularly in later stages, uncertainty arose as to whether the original Type A domain was still being addressed; that is, the items selected and the factors produced may have become a product of statistical manipulation and sample idiosyncracies. Each step in the construction phase appeared to move the instrument further away from the original base in the structured interview.

5.1.4. Criteria for Utilization with Medical Populations

The JAS was specifically developed to address the issue of Type A behavior, a pattern that is strongly implicated in coronary heart disease. Although the developers recommend that it be used primarily for research in group differences, it can be and has been utilized for assigning individuals to preventive intervention groups. It has been employed as a predictor of CHD with some success, although recent literature shows that it does not improve on the predictive accuracy of the structured interview itself (Brand, Rosenman, Jenkins, Stoltz, Zyzanski, in press). The instrument does not propose to provide information on the progress and management of ongoing disease processes.

5.1.5. Current Research

The JAS has been widely used in a number of research studies, in part due to the strong desire of the medical profession to obtain management suggestions. Some studies have addressed differences between Type A and Type B individuals along a variety of medical and nonmedical dimensions (Hiland, 1977; Jenkins, Zyzanski, Rosenman, & Cleveland, 1971; Jenkins, Zyzanski, Ryan, Ethanasivs, & Tannenbaum, 1977). Other studies merely addressed the prevalence (Shekelle, Schoenberger, & Stamler, 1976) and prediction of CHD (Jenkins, Rosenman, & Zyzanski, 1974) and the possibility of inheritance of the pattern (Rahe, Hervig, & Rosenman, 1978). Some studies, such as that of Blumenthal, Knog, Rosenman, Schenberg, and Thompson (1975), failed to obtain the expected correlations. Research has also moved into experimental settings, such as studies of response to challenge (Dembrowski, MacDougall, & Shields, 1977; Glass, 1977; Manuck, Craft, & Gold, 1978). In spite of the instrument's limitations, research does support its utility. It can evaluate broad group differences and provide clinical investigators with a means of assessing an important construct in proneness to CHD.

5.2. Life Experiences Survey (LES)

The Life Experiences Survey, developed by Sarason, Johnson, and Siegel (1978), was formulated to assess an individual's perception of the life stresses experienced during the preceding 12 months. The notion that life stresses lead to an increase in the frequency of illness is well entrenched in the medical literature. Holmes and Rahe (1967) were the first to address this issue in their early Schedule of Recent Experience (SRE), an objective self-report measure of significant events that may have occurred in the subject's life. They posited that each life event, regardless of its positive or negative impact, requires adaptive coping on the part of the individual. Events were chosen for the SRE because their advent required adaptation on the part of the individual. Standardized weights were then determined for each event, reflecting the amount of social readjustment they appeared to require. This absolutist approach to events contrasts with that of Lazarus (1977), who states that the individual's perception of the meaning of the event is of critical importance.

Sarason *et al.* developed the LES as a means of gauging both the occurrence of an event and its perceived significance. The 57-item LES self-report inventory has two sections. The first, completed by all respondents, contains 47 specific events plus three blank spaces where the individual can add unlisted events. These events cover a wide range of experiences. The second section is designed primarily for use with students. In both sections, the respondent is asked to indicate which events were experienced during the past year and, in addition, (1) the positive or negative character of the event as rated on a seven-point scale and (2) the perceived impact of the event at its time of occurrence as rated on a seven-point scale.

5.2.1. Administration, Scoring, and Development of Norms

5.2.1a. Administration. The inventory is self-administered with instructions printed on the first page of the form. Individuals are asked to check which events have occurred, when in the last year these took place, and the type and extent of impact the event may have had. The LES takes approximately 20 minutes to complete.

5.2.1b. Scoring. The respondents themselves provide weights for each event. A positive change score is obtained by summing the impact ratings of events designated as positive; negative change scores are derived by summing the impact of negative events. The total change score is the sum of these.

5.2.1c. Norms. Normative studies involved the administration of the instrument to 345 students in an introductory psychology class (females, $n = 171$; males, $n = 174$). No significant differences between males and females were obtained on any of the three life-change measures.

5.2.1d. Interpretation. The most useful scores appear to be the negative and total change scores. A negative life-change score is often significantly related to several stress-related dependent measures. The higher these scores, the greater the likelihood of future physical and/or psychological problems.

5.2.2. Construction

The LES items were chosen to represent life changes frequently experienced by individuals in the general population. Of the 57 items, 34 are similar in content to those of the SRE. Specific items were clarified or reworded so as to be applicable to both male and female respondents. No further details are given as to the development of the item pool.

As stated, the underlying construct is that stress requires adaptation and that this adaptation will in part rest upon the individual's perception of the event. It is further assumed that this level of adaptive behavior will be related to illness events. Although efforts were made to be representative, it was impossible to tap the entire domain of potentially significant life events. Leaving a section of blanks to be filled in addresses this problem, but recall is a less adequate process than recognition as a means of identifying events. There was no indication that external criteria were utilized in the construction of the instrument, although numerous correlational studies were employed to evaluate the relationship between LES scores and relevant personality indices. One hopes that a formal manual, when published, will address a number of these issues.

5.2.3. Postconstruction Empirical Evaluation

Test–retest data with two samples show that positive change scores correlate .19 and .53 for 5 to 6 weeks, negative scores correlate .56 and .88, and total change scores .63 and .64; the *n*'s were 34 and 58 respectively. It must be noted that test–retest reliability is underestimated, since changes in events will occur with the passage of time.

LES scores were correlated with a number of other instruments. Negative scores correlated .29 with Trait Anxiety on the STAI and .46 with State Anxiety; an almost zero correlation was found between positive scores and State or Trait Anxiety. Crown–Marlowe Social Desirability correlations were also in the zero range, suggesting that the LES is free of social desirability bias. Employing the Psychological Screening Inventory, correlations of .20 were found between social nonconformity and negative LES scores, .23 between neuroticism and negative LES scores, and a correlation of .28 between extraversion and positive LES scores. From these data it would appear that personal maladjustment is associated with negative change scores. Another modest correlation was found between the I-E Scale (.32) and negative LES changes. No studies were reported on the relationship of these scores and illness onset, the posited sequel to life stress.

5.2.4. Applications of Medical Criteria

This instrument proposes to address the issue of life events only. It is posited that these have an impact on the incidence of illness and psychological difficulties. Although no construction studies were reported on the efficacy of this instrument in making such predictions, later research (Yunik, 1979) indicates that negative weighted events and total weighted events tend to have a high correlation with future illness; negative impact scores correlated .42 with the total number of illness problems reported. On the basis of these preliminary studies, it does appear that the LES can serve as a modest predictor of future illness behaviors. Unfortunately, there is no direct application of the instrument to the management of disease.

5.2.5. Current Research

Research reports are relatively sparse, in part due to the recent development of the instrument. Two studies (Johnson & Sarason, 1978; Head, 1979) focus on depression, while Yunik (1979) evaluated health in relation to the interaction of life events and personality. Further evaluation of the instrument must be completed before conclusions can be drawn about its promising current utility.

6. Personality Inventories

The following instruments deal with the total realm of personality functioning and not with single traits or dimensions. They represent different conceptions of personality and different development procedures. The instruments in this sphere include the 16 Personality Factor Inventory, the Minnesota Multiphasic Personality Inventory, and the Millon Behavioral Health Inventory.

The 16PF (Cattell, Eber, & Tatsouka, 1970), one of the oldest personality tests currently in use, was first published in 1949. It is composed of a multidimensional set of 16 scales arranged in omnibus form. If the supplement is used, it is supposedly capable of tapping 23 personality dimensions. The most commonly used form comprises of 187 trichotomous items and is designed to tap what Cattell terms "source traits" rather than syndromes. The traits evaluated are said to have withstood the critical examination of over thirty years of factor-analytic research. Since the scales are claimed to be factorially pure, there is no item overlap; consequently, each scale score is gauged by responses to between only 10 and 13 items. Each of its several forms is geared to a seventh-grade reading level and has been translated into numerous foreign languages. Standardized on a stratified sample of 15,000 normal adults, it has been used in a variety of research studies as well as in clinical assessment in both psychiatric and medical settings.

6.1.1. Administration, Scoring, and Development of Norms

6.1.1a. Administration. A paper-and-pencil self-report inventory, the 16PF takes generally less than 45 minutes for the subject to complete and requires no assistance from the individual administering the test.

6.1.1b. Scoring. Hand-scoring templates as well as machine-scoring and computer-generated narratives are available. Raw scores are transformed into sten scores for the 16 traits.

6.1.1c. Norms. A variety of normative samples have been developed over the years. As mentioned earlier, standardization of the instrument involved a sample of 15,000 normal adults; however, the nature and size of the original construction samples is unclear from the manual.

6.1.1d. Interpretation. The traits are viewed as bipolar and scores are evaluated in terms of their location on the trait continuum. A variety of publications are available to help in interpreting scores (Karson & O'Dell, 1976), including a book specifically addressing the issue of the medical patient (Krug, 1977).

6.1.2. Construction

A significant body of literature has been developed utilizing the 16PF; the "meaning" of many of the results is often unclear. Regarding initial construction, Rorer (1972) states that the scales are of indeterminate origin and unknown significance. Data gathered in support of the instrument often employ samples selected in an unknown way and the manual is not very specific as to which form, developmental stage, or population was employed in many of the reported studies. One of the continuing difficulties in evaluating this instrument is the atypical manner in which data are presented in the handbook (Cattell, Eber, & Tatsouka, 1970). Although large quantities of data are presented, they are not comparable to standard psychometric evaluation techniques, often leaving the reader with little choice but to accept blindly the statements made rather than being able to judge them intelligently for themselves. Although they are mathematically and factorially elegant, there is serious question as to whether the scales and profiles derived from the 16PF have any genuine utility in personality or clinical appraisal.

6.1.3. Postconstruction Evaluation

Test–retest reliabilities are reported to be in the .70 to .90 range short term and drop to .50 to .80 at 2 months. Split-half reliabilities have proved disheart-eningly poor and indicate considerable within-factor heterogeneity. There is a high likelihood that several of the supposedly pure factors subsume a number of different traits. This finding is especially troublesome, since the instrument rests on the factorial purity of the 16 traits. Drawn from the world of everyday expression, these source traits have been refined by factor analytic procedures. Although the description of these factors and their empirical support are presented fully in the handbook, this exposition is highly idiosyncratic. Thus, no effort is made to provide correlation data with instruments purported to measure similar traits. Furthermore, the factoring method that Cattell has used is but one of many available, each of which might have produced different results. A serious if not fatal flaw is that correlations between identical scales on different forms of the test are very low, ranging from a low of .15 to .82; in fact some scales correlate more highly with other scales than with their matched scales. This puts into serious question the very meaning and true reliability of these scales; at the very least, it makes comparison across forms impossible.

6.1.4. Applications of Medical Criteria

The 16PF has been proposed as suitable for assessing the personalities of medical patients. If it is valid at all, it may actually be more suitable with so-called normals than with general psychiatric populations, for whom it has also been claimed to be useful. The edited volume *Psychological Assessment in Medicine* (Krug, 1977) is devoted exclusively to the 16PF, but it provides largely anecdotal suggestions on how to interpret the test. These tend to be global and simplistic.

6.1.5. Current Research

In spite of the shortcomings noted above, research with the instrument has been carried out with a number of illness groups. Some merely seek to describe the characteristics of a given patient type (Boleloucky, 1974; Kidson, 1973; Rosenthal, Aitken, & Zealley, 1973), while others address the issue of differences among treatment programs within a given patient group (Chynoweth, 1973; Goble, Gowers, Morgan, & Kline, 1978; Kornfeld, Heller, Frank, & Moskowitz, 1974). Others have sought to evaluate the role of a significant illness in producing personality changes (Barton & Cattell, 1972).

One is left in reviewing this instrument with a sense of considerable methodological sophistication. At the same time, one is struck by the idiosyncratic conception of personality and the reluctance to compare this instrument and its results with anything other than itself. The use of esoteric proofs and the absence of more widely employed techniques seriously hamper the outsider's efforts to evaluate the instrument. These deficits and idiosyncrasies seriously compromises the confidence one may have in the 16PF's construct validity and consequent usefulness.

6.2. Minnesota Multiphasic Personality Inventory (MMPI)

The MMPI is an empirically derived instrument that was constructed by Hathaway and McKinley in 1939 to serve as an objective aid in a psychiatric case workup and as a tool for determining the severity of specific psychiatric conditions. In its original development the MMPI had little to do with personality traits. As stated by Dahlstrom, Welsh, and Dahlstrom (1972), the MMPI was developed and validated as a psychiatric nosologic categorizing device leading to dichotomous discrimination between psychiatric patients and normals. They wrote:

> Although the content covered in the MMPI item pool included by far a larger array of personological topics than in any other instrument then available, subsequent studies have indicated that—while some areas of emotional maladjustment may be overrepresented (Block, 1965)—items referring to values, to primary group relationships, and to mood, temperament, and various special attitudes are probably too scarce to provide a well-balanced coverage of the domain of personality. (Schofield, 1966, p. 6)

The final 566-item true–false questionnaire has 10 clinical scales: hypochondriasis, depression, hysteria, psychopathic deviance, male sexual inversion, paranoia, psychasthenia, schizophrenia, hypomania, and social introversion along with the following validity scales: *cannot say, lie scale, confusion scale* or *straight validity, K* or *suppressor factor.*

6.2.1. Administration, Scoring, and Development of Norms

6.2.1a. Administration. The test was developed so that those 16 years old or above with 6 years of school would be able to complete the inventory. Booklets are available for group testing or for the patient to complete independently. A card-sort format is also available, and the test can be administered orally if required. The instrument takes 1 to 1½ hours to complete on the average, although there are no limits to the time allotted to complete the inventory.

6.2.1b. Scoring. Hand-scoring templates are available, as is machine scoring; these scores may be transformed into profiles or computer generated narratives. Raw scores are converted to T scores with separate norms for males and females. A T score of 50 is the mean score for the normative construction sample, and 10 represents one standard deviation. T-score scaling assumes normal distribution, an unlikely assumption given the highly variable prevalence rates of the syndromes involved.

6.2.1c. Norms. The original normative group was drawn from samples of Minnesota adults, with separate male and female groups. Most lived in rural or semirural areas, worked in skilled or semiskilled trades, and had an eighth-grade education. The test itself has not been renormed since this 1940 sample; numerous local norms have been developed for a variety of settings and special populations.

6.2.1d. Interpretation. Originally, only single-scale elevations were interpreted. Over the years extensive clinical data have led to greater use of the MMPI. A number of code books have been written to aid in profile interpretations. (Gilberstadt & Duker, 1965; Good & Brantner, 1974; Lachar, 1974; Marks & Seeman, 1963.)

6.2.2. Construction

The original item pool of over 1,000 items was drawn from other inventories, clinical reports, interviews, and clinical experiments. It was reduced to 504 to eliminate duplication and maximize readability. Fifty-five items dealing with male sexual inversion (MF) were added at a later date. The original 504-item form was given to subjects in a card-sort task in which they were asked to describe themselves as accurately as possible. Construction criterion groups were selected from adult psychiatric clinics and wards of the University of Minnesota Hospitals; "normal" subjects were families and visitors of the patients. Items were selected for inclusion in a scale on the basis of their capacity to discriminate between normals and each of the criterion groups. No effort was made at that time to examine scale overlap or to develop a rationale for item selection. Cross-validational samples were employed to evaluate the stability of the obtained separation and the generality of initial scale findings. Of the 550 items (16 are repeated), 351 are utilized in scoring the initial 10 clinical scales.

6.2.3. Postconstruction Empirical Evaluation

The MMPI is without doubt the most thoroughly researched personality instrument. One problem in evaluating the inventory is that its manual has not been updated since 1967, and vast quantities of information on the test's empirical utility and validation reside in hundreds of journal articles often beyond the reach of all but the most diligent students. However, a significant amount of data are published concisely in the two-volume handbook (Dahlstrom, Welsh, & Dahlstrom, 1972).

Test–retest reliability in one sample at 3 to 4 days ranged from .56 to .88, with the majority in the low .80s. College student test–retest scores at 8 months yielded correlations of .44 to .73. Psychiatric patients show 1 week test–retest scores ranging from .59 to .86, with the majority in high .70s. At one year, correlations drop to .36 to .72. Test–retest scores can be difficult to interpret because it is not possible to discriminate real change from reliability error, particularly in the case of psychiatric patients undergoing treatment over extended periods of time. Kudner-Richardson internal consistency estimates are reported on a sample employing the KR_{21} formula. These ranged from .36 to .93, with a median of .70.

Validity data are best summarized in the *MMPI Handbook* (Dahlstrom, Welsh, & Dahlstrom, 1972). As one reads through reviews of the MMPI chronologically, one is struck by the responses of individuals utilizing the test clinically. In 1945, reviews such as those by Benton and Probst (1945) state that there is a significant agreement on ratings and test scores on only *psychopathic deviate, paranoia,* and *schizophrenia* but not the other scales. Schmidt (1945) wrote that psychiatric patients can be distinguished from normals but that it is difficult to distinguish between different abnormal populations. Rotter (1945), in his review, thoughtfully notes that reliability and validity are dependent upon the reliability and validity of the criterion disease groups themselves, which appear to have been much less than might be desired. For example, those diagnosed as belonging to one disease group were more likely than not to have their highest scores on scales other than the expected ones. Ellis (1959) stated that the individual diagnostic utility of the instrument was still in question but that it was useful for purposes of group discrimination. Adcock (1965) noted that the instrument failed to demonstrate discriminative validity regarding those who do and do not need help in a normal population. He went on to note that most clinicians assume the validity of the instrument rather than evaluating it as critically as one should. This acceptance often led to misinterpretations of the meaning of scores. Lingoes (1965) continued in his review to note difficulties in discriminating among groups of psychiatric patients. Undoubtedly the best instrument of its generation, it has assumed an almost mystical impregnability as a function of its age. For its time and purpose, its excellence of construction was unmatched. Unfortunately, enthusiastic users have often exceeded the intent of the test developers, misreading meaning into unreliable data and applying the instrument in inappropriate settings.

6.2.4. Applications of Medical Criteria

The MMPI has been employed in a variety of medical settings with rather equivocal results. Most frequently it has been used to differentiate psychosomatic from organic disease, to delineate psychological factors associated with psychosomatic disorders, and to predict the outcome of surgery or recovery from illness (Dahlstrom, Welsh, & Dahlstrom, 1972). As Butcher and Owens (1978) note, however, the MMPI does not appear to differentiate psychosomatic types successfully, and the commonly noted 1-3/3-1 elevation may indicate a general neurotic overlay that does not preclude the diagnosis of organic disease (Schwartz, Osborn, & Krupp, 1972). Although utilized in a number of studies with medical patients, the MMPI appears to serve as an aid only if psychiatric issues are prominent.

6.2.5. Current Research

Research with the MMPI continues apace, and numerous studies with medical populations are being published. Examples of this body of literature are those seeking to characterize specific patient subgroups (Caslyn, Louks, & Freeman, 1976; Jones, Kinsman, Schum, & Resnikoff, 1976; Pierce, Freeman, Lawton, & Fearing, 1973; Verberne, 1972). Others attempt to identify the presence of psychopathology that might be concurrent with a specified medical illness (Kristianson, 1974; Stevens, Milstein, & Goldstein, 1972). The instrument has been utilized to explain disease course (Abram, Meixal, Webb, & Scott, 1976; Henrichs & Waters, 1972; Kilpatrick, Miller, Allain, Huggins, & Lee, 1975; Lair & King, 1976; Schonfield, 1976; Wampler, Lauer, Lantz, Wampler, Evens, & Madura, 1980). Some researchers seek to validate earlier scales and the accuracy of their interpretations (Rhodes, 1973; Fracchia, Sheppard, Ricca, & Merlis, 1973). Despite active research on the instrument, its clinical utility for those who work in nonpsychiatric health care settings remains questionable.

6.3. Millon Behavioral Health Inventory (MBHI)

The MBHI was developed specifically with physically ill patients and medical–behavioral decision-making issues in mind (Millon, Green, & Meagher, 1982). A major goal in constructing the MBHI was to keep the total number of items comprising the inventory small enough to encourage use in all types of medical diagnostic and treatment settings yet large enough to permit the assessment of a wide range of clinically relevant behaviors. Geared to an eighth-grade reading level, the final form of 150 items is well tolerated by medical patients.

Diagnostic instruments such as the MBHI have increased usefulness if they are linked systematically to a comprehensive clinical theory or are anchored to empirical validation data gathered in their construction. The eight basic "coping styles" comprising the first eight scales of the MBHI are derived from a theory of personality (Millon, 1969). The six "psychogenic attitude" scales were developed to reflect psychosocial stressors found in the research literature to be significant precipitators or exacerbators of physical illness. The final six scales comprising the present form were empirically derived for the MBHI either to appraise the extent to which emotional factors complicate particular psychosomatic ailments or to predict psychological complications associated with a number of diseases. The primary intent of the MBHI is to provide information to clinicians—psychologists, physicians, nurses—who must make behavioral assessments and treatment decisions about persons with physical problems.

6.3.1. Administration, Scoring, and Development of Norms

6.3.1a. Administration. The MBHI is self-administered, with instructions printed on the questionnaire; the greatest majority of patients can complete the inventory in 20 to 25 minutes. Thus there is little patient resistance or fatigue.

6.3.1b. Scoring. Multiple-keyed hand-scoring templates are not available, but machine scoring and computer-generated narratives are. The raw scores on the 20 scales are transformed into base-rate scores.

6.3.1c. Base-Rate Scores. There are some conditions for which the traditional method of transforming raw scores into standard scores is inappropriate. Standard scores by definition assume "normal" distributions or comparable frequency spreads of the traits or variables being measured. This assumption is not met when a set of scales represents coping styles, since these are not normally or equally distributed in the population. Furthermore, it is not the primary purpose of a clinical instrument to locate the relative position of a patient on a frequency distribution but rather to identify or calculate the probability that a patient is or is not a member of a particular class. On both grounds—differential base rates and optimal classificatory efficacy—it would be good to employ transformation scores that are more meaningful and useful than standard scores (Meehl & Rosen, 1955).

For the MBHI, these base-rate conversions were determined by known or estimated prevalence data and by utilizing cutting lines that maximize correct classifications—that is, which are calculated in terms of optimal valid-positive to false-positive ratios.

6.3.1d. Norms. Norms for the MBHI are based on several groups of nonclinical subjects and numerous samples of medical patients involved in diagnosis, treatment, or follow-up. The nonclinical group involved in the construction phases of test development consisted of subjects drawn from several settings (e.g., colleges, health maintenance organizations, nursing schools, medical schools, factories, etc.) and was composed of 212 males and 240 females; the test construction patient group, drawn from diverse clinical populations (e.g., surgical clinics, pain centers, dialysis units, cancer programs, etc.), consisted of 1,019 males and 1,094 females.

6.3.1e. Interpretation. Interpretation is based on both profile configurations and single-scale elevations. The first eight scales or the basic coping styles characterize patients as to interpersonal and personality traits. For most patients, these characteristics blend with other features in a configural pattern of several scales.

The psychogenic attitude scales represent the personal feelings and perceptions of the patient regarding different aspects of psychological stress that increase psychosomatic susceptibility or aggravate the course of a current disease. Scores are gauged by comparing these attitudes to those expressed by a cross section of both healthy and physically ill adults of the same sex. Some details concerning these six scales may be useful.

The *Chronic Tension Scale* gauges level of stress, a factor that has repeatedly been found to relate to the incidence of a variety of diseases. More specifically, qualitative studies of chronic stress—such as persistent job tensions or marital problems—have been carried out with particular reference to their impact on heart diseases. Such stress syndromes are often addressed as Type A–Type B behavior (Friedman & Rosenman, 1974; Gersten, Frii, & Lengner, 1976; Jenkins, 1976; Rahe, 1977). High scorers on this scale are disposed to suffer various psychosomatic and physical ailments, notably in the cardiovascular and digestive systems. Constantly on the go, they live under considerable self-imposed pressure and have trouble relaxing.

The *Recent Stress Scale* addresses the patient's perception of recent events that were experienced as stressful. This is a phenomenological assessment similar to the Social Readjustment Rating Scale (Holmes & Rahe, 1967) and the Life Experience Survey of Sarason, Johnson, and Siegel (1978). High scorers on this scale have an increased susceptibility to serious illness for the year following test administration. Recent marked changes in their life predict a significantly higher incidence of poor physical and psychological health than in the population at large (Andrew, 1970; Rahe & Arthur, 1968; Yunik, 1979; Head, 1979).

The *Premorbid Pessimism Scale* represents a dispositional attitude of help-lessness–hopelessness that has been implicated in the appearance or exacerbation of a variety of diseases such as multiple sclerosis, ulcerative colitis, and cancer (Mei-Tal, Meyerowitz, & Engel, 1970; Paull & Hislop, 1974; Schmale, 1972; Stavraky, Buch, Lott, & Wanklin, 1968). It differs from other "depression" indices by noting characterologic tendencies toward viewing the world in a negative manner. High scorers on this scale are disposed to interpret life as a series of troubles and misfortunes and are likely to intensify the discomforts they experience with real physical and psychological difficulties.

The *Future Despair Scale* focuses on the patients' willingness to plan and look forward to the future (Engel, 1968; Wright, 1960). This is more likely than the previous scale to tap the patient's response to current difficulties and circumstances rather than a general or lifelong tendency to view things negatively. High scorers do not look forward to a productive future life and view medical difficulties as seriously distressing and potentially life-threatening.

Social Alienation looks at level of familial and friendship support, both real and perceived, which appears to relate to the impact of various life stressors (Cobb, 1977; Rabkin & Struening, 1976). This sense of aloneness has been detailed in the sociological literature (Berkman, 1969; Comstock & Partridge, 1972; Moss, 1977; Parkes, Benjamin, & Fitzgerald, 1969). High scorers are vulnerable to physical and psychological ailments. A poor adjustment to hospitalization is also common. These patients perceive low levels of family and social support and may not seek medical assistance until illness is extremely discomforting.

All the above stressors seem to be significantly modulated upward or downward by the preoccupations and fears that patients may express about their physical state, a characteristic addressed in the *Somatic Anxiety Scale*. Studies of what may be called somatic anxiety reflect the general concerns that patients have about their bodies (Lipsitt, 1970; Lowy, 1977; Lucente & Fleck, 1972; Mechanic & Volkart, 1961). High scorers on this scale tend to be hypochrondriacal and susceptible to various minor illnesses. They experience an abnormal amount of fear concerning bodily functioning and are likely to overreact to the discomforts of surgery and hospitalization.

The next set of three scales were derived empirically. They have been labeled the *Psychosomatic Correlates Scales* and are designed for use only with patients who have previously been medically diagnosed as exhibiting one of the following specific disease syndromes: allergy, gastrointestinal problems, or cardiovascular difficulties. The scores of each scale gauge the extent to which the patient's responses are similar to comparably diagnosed patients whose illness has been judged substantially psychosomatic or whose course has been complicated by emotional or social factors.

The last three of the empirically derived scales, those labeled *Prognostic Indices*, seek to identify treatment problems or difficulties that may arise in the future course of the patient's illness. The scores of each scale—*Pain Treatment Responsivity, Life Threat Reactivity*, and *Emotional Vulnerability*—gauge the extent to which the patient's responses are similar to those of patients whose course of illness or treatment has been more complicated and unsatisfactory than is typical.

6.3.2. Construction

The MBHI was developed following procedures recommended by Loevinger (1957) and Jackson (1970), who contend that validation should be an ongoing process involved in all the phases of test construction, not merely a procedure for assessing or corroborating an instrument's accuracy after completion. The three aspects of this validation procedure are labeled *theoretical–substantive, internal–structural,* and *external-criterion.*

6.3.2a. Theoretical–Substantive Validation Stage. Over 1,000 items were gathered from numerous sources—including other psychological tests and abnormal and personality texts—and some were written specifically for item pool purposes. Items were developed so as to cover the full range of characteristics to be tapped by both the personality and psychogenic scales. At this stage the number of items in the personality-style scales ranged from 60 to 135. The psychogenic-attitude scale items ranged in number from 37 to 57. The item set for the six empirically derived scales was drawn entirely from the final pool based on the 14 personality and psychogenic scales; they were not subject to initial theoretical–substantive analysis. Items were balanced at this stage so that approximately half of them could be answered so that the response "true" would signify the style or attitude and half so that the response "false" would do so; balance of this type was built in so as to attempt to correct for "acquiescent" bias (Jackson & Messick, 1960).

Items were deleted according to the following general criteria: too complicated for patient understanding, obvious desirability bias, lack of clarity in phrasing, probable extreme endorsement frequency. Items were retained if they exemplified the traits of the scale for which they were written, and efforts were made to cover the full range of behaviors and attitudes typified by a given scale. To achieve this, ten health professionals with knowledge of personality theory and experience in psychological traits among medical patients were asked independently to sort these items into their theoretically appropriate personality and psychogenic categories. The criteria for inclusion required that the item be sorted into the "correct" scale by at least seven of the judges.

6.3.2b. Internal–Structural Validation Stage. To accord with the theoretical model, items should give evidence not only of substantial within-scale homogeneity but also of selective overlap with theoretically related scales. Item and scale overlap within the MBHI was both expected and constructed in line with theoretical considerations; this contrasts with other instruments, such as the MMPI, where overlap among items on different scales is solely a function of empirically obtained covariations. A detailed explanation of this rationale may be found in the MCMI manual (Millon, 1977).

According to the theory underlying both the MCMI (Millon, 1969) and the MBHI, no personality style or psychogenic attitude is likely to consist of entirely homogeneous and discrete psychological dimensions. Rather, these styles and attitudes comprise complex characteristics, as well as having distinctive features sharing many traits. Items are expected to exhibit their strongest but not their only association with the specific scale for which they were developed. The ultimate test of an item's or scale's efficiency is not statistical but discriminatory or predictive; procedures that enhance high item–scale homogeneity through studies of internal consistency are the best methods for optimizing, rather than maximizing, discriminations among scales.

The initial items had been chosen to accord with theoretical–substantive validation data and were reduced on grounds of preliminary internal consistency and structural validation to the 289 "best." This 289-item "personality" form was administered to over 2,500 persons in a variety of settings, somewhat over half being students at urban universities; medical populations were not included in this evaluation phase.

Several procedures were followed after this form had been administered to these subjects. Most importantly, item–scale homogeneities were again calculated using measures of internal consistency; additionally, true and false endorsement frequencies were obtained. Point–biserial correlations (corrected for overlap) were calculated between each item and each personality scale. To maximize scale homogeneity, only items that showed their highest correlation with the scale to which they were originally assigned were retained for further evaluation. With few exceptions, items showing a correlation below .30 were eliminated. The median biserial correlation for all items for all personality scales was .47. The final number of items retained for inclusion in the MBHI from the provisional 289-item inventory was 64; these comprised the core group of coping-style items for the final 150-item inventory.

Items for the six psychogenic attitude scales were developed on theoretical–substantive grounds, following the development of the core 64 personality items. Lists of approximately 35 to 60 items were developed for each of the six scales on the basis of previous research by other investigators into the characteristics to be measured. These item lists were then rated by clinicians with experience in assessing the effects of psychological influences upon physical illness. Only items "correctly" placed by more than 75% of the raters were considered for inclusion in the inventory. Efforts were made to include some representation of the several diverse traits comprising each scale. By this procedure, 83 items in total were added to the core group of 64 personality items; an additional 3 "correction" items were also included, resulting in a final form of 150 items.

6.3.2c. External-Criterion Stage. The final 150-item form of the inventory was administered in a large number of medical settings to develop a series of empirically derived scales. The central idea behind this step, both as a construction approach and as a method of validation, is that items comprising a test scale should be selected on the basis of their empirically verified association with a significant and relevant criterion measure. The procedure by which this association is gauged is also direct. Preliminary items are administered to two groups of subjects who differ on the criterion measure. The "criterion" group exhibits the trait with which the item is to be associated, the "comparison" group does not. In the case of the MBHI, all subjects were patients with a given diagnosis, but they varied according to clinical judgments regarding the degree to which various psychological or social complications were involved. After administration, true–false endorsement frequencies obtained with each group were calculated on every item. Items that differentiated the criterion group statistically from the comparison group were judged "externally valid." This was the approach followed in attempting to construct empirical scales that would either identify (correlate) or predict (prognose) certain clinically relevant criteria.

Point–biserial correlations between each of the 150 items and all scales were recalculated and reexamined. Items that showed high correlations (usually .30 or more) with any scale other than a theoretically incompatible one were added as items to that scale.

A central factor in the evaluation of any psychological instrument is whether the results obtained with it are reliable. It is particularly difficult to address this question with instruments designed to measure personality traits; it is even more difficult when attitudes that may reflect transient or situational concerns are being appraised. Change is inevitable in these states. Thus, low test–retest reliabilities may be a function of changing circumstances rather than intrinsic measurement errors.

At 4½ months the coping style scales show reasonably high test–retest reliabilities, with most in the range of .77 to .88 and a mean of .82. The psychogenic attitude scales also show high reliabilities, averaging around .85, as do the empirically derived scales at about .80 with the single exception of emotional vulnerability.

KR_{20}s were calculated as the optimal method for addressing internal consistency. The KR_{20} coefficients for all scales ranged from .66 to .90, with a median of .83.

Correlational data have been obtained through the use of a variety of different and often homogeneous patient and nonpatient samples. Among the inventories used were the MMPI, SCL-90, I-E Scale, Beck Depression Inventory, Personal Orientation Inventory, Life Events Survey, Webber-Johansson Temperament Survey, and California Personality Inventory. The results are reported at length in the MBHI manual (Millon, Green, & Meagher, 1982).

6.3.3. Applications of Medical Criteria

The MBHI addresses interpersonal style, attitudes shown to be significant to the management of health concerns, likelihood of psychological components being involved in medical problems, and specific prognostic issues. It uses this information to make probabilistic statements about the patient's behavior in relation to illness, to its management, and to health care personnel. Directly addressing specified disease processes and their management, it provides the basis for making clear recommendations across a variety of medical problems regarding the likelihood of illness occurring and probable progress as well as optimal management of the disease process.

6.3.4. Current Research

A number of research projects have been carried out with the MBHI in both clinical and analog settings. The effect of coping styles on outcome and patient management in an inpatient pain unit has been studied by Green, Meagher, and Millon (1981). Other studies have found the MBHI successful in predicting behaviors such as isolation, hostility toward health personnel, and excessive complaining and emotionality; these data enabled clinicians to modify treatment procedures so as to minimize difficulties. Another clinically relevant study evaluated the impact of presurgical counseling sessions on coronary bypass patients (Levine, 1980). It was found that MBHI-obtained coping style ratings and depression scores were significantly correlated with the speed and level of recovery. Another study evaluated outcome in a traditional outpatient medical program for chronic pain (Rabinowitz, 1979). Here again, coping style was highly predictive of outcome efficacy.

Recent predictive studies with "healthy" college students were carried out to identify those with subsequent physical and mental health difficulties. The dissertations by Head (1979) and Yunik (1979) relate coping styles to subsequent depression and utilization of health care services. Both studies uncovered similar and highly predictive coping style patterns.

7. Discussion

The process of evaluating the medical patient is currently evolving from a strictly medical–diagnostic approach to one encompassing the presenting symptoms along with events, actions, reactions, and personality interactions in an ever-changing presentation. Psychologists employing interview and diagnostic testing contribute to this evaluation by delineating psychosocial aspects of the patient's life as well as developing diagnostic and prognostic statements.

This review of self-report inventories widely used with medical patients provides the practitioner with an overview of the state of the art. Ranging from simple checklists to single-trait assessments and multidimensional personality inventories, these instruments provide a variety of diagnostic options for the clinician. Unfortunately, even within this selected group, construction and post-construction validation results have often proved disappointing. It is critical that the clinician utilizing a given instrument demonstrate caution in both application and interpretation. Employing tests developed and normed with psychiatric populations may fit old habits and be expedient, but only rarely have such instruments proved useful in nonpsychiatric health care settings. Psychological assessment is new to the nonpsychiatric medical world and our instruments must be carefully evaluated regarding not only their construction but also their suitability to provide solutions to the diagnostic and decision-making problems of the medical staff. It is hoped that this review will aid the clinician in making sound choices among the tools currently available.

8. References

Abeloff, M. D., & Derogatis, L. R. Psychological aspects of the management of primary and metastatic breast cancer. *Proceedings of the International Conference on Breast Cancer.* New York: A. R. List, Inc., 1977.

Abram, H. S., Meixal, S. A., Webb, W. W., & Scott, H. W. Psychological adaptation to jejunoileal bypass for morbid obesity. *Journal of Nervous and Mental Disease*, 1976, *62*, 151–157.

Adams-Webber, J. *Perceived locus of control of moral sanctions.* Unpublished master's thesis, Ohio State University, 1963.

Adcock, C. J. In O. Buros (Ed.), *Review of the MMPI; 6th Mental Measurements Yearbook.* Highland Park, N.J.: Gryphon Press, 1965.

American Psychological Association, American Educational Research Association and National Council on Measurement in Education. *Standards for Educational and Psychological Tests*, Washington D.C.: American Psychological Association, 1974.

Andrew, J. M. Recovery from surgery, with and without preparatory instruction, for three coping styles. *Journal of Personality and Social Psychology*, 1970, *15*(3), 223–226.

Auerbach, S., Kendall, P., Cuttler, H., & Levitt, N. Anxiety, locus of control, type of preparatory information, and adjustment to dental surgery. *Journal of Consulting and Clinical Psychology,* 1976, *44,* 809–818.

Barrios, B., Barrios, Z., & Topping, J. Locus of control of what? *Psychology,* 1977, *14*(3), 51–54.

Barton, K., & Cattell, R. B. Personality before and after a chronic illness. *Journal of Clinical Psychology,* 1972, *28,* 464–467.

Beck, A. T. *Depression: Causes and treatment.* Philadelphia: University of Pennsylvania Press, 1972.

Bellack, A. S., Rozensky, R., & Schwartz, J. A. Comparison of two forms of self-monitoring in a behavioral weight reduction program. *Behavior Therapy,* 1974, *5,* 523–530.

Benton, A. L., & Probst, K. A. A comparison of psychiatric ratings with MMPI scores. *Journal of Abnormal and Social Psychology,* 1945, *41,* 75–78.

Berggren, T., Ohman, A., & Fredrickson, M. Locus of control and habituation of the electrodermal orienting response to nonsignal and signal stimuli. *Journal of Personality and Social Psychology,* 1977, *35,* 708–716.

Berkman, P. L. Spouseless motherhood, psychological stress, and physical morbidity. *Journal of Health and Social Behavior,* 1969, *10, 323*–334.

Block, J. *The challenge of response sets: Unconfounding meaning, acquiescences and social desirability in the MMPI.* New York: Appleton Century Crofts, 1965.

Blumenthal, J. A., Knog, Y., Rosenman, R. H., Schenberg, S. M., & Thompson, L. W. *Type A behavior pattern and angiographically documented coronary disease.* Paper presented at the meeting of the American Psychosomatic Society, New Orleans, March 1975.

Boleloucky, Z. Cattell's personality factors in ulcerative colitis male patients. *Activitas Nervosa Superior,* 1974, *16,* 116–117.

Brand, R. J., Rosenman, R., Jenkins, C., Stoltz, R., & Zyzanski, S. Comparison of coronary heart disease prediction in the VCGS using the structured interview and the JAS assessments of the coronary-prone Type A behavior pattern. *Journal of Chronic Diseases,* in press.

Brodman, K., Erdman, A. J., & Wolff, H. G. *Cornell Medical Index Health Questionnaire.* New York: Cornell University Medical College, 1949.

Bruhn, J. G., Chandler, B., Lynn, T. N., & Wolf, S. Social characteristics of patients and coronary heart disease. *American Journal of Medical Science,* 1966, *251,* 629–637.

Butcher, J. N., & Owens, P. L. Objective personality inventories: Recent research and some contemporary issues. In B. Wolman (Ed.), *Clinical diagnosis of mental disorders: A handbook.* New York: Plenum Press, 1978.

Cardi, M. *An examination of internal versus external control in relation to academic failures.* Unpublished master's thesis, Ohio State University, 1962.

Caslyn, D. A. Louks, J., & Freeman, C. W. The use of the MMPI with chronic low back pain patients with mixed diagnosis. *Journal of Clinical Psychology,* 1976, *32,* 532–536.

Cattell, R. B., Eber, H. W., & Tatsouka, M. M. *Handbook for the Sixteen Personality Factor Questionnaire (16PF).* Champaign, Ill.: Institute for Personality and Ability Testing, Inc., 1970.

Chapman, C., & Cox, G. Anxiety, pain and depression surrounding elective surgery: A multivariate comparison of abdominal surgery patients with kidney donors and recipients. *Journal of Psychosomatic Research,* 1977, *21,* 7–15.

Chynoweth, R. Psychological complications of hysterectomy. *Australian and New Zealand Journal of Psychiatry,* 1973, *7,* 102–104.

Coan, R. W. Personality variables associated with cigarette smoking. *Journal of Personality and Social Psychology,* 1973, *26,* 86–104.

Cobb, S. Epilogue: Meditation on psychosomatic medicine. In Z. J. Lipowski, D. R. Lipsitt, & P. C. Whybrow, (Eds.), *Psychosomatic medicine: Current trends and clinical applications.* New York: Oxford University Press, 1977.

Comstock, G. W., & Partridge, K. B. Church attendance and health. *Journal of Chronic Disease,* 1972, *25,* 665–672.

Craig, T. J., & Abeloff, M. Psychiatric symptomatology among hospitalized cancer patients. *American Journal of Psychiatry,* 1974, *131,* 1323–1327.

Cromwell, R. L., Butterfield, E. C., Brayfield, F. M., & Curry, J. L. *Acute myocardial infarction: Reaction and recovery.* St. Louis: Mosby, 1977.

Dahlstrom, W. G., Welsh, G. S., & Dahlstrom, L. E. *An MMPI Handbook* (Vols. I & II). Minneapolis: University of Minnesota Press, 1972.

Danakher, B. G. Rapid smoking and self-control in the modification of smoking behavior. *Journal of Consulting and Clinical Psychology,* 1977, *45,* 1068–1075.

Dembrowski, T. M., MacDougall, J. M., & Shields, J. L. Physiologic reactions to social challenge in persons evidencing the Type A coronary-prone behavior pattern. *Journal of Human Stress*, 1977, *3*, 2–10.

Derogatis, L. R. *SCL-90 R (Revised) Version Manual—I*. Baltimore: 1977.

Derogatis, L. R., Abeloff, M., & McBeth, C. Cancer patients with their physicians in the perception of psychological symptoms. *Psychosomatics*, 1977, *17*, 197–201.

Derogatis, L. R., Lipman, R. S., Rickels, K., Uhlenhuth, E. H., & Covi, L. The Hopkins Symptom Checklist (HSCL): A self-report symptom inventory. *Behavioral Science*, 1974, *19*, 1–15. (a)

Derogatis, L. R., Lipman, R. S., Rickels, K., Uhlenhuth, E. H., & Covi, L. The Hopkins Symptom Checklist (HSCL): A measure of primary symptom dimensions. In P. Pichot (Ed.), *Psychological measurements in psychopharmacology*. Basel: Karger, 1974. (b)

Derogatis, L. R., Meyer, J., & Gallant, B. The invested partner in sexual disorders: Male and female. *American Journal of Psychiatry*, 1977, *134*, 385–390.

Derogatis, L. R., Rickels, K., & Rock, A. F. The SCL-90 and the MMPI: A step in the validation of a new self-report scale. *British Journal of Psychiatry*, 1976, *128*, 280–289.

Derogatis, L. R., Yevzeroff, H., & Wittelsberger, B. Social class, psychological disorder, and the nature of the psychopathologic indicator. *Journal of Consulting and Clinical Psychology*, 1975, *43*, 183–191.

Dinardo, Q. E. *Psychological adjustment to spinal cord injury*. Doctoral dissertation, University of Houston, 1971.

Edwards, K. R. *Psychological changes associated with pregnancy and obstetric complications*. Unpublished doctoral dissertation, University of Miami (Florida), 1969.

Efran, J. S. *Some personality detriments of memory for success and failure*. Unpublished doctoral dissertation, Ohio State University, 1963.

Ellis, A. In O. Buros (Ed.), *Review of the MMPI; 5th Mental Measurements Yearbook*. Highland Park, N.J.: Gryphon Press, 1959, 166–167.

Engel, G. L. A life setting conducive to illness: The given-up—giving-up complex. *Bulletin of the Menninger Clinic*, 1968, *32*, 355–365.

Fracchia, J., Sheppard, C., Ricca, E., & Merlis, S. MMPI performance in chronic medical illness: The use of computer-derived interpretations. *British Journal of Psychiatry*, 1973, *122*, 242–243.

Friedman, M., & Rosenman, R. H. *Type A behavior and your heart*. New York: Knopf, 1974.

Garron, D., & Leavitt, F. Demographic and affective covariates of pain. *Psychosomatic Medicine*, 1979, *41*(7), 525–534.

Gersten, J. C., Frii, S. R., & Lengner, T. S. Life dissatisfactions, job dissatisfaction and illness of married men over time. *American Journal of Epidemiology*, 1976, *103*, 333–341.

Gilberstadt, H., & Duker, J. *A handbook for clinical and actuarial MMPI interpretation*. Philadelphia: Saunders, 1965.

Glass, D. C. *Behavioral patterns, stress and coronary disease*. Hillsdale, N.J.: Lawrence Erlbaum Associates, 1977.

Goble, R., Gowers, J., Morgan, D., & Kline, P. Artificial pacemaker patients—treatment outcome and the 16PF questionnaire. *Journal of Psychosomatic Research*, 1978, *22*, 467–472.

Goldstein, A. M. Denial and external locus of control as mechanisms of adjustment in chronic medical illness. *Essence*, 1976, *1*, 5–22.

Good, P., & Brantner, J. *A practical guide to the MMPI*. Minneapolis: University of Minnesota Press, 1974.

Green, C., Meagher, R., & Millon, T. *The management of the "problem" patient in the milieu setting*. Paper presented at the Society of Behavioral Medicine Meetings, New York, November 1981.

Gunderson, E. K., & Arthur, R. J. A brief mental health index. *Journal of Abnormal Psychology*, 1969, *74*(1), 100–104.

Head, R. *The impact of personality on the relationship between life events and depression*. Unpublished doctoral dissertation, University of Miami, 1979.

Henrichs, T. F., & Waters, W. F. Psychological adjustment and response to open-heart surgery: Some methodological considerations. *British Journal of Psychiatry*, 1972, *120*, 491–496.

Hiland, D. *Behavioral characteristics of male VA patients with and without CHD*. Unpublished doctoral dissertation, University of San Francisco, 1977.

Holmes, T. H., & Rahe, R. The social readjustment rating scale. *Journal of Psychosomatic Research*, 1967, *11*, 213.

Houpt, J., Gould, B., & Norris, F. Psychological characteristics of patients with amyotrophic lateral sclerosis (ALS). *Psychosomatic Medicine,* 1977, *39*(5), 299–303.

Jackson, D. N. A sequential system for personality scale development. In C. D. Spielberger, (Ed.), *Current topics in clinical and community psychology* (Vol. 2). New York: Academic Press, 1970.

Jackson, D. N., & Messick, S. Acquiescence and desirability as response determinants in the MMPI. *Educational and Psychological Measurement,* 1961, *21,* 771–790.

James, W. H. *Internal versus external control of reinforcement as a basic variable in learning theory.* Unpublished doctoral dissertation, Ohio State University, 1957.

Jenkins, C. D. Psychologic and social precursors of coronary disease. *New England Journal of Medicine,* 1976, *284*(6), 307–317.

Jenkins, C. D., Rosenman, R. H., & Zyzanski, S. J. Prediction of clinical coronary heart disease by a test for the coronary-prone behavioral pattern. *New England Journal of Medicine,* 1974, *290,* 1271–1275.

Jenkins, C. D., Zyzanski, S. J., Rosenman, R. H., & Cleveland, G. L. Association of coronary-prone behavior pattern scores with recurrence of CHD. *Journal of Chronic Disease,* 1971, *24,* 601–611.

Jenkins, C. D., Zyzanski, S. J., & Rosenman, R. H. *Jenkins Activity Survey Manual.* New York: The Psychological Corporation, 1979.

Jenkins, C., Zyzanski, S., Ryan, T., Ethanasios, F., & Tannenbaum, S. Social insecurity with coronary-prone Type A responses as identifiers of severe atherosclerosis. *Journal of Consulting and Clinical Psychology,* 1977, *45*(6), 1060–1067.

Johnson, J., & Sarason, I. Life stress, depression and anxiety: I-E control as moderator variable. *Journal of Psychosomatic Research,* 1978, *22,* 205–208.

Jones, N. F., Kinsman, R. A., Schum, R., & Resnikoff, P. Personality profiles in asthma. *Journal of Clinical Psychology,* 1976, *32,* 285–291.

Karson, S., & O'Dell, J. *Clinical use of the 16PF.* Champaign, Ill.: Institute for Personality and Ability Testing, 1976.

Kidson, M. A. Personality and hypertension. *Journal of Psychosomatic Research,* 1973, *17,* 35–41.

Kilpatrick, D. G., Miller, W. C., Allain, N., Huggins, M. B., & Lee, W. H. The use of psychological test data to predict open-heart surgery outcome: A prospective study. *Psychosomatic Medicine,* 1975, *37,* 62–73.

Kornfeld, D. S., Heller, S. S., Frank, K. A., & Moskowitz, R. Personality and psychological factors in post-cardiotomy delirium. *Archives of General Psychiatry,* 1974, *31,* 249–253.

Kristianson, P. The personality in psychological motor epilepsy compared with the explosive and aggressive personality. *British Journal of Psychiatry,* 1974, *125,* 221–229.

Krug, S. E. *Psychological assessment in medicine.* Champaign, Ill.: Institute for Personality and Ability Testing, 1977.

Lachar, P. *The MMPI: Clinical assessment and automated interpretation.* Los Angeles: Western Psychological Services, 1974.

Lair, C. V., & King, G. D. MMPI profile predictors for successful and expired open heart surgery patients. *Journal of Clinical Psychology,* 1976, *32,* 51–54.

Lambley, P., & Silbowitz, M. Rotter's internal-external scale and prediction of suicide contemplators among students. *Psychological Reports,* 1973, *33,* 585–586.

Lazarus, R. Cognitive and coping processes in emotion. In A. Monar & R. Lazarus (Eds.), *Stress and coping.* New York: Columbia University Press, 1977.

Leavitt, F. In O. Buros (Ed.), *Review of the Cornell Medical Index; 7th Mental Measurements Yearbook.* Highland Park, N.J.: Gryphon Press, 1972.

Leavitt, F., Garron, D., & Bielauskas, L. Stressing life events with the experience of low back pain. *Journal of Psychosomatic Research,* 1979, *23*(1), 49–55.

Levine, R. *The impact of personality style upon emotional distress, morale and return to work in two groups of coronary bypass surgery patients.* Unpublished master's thesis, University of Miami, 1980.

Lingoes, J. C. In O. Buros (Ed.), *Review of the MMPI; 6th Mental Measurements Yearbook.* Highland Park, N.J.: Gryphon Press, 1965.

Lipsitt, D. R. Medical and psychological characteristics of "crocks." *International Journal of Psychiatry in Medicine,* 1970, *1,* 15–25.

Loevinger, J. Objective tests as instruments of psychotherapy. *Psychological Reports,* 1957, *3,* 635–694.

Lowy, F. H. Management of the persistent somatizer. In Z. J. Lipowski, D. R. Lipsitt, & P. C. Whybrow,

(Eds.), *Psychosomatic medicine: Current trends and clinical applications.* New York: Oxford University Press, 1977.

Lucente, F. E., & Fleck, S. A study of hospitalization anxiety in 408 medical and surgical patients. *Psychosomatic Medicine,* 1972, *34* 304–312.

Magarey, C., Todd, P., & Blizard, P. Psychosocial factors influencing delay in breast self-examination in women with symptoms of breast cancer. *Social Science and Medicine,* 1977, *11*(4), 229–232.

Manuck, S. B., Craft, S., & Gold, K. J. Coronary-prone behavior pattern and cardiovascular response. *Psychophysiology,* 1978, *15*, 403–411.

Marks, P., & Seeman, W. *The actuarial description of abnormal personality.* Baltimore: Williams & Wilkins, 1963.

Marston. Compliance with medical regimens as a form of risk taking in patients with myocardial infarctions. *Dissertation Abstracts International* 1969, *30*, 2151A–2152A.

Mechanic, D., & Volkart, E. H. Stress, illness behavior and the sick role. *American Sociological Review,* 1960, *26*, 51.

Meehl, P. E., & Rosen, A. Antecedent probability and the efficiency of psychometric signs, patterns or cutting scores. *Psychological Bulletin,* 1955, *52*, 194–216.

Mei-Tal, V., Meyerowitz, S., & Engel, G. L. The role of psychological process in a somatic disorder: Multiple sclerosis. 1. The emotions of illness onset and exacerbation. *Psychosomatic Medicine,* 1970, *32*, 67–86.

Millon, T. *Modern psychopathology.* Philadelphia: Saunders, 1969.

Millon, T. *Millon Clinical Multiaxial Inventory manual.* Minneapolis: National Computer Systems, Inc., 1977.

Millon, T., Green, C., & Meagher, R. *Millon Behavioral Health Inventory manual.* Minneapolis: National Computer Systems, Inc., 1982.

Mlott, S., R., & Mlott, Y. D. Dogmatism and locus of control in individuals who smoke, stopped smoking and never smoked. *Journal of Community Psychology,* 1975, *3*, 53–57.

Moss, E. Biosocial resonation: A conceptual model of the links between social behavior and physical illness. In Z. J. Lipowski, D. R. Lipsitt, & P. C. Whybrow, (Eds.), *Psychosomatic medicine: Current trends and clinical applications.* New York: Oxford University Press, 1977.

Osler, W. In W. P. D. Wrightsman (Ed.), *The emergence of scientific medicine.* Edinburgh: Oliver & Boyd, 1971.

Parkes, M., Benjamin, B., & Fitzgerald, R. G. Broken heart: A statistical study of increased mortality among widowers. *British Medical Journal,* 1969, *1*, 740–743.

Paull, A., & Hislop, I. G. Etiologic factors in ulcerative colitis: Birth, death and symbolic equivalents. *International Journal of Psychiatry in Medicine,* 1974, *5*, 57–64.

Phares, E. J. Expectancy changes in skill and chance situations. *Journal of Abnormal and Social Psychology,* 1957, *54*, 339–342.

Pierce, D. M., Freeman, R., Lawton, R., & Fearing, M. Psychological correlations of chronic hemodialysis estimated by MMPI scores. *Psychology,* 1973, *10*, 53–57.

Pilowsky, I, & Bond, M. R. Pain and its management in malignant disease: Elucidation of staff-patient transactions. *Psychosomatic Medicine,* 1969, *31*(5), 400–404.

Rabinowitz, S. *Psychological, biographical and medical data as predictors of successful treatment of chronic pain.* Unpublished doctoral dissertation, University of Miami, 1979.

Rabkin, J. C., & Struening, E. L. Life events, stress and illness. *Science,* 1976, *194*, 1013–1020.

Rahe, R. H. Subjects' recent life changes and their near future illness susceptibility. *Advances in Psychosomatic Medicine,* 1977, *8*, 2–19.

Rahe, R. H., & Arthur, R. J. Life change patterns surrounding illness experience. *Journal of Psychosomatic Research,* 1968, *11*, 341–345.

Rahe, R., Hervig, L., & Rosenman, R. Heritability of Type A behavior. *Psychosomatic Medicine,* 1978, *40*(6), 478–486.

Rhodes, R. J. Failure to validate an MMPI headache scale. *Journal of Clinical Psychology,* 1973, *29*, 237–238.

Rorer, L. G. In O. Buros (Ed.), *Review of the 16PF; 7th Mental Measurements Yearbook.* Highland Park, N.J.: Gryphon Press, 1972.

Rosenbaum, M., & Rez, D. Denial, locus of control and depression among physically disabled and non-disabled men. *Journal of Clinical Psychology,* 1977, *33*(3), 672–676.

Rosenman, R. H., Friedman, M., Straus, R., Wurm, M., Kositchek, R., Hahn, W., & Werthessen,

N. T. A predictive study of coronary heart disease: The Western Collaborative Group Study, *Journal of the American Medical Association*, 1964, *189*, 15–22.

Rosenthal, S. V., Aitken, R. C., & Zealley, A. K. The Cattell 16PF personality profile of asthmatics. *Journal of Psychosomatic Research*, 1973, *17*, 9–14.

Rotter, J. B. In O. Buros (Ed.), *Review of the MMPI, 3rd Mental Measurements Yearbook*. Highland Park, N.J.: Gryphon Press, 1945.

Rotter, J. B. Generalized expectancies for internal versus external control of reinforcement. *Psychological Monographs*, 1966, *80*(1), 1–28.

Rotter, J. B., Leverant, S., & Crowne, D. P. The growth and extinction expectancies in chance controlled and skilled tests. *Journal of Psychology*, 1961, *52*, 161–177.

Sarason, I. G., Johnson, J. H., & Siegel, J. M. Assessing the impact of life changes. *Journal of Consulting and Clinical Psychology*, 1978, *46*, 932–946.

Schmale, A. H. Giving up as a final common pathway to changes in health. In Z. J. Lipowski, (Ed.), *Psychological aspects of physical illness*. Basel, Switzerland: Karger, 1972.

Schmidt, H. O. Test profiles as a diagnostic aid: The MMPI. *Journal of Applied Psychology*, 1945, *29*, 115–131.

Schofield, W. Clinical and counseling psychology: Some perspectives. *American Psychology*, 1966, *21*, 122–131.

Schonfield, J. Psychological factors related to delayed return to an earlier life-style in successfully treated cancer patients. *Journal of Psychosomatic Research*, 1976, *20*, 41–46.

Schwartz, M. S., Osborne, D., & Krupp, N. E. Moderating effects of age and sex on the association of medical diagnoses and 1-3/3-1 MMPI profiles. *Journal of Clinical Psychology*, 1972, *28*, 502–505.

Seymour, G. The structure and predictive ability of the CMI for a normal sample. *Journal of Psychomatic Research*, 1976, *20*, 469–478.

Shaw, B. F., Steer, R. A., Beck, A. T., & Schut, J. The structure of depression in heroin addicts. *British Journal of Addiction*, 1979, *74*, 295–303.

Shekelle, R. B., Schoenberger, J. A., & Stamler, J. Correlates of the JAS Type A behavior score. *Journal of Chronic Disease*, 1976, *29*, 381–394.

Spielberger, C. D., Gorsuch, R. L., & Lushene, R. *The State–Trait Anxiety Inventory manual*. Palo Alto, Calif.: Consulting Psychologists Press, 1970.

Stavraky, K. M., Buch, C. N., Lott, J. S., & Wanklin, J. M. Psychological factors in the outcome of human cancer. *Journal of Psychomatic Research*, 1968, *12*, 251–259.

Stevens, J. R., Milstein, V., & Goldstein, S. Psychometric test performance in relation to the psychopathology of epilepsy. *Archives of General Psychiatry*, 1972, *26*, 532–538.

Stout, C., Wright, M., & Bruhn, J. G. The Cornell Medical Index in disability evaluation. *British Journal of Preventive and Social Medicine*, 1969, *23*(4), 251–254.

Teuramaa, E. Psychosocial and psychic factors and age at onset of asthma. *Journal of Psychosomatic Research*, 1979, *23*(1), 27–37.

Verberne, T. J. MMPI performance in chronic medical illness. *British Journal of Psychiatry*, 1972, *121*, 235.

Wallston, B. S., Wallston, K. A., Kaplan, G. D., & Maides, S. A. Development and validation of the health locus of control scale. *Journal of Consulting and Clinical Psychology*, 1976, *44*, 580–585.

Wampler, R. S., Lauer, J. B., Lantz, J. B., Wampler, K. S., Evens, M. G., & Madura, J. A. Psychological effects of intestinal bypass surgery. *Journal of Counseling Psychology*, 1980, *27*(5), 492–499.

Weiss, S. Psychosomatic aspects of symptom patterns among medical surgical patients. *Journal of Psychosomatic Research*, 1969, *13*(1), 109–112.

Wendland, C. J. Internal–external control expectancies of institutionalized physically disabled. *Rehabilitation Psychology*, 1973, *20*, 180–186.

Whitehead, W., Blackwell, B., DeSilva, H., & Robinson, A. Anxiety and anger in hypertension. *Journal of Psychosomatic Research*, 1977, *21*(5), 383–389.

Wider, A. *The Cornell Medical Index*. New York: The Psychological Corporation, 1948.

Wise, T. N., & Fernandez, F. Psychological profiles of candidates seeking surgical correction for obesity. *Psychosomatics*, 1977, *18*, 372–375.

Wright, B. A. *Physical disability: A psychological approach*. New York: Harper, 1960.

Yunik, S. *The relationship of personality variables and stressful life events to the onset of physical illness*. Unpublished doctoral dissertation, University of Miami, 1979.

Assessing the Impact of Life Changes

IRWIN G. SARASON, HENRY M. LEVINE,
AND BARBARA R. SARASON

This chapter reviews the literature on life changes, particularly as they relate to health, disease, and recovery from illness. One of the areas of greatest current activity concerns the quantitative assessment of these changes, which are often referred to as stressful life events. We shall review this topic and provide a theoretical perspective for future research.

Clinical observations have long suggested that major life changes, such as the loss of a job, often precede illness and psychological maladjustment. Changes that seem especially conducive to later illness or maladjustment are those that involve losses (such as the death of a loved one), sudden environmental changes (natural catastrophes), war, threats to and loss of control over one's life (as experienced, for example, by people in concentration camps), and personal failures.

Although the mechanisms involved are still obscure, researchers have observed that stressful events in a person's life and unwanted outcomes (maladjustment, illness) are linked. These observations led Adolf Meyer to introduce the concept of the *life chart*, a recording of significant biographical and medical events in a person's life (Leif, 1948). Later, Harold Wolff (1953) introduced the term *life stress* by which he meant the responses of people to noxious stimulation

IRWIN G. SARASON • Department of Psychology, University of Washington, Seattle 98195. HENRY M. LEVINE • Department of Psychology, University of Washington, Seattle 98195. BARBARA R. SARASON • Department of Psychology, University of Washington, Seattle 98195.
Preparation of this chapter was supported in part by the U.S. Office of Naval Research Contract N00014-80-C-0522, NR 170-908, and by the National Institutes of Health Training Grant GMO 7266.

and ego threats. Both Walter Cannon (1932) and Hans Selye (1946) gave special emphasis to the body's reaction to environmental events that call for action and the mobilization of bodily resources. Hinkle (1973), recognizing that similar life events do not lead to symptoms in all people, pointed out the need to take account of personal variables (personality, general level of health) along with situational variables (life events). It is now clear that a complete understanding of the effects of stressful life events will require investigations at several levels, including the delineation of influential situations, the identification of responses, and a mapping of the psychological and physiological mechanisms that link the two.

This chapter is particularly concerned with the first level, the events in people's lives that appear to be stressful and to influence future functioning. It begins with a survey of measurement approaches, continues with a review of the relation between life change and onset of physical illness, proceeds to an examination of methodological issues surrounding the assessment of stressful life events, and analyzes the role of moderator variables that help determine how these events influence behavior. The chapter concludes with a discussion of theoretical considerations and suggestions for future research.

1. Assessing Life Changes

Measures of life changes are becoming so numerous that any comprehensive survey of them would soon be doomed to incompleteness. Our aim is to illustrate approaches that have been taken in this assessment.

1.1. Schedule of Recent Events

The publication by Holmes and Rahe (1967) of an article describing their attempt to quantify the importance of life changes provided a major impetus to research. Their Schedule of Recent Experiences (SRE) has been widely used in research investigations and clinical practice, providing a convenient measure of the cumulative effects of life changes.

The SRE consists of a list of 42 events. Subjects respond to it by indicating for each item whether they experienced that event during the recent past and—if so—the number of times the event was experienced. To determine scoring weights for specific events, Holmes and Rahe had subjects rate each of the 42 events with regard to the amount of social readjustment each would require, regardless of the desirability of the event. The item "Marriage" was employed as a standard or anchor point in these ratings. This item was given an arbitrary value of 50, and subjects were asked to rate the other items by assigning values of above or below 50 to reflect the degree to which events required more or less readjustment than marriage. Mean adjustment ratings were obtained for each of the items. These values, termed *life change units*, when divided by the constant 10, were taken to represent the average amount of social readjustment considered necessary in response to the SRE events. To illustrate, the event "Death of spouse" is given a value of 100, "Pregnancy" a value of 40, "Change in financial state" a value of 38, and "Christmas" a value of 12. A total life stress score for the SRE is obtained by determining the events experienced by the respondent and summing the life change units associated with these events.

Since its initial development, the SRE has been used in numerous studies designed to determine relationships between life changes and indices of health and adjustment. Retrospective and prospective studies have provided support for a relationship between SRE scores and a variety of health-related variables. Life stress has, for example, been related to sudden cardiac death (Rahe & Lind, 1971), myocardial infarction (Edwards, 1971; Theorell & Rahe, 1971), pregnancy and birth complications (Gorsuch & Key, 1974), chronic illness (Bedell, Giordani, Amour, Tavormina, & Boll, 1977; Wyler, Masuda, & Holmes, 1971), and other major health problems such as tuberculosis, multiple sclerosis, diabetes and a host of less serious physical conditions (Rabkin & Struening, 1976). Although they do not provide conclusive evidence, these studies have provided support for the position taken by Holmes and Masuda (1974) that life stress serves to increase overall susceptibility to illness.

1.2. The Life Experiences Survey

Another attempt to quantify the effects of life changes is the Life Experiences Survey developed by Sarason, Johnson, and Siegel (1978). Two major features distinguish the Life Experiences Survey (LES) from the Schedule of Recent Experiences (SRE). First, it provides both positive and negative life change scores. Second, it permits individualized ratings of the impact of events and their desirability. These individualized measures have the advantage of providing reflections of person-to-person differences in the perception of events. Evidence in support of this approach was provided by Yamamoto and Kinney (1976), who found life stress scores, based on self-ratings, to be better predictors than scores derived by employing mean adjustment ratings similar to those used with the SRE. Other investigators have also found that individualized self-ratings of the impact of life events aid in the prediction of clinical course (Lundberg, Theorell, & Lind, 1975).

The LES is a 47-item self-report measure that allows subjects to indicate events they have experienced during the past year. Subjects can also indicate the occurrence of significant events they have experienced that are not on the LES list. A special supplementary list of 10 events relevant primarily to student populations is available. Adaptations for other special groups are possible. The LES items were chosen to represent life changes frequently experienced by individuals in the general population. Thirty-four of the events listed in the LES are similar in content to those found in the SRE. However, certain SRE items were made more specific. For example, the SRE contains the item "Pregnancy," which might be endorsed by a woman but perhaps not by a man whose wife or girlfriend has become pregnant. The LES allows both men and women to endorse the occurrence of pregnancy in the following manner: "*Female:* Pregnancy; *Male:* Wife's/girlfriend's pregnancy." The Schedule of Recent Experiences includes the item "Wife begins or stops work," an item which fails to assess the impact on women whose husbands being or cease working. The present scale lists two items: "*Married male:* Change in wife's work outside the home" (beginning work, ceasing work, changing to a new job, etc.), and "*Married female:* Change in husband's work" (loss of job, beginning of a new job, etc.). Examples of events not listed in the SRE but included in the LES are male and female items dealing with abortion and concerning serious injury or illness of a close friend, engagement, and breaking up with boyfriend/girlfriend. Of the 10 special school-related items, 9 are unique to the LES.

Subjects respond to the LES as originally constructed by separately rating the desirability and impact of events they have experienced (Sarason, Johnson, & Siegel, 1978). Ratings are on a 7-point scale ranging from -3 to $+3$. A rating of -3 indicates a negative event judged to have had an extreme impact on the respondent. A rating of $+3$ indicates a positive event having an extreme impact. Summing the impact ratings of events designated as positive by the subject provides a *positive change score*. A *negative change score* is derived by summing the impact ratings of those events experienced as negative by the subject. Scores on the LES do not seem to be influenced by the respondent's mood state at the time of filling out the questionnaire (Siegel, Johnson, & Sarason, 1979b).

Research is now being carried out on a revised version of the LES on which subjects indicate whether recent life events were "good" or "bad" and, then, rate (1) how much the events affected their lives, (2) the extent to which the events were expected to happen, and (3) how much control the respondents had over the event's occurrence. Copies of the revised LES are available from the authors.

Negative life changes have been found to relate significantly and in a positive direction with both state and trait anxiety, while the positive change score was unrelated to either measure (Sarason *et al.*, 1978). No significant correlations were obtained between LES scores and social desirability, indicating that LES scores are unbiased by a social desirability response set. One replicated finding is that negative change correlates significantly with grades; higher levels of negative life change are related to poorer academic performance (Knapp & Magee, 1979). Block and Zautra (1981) have found that positive and negative life changes are uncorrelated and that distress effects of positive events can be accounted for by negative events that may be associated with them.

The relationship between stressful life events and personal maladjustment has been estimated by correlating the LES with the Psychological Screening Inventory (PSI), using a student sample (Sarason *et al.*, 1978). The PSI (Lanyon, 1970, 1973) is a 130-item true–false inventory which yields scores on five subscales; Alienation (Al), Social Nonconformity (Sn), Discomfort (Di), Expression (Ex), and Defensiveness (De). The Al scale was designed for "assessing similarity to psychiatric patients" and the Sn scale for "assessing similarity to incarcerated prisoners." The Di scale measures neuroticism, the Ex scale measures introversion–extraversion, and the De scale measures test-taking attitude. Correlations between the LES and the PSI showed a significant relationship between negative life change and two measures of maladjustment, the Social Nonconformity and Discomfort scales. Only the PSI Expression scale correlated significantly with positive change. Extraverts appear to experience greater degrees of positive change than do introverts.

Sarason *et al.* (1978) have reported a significant relationship between negative change and scores on the Beck Depression Scale (Beck, 1967), high negative change scores being associated with depression. Positive change was not significantly correlated with depression. Using Rotter's (1966) locus-of-control measure, these researchers also found that subjects who experienced high levels of negative change appear to be more externally oriented, perceiving themselves as being less capable of exerting control over environmental events. No relationship between positive change and locus of control was found. The findings relating to depression are consistent with evidence presented by Vinokur and Selzer (1975), who found negative change to be related to self-ratings of depression.

Although it is a newer instrument and consequently has given rise to a less extensive array of evidence concerning its correlates, the LES has certain advantages over the SRE. Its positive and negative change scores have not been found to correlate significantly with the same dependent measures in the same direction. This, together with evidence of the validity of the negative change score, suggests that the distinction between negative and positive events is a meaningful one. Recent studies have found the LES negative change score to be related to myocardial infarction (Pancheri, Bellaterra, Reda, Matteoli, Santarelli, Pugliese, & Mosticoni 1980), menstrual discomfort (Siegel, Johnson, & Sarason, 1979a), the attitudes of mothers of at-risk infants (Crnic, Greenberg, Ragozin, & Robinson, 1980), and job satisfaction (Sarason & Johnson, 1979).

For example, Pancheri *et al.* (1980) obtained psychological and biochemical measures on male patients with an acute myocardial infarction (MI) within two days of admission. A severity of MI rating was determined following release from the coronary care unit. Significant positive correlations were found between the negative LES scores and severity of MI rating as well as between negative LES scores, plasma cortisol, and cyclic-AMP levels.

1.3. The Diversity of Approaches to Assessing Stressful Life Events

Research on the assessment of stressful life events has explored a wide variety of both populations and assessment devices. Several recent instruments, like the LES, have gone beyond a mere count of life changes in the recent past to provide measures of the undesirability and impact of the events. There seems to be increasing agreement that the perceptions of life events may be as significant as the events themselves (Masuda & Holmes, 1978). Redfield and Stone (1979) have provided striking indications of individual differences in how people perceive life events. Tennant and Andrews (1978), using a specially devised list of events, found that the distressing quality of life events rather than the events themselves is associated with the onset of neurotic symptoms. Horowitz, Wilner, and Alvarez (1979) were successful in developing a measure of the subjective impact of major life events that reflects psychiatric decompensation.

Several researchers have used interviews to assess stressful life events. Interviews have the advantage of permitting greater individualization and depth than do questionnaires. For example, Paykel (1979) used the interview method in studies of the risk for depression and suicide attempts. On the other hand, the interview method does not lend itself to surveys of large samples because of its cost—primarily in the need for qualified and specially trained personnel and the length of time involved in gathering the data on an individual basis. Furthermore, even standardized interviews by carefully trained interviewers introduce variations that increase the unreliability of the result. Sometimes it is not possible either to interview subjects or to administer a questionnaire to them. In such cases, Schless and Mendels (1978) have found that "significant others" (family members, friends) can provide useful, quantifiable information about subjects' recent life events.

Whereas some researchers have been concerned with the development of measures of these events experienced in the general population, others have been concerned with particular groups within the population. Children have been the most widely studied special population, and there are a number of instruments available that can be used with children ranging from preschoolers through adolescents (Coddington, 1972; Monaghan, Robinson, & Dodge, 1979; Sandler & Block, 1979). Johnson and McCutcheon (1980) and Yeaworth, York, Hussey, Ingle, and Goodwin (1980) have developed measures specifically directed toward stressful events in the lives of adolescents. These measures include content related to such topics as new school experiences, dating, and work.

The development of methods of recording life events and their impact on people allows researchers to explore personal crises more objectively and conveniently than was the case in the past. Despite a number of methodological problems, life stress scores have been linked to a variety of physical and psychological conditions. Often these linkages have been statistically significant but of limited practical applicability. As solutions to methodological problems are found, the number of practical applications should increase.

2. Life Change and the Onset of Illness

In a variety of retrospective and prospective studies, stressful life events have been implicated in contributing to the onset of physical illness (Holmes & Masuda, 1974; Petrich & Holmes, 1977). To what extent can one predict an individual's future illness from a score on a measure of life changes? Are negative events more significant than positive events?

Most prospective studies indicate a small but significant correlation between prior life changes and onset of physical illness. Garrity, Marx, and Somes (1977) administered the SRE to over 300 entering college freshmen, asking about events in the preceding year. After another 9 months, they then asked the freshmen questions about their physical health in the prior 2 months. Number of health problems, number of days with a health problem, and number of disability days all correlated with prior life changes. Similar findings were reported by Rahe (1968) in his prospective study of 2,500 American naval personnel.

Johnson and McCutcheon (1980), using a specially devised measure for adolescents similar to the LES, have described their retrospective findings on the relationship between positive and negative life events and illness ratings in children 12 to 14 years old. For males only, increased *negative* life changes were associated with more school days missed because of illness ($r = .36$) and lower self-ratings of present physical health ($r = -.31$). Positive changes did not correlate with illness ratings. No significant relationships were found for females.

Two correlational studies with introductory psychology undergraduates have shown both positive and negative life changes to be associated with self-rated illness. In one study (Sarason, Levine, & Basham, 1980) using the LES, the number of symptoms checked was correlated with number of positive events listed ($r = .21$), number of negative events listed ($r = .26$), and total events ($r = .32$). The second study (Coppel, 1980) found similar results, with significant correlations of positive, negative, and total life changes with the medical items on the Cornell Medical Index (r's of .19, .16, and .21, respectively).

In an admirable study of brewery workers, Thurlow (1971) obtained both retrospective and prospective correlations of SRE with number of illnesses and days off from work due to illness. He divided SRE scores into subjective and objective measures based on his arbitrary evaluation of 20 SRE items as highly objective (e.g., "Changing place of residence") and 17 items as subjective or difficult to verify externally (e.g., "Change of eating habits"). Using bivariate Pearson correlations, the 5-year SRE subjective score correlated significantly with number of illnesses in the *prior 5 years* ($r = 23$) and with number of days off work in the first and second *prospective* years ($r = .31$ and .52 respectively).

With partial correlation and regression analysis, Thurlow showed that in *prospective* associations of SRE with company-documented illness, SRE objective or subjective scores each accounted on their own for less than 1% of the variance. In this situation, *previous* number of illnesses or days off accounted for the greatest amount of variance, with variability in a semantic differential rating scale and socioeconomic status each accounting for more variance than the SRE score. *Retrospectively*, however, SRE subjective scores had significant partial correlations of .25 and .23 with number of illnesses and number of days off. In short, SRE data correlated with prospective illness using bivariate analysis; but multiple regression analysis showed its independent contribution to the overall variance to be minimal.

A study of members of a prepaid health maintenance organization (Harrington, Burnell, & Korenoff, 1975, 1980) sheds light on the relation between life changes and illness when self- and physician-rated illness are differentiated. On the basis of independent ratings of physical well-being by patients and physicians, patients were placed in one of four health categories: *Well, Worried Well, Asymptomatic Sick,* and *Sick.* Worried well and Asymptomatic Sick patients were discordant for self- and physician-ratings, with both the Worried and Asymptomatic describing self-ratings. At this time, they also completed several scales, including the SRE.

Scores on the SRE differed between groups, as did average number of clinic visits. Of the four groups, the Worried Well rated themselves as having the most life changes, followed by the Sick, Well, and Asymptomatic Sick. Similarly, the Worried Well and Sick patients had more clinic visits than did the Asymptomatic Sick and Well patients. This was true both retrospectively and prospectively. Patients with higher SRE scores also had more average clinic visits each year.

Thus, self-rating of illness overrode physician-rating of illness in determining the increased associations between life change and illness as well as between rated illness and future number of clinic visits.

Extensive research will be needed to evaluate the relationship between life change and illness onset. Specifically, more studies are required which investigate life changes and future illness prospectively, using the LES or other measures that yield separate measures of positive and negative life changes.

It may be that positive and negative life changes do not have the same relationship to physical illness and to emotional malfunction. It is interesting that, as described above, only negative life events tend to correlate with emotional malfunction, such as general psychological distress, depression, and anxiety (Johnson & Sarason, 1978), as well as with behavioral problems, such as lowered grade point average (Knapp & Magee, 1979).

On the other hand, a number of studies suggest that both positive and negative life changes contribute to physical illness. This may be due to life changes, in general, stressing the body's physiological homeostasis (Holmes & Rahe, 1967); whereas only negative life changes may be associated with future dissatisfaction and emotional well-being. Petrich and Holmes (1977) have suggested that patients should be advised to pace the occurrence of positive and negative life events wherever possible. It may be that such a maneuver would be advantageous only for patients with physical problems. Controlling the occurrence of positive events might be counterproductive for individuals experiencing emotional problems.

Because of the theoretical and practical relevance of this issue, more prospective research is required to elucidate the relationships between positive and negative life changes and future physical and emotional problems.

3. Moderators of Stressful Life Events

People vary considerably in how they are affected by potential stressors. Some individuals who get divorced, lose their jobs, or experience financial hardships, death, and illness in their families appear to suffer few serious long-term physical or psychological setbacks. Others, however, feel physical and psychological distress even though they have experienced what would objectively seem to be a relatively low level of stress. An important question concerns the nature of those variables that may determine which individuals are likely to be most adversely affected by life change.

Although several authors (Jenkins, 1979; Johnson & Sarason, 1979; Rahe & Arthur, 1976) have pointed to the important role of moderator variables, previous studies of life events have usually been designed simply to assess the relationships between life change and other variables without considering that individuals may vary in how much they are affected by life changes. Lack of attention to moderator variables constitutes a major limitation of much of the research in this area. One might argue that it is unreasonable to expect to find strong correlates of life events unless such variables are examined and taken into account. As the mediators of life stress are identified, measured reliably, and included in research designs, increased effectiveness in prediction is likely to result.

There are three broad categories of moderator variables: (1) relatively stable

personal characteristics, such as internal-external locus of control; (2) prior experiences that influence how a person responds to stress; and (3) environmental
factors, such as social support. Each type can influence how a person responds
to problematic situations. Although the nature of the particular influence processes is often not clear, these moderators can generally be thought of as affecting
vulnerability to life events.

Three variables that illustrate how moderators influence behavior will now
be described. Two are personality characteristics (sensation seeking and locus
of control) and one is an environmental factor (social support).

3.1. Sensation Seeking

Sensation seeking provides an example of how a personality characteristic
can moderate response to stressful events. Some people appear to thrive on
activities that are exciting and stimulating and that might be expected to increase
arousal level. They may enjoy traveling to strange places, prefer the unfamiliar
to the familiar, and participate in activities such as skydiving, automobile racing,
motorcycle riding, and water skiing. On the other hand, many individuals shy
away from the unfamiliar, would never think of racing cars or going skydiving,
and find some everyday situations more arousing than they would like. There
are, of course, many people who fall somewhere between these two extremes.
They neither consistently seek out nor attempt to avoid stimulation.

Given that individuals vary in their desire for or need to seek out stimulation
as well as in their tolerance for stimulation, sensation seeking as a personality
attribute may well serve as an important moderator of life stress. High sensation
seekers might be expected to be relatively unaffected by life changes, particularly
if they are not too extreme. These individuals may be better able to deal with
the increased arousal involved in experiencing such changes. On the other hand,
life changes might have a negative effect on people low in sensation seeking
who are less able to cope with arousing stimulus input. To the extent that
stimulation seeking mediates the effects of life change, one might expect to find
significant correlations between life change and problems of health and adjustment with low but not with high sensation seekers.

Smith, Johnson, and Sarason (1978) have examined the relationship between
the LES, sensation seeking, and psychological distress. Sensation seeking was
measured using the Sensation Seeking Scale (Zuckerman, 1979). Distress was
assessed by means of the Psychological Screening Inventory (Lanyon, 1973), a
self-report measure of neuroticism. The LES positive change score, either alone
or in conjunction with sensation seeking, was unrelated to the individual's psychological discomfort. The major result was that people with high negative
change scores who were also low in sensation seeking reported high levels of
distress. Subjects with high negative change scores but also high scores in sensation seeking did not describe themselves as experiencing discomfort.

Similar results were obtained by Johnson, Sarason, and Siegel (1978), who
were specifically interested in anxiety, depression, and hostility. They found that
positive change was unrelated to dependent measures regardless of arousal-
seeking status. Negative change, on the other hand, was significantly related to

measures of both anxiety and hostility. As in the study by Smith *et al.* (1978), this relationship held only for subjects low in sensation seeking. It is possible that individuals low on the sensation-seeking dimension are much more likely to be affected by life stress than are those high in sensation seeking.

3.2. Locus of Control

Predictability and controllability are aspects of situations that influence how people respond to them. The more predictable an event and the more confident a person feels about how to handle it, the greater the likelihood of an adaptive response. Are individuals who perceive themselves as having little control over events more adversely affected by stressful events than individuals who feel capable of exerting control over these events?

Johnson and Sarason (1978) have provided some evidence concerning this issue. They administered the LES, the Locus of Control Scale (Rotter, 1966), the State–Trait Anxiety Inventory (Spielberger, Gorsuch, & Lushene, 1970), and the Beck Depression Inventory (Beck, 1967) to college students. The Locus of Control Scale is a self-report measure that assesses the degree to which individuals view environmental events as being under their personal control. Subjects scoring low on the measure (internals) tend to perceive events as being controllable by their own actions: those scoring high on the scale (externals) tend to view events as being influenced by factors other than themselves. The State–Trait Anxiety Inventory assesses anxiety as a relatively stable dispositional variable (trait anxiety) as well as more transient reactions to specific situations (state anxiety). The Beck scale is a self-report measure of depression.

Based on research findings concerning the controllability or uncontrollability of aversive stimuli, it was predicted that anxiety and depression would correlate with stressful life events only among subjects external in their locus-of-control orientation. This prediction seemed reasonable, as one might expect undesirable life events to be more threatening and hence exert a more negative impact on people perceiving themselves as having little control over such events. Johnson and Sarason found that negative life changes were significantly related to both trait anxiety and depression: but as predicted, this relationship held only for external subjects. Although this study does not allow for cause–effect conclusions, its results are consistent with the view that people are more adversely affected by life stress if they perceive themselves as having little control over their environment.

3.3. Social Support

Although methodological rigor has not marked the literature on social supports, there is evidence that close social ties have a protection, stress-buffering effect and that their effect may be more important for some individuals than for others. This social-support effect may be particularly noticeable among people who bring to certain situations such cognitions as, "I'll fail," "I'm all alone," "No one cares about me." To the extent that this is true, social support may play powerful preventive and therapeutic roles in such areas as personality development, mental health, and physical well-being. However, these are merely suggestions. At the present time, neither the situations and circumstances conducive to a social support effect nor the mechanisms by which such an effect comes about can be specified. Heller (1979) has recently emphasized the need for extensive research into the ingredients and effects of social support. Experimental studies are needed to answer such questions as: Is lack of social support a cause of personal or social unhappiness, or are people low in personal or social competence deficient in skills needed to elicit supportive social relationships?

Social support is usually defined as the existence or availability of people on whom we can rely and of people who let us know that they care about, value, and love us. As Cobb (1976) has pointed out, someone who believes he or she belongs to a social network of communication and mutual obligation experiences social support. Available evidence suggests that social support may facilitate coping with crisis and adaptation to change. Its absence or withdrawal seems to have a negative effect. In this regard it is interesting that soldiers who have lost many of their buddies in combat are more likely to develop combat exhaustion than soldiers who belong to intact units.

There is by no means agreement about how to assess a person's level of social support. Both interviews and questionnaires have been used as a basis for identifying social networks and estimating social-support levels. Tolsdorf (1976) content-analyzed interviews to assess subjects' relationships with kin and friends and with religious, political, and fraternal groups. Caplan, Cobb, and French (1975) constructed a 21-item self-report index of the support received from three types of work-related sources: immediate supervisor, work group or peers, and subordinates. Two factors may be especially important aspects of social support: (1) the amount of social support available and (2) individual's satisfaction with the available support.

3.3.1. Social Support and Health

One study of pregnant women investigated the role of psychosocial assets—an important component of which was defined as social support—in complications of pregnancy (Nuckolls, Cassell, & Kaplan, 1972). The women were assessed in two ways: (1) frequency and severity of recent life changes and (2) psychosocial assets, a combined score of satisfaction with factors involving self, early childhood, family, friends, and pregnancy. These psychological assets include both childhood and current social support as well as personal resource ratings. Women who had few psychosocial assets and who experienced high levels of life change had significantly more pregnancy complications than women who had relatively few assets with either high or low levels of life changes. For the former group, 91% of women who were low in psychosocial assets had birth complications; the comparable figure for those high in psychosocial assets was 33%. In this study, it appeared that social support was particularly important among women high in life stress.

De Araujo, Dudley, and Van Arsdel (1972) and De Araujo, Van Arsdel, Holmes, and Dudley (1973) studied the interaction of psychosocial support and life changes as they relate to the amount of steroid medication required by adult asthmatics. They found that patients with high life change and *high* support required no more medication than patients with low life changes. However, patients with high life changes and *low* social support required three times as many steroids.

In a prospective study of over 7,000 men evaluating the onset of angina pectoris (chest pain due to insufficient cardiac blood flow, associated with future myocardial infarction), Medalie and Goldbourt (1976) found that wife's love and support was an important predictor. Specifically, where patients were already high on anxiety, those men with low spouse support had a 68% increase in onset of angina as compared with those having high spouse support.

There may be sex differences or other individual differences in response to social support. In a recent study, Whitcher and Fisher (1979) found that for hospitalized women, the warm physical touch of a caring nurse prior to surgery resulted not only in lowered anxiety but also in a faster return to preoperative blood pressure levels. For male patients, however, Whitcher and Fisher obtained results inconsistent with and in some cases opposite to those for women.

Several other studies also indicate that social support functions as a moderator of stressful life events. Lyon and Zucker (1974) found that the posthospitalization adjustment of discharged schizophrenics was better when social support (friends, neighbors) was present. Burke and Weir (1977) found that the husband–wife helping relationship is an important moderator between experiencing stressful life events and psychological well-being. A helping spouse seems to be particularly valuable in contributing to self-confidence and a sense of security in dealing with the demands of daily living. Brown, Bhrolchain, and Harris (1975) found that the presence of an intimate but not necessarily sexual relationship with a male reduced the probability of depression in women following stressful life events. Consistent with these findings, Miller and Ingham (1976) showed that social support (presence of a confidant and friends) reduced the likelihood of psychological and physical symptoms (anxiety, depression, heart palpitations, dizziness) during stress. Gore (1978) studied the relationship between social support and worker's health after being laid off and found that a low sense of social support exacerbated illnesses following the stress of job loss.

In a large-scale epidemiological investigation, Berkman and Syme (1979) found that people who lacked social and community ties were more likely to die during the 9-year period they were studied than those with more extensive contacts. The association between social ties and mortality was independent of self-reported physical health status at the beginning of the 9-year period. It was also independent of physical activity, socioeconomic status, and utilization of preventive health services.

Although social support seems clearly related to physical and emotional health, the precise relationship is unclear. In some of the studies cited above, social support acts only as a moderator variable, counteracting the negative effects of adverse life changes. In other studies, social support acts independently in its relation to health outcomes. More longitudinal, prospective research is required to clarify the direction of causality between the variables.

3.3.2. Social Support and Effective Behavior

Maladaptive ways of thinking and behaving are more common among those with little social support (Silberfeld, 1978). Reliance on others and self-reliance may be not only compatible but also complementary to one another. Although the mechanism by which an intimate relationship is protective has yet to be worked out, the following factors are probably involved: intimacy, social integration through shared concerns, reassurance of personal worth, the opportunity to be nurtured by others, a sense of reliable alliance, and guidance (Weiss, 1974).

There are data consistent with the view that adults who are self-reliant, adept at coping with stress, and able to maintain a task-oriented attitude in the face of challenges frequently had childhoods marked by the personal security that goes along with warm relationships and shared experiences and responsibilities. For example, Ruff and Korchin (1967), in their study of astronauts, found that these self-reliant, adaptable men come from families that provided stable, supportive environments. Reinhardt (1970), in a study of exemplary Air Force fighter pilots, found that as children they had spent more time in joint activities with their fathers (fishing, making things) than did other pilots.

3.3.3. Preventive Measures Based on Social Support

The concept of social support is applicable to both medical and psychological processes. Auerbach and Kilmann (1977) have summarized findings from 13 studies of presurgical interventions with pediatric and adult patients. *All* of the studies where emotional support was a component of the intervention demonstrated significant improvement in patient outcome (e.g., amount of anesthesia required, number of postsurgery hospital days). This is contrasted with 43% of the studies whose interventions included information alone. Sosa, Kennell, Klaus, Robertson, and Urrutia (1980) have described major effects on the outcome of labor by randomly assigning a supportive lay woman (*doula*) to pregnant women throughout their deliveries. In the Guatemalan hospital where the study was conducted, no family members or friends were allowed to be in the room with the woman. They found that 81% of mothers without a support person present had subsequent perinatal problems, whereas only 40% of mothers who *did* have a supportive person had such problems. Mothers with a *doula* present during labor were more often awake after delivery, smiled more at their babies, and talked more to them.

Henderson (1980) has recently pointed out three competing hypotheses that have been offered by researchers who study social support: (1) a deficiency in social support is a cause of morbidity; (2) a deficiency in social support is a cause of morbidity only when adverse circumstances and events are present; and (3) a deficiency of social support is a consequence of a low level of social competence. Although some discrepant findings and the need to identify the causes of different levels of social support are acknowledged, the available evidence suggests that high levels of social support may play a stress-buffering role and to some degree protect an individual from the effects of cumulative life changes. If this is true, there are some important implications for preventative action. As Dean and Lin (1977) have suggested, although it may not be possible for people to avoid experiencing stressful life events, it may be possible to help them mobilize support within the community and thus to some extent protect themselves against the effects of stress. Furthermore, training in the social skills needed to get help from friends, relatives, and the community when stress reaches high levels might protect a significant number of individuals from personal difficulties.

3.3.4. Personality, Social Support, and Health

An important question concerning which there is little evidence is the matter of the relative contributions of personality, experience, and social support to health and adjustment. Because both experience and social support influence personality, it would seem important, wherever possible, to incorporate all three types of variables in research designs. One useful starting point is the identification of exemplary people—those who are particularly stress-resistant. Kobasa (1979) took this tack in a study of middle- and upper-level executives who had had comparably high degrees of stressful life events during the previous 3 years. She found that executives who had high levels of life stress but little illness seemed more hardy than high-stress–high-illness executives. The defining properties of *hardiness* seemed to include a strong commitment to self, an attitude of vigorousness toward the environment, a sense of the meaningfulness of life, and an internal locus of control. Kobasa's findings seem consistent with Antonovsky's (1979) concept of *resistance resources*, according to which stress-resistant people manage their tensions well and have a feeling of social belongingness. According to Antonovsky, stress-resistant people have a *sense of coherence*, a general orientation that sees life as meaningful and manageable. The sources of the sense of coherence, according to Antonovsky, are to be found in people's upbringing, social relationships, and cultural background. He believes people who have resistance resources are high in flexibility, which includes the capacities to (1) tolerate differences in values and (2) adapt quickly to misfortune.

4. Methodological Issues in Assessing Stressful Life Events

Despite numerous medical and psychological correlates of stressful life events as well as several postulated moderators of stressful events, a certain degree of caution is warranted in interpreting available findings. Studies in this area have been primarily correlational in design, so cause–effect conclusions cannot be drawn with a high level of confidence.

In addition to considering the nature of the relationships found in studies of stressful life events and physical or emotional health, it is also necessary to examine their magnitude. Although exceptions are to be found, correlations between measures of stressful life events and dependent variables have typically been low, often in the .20 to .30 range. These significant relationships are of theoretical interest, but life stress seems to account for a relatively small proportion of the variance in the dependent measures that have been studied. It would seem that, by themselves, life stress measures are not likely to be of much practical value as predictors. A logical question is whether this poor predictive ability is due to the inadequacies of life stress measures (unreliability of measurement, failure to assess separately positive and negative life changes, insensitive methods of quantifying the impact of events) or to other factors, such as the need to include important moderator variables. As has been noted, several approaches to the assessment of stressful life events have been employed in the studies published to date. Although instruments that distinguish between positive and negative events typically yield somewhat higher correlations with dependent variables, even these correlations tend to be relatively low in magnitude.

In addition, people may experience stress that is not a product of life change. For example, ecological factors such as crowding and noise pollution are constants for many people, not sudden life changes. There are also a host of other stressors that impinge on people's lives that are not experienced as sudden life events. Examples of these stressors include the knowledge that one has some probability of developing a genetically related disease or the gradual realization that one will not reach goals set earlier in life. Finally, there are undoubtedly a variety of day-to-day situations that do not bring about major life changes but nevertheless serve as stressors (Coppel, 1980). Examples might be friction with teenage children over responsibilities and privileges or work deadlines that involve periodic pressures to produce material by a certain date. To the extent that health and adjustment are influenced by stressors other than those assessed by life change measures, one might expect to find lower correlations between stressful life events and dependent variables.

An example of the critical role played by methodological issues in discussions of life stress is provided by research on the relationship between life events and coronary heart disease. Over fifty studies have examined this relationship, yet no unifying explanation has emerged to account for all the reported findings. Although life events and coronary heart disease seem to be linked, most studies have been retrospective, life events being assessed *after* occurrence of the heart attack. Brown (1974) has pointed out the confounding role played by *retrospective contamination* or distortion in the assessment of life events. Some heart attack victims may want to "blame" their attacks on certain circumstances in their lives. On the other hand, stressful life events can lead to life-style changes that aggravate an existing predisposition to coronary heart disease. A sudden change in one's life, such as a heart attack, produces all manner of psychological reactions and behavioral changes (sleep disturbances, alteration in food intake, confusion, and increased suggestibility) which may produce observable clinical symptoms. A heart attack may then be both a consequence of stressful life events and a stressful life event in its own right.

Some methodological issues concerning which clarifications or improvements in research design are needed are outlined below.

4.1. Types of Events

A wide variety of events may be considered as stressful. Very little is known about the particular types of events that are related to particular types of outcome. The work of Holmes and Rahe (1967) was based on the assumption that symptoms are caused by the total amount of change in a person's life. Later research has suggested that psychological maladjustment, at least, is related more to negative (unwanted, undesirable) than to positive (wanted, desirable) change (Mueller, Edwards, & Yarvis, 1977; Ross & Mirowsky, 1979). Within the category of negative life events there may be certain types of events that are more important than others. Research on this possibility is needed. These are some types of events whose properties, correlates, and consequences need to be better understood:

1. Physical illness and injuries
2. Personal failures (e.g., loss of job due to inadequate performance)
3. Loss of attachments (e.g., bereavement, divorce)
4. Interpersonal changes (e.g., a new supervisor, entrance of new member into one's social group)
5. Victimization (e.g., being burglarized)
6. Natural disasters (e.g., earthquake, volcano eruption)

In addition to categorizing types of events, it also seems important to determine the degree to which they are or might be *predictable* or *controllable*. Unpredictable events and those over which people have little or no control are among the most distressing of all experiences. Predictability or the lack of it is a major factor in the stress experienced from an event (Pennebaker, Burnam, Schaeffer, & Harker, 1977).

4.2. Magnitude of Events

What contributions do particular individual events make to the total level of stressfulness experienced by the individual? Research is needed to determine the ways in which events differing in personal significance combine to produce behavioral and physical effects. Is it worse to experience one really major undesirable event or six medium-sized ones? How might events differing in magnitude of stress arousal be optimally weighted and combined?

4.3. Timing of Events

The incubation time for the impact of life events is probably not a constant. It seems reasonable that different types of events exert their influence in different ways and over different periods of time. A tantalizing question concerns the impacts exerted by remote events. At what points do the effects of stressful life events begin to wear off (Garrity *et al.*, 1977)? Brown and Harris (1978) found that one of the major distinguishing features of women who were depressed in middle age was the loss of their mothers in childhood through death or separation. The interests of psychoanalysts and stress researchers overlap with regard to stressful life events. Stress researchers are more interested in recent events, psychoanalytically oriented researchers in events that occurred early in life.

4.4. Meaning of Events

Lazarus and others have pointed out the distinction between events *per se* and how they are appraised (Folkman, Schaefer, & Lazarus, 1979). It would seem desirable to assess both the things that happen to people and how they are appraised. Some events may be *overappraised* in that the individual attaches more significance to them than they really merit. Other events may be *underappraised*, with the individual failing to appreciate present or future implications.

4.5. Causality versus Correlation

Given that it is desirable ultimately to reach the point where causal inferences can be made and that, for ethical reasons, we will continue to be unable to manipulate life stress experimentally, how then does one proceed? It is likely that any one study, no matter how well designed, will be capable of providing data sufficient to justify the conclusion that a causal relationship exists. It is, in fact, impossible to "prove" the existence of a causal relationship from correlational data. However, by conducting a variety of studies particularly designed to investigate and control for specific variables, it may be possible to accumulate a body of information which, when taken together, would allow an inference of causality to be made with some justification.

A large number of studies of life events are retrospective, with all the limitations of that type of research. Prospective or longitudinal studies are valuable both practically and theoretically because assessment of stressful life events takes place before the appearance of symptoms.

One potentially fruitful approach to investigating the possibility of a causal relationship in the life-stress area would involve the use of a cross-lagged correlational methodology. This quasi-experimental approach, originally suggested by Simon (1954), involves obtaining data on two variables of interest at two points in time and comparing the correlations among these variables from one time period to another.

Johnson and Sarason (1979) measured stressful life events (previous 6 months) and obtained several self-report indices of health and adjustment on a sample of undergraduate psychology students. Using a cross-lagged correlational design, subjects were contacted 7 months later and these same measures were used a second time. Negative life change scores at Time 1 were significantly correlated with the reporting of physical symptoms at Time 2. No significant relationship was found between physical symptoms at Time 1 and subsequent life-stress scores. Vossel and Froehlich (1979) examined the relationship between negative life changes as assessed by the LES and measures of job tension and effectiveness in task performance. The findings of this study were interpreted as being consistent with a causal relationship in which life stress leads to job tension and decreased performance effectiveness.

4.6. Moderator Variables

How events are appraised depends on the personality and circumstances of the individual experiencing them. This topic has been discussed in the section on moderator variables. In addition, life-stress and indicators of illness and maladjustment may both be influenced by other moderator variables that are usually not examined. Socioeconomic status (SES) may function in this way (Syme

& Berkman, 1976; Uhlenhuth, Lipman, Balter, & Stern, 1974). People low in SES may be more likely to experience negative life changes and also, for a variety of reasons, to be more prone to develop health-related and adjustment problems. Correlations between life stress and illness in this instance might simply result from the fact that both variables covary with SES. Neglected variables may play important roles in associations among independent and dependent variables.

5. Cognitive Appraisal and the Experience of Stress

An important area of research that should be explored in order to increase our understanding of the effects of life events concerns the individual's *cognitive* appraisal of situations. The chain of events involved in the experience of stress begins with a problematic situation. A call for action is issued when either the environment or personal concerns identify the need to do something. The actual experience of stress follows when, after the call for action, one's capabilities and personal resources are perceived as falling short of the need. For example, in automobile driving, personal ability is usually perceived as commensurate with the situational challenge and the call for action is handled in a routine, task-oriented manner. However, stressful reactions may well up on treacherous mountain roads among persons who are not confident of their abilities in that situation.

People usually differ in the *salience* or pull value that events have for them. Some situations are universally salient because most people have learned the same meaning for a particular cue. For example, when a stop light turns red, most automobile drivers stop. Other situations are universally salient because their overwhelming characteristics evoke similar stress reactions in large numbers of people. Severe earthquakes, catastrophic fires, bridge collapses, mass riots, and nuclear explosions are examples of this type of stress-producing situation. For many situations, however, when environmental conditions are not stereotyped or extreme, *personal salience* describes the major role that individual's cognitions play in directing attention to particular aspects of a situation that have personal significance. Hearing a particular song may evoke a grief reaction, feelings or nostalgia, or a relaxed state depending on whether it was associated with someone who died recently, someone who is away and whose return is uncertain, or with happy memories of a high school romance. Some situations may not initially be experienced as stressful. With subsequent experiences, however, the situation will tend to arouse stress responses because of the cognitions it elicits.

Another example of the importance of cognitive sets follows from research by Graham, Lundy, Benjamin, Kabler, Lewis, Kunish, and Graham, (1962). Through many interviews with patients suffering various diseases, the authors identified common cognitions among individuals from each disease category. For example, cognitions for hives included feeling "mistreated, unfairly treated" and being a "helpless, innocent victim of unfair, unjust treatment." Cognitions for hypertension included feeling "threatened every instant" and the need "to be ready, on guard, prepared." When these cognitions were hypnotically suggested to normal subjects, predicted physiological changes occurred; that is, there was a rise in skin temperature with the hives-related cognitions and a rise in blood pressure with the hypertension-related cognitions. Thus, it appears that certain cognitions, whether induced experimentally or a function of individual differences, may be associated with specific physiological responses.

Experimental and anecdotal evidence from many sources suggests that individuals use different cognitive strategies in stressful situations and that these cognitions may be important in determining the degree to which ensuing behavior will be adaptive. Although some people are able to maintain a *task-orientation* during such situations, for others, *self-preoccupation* often interferes with realistic planning and weighing of alternatives. There are wide individual differences in the frequency and preoccupying character of stress-related cognitions. The most adaptive cognitive response to stressful situations is generally a task orientation that directs the individual's attention to the task at hand, rather than cognitions focusing on emotional reactions. The ability to set aside unproductive worries and preoccupations seems to be crucial in functioning well under pressure.

It may be that the people most vulnerable to maladaptive, self-preoccupied cognitions can be identified on the basis of moderator variables such as those discussed above. These include both personal characteristics (e.g., locus of control, sensation seeking) and environmental factors (e.g., social support). In fact, it may even be possible to utilize these variables to predict which individuals will be most vulnerable to the negative effects of particular stressors (Zubin & Spring, 1977).

Beyond influencing vulnerability, personal and environmental factors may also affect the mobilization of resources to cope with problems posed by an event. For example, an entering freshman with much social support and an internal locus of control may perform better and feel happier than a freshman with little social support and an external locus of control.

These factors may operate by influencing a person's cognitive appraisal of the demands placed on him or her by various situations as well as the individual's appraisal of his or her ability to meet these demands. In this way, the interactions between a person and situational variables are seen as important in affecting the experience of various life events and in determining the unique personal responses to them.

Research on stressful life events may be on the threshold of progressing from merely assessing whether or not certain events have taken place and correlating the events with outcomes such as illness to integrating the occurrence of life events into a cognitive theory of stress that will account for relevant moderator variables and clarify specific causal models.

6. References

Antonovsky, A. *Health, stress, and coping.* San Francisco: Jossey-Bass, 1979.
Auerbach, S. M., & Kilmann, P. R. Crisis intervention: A review of outcome research. *Psychological Bulletin*, 1977, *84*, 1189–1217.
Beck, A. T. *Depression: Clinical, experimental, and theoretical aspects.* New York: Harper & Row, 1967.

Bedell, J. R., Giordani, B., Amour, J. L., Tavormina, J., & Boll, T. Life stress and the psychological and medical adjustment of chronically ill children. *Journal of psychosomatic Research*, 1977, *21*, 237–242.

Berkman, L. F., & Syme, S. L. Social networks, host resistance, and mortality: A nine-year follow-up study of Alameda County residents. *American Journal of Epidemiology*, 1979, *109* (2), 186–204.

Block, M., & Zautra, A. Satisfaction and distress in a community: A test of the effects of life events. *American Journal of Community Psychology* 1981, *9*, 165–180.

Brown, G. W. Meaning, measurement, and stress of life events. In B. S. Dohrenwend & B. P. Dohrenwend (Eds.), *Stressful life events: Their nature and effects*. New York: Wiley, 1974.

Brown, G. W., Bhrolchain, M., & Harris, T. Social class and psychiatric disturbances among women in an urban population. *Sociology*, 1975, *9*, 225–254.

Brown, G. W., & Harris, T. *Social origins of depression: A study of psychiatric disorder in women*. New York: Free Press, 1978.

Burke, R., & Weir, T. Marital helping relationships: Moderators between stress and well-being. *Journal of Psychology*, 1977, *95*, 121–130.

Cannon, W. B. *The wisdom of the body*. New York: Norton, 1932.

Caplan, R. D., Cobb, S., & French, J. Relationship of cessation of smoking with job stress, personality, and social support. *Journal of Applied Psychology*, 1975, *60* (2), 211–219.

Cobb, S. Social support as a moderator of life stress. *Psychosomatic Medicine*, 1976, *38* (5), 300–313.

Coddington, R. D. The significance of life events as etiological factors in the diseases of children: I. A survey of professional workers. *Journal of Psychosomatic Research*, 1972, *17*, 7.

Coppel, D. *The relationship of perceived social support and self-efficacy to major and minor stresses*. Unpublished doctoral manuscript, University of Washington, 1980.

Crnic, K. A., Greenberg, M. T., Ragozin, A. S., & Robinson, N. M. *The effects of life stress and social support on the life satisfaction and attitudes of mothers of newborn normal and at-risk infants*. Paper presented at Western Psychological Association Convention, Honolulu, Hawaii, May 1980.

Dean, A., & Lin, N. The stress-buffering role of social support. *Journal of Nervous and Mental Disease*, 1977, *165*, 403–417.

De Araujo, G., Dudley, D. L., & Van Arsdel, P. P., Jr. Psychosocial assets and severity of chronic asthma. *Journal of Allergy and Clinical Immunology*, 1972, *50*, 257–263.

De Araujo, G., Van Arsdel, P. P., Jr., Holmes, T. H., & Dudley, D. L. Life change, coping ability, and chronic intrinsic asthma. *Journal of Psychosomatic Research*, 1973, *17*, 359–363.

Edwards, M. K. *Life crisis and myocardial infarction*. Unpublished master's thesis, University of Washington, 1971.

Folkman, S., Schaefer, C., & Lazarus, R. S. Cognitive processes as mediators of stress and coping. In V. Hamilton & D. M. Warburton (Eds.), *Human stress and cognition: An information processing approach*. Chichester, England: Wiley, 1979.

Garrity, T. F., Marx, M. B., & Somes, G. W. The influence of illness severity and time since life change on the size of the life change–health change relationship. *Journal of Psychosomatic Research*, 1977, *21*, 377–382.

Gore, S. The effect of social support in moderating the health consequences of unemployment. *Journal of Health and Social Behavior*, 1978, *19*, 157–165.

Gorsuch, R. L., & Key, M. K. Abnormalities of pregnancy as a function of anxiety and life stress. *Psychosomatic Medicine*, 1974, *36*, 352.

Graham, D. T., Lundy, R. M., Benjamin, L. S., Kabler, J. D., Lewis, W. C., Kunish, B. A., & Graham, F. K. Specific attitudes in initial interviews with patients having different "psychosomatic" diseases. *Psychosomatic Medicine*, 1962, *24*, 257–266.

Harrington, R. L., Burnell, G. M., & Korenoff, C. *Systems approach to mental health care in a HMO model*. Project Report, May 19, 1975, NIMH Grant MH24109, Kaiser-Permanente Medical Office, San Jose, California.

Harrington, R. L., Burnell, G. M., & Korenoff, C. *Systems approach to mental health care in a HMO model*. Project Report, March 13, 1980, NIMH Grant MH24109, Kaiser-Permanente Medical Office, San Jose, California.

Heller, K. The effects of social support: Prevention and treatment implications. In A. P. Goldstein & F. H. Kanfer (Eds.), *Maximizing treatment gains: Transfer enhancement in psychotherapy*. New York: Academic Press, 1979.

Henderson, S. A development in social psychiatry: The systematic study of social bonds. *Journal of Nervous and Mental Disease*, 1980, *168*, 63–69.

Hinkle, Jr., L. E. The concept of "stress" in the biological and social sciences. *Science, Medicine, and Man*, 1973, *1*, 31–48.

Holmes, T. H., & Masuda, M. Life change and illness susceptibility. In B. S. Dohrenwend & B. P. Dohrenwend (Eds.), *Stressful life events: Their nature and effects*. New York: Wiley, 1974.

Holmes, T. H., & Rahe, R. H. The Social Readjustment Rating Scale. *Journal of Psychosomatic Research*, 1967, *11*, 213–218.

Horowitz, M., Wilner, N., & Alvarez, W. Impact of Event Scale: A measure of subjective stress. *Psychosomatic Medicine*, 1979, *41* (3), 209–218.

Jenkins, C. D. Psychosocial modifiers of response to stress. In J. E. Barrett (Eds.), *Stress and mental disorder*. New York: Raven Press, 1979.

Johnson, J. H., & McCutcheon, S. Assessing life stress in older children and adolescents: Preliminary findings with the Life Events Checklist. In I. G. Sarason & C. D. Spielberger (Eds.), *Stress and anxiety* (Vol. 7). Washington, D.C.: Hemisphere Publishing Corp., 1980.

Johnson, J. H., & Sarason, I. G. Life stress, depression, and anxiety: Internal–external control as a moderator variable. *Journal of Psychosomatic Research*, 1978, *22*, 205–208.

Johnson, J. H., & Sarason, I. G. Recent developments in research on life stress. In V. Hamilton & D. M. Warburton (Eds.), *Human stress and cognition: An information processing approach*. Chichester, England: Wiley, 1979.

Johnson, J. H., Sarason, I. G., & Siegel, J. M. *Arousal seeking as a moderator of life stress*. Unpublished manuscript, University of Washington, 1978.

Knapp, S. J., & Magee, R. D. The relationship of life events to grade point average of college students. *Journal of College Student Personnel*, November 1979, pp. 497–502.

Kobasa, S. C. Stressful life events, personality, and health: An inquiry into hardiness. *Journal of Personality and Social Psychology*, 1979, *37* (1), 1–11.

Lanyon, R. I. Development and validation of a psychological screening inventory. *Journal of Consulting and Clinical Psychology*, 1970, *35*, 1–24.

Lanyon, R. I. *Psychological Screening Inventory manual*. Goshen, N.Y.: Research Psychologists Press, 1973.

Leif, A. (Ed.). *The commonsense psychiatry of Dr. Adolf Meyer*. New York: McGraw-Hill, 1948.

Lundberg, V., Theorell, T., & Lind, E. Life changes and myocardial infarction: Individual differences in life change scaling. *Journal of Psychosomatic Research*, 1975, *19*, 27–32.

Lyon, K., & Zucker, R. Environmental supports and post-hospital adjustment. *Journal of Clinical Psychology*, 1974, *30* (4), 460–465.

Masuda, M., & Holmes, T. H. Life events: Perceptions and frequencies. *Psychosomatic Medicine*, 1978, *40* (3), 236–261.

Medalie, J. H., & Goldbourt, U. Angina pectoris among 10,000 men: II. Psychosocial and other risk factors as evidenced by a multivariate analysis of a five year incidence study. *American Journal of Medicine*, 1976, *60*, 910–921.

Miller, P. McC., & Ingham, J. G. Friends, confidants, and symptoms. *Social Psychiatry*, 1976, *11*, 51–58.

Monaghan, J. H., Robinson, J. O., & Dodge, J. A. The children's Life Events Inventory. *Journal of Psychosomatic Research*, 1979, *23*, 63–68.

Mueller, D. P., Edwards, D. W., & Yarvis, R. M. Stressful life events and psychiatric symptomatology: Change or undesirability? *Journal of Health and Social Behavior*, 1977, *18* (3), 307–317.

Nuckolls, K. B., Cassell, J., & Kaplan, B. H. Psychosocial assets, life crisis, and the prognosis of pregnancy. *American Journal of Epidemiology*, 1972, *95*, 431–441.

Pancheri, P., Bellaterra, M., Reda, G., Matteoli, S., Santarelli, E., Pugliese, M., & Mosticoni, S. *Psycho-neural-endocrinological correlates of myocardial infarction*. Paper presented at the NIAS International Conference on Stress and Anxiety, Wassenaar, Netherlands, June 1980.

Paykel, E. S. Causal relationships between clinical depression and life events. In J. E. Barrett (Eds.), *Stress and mental disorder*. New York: Raven Press, 1979.

Pennebaker, J. W., Burnam, M. A., Schaeffer, M. A., & Harper, D. C. Lack of control as a determinant of perceived physical symptoms. *Journal of Personality and Social Psychology*, 1977, *35* (3), 167–174.

Petrich, J., & Holmes, T. H. Life change and onset of illness. *Medical Clinics of North America*, 1977, *61* (4), 825–838.

Rabkin, J. G., & Struening, E. L. Life events, stress, and illness. *Science*, 1976, *194*, 1013–1020.

Rahe, R. H. Life-change measurement as a predictor of illness. *Proceedings of the Royal Society of Medicine*, 1968, *61*, 1124–1126.

Rahe, R. H., & Arthur, R. J. *Life change and illness studies: Past history and future directions.* Technical Report No. 76-14, Naval Health Research Center, San Diego, Calif., March 1976.

Rahe, R. H., & Lind, E. Psychosocial factors and sudden cardiac death: A pilot study. *Journal of Psychosomatic Research,* 1971, *15*, 19.

Redfield, J., & Stone, A. Individual viewpoints of stressful life events. *Journal of Consulting and Clinical Psychology,* 1979, *47* (1), 147–154.

Reinhardt, R. F. The outstanding jet pilot. *American Journal of Psychiatry,* 1970, *127*, 732–736.

Ross, C. E., & Mirowsky J. II. A comparison of life-event-weighting schemes: Change, undesirability, and effect-proportional indices. *Journal of Health and Social Behavior,* 1979, *20*, 166–177.

Rotter, J. B. Generalized expectancies for internal versus external control of reinforcement. *Psychological Monographs,* 1966, *80* (1), 1–28.

Ruff, G. E., & Korchin, S. J. Adaptive stress behavior. In M. H. Appley & R. Trumbull (Eds.), *Psychological stress.* New York: Appleton Century Crofts, 1967.

Sandler, I. N., & Block, M. Life stress and maladaptation of children. *American Journal of Community Psychology,* 1979, *7* (4), 425–440.

Sarason, I. G., & Johnson, J. H. Life stress, organizational stress, and job satisfaction. *Psychological Reports,* 1979, *44*, 75–79.

Sarason, I. G., Johnson, J. H., & Siegel, J. M. Assessing the impact of life changes: Development of the Life Experiences Survey. *Journal of Consulting and Clinical Psychology,* 1978, *46*, 932–946.

Sarason, I. G., Levine, H., & Basham, R. *The development of the Social Support Questionnaire: Reliability and validity.* Unpublished manuscript, 1980.

Schless, A. P., & Mendels, J. The value of interviewing family and friends in assessing life stressors. *Archives of General Psychiatry,* 1978, *35*, 565–567.

Selye, H. The general adaptation syndrome and the diseases of adaptation. *Journal of Clinical Endocrinology,* 1946, *6*, 117.

Siegel, J. M., Johnson, J. H., & Sarason, I. G. Life changes and menstrual discomfort. *Journal of Human Stress,* 1979, *5* (1), 41–46. (a)

Siegel, J. M., Johnson, J. H., & Sarason, I. G. Mood states and the reporting of life changes. *Journal of Psychosomatic Research,* 1979, *23*, 103–108. (b)

Silberfeld, M. Psychological symptoms and social supports. *Social Psychiatry,* 1978, *13*, 11–17.

Simon, H. A. Spurious correlation: A causal interpretation. *Journal of the American Statistical Association,* 1954, *49*, 467–479.

Smith, R. E., Johnson, J. H., & Sarason, I. G. Life change, the sensation seeking motive, and psychological distress. *Journal of Consulting and Clinical Psychology,* 1978, *46*, 348–349.

Sosa, R., Kennell, J., Klaus, M., Robertson, S., & Urrutia, J. The effect of a supportive companion on perinatal problems, length of labor, and mother–infant interaction. *New England Journal of Medicine,* 1980, *303*, 597–600.

Spielberger, C. D., Gorsuch, R. L., & Lushene, R. E. *Manual for the State–Trait Anxiety Inventory.* Palo Alto, Calif.: Consulting Psychologists Press, 1970.

Syme, S. L., & Berkman, L. F. Social class, susceptibility and sickness. *American Journal of Epidemiology,* 1976, *104*, 1–8.

Tennant, C., & Andrews, G. The pathogenic quality of life event stress in neurotic impairment. *Archives of General Psychiatry,* 1978, *35*, 859–863.

Theorell, T., & Rahe, R. H. Psychosocial factors and myocardial infarction: 1. An inpatient study in Sweden. *Journal of Psychosomatic Research,* 1971, *15*, 25–31.

Thurlow, H. J. Illness in relation to life situation and sick-role tendency. *Journal of Psychosomatic Research,* 1971, *15*, 73–88.

Tolsdorf, C. Social networks, support, and coping: An exploratory study. *Family Process,* 1976, *15* (4), 407–417.

Uhlenhuth, E. H., Lipman, R. S., Balter, M. B., & Stern, M. Symptom intensity and life stress in the city. *Archives of General Psychiatry,* 1974, *31*, 759–764.

Vinokur, A., & Selzer, M. L. Desirable versus undesirable life events: Their relationship to stress and mental distress. *Journal of Personality and Social Psychology,* 1975, *32*, 329–337.

Vossel, G., & Froehlich, W. D. Life stress, job tension, and subjective reports of task performance effectiveness: A cross-lagged correlational analysis. In I. G. Sarason & C. D. Spielberger (Eds.), *Stress and anxiety* (Vol. 6). New York: Wiley, 1979.

Weiss, R. S. The provisions of social relations. In Z. Rubin (Ed.), *Doing unto others.* Englewood Cliffs, N.J.: Prentice-Hall, 1974.

Whitcher, S. J., & Fisher, J. D. Multidimensional reaction to therapeutic touch in a hospital setting. *Journal of Personality and Social Psychology*, 1979, *36*, 87–96.

Wolff, H. G. *Stress and disease.* Springfield, Ill.: Charles C Thomas, 1953.

Wyler, A. R., Masuda, M., & Holmes, T. H. Magnitude of life events and seriousness of illness. *Psychosomatic Medicine*, 1971, *33*, 115–122.

Yamamoto, K. J., & Kinney, O. K. Pregnant women's ratings of different factors influencing psychological stress during pregnancy. *Psychological Reports*, 1976, *39*, 203–214.

Yeaworth, R. C., York, J., Hussey, M. A., Ingle, M. E., & Goodwin, T. The development of an adolescent life change event scale. *Adolescence*, 1980, *25* (57), 91–98.

Zubin, J., & Spring, B. Vulnerability—A new view of schizophrenia. *Journal of Abnormal Psychology*, 1977, *86*, 103–126.

Zuckerman, M. *Sensation seeking: Beyond the optimal level of arousal.* Hillsdale, N.J.: Lawrence Erlbaum, 1979.

Behavioral Indicators of Client Progress after Spinal Cord Injury
An Ecological-Contextual Approach

EDWIN P. WILLEMS AND JAMES L. ALEXANDER

1. Background

During each day and throughout the life span of the individual, various processes of adaptation lead to the development of a repertoire of behavioral performances in the everyday environment. This repertoire is part of the substance of everyday life and is critical to survival, but it is usually overlooked by the healthy person because it is taken for granted. Onset of a severe physical disability such as spinal cord injury eliminates or alters this repertoire; the person's major means of coming to terms with the everyday environment are impaired, often drastically.

The overall objective of rehabilitation programs in general is to return clients to the mainstream of society with satisfying and functional life-styles. Typically, the rehabilitation process consists of helping clients to learn to live with their disabilities in their own environments. This is a teaching-learning process in the behavioral domain that begins with onset of disability and continues for the client's lifetime. Most handicapping conditions—such as sensory impairment, birth defects, learning disabilities, stroke, traumatic injury, orthopedic impair-

EDWIN P. WILLEMS • Department of Psychology, University of Houston, Houston, Texas 77004.   JAMES L. ALEXANDER • Department of Rehabilitation, Baylor College of Medicine, Waco, Texas 76703.

ment, or the infirmities of advancing age—eliminate or restrict clients' behavioral performances in the everyday environment and impair their major means of adapting to their environments. Thus, philosophically and practically, most rehabilitation programs are concerned with adapting to loss, improving functional capability, enhancing self-reliance, and enriching the client's repertoire of and proficiency in everyday practical skills. For the specific types of disability associated with spinal cord injury, rehabilitation means intensive, goal-oriented, programmatic arrangements designed to restore a person's lost or altered repertoire of functional abilities as much as possible (or to find substitutes for it), to teach clients new forms of performance and new kinds of relationships to their environments, and to alter environments in appropriate ways. When such performance is effected in the most timely, positive, and effective manner, waste of human resources is minimized for society, for the service system, and—most importantly—for the client.

Among the major goals of rehabilitation for the spinal cord patient is the restoration of optimal functional performance in both the institutional and community environments. A goal frequently voiced in rehabilitation for spinal injury is to "help the person become maximally independent." Independence is a behavioral issue because it involves performances which clients can carry out in their usual environments with a minimum of intervention and support from others.

Since issues of functional performance in the context of everyday living in the clients' own environments over long periods of time are central to the objectives of most rehabilitation efforts, it follows that assessment and evaluation of the efficacy of rehabilitation programs must necessarily include measures of behavioral or functional health status. Such measures of functional health status provide the criteria for evaluating both the quality of health care services delivered and the outcome of rehabilitation programs. For example, if independence is a major goal of rehabilitation programs, then actual levels of patients' independent functioning should serve as a criterion for the assessment and evaluation of rehabilitation programs. This requires that accurate and objective quantitative data on patients' independent functioning—in both the institutional and community environments—be included in the assessment and evaluation process.

For the past several years, we have been developing a new approach to the measurement of health status and functional performance in rehabilitation. This approach, called Longitudinal Functional Assessment (LFA), is based on the continuous and direct measurement of client performance in various settings from admission to discharge in a rehabilitation center and well past discharge. The major advantages of the LFA over more traditional measures are that it focuses directly on the behaviors that are most relevant to the long-term adjustment of patients and that it provides a far more detailed and objective basis for assessing the status of clients and their progress over time. This kind of information is essential if rehabilitation is to develop a more scientific foundation and become more cost-effective.

The purpose of this chapter is to describe a few high points along the route we and our colleagues have taken toward such measures. Readers should keep several features of this description in mind. First, we will emphasize the development of measures. This thread through our work of 7 years leaves out many substantive issues, false starts, dead ends, demonstrations, and methodological side roads. Second, and closely related, there are many articles, book chapters, and technical reports that describe the work. We will be glad to share reference lists and materials with readers who are interested. Here, we will tell a sequential story; we will not distract readers with reference citations. Third, approximately a hundred people have contributed to this work over the years. Thus, when we say "we" in this chapter, we usually are referring to a larger group than the two of us.

403

BEHAVIORAL
INDICATORS OF
CLIENT PROGRESS
AFTER SPINAL
CORD INJURY

2. Observational Developments

From the beginning of our work, we have sought to develop an LFA that would be (1) reliable (both within and between raters); (2) valid; (3) convenient, so that it might be used by busy professionals; (4) sensitive and powerful enough to discriminate clearly among levels of status and stages of progress; (5) applicable to longitudinal and continuous measurement over time; (6) intelligible and communicable to a variety of users; (7) applicable to a variety of client groups; and (8) usable with both individual clients and groups of clients. One facet of the state of the art in the early seventies, when we started this work, was that almost nothing was known systematically and quantitatively about the behavioral aftermath of spinal cord injury. This meant that there was no clear, consensual set of behavioral measures on which we could focus. As a result, we approached the problem much as ethologists might approach a strange new organism.

Teams of trained observers followed patients. Using a small, battery-operated cassette recorder, the observer dictated a continuous narrative description of the target patient's behavior and enough of the immediate situation to add intelligibility to the narrative. Few strictures were placed on the observational process, but observers were instructed to dictate clock time into the narratives in terms of minutes and fractions of minutes. After typists had transcribed the narratives, observers and checkers screened the transcripts for technical accuracy, after which coders analyzed the narratives.

Our analysis of the protocols assumed that they had captured and described the patient's sequential behavior streams and that the events in these behavior streams included things patients did, things that were done to or with them, and periods during which they were idle or passive. Our major coding unit, a *chunk*, demarcated a molar event in a patient's behavior stream. The analysis was designed to minimize the coder's inferential burden and to provide the means to retrieve systematic and quantitative information regarding the common, everyday behaviors of patients. Direct involvement by the patient was a necessary condition for marking a chunk. Thus, if the patient was described clearly as having been involved in two distinct principal activities at the same time (for instance, eating lunch and playing cards), two chunks were demarcated as having occurred simultaneously. Examples of chunks include *Lying in Bed, Eating Scheduled Meal, Transporting to Lobby, Passive Range of Motion—Arms, Waiting, Transferring,* and *Reading Magazine.*

Chunks were marked on the protocols by means of marginal brackets. The information on each chunk was then transferred to computer files, with the following codes: (1) patient identifying number; (2) where the chunk occurred in terms of behavior setting; (3) starting time; (4) ending time; (5) numerical code for the kind of behavior; (6) who else, if anyone, was directly involved in the principal activity of the chunk, and how many persons were involved; and (7) who instigated or initiated the chunk. Thus, for each chunk, it is possible to retrieve information regarding *who* did it, *what* kind of behavior it was, *where* it occurred, *when* it occurred, for *how long* it occurred, *who else* was directly involved in it or whether the patient did it alone, and who *instigated* it. When these measures were taken singly and in combination and when the overall distributions of chunks were considered, a great many analyses and descriptive statistics became possible.

The LFA observations measured patient functioning at the molar level of behavior—the level characteristic of common conversational usage. Research in other areas suggests that the molar level corresponds to what is discriminated naturally in day-to-day life. This level of behavior represents the kinds of performances that are crucial to everyday functioning; for example, eating a meal, moving from the ward to physical therapy, getting dressed, brushing teeth. The molar level of behavior is an appropriate level at which to measure patient functioning for two reasons, one theoretical and the other methodological. Theoretically, the challenge of rehabilitation is to restore function at the molar level. Much time and effort in rehabilitation programs are spent fostering skills in activities of daily living and enhancing autonomous functioning across the range of day-to-day behaviors. This is so because independent functioning involves executing such molar acts with minimal hands-on assistance from others. Since the reduction of dependency occurs at the molar level of performance, it is these functional endpoints that count most in effective rehabilitation.

Second, our work has focused on behavior at the molar level for methodological reasons. More molecular or fine-grained levels (e.g., eye blinks, muscle movements) are virtually impossible to measure in the course of everyday activities and over long periods of time. Conversely, the much more global levels, such as marital adjustment or vocational development, do not provide enough information to provide accurate assessments or to aid future interventions. Our research has demonstrated that ongoing molar behavior in natural settings can be observed, coded, and classified reliably.

The in-hospital phase of observation started on the day the patient was admitted to the hospital. After fully informed consent was obtained from such patients, trained personnel began to observe them on a prearranged schedule. Ten 90-minute observations were spaced across each week in such a way that all the 15 hours between 7 A.M. and 10 P.M. were observed during the week.

For one-tenth of all observations, two observers generated independent paired protocols. After these protocols had been processed by separate coders, estimates of interobserver and intercoder agreement were available. Agreement was tallied in terms of the number of seconds accounted for in exactly the same fashion by the two accounts. With this rather stringent procedure, intercoder agreement averaged 98.4% across 96 hours of paired protocols. Across the same paired protocols, interobserver agreement averaged 92.8%.

405

BEHAVIORAL
INDICATORS OF
CLIENT PROGRESS
AFTER SPINAL
CORD INJURY

This observational system yielded the information we needed for our next step, but it was very costly and inefficient. Approximately six or seven people were required from beginning to end to acquire and process the data from a protocol. After completion of an observation, approximately 12 person-hours were required to analyze and reduce the data, and the entire sequence for a protocol took 5 to 7 days before the data were ready to use.

For these reasons, we developed the *standard-form* observation as an alternative to the *narrative* observation system with which the work began. Since this new approach placed more judgmental responsibility on the observer and eliminated the transcribing of narrative transcripts, the standard-form technique represented an important saving of time, effort, and expense. Most important, the turnaround time from observation of a patient to the point at which data were available for use was reduced from days down to as little as 2 hours. Thus, the standard form was designed to yield the same performance data, but with much greater efficiency.

In the form technique, the observer was given a form on which columns were labeled as follows: (1) *time,* (2) *activity* (patient behavior), (3) *others directly involved,* (4) *who instigated the behavior,* (5) *conversation,* and (6) *location.* Ninety rows, one for each minute of observation, were premarked on the form. While observing the patient, the observer wrote in the major types of information for each minute (row). The observer and a coder reviewed this account to clarify ambiguous entries and to collect the various row entries into performance units (chunks) by the coding system that we had developed. Then, the coder alone continued by supplying numerical information for each performance unit.

For a time, the standard form and the older narrative approach were used on alternate weeks during the hospital stays of given patients. One purpose was to measure the reliability of the standard form. Once during each week on which the form was used, two observers monitored the patient simultaneously. On the basis of independent coding processes for the two forms, we could measure intercoder and interobserver reliability in terms of the percentage of seconds that agreed exactly.

The second purpose of this test of the form was to determine the extent to which it yielded the same data as the older narrative system. Once each week during the hospital stays of patients, two observers (one with narrative procedure and one with standard-form procedure) monitored the patient simultaneously. Coded data from the two procedures were used to make cross-modal comparisons (form-narrative) of the percentage of seconds that agreed exactly. Across 25.5 hours of paired-form observations, the intercoder agreement for the form method averaged 98.3%. Across the same paired hours, interobserver agreement averaged 92.1%. More importantly, across 48 hours of paired narrative-form observations, intermodal agreement averaged 93.9%. The importance of this finding lay in the fact that we had achieved a much more efficient monitoring technique of high quality.

Finally, we tested the simultaneous acquisition of two types of instrument-based measures. The first was gathered by means of a series of pressure-sensitive pads placed under the patient's mattress and connected to a continuous recorder in one of the hospital laboratories. This device provides a sensitive, continuous recording of motility on the bed surface and, more importantly, an exact measure of time out of bed. The second was gathered by means of a mechanical odometer attached to the wheel of the patient's wheelchair. These odometers provide a measure of patient mobility. We tested the reliability of the odometers and the adequacy with which periodic readings estimate total mobility. Data from the bed monitor and odometers then were mapped onto the observational data to ascertain which observational measures are approximated best, or estimated best, by the instrumented measures. These efforts were motivated by the potential saving in time and effort that would come from using instrumented measures as much as possible to supplement or replace the more cumbersome observational measures.

In these developmental phases, we cast a wide net for patient activity. What we got back was a very rich and diverse representation of the behavioral aftermath of spinal cord injury. The next problem was to reduce this very large set of longitudinal measures and select those that would serve as indicators of patient progress and yet be cost-efficient to obtain.

3. Reduction and Selection

With 215 measures of molar patient behavior available on a nearly continuous basis (i.e., 10 times per week) throughout the patients' hospital stays plus continuous data from the wheelchair odometer (mobility) and rest-time monitors (time out of bed), we felt we had obtained good coverage. However, we had to decide which measures to obtain and which to leave behind, because we were pressing toward a version of the LFA that would be usable clinically. We chose the logic of eliminating redundancy. The domain of patient behavior represented by this data set was analyzed from what we call a cartographic point of view in order to map out the dominant terrain features. The analytic procedures were based on a Euclidean dimensionalization of the measurement space followed by an empirical identification of natural groupings or clusters of measures. Employing the reduction logic, the analysis worked upward in pyramid fashion to the point where far fewer data had to be collected to provide measurements indicative of the larger domain. Since the process began with complete descriptions and worked up the pyramid based on the data below, fewer and fewer data were needed to provide an adequate description of the whole domain. The objective was to chart the dominant features (clusters) in the measurement domain and then select one or a few key indicators of each cluster. This was a way to determine key behaviors indicating the functional health status of patients.

The analytic procedure developed to map out the data set was based on a geometric or dimensional approach. First, the variables were intercorrelated in order to locate obvious redundancy and to establish a common metric among the variables. A matrix of paired correlations represented the variance in the data set with a single measurement form (the correlation coefficient), while the variables were based on many measurement forms (e.g., frequency counts, elapsed time, proportions or rates, feet, hours, etc.). Raymond B. Cattell's logic for creating a correlation matrix with the chain P technique was used to link patients across occasions (weeks). Thus, the correlation matrix became a variables-by-variables square matrix with the n for each correlation being the total n of occasions (162 weeks).

407

BEHAVIORAL
INDICATORS OF
CLIENT PROGRESS
AFTER SPINAL
CORD INJURY

The second step in the mapping procedure was a principle-components factor analysis. This step had two purposes: to serve (1) as a descriptive aid in understanding the interrelations among the variables and (2) as a prelude to cluster analysis. Principal-components analysis as a prelude to clustering accomplished three important things. First, it provided a means for establishing an appropriate Euclidean dimensionalization of the measurement space based on the variance in the data matrix. Second, the loadings of the variables on the factors provided a standardized metric for scaling all of the variables in the n space uniformly. Finally, each variable could be located precisely in the Euclidean n space by a set of coordinates, the loadings on the factors. The output of the factor analysis was analyzed with a hierarchical cluster-analysis routine that operated on the straight-line Euclidean distance between the variables in the n space.

The correlation-factor-cluster procedure was keyed to the relationships among variables: it was a technique for establishing the topography of the whole domain of variables in the analysis. Given the direct monitoring of actual patient behavior, this technique provided the information needed to determine the smallest set of measures that represented the essential features of the larger domain.

The last step in the mapping analysis was to iterate the factor-cluster procedure on two partitionings of the data (early vs. late patients, paraplegics vs. quadriplegics), in order to check the stability or internal consistency of the structure of patient behavior.

Overall, the structure of patient performance revealed by these iterations of the factor–cluster procedure was remarkably clear. There was a tight and well-defined group of variables based on the unaided and patient-instigated bits of information in the chunk activity unit. Conceptually, these can be called measures of the dynamics of behavior. The second group of variables in the structure was not as tight and well defined as the behavior dynamics facet. The combination of these variables made a powerful conceptual argument for a second major facet in the measurement domain: environmental diversity or a behavioral/spatial facet. The clearest and most stable of the remaining minor facets was composed of involvement by family members in the behavior of the patients. These variables were included in the analysis in response to input by clinical personnel about what was considered important in rehabilitation. That they mapped as a clear and stable minor facet in the overall structure perhaps reflected the wisdom of accumulated clinical experience.

The map of the domain of patient performance was stable. That is, similar structure prevailed across the para–quad and early–late partitioning of the cases. There were some differences between the clusterings, but these differences only served to highlight and confirm the overall structure. For example, the changes in the clusterings were in the second major facet (behavioral/spatial or environmental diversity), demonstrating that the behavior of paraplegics and patients nearing discharge is more differentiated than the behavior of quadriplegics or patients near admission.

One constiuent measure was selected from each major cluster, yielding five key indicators of patient progress, that is, five behavioral vital signs: (1) independence (number of activities conducted without the help of anyone else); (2) activity level (number of activities); (3) time out of bed (number of hours per day out of bed, as measured by the instrumented rest time monitor); (4) mobility (number of feet traveled, as measured by the wheelchair odometer); and (5) family involvement (number of in-hospital activities in which members of the patients' families were involved).

In summary, we used a variety of unobtrusive direct-monitoring techniques, including direct behavioral observation and instrumented measures, to build a comprehensive and detailed data base describing the longitudinal behavior of patients during first hospitalization for comprehensive rehabilitation. The emphasis during this phase was on developing and refining direct monitoring procedures that produced data with high levels of reliability and accuracy. Since the analytic strategy began with complete descriptions (not assumptions) and worked up the reduction pyramid on the basis of data aggregated below, selecting indicator variables meant that fewer and fewer data were needed to provide a useful description of the whole domain. Once the topography of the data was established, benchmark measures could be selected for continued measurement. We refer to these indicator variables as *behavioral vital signs* indicating the functional health status of patients.

Having identified a manageable set of measures which, we hypothesized, would disclose important aspects of patient progress, we were confronted by two important questions: (1) How should the information be obtained in order to optimize yield per unit of effort and yet make the procedures usable by busy health care professionals? (2) How could we be sure that these candidates for inclusion in the LFA measured something meaningful? In sections 4 and 5, we deal with the first question; in section 6, we deal with the second.

4. Clinical Personnel as Estimators

We were led to members of the clinical staff as possible data gatherers by several factors: (1) many traditional modes of patient assessment are based on staff estimates or ratings of patients, (2) many treatment decisions seem to be based quite directly on the informal impressions and judgments of staff members, and (3) staff assessments promised to meet our requirements of efficiency because staff members work near patients and should be quite trainable.

We investigated the quality of staff estimates by obtaining both staff ratings and independent observational records of patient behavior. In the first phase, we measured the degree of consensus among treatment-team members and the degree of agreement between staff ratings and the observational records. In the second phase, we analyzed patterns of bias in staff judgments.

We compared staff members' weekly ratings of three behavioral criteria to observational measures of the same behaviors. The variables rated by the staff were *mobility* (the extent to which the patient gets around the hospital environment); *diversity* (the number of different kinds of activities the patient engages in); and *independence* (the rate at which the patient takes initiative for activities and does them without direct help).

409

BEHAVIORAL
INDICATORS OF
CLIENT PROGRESS
AFTER SPINAL
CORD INJURY

Treatment teams of patients with spinal cord injuries who were undergoing comprehensive rehabilitation made the ratings. A patient's treatment team consisted of six different types of staff members: physicians, physical and occupational therapists, social workers, and representatives of the nursing staff from the day and evening shifts. The instrument used to collect staff assessments of patient progress was a one-page form on which the raters indicated whether the patient's actual performance was better, the same as, or worse than during the previous week. Once a week, on Friday afternoons, the staff members made these assessments for each of the criterion variables. We compared these ratings to similar behavioral data generated from direct, concurrent observational monitoring of patients performed by an independent team of observers. Forty-eight patient-weeks of data were gathered.

Since staff members were asked to rate changes in levels of patient performance, corresponding measures of behavioral change were used for comparison, where a change score was the value of a measure for the present week minus its value the previous week. Staff ratings were coded 1 for positive change, 0 for no change, and -1 for negative change. Some data transformations were necessary in order to compare the trichotomous ratings with the continuous behavioral measures. The comparisons were based on two different strategies designated *absolute* and *arbitrary*. First, the observational data were trichotomized along absolute guidelines. That is, positive or negative changes in measures of performance were labeled *positive* or *negative* and only true zero changes were labeled *no change*. Because it seemed unreasonable to expect staff raters to detect very small changes in levels of performance, an arbitrary strategy was used to increase the probability of agreement. This second trichotomy subdivided each distribution of observational data to match the proportion of positive, negative, and no-change ratings observed in the staff assessments. For each distribution of change scores, the upper 58% were scored positive, the lower 5% negative, and the middle 37% no change.

Among results, it was possible to measure consensus or agreement among staff groups. The agreements were moderate at best; staff members' judgments displayed a great deal of disagreement.

To examine the relationship between staff ratings and corresponding behavioral measures, each week of hospital stay was regarded as a single data point. Measures of the three staff ratings and the corresponding behavioral measures were correlated. The correlations were all low and none were statistically significant (the median correlation was .14). In raw terms, staff ratings of change in patient performance showed very little agreement with independently observed measures of such change.

Since high interobserver agreement and rigorous sampling procedures supported the construct validity and sampling validity of the behavioral observation of patient performance, we next sought to determine how and why staff judgments differed from the behavioral standards.

First, we found the staff assessments to be insensitive to changes, especially negative changes. Although the treatment teams reported no change in patient performance 37% of the time, the behavioral measures showed no change only 8% of the time. Further, the staff ratings were negative 5% of the time, while the observational change scores were negative 37% of the time. Perhaps staff members perceive change in patient performance as a continuous, unidirectional progression. The staff are likely to be insensitive to deviations from this pattern, especially deviations that reflect decreasing performance. To examine these hypotheses, we calculated two new indices for each of 17 treatment-team members who had made at least five ratings: (1) the percentage of patient-weeks for which change in the direction of the patient's performance was rated and (2) the percentage of patient-weeks for which a negative rating was recorded. Typically, the staff members reported a lower percentage of change in patient performance than the observations indicated. In addition, the staff members reported a lower percentage of negative change than the behavior scores indicated. The median change percentage as assessed by the staff was only 42%, while the median change percentage derived from the behavioral change scores was 64%. Thus, the staff underestimated change in patient performance. The median negative change percentage assessed by the staff was only 4%, while the median negative change percentage derived from the behavioral change scores was 36.5%. Thus, the staff was insensitive to negative change in patient performance.

This test of staff members as estimators of patient behavior led us to several important conclusions:

1. Patient mobility yielded the highest rates of consensus, followed by diversity and independence. This may have been due to the fact that the behaviors associated with mobility are easily recognized and happen in more places, providing greater opportunity for recognition.
2. From the consensus data and from anecdotal information, there appeared to be a bias in levels of consensus according to how well individual patients were liked or disliked. The patient who was most liked by staff yielded the highest rates of consensus; the patient who seemed to give staff members the most difficult time yielded the lowest rates.
3. Little agreement was demonstrated between treatment-team ratings of mobility, diversity, and independence and corresponding behavioral measures obtained by observers.
4. Clinical personnel were more inclined to rate positively and much less inclined to rate negatively than was warranted by direct observations of patient behavior.

The insensitivity of treatment-team members to negative changes in levels of patient performance and the lack of congruence between team ratings and independent measurements were clear. Thus, it seems that recognition and rating of functional performance are skills which simply are not taught systematically to rehabilitation health care professionals. Although the various staff groups are skilled at providing their specific varieties of care, it does not seem that they are very adept at recognizing, measuring, or providing estimates of the very functional performances which they themselves are trying to teach. As long as staff members are not depended upon to evaluate the progress of patients in the domain of functional performance, this will not be problematic. However, the study does call into serious question the validity of any assessment system designed to measure patients' functional performance in rehabilitation that depends strictly upon estimates by raters who are also providers of care.

No matter what the precise explanation for the inability of clinical personnel

411

BEHAVIORAL
INDICATORS OF
CLIENT PROGRESS
AFTER SPINAL
CORD INJURY

to give accurate estimates of ongoing patient behavior, it was clear that our search for efficient data-gathering techniques would have to lead elsewhere. We were very much aware of the strengths of our original approach using independent observers and were somewhat attached to it, having spent so much time with it. However, its greatest liabilities for purposes of clinical application were that it required separate personnel as well as a relatively large investment of time and effort. Thus, we finally turned to the major remaining possibility: the patient.

5. Self-Observation and Report of Behavior

In our follow-up work with clients after discharge, we had had some positive experience with telephone contacts. Research personnel initiated phone calls to clients during evening hours and asked the clients to describe their activities of the day. Comparisons of data from the phone calls to data from continuous diaries kept by clients yielded high agreement. One of our colleagues had used independent observations to test the quality of data from self-reports in the form of describing daily behavior in evening interviews and had found the accuracy to be high. Encouraged by these experiences and sensing that depending on clients for self-reports of behavior would increase flexibility (because the observer is always with the target) and efficiency (the reporting time tends to be quite short), we developed a formal evaluation of clients as observers and reporters of their own behavior.

The Self-Observation and Report Technique (SORT) developed by our staff required the target person to monitor characteristics of his or her own molar behavior during designated periods of time and to report those events to a researcher retrospectively. The target person described, in a continuous manner, his or her ongoing behavior stream, in which the major parts could be (1) something he or she did (in the active sense); (2) something that was done to, happened to, or was done with the target person; and (3) segments in which the target person was overtly idle or passive. The researcher recorded this information as it was reported by the target person. The researcher's primary purpose, other than to record the reported information, was to provide prompts to assist the target person to reconstruct his or her own behavior stream during the designated period of time. The target person also supplied supportive information by indicating what other people did within that behavior stream. The resulting protocol appeared as a shorthand account of the activities of the target person. The coding process combined and condensed the information from the protocol into numerical form.

In order to test the adequacy of self-reports as a method for patient monitoring, we collected data on 10 patients. All participating patients were male, with an average age of 25.2 years. The monitored patients included some who were just beginning comprehensive rehabilitation and others who were near completion of their programs. Patients were trained in the monitoring technique and then were asked to monitor various characteristics of their own behavior and to report these events chronologically to a researcher at the end of a $4\frac{1}{2}$

hour period. Patients described the kind of activity performed, where it occurred, and whether assistance was given and by whom. The descriptions included such behaviors as dressing, medical treatments, and physical therapy exercises. In general, only behaviors lasting 5 minutes or more were reported. For each patient, the following types of data were gathered over a period of 2 weeks: (1) eight self-report records, each covering 4½ hours; (2) eight 90-minute observations by independent observers, superimposed on the periods of patient self-report: (3) ten 5-minute observations by independent observers, conducted during the periods of patient self-report; (4) continuous recording of out-of-bed time by means of the rest-time monitor placed under the patient's mattress; and (5) two retrospective 90-minute reports of patient behavior, made by independent observers and superimposed on the patient self-reports and the continuous monitoring by independent observers.

The picture that emerged was quite clear and full of implications for our effort to develop clinically usable tools. For example, the single self-report periods, the four self-reports for a whole week, and the eight self-reports for a given subject all agreed with independent observers on the number of patient activities at percentage rates ranging from 83% to 86%. All three modes for sampling self-reports yielded data of acceptable quality. Similarly, patient self-reports and independent observers agreed at about a 90% rate on whether or not help (aid) was given by someone else. This high agreement on aid was gratifying because we have placed a great deal of emphasis on the rate of activities without aid as a measure of behavioral independence.

Hospital staff members often report to each other about patient progress in terms of week-long periods, and we have developed the habit of rendering LFA information for clinical personnel in terms of weeks. The extent of correlation between self-reports and independent observers for a number of important measures derived for each week was generally high (ranging from .60 to .88). In terms of a very different criterion of accuracy, the number of bed transfers reflected in self-reports agreed quite well with the number of transfers indicated by the unobtrusive instrumentation. More importantly, comparisons of instrumented measures and independent observations on days when patients made self-reports to days on which they made no self-reports indicated that the process of self-reporting is not reactive.

We calculated paired agreements for self-reports, continuous independent observations, and retrospective independent observations for the percentage of monitored time accounted for in exactly the same way. The fact that the two comparisons involving self-reports yielded slightly lower percentages than the comparison involving only independent observations suggested that self-reporting produces a slight error rate, but this is clearly not large enough to rule out self-reporting as an acceptable means of patient monitoring. This conclusion was supported by paired correlations among self-reports, continuous independent observations, and retrospective independent observations for six derived behavioral measures. Overall, it seems clear that retrospective reporting as a part of the self-reporting process was not injurious to the quality of data. When there was a problem (never serious), it seemed to be associated with the self-reporting component.

Overall, self-reports of behavior by patients held up well as a means for

413

BEHAVIORAL
INDICATORS OF
CLIENT PROGRESS
AFTER SPINAL
CORD INJURY

gathering LFA data. This finding was extremely important for two reasons. First, it meant that good data on functional performance by patients could be gathered on a relatively continuing basis in clinical settings where members of the hospital staff would find it impossible to carry out independent observations. Second, the finding meant that we could, with some confidence, now use a method that enhanced the flexibility of data gathering to a remarkable extent. That is, reports could come from times and places and for extended periods that would be very hard to monitor by means of independent observations. All in all, this finding was one of the most important in our whole program of research, since we could now package our point of view and a usable technique for clinical application. In fact, we are using the SORT approach exclusively in several clinical demonstrations now under way. Patients and clinical personnel all seem quite comfortable with the procedure.

Two other facets of our use of self-reports are worth mentioning. First, the patients *describe* behavior (as well as locations and other persons involved) and do *not* provide estimates of quantity or magnitude (e.g., "How often did you . . .," "How much can you . . ."). It just may be that people are good describers but poor estimators. Second, the behavior that patients reported varied remarkably from one hospital setting to another. This powerful setting dependency of behavior is one of the most common findings of our research program. The independent observers in our evaluation of the SORT observed patients in many different settings, but the amount of agreement between SORT data and observational data did not vary appreciably with the setting in which the observed or reported behavior occurred. In other words, although patient behavior was very setting-dependent, the intermodal agreement between self and observer *about* that behavior was not. This is a very important finding in our overall evaluation of the SORT.

Having selected key indicators of patient behavior in terms of the extent to which they represented the aftermath of spinal cord injury, having explored several ways to obtain the data, and having found the patient to be a dependable and efficient reporter of the data, we were confronted next by the question of how worthwhile the data were.

6. Prediction of Outcomes

We had found the LFA measures to be valued by clinical personnel and to relate in sensible and meaningful ways to other phenomena, such as patient mood, medical complications, and other significant events in the lives of patients. The logic of our next evaluation was that the extent to which LFA measures predicted meaningful long-range outcomes would be a crucial basis for assessing their validity and their usefulness as indicators of patient progress.

The objective of our evaluation was to identify LFA measures during hospitalization that would predict performance after discharge. The indicators of outcome included a measure of independence in activities, a measure of mobility and participation in the larger community, and a measure of medical status.

We observed and calculated three measures of performance for each week of 14 patients' hospitalizations—independence, diversity, and level of activity— on the basis of the results of the previous selections (see section 3). *Independence* is the proportion of behavior units that patients completed without assistance. *Diversity* is the number of different kinds of behaviors. *Level of activity* is the total number of behavior units performed by patients for a specified period of time. Our previous research had demonstrated that (1) patient behavior varied widely from one setting to another within the hospital, (2) the way patients carried out behaviors also varied, and (3) there were powerful variations among settings in the rate of growth and behavioral development displayed by patients over time. On the basis of these findings, we focused on three major settings within the hospital—the ward, physical and occupational therapy, and public areas—which accounted for over 90% of the activities patients completed in all hospital settings. Measuring the three kinds of behavior within the three settings yielded a 3 × 3 matrix. In addition to the matrix of intrasetting indicators, the observations yielded an intersetting index of mobility, or the movement of patients from setting to setting within the hospital.

Data from two intervals during hospitalization were analyzed in order to determine the relative predictive power of measures obtained early in hospitalization and close to discharge. The early interval sampled each patient's performance during the first three weeks after the patient began using a wheelchair. The later interval sampled each patient's performance during the last 3 weeks prior to discharge from the hospital. After the patients were discharged, self-reports of behavior were used to document their daily activities. Independence and the proportion of activities completed away from home were calculated from these records. (The proportion of activities conducted away from home provides one indicator of patients' involvement in the community.) The third indicator was obtained from the records of the rehabilitation center: the number of readmissions to the center during the 18-month interval after the initial discharge from the comprehensive rehabilitation program. The readmissions represented the frequency of medical problems such as urinary tract infections, decubitus ulcers, or phlebitis.

The behaviors observed during hospitalization predicted postdischarge outcomes to a dramatic extent. For example, the higher the patients' behavioral diversity and independence in the hospital, the lower (more favorable) the rate of medical complications and unscheduled readmissions after discharge (multiple r of .62). The more diverse the patients' behaviors during hospitalization, the greater was their involvement in the community after discharge (multiple r of .66). Mobility during hospitalization also predicted community involvement.

These findings suggested that the behavior of patients during hospitalization for comprehensive rehabilitation is a powerful predictor of behavioral and medical outcomes after discharge. In general, higher levels of performance, especially in therapies, were associated with higher levels of independence after discharge and lower levels of medical complications requiring readmission to the rehabilitation center. High levels of performance, especially mobility, during hospitalization were related to high levels of participation in the larger community after discharge. The signs of these relationships were all in the expected directions, but it is worth noting that the magnitudes of these relationships were unusually large. Even after adjustment for the size of the sample, relatively large portions

415

BEHAVIORAL
INDICATORS OF
CLIENT PROGRESS
AFTER SPINAL
CORD INJURY

of variance in the outcome variables were accounted for by behavioral measures obtained during hospitalization. If personnel and funds were in short supply, our results suggest that two indicators alone could be used for monitoring. Tallying the number of different kinds of behaviors the patient completed in therapies and recording mobility with a wheelchair odometer would provide at least an approximation of the essence of behavioral progress and prediction of outcomes for patients with spinal cord injuries.

7. Concluding Comments

We have described some benchmarks in our attempt to develop a new set of measures of client progress after spinal cord injury. We started by measuring very extensively because so little was known about which measures were best. We developed a good deal of confidence in that early measurement system, but we knew that we could not use it forever, especially not for clinical purposes. We took some significant steps toward determining which were the most significant measures. Then, after making several attempts to develop manageable and cost-efficient ways to get the data, we came back to self-observation and report by clients themselves as the optimal method.

Experienced workers in rehabilitation who see the same patient one or more times a day develop a general feel for how the patient is performing. However, what is usually lacking is a reliable, quantitative, composite picture of how the patient performs throughout a given day, the size of daily fluctuations, and the trends from week to week for various activities. By the nature of the rehabilitation process (which divides patient activity and assessment among a variety of team members), no single person or discipline is in a position to have firsthand information concerning how a patient performs during a 24-hour period or even an 8-hour shift. Staff meetings, the patient's record, and even team rounds that include the patient generally provide only a partial and rather static view of what is essentially a dynamic process. Team rounds attempt to construct an overall picture of the patient by bringing together the bits and pieces of information scattered among the various disciplines and individual staff members. This mosaic approach to assessing the patient is at best incomplete and fragmentary; some groups are not represented at rounds (e.g., nurses' aides), and often the staff members at rounds report on patients they are not personally treating. This fragmented view of the patient and lack of continuity in how the patient is monitored all preclude a composite picture of performance. Traditional techniques for the collection, storage, retrieval, and exchange of information are limited and imperfect. Nowhere under traditional procedures can a professional obtain the thread of patient performance that runs through the various components of delivery and experience.

Within this fragmentation and lack of true functional assessment, techniques that fill the gaps will improve patient care by attuning it more directly to patient performance. No professional person's role spans the gaps, but we offer a reliable information-assessment system that will. With a continuous, explicit, and integrated data system, decisions (e.g., regarding discharge) can become more direct, timely, and personalized. By adding continuity, objectivity, and reliability where there is now only rather global, diffuse, and frequently subjective judgment, the LFA provides a unique information base to make major decisions regarding the rehabilitation process more rational, more coordinated, more integrated, and more individualized.

To date, our work has produced a number of developments and conclusions that bear on these issues in important ways. Illustrations, data, demonstrations, or descriptions are available for most of these conclusions:

1. It is possible to obtain longitudinal measures that are theoretically, clinically, and intuitively sound (i.e., they chart the course of patient performance over time in ways that are interpretable and useful).
2. Such measures can be obtained throughout hospitalization and for an extended period after discharge.
3. The measurements are reliable and valid.
4. The time and effort required to gather and analyze the measures have been reduced to a clinically manageable level.
5. The techniques are ready for use by professionals in rehabilitation.
6. There are distinctive patterns of change in performance over time that permit patients and their outcomes to be classified in terms of performance profiles.
7. It is possible to construct longitudinal norms of performance against which the status and progress of individual patients can be evaluated.
8. The conceptualization of the LFA and the methods and data involved in its development have proved useful to professionals in a number of areas.
9. With the LFA, a distinctive viewpoint has emerged regarding rehabilitation, health status, and assessment for spinal cord injury.
10. A relatively small number of measures are key indicators of progress (behavioral vital signs). Thus, it is feasible to construct an efficient and practical tool based on these measures.
11. Data on patient performance can be used to evaluate hospital programs.
12. Measures of patient performance yielded by the LFA are useful to clinical teams in judging patient progress. There is promise that the LFA will provide the unifying thread among the rehabilitation staff which will permit the development of truly coordinated, integrated, and individualized programs for clients.
13. The strategy for development of the LFA, as well as its specific measures, are applicable to various client groups.

Issues in Patient Compliance

PARK O. DAVIDSON

The literature on compliance is extensive, and an exhaustive review of its substance would probably only have the singular effect of forcing Peter Suedfeld
to consider revising his publication (1975) on the benefits of boredom. Reviews
of the compliance literature have recently been published (Haynes, Taylor, &
Sackett, 1979: Stuart & Davidson, 1981) for those who wish to learn from the
details. I would prefer instead to draw attention to some important issues of this
literature. In doing so we must also note some favored "hobbyhorses"* that need
to be either exorcized or written about (depending on your verbal acuity).

Actually there is not one literature on compliance but four or five—generally
mutually exclusive in regard to cross-referencing, professional orientation, and
even definition of the term *compliance*.

Perhaps I can attune you to the discordance of this literature by recalling
the comments of four colleagues who represent what we were taught in Sunday
school to call "friends of different persuasions" regarding the nature of compliance. To protect the professional anonymity of my friends, let's just call them
a prepaid practitioner, a prisoner of a dilemma, a professional "person," and
. . . a token freak.

Their comments (*verbatim*) to my expressed interest in therapeutic compliance were as follows. The practitioner: "Did you not advise us just last week,
Mr. Davidson, that the Ontario psychologists were only joking about wanting to
administer drugs?" The prisoner: "An explanation of dyadic interactions for
therapeutic compliance requires a specification of the equity behaviors of the
parties involved in the exchange." The professional: "Who the hell do you think

This chapter is based on the author's presidential address to the Canadian Psychological Association, published in the *Canadian Psychological Review*, 1976, *17*, 247–259.

*An unfortunate choice of words from an earlier source (Davidson, 1970).

PARK O. DAVIDSON   •   Late of the Department of Psychology, University of British Columbia,
Vancouver, British Columbia, Canada.

compliance is therapeutic *for*, sir?" And you can easily anticipate the token freak: "S delta, S delta, man. What are the contingencies?"

Well, where does one begin? With *more* anonymous friends I suppose. I looked up *compliance* in an unabridged dictionary and it was like renewing old acquaintances. Four different meanings are given for the term. See if you recognize them *pari passu*.

1. The act of acquiescing, yielding or obeying
2. To act in accordance, to cooperate, or to conform
3. A tendency to yield to others, especially in a weak or subservient way
4. A coefficient expressing the responsiveness of a mechanical system to a periodic force

I should note parenthetically that I also looked up *compliance* in Chaplin's *Dictionary of Psychology* (1968) and found "making one's desires conform to the wishes of others"—a definition so removed from the unabridged versions that I had to glance at the cover to see if I hadn't picked up Alex Comfort's thesaurus by mistake.

Clearly we must decide whether these disparate viewpoints on compliance represent views through a looking glass or blind men groping at an elephant.

Let us begin with the tale from medical literature.

1. Medical Compliance

For as long as we have records of human behavior, people troubled in body or mind have sought help from medical practitioners and complied or not complied with the various treatments proferred. One thing the history of medicine has clearly demonstrated is that compliance is not a simple function of treatment efficacy. Indeed, many early examples may suggest that *non*compliance was often a necessary precursor to survival. As late as 1898, Sir William Osler was recommending mercury for the treatment of influenza and full-dosage strychnine for the convalescent period.

Prior to the Renaissance, the question of compliance was not usually open to the patient in medicine. Physicians had little interest in whether a patient complied or not because the treatments (e.g., trephining, leeching, bloodletting, purgatives, alchemy) were administered (by force if necessary) rather than being prescribed.

The major medical interest in compliance arose partly out of sociopolitical change (recognition of individuals' rights) and partly out of increased use of drugs in medical treatment—both changes that occurred in the 1800s. Medical practice increasingly involved the now familiar procedure of doctor prescribing, pharmacist supplying, and patient swallowing. If we look at the *Codex medicamentarius* of 1758 we may, with 20th-century hindsight, express amazement that any rational patient would *want* to comply. Obsolete preparations such as mummy skull, ground placenta, and urine had been removed during the previous decade, but the authors were proud of their increased ability to standardize varieties of animal dung (cf. Grinnel & Sweeney, 1974). It is appalling to read of the different kinds of guava, bird droppings, mice, lizards, and so on that were used as medications. The commonly known bovine variety of dung was notably absent from the typology. I guess that it wasn't considered therapeutic until closer to the time of Freud.

Although one might silently hope that compliance rates were very low in those times, any condescension toward those regimens must be dampered by the realization that, over 200 years later, the *Vademecum International* was listing substances such as thalidomide.

Which brings me to my first proscription. We have a much greater (and prior) ethical requirement to assure the efficacy of a treatment than to ensuring compliance. The worst combinations of coerced compliance with ethically and therapeutically questionable techniques have created problems of professional practice for some of our colleagues that can and should be avoided in the future.

Reviewing the *current* medical literature on therapeutic compliance, one is left with the uneasy feeling that noncompliance is considered vaguely sinful. From the physicians' viewpoint, there must be something wrong with the patient who does not comply with a medical regimen, and much research is designed to find out what. According to this viewpoint, the definition of *compliance* is "the extent to which the patient adheres to the treatment as prescribed." Obviously this definition gives all the blame (or credit) to the patient (cf. Sackett, 1974). Furthermore, it assumes that compliance is a consistent trait or behavior in a given individual.

I am surprised that there are extremely few compliance studies (in any of the literature reviewed) that address the question of personal consistency. One study (Caron & Roth, 1968) reported that ulcer patients' compliance with diet restrictions was not related to their faithfulness in taking antacid therapy. Bowers (1977) cautions us that psychologists (like Othello) are sometimes misled by what meets the eye. Personal consistency has been resurrected by Bowers in the character of Iago (more or less) when some of us would have preferred a characterization of, alas, poor Yorick.

Attempts have been made recently to develop a nonjudgmental definition of medical compliance as "the extent to which a person's behavior coincides with medical or health advice" (Haynes, 1979). Such a definition attempts to place no specific blame on the dispositions of the patient, the behaviors of the physician, or the characteristics of the situation. However, physicians are clearly on the trait side of the dispositional–situational controversy (Bowers, 1973) when it comes to explaining compliance. This is evidenced by the kinds of variables they look for to explain the phenomena and also, I guess, by the consistent lack of results they obtain.

Therapeutic compliance is reported in the medical literature as unrelated to—among other things—the following:

1. Age (cf. Borofsky, Louis, Kutt, & Roginsky, 1972; Wilcox, Gillan, & Hare, 1965)
2. Sex (cf. Becker, 1974; Bynum, Eldredge, Frank, MacWhinney, McNabb, Scheiner, Sumpler, & Iker, 1967) but more about that later
3. Race (cf. Blackwell, 1972; Neely & Patrick, 1968)
4. Religion (cf. Davis, 1968; Morrow & Rabin, 1966)

5. Education (cf. Francis, Korsch, & Morris, 1969; Maddock, 1967)
6. Socioeconomic status (cf. Becker, Drackman, & Kirscht, 1972; Kasl, 1975; Wilson, 1973)
7. Type of illness (cf. Lendrum & Kobrin, 1956; Roth & Berger, 1960)
8. Onset of illness (cf. Gordis, Markowitz, & Lilienfeld, 1969; Marston, 1970)
9. Attitudes toward doctor (cf. Korsch, Gozzi, & Francis, 1968; Zola, 1972, 1973), illness (cf. Hochbaum, 1958; Taylor, 1979; Watts, 1966), death (cf. Davis, 1968; Vincent, 1971)
10. Personality measures such as the MMPI, Rorschach, TAT (cf. Becker, 1974a,b; and Hellmuth, 1966) tests of introversion/extraversion (cf. Davis, 1968), locus of control (cf. Best & Steffy, 1975; Hall & Hall, 1974), and willingness to take risks (cf. Marston, 1969)

In case any of you are tempted to take futures in situationalism because the dispositional group has a corner on the market for nonsignificant differences, I should also note that therapeutic compliance is reportedly unrelated to such a diversity of situations as:

1. Doctor–patient interaction (cf. Davis, 1968; Kasl, 1975)
2. Type of agency the client attends (cf. Davis, 1967; Wilson, 1973)
3. Family interaction of the patient (cf. Oakes, Ward, & Gray, 1970; Porter, 1969)
4. Distance to the site of treatment (cf. Francis *et al.*, 1969)

To this list might be added a master's degree at Yale Medical School that was awarded for the failure to demonstrate a relationship between compliance and weather conditions (Jonas, 1973). General reviews of this medical literature are available in Haynes *et al.* (1979) and Stuart and Davidson (1981).

This litany of failure does not mean that variables significantly affecting compliance cannot be found. As a matter of fact, the very first research I conducted after my Ph.D. was to examine compliance by parents with recommendations given to them by child psychiatrists in a child guidance clinic consultation (Davidson & Schrag, 1969). Factors which we found to affect compliance were (in order of importance) parental attitude toward the child's problem, amount of the psychiatrist's experience, whether both parents accompanied the child, and (most interesting to me) how long they had to wait in the waiting room on the day of the appointment. It didn't matter how many days (or months!) they had to wait to get the appointment, but if they were kept cooling their heels in the waiting room more than an hour, compliance dropped 40% below what it was with less than a half-hour wait. [This finding has an interesting relationship to social exchange theories of compliance, to be discussed later (cf. Schwartz, 1974).]

In our study of almost 800 children, fewer than 50% of the families had carried out the recommendations made to them at the initial consultation. This figure is not unusually low in comparison to the available literature on the magnitude of compliance. Haynes *et al.*, reviewing this literature to 1979, reported the degree of compliance of patients to appointment-keeping was only 50%. Taking medication for prevention when short-term compliance is required,

60% to 80% were compliant; for long-term prophylaxis, a mean of 50%. For long-term medication to *cure* a disorder, the mean is about 50%. It seems that about one-third of the patients are always compliant, one-third sometimes, and one-third never. The reviews available report compliance ranging from 87% down to a low of 7% (Gillum & Barsky, 1974; Sackett, 1974; Wilson, 1973).

The magnitude of noncompliance has important implications for the health delivery system, with its increased emphasis on prevention and on home care. The increasing concern about costs in the health delivery system these days has resulted in a few studies examing cost figures of noncompliance (Becker & Maiman, 1975). The compliance rates reported in the medical literature are oversimplified. There is often an implicit assumption that noncompliance represents an occurrent phenomenon somewhat like an infectious disease, for which we need only find the proper prescription for cure independent of context. A number of nostrums are peddled under trade names such as "will power" and "motivation" or in such catch phrases as "the patient's need for increased trust in competent medical authority." These restoratives usually come candy-coated for oral ingestion—and sometimes, I'm afraid, as suppositories.

In those instances where compliance is seen as a dispositional construct rather than an occurrent event, almost invariably it is conceptualized as having a unidimensional exemplar (i.e., doing exactly what the authority—read "doctor"—told you to do).

Quite apart from the empirical question of whether compliant behavior is multidimensional, this view ignores differences in the conditions antecedent to compliance and in the nature of the request. Thus, in calculating noncompliance you can presumably score as high for failing to make one phone call to a consultant's secretary as for failing to inject yourself with insulin 3,000 times over a period of years. The development of more systematic and objective methods for classifying patients as compliant or noncompliant has just begun (Feinstein, 1979; Gordis, 1979).

In addition to the concern with more accurate measurement of compliance and its effects, there is an increasing interest in improving compliance behavior. To do this, we may need to identify and examine antecedent conditions to compliant behavior more systematically.

2. Social Compliance

Probably the most systematic attempts to control, manipulate, and measure antecedents occur in the social psychology literature on compliance. This literature (almost totally divorced from the clinical literature) grew out of early attempts to understand dyadic interactions—particularly as they related to opinion or attitude change.

Many theorists (e.g. Adams, 1965; Blau, 1964; Homans, 1974; Thibaut & Kelley, 1959) have analyzed dyadic interaction in terms of a reciprocal exchange of rewards and costs. A proposition that is common to these theories is that individuals in an interaction try to ensure that the rewards or gains from a relationship exceed the costs of the exchange (Chadwick-Jones, 1976). For example, Homans (1974) assumes that an interaction will cease if it is not mutually reinforcing for the parties involved. Homans, however, noted that the experience of mutual reward did not guarantee satisfaction with the exchange unless the distribution of reward was such that the reward received by the parties was in proportion to their contributions to the exchange.

Consideration of the theoretical and practical importance of perceived justice or injustice in dyadic exchange resulted in the Adams (1965) formulation of equity theory. Adams's theory was developed with employer–employee exchanges in mind, but he pointed out that the theory was also applicable to other social situations.

2.1. Social Exchange

Much of the equity research has been concerned with simulated crimes against victims (although the subjects of some of these studies might charitably be designated as simulated victimless crimes). Walster, Berscheid, and Walster (1973) have hypothesized the applicability of equity theory to intimate relationships and helping relationships. Empirical tests of social exchange theory predictions in these areas are scarce (cf. Lupri, 1969; Scanzoni, 1970, 1972), but a number of potentially valuable ideas for understanding therapeutic compliance do emerge. Most obvious is the need to analyze the inputs and outputs of the exchanges that lead to compliant behavior. Although behavior modification types would be happier talking about an applied behavioral analysis of compliant behavior (see Zifferblatt, 1975), the social exchange theorists point out a number of critical variables that would probably be overlooked by the behaviorist crowd.

In social exchange terms, compliance by a subordinate with a superior's task norms represents a type of social exchange gift to the superior (Nord, 1969). When a superior confers social gifts on a subordinate, the subordinate is obligated (according to the norms of social exchanges) to reciprocate. A salient mode of reciprocation is compliance with the superior's directions. However, if the subordinate believes that the gift was conferred with manipulative intent, then, according to Brehm's (1966) theory of social reactance, it should lead to the subordinate's refusal to return the favor (i.e., noncompliance). Let's translate this into an example of therapeutic compliance. Suppose a therapist expressed high confidence in a patient's ability to follow a regimen (pill taking, new diet, whatever). One could ask what situational parameters would determine whether this high-confidence expression would have a social exchange effect (compliance by the patient) or a psychological reactance effect (noncompliance). As an example, one such parameter might be the amount of surveillance maintained by the therapist over the patient. High surveillance has been demonstrated to reduce compliance in a variety of organizational studies (cf. Organ, 1974), and Lepper and Greene (1975) have shown that adult surveillance leads to significant reductions in target behaviors for classroom settings. Paradoxically, the medical literature (Gillum & Barsky, 1974) suggests high surveillance as significant for increased compliance. Perhaps patient playing sick roles in present-day society perceive high surveillance by their doctors as an unexpected social favor that obligates them to increased compliance by way of reciprocity. Clearly, an empirical test of surveillance effects could help to resolve the apparent paradox.

Social power theory (French & Raven, 1959) draws our attention to the power base of the influencing individual in producing compliant behavior. A variety of power bases have been identified—including expert, legitimate, referent, coercive, reward, and informational power (Leet-Pellegrini & Rubin, 1974, rated the latter three as most likely to elicit compliance). Ross (1973) investigated parental compliance utilizing two different power sources—expert and referent. Using lower-class black mothers of preschool children as subjects, recommendations were made to each of them to send away for free aids to improve her child's perceptual–motor development. Ross found compliance was greater with recommendations given by white experts than with those made by a black peer. Crisci and Kassinove (1973) demonstrated that recommendations made by a psychologist who called himself "Doctor" were complied with by mothers significantly more often than when he called himself "Mister" (a finding that should have some relevance to discussion of legislative changes for registration of psychologists!). Incidentally, teachers are not responsive to the expert power implied by "Doctor" (for psychologists at least), according to Frankel and Kassinove, 1974. A few politicians have a similar conceptual handicap.

Some readers will also be interested to note that sex of the psychologist or therapist apparently does not represent a differential power base in influencing behavior compliance. While we are looking at power bases, I should comment further on sex roles. (The literature on sex differences in compliance has generally been concerned with the kind of compliance that is modified by the attribute *dominance* rather than by the adjective *therapeutic*.) There is considerable evidence (Macoby & Jacklin, 1974) that preschool girls are more likely to comply with adults' directions. This difference disappears and perhaps even reverses with either school age or school environment. Some studies are now showing that boys are more compliant than girls in the school-age range (cf. Redd, Amen, Meddock, & Winston, 1974). In compliance to pressure from age mates, studies across six cultures showed neither sex as more compliant. In the relatively impersonal situation that is involved in persuasive communication, no consistent sex differences are found (Macoby & Jacklin, 1974). Finally, I should note, for those of you who don't already know, that married women are reported to be more noncompliant than single women and single men are more noncompliant than married men (Vincent, 1971).

2.3. Social Influence

Kelman (1961), in his classical work on processes of opinion change, tried to identify the mechanisms through which social influence operates.

He called his three sources of social influence:

1. Compliance—said to occur when an individual accepts influence from another because he or she hopes to achieve a favorable reaction from the other.
2. Identification—occurs when an individual accepts influence from another because the behavior is associated with a satisfying relationship to

the other. The agent's attractiveness is seen as the critical source of power for this kind of influence.

3. Internalization—involves accepting influence because the induced behavior is useful for solving a problem or maximizing one's values. The agent's credibility is crucial to this kind of influence.

Although clinicians would tend to lump these three sources together under the generic term *compliance,* the distinction has persisted in the social psychology literature, based on the type of behavior in which the induced response is embedded. Compliance in Kelman's sense involved studying the effects of external demands and coercion on attitude change. The most prolific exemplification of this process is the literature on forced compliance.

2.4. Forced Compliance

Studies of the ways in which novel "counterattitudinal" coerced behaviors might produce attitude change became doubly fashionable in the late '50s and early '60s, because the studies appeared consistent with the development of cognitive dissonance theory (Festinger, 1957). The literature on forced compliance and all its complexities has been reviewed elsewhere (cf. Collins & Hoyt, 1972). Much of this literature may appear to be irrelevant to the problems of clinical compliance (being concerned more with the essay-writing behaviors of university sophomores and with what constitute dissonance-producing underpayments or overpayments in these days of changing social and dollar values). The kind of forced-compliance paradigm that *does* appear to be relevant relates to the studies which demonstrate a negative relationship between the amount of pressure exerted and the amount of change produced. (Such studies could more properly be labeled *subtly induced compliance—forced compliance* is clearly a misnomer.) This compliance paradigm was originally thought by Kelman (1958) and also Festinger (1957) to relate to the kind of temporary situation-specific attitude change that would disappear as soon as the social pressure was removed. Ironically, subsequent research has demonstrated that these procedures produce enduring changes not only in attitudes but also in behavior. Schoolchildren have been enticed to eat disliked vegetables and to give up favored toys; equipment has been recalibrated to entice subjects to withstand more pain; housewives have been enticed to sign safe-driving petitions and to have large, unattractive safe-driving signs planted on their lawns; and sexually dysfunctional females have been made vibrantly orgasmic!

It has been difficult to predict whether and under what circumstances a particular forced-compliance procedure would produce attitude or behavior change, but there is ample evidence that once established, the changes that result are stable over time, over differing situations, and over differing environments. Collins and Hoyt (1972) provide an interesting explanation of the necessary conditions under which forced compliance produces behavioral change. They propose that the necessary condition for demonstrating this compliance effect is that the subject must feel personally responsible for an act which appears to have important consequences. Compliance to a therapeutic regimen in a clinical setting should have important consequences for the patient, but one of the implications of defining oneself in a sick role is abrogation of personal responsibility. To obtain the desired long-term generalized behavior changes with minimal surveillance or coercion, we may have to manipulate the therapist–patient relationship in ways that encourage the individual to accept responsibility for complying with the therapuetic regimen. The most promising approaches for increasing personal responsibility for compliance seem to be behavioral self-management strategies. These include Meichenbaum's (1977) self-instructional methods and Kanfer's (1979) transfer-enhancing procedures. A number of self-management programs have been specifically designed to enhance compliance, and I will review their success in a later section.

2.5. Attribution Processes

Attribution theory and research (Kelley, 1967) have suggested that self-attributed behavior changes are maintained to a greater extent than behavior changes attributed to an external agent or force. A classic experiment by Davison and Valins (1969) demonstrated this principle with an experimental analogue of drug therapy. Pain-tolerance levels for shock were obtained, then all subjects were given a drug (actually a placebo) and the shock test was readministered with the intensities surrepititiously halved. Thus all subjects believed that the drug had increased their pain tolerance. Half the subjects were told that the drug was in fact a placebo. This group then attributed the behavior change to themselves. On follow-up testing, when neither group was under the influence of drugs, the self-attribution group tolerated significantly more shock than the external-attribution group. The authors argued that self-attribution permitted the subjects to infer that something about their shock-taking ability had changed— as opposed to inferring that a temporary state had been brought about by the drug. Bowers (1975), in an ingenious study, led subjects to observe a change in their preference behavior using posthypnotic suggestion. Half the subjects received concurrent verbal reinforcement for their observed behavioral change; the other subjects had no external cues to explain their new behavior. The self-attribution group showed significantly greater persistence of behavior than the group who attributed the change to the contingent reinforcement. Kopel and Arkowitz (1975) provide a good review of the role of attribution in behavior change.

Two concepts closely related to self-attribution are internal locus of control (Lefcourt, 1976) and sense of self-efficacy (Bandura, 1977). Studies by Dweck (1975) and Hanel (1974, as cited in Heckhausen, 1975) have shown successful alteration of children's attributions and cognitive style by using self-instructional training procedures. There are suggestions in the literature that an external locus-of-control orientation in adults can also be changed by "attribution therapy" (cf. Valins & Nisbett, 1976).

Increasing a patient's feelings of self-efficacy generally involves teaching specific self-management skills that give the patient alternate perceptions of (and responses to) situations that otherwise evoke the conclusion "I can't do this." An increased sense of self-efficacy partly determines the persistence with which coping behavior will be sustained and hence has obvious relevance to compliance (Wilson, 1980a). For example, conceptualizing compliance behavior as a skill-acquisition process would encourage self-attribution (cf. Cameron, 1978).

Some social psychologists have made distinctions between intrinsic and extrinsic motivation (see Deci, 1975, and Staw, 1975, for current reviews of this area). Bem (1967, 1972) suggests that one will be more likely to perceive oneself to be extrinsically motivated if one is provided with a strong reward for the behavior. This *self-perception* effects subsequent behavior changes. A number of studies—variously called "forbidden toy" studies, "resistance to temptation" studies, or self-control studies—have demonstrated that (for children, at least) mild threats are superior to severe threats for long-term response inhibition, which represents the compliant behavior in these studies (Freedman, 1965; Pepitone, McCauley, & Hammond, 1967). Lepper and his associates (cf. Lepper & Greene, 1976) suggest that the mild threat permits the child to make self-attributions that facilitate compliance to the task, be it to refrain from cheating, playing with a favored toy, or disrupting a classroom.

A number of conceptually similar studies have demonstrated that over-emphasis on external rewards decreases behavioral persistence—presumably because of decreased intrinsic motivation. Ross (1975) has recently demonstrated that children's continued interest in a play activity declined with increased salience of the reward associated with that activity. Ross, therefore, questions the efficacy of using anticipated contingent rewards to control behavior.

I think Ross is addressing an important issue here, but not quite specifically enough for our interest. He is not, I am sure, implying that we should abandon contingent reinforcement for behavioral control but that we need to rethink the principles of its use. Kopel and Arkowitz (1975) argue for the adoption of a principle of least powerful reward or punishment for therapeutic behavior change. Although powerful rewards and punishments may be useful to initiate a new behavior or change a well-established one, continued compliance to the new regimen may require decreasing the relevant stimuli so that patients or clients have a greater opportunity to attribute their behavior control to themselves. Kanfer (1977, 1979) recognizes a similar need in suggesting that low extrinsic reinforcement may facilitate maintenance of behavior under self-regulation.

3. Behavioral Compliance

Clearly, if behaviorists were to embrace the findings from attribution studies by their social colleagues, efforts should be made to maximize self-control strategies for fulfilling the requirements of therapeutic regimens. Indeed, self-management technology is becoming a very fashionable research area in clinical psychology (cf. Mahoney & Thoreson, 1974; Schmidt, 1976; Stuart, 1977). I am sorry to report, however, that this self-management technology has proceeded without much attention to the social literature. It appears as if the research on self-management procedures had succeeded in rediscovering the original forced-compliance effect; many situational pressures are situation-specific and remain effective only so long as surveillance and social pressure are maintained. Although there are notable exceptions in the work of Kanfer (1977) and Meichenbaum (1977), most of the studies of maintenance of behavior change have focused on broadening the range of situations over which surveillance and reward contingencies could be operated. Many therapists and clinical researchers have yet to learn the lessons available in the literature on forced compliance. The very stimulus and reinforcement conditions which maximize response training (maximal reinforcement, restricted freedom of alternate responses, etc.) inhibit compliance with maintenance of the changed behavior once it passes beyond the direct control of therapy.

Several current reviews of the self-management literature are available (cf. Stuart, 1977). We can extract from this literature four relevant themes, two of which are generally consistent in increasing compliance and two which should be relevant but are conceptually and empirically problematic.

3.1. Self-Reinforcement

To deal with problems first, let us look at the self-reinforcement literature developed and maintained by Kanfer and his associates. One could expect that compliant behavior followed by pleasant consequences, or reduction of aversive consequences, should be more likely to recur—particularly if generation of the behavior *and* the consequences are self-attributed. Kanfer has demonstrated this to be the case in a number of laboratory studies involving ambiguous tasks and "self-reinforcements" such as pushing a button to turn on a light (cf. Kanfer & Seidner, 1973). A number of investigators have demonstrated the efficacy of self-reward procedures, and others have demonstrated self-punishment effectiveness. Increasingly, however, these researchers are finding that the subjects tend to reward themselves excessively when they haven't complied and also consistently fail to punish themselves (cf. Hiebert, 1973; Kanfer & Duerfeldt, 1968; Rozensky & Bellack, 1974).

When one moves out of the laboratory to deal with real clinical situations, a number of problems in the use of self-reinforcement emerge. One of the major problems is the extreme difficulty that most people have in generating effective self-rewards and self-punishments. Another problem is the lack of efficacy of the procedure in maintaining the behavior changes.

One of my students (Hiebert, 1973) developed a program to increase physical exercise using four alternate treatments: self-reinforcement or experimenter reinforcement for compliance and self-imposed or experimenter-imposed penalties. The results indicated that both penalty procedures but neither of the reinforcement procedures were effective in increasing the amount of exercise. In addition, experimenter-penalty procedures were more effective than self-penalty procedures. An examination of trends across weeks indicated that the average cycling frequencies decreased progressively across all weeks except for the experimenter-penalty group. Subjects in the self-punishment group paid progressively smaller penalties as the program continued. By the sixth week, they were paying only one-sixth as much as they would have paid in the experimenter-penalty group.

These findings, which are troublesome for behavior modifiers to explain, are, of course, directly consistent with social-exchange theory in that the subjects will try to maximize their gains in their interactions with the experimenter. (Notice that the self-rewards and punishments in these studies are usually not self-generated, only self-administered.) Social-exchange theory suggests that the behavioral strategy of response cost for noncompliance should be more effective than self-reinforcement for compliance, and the experimental evidence supports this contention (cf. Epstein & Masek, 1978).

3.2. Self-Monitoring

Self-monitoring should be preferable to therapist surveillance for a number of reasons I have already discussed. It should be particularly desirable for identifying those antecedent cues and situations that are uniquely compatible with the performance of compliant behavior. From the few studies that are available, self-monitoring alone appears to be of limited utility for improving compliance (Carnahan & Nugent, 1975). However, it may be a useful or necessary component of multiple-component compliance strategies (Haynes, in press).

3.3. Behavioral Contracting

One of the main advantages of contracting procedures is that they force the clients out of the "sick patient" role and require them to assume and specify their responsibility for their own behavior. It has been found, for example, that patients who made compliance contracts dropped out of treatment at a lower rate and maintained treatment goals to a significantly better degree than control patients or patients receiving an educational program for compliance. To the extent that patients see the contract as giving them some choice in compliance, social reactance (Brehm, 1966) may be reduced.

A strategy that works particularly well to increase compliance in children is to have the parents participate in establishing a behavioral contract to reinforce compliant behavior (cf. McMahon, Forehand, & Griest, in press). Involving family support may also improve compliance in adult patients (Levine, Green, Deeds, Chwalow, Russell, & Finlay, 1979), at least when combined with other methods. An advantage of family involvement is that it places the reinforcement of compliance in the patient's immediate environment.

3.4. Self-Instructional Training

Meichenbaum and his students have demonstrated the effectiveness of modifying self-statements in controlling a variety of behaviors—from impulsiveness to pain tolerance (Meichenbaum & Turk, 1976). A number of Kanfer's students are now working in this area. Hartig and Kanfer (1973), for example, have demonstrated that teaching children to increase verbal self-commands enables them to increase their self-control.

There is no theoretical reason why changing self-statements should produce better compliance than the modification of overt behavior. To the extent that self-instructional (or other cognitive mediating) processes alter self-efficacy, increased compliance should occur. As discussed above, efficacy expectations affect the persistence with which patients will continue to try to cope with stressful life events (Wilson, 1980b). Complying with a therapeutic regimen can certainly be stressful. It is important that the expectations of the process of therapeutic compliance be congruent with what the patient experiences; otherwise compliance will be diminished (Dunbar & Stunkard, 1979). Encouraging appropriate compliance expectations may reduce negative feelings of demoralization and hopelessness. Self-instructional training can help to reduce these negative feelings by allowing the patient to relabel or reinterpret the reason for his or her problem (Wilson, 1980a).

4. Other Compliance-Improvement Strategies

Dunbar, Marshall, and Hovell (1979) have classified compliance procedures into educational, organizational, and behavioral strategies. I have already outlined the major behavioral strategies (with one exception) that appear to hold promise for improving compliance. Several studies have employed token economies to improve compliance with long-term regimens in pediatric populations. These studies have been reviewed in detail elsewhere by Rapoff and Christophersen (in press), who suggest adding a response-cost component.

Educational strategies (e.g., explicit written instructions) appear to be useful in improving compliance with short-term regimens, but these strategies have not been effective with long-term regimens (Haynes, in press).

The results of organizational strategies (modifying service delivery) have been equivocal. Further study is necessary to determine whether more frequent supervision, for example, can reliably increase and maintain compliance (Rapoff & Christophersen, in press).

Three recent reviews of the compliance literature have all recommended multiple-component strategies as the most efficacious approach to improving patient compliance, given the current state of our knowledge (Dunbar *et al.*, 1979; Haynes *et al.*, 1979; Stuart & Davidson, 1981).

5. Some Paradoxes

Before leaving the discussion of improving compliance, I would like to present you with a seeming paradox. Some of my colleagues are involved in assertiveness training programs to deal with the perceived social problems of "excessive" compliance. (The paradox is not that we are at cross purposes— that's simply the *modus operandi* in our clinic. Besides, paradoxes always lie in other people; they are never attributed to oneself.) No, the problem is that *they*, in teaching assertiveness skills, are asking their clients to demonstrate their ability to be noncompliant as evidence of learning; at the same time, however, these clients are being asked to demonstrate the ability to be compliant with the procedures of assertiveness training.

In examining the costs and benefits of compliance, I would like to draw your attention to a second apparent paradox based on an extensive analysis by Vincent (1971) of compliance in a glaucoma clinic. Her sample included a number of patients who had originally contacted their family physician because they had noted loss of vision. After a diagnosis of glaucoma, they were told by the clinic to use eyedrops three times a day for an extended period or "go blind." (I would like you to note those instructions so that you can see how dissonant they are from what social psychologists who study forced compliance would recommend.) The clinic believed that the phrase "go blind" would increase compliance. In this kind of either/or situation, 58% of the clients responded exactly as we would predict for an avoidance–avoidance conflict situation—they did nothing, at least often enough to create medical complications. At the point at which subjects became legally blind in one eye, compliance improved, but only by 17% (from 42% to 59%). To the health professionals studying these cases, it appeared that there must be something wrong with people who would choose (note the value judgment here) to go blind rather than follow a relatively simple (but not quite innocuous) preventive regimen. Compare this study with the Milgram studies (1974) from the social psychology literature. What factors make one individual choose noncompliance at a cost of going blind and another individual to choose compliance at a cost of severe pain to a fellow human being? If you can answer that question, you may know more about the nature of compliance, or perhaps you will just learn something about the differences between laboratory and applied research.

6. References

Adams, J. S. Inequity in social exchange. In L. Berkowitz (Ed.), *Advances in experimental social psychology* (Vol. 2). New York: Academic Press, 1965.

Bandura, A. Self-efficacy: Toward a unifying theory of behavior change. *Psychological Review*, 1977, *84*, 191–215.

Becker, M. H. Sociobehavioral determinants of compliance. In D. L. Sackett (Ed.), *A workshop/symposium: Compliance with therapeutic regimens*. Hamilton, Ontario: McMaster University, 1974. (a)

Becker, M. H. The health belief model and sick role behavior. *Health Eduction Monographs*, 1974, *2*, 409. (b)

Becker, M. H., Drackman, R. H., & Kirscht, J. P. Predicting mothers' compliance with pediatric medical regimen. *Journal of Pediatrics*, 1972, *81*, 843.

Becker, M. H., & Maiman, L. A. Sociobehavioral determinants of compliance with health and medical care recommendations. *Medical Care*, 1975, *13*, 10–24.

Bem, D. J. Self-perception: An alternative interpretation of cognitive dissonance phenomena. *Psychological Review*, 1967, *74*, 183–200.

Bem, D. J. Self-perception theory. In L. Berkowitz (Ed.), *Advances in experimental social psychology* (Vol. 6). New York: Academic Press, 1972.

Best, J. A., & Steffy, R. A. Smoking modification procedures for internal and external locus of control clients. *Canadian Journal of Behavioural Science*, 1975, *7*, 155–165.

Blackwell, B. The drug defaulter. *Clinical Pharmacological Therapy*, 1972, *13*, 841.

Blau, P. M. *Exchange and power in social life*. New York: Wiley, 1964.

Borofsky, L. G., Louis, S., Kutt, H., & Roginsky, M. Diphenylhydantoin: Efficacy, toxicity, and dose-serum level relationships in children. *Journal of Pediatrics*, 1972, *81*, 995.

Bowers, K. S. Situationalism in psychology: An analysis and critique. *Psychological Review*, 1973, *80*, 307–336.

Bowers, K. S. The psychology of subtle control: An attributional analysis of behavioral persistence. *Canadian Journal of Behavioural Science*, 1975, *7*, 78–95.

Bowers, K. S. There's more to Iago than meets the eye: A clinical account of personal consistency. In D. Magnusson & N. S. Endler (Eds.), *Personality at the crossroads: Current issues in interactional psychology*. Hillsdale, N.J.: Lawrence Erlbaum, 1977.

Brehm, J. W. *A theory of psychological reactance*. New York: Academic Press, 1966.

Cameron, R. The clinical implementation of behavior change techniques: A cognitively oriented conceptualization of therapeutic "compliance" and "resistance." In J. P. Foreyt & D. P. Rathjen (Eds.), *Cognitive behavior therapy: Research and application*. New York: Plenum Press, 1978.

Carnahan, J. E., & Nugent, C. A. The effects of self-monitoring by patients on the control of hypertension. *The American Journal of Medical Sciences*, 1975, *269*, 69–73.

Caron, H. S., & Roth, H. P. Patients' co-operation with a medical regimen. *Journal of the American Medical Association*, 1968, *203*, 922.

Chadwick-Jones, J. K. *Social exchange theory: Its structure and influence in social psychology*. New York: Academic Press, 1976.

Chaplin, J. P. *Dictionary of psychology*. New York: Dell, 1968.

Charney, E., Bynum, R., Eldredge, D., Frank, D., MacWhinney, J. B., McNabb, N., Scheiner, A., Sumpter, E. A., & Iker, H. How well do patients take oral penicillin? A collaborative study in private practice. *Pediatrics*, 1967, *20*, 188.

Collins, B. E., & Hoyt, M. F. Personal responsibility-for-consequences: An integration and extension of the "forced compliance" literature. *Journal of Experimental Social Psychology*, 1972, *8*, 558–593.

Crisci, R., & Kassinove. H. Effect of perceived expertise, strength of advice, and environmental setting on parental compliance. *Journal of Social Psychology*, 1973, *89*, 245–250.

Davidson, P. O. Graduate training and research funding for clinical psychology in Canada: Review and recommendations. *Canadian Psychologist*, 1970, *11*, 101–127.

Davidson, P. O., & Schrag, A. R. Factors affecting the outcome of child psychiatric consultations. *American Journal of Orthopsychiatry*, 1969, *39*, 774–778.

Davis, M. S. Discharge from hospital against medical advice: A study in reciprocity in the doctor–patient relationship. *Social Science Medicine*, 1967, *1*, 336–346.

Davis, M. S. Physiologic, psychological and demographic factors in patient compliance with doctors' orders. *Medical Care*, 1968, *6*, 115–122.

Davison, G. C., & Valins, S. Maintenance of self-attributed and drug-attributed behavior change. *Journal of Personality and Social Psychology*, 1969, *11*, 25–33.

Deci, E. L. *Intrinsic motivation*. New York: Plenum Press, 1975.

Dunbar, J. M., Marshall, G. D., & Hovell, M. F. Behavioral strategies for improving compliance. In R. B. Haynes, D. W. Taylor, & D. L. Sackett (Eds.), *Compliance in health care*. Baltimore: John Hopkins University Press, 1979.

Dunbar, J. M., & Stunkard, A. J. Adherence to medical regimens. In R. Levy, B. Rifkind, B. Dennis, & N. Ernst (Eds.), *Nutrition, lipids, and coronary heart disease*. New York: Raven Press, 1979.

Dweck, C. The role of expectations and attributions in the alleviation of learned helplessness. *Journal of Personality and Social Psychology*, 1975, *31*, 674–685.

Epstein, L. H., & Masek, B. N. Behavioral control of medicine compliance. *Journal of Applied Behavior Analysis*, 1978, *11*, 1–9.

Feinstein, A. R. "Compliance bias" and the interpretation of therapeutic trials. In R. B. Haynes, D. W. Taylor, & D. L. Sackett (Eds.), *Compliance in health care*. Baltimore: John Hopkins University Press, 1979.

Festinger, L. *A theory of cognitive dissonance*. Stanford: Stanford University Press, 1957.

Francis, V., Korsch, B. M., & Morris, M. J. Gaps in doctor–patient communication: Patients' response to medical advice. *New England Journal of Medicine*, 1969, *280*, 535–540.

Frankel, E., & Kassinove, H. Effects of required effort, perceived expertise, and sex on teacher compliance. *Journal of Social Psychology*, 1974, *93*, 187–192.

Freedman, J. L. Long-term behavioral effects of cognitive dissonance. *Journal of Experimental Social Psychology*, 1965, *1*, 145–155.

French, J. R. P., Jr., & Raven, B. H. The bases of power. In D. Cartwright (Ed.), *Studies in social power*. Ann Arbor, Mich.: University of Michigan, Institute for Social Research, 1959.

Gillum, R. F., & Barsky, A. J. Diagnosis and management of patient compliance. *Journal of the American Medical Association*, 1974, 228, 1563–1567.

Gordis, L. Conceptual and methodologic problems in measuring patient compliance. In R. B. Haynes, D. W. Taylor, & D. L. Sackett (Eds.), *Compliance in health care*. Baltimore: John Hopkins University Press, 1979.

Gordis, L., Markowitz, M., & Lilienfeld, A. M. The inaccuracy of using interviews to estimate patient reliability in taking medications at home. *Medical Care*, 1969, 7, 45–54.

Grinnel, G. J., & Sweeney, G. D. Historical perspectives on the determinants of compliance. In D. L. Sackett (Ed.), *Compliance with therapeutic regimens*. Hamilton, Ontario: McMaster University Medical Centre, 1974.

Hall, S. M. & Hall, R. G. Outcome and methodological considerations in behavioral treatment of obesity. *Behavior Therapy*, 1974, 5, 352–364.

Hartig, M., & Kanfer, F. The role of verbal self-instructions in children's resistance to temptation. *Journal of Personality and Social Psychology*, 1973, 25, 259–267.

Haynes, R. B. Introduction. In R. B. Haynes, D. W. Taylor, & D. L. Sackett (Eds.), *Compliance in health care*. Baltimore: John Hopkins University Press, 1979.

Haynes, R. B. Improving patient compliance: An empirical view. In R. B. Stuart & P. O. Davidson (Eds.), *Compliance, generalization and maintenance in behavioral medicine*. New York: Brunner/Mazel, 1981.

Haynes, R. B., Taylor, D. W., & Sackett, D. L. *Compliance in health care*. Baltimore: John Hopkins University Press, 1979.

Heckhausen, H. Fear of failure as a self-reinforcing motive system. In I. Sarason & C. Spielberger (Eds.), *Stress and anxiety* (Vol. 2). Washington, D.C.: Hemisphere, 1975.

Hellmuth, G. A. Psychological factors in cardiac patients: Distortion of clinical recommendations. *Archives of Environmental Health*, 1966, 12, 771–775.

Hiebert, S. F. *The effectiveness of self-determined consequences for increasing the frequency of desired behaviour*. Unpublished doctoral dissertation, University of Calgary, 1973.

Hochbaum, G. M. *Public participation in medical screening programs: A sociological study*. Washington, D.C.: U.S. Government Printing Office, 1958.

Homans, G. C. *Social behavior: Its elementary forms* (Rev. ed.). New York: Harcourt, Brace, Jovanovich, 1974.

Jonas, S. Influence of the weather on appointment-breaking in a general medical clinic. *Medical Care*, 1973, 11, 72–74.

Kanfer, F. H. The many faces of self-control. In R. B. Stuart (Ed.), *Behavioral self-management*. New York: Brunner/Mazel, 1977.

Kanfer, F. H. Self-management: Strategies and tactics. In A. P. Goldstein & F. H. Kanfer. *Maximizing treatment gains*. New York: Academic Press, 1979.

Kanfer, F. H., & Duerfeldt, P. H. Comparison of self-reward and self-criticism as a function of types of prior external reinforcement. *Journal of Personality and Social Psychology*, 1968, 8, 261–268.

Kanfer, F. H., & Seidner, M. L. Self-control: Factors enhancing tolerance of noxious stimulation. *Journal of Personality and Social Psychology*, 1973, 25, 381–389.

Kasl, S. V. Issues in patient adherence to health care regimens. *Stress*, 1975, 1, 5–17.

Kelley, H. H. Attribution theory in social psychology. *Nebraska Symposium on Motivation*, 1967, 15, 192–241.

Kelman, H. C. Compliance, identification, and internalization: The processes of attitude change. *Journal of Conflict Resolution*, 1958, 2, 51–60.

Kelman, H. C. Three processes of social influence. *Public Opinion Quarterly*, 1961, 25, 57–78.

Kopel, S., & Arkowitz, H. The role of attribution and self-perception in behavior change: Implications for behavior therapy. *Genetic Psychology Monographs*, 1975, 92 (2), 175–212.

Korsch, B. M., Gozzi, E. K., & Francis, V. Gaps in doctor–patient communication. *Pediatrics*, 1968, 42, 855–860.

Leet-Pellegrini, H., & Rubin, J. Z. The effects of six bases of power upon compliance, identification, and internalization. *Bulletin of the Psychonomic Society*, 1974, 3, 68–70.

Lefcourt, H. M. *Locus of control*. Hillsdale, N. J.: Lawrence Erlbaum, 1976.

Lendrum, B., & Kobrin, C. Prevention of recurrent attacks of rheumatic fever: Problems revealed in long-term follow-up. *Journal of the American Medical Association*, 1956, 162, 13–16.

Lepper, M. R., & Greene, D. Turning play into work: Effects of adult surveillance and extrinsic rewards on children's intrinsic motivation. *Journal of Personality and Social Psychology*, 1975, *31*, 479–486.

Lepper, M., & Greene, D. On understanding "overjustification": A reply to Reiss and Sushinsky. *Journal of Personality and Social Psychology*, 1976, *33*, 25–35.

Levine, D. M., Green, L. W., Deeds, S. G., Chwalow, J., Russell, P., & Finlay, J. Health education for hypertensive patients. *Journal of the American Medical Association*, 1979, *241*, 1700–1703.

Lupri, E. Contemporary authority patterns in the West German family: A study in cross-national validation. *Journal of Marriage and Family*, 1969, *31*, 34–44.

Macoby, E. E., & Jacklin, K. N. *The psychology of sex differences*. Stanford, Calif.: Stanford University Press, 1974.

Maddock, R. K. Patient cooperation in taking medicine: A study involving isoniazid and aminosalicylic acid. *Journal of the American Medical Association*, 1967, *199*, 169–172.

Mahoney, M. J., & Thoresen, C. E. *Self-control: Power to the person*. Monterey, Calif.: Brooks/Cole, 1974.

Malohy, B. The effect of instruction and labeling on the number of medication errors made by patients at home. *American Journal of Hospital Pharmacology*, 1966, *23*, 283.

Marston, M. V. *Compliance with medical regimens as a form of risk taking in patients with myocardial infractions*. Boston: Boston University Press, 1969.

Marston, M. V. Compliance with medical regimens: Review of the literature. *Nursing Research*, 1970, *19*, 312–323.

McMahon, R. J., Forehand, R., & Griest, D. L. Parent behavioral training to modify child noncompliance: Factors in generalization and maintenance. In R. B. Stuart & P. O. Davidson (Eds.), *Compliance, generalization and maintenance in behavioral medicine*. New York: Brunner/Mazel, 1981.

Meichenbaum, D. *Cognitive behavior modification*. New York: Plenum Press, 1977.

Meichenbaum, D., & Turk, D. The cognitive behavioral management of anxiety, anger and pain. In P. O. Davidson (Ed.), *The behavioral management of anxiety, depression and pain*. New York: Brunner/Mazel, 1976.

Milgram, S. *Obedience to authority*. New York: Harper & Row, 1974.

Morrow, R., & Rabin, D. L. Reliability of self-medication with isoniazid. *Clinical Research*, 1966, *14*, 362.

Neely, E., & Patrick, M. L. Problems of aged persons taking medication at home. *Nursing Research*, 1968, *17*, 52–55.

Nord, W. R. Social exchange theory: An integrative approach to social conformity. *Psychological Bulletin*, 1969, *71*, 174–208.

Oakes, T. W., Ward, J. R., & Gray, R. M. Family expectations and arthritis patient compliance to a hand resting splint regimen. *Journal of Chronic Diseases*, 1970, *22*, 757–764.

Organ, D. W. Social exchange and psychological reactance in a simulated superior–subordinate relationship. *Organizational and Human Performance*, 1974, *12*, 132–142.

Pepitone, A., McCauley, C., & Hammond, P. Change in attractiveness of forbidden toys as a function of severity of threat. *Journal of Experimental Social Psychology*, 1967, *3*, 221–229.

Porter, A. M. W. Drug defaulting in general practice. *British Medical Journal*, 1969, *1*, 218–222.

Rapoff, M. A., & Christophersen, E. R. Compliance in pediatric patients with medical regimens: A review and evaluation. In R. B. Stuart & P. O. Davidson (Eds.), *Compliance, generalization and maintenance in behavioral medicine*. New York: Brunner/Mazel, 1981.

Redd, W. H., Amen, D. L., Meddock, T. D., & Winston, A. S. Children's compliance as a function of type of instructions and payoff for noncompliance. *Bulletin of the Psychonomic Society*, 1974, *4*, 597–599.

Ross, J. Influence of experts and peers upon Negro mothers of low socioeconomic status. *Journal of Social Psychology*, 1973, *89*, 79–84.

Ross, M. Salience of reward and intrinsic motivation. *Journal of Personality and Social Psychology*, 1975, *31*, 1116–1125.

Roth, H. P., & Berger, D. G. Studies on patient cooperation in ulcer treatment. *Gastroenterology*, 1960, *38*, 630–633.

Rozensky, R. H., & Bellack, A. S. Behavior change and individual differences in self-control. *Behavior Research and Therapy*, 1974, *12*, 267–268.

Sackett, D. L. *Compliance with therapeutic regimens*. Hamilton, Ontario: McMaster University Medical Centre, 1974.

Scanzoni, J. *Opportunity and the family*. New York: The Free Press, 1970.

Scanzoni, J. *Sexual bargaining: Power politics in the American marriage*. Englewood Cliffs, N.J.: Prentice-Hall, 1972.

Schmidt, J. A. *Help yourself: A guide to self change*. Champaign, Ill.: Research Press, 1976.

Schwartz, B. Waiting, exchange and power: The distribution of time in social systems. *American Journal of Sociology*, 1974, *79*, 841–870.

Staw, B. M. *Intrinsic and extrinsic motivation*. New York: General Learning Press Module, 1975.

Stuart, R. B. *Behavioral self-management*. New York: Brunner/Mazel, 1977.

Stuart, R. B., & Davidson, P. O. (Eds.). *Compliance, generalization and maintenance in behavioral medicine*. New York: Brunner/Mazel, 1981.

Suedfeld, P. The benefits of boredom: Sensory deprivation revisited. *American Scientist*, 1975, *63*, 60–69.

Taylor, D. W. A test of the health belief model in hypertension. In R. B. Haynes, D. W. Taylor, & D. L. Sackett (Eds.), *Compliance in health care*. Baltimore: John Hopkins University Press, 1979.

Thibaut, J., & Kelley, H. H. *The social psychology of groups*. New York: Wiley, 1959.

Valins, S., & Nisbett R. Attribution processes in the development and treatment of emotional disorders. In J. Spence, R. Carson, & J. Thibaut (Eds.), *Behavioral approaches to therapy*. Morristown, N.J.: General Learning Press, 1976.

Vincent, P. Factors influencing patient noncompliance: A theoretical approach. *Nursing Research*, 1971, *20*, 509–516.

Walster, E., Berscheid, E., & Walster, G. W. New directions in equity research. *Journal of Personality and Social Psychology*, 1973, *25*, 151–176.

Watts, D. D. Factors related to the acceptance of modern medicine. *American Journal of Public Health*, 1966, *56*, 1205–1212.

Wilcox, D. R. C., Gillan, R., & Hare, E. R. Do psychiatric patients take their drugs? *British Medical Journal*, 1965, *2*, 790.

Wilson, G. T. Cognitive factors in lifestyle change. In P. O. Davidson & S. M. Davidson (Eds.), *Behavioral medicine: Changing health lifestyles*. New York: Brunner/Mazel, 1980. (a)

Wilson, G. T. Toward specifying the "nonspecific" factors in behavior therapy. In M. J. Mahoney (Ed.), *Psychotherapy process: Current issues and future directions*. New York: Plenum Press, 1980. (b)

Wilson, J. T. Compliance with instructions in the evaluation of therapeutic efficacy. *Clinical Pediatrics*, 1973, *12*, 333–340.

Zifferblatt, S. M. Increasing patient compliance through applied analysis of behavior. *Preventative Medicine*, 1975, *4*, 173–182.

Zola, I. K. Studying the decision to see a doctor. In Z. J. Lipowski (Ed.), *Psychosocial advances in psychosomatic medicine*. Basel, Switzerland: S. Karger, 1972.

Zola, I. K. Pathways to the doctor—from person to patient. *Social Science Medicine*, 1973, *7*, 677.

Psychomaintenance of Chronic Physical Illness
Clinical Assessment of Personal Styles Affecting Medical Management

ROBERT A. KINSMAN, JERALD F. DIRKS, AND NELSON F. JONES

1. Psychomaintenance of Physical Illness

Psychomaintenance refers to the psychologic and behavioral perpetuation and exacerbation of physical illness (Dirks, 1978; Jones, Kinsman, Dirks, & Dahlem, 1979). In this regard, it should be noted that psychomaintenance does not address the etiology of illness as an area of interest but instead focuses on how psychologic and behavioral factors maintain and increase both perceived severity and medical intractability of the illness once it has already developed. How is it that the patient continues to be functionally incapacitated by illness, despite medical treatment that is effective in most other cases? How is it that the patient appears to require a disproportionately intense medication regimen? How is it that the patient continues to be hospitalized longer and more frequently than

ROBERT A. KINSMAN ● Division of Psychobiology, National Jewish Hospital and Research Center, Department of Psychiatry, University of Colorado School of Medicine, Denver, Colorado 80206.   JERALD F. DIRKS ● Division of Psychobiology, National Jewish Hospital and Research Center, Department of Psychiatry, University of Colorado School of Medicine, School of Professional Psychology, University of Denver, Denver, Colorado 80206.   NELSON F. JONES ● School of Professional Psychology, University of Denver, Denver, Colorado 80206.   Supported in part by grants AI-10398, HL-22065, and AI-15392 from the National Institutes of Health.

would be indicated by the objective medical parameters of the illness? What is the patient doing to contribute adversely to his or her medical response? What is the patient not doing in relation to the illness, and what negative effects does that have on medical management and treatment? These are questions whereby the specific mechanisms of psychomaintenance can be isolated. The mechanisms of psychomaintenance appear to be general across illness types and often so commonplace as to be overlooked.

Increasing health care costs (Kristein, Arnold, & Wynder, 1977) and the practical realities implied by an aging population now make psychomaintenance issues as timely and as compelling concerns for medical psychologists as understanding the personal habits and styles that contribute to illness onset. In this sense, psychomaintenance theory is entirely congruent with the best objectives of preventive medicine: to understand, explain, and resolve (psychologic) factors that contribute to the maintenance of illness and the defeat of medical management.

2. Two Assumptions Relating to Assessment

The ultimate resolution of psychomaintenance issues depends on the assessment and identification of personal styles underlying specific behavioral mechanisms that contribute to medical treatment failure. This chapter will provide an approach to assessment that makes possible focused recommendations and interventions to resolve psychomaintenance. The approach can be generalized to any chronic illness, although the principal clinical examples are drawn from asthma.

At the heart of psychomaintenance theory and assessment are two assumptions that need to be made explicit. First, any behavior that can maintain illness and defeat medical management (e.g., noncompliance to therapeutic regimens) may arise from numerous and different psychologic bases. For example, one patient with severe memory problems due to brain damage or mental retardation may repeatedly forget to take medications. A second patient, who has taken pride in an ability to cope with any difficulty throughout life, may be noncompliant because he or she regards all medications as a crutch or sign of weakness. A third patient, extremely pessimistic about the illness, may not take medication because of a sense of hopelessness and an attitude that "it doesn't matter anyway." A fourth patient may be noncompliant because of a profound need to deny that he or she is ill and therefore often disregards the need to take medication or other appropriate action. A fifth patient may fail to take medications merely because the importance of adhering to the medication regimen is not clearly comprehended. A sixth patient may fail to do so because the rewards for being ill provide a release from the responsibilities coincidental with being healthy. To complicate matters even further, two or more of the above reasons may combine to contribute to a given patient's noncompliance.

This brings us to the second assumption: focused assessment to clarify the basis of psychomaintenance mechanisms is a prerequisite for the resolution of these issues. In effect, the approach is analogous to that of a physician confronted with a patient complaining of fatigue. Fatigue is only a symptom. The physician cannot properly treat the patient until medical evaluation reveals whether the cause of the fatigue is an acute viral or bacterial infection, hypoglycemia, or a wide array of other physiologic possibilities. Once the medical evaluation reveals the basis of the fatigue, appropriate treatment can be specified. In much the same way, assessment of psychomaintenance enables prescription of effective, focused treatment and recommendations.

3. Examples of Psychomaintenance

A middle-aged woman consults her physician about a chronic arthritic condition. The physician prescribes a proven medical regimen and instructs the patient on proper self-care procedures. She leaves the office and the next day has forgotten or distorted most of what her physician has said. Needless to say, there is a high risk for psychomaintenance. Yet, a poor memory for medical information is a common problem among patients with chronic physical illness. Ley (1979) has amply demonstrated how very little physician advice and instruction is remembered by the average patient. More recently, Schraa, Dirks, Jones, and Kinsman (1981) have documented that over 50% of the patients in some chronic illness groups may suffer from clearly impaired short-term memory. If untreated or uncompensated for, such neuropsychologic dysfunction can have an unequivocably negative effect on medical prognosis.

Suppose, however, that our hypothetical patient does remember what her physician has told her. For whatever reason, however, she does not comply with her medication regimen. That the patient is noncompliant should not be surprising. In his review of compliance studies, Sackett (1976) found that medication compliance is a universal and serious problem across illness types. Vincent (1971) reported 58% noncompliance among glaucoma patients taking eyedrops to prevent incipient blindness. Noncompliance with insulin therapy for diabetes has been reported to be as high as 52% (Watkins, Williams, Martin, Hogan, & Anderson, 1967), 46% for antituberculosis antibiotics (Zaki, Edelstein, Josephson, & Weisberg, 1968), and 45% for dietary restrictions recommended for patients on chronic hemodialysis (Kaplan De-Nour & Czacakes, 1972). None of these diseases is in any way classically "psychologic," yet the rates of noncompliance for them are essentially similar to the 52% noncompliance rate for clearcut psychiatric patients on tranquilizers (Michaux, 1961). Among asthmatic patients, medication noncompliance has been variously reported between 54% (Kleiger & Dirks, 1979) and 67% (Kinsman, Dirks, & Dahlem, in 1980a), depending on the type of medication studied. These and similar findings are alarming for at least two reasons. First, noncompliance is a major cause of medical treatment failure across disease types (Addington, 1979). Second, physicians are generally unable or unwilling to discern which of their patients are compliers and which are noncompliers (Canon & Roth, 1968). At one hospital, by their own report, more than half of the patients with respiratory disease failed to comply to medication regimens, yet only about one in four physicians routinely inquired about the patients' medication usage (Kleiger & Dirks, 1979).

Another psychomaintenance issue is how the patient presents to the physician. Minimization or exaggeration in patient presentation of illness severity is common, prompting Pilowsky (1969) to classify abnormal illness behavior along this bipolar dimension. Minimization or denial often leads to undertreatment by the physician and to subsequent exacerbation of the illness. Exaggeration can contribute to needless functional incapacitation of the patient (Bellak, 1952; Fross, Dirks, Kinsman, & Jones, 1980). In terms of the patient–physician relationship, exaggeration during symptom presentation contributes to overmedication, with its concomitant risks of medication side effects, toxicity, and paradoxical reactions.

4. The Context of Psychomaintenance

Although numerous other examples could be listed, it is time to consider what sort of perspective the medical psychologist should bring to bear on psychomaintenance. Psychomaintenance is not merely dependent upon isolated behaviors, nor can these be studied in a vacuum. For example, medication noncompliance, though a very real and very serious problem, is not a behavior that can be identified, studied, and treated outside of a known context. In the first place, the term *medication noncompliance* does not refer to a discrete behavior: it is a generic term covering a gamut of behavioral patterns. A patient could underuse medications, overuse medications, or take the medications in an erratic and arbitrary fashion (Kinsman *et al.*, 1980; Kleiger & Dirks, 1979). Although all three usage patterns are properly designated as noncompliant, they are very different behavioral patterns, each occurring for a potentially different psychologic reason for any given patient and each requiring its own particular resolution. These last two points bring us face to face with the context in which psychomaintenance behaviors must be studied, that is, primarily the patient's psychological makeup and secondarily the nature of the patient–physician relationship.

Psychomaintenance behaviors are congruent with and can be best studied within the context of the patient as a whole person. The assessment, study, and treatment of psychomaintenance cannot proceed simply by focusing on one or two discrete behaviors but only by applying psychologic assessment to the chronically ill. As such, the assessment of psychomaintenance potentials in any given patient is the study of the patient at each of several levels of functioning.

Figure 1 illustrates, in a simplified fashion, the levels of involvement for any given patient with a chronic illness. As we can see, the premorbid, basic, predisposing personality style interacts with the onset, type, and severity of illness to result in the patient personality. For example, a person predisposed to dependency is likely, in the face of illness, to become an excessively dependent, clinging, demanding, and fearful patient. In turn, this patient's personality predisposes to a helpless, pessimistic attitude toward the illness, in which medical caregivers are seen as being totally responsible for medical care and treatment.

In other words, the patient may believe that "It's all up to the doc . . . I can do nothing." These attitudes, combined with the patient's personality, are likely to influence the way in which the symptoms of the illness are experienced subjectively. Such a patient may respond with acute anxiety attacks during each illness exacerbation. It is only when the patient's personality, attitudes toward illness and its treatment, and subjective experience of the illness are combined that the patient's resulting illness behavior can be properly understood. Thus, in our present hypothetical example, such abnormal illness behaviors as overuse of medications, exaggeration of physical distress, and inability or unwillingness to care for oneself are not only understood but to be expected. Hence the medical psychologist is not limited to assessing the presence or absence of a discrete behavior. Instead, assessment is made at the levels of *patient personality, attitudes toward illness and its treatment*, and the *subjective experience of the illness*. These integrated assessments, coupled with knowledge of the medical characteristics of the illness, allow for predictions to be made as to the probability of present or future psychomaintenance and its form.

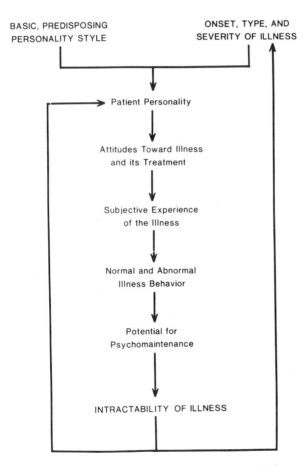

Figure 1. A schema for psychomaintenance in chronic illness.

Needless to say, this description is oversimplified. For example, the nature of the physical illness affects not only the patient's personality but also his or her attitudinal level as well as the level of subjective experience, feasibility of defining of abnormal illness behavior, potential for psychomaintenance, and intractability of the illness. Likewise, Figure 1 fails to address the role of medical care givers and significant others. Figure 2 corrects these oversimplifications, highlighting the numerous feedback loops that exist.

So far, we have confined our remarks to chronic illness. That limitation is not without reason. Considering Figures 1 and 2, it is easily seen that a simple cold lasting only a day or a broken bone that knits as expected hardly has the impact or duration necessary to set a psychomaintenance schema easily and

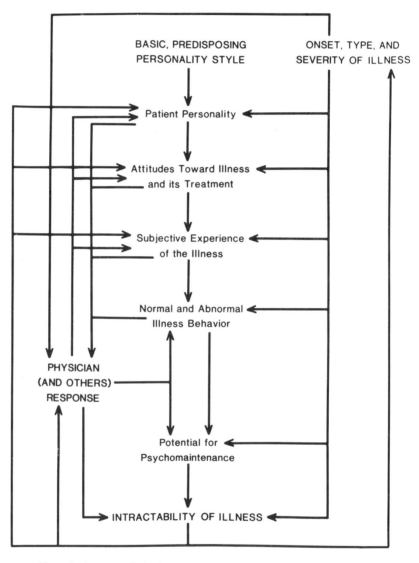

Figure 2. An expanded schema for psychomaintenance in chronic illness.

completely into effect. It is only with the chronic illness that the full impact and complexity of psychomaintenance can be appreciated. In what follows, an in-depth look at psychomaintenance in one chronic illness, asthma, is presented. It is hoped that both the methodology and the results of this endeavor will serve as catalysts in the further exploration of psychomaintenance across diverse chronic illnesses.

5. Psychomaintenance and Its Assessment in Asthma

5.1. Characteristics of Asthma and Its Treatment

Asthma is a heterogeneous chronic illness, functionally defined as "inter-mittent, reversible obstructive airways disease." Asthma is often experienced as periodic episodes of acute breathing difficulty—attacks that are separated by periods of relative freedom in breathing. For the patient, it may be difficult or impossible to predict the onset of attacks, difficult to identify specific causes of an attack, and difficult to resolve an attack once it has begun. Almost all asth-matics share the common physiologic feature of hyperreactivity of the airways (Nadel, 1965, 1976), although variations in the degree of airways hyperreactivity exist which can affect ease of medical management and treatment outcome (Staudenmayer, Kinsman, Dirks, Spector, & Wangaard, 1979). This inherent hyperreactivity of the airways enables a variety of irritants (e.g., dust, cold air, fumes) to trigger the airways obstruction that is the hallmark feature of asthma attacks. Minden and Farr (1969) have graphically depicted how two basic fac-tors—allergic (reaginic) predisposition and organ reactivity, which exist in vary-ing degrees in each patient—combine to elicit symptoms. Skin tests, standardized inhalation challenges with antigens and irritants (e.g., methacholine and hista-mine), and pulmonary function tests enable asthma to be characterized and its objective severity to be evaluated (Comroe, Forster, DuBois, Briscoe, & Carlsen, 1962: Spector, Kinsman, & Farr, 1975).

Important medical decisions in the treatment of asthma center on the iden-tification of potential immunologic or environmental triggers for airways ob-struction and the tailoring of a medication regimen (which may or may not involve oral corticosteroids) to manage the illness. As in most chronic illnesses, the patient is required to assume an active role in self-management. Medications must be taken according to a prescribed schedule and/or on an as-needed (p.r.n.) basis to relive acute episodes of breathing difficulty. Exposure to certain environmental triggers may have to be minimized. The patient's strategies and modes of reacting to the illness and its treatment become important at these and many other points.

From the standpoint of psychomaintenance, it is assumed that the patient brings to the illness a personal style that may either defeat, have no effect on, or facilitate medical management. Assessment of psychomaintenance potentials and these styles begins at the level of personality and then proceeds to explore the linkages among personality factors and the more illness-specific attitudes and symptom reports. The linkages between these levels reveal much about how

Table 1. Battery of Asthma Illness Behavior (BAIB)

Assessment level	Assessment locus	Psychometric instrument
1. General	Patient personality	Minnesota Multiphasic Personality Inventory (MMPI)
2. Intermediate	Attitudes toward illness and treatment	Respiratory Illness Opinion Survey (RIOS)
3. Illness-specific	Asthma subjective symptom reports	Asthma Symptom Checklist (ASC)

the person is apt to regard asthma, experience it, and behave during its treatment. In asthma, this approach has been put to use psychometrically by the Battery of Asthma Illness Behavior (Jones, Dirks, & Kinsman, 1980).

5.2. The Battery of Asthma Illness Behavior (BAIB)

The Battery of Asthma Illness Behavior (BAIB) consists of three psychometric instruments summarized briefly in Table 1 (Jones *et al.*, 1980). At the most general level, the MMPI is used, augmented by Barron's (1953) ego strength scale (Es): Navran's (1954) manifest dependency scale (Dy); Drake's (1946) social introversion scale (Si); and Dirks, Jones, and Kinsman's (1977b) Panic–Fear personality scale.

At a more illness-specific level, the BAIB assesses attitudes toward illness and its treatment using the Respiratory Illness Opinion Survey (RIOS). The RIOS consists of 76 statements, each of which is an expression of various attitudes about being ill, being in treatment, and regard for physicians. Patients can agree or disagree with each statement by choosing some point along a five-point scale (1 = strongly agree; 5 = strongly disagree). The RIOS attitude statements organize empirically into the five reliable clusters shown in Table 2. Each RIOS attitude category score yields a T-score with a mean of 50 and a standard deviation of 10. The development and psychometric characteristics of the RIOS

Table 2. Respiratory Illness Opinion Survey (RIOS)

Attitude category	Attitude category description
1. Optimism (O)	Professed ability to cope with and master the asthma
2. Negative Staff Regard (NSR)	Dissatisfaction about treatment and toward medical caregivers
3. Specific Internal Awareness (SIA)	Degree to which the patient reports being aware of the early bodily signals of an asthma attack
4. External Control (EC)	Extent to which the patient regards treatment as being exclusively in the hands of others
5. Psychological Stigma (PS)	Extent to which asthma is regarded as a psychological flaw

have been described (Kinsman, Jones, Matus, & Schum, 1976; Staudenmayer, Kinsman, & Jones, 1978).

Finally, at a highly illness-specific level, the BAIB assesses subjective experiences and symptoms during an asthma attack using the Asthma Symptom Checklist (ASC). The ASC is a checklist of 77 heterogeneous symptoms and experiences. Next to each symptom, patients indicate the frequency with which that symptom typically occurs during asthma attacks by choosing a point along a five-point scale of frequency (1 = always; 5 = never). The ASC symptoms organize empirically into the 10 symptom categories shown in Table 3. Like the MMPI and the RIOS, each ASC symptom category yields a T-score with a mean of 50 and a standard deviation of 10. The development and psychometric characteristics of the ASC have been described (Kinsman, Luparello, O'Banion, & Spector, 1973a; Kinsman, O'Banion, Resnikoff, Luparello, & Spector, 1973b; Kinsman, Spector, Shucard, & Luparello, 1974; Kinsman, Dahlem, Spector, & Staudenmayer, 1977).

Extensive research using all or part of the BAIB has enabled the battery's application to assess psychomaintenance potentials among chronic asthmatic patients on a clinical basis. Research has suggested that nine patient styles provide a starting point for assessment application with the BAIB.

5.3. The Empirical Bases of the BAIB: Nine Personal Styles

Applying the BAIB to assess psychomaintenance and understanding its empirical bases are simplified by using just two of the BAIB measures to identify nine psychologic subtypes of asthmatic patients. These nine subtypes are shown in Table 4. Each subtype represents a specific personal style that is the result of the interaction of two distinct levels of psychologic functioning. One level is based on characteristics of the patient's general personality (high, moderate, and low MMPI Panic–Fear personality). The second level is based on subjective symptom reports (high, moderate, and low Panic–Fear symptomatology) that index the level of attention the patient gives to asthmatic symptoms (Dirks, Kinsman, Staudenmayer, & Kleiger, 1979). Patients belonging to these types

Table 3. Asthma Symptom Checklist (ASC)

Symptom category	Symptom category description
1. Panic–Fear (P-F)	Panic and anxiety focused upon asthma attacks
2. Irritability (I)	Feelings of irritation
3. Fatigue (F)	Reduced energy level and fatigue
4. Hyperventilation–Hypocapnia (H-H)	Hyperventilation symptoms
5. Airways Obstruction/Dyspnea (AO/D)	Breathing difficulty symptoms
6. Airways Obstruction/Congestion (AO/C)	Chest congestion symptoms
7. Worry (W)	Worry and concern about self
8. Anger (A)	Feelings of anger
9. Loneliness (L)	Feelings of loneliness and isolation
10. Rapid Breathing (RB)	Symptoms of rapid breathing, heart pounding, and panting

Table 4. Patient Styles Based on Panic–Fear Personality (PF-P) and Attention to Breathing Difficulties (PF-S) and Their Influence on Medical Treatment and Its Outcome

Pattern no.	Patient personality (PF-P)	Attention to symptoms (PF-S)	Patients[a] %	Typical attitude to asthma	Medication compliance			Influences and outcome		
					Routinely scheduled medications	As-needed (p.r.n.) medications	Frequency hospitalized	Length of hospital stay	Intensity of prescribed medications	Long-term medical outcome
1	Anxious dependency	Vigilant	11.6	Pessimism & lack of self-reliance	Erratic over- & underuse	Overuse/arbitrary use	High	Long	Increased	Poor
2	Anxious dependency	Typical	8.3	Pessimism & lack of self-reliance	Erratic over- & underuse	Overuse/arbitrary use	High	Long	Increased	Poor
3	Anxious dependency	Disregarding	2.0	[b]	[b]	[b]	High	[b]	[b]	Poor
4	Generally adaptive	Vigilant	12.2	Appropriate optimism	Compliant	Appropriate use	Low	Moderate	Moderate	Good
5	Generally adaptive	Typical	33.4	Appropriate optimism	[c]	[c]	Moderate	Moderate	Moderate	No effect
6	Generally adaptive	Disregarding	16.4	Appropriate optimism	[c]	Underuse	Moderately high	Moderate	Moderate	Poor
7	Driven counter-dependency	Vigilant	1.3	[b]	[b]	[b]	[b]	[b]	[b]	[b]
8	Driven counter-dependency	Typical	6.3	Unrealistic optimism and self-reliance	Underuse	[c]	High	Short	Moderate	Poor
9	Driven counter-dependency	Disregarding	8.5	Unrealistic optimism and self-reliance	Underuse	Underuse	High	Short	Decreased	Poor

[a]These percentages reflect incidence for asthmatic patients at NJHRC.
[b]These patients are too few in number to permit documentation of the effect.
[c]Compliance cannot be predicted solely on the basis of this style.

and subtypes do not differ in the objective severity of their asthma as determined either by longitudinal spirometric pulmonary function measures (Dirks *et al.*, 1977b; Dirks, Kinsman, Horton, Fross, & Jones, 1978b; Kinsman *et al.*, 1977) or by methacholine and histamine inhalation challenge tests to determine airways hyperreactivity (Dirks, 1978: Dirks, *et al.*, 1979b: Staudenmayer *et al.*, 1979). As such, the differing medical outcomes, medical decisions, and patient attitudes associated with the nine subtypes cannot be accounted for by differences in the actual severity of the asthma. The purpose here is to provide a conceptual understanding and a brief review of the relevant research. Clinical application of the full BAIB will be presented subsequently.

5.3.1. High Panic–Fear Personality

On the BAIB, these patients score one standard deviation above the mean of asthmatic patients on the MMPI Panic–Fear personality scale (Dirks, Kinsman, Jones, Spector, Davidson, & Evans, 1977c). Primarily, the Panic–Fear personality scale measures characterological or trait anxiety while only secondarily relating to illness-focused anxiety (Kinsman, Dirks, Dahlem, & Heller, 1980a). Extremely high characterological anxiety is typical of asthmatics who are dependent, tend to feel helpless, emphasize their distress, and give up easily in many situations. As represented by the first three patterns of Table 4, their personality type might be characterized as anxious–dependent. Typically, these patients were overprotected during childhood (Dirks, Paley, & Fross, 1979). Relative to others, they are pessimistic about their own ability to control and to cope with their asthma and tend to see their illness as being totally in the hands of medical care givers (Kinsman, Dirks, & Jones, 1980b). These characteristics are consistent with a maladaptive reaction to breathing difficulties: extreme anxiety, exaggeration of affective distress, and helplessness, all of which could prevent the patient from taking effective action when experiencing breathing difficulties, leading him or her to become excessively dependent upon medical assistance (Dirks, Jones, & Fross, 1979a). As a group, twice the percentage of these patients were found to be rehospitalized within 6 months and again at 12 months following intensive treatment as compared with patients with only moderate levels of this form of anxiety (Dirks *et al.*, 1978b). Among these anxious–dependent patients, the same 2:1 ratio existed 2 years after discharge from intensive medical treatment (Dirks, Schraa, Brown, & Kinsman, 1980). The effect of this personality style on medical utilization is seen in the almost $200,000 in estimated excess hospital costs generated by 42 of these patients followed for a 2-year period. There were no differences in the actual severity of the asthma to account for this disparity (Dirks *et al.*, 1980).

Despite the commonalities among these characterologically anxious–dependent patients, important differences exist in regard to whether they attend to their asthmatic symptoms in vigilant, typical, or disregarding ways.

5.3.1a. Vigilant Responders. Asthmatic patients are classified as vigilant responders if they score at least 0.5 standard deviation above the normative mean on the Asthma Symptom Checklist (ASC) Panic–Fear symptom scale (Kinsman *et al.*, 1977). Vigilance about one's asthma is a by-product of anxiety that is specifically focused upon breathing difficulties. Such illness-focused anxiety appears to serve as a signal (i.e., signal anxiety) warning of potential problems, and thereby motivating the patient to take action (Dirks *et al.*, 1979b; Staudenmayer *et al.*, 1979). Approximately 11.6% (Table 4, Pattern 1) of the asthmatic patients studied have personalities characterized by anxious dependency and are vigilant about their symptoms.

Unfortunately, high Panic–Fear personality patients lack effective strategies to react adaptively when alerted by the signal aspects of their illness-focused anxiety. It is as if their illness-focused anxiety triggered the fears, anxieties, dependency, and feelings of helplessness that are part and parcel of their psychologic being. In brief, when confronted by an asthma attack, they panic. Their overwhelming anxiety at these times interferes with the reasonably expeditious care needed to alleviate asthmatic distress. Their exaggerated presentation of distress and their conveyed helplessness influences the physician's judgment to prescribe more intensive (and thereby risky) medication regimens (Dirks, Fross, & Evans, 1977a), to hospitalize them longer (Dirks *et al.*, 1977c), and generally to regard them as more seriously ill than they actually are (Dirks, Horton, Kinsman, Fross, & Jones, 1978a). Physicians can be further misled by these patients' tendency to vary between erratic overuse and underuse of medications prescribed on a regular basis (Kleiger & Dirks, 1979) and by their tendency to overuse p.r.n. medications (e.g., aerosolized bronchodilators) or to use p.r.n. medications in an arbitrary way relative to their actual airways obstruction (Dahlem, Kinsman, & Horton, 1977; Kinsman *et al.*, 1980). Such p.r.n. overusage is known to affect physician judgment (Dahlem, Kinsman, & Horton, 1979), and overusage of aerosolized bronchodilators can lead to serious, life-threatening consequences (Bierman & Pierson, 1974). Finally, possibly as a result of their extreme anxiety, these patients tend to breathe rapidly and to hyperventilate during asthma attacks (Kinsman *et al.*, 1980b), a behavior which can exacerbate asthma directly (Zeballos, Shturman-Ellstein, McNally, Hirsch, & Souhrada, 1978). Predictably, they experience their asthma as more of an interference in their physical, social, and vocational lives than do other patients (Fross *et al.*, 1980).

In summary, this style serves to maintain the asthma and to increase the frequency of hospitalization, the length of hospital stay, and the intensity of medication regimens prescribed (and thus the risk of medication side effects). Ultimately, this style undermines the long-term success of medical management.

5.3.1b. Typical Responders. These patients score within ±0.5 standard deviations of the normative mean on the ASC Panic–Fear symptom scale (Kinsman *et al.*, 1977). Although their level of illness-focused anxiety is not as high as that of the vigilant responders, they are at least attentive to their symptoms. However, they share the same psychologic pattern as other high Panic–Fear personality patients, and they respond equally ineffectively to their breathing difficulties. Comprising approximately 8.3% of the asthmatic population studied (Table 4, Pattern 2), they are in all other respects (e.g., attitudes, medication compliance, and medical outcome) essentially similar to their vigilant, high Panic–Fear personality counterparts.

5.3.1c. Symptom Disregarders. These patients score below 0.5 standard deviation from the normative mean on the ASC Panic–Fear symptom scale (Kinsman *et al.*, 1977). Despite the fact that they share the high Panic–Fear personality style, they report unusually low levels of anxiety during their asthma attacks.

Such low levels of illness-focused anxiety are associated with a maladaptive symptom disregard (Dahlem *et al.*, 1977; Dirks *et al.*, 1979b; Staudenmayer *et al.*, 1979) that leads the patient to delay acting expeditiously when breathing difficulties occur. Since these patients comprise only 2.0% of the asthmatic population studied (Table 4, Pattern 3), little has been confirmed about their behavior during treatment, although their hospitalization rate is high and their long-term treatment outcome is poor.

5.3.2. Low Panic–Fear Personality

These patients are identified by scores more than one standard deviation below the normative mean on the MMPI Panic–Fear personality scale (Dirks *et al.*, 1977c). Their basic personality contrasts sharply with the high Panic–Fear personality patients. As a group, they report growing up in family environments characterized by parental underprotection, a rigid emphasis on independence, and a lack of warm interpersonal relationships (Dirks *et al.*, 1979c). They see themselves as persistent in the face of difficulty, as self-contained during stress, and as coping in a highly self-reliant manner (Dirks *et al.*, 1977b). Compared to other asthmatic patients, they are often rigid and constricted and so independent as to be counterdependent (Kinsman *et al.*, 1980b). Their extreme need to be strong, independent, and capable forms the most notable basis for the adult personality of these low Panic–Fear personality patients.

At more illness-specific levels, the maladaptive features of this style become more apparent. Thus, these patients have unusually stong attitudes about self-management of their asthma, are unrealistically optimistic about their ability to master their asthma on their own, and see the role of medical caregivers as less remarkable than others perceive it to be (Kinsman *et al.*, 1980b). They generally report very reduced affective responses to their breathing difficulties (Kinsman *et al.*, 1980b).

Behaviorally, their need to be self-reliant is reflected by avoidance of medical assistance even when needed (Dirks *et al.*, 1978b), by underuse (noncompliance) of routinely scheduled medications (Kleiger & Dirks, 1979), and by underuse of p.r.n. medications (Kinsman *et al.*, 1980a). As a result of their style of presenting minimal affective distress, they are typically prescribed less intensive medication regimens than are others in the short run (Dirks *et al.*, 1977b; Dirks, Kinsman, Jones, & Fross, 1978c) and are hospitalized more briefly (Dirks *et al.*, 1977c). Their long-term outcome is, however, dismal, and they are hospitalized following intensive treatment at exceptionally high rates (Dirks *et al.*, 1978b; Dirks *et al.*, 1980). The financial and personal impact of this general style can be seen by the estimated $86,500 in excess hospitalizations for 29 low Panic–Fear personality patients studied during a 2-year period (Dirks *et al.*, 1980).

The similarities among the basic personality types of these patients do not prevent them from attending to breathing difficulties in vigilant, typical, or disregarding ways.

5.3.2a. Vigilant Responders. Given their basic personality, it is not surprising that only 1.3% of the asthmatic patients studied have low Panic–Fear personalities and the high illness-focused anxiety that is a prerequisite to symptom vigilance (Table 4, Pattern 7). Therefore, little is known about those low Panic–Fear personality patients who generally seem to be very self-reliant but who, in regard to periods of illness exacerbation, are vigilant toward breathing difficulties.

5.3.2b. Typical Responders. Nearly half of the low Panic–Fear personality patients are attentive to breathing difficulties. However, this attentive stance is channeled by a rigidly independent style which prevents adaptive action (such as seeking appropriate medical attention when needed). Their need to see themselves as strong, self-reliant, and independent causes them to minimize the significance of their own awareness of discomfort. The frequency of low Panic–Fear personality patients studied who are typical responders is estimated to be 6.3% (Pattern 8, Table 4).

Since these patients typically avoid medical assistance, they may allow asthma attacks to develop to the point that any treatment short of hospitalization is ineffective. The unnecessary delays caused by their excessive independence may transform a minor episode of breathing difficulty into a major one. These patients are likely to withhold pertinent information during medical treatment, to minimize their symptoms, and to present themselves as more calm and less worried than others (Dirks *et al.*, 1979a; Kinsman *et al.*, 1980b). This style can initially cause underestimation of severity and undertreatment of their asthma (Dirks *et al.*, 1978a; Jones *et al.*, 1979). The eventual effect of this style is to increase the hospitalization rate for these patients markedly (Dirks *et al.*, 1978b; Dirks, Fross, & Paley, 1978d).

5.3.2c. Symptom Disregarders. These patients have a double-barreled problem. First, the low level of anxiety they focus upon their illness leads to an initial disregard of breathing difficulties, thereby delaying action. This disregard is reflected behaviorally by their underusage of p.r.n. medications even when they are experiencing airways obstruction (Dahlem *et al.*, 1977: Kinsman *et al.*, 1980). Second, when their breathing difficulties become impossible to disregard, their extreme need to be independent leads them to try to tough out their distress on their own without seeking appropriate assistance. Approximately 8.5% of the asthmatic patients studied (Pattern 9, Table 4) respond with initial symptom disregard and subsequent avoidance of appropriate action (Jones *et al.*, 1979).

The effects of this response style are varied and dramatic, underscoring the serious implications of this posture in asthma. As noted, use of p.r.n. medications (e.g., aerosolized bronchodilators) to relieve acute breathing distress is infrequent even in the face of severe airways obstruction (Dahlem *et al.*, 1977; Jones *et al.*, 1979). In the short run, such underusage of p.r.n. medications influences physicians, who monitor reported p.r.n. usage as one index of the effectiveness of ongoing therapy, to judge them as less severely ill than others. These patients also tend to underuse regularly scheduled medications (Kleiger & Dirks, 1979). Additionally, since these patients also report little interference with their life due to illness and tend to minimize their distress, their physicians typically prescribe less intensive medication regimens for them (Dirks *et al.*, 1977a). This doubly maladaptive style is defeating at best and results in excessively high rates of hospitalization for asthma (Dirks *et al.*, 1978b; Dirks *et al.*, 1978d). There is reason to believe that death in asthma, a relatively rare occurrence, can be the end result of the interplay of such symptom denial and unrealistic independence combined with severe disease that is characterized by rapid-onset asthma attacks (Dirks, & Kinsman, 1980; Read, 1968).

Moderate Panic–Fear personality patients (Dirks *et al.,* 1977b; Dirks *et al.,* 1978b) have the best potential for adapting appropriately to asthma and its treatment. Unlike the extreme low and high Panic–Fear personality patients, they generally perceive their family environment to have been as warm, supportive, and secure. Issues related to dependency are less likely to color the ways that they behave during stress in general or specifically during the stress of chronic asthma. They neither spend a great deal of time anxiously seeking dependent relationships (as the high Panic–Fear personality patients do) or religiously avoiding any taint of dependency (as the low Panic–Fear personality patients do). Relieved of these issues, they generally adopt more flexible, adaptive, and appropriate strategies in mastering life's crises, including the crisis of a chronic illness.

In regard to their asthma, their level of optimism is generally appropriate and they can accept medical guidance while being able to assume appropriate responsibility for their own self-management (Dirks *et al.,* 1979b; Kinsman *et al.,* 1980b). However, these generalities must be tempered, since differences do exist in regard to the degree of attention that these patients give to their breathing difficulties.

5.3.3a. Vigilant Responders. Approximately 12.2% of the patients studied show a moderate Panic–Fear personality pattern and are vigilant responders (Pattern 4, Table 4). It is here that we see the real value of appropriate anxiety about breathing difficulties as a signal to warn the patient that action needs to be taken. For these patients, this high level of anxiety specifically focused on breathing difficulties is highly adaptive by serving as an early warning system. Moreover, this early warning to act is likely to be followed by appropriate action. As a result of this adaptive style—initial vigilance and subsequent effective action—their rate of hospitalization is much lower than that of any other patient group, despite the fact that they have asthma of similar objective serverity (Dirks *et al.,* 1978b; Dirks *et al.,* 1978d; Dirks *et al.,* 1979b). Thus, the high levels of anxiety they focus on their breathing difficulties are linked to an appropriate symptom vigilance that should be encouraged. This is an important point which appears to go against a common inclination to reduce anxiety in asthma, no matter what its form or focus (Kinsman, Dirks, Jones, & Dahlem, 1980b). Illness-focused anxiety combined with adequate resources to react effectively to its signal value is an exceptionally adaptive stance in severe asthma. For mild to moderately severe asthmatics, this vigilant stance leads to a notably good prognosis and low rates of medical utilization (Dirks *et al.,* 1979b; Staudenmayer *et al.,* 1979).

5.3.3b. Typical Responders. Although not precisely vigilant, these patients are at least attentive about their breathing difficulties, and this attentiveness needs to be fostered (Dirks *et al.,* 1978d; Dirks *et al.,* 1979c). Since they react effectively to their breathing difficulties, their medical course is generally uncomplicated by psychomaintenance issues. Approximately 33.4% of the patients studied have moderate Panic–Fear personalities and are typical responders (Pattern 5, Table 4).

5.3.3c. Symptom Disregarders. Patients within this subtype have the ability and resources to react effectively to breathing difficulties, but they fail to act expeditiously because of a low level of anxiety—which is linked with a maladaptive symptom disregard—about their breathing difficulties. Thus, by the time action is initiated, their symptoms have often progressed beyond the point of easy resolution. For example, their use of p.r.n. medications is typically low even when their breathing difficulties are quite pronounced (Dahlem *et al.*, 1977: Jones *et al.*, 1979). Despite their potentially flexible and adaptive style of reacting to breathing difficulties, they simply get started too late, and their medical treatment is less effective than it would be given expeditious action. In severe asthma characterized by highly hyperreactive airways, such disregard contributes greatly to treatment failure (Staudenmayer *et al.*, 1979). Approximately 16.4% of the patients studied have moderate Panic–Fear personalities and are symptom disregarders (Pattern 6, Table 4).

6. Examples of Assessment and Treatment

These nine types provide a useful initial starting point for the clinical application of the BAIB in psychomaintenance assessment. Use of the full BAIB provides a richer source of information about the patient styles through clarifying linkages between patient personality, attitudes, and symptom experiences. Using the BAIB, two psychologists correctly predicted rehospitalization for 70% to 84% of the asthmatic patients studied while blind to all demographic and medical characteristics of these patients (Dirks & Kinsman, 1981). More recently, Bayesian models (Dirks, 1980a,b) based on test scores from the BAIB have provided the subjective likelihood of (1) rehospitalization for asthma and (2) specific patterns of p.r.n. medication usage (appropriate, overusage, underusage, and arbitrary usage). For each of the four clinical examples that follow, these subjective likelihoods are given. For these examples, the BAIB is used to provide assessment in a way that treatment recommendations can be tailored both to the psychomaintenance issues identified and to the medical treatment context.

6.1. Patient A: A Low Panic–Fear Personality, Symptom Disregarder

The patient was a 33-year-old female with a diagnosis of bronchial asthma. Shortly after admission to intensive, long-term hospital treatment, she was given the BAIB. The results are presented in Figure 3. In order of analysis, we will examine the MMPI, the RIOS, and then the ASC.

6.1.1. Psychomaintenance Assessment for Patient A

An examination of the MMPI reveals several potential problem areas. First, this patient's Panic–Fear personality, a T-score of 38, is low. Coupled with her excessively low Dependency score of 35, her low Panic–Fear personality status suggests a definite counterdependent potential which could lead to avoidance of physicians and reluctance to follow medical advice. One could well imagine that for her, asthma represents a threat to both her independence and her competence. Her manner of responding to that threat is to "dig in her heels," to become excessively and perhaps dangerously independent of medical care givers, and to drive herself inappropriately in an attempt to reaffirm her competence. Confirmation of these hypotheses are found throughout her testing. Second, her F minus K index (raw score = −16) suggests the probability that she characteristically withholds negative information while attempting to maintain a smiling facade. The danger here is that she will withhold medically relevant information and symptoms from her medical care givers. This hypothesis is consistent with her aforementioned counterdependence and her Hs score. Third, her Hs score of 58 is about 10 T-score points below the average for asthmatics in this population. It is as though, given her excessive preoccupation with independence and competence, she doesn't have enough energy left to be properly focused on and properly concerned about her illness. Fourth, this last hypothesis derives some support from her Hy score. With a T-score of 72, Hy is her highest scale on the MMPI, suggesting that she simply does not perceive what she wishes to ignore (e.g., the realistic constraints her illness places upon her). Fifth, her

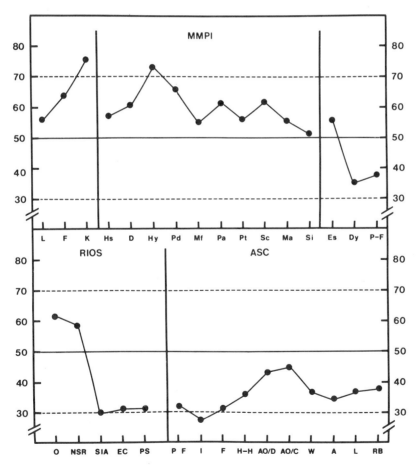

Figure 3. General and illness-specific profiles on the Battery of Asthma Illness Behavior (BAIB) for Patient A.

Pd score of 67—and the pattern of her Hy, Pd, and Mf scores—raises the possibility of conflict with authority figures. Given her counterdependence, authority conflict may further interfere with her relations with her physician and medical care givers. Sixth, with Pd at 67 and Ma at 57, we have to wonder about occasionally impulsive behaviors. Finally, two good signs should be mentioned. Pa is low enough (T-score = 62) and Es is high enough (T-score = 56) to suggest that she can come to understand her own psychomaintenance potential and that information about her style and its implications can be profitably presented to her as long as her need for independence is respected.

Given these considerations about her personality, this patient's RIOS findings are consistent, offer confirmation, and allow us to expand our understanding of the patient. First, her high score on Optimism (T-score = 62) combined with her lack of focus on her general health (low Hs) and her tendency to repress and deny (high Hy) indicate that she may well be engaged in a rather Pollyannish denial of the actual severity of her illness. Second, her high Negative Staff Regard (T-score = 58) suggests that our earlier concern that authority conflict may generalize to her relationship with medical care givers is correct. Third, her lack of awareness of the prodromal signs of an asthma attack (Specific Internal Awareness T-score = 30) is troublesome and may indicate the extent and rigidity of her denial of the illness. Fourth, her excessively low score on External Control (T-score = 31) confirms that her counterdependent style interferes with her ability to accept medical directives and care. It's as though she's determined to go it alone in the treatment of her illness. Finally, her Psychological Stigma level (T-score = 31) is so low as to suggest that she is strangely comfortable with her illness. Again, this is indicative of her counterdependence and denial.

The ASC demonstrates her remarkably mild affective response to periods of acute breathing difficulty. Her Panic–Fear symptomatology T-score of 32 suggests that she disregards her symptoms of breathing difficulty. Additionally, Irritability at 27, Worry at 37, and Anger at 34 all attest to a blanket denial of affect during asthmatic attacks. This finding, coupled with the sum of the above, makes a strong case for predicting underusage of medications. However, despite her denial of anxiety secondary to an asthmatic attack, this underlying anxiety probably does surface in her behavior. For example, with her Fatigue score at 31 being 15 T-score points lower than her Airways Obstruction/Congestion score, there is a very strong possibility that she becomes overly active and pushes herself physically during acute exacerbations of her asthma. This behavioral pattern will no doubt exacerbate any attack and is consistent with our MMPI-derived hypothesis of occasionally impulsive behaviors.

The picture that emerges of this patient becomes progressively consistent and more refined as we move across the three assessment levels of the BAIB. In summary, this patient is at extremely high risk of asthma-related rehospitalization due to psychomaintenance issues. Specific potential issues of concern with this patient are the following:

1. Her relationships with medical care givers are characterized by:
    a. Counterdependent avoidance and need for excessive patient control
    b. Withholding of medically relevant information and minimization of her symptom picture
2. Her relationship to her illness is characterized by:
    a. Denial and lack of concern

b. Lack of awareness of the prodromal signs of an impending attack, thus preventing the use of preventive measures

3. She becomes overly active during attacks, thus exacerbating her breathing distress.

4. She is at extreme risk to underuse p.r.n.-type medications and is likely to underuse all medications. Based on the Bayesian model, the subjective probability of underuse of p.r.n. medications is 91%: the likelihood of appropriate use is only 7% (Dirks, 1980a).

5. Unless these problems are resolved, rehospitalization for psychomaintenance issues is highly likely for this patient, the subjective probability of such an outcome being equal to 88% (Dirks, 1980b).

6.1.2. Treatment Recommendations for Patient A

Several recommendations can be made for this patient. In each case, the intervention focuses on specific problems and is tailored to be compatible with the patient as a whole person:

1. As already noted, the patient's moderate Pa and high Es scores indicate that she could benefit from an open discussion of her psychomaintenance potentials. Thus, it is recommended that she receive a one-session test feedback on her BAIB scores. Two points will have to be remembered in the test feedback. First, it is vital to avoid any judgmental, authoritarian, domineering, or paternalistic approach to the patient, as this would only mobilize her counterdependence. Second, while sticking to the problem list generated, the psychologist should get the patient to verbalize her psychomaintenance behaviors rather than telling them to her. This accomplished, the psychologist can then integrate her report and show her the consequences of her behavior. This may well result in substantial behavioral change.

2. All medical caregivers should avoid an authoritarian, domineering, and/or paternalistic approach to the patient, although the physician should also be firm and open. In this way, the patient's counterdependence can be diffused and her authority conflict with the physician alleviated.

3. Where possible, the physician should give the patient choices about her treatment. For example, if it has been determined that the patient should take aminophylline 200 mg four times a day, the physician can ask the patient whether she'd rather take her aminophylline at 6-12-6-12 or 8-2-8-2. Such a procedure channels the patient's independence into constructive compliance rather than avoidance and noncompliance.

4. Recognizing the patient's tendency to withhold information and to minimize her illness, medical staff should pay special attention to even minimal reports of symptom complaint. Objective medical tests instead of patient reports should be used wherever possible.

5. The patient should be taught to recognize the prodromal signs and symptoms of acute asthmatic distress and the need to act expeditiously. Such education could make it possible to abort potential attacks through early action.

6. The patient must be informed about the realistic severity of her illness.

7. The patient and physician must jointly plan a behavioral strategy to be implemented by the patient when she has an attack. Such a strategy should be aimed at reducing overactivity.

8. The patient must be educated about proper medication usage. If such education and the insight gained through test feedback is insufficient to insure p.r.n. compliance, then a more rigorous plan can be instituted. The patient can be given a minipeak flow meter with instructions to take twice-daily readings and to take a certain p.r.n. regimen whenever her readings drop below a predetermined level.

6.2. Patient B. A High Panic–Fear Personality, Vigilant Patient

The BAIB profiles for this 34-year-old female with bronchial asthma are presented in Figure 4.

6.2.1. Psychomaintenance Assessment for Patient B

This patient's MMPI appears valid, although there is some tendency for her to exaggerate her distress when responding to the test items (moderately

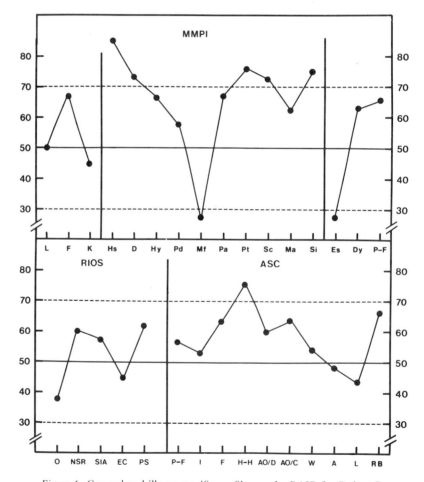

Figure 4. General and illness-specific profiles on the BAIB for Patient B.

high F-scale). More notably, she has an unusually strong focus on diffuse bodily symptoms (high Hs) that cannot be accounted for solely on the basis of her asthma. This strong, diffuse symptom focus combines with exceptional passivity (low Mf) and leads to the expectation that she deals with many issues, particularly those apt to generate angry affect, by avoidance and withdrawal (high Si). At times, such withdrawal may take the form of a flight into illness. Her perceived lack of resources to deal with many of her personal problems (low Es) and her dependency (high Dy) suggest that she will react in a helpless, characterologically anxious, and dependent way to many situations. Such a highly anxious, helpless, and clingingly dependent style is further suggested by her high score on the Panic–Fear personality scale. Combined with her strong focus upon a diffuse array of bodily symptoms, her high Panic–Fear personality score suggests that she will run to the physician for treatment of a wide range of physical complaints, present these physical complaints in an intensely anxious way, and demand immediate relief. This style may ultimately wear her physician's patience thin and thereby increase her own dissatisfaction with her medical treatment, ultimately compounding her sense of interpersonal alienation (high Sc) and discomfort (high Pt).

At a more illness-specific level measured by the RIOS, her attitudes toward her asthma reflect her general personality style and tell more about the way in which she regards her asthma and its treatment. In line with her general sense of helplessness, suggested at the level of personality, she is very pessimistic about her own ability to help master her asthma (low Optimism). Such pessimism may lead her to exert little constructive, independent effort to manage her illness on her own. Given her extreme dependency, her intolerance of discomfort, and her demandingness, it is not surprising that she is currently dissatisfied with her physicians (high Negative Staff Regard). Her passivity suggests that she is unlikely to express her anger and dissatisfaction directly to her physicians, but she may (1) fail to comply with therapeutic regimens and (2) change physicians frequently ("doctor shop"). It is not surprising that she perceives asthma as a stigma that makes her "psychologically different" from others (high Psychological Stigma) and blames many of her personal difficulties on her illness.

Her ASC profile indicates that this patient experiences relatively high levels of anxiety specifically focused on her breathing difficulties (high Panic–Fear symptomatology). Given adequate resources to react effectively, such high levels of this form of anxiety are beneficial by signaling the patient to react in a rapid, expeditious way to incipient asthma attacks. However, for this patient, the high level of illness-focused anxiety is apt to trigger a sequence of ineffective, anxious, and dependent behaviors that are typical of such characterologically anxious and helpless patients (high Panic–Fear personality). She reports rapid breathing (high Rapid Breathing) and hyperventilation (high Hyperventilation–Hypocapnia) at unusually high levels relative to other asthma patients. This hyperventilation may lead to two additional psychomaintenance potentials: (1) hyperventilation may directly exacerbate the asthma and (2) she may misinterpret an episode of hyperventilation as an asthma attack. The latter possibility is supported by the fact that Hyperventilation–Hypocapnia is the highest symptom scale reported to occur during asthma attacks, fully 20 T-score units above either of the target-symptom categories that characterize asthma attacks (Airways Obstruction/Congestion and Airways Obstruction/Dyspnea).

Given the test scores on the Battery of Asthma Illness Behavior, this patient is at extremely high risk for psychomaintenance of her asthma. The following problems can be summarized:

1. Her extremely strong symptom focus, her emphasis on her affective distress, her demands for immediate relief, and her excessive running to physicians will lead her to be treated more intensively by her physicians than the objective severity of her illness actually requires. Overly intensive medication dosages are likely to be prescribed, and these will increase the risk of side effects. Such side effects may require further treatment in their own right, setting up a vicious circle.

2. Her characterologically helpless reactions to her breathing difficulties, her intense anxiety about these, her sense of helplessness, and her demand for instant relief will lead her to overuse p.r.n. medications (e.g., aerosolized bronchodilators) even when her breathing is not at all impaired. In asthma, such PRN overusage had led to paradoxical reactions (e.g., increased airways obstruction) and even to death. The Bayesian model based on her BAIB scores yields a 95.6% subjective probability of p.r.n. overusage (Dirks, 1980a).

3. Her intense anxiety about her breathing difficulties, her tendency to withdraw into illness, and her likely noncompliance as an expression of her anger with her physician may lead her to take regularly scheduled medications in an erratic manner.

4. Her tendency to breathe rapidly and to hyperventilate as an anxiety equivalent can exacerbate asthma attacks that might otherwise abate with minimal treatment.

5. Her diffuse symptom focus and her extreme likelihood of hyperventilation may also lead her to mislabel episodes of hyperventilation as asthma attacks, thereby further increasing the likelihood of intensive medical treatment.

Based on these considerations and the Bayesian model using the BAIB scores, the subjective likelihood of this patient's rehospitalization within a 6-month period following discharge from treatment is 88% (Dirks, 1980b).

6.2.2. Treatment Recommendations for Patient B

This patient will require a focused intervention package tailored to structure her medical treatment and to resolve the unique psychomaintenance potentials that would otherwise defeat her medical management.

1. Due to this patient's tendency to present diffuse symptoms in an exaggerated way, the physician will have difficulty discerning what is asthma and what is not and how serious the asthma actually is. The patient's self-report of breathing difficulties should be carefully monitored with obtained pulmonary functions so that the physician will not to be misled by the patient's tendency to exaggerate her distress or to present other symptoms (e.g., hyperventilation) as manifestations of the airways obstruction characteristic of asthma. Her physician may need to work with

her to teach her to differentiate between hyperventilation and asthmatic symptoms.

2. Her physician must be cautioned to avoid regarding her usage of p.r.n. medications as an index of the effectiveness of ongoing therapy, since this patient is at extreme risk to overuse these medications. It may be useful to equip her with a minipeak flow meter and to instruct her not to take a p.r.n. medication unless her values fall below some established level.

3. The patient's adherence to routinely scheduled medications should be monitored carefully: special efforts are needed to educate her as to proper usage of medications and compliance with her regimen.

4. The patient should be taught diaphragmatic breathing, both to alleviate anxiety and to combat potential hyperventilation.

5. Relaxation training techniques may be helpful in containing the patient's anxiety. However, the real benefit may actually lie in encouraging her to believe that she has some self-control. As such, any relaxation training used should also heavily stress her ability to control and master her own reactions. Note that this should not be intended as a direct means to control her asthma.

6. For long-term management, it must be remembered that this patient has fairly serious psychological problems. Long-term therapy is desirable and should be aimed at resolving her characteristic maladaptive means of coping with various issues in her life. Although it must be understood that this style affects her illness enormously, the therapy should not be aimed at "resolving her asthma." That is an issue of medical management. Psychotherapy must address her self-defeating ways of reacting to stresses and problems.

6.3. Patient C: A Moderate Panic–Fear Personality, Vigilant Patient

This 52-year-old male was admitted to long-term intensive treatment with a diagnosis of bronchial asthma. Findings on the BAIB, administered shortly after admission, are presented in Figure 5.

6.3.1. Psychomaintenance Assessment for Patient C

The MMPI profile suggests depression (high D), which does not appear to be exclusively attributable to the patient's illness or physical symptoms (D is high relative to Hs and Hy). To some extent, this depression may be fostered by his tendency to repress anger (low Pd) and a somewhat passive style (slightly elevated Mf). These observations must be made cautiously in view of the absence of clearly extreme scale deviations: they require further substantiation. Notably, this patient has important strengths. Dependency (Dy) is not an issue for him, and he has the resources to react adaptively to difficulties in his life, including those posed by his illness (moderate Panic–Fear personality). Behavioral controls and ability to delay gratification appear to be good (Hy, Pd, Ma), and it is unlikely that his repressed anger will surface in any sudden explosive outbursts.

On the RIOS, his attitudes reflect an unusually positive regard for his medical care givers (low Negative Staff Regard). Although it is possible that such a favorable view is partially secondary to difficulty in expressing anger directly, such high regard for his medical care givers may help to cement a good patient–physician working alliance. Given this favorable view of the medical staff and the absence of any noticeable dependency conflicts, his tendency to assume major responsibility for his self-care (low External Control) should be seen to imply adaptive and responsible behavior. He reports good prodromal awareness of his acute breathing difficulties. Finally, his excessively low score on Psychological Stigma (PS) may indicate either an unusually good adjustment to his illness or a tendency to deny that his illness is a source of psychologic discomfort.

On the ASC, his vigilance toward breathing difficulties (high Panic–Fear symptomatology) combined with his reported prodromal awareness (high RIOS Specific Internal Awareness), will help ensure that he reacts quickly when breathing difficulties occur. Since he has a good ability to respond adaptively (moderate Panic–Fear personality), such early action is likely to be both expeditious and

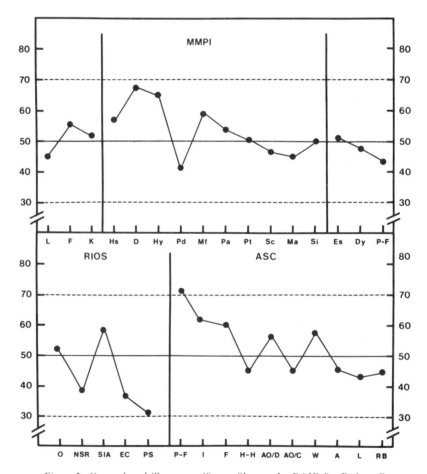

Figure 5. General and illness-specific profiles on the BAIB for Patient C.

effective. These are two primary ingredients of a highly beneficial style in asthma— initial vigilance and subsequent effective responses. Two minor problems are suggested. First, he tends to become quite irritable during attacks (high Irritability), which may occasionally drive others away at these times. Second, his low energy level (high Fatigue) during asthma attacks, consistent with a somewhat characteristically low energy level (MMPI Ma), may retard his otherwise effective reactions. In summary:

1. This patient has a highly adaptive style, combining vigilance and effective reactions to breathing difficulties, which places him at low risk for psychomaintenance. The Bayesian model for rehospitalization (Dirks, 1980b) yields a 26% subjective likelihood of rehospitalization for psychomaintenance.
2. His depressive tendencies and fatigue may somewhat blunt his adaptive style and reactions.
3. Although it is clinically unexpected, the Bayesian model for p.r.n. medication usage (Dirks, 1980a) yields a 76% subjective likelihood for arbitrary PRN medication usage.

6.3.2. Treatment Recommendations for Patient C

1. There should be no attempt to reduce this patient's illness-focused anxiety, for this anxiety is the basis of his adaptive symptom vigilance (Kinsman et al., 1980b).
2. Usage of p.r.n. medication should be monitored to assess the accuracy of the predicted pattern of arbitrary usage. If confirmed, given the patient's resources, any noncompliance should be readily resolved by educating the patient.
3. This patient could benefit from a few counseling sessions aimed at alleviating his depression and actualizing his potential assertiveness. It should be noted, however, that this will have little if any direct impact on his asthma.

6.4. Patient D: A Moderate Panic–Fear Personality, Typical Patient

Results on the BAIB for this 26-year-old female with bronchial asthma are summarized in Figure 6.

6.4.1. Psychomaintenance Assessment for Patient D

At the level of general characteristics pertinent to the maintenance of her illness, one would predict an adaptive approach from this patient's moderate Panic–Fear personality score. Her Hs-Hy-D pattern indicates a style characterized by a clear focus on nonsalient somatic complaints. Coupled with the prominent elevation (T-score = 86) of Ma, which indicates a tendency to handle anxiety by hyperactivity, the Hs-Hy-D pattern probably results in a bland, indifferent presentation of her symptoms to care givers while further obscuring and complicating her problems by overactivity.

At the level of attitudes toward illness, she maintains a highly optimistic stance (Optimism T-score = 60), which is quite consistent with the personality style just described and may well represent an expectation of some magical cure to be provided during medical treatment. Her presentation of herself as very much in control of her problems (External Control T-score = 40) supports the earlier hypothesis that she presents her situation as "just fine."

On the symptom-specific measures, she is clearly irritable (Irritability T-score = 64) during the course of an attack, but of most interest is the fact that her breathing pattern, though described as very labored (Airways Obstruction/Dyspnea T-score = 60), involves notably less congestion (Airways Obstruction/Congestion T-score = 49) but considerable Hyperventilation (T-score = 64). The only other dimension of symptom experience of special interest is the low score on Anger. She cannot express her frustration very directly.

In summary, this woman has some psychologic strengths but also some specific liabilities from the point of view of her illness:

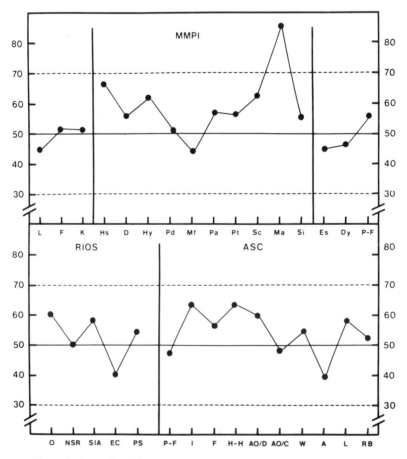

Figure 6. General and illness-specific profiles on the BAIB for Patient D.

1. She is not given to panicky reactions at any level, and she shows few signs of psychological maladjustment.
2. She does not appear to be particularly uncomfortable with her present situation. By the same token, she exercises no particular vigilance about her symptoms (moderate Panic–Fear symptomatology), presents herself in a rather bland way, and tends to allay her anxiety by engaging in a great deal of activity. This latter pattern is generally maladaptive for asthmatics, who profit by conserving energy during periods of breathing difficulty.
3. Her report of hyperventilation as an asthmatic symptom may be interpreted in two ways. First, it may be that she is responding to unrecognized anxiety with hyperventilation and confusing that with asthma; more likely, she may respond to the onset of a genuine asthma attack with anxiety channeled to hyperventilation and thus may significantly worsen the problem. Her experience of irritability during her attacks suggests the latter.

The Bayesian model yields an almost equal subjective likelihood of arbitrary usage (34%) and underusage (37%) of p.r.n. medications but only an 11% subjective likelihood of appropriate usage (Dirks, 1980a). Finally, her subjective likelihood of rehospitalization due to psychomaintenance issues is 69%.

6.4.2. Treatment Recommendations for Patient D

1. There is little reason to approach this patient on a general psychotherapeutic basis. However, she is quite competent to profit from education about the handling of her illness, including an explanation of the maladaptive quality of her high activity level.
2. She should be taught diaphragmatic breathing to help her control the hyperventilation, and she should be encouraged to give her reports of experienced breathing problems less "offhandedly" in order to impress her situation on medical staff.
3. She might profit from being given permission to be angry about her situation.

Without help in dealing with these issues, she seems a likely candidate for psychomaintenance. With some appropriately focused help, however, she may avoid rehospitalization.

6.5. Summary of the Psychomaintenance Assessment Approach and Its Implications for Treatment

Among the four patients presented, there were different risks for psychomaintenance. Yet, even where the likelihood of rehospitalization, for example, appeared to be essentially equal (e.g., Patients A and B), the reasons for the potential defeat of medical management differed enormously. Assessment is aimed at understanding patient styles and taking into account the patient's personality as well as the more illness-specific attitudes and symptom experiences that together make it possible to predict behaviors and outcome during medical treatment (Jones *et al.*, 1979).

Treatment recommendations that flow from this assessment approach must be individualized, tailored to the psychomaintenance issues suggested, and conform to the context of medical treatment. Information must be directed to the physician in order to mesh the findings with medical treatment planning. It also needs to go to the patient directly so as to improve the patient's own understanding of how his or her style may contribute to the maintenance of illness. Direct psychological intervention (e.g., focused psychotherapy) may or may not be warranted. But whenever specific psychomaintenance issues arise for a patient, it is always appropriate to involve the patient and the physician in such a way as to ensure that these issues will be considered in treatment planning. Application of across-the-board treatment approaches is unwarranted (e.g., Kinsman *et al.*, 1980b).

7. Relevance and Generality of Psychomaintenance

Our own experience has led us to concentrate on one chronic physical illness, asthma, where assessment of psychomaintenance potentials is increasingly possible and leads to focused recommendations congruent with the goals of medical management. The larger issues raised by this type of research and clinical assessment are relevant to many chronic physical illnesses, although the approach must be tailored to each illness and its form of medical management.

Kristein *et al.* (1977) maintain that the American health care industry is becoming progressively less cost-effective. In 1950, only 4.6% of the gross national product was spent on health care; in 1975, 8.3%—an increase of 80.4% in 25 years—was spent. Hospital admissions have increased 50% since 1950, and elective surgery in the United States is among the highest in the world. Kristein *et al.* (1977) note that these health care costs add "to the consumer costs of nearly all American goods and services, making them less available to the poor and less competitive on the world market. As a consequence, nationally we face curtailment of other basic services and goals in order to pay for a medical care system that does not concurrently improve our health" (p. 459). Expenditures on the treatment of chronic disease is a major factor in the deterioration of present health economics (Wilder, 1976).

The continuance of this trend can be predicted. The neglect of psychomaintenance issues accentuates this cost-ineffectiveness, as there is no way to deal with chronic illness on a biomedical basis alone. Engel (1977, 1980) described the need for a biopsychosocial model for medicine—instead of a more exclusively biomedical model—that takes into account the psychosocial realities of people who are ill. More than ever before, modern medicine is a very highly specialized and technique-oriented enterprise, attempting a biomedical resolution of disease by way of medications as well as specialized procedures such as radiation therapy, surgery, and many other highly focused forms of intervention that may be increasingly effective *per se*. But such focused medical interventions all too often target only the affected organ, the chemical defect, or the offending pathogen to the exclusion of the affected person. Engel's view is highly relevant to treating chronic illness, since a relatively small proportion of individuals whose psychological styles serve to perpetuate illness account for an enormous proportion of medical services and costs. This has been well documented in asthma, where a significant proportion of chronically ill patients—easily ignored and not readily identifiable—have styles of reacting to illness that are maladaptive in ways that increase medical utilization, increase the apparent impairment, and contribute greatly to medical treatment failure. For these most notably, the biopsychosocial approach to medical treatment is needed. But all too often, the patient's psychological problems are interpreted as another manifestation of the physical problem *per se,* and if the patient does not improve, further efforts toward resolution often involve increases in medication, diagnostic procedures, hospitalization, and other forms of intensified medical treatment. The increased utilization of medical services in these cases can be initiated both by the patient looking for a medical resolution to his psychologically exacerbated medical problem or by the physician who is puzzled about the failure of current medical treatment plans.

If psychologic factors contribute to increased utilization of medical services, what can be done to resolve these problems? We would argue that broad-based research relating to psychomaintenance issues is needed across various physical illnesses, and that this will lead to the development of focused assessment procedures as the prerequisite to resolution. But it is well to keep in mind that at least two general views are held among psychologists and physicians in regard to the role of psychological factors in illness. The first, most general, and most traditional view merely notes that medical and psychological problems (in the classical sense of personality or thought disorders or mental deficits) often exist side by side with medical problems. Although such parallelism of psychological and medical problems can increase utilization of medical services (e.g., APA Task Force on Health Research, 1976), no concerted effort is made to discern exactly how they do so. Psychological assessment and intervention are often aimed at identifying "classical" psychological problems and resolving these with only incidental consideration of precisely how psychological issues can influence medical management. Nonetheless, even for this conservative approach, there is evidence that psychological intervention can dramatically reduce the utilization of medical services (Cummings, 1977; Follette & Cummings, 1967; Olbrisch, 1977; Rosen & Weins, 1979). In the recent article by Rosen and Weins (1979), despite consideration of this traditional approach, a convincing argument is made that it is not so much direct intervention with the patient that produces lower medical utilization rates but rather clarification for the physician of the role that psychological factors play in a particular patient's case.

This brings us to the psychomaintenance position that we have described in this chapter. In contrast to the above, the issues that need to be addressed are precisely how psychological factors act to maintain illness and defeat medical management in a given patient's case. As we have described, this position promotes the understanding of psychomaintenance and encourages focused recommendations aimed at ensuring that the patient realizes maximum benefit from medical management.

The authors wish to thank Sharon Robinson and Jim Schraa for their contributions to this manuscript.

8. References

Addington, W. W. Patient compliance: The most serious remaining problem in the control of tuberculosis in the United States. *Chest*, 1979, *6*, 741–743.

American Psychological Association Task Force on Health Research. Contributions of psychology to health research: Patterns, problems, and potentials. *American Psychologist*, 1976, *31*, 263–274.

Barron, F. An ego-strength scale which predicts response to psychotherapy. *Journal of Consulting and Clinical Psychology*, 1953, *17*, 327–333.

Bellak, L. Introduction. In L. Bellak (Ed.), *Psychology of physical illness: Psychiatry applied to medicine, surgery, and the specialties.* New York: Grune & Stratton, 1952.

Bierman, C. W., & Pierson, W. E. Hand nebulizers and asthma therapy in children and adolescents. *Pediatrics*, 1974, *54*, 668–673.

Canon, H. S., & Roth, H. P. Patients' cooperation with a medical regimen. *Journal of the American Medical Association*, 1968, *203* (11), 120–124.

Comroe, J. H., Forster, R. E., DuBois, A. B., Briscoe, W. A., & Carlsen, E. *The lung: Clinical physiology and pulmonary function tests.* Chicago: Year Book Medical Publishers, 1962.

Cummings, N. A. The anatomy of psychotherapy under national health insurance. *American Psychologist*, 1977, *32*, 711–718.

Dahlem, N. W., Kinsman, R. A., & Horton, D. J. Panic–Fear in asthma: Requests for as-needed (PRN) medications in relation to pulmonary function measurements. *Journal of Allergy and Clinical Immunology*, 1977, *60*, 295–300.

Dahlem, N. W., Kinsman, R. A., & Horton, D. J. Requests for as-needed (PRN) medications by asthmatic patients: Relationships to prescribed oral corticosteroid regimens and length of hospitalization. *Journal of Allergy and Clinical Immunology*, 1979, *63*, 23–27.

Dirks, J. F. *The psychomaintenance of bronchial asthma: A review and preliminary theoretical integration of Panic–Fear research in asthma.* Report No. 54. Denver, Colo.: Psychophysiology Research Laboratories, National Jewish Hospital and Research Center, July 1978.

Dirks, J. F. *An automated Bayesian model for predicting psychomaintenance: As-needed (PRN) medication usage patterns and the Battery of Asthma Illness Behavior.* Report No. 86. Denver, Colo.: Division of Psychobiology, National Jewish Hospital and Research Center, August 1980. (a)

Dirks, J. F. *An automated Bayesian model for predicting psychomaintenance: Rehospitalization and the Battery of Asthma Illness Behavior.* Report No. 85. Denver, Colo.: Division of Psychobiology, National Jewish Hospital and Research Center, August 1980. (b)

Dirks, J. F., & Kinsman, R. A. *Death in asthma: A psychosomatic autopsy.* Report No. 72. Denver, Colo.: Psychophysiology Research Laboratories, National Jewish Hospital and Research Center, January 1980.

Dirks, J. F., & Kinsman, R. A. Clinical prediction of medical rehospitalization: Psychological assessment with the Battery of Asthma Illness Behavior. *Journal of Personality Assessment*, 1981, *45*, 608–613.

Dirks, J. F., Fross, K. H., & Evans, N. W. Panic–Fear in asthma: Generalized personality trait vs. specific situational state. *Journal of Asthma Research*, 1977, *14*, 161–167. (a)

Dirks, J. F., Jones, N. F., & Kinsman, R. A. Panic–Fear: A personality dimension related to intractability in asthma. *Psychosomatic Medicine*, 1977, *39*, 120–126. (b)

Dirks, J. F., Kinsman, R. A., Jones, N. F., Spector, S. L., Davidson, P. T., & Evans, N. W. Panic–Fear: A personality dimension related to length of hospitalization in respiratory illness. *Journal of Asthma Research.* 1977, *14*, 61–71. (c)

Dirks, J. F., Horton, D. J., Kinsman, R. A., Fross, K. H., & Jones, N. F. Patient and physician characteristics influencing medical decisions in asthma. *Journal of Asthma Research*, 1978, *15*, 171–178. (a)

Dirks, J. F., Kinsman, R. A., Horton, D. J., Fross, K. H., & Jones, N. F. Panic–Fear in asthma: Rehospitalization following intensive long-term treatment. *Psychosomatic Medicine*, 1978, *40*, 5–13. (b)

Dirks, J. F., Kinsman, R. A., Jones, N. F., & Fross, K. H. New developments in panic–fear research in asthma: Validity and stability of the MMPI panic–fear scale. *British Journal of Medical Psychology*, 1978, *51*, 119–126. (c)

Dirks, J. F., Fross, K. H., & Paley, A. Panic–Fear in asthma: State–trait relationship and rehospitalization. *Journal of Chronic Disease*, 1978, *31*, 605–609. (d)

Dirks, J. F., Jones, N. F., & Fross, K. H. Psychosexual aspects of the Panic–Fear personality types in asthma. *Canadian Journal of Psychiatry*, 1979, *24*, 731–739. (a)

Dirks, J. F., Kinsman, R. A. Staudenmayer, H., & Kleiger, J. H. Panic–Fear in asthma: Symptomatology as an index of signal anxiety and personality as an index of ego resources. *Journal of Nervous and Mental Disease*, 1979, *167*, 615–619. (b)

Dirks, J. F., Paley A., & Fross, K. H. Panic–Fear research in asthma and the nuclear conflict theory of asthma: Similarities, differences, and clinical implications. *British Journal of Medical Psychology*, 1979, *52*, 71–76. (c)

Dirks, J. F., Schraa, J., Brown, E. L., & Kinsman, R. A. Psychomaintenance in asthma: Hospitalization rates and financial impact. *British Journal of Medical Psychology*, 1980, *53*, 349–354.

Drake, L. E. A social I-E scale for the MMPI. *Journal of Applied Psychology*, 1946, *30*, 51–54.

Engel, G. L. The need for a new medical model: A challenge for biomedicine. *Science*, 1977, *196*, 129–136.

Engel, G. L. The clinical application of the biopsychosocial model. *American Journal of Psychiatry*, 1980, *137*, 535–544.

Follette, W., & Cummings, N. A. Psychiatric services and medical utilization in a prepaid health plan setting. Part I. *Medical Care*, 1967, *5*, 25–35.

Fross, K. H., Dirks, J. F., Kinsman, R. A., & Jones, N. F. Functionally determined invalidism in chronic asthma. *Journal of Chronic Disease*, 1980, *33*, 485–490.

Jones, N. F., Kinsman, R. A., Dirks, J. F., & Dahlem, N. W. Psychological contributions to chronicity in asthma: Patient response styles influencing medical treatment and its outcome. *Medical Care*, 1979, *17*, 1103–1118.

Jones, N. F., Dirks, J. F., & Kinsman, R. A. Assessment in the psychomaintenance of chronic physical illness. *Journal of Psychiatric Treatment and Evaluation*, 1980, *2*, 303–312.

Kaplan De-Nour, A., & Czacakes, J. W. Personality factors in chronic hemodialysis patients causing noncompliance with medical regimens. *Psychosomatic Medicine*, 1972, *34*, 333–344.

Kinsman, R. A., Luparello, T. J., O'Banion, K., & Spector, S. L. Multidimensional analysis of the subjective symptomatology of asthma. *Psychosomatic Medicine*, 1973, *35*, 250–267. (a)

Kinsman, R. A., O'Banion, K., Resnikoff, P., Luparello, T. J., & Spector, S. L. Subjective symptoms of acute asthma within a heterogeneous sample of asthmatics. *Journal of Allergy and Clinical Immunology*, 1973, *52*, 284–296. (b)

Kinsman, R. A. Spector, S. L., Shucard, D. W., & Luparello, T. J. Observations on patterns of subjective symptomatology of asthma. *Psychosomatic Medicine*, 1974, *36*, 129–143.

Kinsman, R. A., Jones, N. F., Matus, I., & Schum, R. A. Patient variables supporting chronic illness: A scale for measuring attitudes toward respiratory illness and hospitalization. *Journal of Nervous and Mental Disease*, 1976, *163*, 159–165.

Kinsman, R. A., Dahlem, N. W., Spector, S. L., & Staudenmayer, H. Observations on subjective symptomatology, coping behavior, and medical decisions in asthma. *Psychosomatic Medicine*, 1977, *39*, 102–119.

Kinsman, R. A., Dirks, J. F., Dahlem, N. W., & Heller, A. S. Anxiety in asthma: Panic–Fear symptomatology and personality in relation to manifest anxiety. *Psychological Reports*, 1980, *46*, 196–198. (a)

Kinsman, R. A., Dirks, J. F., & Jones, N. F. Levels of psychological experience in asthma: General and illness-specific concomitants of Panic–Fear personality. *Journal of Clinical Psychology*, 1980, *36*, 552–561. (b)

Kinsman, R. A., Dirks, J. F., & Dahlem, N. W. Noncompliance to prescribed as-needed (PRN) medication use in asthma: Usage patterns and patient characteristics. *Journal of Psychosomatic Research*, 1980, *24*, 97–107. (a)

Kinsman, R. A., Dirks, J. F., Jones, N. F., & Dahlem, N. W. Anxiety reduction in asthma: Four catches to general application. *Psychosomatic Medicine*, 1980, *42*, 397–405. (b)

Kleiger, J. H., & Dirks, J. F. Medication compliance in chronic asthmatic patients. *Journal of Asthma Research*, 1979, *16*, 93–96.

Kristein, M. M., Arnold, C. B., & Wynder, E. L. Health economics and preventive care. *Science*, 1977, *195*, 457–462.

Ley, P. Memory for medical information. *British Journal of Social and Clinical Psychology*, 1979, *18*, 245–255.

Michaux, W. W. Side effects, resistance, and dosage deviations in psychiatric patients treated with tranquilizers. *Journal of Nervous and Mental Disease*, 1961, *133*, 203–212.

Minden, P., & Farr, R. S. The management of allergic disorders in children. *Pediatric Clinics of North America*, 1969, *16*, 305–320.

Nadel, J. A. Structure–function relationships in the airways: Bronchoconstriction mediated via vagus nerves on bronchial arteries, peripheral lung constriction mediated via pulmonary arteries. *Medical Thoracics*, 1965, *22*, 231–238.

Nadel, J. A. Airways: Autonomic regulation and airway responsiveness. In E. B. Weiss & M. S. Segal (Eds.), *Bronchial asthma: Mechanisms and therapeutics*. Boston: Little, Brown, 1976.

Navran, L. A rationally derived MMPI scale for dependence. *Journal of Consulting and Clinical Psychology*, 1954, *18*, 192.

Olbrisch, M. E. Psychotherapeutic intervention in physical health. Effectiveness and economic efficiency. *American Psychologist*, 1977, *32*, 761–777.

Pilowsky, I. Abnormal illness behavior. *British Journal of Medical Psychology*, 1969, *42*, 347–351.

Read, J. The reported increase in mortality from asthma: A clinicofunctional analysis. *Medical Journal of Australia*, 1968, *1*, 879–884.

Rosen, J. C., & Weins, A. N. Changes in medical problems and use of medical services following psychological intervention. *American Psychologist*, 1979, *34*, 420–431.

Sackett, D. L. The magnitude of compliance and noncompliance. In D. L. Sackett & R. B. Haynes (Eds.), *Compliance with therapeutic regimens*. Baltimore: Johns Hopkins University Press, 1976.

Schraa, J. C., Dirks, J. F., Jones, N. F., & Kinsman, R. A. Bender-Gestalt performance and recall in an asthmatic sample. *Journal of Asthma Research*, 1981, *18*, 7–9.

Spector, S. L., Kinsman, R. A., & Farr, R. S. A scheme to characterize asthma. In M. Stein (Ed.), *New directions in asthma*. Park Ridge, Ill.: American College of Chest Physicians, 1975.

Staudenmayer, H., Kinsman, R. A., & Jones, N. F. Attitudes toward respiratory illness and hospitalization in asthma: Relationships with personality, symptomatology, and treatment response. *Journal of Nervous and Mental Disease*, 1978, *166*, 624–634.

Staudenmayer, H., Kinsman, R. A., Dirks, J. F., Spector, S. L., & Wangaard, C. Medical outcome in asthmatic patients: Effects of airways hyperreactivity and symptom-focused anxiety. *Psychosomatic Medicine*, 1979, *41*, 109–118.

Vincent, P. Factors influencing patient noncompliance: A theoretical approach. *Nursing Research*, 1971, *20*, 509–516.

Watkins, J. D., Williams, T. F., Martin, D. A., Hogan, N. D., & Anderson, E. A. A study of the diabetic patient at home. *American Journal of Public Health*, 1967, *57*, 452–459.

Wilder, C. S. Health characteristics of persons with chronic activity limitation. (U.S. Department of Health, Education, and Welfare, Publication No. (HRA) 77-1539). Washington, D.C.: U.S. Government Printing Office, 1976.

Zaki, M. H., Edelstein, S., Josephson, R. A., & Weisberg, S. R. Regularity of drug administration among hospitalized and ambulatory tuberculosis patients. *American Review of Respiratory Disease*, 1968, *97*, 136–139.

Zeballos, R. J., Shturman-Ellstein, R., McNally, J. F., Hirsch, J. E., & Souhrada, J. F. The role of hyperventilation in exercise-induced broncho-constriction. *American Review of Respiratory Disease*, 1978, *118*, 877–884.

Behavioral Health Care in the Management of Chronic Pain

Jeffrey C. Steger and Wilbert E. Fordyce

1. Some Behavioral Concepts in Pain Treatment

The health care system has long been plagued by difficult and persistent problems. Recently, it has been suggested that a major problem facing health care professionals is the lack of follow through with treatment regimens; it is claimed that as much as 85% of chronic health problems are partially the result of noncompliance with therapeutic and preventive treatments (Sackett & Haynes, 1976). It is not surprising, then, that behavioral psychologists specializing in enhancing treatment compliance (e.g., Steger, Shelton, Beukelman, & Fowler, 1981) have begun to appear more frequently in the constellation of health care providers, especially where long-term and chronic problems are being treated. Psychologists have successfully applied behavioral and environmental contingency models in treating such health care problems as life-style adjustment following severe disability (Treischmann, 1979), cardiac complications (Engel, 1973), pulmonary dysfunction secondary to smoking (Lichtenstein, Harris, Birchler, Wahl, & Sehmahl, 1973; Pomerleau & Pomerleau, 1977), and hypertension (Elder & Eustis, 1975; Haynes, Gibson, Hockett, Sackett, Taylor, Roberts, & Johnson, 1976).

Chronic pain is one of the more complex problems faced by the health care establishment. Although pain is most often associated with the feelings accompanying tissue damage, it is a multifaceted phenomenon. To the neurophysiol-

JEFFREY C. STEGER AND WILBERT E. FORDYCE ● Department of Rehabilitation Medicine, University of Washington School of Medicine, Seattle, Washington 98195.
This study was supported in part by Research Grant #NIHR 16-P-56818/0-18 from the National Institute of Handicapped Research, Department of Education, Washington, D.C. 20202

ogist, it may be the firing of a particular type of nerve ending; to the physician, an indication of tissue damage requiring healing; to the experimental psychologist, an estimate of threshold of sensation; and to the patient, an unpleasant feeling often causing despair and suffering. The difficulty of defining pain has been readily admitted (e.g., Melzack, 1973; Sternbach, 1974; Weisenberg, 1977); it is important to note that many definitions focus on the physiological components of pain, but pain is more than a physiological stimulus.

Specifically, a large body of literature has suggested that the experience of pain can be a function of past conditioning experiences, cognitive expectations, pain history, anxiety or fear level, the perceived consequences of pain, various personality and psychological factors, as well as tissue damage. Sternbach (1974) has referred to pain as an abstraction concerning feelings associated with some physical injury, and Weisenberg (1977) has labeled pain as a sensation that is in some respects an emotional–motivational phenomenon leading to avoidance behavior. Finally, individual reactions to acute traumatic injury have been shown to vary dramatically according to environmental factors. Beecher (1972) demonstrated that use of analgesics and complaints of pain were significantly less in a combat situation, where a wound is a signal for being taken out of danger; in the safer environment of a hospital, however, where a wound only signals continued noxious stimulation and the presence of fear and anxiety, there were more complaints of pain and more analgesics were used. These varying reports combine to suggest strongly that the concept of pain is a complex network of phenomena which may relate to severity of tissue damage but also to emotional, physiological, psychological, and historical factors.

The focus of this chapter is to contrast traditional health care with behavioral health care approaches in the management of chronic pain. In this chapter, the term *behavioral health care* refers to those techniques—often called *behavioral medicine*—that involve the applications of learning theory and contingency management in medical settings. In this context, *chronic pain* will refer primarily to long-standing complaints of trauma-induced discomfort and pain that have persisted beyond the expected healing time and have resisted more conservative and traditional health care intervention strategies. Prior to reviewing various treatment approaches, several conceptual issues inherent to any discussion of pain need to be addressed.

1.1. Pain as Behavior

It has been remarked that, in order to infer nociception and tissue damage, one must exhibit some behavior labeled as pain. According to Sternbach (1968), "In order to describe pain, it is necessary for the patient to do something . . . in order for us to determine that he is experiencing pain" (page 13). Thus, the patient must provide some signal to the health care system that he or she is in some form of distress that may be related to tissue pathology requiring treatment. Typical signals interpreted by observers as relating to pain are grimaces, moans, limps, medication use, and requests for prosthetic or assistive devices like canes, crutches, or wheelchairs. The emitting of such observable behavior is typically understood by health professionals as relating to a person's experience of some pain sensation which, in turn, requires treatment. Unfortunately, verbal reports and other forms of communication from one person to another have been demonstrated to be susceptible to biasing effects (Orne, 1962; Rosenthal, 1966). These biasing effects can yield inappropriate health care decisions. Furthermore, the assumption that a communication—verbal or nonverbal—is somehow related to an underlying physical pathology leads the traditional health care system to focus on the "cause or source" of the pain verbalization, or other nonverbal communications, rather than on the communication in and of itself. Indeed, traditional health care treatment has tended to focus specifically on assumed or inferred physiological concomitants of the pain communications. All too often their alleged presence has been accepted as a given. The point here is that pain as a set of observed communications in the clinical setting is a set of behaviors that may or may not be related to *tissue damage*. Those communications or pain behaviors need to be evaluated from all aspects, including the notion that the verbal report may serve a purpose in and of itself unrelated to physiological processes.

1.2. Respondent versus Operant Pain Behavior

A behavioral approach to the treatment of chronic pain typically utilizes the concept that there are at least two types of pain behavior—respondent and operant—just as virtually all behavior can be classified as respondent or operant. Simply stated, respondent behavior is a type of reflex response occurring as a result of a specific stimulus. In this kind of behavior, there is a high correlation or covariation between stimulus and response. Respondent behavior often falls into the patterns associated with the classical or reflex conditioning paradigms described by Pavlov (1927). Respondent behaviors include actions like the "startle" response associated with a loud unexpected auditory stimulus, the patellar-tendon reflex response, and paralysis following the injection of curare. The critical aspect of respondent behavior is that it occurs regardless of whether the organism wishes or does not wish the response to happen: it is automatic. In the context of pain, *respondent pain* is pain behavior controlled by specific antecedent nociceptive stimuli. Examples of respondent pain behavior include the discomfort associated with an acute fracture, the burning sensation associated with a muscle or nerve injury, or the specific painful experience generated by a needle piercing the skin. Any mechanical or thermal energy impinging on specialized peripheral nerve endings is a nociceptive stimulus which, in turn, activates A-delta and C fibers and is likely to produce respondent pain.

Operant behavior, in contrast to respondent, is not necessarily associated with a specific antecedent stimulus. According to Skinner (1938), operant behaviors are those that either increase or decrease in probability of occurrence when followed by a rewarding or punishing consequence. Another way of stating this is that operants come under the influence of learning and conditioning; key elements to that phenomenon may be external to the organism. In this view, operant pain behaviors could initially be related or "caused" by nociception and tissue damage (as with respondent pain); subsequently, however, they come under the control of the environment and other behavior-consequence relationships. Operant pain behaviors may be increased by positive consequences from the environment or be decreased by negative ones.

One important implication of this formulation for the health care system is that the longer a pain problem persists, the more opportunity there is for pain behavior to be influenced by the environment. Clinically, one observes that operant pain does not occur in the total absence of tissue damage. It may relate to the experience of discomfort arising from body damage but is magnified beyond that which might be predicted by the tissue damage or persists after healing. A not unusual example of this might occur in a patient following a recent car injury in which there was both low-back and neck strain. The pain behaviors associated with the acute tissue damage situation (i.e., respondent pain behaviors) could involve wearing a neck brace, taking pain medication for low-back discomfort, and adapting certain body postures which would not exacerbate the low-back and neck pain. Also, certain heavy physical activities would be avoided and those around the patient may make adjustments (i.e., they may sanction and reinforce the change in activity level following this type of injury). However, even though the pain behaviors in this situation are to a large degree historically related to the nociception involved, the muscle and nerve damage related to the accident in this situation provide an ideal opportunity for conditioning and the emergence of operant pain. Continued wearing of the neck brace beyond healing time and continued avoidance of selected physical activities with continued environmental sanctioning or reinforcement, even though physical evidence of tissue damage has decreased, may indicate that the pain behaviors have come under the influence of environmental factors. Those pain behaviors may be more extreme or last longer than the initial tissue damage would predict. It has become, at least in part, a problem of operant pain.

To recapitulate, respondent pain behaviors are directly related to the presence of a nociceptive stimulus. Operant pain behaviors can be independent of nociception. They have come to be affected by positive and negative consequences from the environment, including the health care system.

Given the increasing scientific data base regarding voluntary and involuntary response systems in the human organism, the relevance of the distinction between operant and respondent pain is particularly important. Specifically, biofeedback literature has demonstrated the fallacy of traditional notions about the existence of a set of involuntary physiological response systems in the body that are immune to conditioning effects. The ability of external factors to affect previously assumed involuntary responses (e.g., heart rate, blood flow) suggests that consideration of the operant option in any pain problem is essential. Bodily behaviors and sensations previously assumed to be reflexive can come under the influence of environmental conditioning and, therefore, become partly operant in nature (e.g., EEG biofeedback facilitated brain-wave-pattern alteration; Sterman, 1973).

1.3. Acute versus Chronic Pain

The distinction between acute and chronic pain is a critical one for the health care professional attempting to diagnose or treat a pain problem. It is particularly important because acute and chronic pain problems require significantly different treatment strategies; improper intervention, as will be discussed later, can often yield a worsened condition.

In acute pain, a specific and identifiable tissue damage site can typically be found (e.g., a fractured femur, laceration, or burn). In such situations, the course of treatment is usually based on the specific nociceptive stimulus leading to pain. It is typically identifiable, and pain usually does not persist beyond the expected therapeutic or healing time interval. The pain is time limited.

Chronic pain, on the other hand, will typically begin with an acute episode similar to the situation just described, but health care intervention over a prolonged period of time has not, for whatever reason, resulted in reduction of pain. Often, in fact, the discomfort may be increased by repeated surgical intervention or prolonged use of analgesics. In these situations, the health care system has failed to resolve the patient's pain problem and a chronic situation has developed.

Another factor differentially affecting acute and chronic pain is anxiety. Researchers have demonstrated that anxiety is significantly related to many pain situations regardless of the extent of chronicity (Beecher, 1972; Merskey & Spear, 1967; Sternbach, 1968). Anxiety is also a function of uncertainty. In the acute pain problem, uncertainty is typically short-lived and anxiety decreases or is discontinued as soon as the effective and appropriate treatment is applied and the pain decreases. Conversely, chronic pain is often associated with high levels of persisting uncertainty. In the face of failure of the health care system to solve the problem or the impact of potent environmental conditioning combined with prolonged periods of sleeplessness and resulting fatigue due to the pain experience, the patient understandably begins to become increasingly angry and frustrated. In such a situation, the patient begins to feel that his or her discomfort may be eternal. Anxiety and uncertainty are increased. Both serve to increase the subjective experience of pain. The burden is made heavier if, as often happens, one of the practitioners within the health care system suggest to the patient that the pain is "in your head" or "psychosomatic." That serves little to decrease the anxiety and uncertainty the patient is experiencing.

The importance of distinguishing between acute and chronic pain is supported empirically by the work of several clinical researchers. In one study, the efficacy of transcutaneous nerve stimulation (TNS) in treating chronic and acute pain was investigated. The results suggested that TNS was effective for 80% of the acute pain sufferers, while only 25% of the chronic pain patients achieved similar relief (Shealy & Maurer, 1974). In a similar comparison, Loeser (1974) demonstrated that when applied to chronic pain sufferers, traditional medical interventions for acute pain are less than 60% effective. Also, he demonstrated that the long-term benefit from such traditional health care applications in chronic pain was less than 30%. These data suggest that intervention strategies for chronic and acute pain should be quite different.

1.4. Behavioral Health Care Goals

The primary goal in most health care is to provide treatment that reestablishes and maintains appropriate, healthy behaviors. Typically, it is assumed that identifying the underlying cause for treatment will lead to a "cure," resulting in decreased health care utilization. Unfortunately, traditional approaches to chronic pain often do not have this effect. This is partly a function of the complex nature of chronic pain. Many approaches in the treatment of chronic pain misidentify the nature of the problem being treated. This seems to arise primarily through a failure to consider behavioral as well as physiological components in chronic pain problems.

In treating pain, one must differentiate between pain as a sensation arising from a noxious or nociceptive stimulus, suffering as a negative affective state, and pain behavior as the observable manifestations of a pain problem (Loeser, 1978). When using the word *pain*, the traditional health care practitioner and patients and family as well typically think about and speak of these three as if they were one. They tacitly assume that the behaviors indicating suffering or distress are associated with nociceptive stimulation leading to the experience of pain. Failure to make these distinctions is perhaps the major reason for the ineffectiveness of traditional health care approaches to chronic pain.

One implication of the above discussion is that behavioral health care approaches to chronic pain distinguish between nociception pain, suffering, and pain behavior. Treatment goals focus on pain behaviors and their converse, functional activity and "well" behavior. There is also focus on training family and environmental agents to maintain increased function and well behavior and to reduce excessive and possibly risky health care utilization. This concept goes beyond the traditional health care approach, which assumes that treatment of the underlying pathology will facilitate increased function and activity. It addresses the behavioral and environmental issues apparent in most chronic pain. Such an approach leads to multifarious treatment strategies. The following review is designed to give the reader an overview of behavioral strategies that have been effectively applied to chronic pain populations.

1.5. Review of Behavioral Strategies in Pain Treatment

Although there are well over one hundred pain clinics in operation in the United States, only a small number have published objective outcome data from which their procedures can be evaluated. The treatment strategies used tend to range from somewhat narrowly applied behavioral to more eclectic approaches. Most effective treatment programs are administered on an inpatient basis and involve medication management, activation through physical and occupational therapy, and various interventions designed to facilitate follow-through. For the purpose of this brief review, the distinctions among approaches are based mainly on the extent to which the psychological components of treatment strategy involve more than reinforcement programming for well behavior. For example, group therapy, stress-management and relaxation techniques, placebo treatment, or family therapy related to issues other than pain might be added.

The prototype operant pain treatment program for chronic pain involves several (e.g., 4 to 6) weeks of inpatient hospitalization. It emphasizes increases in general activity and socialization and decreases in medication and pain-related health care services. A detailed description of this program (the operant pain treatment component of the Department of Rehabilitation Medicine at the University of Washington) will be presented following this review. Using this approach, Fordyce, Fowler, Lehmann, DeLateur, Sand, and Treischmann (1973) demonstrated significant increases in up time and activity level, significant decreases in medication usage, decreased reports of interference with daily activities, and maintenance of such changes after 22 months. That program includes family training and vocational rehabilitation. A similar program has been implemented at Rancho Los Amigos Hospital, where significant treatment gains were observed in 70% to 80% of the patients treated. Decreases in medication were reported to maintain at follow-up for 58% of the patients, with 74% of low-back-pain patients seeking no further health care and 75% involved in some vocation-related training program (Cairns, Thomas, Mooney, & Pace, 1976). Another heavily behavioral program at the University of Minnesota demonstrated that 75% to 80% of treatment gains were maintained in "most" of their patients over follow-up intervals varying from 1 to 8 years (Anderson, Cole, Gullickson, Hudgens, & Roberts, 1977) and that 77% of those treated were leading normal lives without pain medication (Roberts & Reinhardt, 1980).

An example of a more mixed approach is reported from the Mayo Clinic (Swanson, Floreen, & Swenson, 1976). In addition to the treatment components just described, the Mayo approach involves group exercises, group therapy, and discussion among pain patients. They also use biofeedback and relaxation techniques during physical and occupational therapy as well as for general stress coping. Ignoring those patients who did not complete treatment, the results of this program suggest that approximately 79% of the patients showed improvement. Unfortunately, at 6-month follow-up, only 50% of these maintained the same level of treatment gains (Swanson *et al.*, 1976). A similar mixed approach is used in Oregon by Newman, Seres, Yospe, and Garlington, (1978); there, a multidisciplinary program demonstrated that treatment gains were maintained for chronic low-back pain patients in analgesic use and four measures of physical functioning. This was particularly significant, since this study used an 80-week follow-up which was done through direct in-hospital observation (Newman *et al.*, 1978). A final example of a "mixed" inpatient treatment approach similar to the Mayo program occurs in the chronic-back-pain management program of Casa Colina Hospital for Rehabilitation in Pomona, California. In addition to the group physical and occupational therapy and stress-management techniques used at the Mayo Clinic, the Casa Colina program emphasizes self-regulation of stress management, assertiveness training, patient-regulated medication programs, and information sessions. Vocational planning and individual marital counseling are also provided. Of the patients in this program, 66% demonstrated significant improvement which was maintained at the 1-month follow-up (Gottlieb, Strite, Killer, Madorsky, Hockersmith, Kleeman, & Wagner, 1977).

The above results combine to suggest that several weeks of inpatient behavioral health care can generate significant improvement in many variables related to chronic pain, especially regarding objective treatment outcome measures related to specific behaviors (e.g., medication levels, percentage of involvement in vocational activities, percentage of physical return, etc.). Unfortunately, there is as yet no report of a systematic study that separates treatment components to identify which components contribute most to treatment outcome. It is virtually impossible to carry out such studies in clinical settings; yet pragmatically, until such studies are done, the available evidence suggests that a number of variations of behavioral approaches appear to be useful.

There are, in the literature, many outpatient treatment programs for chronic pain but few reported studies of treatment efficacy. Typically, the outpatient approaches comprise the same procedures as described in the inpatient, but follow-through with treatment is done in the environment or *in vivo* home situation. The previously discussed methodological problems in obtaining accurate and unbiased data on activity and medication on an outpatient basis moderate outpatient pain treatment efficacy and place these programs at a greater risk for failure. This may account for the limited number of systematic studies of comprehensive mixed or pure behavioral outpatient approaches to chronic pain.

Several recently developed treatment strategies are worth mentioning. In isolation, they may not be appropriate for the treatment of complex chronic pain problems, but they do seem to show promise in treating specific types of chronic pain. Specifically, "cognitive–behavioral" approaches (Turk, 1978) are designed to reduce anxiety and to affect self-statements concerning the experience of pain. The assumption is that this approach can be used to alter the individual's perception of pain and therefore increase pain tolerance to allow increased activity levels and decreased use of medication. With this method, outcome research involving complex chronic pain has been only preliminary. However, cognitive behavioral treatment like "stress inoculation" (Meichenbaum & Turk, 1976) has been applied to the outpatient treatment of stress reactions and tension. This outpatient strategy appears to incorporate many of the effective inpatient strategies for the treatment of chronic pain (e.g., identifying antecedent and consequent stress and pain behaviors, generating alternative ways of coping with stress and pain, and implementing these skills), so that future research may demonstrate the efficacy of this approach applied to outpatient treatment of chronic pain. The use of self-control and cognitive–behavioral strategies appears to be particularly relevant for outpatient treatment, since the decreased external structure of treatment dictates a much more rigorous and consistent self-monitoring process for the patient. Patients must understand clearly the nature and specifics of the treatment and involve themselves in conceptualizing the strategies of treatment. The relevance of patient involvement was apparent in one study of outpatient pain treatment for tension headaches (Steger & Harper, 1980). Here the investigators demonstrated that both a relaxation and biofeedback group were equally effective in decreasing muscle tension, which was one of the major factors assumed to be related to the muscle-contracture headaches. However, it appeared that the stress inoculation and self-monitoring training of the comprehensive outpatient biofeedback group was significantly more effective in encouraging patient follow through and thereby resulted in more improvement in pain ratings and general feelings of anxiety and distress (Steger & Harper, 1980). This study and the findings of other cognitive types of behavioral research suggest that the failure of inpatient programs to provide as much improvement in subjective pain ratings may stem from their failure to focus specifically on the cognitive issues of subjective pain perception. Furthermore, it appears that this may be particularly important in an outpatient treatment setting where structure and external monitoring is minimal and self-monitoring and comprehension of behavioral treatment strategies must play a greater role.

2.1. Evaluation Procedures

Based upon the previous discussion, it can be seen that it is critical to diagnose acute versus chronic pain situations accurately. Also, the reliance upon a strictly stimulus–response conceptualization of clinical pain is inadequate and, as shown by the research on acute versus chronic pain applications, leads to ineffective treatment strategies.

The initial phase of chronic pain evaluation should involve a traditional and thorough medical evaluation. Physiological or "organic" etiological factors are evaluated and an attempt is made to identify all medical problems that might be contributing to the pain complaints. When respondent or acute pain problems are identified, they should be treated with appropriate strategies, just as the health care system would deal with acute medical problems. The importance of a thorough and accurate medical diagnostic procedure at this point can hardly be overstated. It is this procedure that determines whether surgical intervention, rest, rehabilitation, or some other treatment is appropriate. A paucity or absence of positive physical findings does not, however, indicate that the pain problem being evaluated is definitely operant in nature. Such a determination can only be made by adding a thorough behavioral analysis.

A behavioral health care analysis following the traditional health care workup is indicated when (1) the physiological results of the medical evaluation are inconsistent with the intensity or duration of observed pain behaviors and (2) when physical findings leading to inferred nociception are implied or speculative.

2.1.1. Behavioral Analysis

A first objective of the behavioral analysis of a problem of chronic pain is to explore the correlation between pain behaviors and activities or social consequences. Identification of antecedent and subsequent events relative to pain behaviors are examined. It is important to understand clearly that a behavioral analysis says nothing about the extent to which the problem is respondent. It serves only to assess the extent to which learning and conditioning explanations of the problem are viable alternatives. Even where a patient's pain behavior is being reinforced by environmental consequences and where learning factors appear to be pervasive, much of the patient's pain behavior could still be controlled to a significant degree by nociception and organic pathology.

It is helpful for the psychologist or other health care professional performing a behavioral analysis to remember that most chronic pain sufferers have a history of negative interaction with the health care system. It is critical to generate a positive and supportive atmosphere during the behavioral analysis interview so as to obtain accurate data and identify relationships between pain behaviors and activity patterns. Since many pain patients have been told directly or indirectly by the health care system that their pain experience is "imagined" or psychogenic, the patient often enters the evaluation situation with a distrustful, defensive stance from which there is a felt need to prove the authenticity of the pain experience. It is imperative to impart to the patient the feeling that the examiner understands and accepts the patient's suffering. The main purpose of the evaluation is to identify the factors that influence suffering, not whether there "really" is pain.

A preliminary orientation can be valuable in helping the patient understand the reasons behind a behavioral pain analysis and can facilitate his or her acquisition of an accurate behavior–pain relationship. The following clarifications are often useful.

1. There is no question about the authenticity of the patient's suffering—it is real and not "imagined" (only in rare cases where psychotic hallucinations take the form of pain experience does this fail to be accurate).
2. Most pain problems originate with tissue damage or nociception; however, in any chronic illness, the experience of discomfort can be maintained by learning and conditioning.
3. The effect of learning or conditioning on chronic pain is automatic and independent of the patient's desires.
4. Where there is or has been opportunity for learning and conditioning of chronic pain behaviors, the patient often suffers more than is necessary; then a relearning process can help improve the chronic pain situation.

The specific goal of the behavioral analysis is to identify factors linked to the environment and correlated with pain behaviors. These include detailed information about the activity level, rest requirements, mechanisms of avoidance, sleep disturbance pattern, time pattern of the pain, and the interrelationship of these various factors with the patient's experience of discomfort. Table 1 presents prototypical questions and an interview format for the evaluation of chronic pain. In gathering this type of information, it is often useful to draw on varying information sources, including the patient's spouse or other significant environmental agents (past physicians, employers, etc.).

It is also important to identify those procedures in the past which have been helpful in reducing the pain and discomfort, since these may be incorporated into the operant pain treatment being devised; they may also point toward possible sources of reinforcement that are maintaining pain behaviors. A more extensive description of the behavioral analysis technique is available in other sources (Fordyce, 1976; Fordyce & Steger, 1979). The following, however, are the main areas of information necessary to complete an effective health care behavioral analysis.

2.1.2. Baseline Techniques

Baseline data are essential to effective treatments. They provide specific and objective information about the patient's current ability level and the extent to which pain is influenced by various activities. Baseline observation—whether it be in the hospital or through a systematic self-monitored home diary—is more accurate and reliable than subjective or retrospective recall by the patient at the time of an interview. Verbal reports as to how much one can do should never suffice. Find out by observing and recording actual performance.

During baseline evaluation, it is possible to document exact levels of activity

Table 1. Behavioral Analysis Outline

General topics and key phrases	Relevant details and guidelines[a]
Time Patterns "Describe your pain experiences throughout a typical day."	Constant and unchanging = operant Intermittent with fluctuating but existing pain-free intervals = respondent Pain at night or during other environmental "shutdown" periods suggests respondent Nocturnal pain ↑ corresponding to analgesic intake schedules suggests medication habituation rather than respondent pain.
Pain Exacerbation "Which activities or events bring on or increase your pain?" Pain Reduction "List the activities or techniques which decrease your experience of pain."	Get specifics like lifting 15 kg parcels to waist level or higher rather than "lifting anything" or "any type of movement." Specify rest intervals and time out from work in units of time required to consistently ↓ pain. List all medications (prescribed & "street" drugs) used for pain and the time delay before pain reduction occurs. Immediate relief following medication or rest = conditioned or operant pain. Switching from one productive strategy to another for pain relief suggests respondent pain.
Pain Related Activity Changes "What physical, social, and work activities have been altered because of your pain problem?" "Which of these would you like to resume?"	Identify discrepancies between avocational and vocational behavior change, given comparable physical demands. For example, in sitting tolerance at work with no change in sitting tolerance at the movies = operant pain. Specify individual and couple activity changes in work and intercourse due to low-back pain (where sexual activity has been enjoyable) suggests respondent pain.
Pain Behavior "If I were in the room and you were in pain, how would I know? What would you do or say?" Environmental Consequences of Pain Behaviors "How does your spouse react when you're in pain?" "What do you (spouse) do in response to his or her pain?"	Specify sounds, grimaces, and body movements used to indicate pain. Medication usage or health care utilization = pain behavior. List direct and indirect (via avoidance of stress or responsibility) reinforcement of pain behavior. No spouse and no job payoffs for pain suggest respondent pain. Angry or resentful spouse reactions can be reinforcing. The more responsibilities or unpleasant activities assumed by the environment in response to pain, the higher the probability of operant pain.

[a]Many factors need to be considered in discriminating between operant and respondent pain; the examples listed should be treated as diagnostic signs, *not* proven indicators.

and physical energy tolerance levels, specific doses and schedules of medication, and effects of various emotional and postural stress on the patient's report of pain. The following are additional data-acquisition techniques that can provide important information as part of a behavioral analysis and the baseline evaluation procedure.

2.1.3. Activity Diaries

Activity or pain diaries have been used to monitor the effects of various pain treatment approaches, including biofeedback (Budzynski, Stoyva & Adler, 1970; Steger & Harper, 1980) and behavioral therapy (Fordyce et al., 1973; Fowler, 1975) and serve to augment information gathered in the clinical interview. Typically, the patient monitors activities during each hour of the day and indicates the extent to which time was spent sitting, walking, or reclining; the amount of analgesic used; and the rating of subjective pain. When these data are recorded at least reasonably accurately, they can provide useful information regarding the patterns of pain and activity covariation and the extent to which the patient is engaging in a dysfunctional life-style. Also, this type of information can be used as an indication of pretreatment status and to provide reference points against which to assess treatment effects.

2.1.4. Medication Baseline

Medication use is not always a problem in chronic pain sufferers. However, Maruta, Swanson, and Finlayson (1979) showed that out of 144 sufferers from chronic pain with a nonmalignant cause, 24% were drug-dependent, 41% drug abusers, and 35% nonabusers. Thus, the behavior of taking analgesics can be one of the most important aspects in controlling a chronic pain problem. Physiological addiction is common. Moreover, the long-term benefit of continued analgesic use for chronic pain problems is highly questionable, at best.

Retrospective reports of analgesic use among users of heavy medication use are often inaccurate. Some of these patients are too toxic to be able to remember. Others are too ashamed to be candid. Yet others fear that their supply will be cut and so overstate need as a hedge against reduction. In our experience, when medication use or abuse appears to be a major factor in the pain problem, the patient must usually be hospitalized if one is to make an accurate assessment of the actual use of medication. The management of medication problems again illustrates the symbiotic interplay between traditional health care and behavioral health care.

A patient hospitalized for medication evaluation typically undergoes a 24- to 48-hour observation period of *ad lib* medication ingestion. This usually provides sufficient information to establish a regimen for the reduction of pain medication. The patient is instructed to bring all of his or her medication to the hospital for the primary nurse to dispense. Then the free operant or *ad lib* medication evaluation period is initiated. The patient is instructed to continue using medication on an as-needed (p.r.n.) basis just as he or she has been doing at home. It is critical that the staff not give the patient the impression that use is being controlled during this period. The goal of the evaluation is to obtain an accurate assessment of the amount of medication currently being used by the patient.

Inpatient observation is also critical from a medical and health standpoint, since a patient who has been taking high levels of medication may attempt to "put on a good show" by underutilizing relative to recent levels. Such a patient can have withdrawal symptoms, with potentially dire physiological consequences. For the same reason, prescribing exercise in physical therapy and occupational therapy can be very helpful. The stress of exercise tends to ensure representative levels of medication ingestion.

Chronic pain patients with medication use problems are usually "experts" concerning their own physical medication level limitations. We have yet to observe dangerous overdosing. However, inpatient observation in cases of high medication usage provides a medically prudent safeguard.

The type and amount of medication and the schedule of use throughout the day and night are the important data for the patient. Inpatient evaluation of medication use may not always be necessary if there is an accurate and persistent observer available in the patient's home environment and one feels confident the information obtained will be precise. Under these conditions, the same procedure can be used and analgesic use recorded on the activity diary. However, medication baseline data obtained at home may lead to an added problem. When it comes time to embark on a pain medication reduction regimen, there is often a significant shift in form (from I.M. to P.O.) or content (e.g., codeine to methadone). Great care must be taken at that point to ensure that the altered analgesics are at proper levels and severe withdrawal symptoms or respiratory embarrassment does not occur. Rare is the home which can provide that kind of meticulous surveillance.

2.1.5. Activity Baselines

As with medication, accurate baseline levels of activity are prerequisites for effective chronic pain treatment. To obtain baselines of physical strength and endurance, the patient should be observed in daily physical and occupational therapy sessions. A set of individualized exercises and activities is prescribed and the patient attempts all exercises with the instruction to work until pain, fatigue, or discomfort cause him or her to want to stop. This type of monitoring repeated over several days provides an estimate of pretreatment tolerance levels and is more accurate and reliable than a "one shot" evaluation. Hospitalization is not necessary in all cases for activity baseline evaluation. When a spouse or significant other is capable and willing to monitor activities in the home, this type of baseline evaluation can be performed in that setting. There are limitations to this approach however. The paucity of specialized equipment limiting range of exercises for baseline evaluation, the availability of trained observers, and the susceptibility of family or others to bias in observation cannot totally be circumvented. When, however, financial or other practical limitations make the inpatient observation impossible, the *in vivo* home observation is a better alternative to activity diaries or retrospective self-report as a basis for estimating current tolerance levels for specific exercises.

2.1.6. Stress Level Baselines

The relationship between stress and anxiety and the experience of pain is often significant. Since increased situations of stress can increase anxiety, which, in turn, may increase the subjective experience of pain in a chronic sufferer, it is important to identify specific activities and situations that generate stress. One potentially stressful situation is the transition from the home to the hospital environment. When baseline observation is being done in the hospital, it is possible to use this situation as a stress evaluation and to observe the patient's responses in this setting. For some patients, engaging in social and recreational activities with strangers in the hospital setting can be stressful. The activity and pain diaries can be used as an ongoing monitor of stress or discomfort during various hospital activities, and antecedent and consequent events in such situations can be identified. Furthermore, a specific physiological assessment of musculoskeletal reactions under conditions of general bodily stress (e.g., EMG biofeedback) can also be helpful. The extent to which muscle tension, blood pressure, and heart rate are affected by various body positions or social activities can be monitored (e.g., during physical or recreational therapy with a portable EMG monitor). The important consideration is to record multiple baseline measures of stress and muscle tension over varying conditions to obtain a valid assessment of the patient's baseline stress coping mechanisms.

2.1.7. Identification of Target Behavior

One of the most important aspects of behavioral treatment involves the specification of target behaviors and goals. One of behavioral science's major contributions to health care has been its emphasis on the pinpointing of tasks and goals that are observable, measurable, and related to treatment objectives (Battle, Imber, Hoehn-Saric, Stone, Nash, & Frank, 1966; Kiresuk & Sherman, 1968; Waskow & Parloff, 1975). To accomplish this, it is important to work closely with the patient to identify specific goals and specific therapy tasks that will facilitate the achievement of these ends. It is also important to identify specific measurement devices and techniques that will monitor these behaviors and when changes or alterations are needed. Obviously, each discipline has the expertise in its own area. The behavioral health care professional can facilitate identification of specific treatment steps related to the goals.

Target behaviors for the treatment of chronic pain typically involve decreasing the use of medication, increasing strength (e.g., the ability to do 25 repetitions on the N/K table set at 50 pounds or to do 20 repetitions of an arm lift with 30 pounds), and increasing walking tolerance. Table 2 describes a subset of target behaviors for the treatment of chronic low-back and abdominal pain. This example indicates the way in which behavioral health care generates specific targets in a multidisciplinary treatment of chronic pain.

Treatment Goals:

Return to work as an engineer.

Travel 150 miles to farm for recreation on weekends and return.

Goals require the following:

Ability to sit for at least an hour at a time.

Ability to stand for at least an hour at a time.

Ability to drive a car for at least an hour at a time.

Ability to walk a mile at a time twice a day.

Selected exercises	Beginning quota	Increment	Plateau
a. Ride bicycle	0.4 miles	.1 miles/day	2.5 miles
b. Walk 50 meter laps	4 laps	1 lap/day	30 laps
c. Walk up and down stairs	1 flight (2 flights = 1 floor)	1 flight/day	8 flights
d. Partial situps	10	1 situp/day	25 situps
e. Knee extension with weight	10 pounds, 4 repetitions	2 repetitions/day to 10 repetitions, then add 2.5 lbs. and begin again at 4 repetitions.	40 pounds, 10 repetitions
f. Weaving (sitting)	10 rows (rate approximately 2 rows/minute)	6 rows/day	90 rows
g. Macramé (standing)	12 knots (rate approximately 2 knots per minute)	4 knots/day	120 knots

1. Initially, the above exercises were each done twice a day. Exercises a through e were done in physical therapy; exercises f and g were done in occupational therapy.
2. When walking reached 10 laps, one walk per day was done outside to the canal to generalize walking ability to other environments.
3. When walking reached 15 laps, one walk per day was done outside to the fountain to further generalize walking ability.
4. After walking reached 30 laps, walking time was increased 5 minutes per day until a 20-minute walk of approximately a mile, the goal for walking, was achieved.
5. Macramé and weaving were both done during each of two sessions per day. When time spent on the two activities combined reached 60 minutes, weaving became the primary activity one session per day and macramé became the primary activity the second session.
6. When weaving reached 60 rows (sitting about 30 minutes), the patient began a job station for an hour per day. The job station required primarily sitting, but he did not have to sit for more than 30 minutes at any one time.
7. When weaving reached 90 rows, the patient began to ride in a car for 20 minutes, increasing 10 minutes per day until 50 minutes' riding time was reached. Then the patient began driving the car 10 minutes and riding 20 minutes, increasing driving time 10 minutes per day to driving goal of 1 hour, eliminating riding time when driving time reached 30 minutes.
8. When driving began, it took the place of the sitting occupational therapy session. Thus, sitting time was increased to 1 hour during driving, thereby achieving the sitting goal.
9. When macramé reached 80 knots, patient began a job station which required primarily standing but allowed for some sitting, so that he did not have to stand more than 40 minutes at a time.
10. Job-station time increased 1 hour per week to a total of 6 hours.
11. When job-station reached 3 hours per day, one physical therapy session was dropped. When job-station reached 4 hours, one occupational therapy session was eliminated; the patient alternated sitting and standing activities in occupational therapy, sitting one day and standing the next.

(continued)

Table 2. (continued)

12. After the patient completed 4 hours per day on job station for a week, he was discharged. On the outpatient program, he built up job-station time to 6 hours plus 1 hour of occupational therapy and 1 hour of physical therapy. He then gradually resumed his former job, beginning at 4 hours on the job plus 2 hours at the job station and 1 hour of physical therapy for 2 weeks, then increasing by an hour a day every 2 weeks until he had returned to an 8-hour day at work. As he increased his job time, job-station training and therapies were reduced.

*^aThe treatment program described is for a 41-year-old man with chronic low-back and left-leg pain.

2.2. Treatment Strategies

As the literature review suggests, typical behavioral health care interventions in chronic pain involve a multidisciplinary team and multiple treatment components. Clearly, such intervention requires a coordinated and comprehensive treatment team. This coordination can be facilitated by the health care professional who is trained in behavioral methods. Typically, the psychologist most often has expertise and experience in this area. However, people in other disciplines (e.g., social work and psychiatry) are often trained in behavioral methods as well and can help to coordinate a complicated behavioral intervention.

Regardless of the discipline or speciality involved in coordinating the comprehensive treatment of chronic pain, this system of intervention requires careful communication and coordination. Frequent conferences or team meetings—at which all the individuals involved in patient care coordinate their efforts—are essential. In addition, conferences with patient and family are often used to clarify the treatment rationale and update changes in therapeutic regimens. The following description of a typical inpatient treatment program is based on the University of Washington Operant Pain Treatment Program.

2.2.1. Establishing Quotas

Initially, there is a medical work-up to assess underlying tissue pathology and constraints on activity potential. This is accompanied by a behavioral analysis identifying social, emotional, or environmental contingencies that support the patient's pain behaviors. Baseline levels of activity tolerance are then established by direct observation of exercise performance. Then, this comprehensive set of information (including the specific goals of each patient) is combined with a set of treatment quotas (for each of the different activities involved in treatment). The selection of exercises and activities is a critically important part of any contingency management treatment of pain, since both increase physiological tolerance and functional abilities and both are virtually always incompatible with pain behavior. Moreover, increased activities and exercises are in themselves "well" behavior, and they, as opposed to displays of pain behavior, often elicit positive reinforcement from the environment. Thus, exercise and activity selection are designed to choose behaviors that have been observed to be associated with or restricted by pain, that will increase physical conditioning and endurance, or that are related to the rehabilitation of a specific acquired disability related to the pain problem (e.g., muscle atrophy).

Quotas for exercises and activities are most often set in terms of repetitions and frequencies rather than time, since these parameters are more readily translated into a rate. That is, in the behavioral treatment of chronic chest pain involving a patient whose goal is to return to a part-time job, therapy quotas would be directed toward increasing his physical endurance to allow him to lift 40 pounds several times a day on his job. Therefore, physical and occupational therapy activities are chosen and quotas are set so that the goals will be reached in the time alloted for treatment.

The goal in setting treatment increments and quotas is based on the notion of reinforcement and success. The initial treatment quotas should allow successful performance; if they are consistently followed by pain behaviors or fatigue, they are by definition too high. There is no simple formula for establishing initial quotas, but one rule of thumb is to set each activity or exercise 10% to 15% below the level of performance during baseline. The guiding principle is to establish the highest possible quota that will generate consistent success.

After initial treatment quotas have been established, rates of increase for each activity are set. There is no simple rule for the calculation of treatment increments, but the guiding concept is that increments should be set at a level that will allow consistent, successful performance across repeated activities and treatment sessions. In inpatient treatment settings, frequent therapist observation is possible and accurate increment monitoring and alteration can be done. Conversely, on an outpatient basis, conservative exercise increments should be established based on the principle that if treatment is to occur over 6 weeks, increment rates must be set so that one-sixth of the treatment goal is accomplished each week. For example, for a patient with chronic chest pain, the goal of 30 minutes of driving would be established as follows. Since the initial baseline for driving was 5 minutes and the alloted treatment duration is 5 weeks, the initial quota for driving was 5 minutes, with an increment rate of 1 minute per day (assuming one treatment session of driving per day). This would allow the patient to achieve a gradual but consistent increase in driving tolerance which would reach a 30-minute tolerance level by the end of 5 weeks. Again, regardless of inpatient or outpatient treatment, frequent monitoring of exercise and activity performance is necessary to ensure that the treatment steps are consistently followed and that increment rates are not set too high or too low.

2.2.2. Behavioral Management Methods

One advantage of using specified quotas and monitoring the increases in activity level is the implied contingency management system. That is, rest and attention to health care have often been reinforcers for pain behavior, but they can be used as reinforcers for success at achieving quotas. In this way, rest and attention to health care can be made contingent on follow-through with "well" behaviors and appropriate activity increases rather than expressions of pain. Furthermore, specific and reliable criteria for improvement are provided by quota measures and staff is instructed to reinforce the patient socially for successful performance. One of the easiest and most effective forms of reinforcement is the activity and performance graph demonstrating increment increases. This is not only an effective reinforcer for the patient and his or her family, but also a form of useful feedback for the health care staff. Such input has been shown to increase staff compliance with treatment regimens, leading to patient compliance (Quilitch, 1975; Steger *et al.* 1981). A typical performance graph is represented in Figure 1.

Another form of behavioral management inherent in an inpatient health care system using quotas involves the use of contingent "free time." Specifically, activities off the ward or outside the hospital (whether evening passes, weekend passes, or hospital privileges) can all be made contingent on successful completion of activity quotas. Obviously, it is critical that the spouse and family are in agreement with this approach in advance and that appropriate consequences and contingencies are applied. Specifically, if the conditions of the contingency system are met (i.e., the patient completes quotas and the reinforcing activity is compatible with his or her demonstrated level of endurance), it is imperative that the family or environmental agents be capable of providing the reinforcer. Conversely, these agents must be willing to withhold this reward when quota failures occur. Obviously, the use of such contingency management strategies can easily be mishandled; therefore this type of management is best left to professionals trained in behavioral management, interpersonal communication, and marital or family therapy. Many treatment dropouts can be attributed to the insensitive application of arbitrary contingencies, without adequate and effective interpersonal or family therapeutic management to back up the contingency system. Finally, the use of such contingency plans is possible on an outpatient basis, but once again the importance of close monitoring of performance is vital to the effectiveness of such an approach.

2.2.3. Quota Failure

This is a common occurrence in any health care intervention, including behavioral therapy for chronic pain. It is important to adapt a systematic and consistent strategy for such situations. The first two or three quota failures—as well as indications of fatigue or inability to comply with the increments—can be

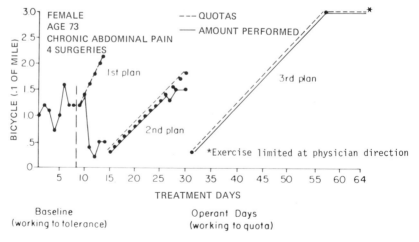

Figure 1. Activity changes following quota failure.

systematically ignored, and the patient can be instructed by the appropriate therapist simply to remember his or her next appointment and to continue with treatment. If, however, failure persists, the patient is informed that the quotas will be lowered. If, following this alteration, quota failure continues, it is possible that a reassessment of the initial exercise level and increment rates will be necessary. This reassessment and recycling of increment rates and quotas is often sufficient to handle most quota failures. Despite this procedure, however, some continued failure can occur, and when this happens in the presence of medical opinion that the quotas and increments of activity are well within physical capabilities of the patient, the patient is given a choice of continuing with treatment at the current rate of increment or terminating the program. In presenting this alternative to the patient, it is important to remind him or her that the experience of discomfort is not the determining factor in completing quotas (since the activities have been deemed as medically safe) and that it is necessary to experience some discomfort if progress is to be made. Consistency of performance is stressed, but if the patient continues to fail, treatment must be terminated. In such cases, either there are insufficient reinforcers available to maintain performance or there is some other factor generating decreased interest in follow-through with treatment. This system requires effective, systematic, and thorough medical evaluation to ensure that quota failures are not somehow related to an ongoing organic pathology.

There is another set of factors which affect quota performance. These relate to avoidance conditioning and its effects. In the situation of chronic pain, movement and activity may easily be followed by aversive consequences (e.g., pain, decreased strength, disapproval from the environment for lowered activity level). This is especially true in those problems of chronic pain that originated with an injury that led to aversive experiences in relation to movement. These situations typically result in some form of avoidance conditioning in which sets of actions become associated with aversive results and are therefore avoided. Clinical chronic pain is similar to experimentally induced traumatic avoidance learning (Solomon & Wynne, 1954). That is, once the avoidance paradigm has been established, the pain patient will not test the set of activities that previously led to discomfort or suffering but will assume that aversive consequences are inevitable. This form of conditioning has been labeled "learned helpnessness" (Seligman, 1975) and partially explains why some pain patients are reluctant or unwilling to attempt quotas even in the face of "new" evidence that these actions will no longer result in aversive experiences. In addition, many superstitious behaviors can be generated in an avoidant conditioning paradigm, and chronic pain patients often develop such apparent "irrational" actions. Unfortunately for the pain patient, these aversive conditioning patterns are difficult to extinguish and can interfere with active and willing participation in treatment. This type of problem has been identified in treatment for sexual dysfunction, where the traditionally applied behavioral rehearsal and *in vivo* desensitization program was not practiced due to the patient's abhorrence for sexual activity of any form. Treatment was effected by administering a cognitive or imaginal desensitization program, so that the patient could participate in the behaviors necessary to decondition the sexual aversion and subsequently relearn appropriate and pleasant sexual activity (Wish, 1975). A similar approach is appropriate when the chronic pain patient is totally unwilling to engage in physical activities due to strong aversion or superstitious beliefs. However, even this tactic will fail for some, and then it is clear that behavioral intervention is not likely to afford assistance.

2.2.4. Medication Management

As indicated earlier, medication is not always a relevant issue in the treatment of chronic pain; when it is, however, a medication management strategy is necessary. This component of treatment, like the other facets of behavioral health care of chronic pain, relies upon learning and conditioning. After the patient has entered the hospital, bringing his or her medication, and the baseline p.r.n. analgesic levels have been established (over a 1- to 2-day interval), intervention begins. To ensure initial success, it is important to reemphasize that it is better to overestimate the patient's dosages of medication than to underestimate them. Two types of medication intervention apply to chronic pain: (1) detoxification and (2) deconditioning. If toxicity due to medication overuse exists, an initial detoxification process is necessary, and this is done through the traditional health care system. This process should be successfully completed before any behavioral intervention or operant approach is attempted, since the medical and physiological implications of toxicity can override most of the learning components involved in a behavioral health care plan. Detailed specifications and guidelines involved in a typical detoxification program are found in Halpern (1974).

Unlike the detoxification process, medication deconditioning is an integral part of the desensitization and deconditioning procedures in behavioral treatment. Analgesic deconditioning is done through the use of a pain cocktail consisting of a taste- and color-masking vehicle (e.g., cherry syrup) administered in a dose consisting of active ingredients and masking vehicle totaling 10 or so milliliters. The patient is reassured that initially daily medication totals will equal or exceed baseline medication use and that the pain cocktail will be administered consistently and promptly over the 24 hours in each day. In behavioral health care, medication is administered on a time-contingent basis rather than a pain-contingent basis; the success of this approach depends on the consistency of delivering the pain cocktail on time. This is as much related to anxiety control as it is to attenuating the physiological and psychological conditioning that has occurred throughout a long history of consistent analgesic use.

As with other aspects of treatment, the goal of medication management is to decrease analgesic use to zero or near-zero levels in a specified treatment interval. In the process of decreasing medication, it is important to eliminate addictive and toxic agents while avoiding the side effects attributable to withdrawal. Symptoms such as severe emotional distress, seizures, acute respiratory failure, and depression have been observed to be associated with rapid withdrawal of analgesics in chronic medication users. Our experience dictates that effective and "safe" deconditioning of medication requires from 7 to 10 weeks.

Another reason for gradually decreasing medication levels is to provide an opportunity to generate and practice "well" behaviors as an alternative to medication use. Thus, crash programs that fade active ingredients at the fastest possible rate often fail, since the opportunity for relearning alternative responses is minimized. Alternative pain control behaviors might include muscle relaxation techniques, meditation, and attention distractions like reading or macramé. Also, if two or more pain medications are used in the cocktail (if this was the patient's baseline pattern), it is not necessary to reduce their levels in equal decrements. Instead, the active ingredients are alternately reduced every 1 to 2 weeks with the goal of decreasing both active ingredients to near-zero levels by the end of treatment. Table 3 provides an example of a typical operant pain cocktail regimen.

The previous discussion implies that all chemical agents related to pain or tension control must be in the pain cocktail. This is particularly true for muscle relaxants or tranquilizers, since these ingredients are rarely of continuing help to chronic pain patients. Often these ingredients have been ingested in conjunction with narcotics or barbiturates and must gradually be eliminated following baseline. As with other behavioral approaches, merely decreasing the target behavior is insufficient; it is important to provide alternative anxiety and muscle relaxing mechanisms when gradually fading out tranquilizers. EMG biofeedback, Jacobsonian muscle relaxation, autogenic self-statements, deep-breathing exercises, or cognitive stress inoculation techniques are appropriate alternatives to chemical intervention.

Medication to treat depression is often prescribed in conjunction with analgesics, since depression is frequently observed in chronic pain sufferers. Antidepressants are rarely given on a p.r.n. basis, yet it is still important to include them in the pain cocktail when depression is being managed chemically. Unlike analgesics and tranquilizers, however, antidepressants need not be tapered throughout the deconditioning program, since the efficacy of these regimens requires consistent medication levels. In a behavioral intervention system, the efficacy of chemical depression intervention should be reevaluated periodically, since it has been shown that increasing depressed patients' physical activities can in and of itself be effective in combating depression (Lewinson, 1975). If it appears that depression decreases as exercise and activity levels increase and these changes maintain when the patient is discharged into the natural environment, antidepressant medication can be tapered and discontinued. This should not be considered, however, until the patient is engaging in reinforcing posttreatment behaviors.

When the active ingredient in the pain cocktail has been reduced to zero, the pain patient should be informed. Usually it is advisable to wait 1 to 2 days after reaching this level before informing the patient, so as to make sure that adequate deconditioning has occurred and that consistent performance of increased activities occurs in the medication-free state. However, conditioning and its effects are potent, and the habitual use of medication associated with pain reduction often generates a conditioned response that must be deconditioned. Therefore, even when the active ingredients in the pain cocktail have been eliminated, it may be necessary to continue a regimen of pain cocktail using only the vehicle, which will allow a continued desensitization and deconditioning response to the ingestion of analgesics. Furthermore, it is particularly important to maintain a post-inpatient medication schedule in those cases where the active ingredient has not been eliminated by the end of treatment or in those few cases where it may never be eliminated (e.g., where a long-standing respondent pain problem is expected and will require some continuing medication). In these

Table 3. Sample Pain Cocktail Regimen[a]

Inpatient days		Pain cocktail format
1–6	**Baseline:**	Patient reports preadmission pattern of "... one or two of the 50 mg tablets of Demerol two or three times a day, as needed, at home."
		Physician orders to nurse: "May have Demerol, *prn* pain, not to exceed three 50 mg tablets every 3 hours. Carefully record amount taken."
		Analysis of baseline data: Patient averaged 600 mg of Demerol per 24-hour period, at average of 3 to 4-hour intervals between requests.
7–9	**First cocktail**	
	℞ to pharmacists:	Demerol, 1920 mg
		Bevisol, Plebex, or other liquid B complex, 12 ml; cherry syrup qs 240 ml
	Sig:	Pain cocktail, 10 ml po q3h, day and night, *not prn*
	Nursing order:	Pain cocktail, 10 ml po q3h, day and night, *not prn*
		Since contents of the pain cocktail are not on the label, a copy of the prescription must be kept in a separate pain cocktail book.
10–12		Decrease each daily total by 64 mg, $\frac{1}{10}$ or original amount. A 3-day ℞ is decreased by 64 × 3 or 192 mg.
	℞ to pharmacists:	Demerol, 1728 mg
		Bevisol, Plebex, or other liquid B complex, 12 ml; cherry syrup qs 240 ml
	Sig:	Pain cocktail, 10 ml po q3h, day and night, *not prn*
	Nursing order:	Pain cocktail, 10 ml po q3h, day and night, *not prn*
13–15	**℞ to pharmacists:**	Demerol, 1536 mg
		Bevisol, Plebex, or other liquid B complex, 12 ml; cherry syrup qs 240 ml
	Sig:	Pain cocktail, 10 ml po q3h, day and night, *not prn*
	Nursing order:	Pain cocktail, 10 ml po q3h, day and night, *not prn*
16–18	**℞ to pharamacists:**	Demerol, 1344 mg
		Bevisol, Plebex, or other liquid B complex, 12 ml; cherry syrup qs 240 ml
	Sig:	Pain cocktail, 10 ml po q3h, day and night, *not prn*
	Nursing order:	Pain cocktail, 10 ml po q3h, day and night, *not prn*
19–21	**℞ to pharmacists:**	Demerol, 1152 mg
		Bevisol, Plebex, or other liquid B complex, 12 ml; cherry syrup qs 240 ml
	Sig:	Pain cocktail, 10 ml po q3h, day and night, *not prn*
	Nursing order:	Pain cocktail, 10 ml po q3h, day and night, *not prn*
22–24	**℞ to pharmacists:**	Demerol 960 mg
		Bevisol, Plebex, or other liquid B complex, 12 ml; cherry syrup qs 240 ml
	Sig:	Pain cocktail, 10 ml po q3h, day and night, *not prn*
	Nursing order:	Pain cocktail, 10 ml po q3h, day and night, *not prn*
37–39	**℞ to pharmacists:**	Demerol 0 mg
		Bevisol, Plebex, or other liquid B complex, 12 ml; cherry syrup qs 240 ml
	Sig:	Pain cocktail, 10 ml po q3h, day and night, *not prn*
	Nursing order:	Pain cocktail, 10 ml po q3h, day and night, *not prn*

(Maintain patient on vehicle for 2 to 10 days; if all is going well, inform patient and ask if continuation of vehicle is desired.)

[a]The assistance of Barbara J. DeLateur, M.D., in preparing the pain cocktail regimen sample and the related discussion is gratefully acknowledged.

situations the pain cocktail is administered on an outpatient basis and a fading schedule is generated. Once again, whether inpatient or outpatient treatment is used, behavioral health care dictates that adjustment of pain medication be made independent of pain behavior. Therefore, if an operant pain problem emerges at a later date (whether triggered by a stressful or physically traumatic event), it is important to reinstitute the pain cocktail and avoid pain-contingent or p.r.n. medication schedules. Also, if an acute or respondent situation arises, pain medication can be used. Its use should, however, only occur over the expected duration of the ailment (e.g., an abscessed wisdom tooth requiring analgesics until proper care is provided) and on a time-contingent basis. These procedures provide opportunity for learning appropriate methods, which do not recondition an operant pain response, of handling recurrent pain problems.

2.2.5. Programming a Therapeutic Health Care Environment

An effective behavioral health care intervention with chronic pain requires more than the availability of multiple specialty areas related to the treatment of chronic pain. That is, it is not sufficient that a chronic pain treatment center has access to specialists in physical therapy, occupational therapy, physiatry, psychology, psychiatry, vocational counseling, social work, nursing, and other disciplines. Although these specialties may be required, it is the way in which all interact with the patient that determines the extent to which a treatment program will be effective. In providing an orientation for a chronic pain behavioral health care team, the psychologist is often called on to present intervention strategies, since he or she typically has behavioral intervention expertise. An important concept imparted to the treatment team is the notion that all of us as human beings are exquisitely sensitive to the interpersonal reactions of others. This is particularly relevant for the chronic pain patient, since health care professionals have, by virtue of their past conditioning and training, learned to respond to patients in a pain-contingent manner, thereby maintaining and accelerating the pain behaviors desired to be decreased. Thus, an important and critical aspect of behavioral health care intervention is to reverse this contingency system by retraining and reprogramming staff responses to be health-contingent and non-reinforcing of pain behavior. Health care team members are instructed to systematically diminish their attention and social responses to pain behaviors through avoiding eye contact or by emitting noncommittal and neutral statements following patient displays of pain behavior. Concomitantly, staff are encouraged to increase social interaction and attention when the patient engages in increased activity levels and effective exercises. It is critical that staff learn the difference between responding to pain behaviors neutrally and punishing pain behaviors through judgmental or negative comments, since the negative side effects of punishment can override other positive aspects of treatment (e.g., anger resulting in depression or discontinuation of the program). Specifically, behavioral health care professionals are encouraged to monitor and record all behaviors, including pain behavior, but to overtly respond only to effective "well" behaviors. In this way, the patient receives the communication that "well" behavior and increased activity levels are the types of things getting support and social approval from the health care system in an operant pain program. Also, the behavioral professional can help impress upon the health care staff the importance of objective data collection regarding pain complaints and "well" behavior, thereby, providing continued encouragement and reinforcement to the patient for success and providing an effective way of monitoring treatment progress.

In reprogramming health care professionals' responses to pain, it is inadvisable and sometimes unethical to completely ignore complaints of pain or indications of discomfort. Once again, the use of time-contingent, periodic medical review of the treatment program (e.g., through weekly or biweekly scheduled appointments) can provide the appropriate opportunity for discussion of new and possibly respondent pain episodes while avoiding pain-contingent discussions. A further advantage of the time-contingent medical review is that it provides a context for appropriate discussion of pain but decreases the focus and preoccupation with discomfort at other treatment times.

An additional part of generating a behavioral treatment milieu involves reinforcing staff for dealing with difficult and sometimes complaining or "whiny" patients. It is important for the behavioral health care professional to remember that most therapists, especially those trained in acute care and traditional health intervention systems, are unaccustomed to patients failing to comply with their treatment regimens. They are particularly unaccustomed to being resented for attempting to provide help. Since this is often the case for chronic pain patients who initially distrust health care professionals, it is essential to provide some form of reinforcement and encouragement for the staff until the effects of reconditioning and increased activity can begin to become reinforcing in and of themselves. As with patient performance, it is possible to monitor and graph staff performance and to provide encouragement and reinforcement through weekly group meetings or periodic social encouragement and professional support. Furthermore, it has been demonstrated that staff follow-through and compliance with therapeutic regimes can be enhanced by simple methods like assigning specific tasks specific thrapists and posting or distributing lists of expected activities for all members of the therapeutic team (Quilitch, 1975; Steger *et al.*, 1981). Additional behavioral techniques designed to increase staff compliance involve reward systems for tasks completed and periodic didactic sessions given by the behavioral professionals to restate and reinforce the concepts and specific techniques involved in behavioral health care of chronic pain. All these can be effective in helping maintain an appropriate milieu for responding positively to "well" behavior and responding neutrally to pain behavior in operant pain treatment.

2.2.6. Maintaining an Effective Pain Control Environment

In the treatment of chronic pain, it has not been unusual for behavioral treatment strategies to generate significant outcome results only to have these remit or disappear at the end of a 1-year follow-up period (Sternbach, Murphy, Akeson, & Wolfe, 1973; Sternbach, 1974; Swanson, *et al.*, 1976). Other results suggest that effective generalization strategies as well as environmental alterations are critical if long-term treatment effects are to be maintained for sufferers from chronic pain (Painter, Seres, & Newman, 1980). Using such strategies, several behavioral pain treatment programs have been successful in decreasing pain medication usage and reported discomfort, increasing activity levels and vocational involvement, and maintaining these results at follow-up intervals from 1 to 3 years (Anderson *et al.*, 1977; Fordyce *et al.*, 1973; Gottlieb *et al.*, 1977). Several methods converge in these effective programs, including self-monitoring procedures, techniques designed to change environmental contingencies permanently, and the use of preventive health care techniques that generalize to other pain problems and thereby reduce the likelihood of future remission.

In those situations where systematic attention from spouse or family have become part of the pain problem, a systematic reprogramming and reconditioning of the family unit is essential. This can usually be provided by a family or marital therapist who is versed in behavioral pain treatment. A behavioral psychologist is often the one to provide such services. As with other aspects of behavioral health care for chronic pain, these interpersonal and environmental changes must be orchestrated so that the patient and family have time to reprogram and integrate their behavior into their daily life-style systematically. For example, one patient suffering from chronic low back and abdominal pain, had discontinued sexual activity (in addition to many other physical activities), and this was a major source of marital discord. Although both the patient and spouse had expressed a desire to increase sexual activity, this interest alone did not suffice to generate a change in behavior. In this particular case, the psychologist provided systematic sexual desensitization and treatment for sexual dysfunction; this gradually increased the amount and type of sexual activity as the patient's physical endurance and capabilities increased. Since this type of treatment often cannot be initiated until the middle or end of an inpatient program, it is not unusual for an outpatient program focusing on this type of environmental change to be instituted. In this particular case, the sexual problem was secondary to the pain problem (both partners had rated their sexual functioning as satisfactory prior to the surgery); following systematic instruction in alternative ways for engaging in sexual activity (considering her altered physical condition and increased physical capabilities), the couple were gradually able to reintroduce sexual activity into their lives. This is not to suggest that specific sexual dysfunction treatment is necessary for all pain patients who develop sexual problems. However, it is essential that the health care system provide the opportunity for such specialized treatment when it is required. In contrast, it is often the case that, in cases of low back pain, a couple can self-monitor the gradual introduction of sexual activity once physical reconditioning has occurred, medication control exists, and the patient and spouse have been instructed in specific body mechanic techniques.

Self-control procedures can also be incorporated across most aspects of behavioral health care as another way to maintain chronic pain control. As mentioned earlier, stress inoculation training, EMG biofeedback, deep breathing exercises, meditation exercises, and other self-control methods for reducing stress and anxiety can be incorporated following treatment. Periodic phone calls to the patient, the keeping of an activity diary and similar cueing systems can be helpful in generating long-term practice of self-control techniques learned in the hospital. Also, the patient may be offered specific didactic and instructional cassette tapes that can serve as cues or "booster treatments" requiring only self-initiation. This approach can be very powerful in maintaining treatment effects gained during the intervention phase. For example, in treating one patient with chronic low back pain, the authors found it to be helpful to provide a cassette tape with specific instructions in EMG relaxation techniques, stress inoculation methods, and a special "acute back-spasm drill." This drill could be used whenever a severe back spasm associated with certain body movements occurred, since this was going to be an ongoing part of the patient's life due to the degenerative pathology resulting from a severe motor vehicle accident. Also, with this particular patient it was mandatory to provide some form of cueing and external input, since he did not read and previous intervention techniques had failed due to reliance upon written instructions. Of equal importance is the fact that the use of cassette tapes and instruction manuals allows self-monitoring of pain-control strategies and prevents environmental agents (like spouses or health care professionals) from providing assistance or treatment that could reinforce pain behavior and health care utilization. Additional self-monitoring methods for treatment generalization are home-monitored physical exercises, home gymnastic systems, and patient-initiated exercise regimens. Furthermore, self-initiated avocational activities involving macramé and other hobbies can be effective ways to maintain "well" behavior that is incompatible with pain behavior.

Further environmental intervention involves the health care system itself. Specifically, it is essential that referring treatment personnel (family physicians, orthopedic surgeons, social workers, etc.) are given specific suggestions relating to the long-term treatment of chronic pain. In the absence of such information, it is likely that the environment will continue to deal with the chronic pain patient as if there had been no behavioral intervention. In our experience, when provided with specific alternatives to a traditional health care intervention system, referring physicians and health care agents have been cooperative in helping to maintain a long-term behavioral maintenance environment. This specifically relates to providing additional pain treatment interventions on a time-contingent rather than a pain-contingent basis. Also, helping the patient cope with agencies that reinforce pain behavior through bureaucracy (e.g., in some states the monetary reward system requires a person to demonstrate illness behavior to receive disability benefits) can provide momemtum to the maintenance of health. Further environmental alteration can accrue through the systematic use of vocational counseling designed to identify appropriate job activities following intervention and to facilitate a systematic reentry into the job market. This aspect of treatment is extremely important and has been shown to make the difference between programs which are able to get people to return to work and those that are not. Specifically, the vocational counselor is often called on to interact with the patient's employer and help that person comprehend the behavioral contingency strategies and the need for systematic but gradual reintroduction of work behavior. This typically takes the form of encouraging an employer to hire a patient (following treatment demonstrating physical capabilities that permit part-time work) for 4 hours per day. Then the *in vivo* job setting provides for gradual incrementing of work time and work responsibilities as dictated by physical abilities and limitations and the counselor's careful analysis and evaluation.

Finally, one of the most important aspects of generating long-term maintenance of treatment gains deals with providing "well" behavior alternatives to pain behavior. That is, although many aspects of the behavioral health care of chronic pain focus on *decreasing* medication and health care use and *increasing* physical and activity tolerance levels, the identification of gaps in "well" behavior is the responsibility of the behavioral psychologist. Specifically, it is important to identify learning disabilities, decreased neuropsychological functioning, social skill deficits, vocational weaknesses, sexual dysfunction, or emotional problems and to provide specific training in the areas of deficit so that alternative ways of approaching these problems are practiced and the retreat into pain behavior is avoided. This is not to suggest that all chronic pain patients are "using pain" to avoid pyschological problems. However, it is not infrequent that the development of a chronic pain problem magnifies those areas of deficiency, especially interpersonal dysfunction. As with other aspects of an operant pain program, the treatment for dysfunctional behaviors (replacing them with "well" behaviors) can begin as part of the behavioral intervention inpatient strategy and develop into long-term therapeutic intervention designed to facilitate permanent environmental and individual change.

2.3. Use of Adjunct Pain Treatment

Occasionally it is necessary that additional pain-related treatment be considered for a chronic pain patient. For example, anyone can fracture a leg and require pain medication secondary to the acute treatment of that problem. In these situations, where a clear underlying pathology is demonstrated, the traditional health care approach can be effectively used and as long as pain medication is judiciously and conservatively prescribed (preferably on a time-contingent rather than p.r.n. basis). Thus the operant pain patient remains at low risk. However, whenever any pain-related strategy is used, operant patients are susceptible to the effects of relearning, and they recondition their original pain problem. Therefore, it is imperative that acute pain strategies used with operant patients be effected in a time-contingent or time-limited fashion. Occasionally, additional pain-related treatments will be considered appropriate in combination with an operant pain approach. For example, transcutaneous nerve stimulations (TNS), nerve blocks, ethylchloride spray, or traction may be considered necessary. In most cases, it is ideal to attempt these procedures first, before initiating the operant pain program, and only after these have proven ineffective to initiate a behavioral approach. However, in some cases (e.g., the use of massage, biofeedback, or procedures with potentially lasting effects on pain), these strategies can be combined as one of the multiple facets in the behavioral health care approach to chronic pain. Similarly, when incorporating psychotherapy for pain-related psychological problems (e.g., depression, or passive-aggressive tendencies), it is imperative that treatment be coordinated with the behavioral contingency framework. Once again, the overriding principle is to consistently reinforce the idea that medical attention and health care treatment for pain control will be prescribed not on the basis of the experience or report but on some specific and time-related schedule.

One of the most important issues to consider when determining the possible efficacy of a behavioral intervention strategy in chronic pain is the extent to which social or rest-related reinforcers are available and to what degree they are within the control of the health care system. The presence of these factors can often be observed during the baseline monitoring period. If the patient exhibits consistent unwillingness to even attempt exercises or activities (when these have been established as medically safe and when rest or praise has been made contingent on successful completion), an operant approach is likely to fail. Problems will be compounded when (1) a patient is unwilling to decrease high medication use; (2) the spouse is unwilling or unavailable and environmental factors are critical; (3) pain- and illness-contingent compensation occurs, providing a comfortable existence in the absence of "well" behavior; and (4) significant physiological or psychological problems interfere with the patient's ability to follow through with a self-monitored and systematic program.

These considerations are, however, not easy to weigh, and the health care professional making the evaluation must be very careful. For example, the fact that a spouse is unwilling to participate or that the patient receives disability compensation does not in itself contraindicate a behavioral approach. The patient may, in fact, be planning to leave the spouse to live alone, or the compensation payments may be at a level so much lower than previously attained through work that the patient's incentive for getting well is high. When these issues are apparent, however, it is essential, if the treatment is to be effective, to identify appropriate reinforcers (e.g., a patient who must work or will feel depressed, or an alternative person in the environment who can provide encouragement and reinforcement for "well" behavior even though the spouse does not).

It is also important to remember that emotional or psychiatric difficulties do not automatically mark a patient as inappropriate for behavioral health care intervention. As Sternbach (1974) has shown, many chronic pain sufferers exhibit psychological difficulties. The critical factor involves the extent to which the patient's problems interfere with consistent application and follow-through with the treatment steps. Specifically, a paranoid patient with a history of chronic medication abuse who will not take the pain cocktail because he feels the health system is "out to poison him" does not qualify. Furthermore, patients with chronic behavior patterns which periodically place them in "time out" (e.g., binge alcoholics, street drug users who require either incarceration or detoxification) cannot be considered until these situations are controlled so that they will not disrupt the deconditioning and desensitization aspects of the behavioral care system. In contrast, the chronically depressed patient or "hysterical patient" often responds well to the structured nature of some behavioral strategies (Steger, 1978). A final and obvious consideration is the extent to which nociception or chronic physical limitations (e.g., rheumatoid arthritis) restrict active participation in the physical reconditioning aspect of behavioral health care. Also, the presence of ongoing pain during activity will severely limit the effectiveness of a desensitization approach to chronic pain. For a thorough review of these factors, see Fordyce (1976).

It has been suggested in this chapter that behavioral intervention strategies can and have been effectively applied to the treatment of chronic pain. The importance of viewing pain as a complex and multifaceted phenomenon related to nociception, sensory–receptor response systems, suffering, and the behavioral and environmental effects of learning principles has been suggested. The health care system typically intuits from behavior and verbalizations of the patient that intervention for pain is needed. In contrast, a behavioral health care approach to the analysis and treatment of chronic pain has been presented, and the importance of such factors as medication use, exercising to quota, vocational counseling, stress coping strategies, interpersonal functioning, and environmental influences has been discussed. Furthermore, it has been suggested that traditional health care intervention focusing only on one or two aspects of chronic pain is inadequate and may, in fact, exacerbate or maintain a chronic pain problem. Thus, it is critical that health care professionals begin to evaluate the treatment of chronic pain more systematically, utilizing advances in behavioral technology as well as the traditional health care system. There no longer appears to be a need for pain-contingent medications and treatment strategies, reliance on self-report of pain and exercise tolerance, and other traditional approaches to chronic pain management, since behavioral health care now provides alternatives that appear to be more effective. Finally, the careful and consistent orchestration of multiple factors has been suggested as critical if the health care system is to apply behavioral technology effectively to help solve chronic pain problems.

4. References

Anderson, T., Cole, T., Gullickson, G., Hudgens, A., & Roberts, A. Behavior modification of chronic pain: A treatment program by a multidisciplinary team. *Journal of Clinical Orthopaedics and Related Research*, 1977, *129*, 96–100.

Battle, C., Imber, S., Hoehn-Saric, R., Stone, A., Nash, E., & Frank, J. Target complaints as criteria of improvement. *American Journal of Psychotherapy*, 1966, *20*, 184–192.

Beecher, H. K. The placebo effect as a non-specific force surrounding disease and the treatment of disease. In R. Janzen, W. D. Keidel, A. Herz, C. Steichele, J. P. Payne & R. A. P. Burt (Eds.), *Pain: Basic principles, pharmacology, therapy*. Stuttgart: George Thieme, 1972.

Budzynski, T., Stoyva, J., & Adler, C. Feedback-induced muscle relaxation: Application to tension headache. *Journal of Behavioral Therapy and Experimental Psychiatry*, 1970, *1*, 205–211.

Cairns, D., Thomas, L., Mooney, V., & Pace, J. B. A comprehensive treatment approach to chronic low back pain. *Pain*, 1976, *2*, 301–308.

Elder, S., & Eustis, N. Instrumental blood pressure conditioning in outpatient hypertensions. *Behavior Research Therapy*, 1975, *13*, 185–188.

Engel, B. Clinical applications of operant conditioning techniques in the control of the cardiac arrhythmias. *Seminars in Psychiatry*, 1973, *5*, 433–438.

Fordyce, W., Fowler, R., Lehmann, J., DeLateur, B., Sand, P., & Trieschmann, R. Operant conditioning in the treatment of chronic clinical pain. *Archives of Physical Medicine and Rehabilitation*, 1973, *54*, 399–408.

Fordyce, W. *Behavioral methods for chronic pain and illness.* St. Louis, Mosby, 1976.

Fordyce, W., & Steger, J. Behavioral management of chronic pain. In O. Pomerleau & J. Brady (Eds.), *Behavioral medicine: Theory and practice.* Baltimore: Williams & Wilkins, 1979.

Fowler, R. Operant therapy for headaches. *Headache,* 1975, *15*(1), 63–68.

Gottlieb, H., Strite, L., Killer, R., Madorsky, A., Hockersmith, V., Kleeman, M., & Wagner, J. Comprehensive rehabilitation of patients having chronic low back pain. *Archives of Physical Medicine and Rehabilitation,* 1977, *58,* 101–108.

Halpern, L. M. Psychotropic drugs and the management of chronic pain. In J. J. Bonica (Ed.), *Advances in neurology: International symposium on pain* (Vol. 4). New York: Raven Press, 1974.

Haynes, R., Gibson, E., Hockett, B., Sackett, D., Taylor, D., Roberts, R., & Johnson, A. Improvement of medication compliance in uncontrolled hypertension. *Lancet,* 1976, 1265–1268.

Kiresuk, T., & Sherman, R. Goal attainment scaling: A general method of evaluating comprehensive community mental programs. *Community Mental Health Journal,* 1968, *4,* 443–451.

Lewinsohn, P. Engagement in pleasant activities and depression level. *Journal of Abnormal Psychology,* 1975, *84*(6), 729–731.

Lichtenstein, E., Harris, D., Birchler, G., Wahl, J., & Schmahl, D. Comparison of rapid smoking, warm smoky air, and attention placebo in the modification of smoking behavior. *Journal of Consulting and Clinical Psychology,* 1973, *40,* 90–98.

Loeser, J. D. Dorsal rhizotomy: Indications and results. In J. J. Bonica (Ed.), *Advances in neurology: International symposium on pain* (Vol. 4). New York: Raven Press, 1974.

Loeser, J. D. Personal communication, 1978.

Maruta, T., Swanson, D., & Finlayson, R. Drug abuse and dependency in patients with chronic pain. *Mayo Clinic Proceedings,* 1979, *54,* 241–244.

Meichenbaum, D., & Turk, D. The cognitive–behavioral management of anxiety, anger, and pain. In P. Davidson (Ed.), *The behavioral management of anxiety, depression, and pain.* New York: Brunner Mazel, 1976.

Melzack, R. *The Puzzle of pain.* New York: Basic Books, 1973.

Merskey, H., & Spear, F. G. *Pain: Psychological and psychiatric aspects.* London: Bailliere, Tindall, & Cassell, 1967.

Newman, R., Seres, J., Yospe, L., & Garlington, B. Multidisciplinary treatment of chronic pain: Long-term follow-up of low-back pain patients. *Pain,* 1978, *4,* 283–292.

Orne, M. On the social psychology of the psychological experiment: With particular reference to demand characteristics and their implications. *American Psychologist,* 1962, *17,* 776–783.

Painter, J., Seres, J., & Neuman, R. Assessing benefits of the pain center: Why some patients regress. *Pain,* 1980, *8,* 101–113.

Pavlov, I. *Conditioned reflexes.* (Trans. G. V. Anrep). London: Oxford University Press, 1927.

Pomerleau, O., & Pomerleau, C. *Break the smoking habit: A behavioral program for giving up cigarettes.* Champaign, Ill.: Research Press, 1977.

Quilitch, H. A comparison of three staff management procedures. *Journal of Applied Behavioral Analysis,* 1975, *8,* 59–66.

Roberts, A., & Reinhardt, L. The behavioral management of chronic pain: Long-term follow-up with comparison groups. *Pain,* 1980, *8*(2), 151–162.

Rosenthal, R. *Experimenter effects in behavioral research.* New York: Appleton Century Crofts, 1966.

Sackett, D., & Haynes, R. *Compliance with therapeutic regimens.* Baltimore: Johns Hopkins University Press, 1976.

Seligman, M. *Helplessness.* San Francisco: W. H. Freeman, 1975.

Shealy, C., & Maurer, D. Transcutaneous nerve stimulation for control of pain. *Surgical Neurosurgery,* 1974, *2,* 45–47.

Skinner, B. *The behavior of organisms.* New York: Appleton Century Crofts, 1938.

Solomon, R., & Wynne, L. Traumatic avoidance learning: The principles of anxiety conservation and partial ineversability. *Psychological Review,* 1954, *61,* 353–385.

Steger, J. Personality and pain ratings in biofeedback treatment. *Archives of Physical Medicine and Rehabilitation,* 1978, *59*(11), 551.

Steger, J., & Harper, R. Comprehensive biofeedback versus self-monitored relaxation in the treatment of tension headache. *Headache,* 1980, *20*(3), 137–142.

Steger, J., Shelton, J., Beukelman, D., & Fowler, R. Pinpointing: One method of improving staff compliance with rehabilitation regimens. *Journal of Behavioral Medicine,* 1981, in press.

Sterman, M. Neurophysiologic and clinical studies of sensorimotor EEG biofeedback training: Some effects on epilepsy. *Seminars in Psychiatry*, 1973, *5*, 507–525.

Sternbach, R. A. *Pain: A Psychophysiological analysis.* New York: Academic Press, 1968.

Sternbach, R. A. *Pain patients: Traits and treatment.* New York: Academic Press, 1974.

Sternbach, R., Murphy, R., Akeson, W., & Wolfe, S. Chronic low back pain: Characteristics of the "low back loser." *Postgraduate Medicine*, 1973, *53*, 135–138.

Swanson, D., Floreen, A., & Swenson, W. Program for managing chronic pain. II. Short-term results. *Mayo Clinic Proceedings*, 1976, *51*, 409–411.

Treischmann, R. *Spinal cord injuries.* New York: Pergamon Press, 1979.

Turk, D. Cognitive–behavioral techniques in the management of pain. In J. Foreyt & D. P. Rathjen (Eds.), *Cognitive behavior therapy: Research and applications.* New York: Plenum Press, 1978.

Waskow, I., & Parloff, M. *Psychotherapy change measures.* Rockville, Md.: National Institute of Mental Health (DHEW Publication No. (ADM) 74-120), 1975.

Weisenberg, M. Pain and pain control. *Psychological Bulletin*, 1977, *84*(5), 1008–1044.

Wish, P. The use of imagery-based techniques in the treatment of sexual dysfunction. *The Counseling Psychologist*, 1975, *5*(1), 52–55.

Cognitive Behavior Therapy in Health Psychology

Robert B. Meagher, Jr.

Cognition is "in"! In developmental psychology, in social psychology, and now in behavior therapy—the bastion of "behavior"—a change is under way whose end has not yet been charted. Behavior therapy, which was developed as a protest against "mentalistic" and "nonscientific" therapies, particularly psychoanalysis, has been recast as cognitive behavior therapy in those "unobservable" terms it so vehemently eschewed 25 years ago. With its progenitor, which has flourished beside it, it shares mainly an interest in behavior as outcome.

The cognitive behavioral approach has now found its way into the rapidly growing area of treatment of medical problems. It has been used with hypertensives (Agras & Jacob, 1979; Bloom & Cantrell, 1978; Seer, 1979; Shapiro, Schwartz, Ferguson, Redmond, & Weiss, 1977), pain (Beers & Karoly, 1979; Girodo & Wood, 1979; Khatami & Rush, 1978; Levendusky & Pankratz, 1975; Meichenbaum & Turk, 1976; Spanos, Horton, & Chaves, 1975; Turk & Genest, 1979), preparation for medical procedures (Auerbach, Kendall, Cuttler, & Levitt, 1976; Fortin & Kirouac, 1976; Horan, 1973; Kendall, Williams, Pechacek, Graham, Shisslak, & Herzoff, 1979; Langer, Janis, & Wolfer, 1975; Shipley, Butt, Horwitz, & Fabry, 1978), smokers (Barbarin, 1978; Berecz, 1976; Chambliss & Murray, 1979a; Nesse & Nelson, 1977; Pechacek & Danaher, 1979; Rozensky, 1974), stomach ulcers and colitis (Brooks & Richardson, 1980; Harrell & Beiman, 1978), Type-A CHD behavior pattern (Glass, 1977; Jenni & Wollersheim, 1979; Roskies, *et al.*, 1978; Roskies, 1980; Suinn, 1975a & b, 1977); headaches (Holroyd, Andrasik, & Westbrook, 1977; Mitchell & White, 1976; Reeves, 1976); obesity (Castro & Rachlin, 1980; Chambliss & Murray, 1979a; Chapman & Jeffrey, 1979;

ROBERT B. MEAGHER • Departments of Neurological Surgery and Psychology, University of Miami School of Medicine, Miami, Florida 33101.

Dunkel & Glaros, 1978; Leon, 1979; Pechacek, 1979; Schreber, Schauble, Eating, & Skovholt, 1979), as well as, in general, stress-management inoculation (Barrios & Shigetoni, 1979; Budzynski, 1978; Horan, Hackett, Buchanan, Stone, & Denchik-Stone, 1977; Meichenbaum, 1975; Sanchez-Craig, 1976; Suinn, 1975a; Suinn & Richardson, 1971), and, finally, to structure the teaching of health-related behavior change (Davidson & Davidson, 1980; Gordon, Friedenbergs, Dillen, Hibbard, Wolf, Levine, Lipkins, Ezrachi, & Lucido, 1980; Stone, Hinds, & Schmidt, 1975; Strickland, 1978).

There are many reasons why those offering treatment for medical patients might elect this approach. One is clearly the therapeutic zeitgeist (see reviews by Wilson, 1978, and by Mahoney & Arnkoff, 1978, for a thorough discussion of the present and past in this field), which now so thoroughly welcomes cognition. Another reason is related to the difficulty of developing behavioral programs for adults over whom therapists have so little environmental control. A related issue is the public acceptability of such programs. A final factor is related to the often cited (e.g., O'Leary & Wilson, 1975) problem of situational specificity encountered in operant programs. Cognitive behavioral therapy offers an answer in the form of self-administered rewards which can be provided anywhere.

This chapter will examine in detail a current theoretical model, show how it is used in several complex behavioral health treatment programs, and then describe an alternative model incorporating aspects of both cognitive control systems as well as medical–behavioral change. First, however, several theoretical issues deserve discussion.

1. Theoretical Issues in Cognitive Behavior Therapy

As cognitive behavior therapy broke free from traditional behavior approaches (e.g., Ayllon & Azrin, 1964; Homme, 1965; Wolpe, 1958, 1961, 1969), it carried traditional ways of conceptualizing behavior and behavior change with it. For example, there could be said to be a camp that applies a cognitive variant of the experimental analysis of behavior, which involves overt "operants" (Skinner, 1953, see definition by Meichenbaum, below). Another group finds its genesis in behavior therapy (Pavlov, 1927), which tended to emphasize covert, classical, or "respondent" learning. Murray and Jacobson (1978) outline these conceptual bases while providing a reinterpretation of learning theory and related therapy along cognitive lines.

Although not all cognitivists' ontological roots can be cleanly categorized, the learning theory lines of development can generally be identified. As the progression occurred, it borrowed from several additional sources. Social psychology has always followed a cognitive model (Bem, 1972; Festinger, 1957; Heider, 1958; Rosenberg, Horland, McGuire, Abelson, & Brehm, 1960; Schachter, 1964). Some of the therapeutic implications of these approaches were developed by Goldstein, Heller, and Sechrest (1966). Cognitive theorists in other areas, like Piaget (1930, 1952, 1971) in developmental psychology, have been embraced less thoroughly. One reason may be that the "structuralist" position has thus far been difficult for learning theory (associationist) approaches to fit into their systems. It has been traditional for proponents of learning theory to make minimal assumptions regarding the structuring (Rosenthal & Zimmerman, 1978) of the mind. For example, in an attempt at *rapprochment*, Turk, a writer in cognitive methodology, discusses "structures" in thought (1978). He is not in the least referring to a model that resembles Piaget's hierarchically ordered system. Moreover, an area in which theory in cognitive behavior therapy is sorely lacking is precisely that comprising the development and integration of structured models of cognition or, for that matter, personality (Rotter, 1978).

A final developmental line comes from such cognitive theorists as Rotter (1954, 1966, 1978) and Ellis (Ellis & Grieger, 1977; Ellis, 1980), Kelley (1977), Bandura (1969, 1977a, 1977b) and, to a lesser extent, Johnson (1946). Bandura has in many ways led the theoretical development in this area with an evolving social learning theory (SLT). Beginning with his observational learning work (Bandura & Walters, 1959; Bandura, Ross, & Ross, 1963), he emphasized internal self-reward mechanisms. His book of 1969 did much to shape the area. The 1977 restructuring of SLT—in which "self-efficacy" becomes a major construct—has done much to influence the direction of the field (Bandura & Adams, 1977).

It should be evident at this point that there is no monolithic cognitive behavior theory of therapy. There exist instead a variety of theorists and therapists working in parallel fashion, having in common a variety of assumptions about the critical variables in therapy and a tremendous enthusiasm. Recently, two new journals were established in which workers in this area could communicate with one another: *Cognitive Therapy and Research* and *Biofeedback and Self-Regulation*. The early issues of the first journal dealt with definitions, commonalities, historical roots, and skirmishes with the "enemy": behavior modification. In an early interchange, Meichenbaum (1979) defined behavior modification with humans out of existence in any practical sense!

2. A Theoretical Model of Behavior Change

2.1. Description of the Model

Among the many theories of cognitive mediation of behavior change, one of the most influential as well as the most clearly articulated is that of Meichenbaum (1977). Central to his system is the concept of the client's "recognition" or "awareness" of his or her own behavior. This "awareness" provides a cue for producing an "internal dialogue" (e.g., Luria, 1961), whose content becomes the focus of the therapy. Often, the client is unaware of the dialogue; behavior is "automatic," or without particular awareness. Before therapy, the dialogue may take the form, "I'm helpless," "I'm the victim of feelings and thoughts over which I have no control." According to Meichenbaum, "rarely does the client consider the role of his own thinking processes and/or the interpersonal meaning of his own behavior as sources of disturbance (1977, p. 217)." During the therapy process, a translation occurs in which the client reconceptualizes the problem and learns to phrase the dialogue in different terms.

For Meichenbaum, the sequence has an end/feedback point in the environment. That is, the client tries the new dialogue, first with the therapist who interprets, clarifies and instructs and then in real-life coping situations in the outside world. Paramount in this process is what the client *says to himself* or *herself.*

> The three basic processes of change have been introduced in the form of (1) the client's behaviors and the reactions they elicit in the environment; (2) the client's internal dialogue or what he says to himself before, accompanying, and following his behavior; and (3) the client's cognitive structures that give rise to the specific internal dialogue. In short, I am proposing that behavior change occurs through a sequence of mediating process involving the interaction of inner speech, cognitive structures, and behavior and their resultant outcomes. If an individual (whether a client, or scientist, or whatever) is going to change his pattern of responding, he must introduce an intentional mediational process. The mediational process involves the recognition of maladaptive behavior (either external or internal) and this recognition must come to elicit inner speech that is different in content from that engaged in prior to therapy. The altered private speech must then trigger coping behaviors. Some clients require explicit teaching of such coping responses and this is where the technology of behavior therapy is of particular value. (1977, pp. 218–219)

For Meichenbaum, the kind of dialogue that is therapeutically appropriate is one in which the client sees self as the active mediator of cognitions rather than a helpless victim. One "notes the opportunities for engaging in adaptive behaviors, behaviors that will be rehearsed and discussed in therapy." "Internal dialogue" is a pregnant construct that refers to attention, appraisal, affect, and physiological responses as well as the initiation of behavior. Changing dialogues are responsible not only for changed directions in behavior but also affect the value ascribed to and the interpretation of reinforcements which come from the environment attendant to changed behavior. Therapeutic success is defined, therefore, not only by changed behavior but also by what the client says to self about the change and to whom it is attributed.

2.2. Assessment

Assessment, for Meichenbaum, is "cognitive–functional." Parallelling Skinner's (1953) "functional analysis of behavior," an important concept is *response class,* defined both topographically and in its frequency in various stimulus configurations. Environmental events are then changed systematically in order to establish functional relationships. In cognitive–functional analysis, client cognitions become not merely one of several response classes under study but also the sphere of paramount concern. Assessment is the act of examining the task (typically coping or initiating behavior) from the point of view of the *cognitive* demands it makes on the client; that is, it seeks to ascertain the "sequentially organized set of cognitive processes" required for adequate performance. Of particular interest are the individual's opportunities to stray from the task, either by allowing or creating interruptions or by the way in which he or she defines the task through self-statements.

In this cognitive–functional approach, assessment becomes indistinguishable from treatment. After the "cognitive" elements of the task are delineated, the manipulative process begins: tasks are modified in the search for changes in cognition which reflects changes in demands. Nontask environmental variables

503

COGNITIVE
BEHAVIOR
THERAPY IN
HEALTH
PSYCHOLOGY

are altered (e.g., changing the type of room, social company, etc.), and then the client is offered various cognitive strategies that may be used to improve task performance. This last procedure is crucial, embodying the idea that strategies can be shared by the therapist and integrated by the client. The assessment process includes the strong suggestion that the client can change his or her own personal dialogue concerning the problem.

2.3. A Critical Appraisal of the Model

In simple terms, inner dialogues are formulated as occasionally connected statements that are "run off" with high probability in certain critical situations. This "simple" model (Bower, 1978) may prove to be complex enough, and it may be all that is needed pragmatically to account for changes in cognitions. On the other hand, there is ample evidence from cognitive theorists favoring the notion of an organization, that is, an ordered or hierarchical structure of thought. Piaget, among others, described cognitive development as being ordered from the very beginning. To him, development during the formal operational stage involves a layering or concatenation of organized concepts. Thought is conceived not merely as a series of discrete self-statements but as a highly organized system. Moreover, there is reason to suppose that behavioral problems of a specific sort may share a common class of cognitions, that is, "typical" self-statements. For example, chronic pain patients typically say that they are helpless to control experienced pain; Type-A clients often say that they have difficulty relaxing. Meichenbaum, however, would take each client's problem *de novo*, as if it were unique. In his approach, the clinician is asked to ascertain where he or she believes the deficit lies and to administer a task to the client. The clinician is in a position at this point to complete the task and to introspect about the "process," that is, the affects, images, and behaviors used to solve the task. An analysis of the cognitive strategies involved in the task is expected to lead to clear hypotheses about its nature. Interesting and illuminating though the process may be, it means that the clinician essentially starts with a clean slate for each new client. Although many personality theorists conceive of persons as fitting categories according to "typical" self-statements, Meichenbaum rejects such views as highly speculative. Very little of what has been established in personality and clinical research finds acceptance in Meichenbaum's model.

Those schooled in operant and experimental behaviorism would have little trouble understanding Skinner's vehement response to this newer approach in his paper "Why I Am Not a Cognitive Therapist" (1978). Meichenbaum's recasting of the concept of functional analysis is especially irksome to behaviorists, given his insistence on calling cognitions "behavior" (Ledwidge, 1978). In view of the radical behaviorists' long historical struggle against "mentalism," with its attendant imprecision, demand characteristics, and circularity, Skinner and his followers find this flagrant misuse of their cherished term an insult to its ostensive "purity."

Another criticism of cognitive behavior therapy, especially as structured by Meichenbaum, is its implicit reliance on the client's "faith." One author (Pecheur, 1978) examined the model presented here and concluded that there exists a striking similarity between this approach to therapy and the religious concept of "sanctification." The concepts may not be similar in content, but they are in their structure. Thus, participants or clients are invited to learn ways to live with difficult situations rather than changing them. Furthermore, and in contrast to the situational focus of most behaviorists, the source of change lies entirely within the client, not in the stimulus environment about him.

A final comment relates to the minor role assigned to the relationship (Morris & Suckerman, 1974) between client and therapist. The model as presented has no room for concepts such as transference/countertransference and the way therapists use their emotional responses as part of the therapeutic intervention (Gill & Hoffman, 1980; Frank, 1959; Freud, 1905; Ford, 1978; Pande & Gant, 1968) or even for such social role aspects as relationship, discussed by Frank (1959, 1972, 1974). In many ways, the system promotes a sterile computer-programming approach devoid of affect.

3. Issues in Cognitive Behavioral Assessment

Consonant with cognitive–functional analysis as described earlier, assessment consists of task analysis as well as an analysis of cognitions the client uses or fails to use. What is not clear is the specification of the standard or most appropriate unit for the analysis. Several questions arise in this regard. To what extent does the particular orientation of the therapist/assessor determine the units of assessment? To what extent do the therapist's own cognitions "pull" or "demand" similar cognitive approaches from the client?

Beyond Meichenbaum's extremely narrow approach to assessment, a variety of specific dimensions have been proposed by other cognitive theorists (Kendall & Kongeski, 1979). These include self-efficacy and internal–external locus of control (Rotter, 1966), attribution theory, beliefs about self, cognitive style (e.g., field dependence/field independence, cognitive tempo, sensation-seeking; Zuckerman, Bushsbaum, & Murphy, 1980), repression sensitization (Heilbrun, 1978), imagery, assessed for both content and vividness by *in vivo* thought sampling, a form of free association. In addition, theories of personality relate constructs to "typical" or expected cognitions. For example, Millon's (1969) active detached type is given to self-derogating statements, to statements which assume that others will not be concerned, or to the expectation that others will be ridiculing him or her, and so on. Equally important are correlated physical parameters such as frequency and intensity of pain behavior (e.g., limping, holding the back, whimpering), the amount and type of "functional" (Fordyce, 1976) behavior engaged in (e.g., "up" or out-of-bed time, number of hours at work, amount of active leisure time), amount of rest time taken by Type-A clients, number of cigarettes smoked, frequency of gastric spasms, and frequency of debilitating headaches.

There is no system that ties assessment categories together. An example of what is needed in this regard may be seen in Keefe and Brown (in press). In addition, the final section in this chapter describes a multidisciplinary pain treatment program that integrates various assessment aspects.

4. Cognitive Behavioral Therapy for Type-A CHD Patients

505

COGNITIVE
BEHAVIOR
THERAPY IN
HEALTH
PSYCHOLOGY

The increased CHD risk associated with membership in the Type-A category (Dembrowski, Weiss, Shields, Haynes, & Feinleib, 1978; Jenkins, 1971, 1976; Roskies, 1980) has in recent years become more clearly established with follow-up research (e.g., Jenkins & Zyzanski 1980). The pattern consists of a constellation of attitudes and behaviors characterized by a "driven" quality. In the work setting, it is the tendency to take on whatever tasks are assigned without regard to realistic time or other constraints (e.g., Glass, Snyder, & Hollis, 1974). There is a pervasive inability to relax, even in situations where the person might agree that it was objectively appropriate to do so. This attitude is generalized to home and leisure settings (Glass, 1977).

Therapeutically, one might ask whether the pattern *could* even be changed. The literature is replete with statements (Friedman & Rosenman, 1977; Rosenman & Friedman, 1977; Suinn, 1978) to the effect that even when the person has experienced an infarct or a CVA, change in style is almost impossible; in the absence of a life-threatening event or its imminence, the movitation to effect change is simply insufficient. The Type-A attitude is perceived as being so highly rewarding that even the threat of loss of life cannot motivate change.

A second question is related to *what* should be changed. Should people be asked to give up productive and fulfilling lives to accept less challenging and less remunerative jobs? Would not the loss of such involvements be a stressor in itself? Alternatively, could not those who display the pattern be helped to moderate the more extreme reactions that are intrinsic elements of the syndrome?

Two of a number of programs that adopt the latter approach will be described in some detail below. The less complex of these programs was developed by Suinn (Suinn & Bloom, 1978). Three questions guided the construction of the regimen: What reinforcers maintain Type-A behavior? What alternative behaviors are desirable? How might these be achieved? According to Suinn, the answer to the first question is primarily "cultural"; that is, society admires and rewards these behaviors. In addition to job-related rewards for aggressive, tireless, "workaholic" behaviors, Type-A people tend to internalize these values and to impose these stresses upon themselves. Timetables are constructed and then adhered to as a means of reducing anxiety. Of course, a change in the rewards of work could, if practiced, help remedy the external sources of stress. However, internal stress creates its own reward for hard work in the form of the negatively reinforcing reduction of anxiety.

Suinn states that Type-A people believe that Type-A behaviors are the *only* way in which they can retain productivity and control an uncertain world. There may be less stressful ways of achieving; however, Type A's appear unwilling to try methods that have not yet been associated with reward.

The treatment approach developed by Suinn emphasizes "stress management training" (Suinn & Richardson, 1971), as well as a number of techniques for the covert rehearsal of these training strategies. Self-imposed habits that produce stress are examined and alternative responses, such as relaxation, are substituted for the problematic ones. Initial results appear promising in some measures of Type-A behavior, such as self-reported stress levels and cholesterol and triglyceride levels. Long-term follow-up studies of these changes and their expected concomitant decreases in CHD risk have not yet been reported.

A second, more complex approach has evolved from a group led by Roskies (Roskies, Sperack, Surkis, Cohen, & Gilman, 1978; Roskies & Avard, in press; Roskies, 1980). Their behavior therapy program, even in its simplest forms, demonstrated 6-month follow-up improvement across several measures. The central issue in their research was that of inducing people to change the behaviors that had been previously so successful and productive. Roskies worked both with people with no clear confirmation of a covert disease process and with others who had had myocardial infarctions. Those who had experienced heart attacks did show greater change in the desired direction than those who had not. Both groups were in a cognitive–behavioral program and did better than controls in a "psychotherapy" program (Roskies *et al.*, 1978).

In an attempt to convince people at risk for CHD who were not yet patients to change their injurious behavior patterns, a complex program was constructed utilizing a large number of integrated concepts and modalities. The Type A's apparent need to control the environments became a strength as the program unfolded. The need was translated into a challenge to patients to learn to control their own behavior so as to maximize productivity and minimize strain. The idea that "modulation of Type A behavior need not diminish performance, but might actually enhance it," became the watchwords. "Personal effectiveness" was the rubric under which treatment was presented. The program combined a variety of techniques, since the problem was seen as a general way of thinking, feeling and behaving that had generalized into several domains, all of which could be usefully modified. The program addressed intellectual, social, emotional, and physical functioning, with the participant having some degree of choice in selecting which combination of approaches he or she wished to utilize to address personal problem areas. Subjects were selected from middle-level managers in a Canadian city; 90% turned out to be Type A.

The goal of this program was to develop a set of techniques suitable for use in a variety of settings both at work and at home, one that could easily be continued and monitored by the participants.

In the latest form, the modes chosen are as follows:

1. Awareness, self-observation. Participants were assisted in developing a schedule and taught techniques of monitoring such events as muscle tension, outbursts of anger, sense of time pressure.

2. Relaxation. Basic skills were first taught in 20-minute sessions, then in condensed 5-minute form, then in instant, interiorized relaxation responses to specific cues. Participants were expected to practice all phases by themselves. External cues were employed initially; participants were provided with 60 stars which they affixed in places at work and at home where stress was frequently encountered. Emphasis was later placed on developing internal cues associated with perceived real-life tension.

3. Rational–emotive thinking (Ellis & Grieger, 1977). Participants were encouraged to examine irrational beliefs (e.g., others should always be perfect, we should always be perfect, others should always love us, etc.) to challenge and change. Each participant was to engage in internal debate in a group setting

that recreated a situation in which he or she had been upset, with the goal of shifting feelings to a "lower key."

4. Communication skills. These business managers were assumed to have skills in this area. However, a model designed to decrease stress responses was taught. Participants were taught to distinguish among three levels of communication: those with a focus on a problem, those that are an attack on the person; and those that reflect an attack on the relationship. The first level was considered the least stressful.

5. Problem-solving skills in personal decision making. Participants were taught to make decisions efficiently, to implement them, and to evaluate them in terms of outcome.

6. Stress inoculation. Participants were taught to value coping with rather than seeking to "cure" feelings of distress. The emphasis was on emitting coping self-statements and practicing general coping behaviors. This stage acted as a conceptual "umbrella," tying the program together philosophically and ultimately integrating all strategies into a single master coping model (Meichenbaum, 1977).

7. Posttraining. Booster sessions were scheduled and informal meetings among participants arranged. The program relied, however, on having inculcated a general approach to problem solving and stress management. Participants were to apply the skills they had already learned or to reach out for additional skill training if warranted.

The initial report on the program was encouraging. Difficulties in meeting participant time schedules, completing homework assignments, and so on were noted as requiring modification. Outcome data have not been reported to date.

This program brings to focus many of the features that characterize cognitive behavior therapy. First, it uses the participants' strengths and previous coping strategies to promote change. Second, it is applicable to adults living in a world where the therapist exerts little control. Third, it attempts to engender a structure whose form can be generalized to a variety of situations. Thus, if it succeeds, the program will minimize situation-specific response patterning. Finally, it treats the problem in a psychological as opposed to a medical fashion; like many cognitive behavioral programs, it is not embedded in the medical treatment delivery system but stands by itself.

Two approaches to cognitive–behavioral treatment of chronic pain will be described below. The first of these can be seen to bear a strong conceptual relationship to the programs already described; the second marks a departure in several important respects.

5. Cognitive Behavioral Approach to Pain Treatment

Turk alone (in press, 1977a,b, 1978) and with coauthors (Genest & Turk, 1979; Meichenbaum & Turk, 1976; Turk & Genest, 1979) has applied the stress-inoculation model of cognitive behavior therapy to pain patients. The general model consists of teaching patients to examine their self-statements in response to pain. For example, one technique involved videotaping the patient while he

507

COGNITIVE
BEHAVIOR
THERAPY IN
HEALTH
PSYCHOLOGY

or she was experiencing induced pain (cold-pressor). The tape was played back while the patient attempted to recapture a variety of self-statements. The vividness of the video as well as audio cues was designed to enhance veridical recall.

Turk has outlined a three-part program. Initially patients are given a rationale for using psychological techniques for pain control. For example, the literature on the relationship between anxiety and experienced pain is explained (Bobey & Davison, 1970). Alternatively, the gate-control theory of Melzack and Wall (1965) is explained. The second phase of the program consists of teaching a variety of self-control techniques. On the assumption that different individuals benefit differentially from specific techniques—owing to differences in their personalities and habitual internal statements—the variety seeks to maximize the probability that an optimal combination will be constructed and utilized by the patient. The third phase consists of implementing self-instructions. These techniques may be summed up as follows:

1. A conceptual framework provides a rationale for treatment. Pain has two components, sensory input and internal reactions to the input. Turk's program incorporates procedures that are understood as addressing both aspects.

2. Relaxation is explained as a treatment that addresses the sensory side of the interaction. Procedures consist of muscle tensing/relaxing, slow, deep breathing, and relaxing images.

3. Attention diversion consisting of a variety of strategies that the client is invited to try. Among these are focusing on aspects of the environment (rather than pain sensations) and focusing on mental images that are incompatible with the experience of pain (e.g., transforming pain by imagining "numbness").

4. Self-instruction is divided into four parts: (a) Anticipation; "what will I be coping with, what plans are needed?" (b) Statements made to self in the midst of a painful situation. For example, "I can cope. I won't think about pain. I'm relaxing.", etc. (c) Rehearsal of coping with thoughts and feelings that arise at "impossible" times. Statements such as "Don't make things worse—pause and collect yourself" fit in at this stage. (d) Self-reflection and self-reinforcement complete this part of the package. Examples here are, "I'm doing well. I'm succeeding."

5. This is followed by an overview of coping processes that are used to alter the perception of intense stimulation.

As in the Roskies program examined earlier, emphasis is given to developing a structure or style of approach that can be used to manage a variety of situations. It should be noted that although the program is certainly a cognitive one, the behavioral component, such as in feedback, is almost totally lacking. Trying and working out behavioral strategies in task simulations is not included as a component. Moreover, the medical aspects of the problem are either ignored or are presumed to be irrelevant. This approach characterizes many cognitive–behavioral interventions to be found in the literature. Studies such as Turk's are laboratory-based and in many respects demand replication in real chronic-pain treatment settings, since chronic pain is different in many ways from acute pain (e.g., Grzesiak, 1980; Fordyce, 1976; Sternbach, 1974). A good way to illustrate different uses of the cognitive approach, especially as these might be addressed in medically based treatment settings, is to describe such a program.

The following describes a program for chronic pain that blends both cognitive and medical–physical aspects of management. The reader's attention is directed to the interplay between both physical and psychological aspects of the process. In many ways, addressing only the cognitive issues would make for a simpler situation, both in terms of analyzing what is going on (i.e., what is effective) and also in terms of the sheer mechanics of interfacing with the medical system. For years, medicine has been singularly unhappy with the results of purely medical interventions for pain problems (Hirsch, 1965). This does not mean, however, that the problem should be addressed exclusively as a psychological issue either.

509

COGNITIVE
BEHAVIOR
THERAPY IN
HEALTH
PSYCHOLOGY

The complex treatment program to be described has grown from a collection of disparate elements into an integrated unit that combines both medical and psychological assessment and treatment. The program is evolving and is not a rigidly fixed one; changes are introduced regularly and appear to be associated with increased effectiveness (Rosomoff, Green, Silbref, & Steele, 1981).

The complexity and highly integrated nature of the program make it difficult to sort out the effective parts from those that may be unimportant or even irrelevant. Some attempts to look at these questions is being made, however. These are described in some detail at a later point. Finally, the program requires the efforts of a large staff of devoted therapists and other professionals. Gottlieb, Laban, Koller, Madorsky, Hackersmith, Kleeman, and Wagner (1977) report the only other program of this type to be found in the literature.

6. Program Blending Cognitive Behavioral Aspects of Chronic-Pain Treatment

6.1. Theoretical Assumptions

This program is based on two assumptions. One is that chronic-pain patients have developed physical changes concomitant with the advancing pain problem (Grzesiak, 1980). These changes must be dealt with physically. The issue of whether a person has "real" pain is never addressed. The second assumption is more complex. Patients have developed a fear of activity based on the cuing function of pain. The program is structured around changing the meaning or consequences of pain. Patients are taught to use a variety of cues to regulate activity, including non-pain bodily cues and non-bodily cues. They are encouraged to expand their scope of awareness to encompass more than a narrow focus on pain. Efforts are made to make pain just one part—and an increasingly minor part—of the patient's focus of awareness and concern. Along with these fears patients often acquire a sense of helplessness about being able to predict or control their feelings. The sense of helplessness becomes embodied in the depression often seen among chronic-pain patients (e.g., Gentry, Shows, & Thomas, 1974; Le Shan, 1964; Levine, 1971; Sternbach, 1974). By being guided through a graded series of activities that offer constant assurance that the pain is manageable (Beck, 1976; Rush, Khatami, & Beck, 1975); by experiencing such mastery in a variety of situations, both internal and external; and by the constant repetition that successful change can be attributed to self-actions rather than external forces, the patient comes to feel an enhanced sense of self-efficacy (Bandura, 1977a).

Information about the patient characteristics and program outcomes are detailed in a recent monograph (Rosomoff, *et al.*, 1981). The summary provided here will give the reader a flavor of these findings.

6.2. Program Overview

Approximately 60% of those treated are receiving workmen's compensation. The large majority had previous surgical intervention and most were taking narcotic pain medications. Most were described as severely limited in their activity levels at admission. The most frequent diagnosis was secondary soft-tissue changes, with or without bony pathology. Ages ranged from the teens to the seventies, with most between 30 and 50. The average length of stay in the program was 48 days, approximately half of which was in inpatient and half as full-day out-patient. At follow-up, with intervals ranging from 6 months to 2½ years, 86% rated themselves as fully functioning, 12% able to perform self-care Activities of Daily Living (ADL) only, and 2% were incapable of self-care.

6.3. Assessment

The initial assessment program consists of thorough evaluation first by a neurosurgeon and then by a physician specializing in physical medicine and rehabilitation. These evaluations are done to assess the likely connections of identifiable physical problems to the pain complaints. Only 1% of patients referred for surgery are, in fact, recommended for surgery in this program. Most are found to have major soft-tissue problems, such as bursitis, tendonitis, trigger points, muscle spasms, and so on. All chronic-pain problems are assumed to require a cognitive–behavioral management program as well as a surgical and/or physical medicine program. Physical diagnosis never has a bearing on the judged *validity* of the patient's pain complaints; rather, it only helps determine certain features of what will be treated in the program. Since many patients whose original pain may not be related to physical disease do develop measurable soft-tissue changes over time, it is clear that cognitive–behavior approaches by themselves will not be sufficient to effect all desired changes.

Psychological assessment is made up of several components: ward observations for 3 days by nurses trained for this purpose; considerable self-report data from the patient on such gauges as the POMS, the Beck Depression Inventory, the SCL-90, and the CMI for psychological discomfort; diaries of daily activities; thoughts related to pain and pain control; a catalogue of approaches the patient has tried in attempts to control pain; the patient's self-rated ability to control discomfort; use of narcotics and other analgesic or mood-altering substances (e.g., alcohol, marijuana). Especially valuable are the assessment data obtained on patient personality and coping style as well as compliance indices from the Millon Behavioral Health Inventory (MBHI). In addition, the patient

511

COGNITIVE
BEHAVIOR
THERAPY IN
HEALTH
PSYCHOLOGY

is interviewed by a psychiatrist or psychologist who is, in part, looking for reasons to exclude patients with severe pathological behaviors. A report from a rehabilitation specialist and an interview with either spouse or close family member for information about the home environment and behavior completes the assessment. This information serves as a starting point for constructing the program's cognitive–behavioral rehabilitation strategy.

Additional assessment, once the patient has been accepted into the program, will be described in the appropriate treatment section. Information from all these data sources is put together in a lengthy staff conference of 1 to 2 hours which includes the participation, where appropriate, of the patient. All patients receive direct feedback that is tape-recorded for later auditions by staff and patient. The patient is given an honest appraisal of the problem. If the patient accepts treatment and agrees to enter the program, the following coordinated plan is put into effect.

6.4. Physical Therapy

Physical therapy is provided to stretch and strengthen debilitated muscles (Cailliet, 1977). Local injections are used to treat inflammation or trigger points. Heat, ice, methylchloride spray, trancutaneous nerve stimulation (TNS), and other modalities are used to ease discomfort temporarily. Patients are taught to use the techniques themselves. Moreover, the emphasis is on dealing with the patient's fear of doing physical activity, of causing severe damage for which pain has served as the signal in the past. The concept of pushing beyond tolerance in a controlled way is explained. Members of the psychological staff often work with patients in the physical therapy setting, not interfering with directed activities but teaching patients self-control techniques during the activity. Patients are taught to monitor and extend their own activities and to become their own therapists. Physical therapy takes place in group sessions, and other patients provide reinforcement in the form of praise (at times this becomes wild applause!) for the achievement of exercise milestones. Patients often given considerable evidence of skills in monitoring and rewarding each other's achievements.

6.5. Occupational/Recreational Therapy

The focus within occupational recreational therapy is on assembling movements into functional patterns. Most chronic-pain patients develop poor postural and movement habits, partly out of fear and self-protective "splinting." Patients learn self-management techniques for "safe" or less injurious ways of using their own bodies. Good body mechanics are observed, fed back, and rehearsed until they become automatic. Patients frequently remind staff as well as each other when they observe incorrect body movement (e.g., bending at the waist to pick up fallen objects), often insisting on correct performance. As the basic motions are routinized, the application to work, self-care, and leisure settings are explored and simulated. Pain behavior is systematically not rewarded; coping, however, is attended to and encouraged.

Tolerances (e.g., sitting, standing, walking, lifting) are assessed, and routines for systematically extending capability are worked out. Patients are taught the concept of "pacing," which in its simplest form consists of stringing together activities without exceeding the tolerance of any one of them. This enables patients with even very short tolerances—that is, *before* pain signals a halt—to put together hours of consistent activity.

Job analysis data provided by the rehabilitation specialists, by employers, and by the patients themselves are used to construct work-simulation tasks. Questions and thoughts that are used to facilitate work-simulation activities are explored by occupational recreational therapists as well as the psychology staff. Psychologists frequently work together with patients in these active settings, helping them find strategies and cognitions to guide their increased physical tolerance.

6.6. Rehabilitation Specialist

Rehabilitation specialists are the patients' link to their home community, including job placement. Many patients are referred to the program by these specialists. They often follow the patient throughout the program, attending weekly conferences, working with families, running interference with insurers, and helping patients find work appropriate to their discharge physical status. They provide a needed link between normal community life and the clinical program.

6.7. Physical Medicine

Physician treatment consists of the management of any concurrent medical problem, supervision of physical and occupational therapy, and the prescription and overseeing of medication. Psychotropic medications are often used to facilitate the treatment of depression as well as some other, less common psychopathological problems. Pain medications are initially stabilized for several days after admission; withdrawal then begins and generally requires 1 to 2 weeks, depending on initial level. The rate of withdrawal is determined by the physician rather than by patients, as is the case in many programs. Weekly conferences as well as daily rounds are used to update plans, share information, and feed information concerning progress back to the patients.

6.8. Psychology Program

The psychology staff's contribution, in addition to what has already been mentioned, may be described as follows. Two modalities are utilized in biofeedback. As noted earlier, patients have often adopted a dysfunctional gait or posture (e.g., using inappropriate muscles, standing in a bent-forward position, scoliosis). Electromyographic (EMG) biofeedback is used to facilitate appropriate muscle use, to inhibit inappropriate tension, or both (Hendler, Derogatis, Arella, & Long, 1977; Jones & Wolfe, in press). As soon as muscle control is achieved in a quiet and relaxed setting, the patient begins to use the EMG machine in an active mode (e.g., work simulation, activities of daily living, group therapy or weekly conference, etc.). Gradually feedback from the machine is faded and, after many hours of training, the patient uses his or her internal cues to signal muscle tension and consequent relaxing response. Beyond learning control of errant muscle activity, chronic-pain patients often adopt an autonomic or musculoskeletal response pattern that becomes habitual. Patients are offered the explanation that these changes are part of the emotional component of pain perception. Patients are helped to learn control of the response system using a temperature biofeedback apparatus, first in a quiet place and then in more active modes. The demonstration that patients can *control* aspects of their responding, particularly ones as covert and ordinarily hidden as these psychophysiologic systems, is a powerful tool for fostering a sense of self-efficacy. All training is pointed toward use of the learned control response in a variety of activity settings. Furthermore, response categories that are easily and unobtrusively monitored (such as finger temperature) are chosen over more disruptive measures.

Individual therapy is used to help patients cope with some of the restrictions and requirements of the program. Information concerning the patient's habitual pattern of response to pain is gathered at intake. These data provide a takeoff point for individual therapy designed to maximize both constructive and creative aspects of coping (Rybstein-Blinchik, 1979; Scott & Barber, 1977) and to examine and change destructive patterns. Pain as a communication mode is explored in these sessions, with emphasis on the development and use of alternative verbal and behavioral styles of communicating wishes and affects. Here also, the lessons derived from activity therapy are examined and reinforced. The goal is to restore premorbid levels of function, not to restructure personality.

Relaxation groups are used to teach basic self-control and relaxation skills (Levendusky & Pankratz, 1975; Scott & Barber, 1977; Turk, 1977b). A number of images and techiniques are suggested (Spanos, Barber, & Lang, 1974; Spanos & Radtke-Bodorik, 1979); patients are also asked to develop their own methods and styles (Goldfried, 1977). Initial meetings are devoted to teaching basic skills. Later sessions concentrate half on relaxation, with patients beginning to lead their own sessions, and half on discussions of how and when patients can and will use their skills. Emphasis is given to employing skills in covert ways. In this way the patient need not feel discomfited by having to let those around him or her know the skill is even being used. Biofeedback and relaxation skills are combined in these sessions.

Group therapy is used to explore cognitions common among chronic-pain patients. Topics are chosen from issues known to be applicable to patients from intake and which are known from research to apply to such patients. The role of goal setting is explored as an antidote to patients' frequent report of few goals or expectations of life. This orientation is related to the depression , which most pain patients exhibit. Socialization is explored, with the isolation (Sternbach, Wolf, Murphy, & Akeson, 1973) of so many chronic-pain patients as a takeoff point. Marital and sexual difficulties stemming from pain problems are explored. Self-concept and communication patterns become frequent topics for group discussion. Men and women who do not "pull their own weight," so to speak, have special problems with feeling in control of themselves (Armentrout, 1979); their felt self-efficacy is also extremely low. Group sessions are used to help integrate

513

COGNITIVE
BEHAVIOR
THERAPY IN
HEALTH
PSYCHOLOGY

changes that are taking place in a variety of settings. Self-responsibility is a major subject. Many pain patients feel victimized by the medical system (Fordyce, 1976; Sternbach, 1974, 1979). Options—the patient having final say in regard to what happens to his or her own body—are explored. As the patient improves his or her role, the change process is explored (e.g., the patient is learning to do for self, rather than what is being done to the patient).

Family groups are held on a weekly basis to acquaint patients' families with aspects of the program that patients must learn to follow at home (Greenhoot & Sternbach, 1974). Among the themes are ways that families deal with pain behavior, how they can encourage the patient to cope with discomforts, and ways to facilitate exercise and body mechanics. Family members are encouraged to spend a day or two following the patients through the therapy program so as to help them, as family members, to understand the patient's changed status and capabilities. The goal is to help families think about the patient differently, to "see" him or her as capable, though perhaps with some special needs and coping techniques. One technique frequently used is to have patients explain the program with their families present. Family members frequently express concern about how much and in what ways they can be supportive and caring.

The milieu structure uses peer pressure to help patients support each other. Meals are given in a communal setting and evening activities are designed to increase "up time." Here, patients make it their responsibility to see that other patients come to card games, dances (movement therapy), and social hours. The staff is trained to observe and, at times, shape these sessions by encouraging participation. Patients are helped to appreciate themselves again as social beings, with skills and warmth to offer others.

6.9. Research

Research studies are carried out in the program. In a system as complex as the one described, it is almost impossible to say what the effective or even the important ingredients may be. At present, half the patients receive a twice-weekly assertiveness group therapy session (Hammen, Jacobs, Mayol, & Cochran, 1980). The other half are involved in a discussion that focuses on feelings, thereby serving as an attention placebo control. Other research studies focus on the relationship of personality and other variables to success in the program (e.g., Rosenbaum, 1980). Predictors of complaint behavior in the setting are being evaluated with two aims. First, failures, if they can be identified early, may prove responsive to alternative intervention methods. Predictors may also be used, where advisable, to establish criteria for exclusion from the program.

7. Conclusion

Cognitive–behavioral programs for the management of medical problems are becoming increasingly sophisticated and have already demonstrated success in achieving their ends. Demonstration of efficacy by itself is no guarantee of survival in a complex medical system that determines which treatments are reinbursable under insurance coverage as well as which techniques are considered allowable. To the extent that these techniques are integrated into the medical system at large, their impact is likely to be powerful and lasting. When medical and nursing education includes courses in the cognitive–behavioral management of chronic medical problems, these techniques will become part of the repertoire of all professionals working in this area, not just the psychological specialists. If treatment in this area is conceived as something foreign, or an intrusion from the "outside," acceptance by the medical community and patients alike is bound to remain marginal.

515

COGNITIVE
BEHAVIOR
THERAPY IN
HEALTH
PSYCHOLOGY

8. References

Agras, S., & Jacob, R. Hypertension. In D. F. Pomerleau, & T. P. Brady (Eds.), *Behavioral medicine: Theory and practice*. Baltimore: Williams & Wilkins, 1979.

Armentrout, D. P. The impact of chronic pain in the self-concept. *Journal of Counseling Psychology*, 1979, *35*, 517–521.

Auerbach, S. M., Kendall, P. C., Cuttler, H. F., & Levitt, R. Anxiety, locus of control, type of preparatory information and adjustment to dental surgery. *Journal of Consulting and Clinical Psychology*, 1976, *44*(5), 809–818.

Ayllon, T., & Azrin, N. H. Reinforcement and instructions with mental patients. *Journal of the Experimental Analysis of Behavior*, 1964, *7*, 327–331.

Barbarin, O. A. Comparison of symbolic and overt aversion in the self-control of smoking. *Journal of Consulting and Clinical Psychology*, 1978, *46*(6), 1569–1571.

Bandura, A., Ross, D., & Ross, S. A. Vicarious reinforcement and imitative learning. *Journal of Abnormal and Social Psychology*, 1963, *67*, 601–607.

Bandura, A. *Principles of behavior modification*. New York: Holt, 1969.

Bandura, A. Self-efficacy: Toward a unifying theory of behavioral change. *Psychological Review*, 1977, *24*, 191–215. (a)

Bandura, A. *Social learning theory*. Englewood Cliffs, N.J.: Prentice-Hall, 1977. (b)

Bandura, A., & Adams, M. E. Analysis of self-efficacy theory of behavioral change. *Cognitive Therapy and Research* 1977, *1*(4), 287–310.

Bandura, A., & Walters, R. H. *Adolescent aggression*. New York: Ronald Press, 1959.

Barrios, B. A., & Shigetoni, C. C. Coping-skills training for the management of anxiety: A critical review. *Behavior Therapy*, 1979, *10*(4), 491–522.

Beck, A. T. *Cognitive therapy and the emotional disorders*. New York: International Universities Press, 1976.

Beers, T. M., & Karoly, P. Cognitive strategies, expectancy, and coping style in the control of pain. *Journal of Consulting and Clinical Psychology*, 1979, *47*(1), 179–180.

Bem, D. J. Self-perception theory. In L. Berkowitz (Ed.), *Advances in experimental social psychology*. New York: Academic Press, 1972.

Berecz, J. Treatment of smoking with cognitive conditioning therapy: A self-administered aversion. *Behavior Therapy*, 1976, *7*, 641–648.

Bloom, L. J., & Cantrell, D. Anxiety management training for essential hypertension in pregnancy. *Behavior Therapy*, 1978, *9*, 377–382.

Bobey, M., & Davidson, P. Psychological factors affecting pain tolerance. *Journal of Psychosomatic Research*, 1970, *14*, 371–376.

Bower, H. Contacts of cognitive psychology with social learning theory. *Cognitive Therapy and Research*, 1978, *2*(2), 123–146.

Brooks, G. R., & Richardson, F. C. Emotional skills training: A treatment program for duodenal ulcer. *Behavior Therapy*, 1980, *11*(2), 198–207.

Budzynski, T. H. Biofeedback applications to stress related disorders. *International Review of Applied Psychology*, 1978, *27*(2), 73–79.

Cailliet, R. *Soft tissue pain and disability.* Philadelphia: Davis, 1977.

Castro, L., & Rachlin, H. Self-reward, self-monitoring, and self-punishment as feedback in weight control. *Behavior Therapy,* 1980, *11*(1), 38–48.

Chambliss, C., & Murray, E. J. Cognitive procedures for smoking redirection: Symptom attribution versus efficacy attribution. *Cognitive Therapy and Research.* 1979, *3*(5), 91–96. (a)

Chambliss, C. A., & Murray, E. J. Efficacy attribution, locus of control and weight loss. *Cognitive Therapy and Research,* 1979, *3*(4), 349–354. (b)

Chapman, S. L., & Jeffrey, D. B. Processes in the maintenance of weight loss with behavior therapy. *Behavior Therapy,* 1979, *10*(4), 566–570.

Davidson, P. O., & Davidson, S. M. *Behavioral medicine: Changing health lifestyles.* New York: Brunner/Mazel, 1980.

Dembrowski, T. M., Weiss, S., Shields, J., Haynes, S. G., & Feinleib, M. (Eds.), *Coronary-prone behavior.* New York: Springer, 1978.

Dunkel, L. P., & Glaros, A. C. Comparison of self-instructional and stimulus control treatments for obesity. *Cognitive Therapy and Research,* 1978, *2*(1), 75–78.

Ellis, A. Rational–emotive therapy and cognitive behavior therapy: Similarities and differences. *Cognitive Therapy and Research,* 1980, *4*(4), 325–340.

Ellis, A., & Grieger, R. (Eds.). *Handbook of rational–emotive therapy.* New York: Springer, 1977.

Festinger, L. *A theory of cognitive dissonance.* Evanston, Ill.: Row, Peterson, 1957.

Ford, J. Therapeutic relationship in behavior therapy: An empirical analysis. *Journal of Consulting and Clinical Psychology,* 1978, *46*(6), 1302–1314.

Fordyce, W. E. *Behavioral methods for chronic pain and illness.* St. Louis: Mosby, 1976.

Fortin, F., & Kirouac, S. A randomized controlled trial of preoperative patient education. *International Journal of Nursing Studies,* 1976, *13,* 11–24.

Frank, J. D. The dynamics of the psychotherapeutic relationship. *Psychiatry,* 1959, *22,* 17–39.

Frank, J. *Persuasion and healing: A comparative study of psychotherapy* (Rev. ed.). New York: Schocken Books, 1974.

Frank, J. D. *Psychotherapy—The human predicament: A psychosocial approach.* New York: Schocken Books, 1972.

Freud, S. *Drei abhandlunger zur sexualtheorie.* Leipzig and Vienna: Deuticke, 1905.

Friedman, M., & Rosenman, R. H. *Modification of the type A coronary-prone behavior pattern.* Paper presented at the clinical meeting of the American Psychological Association, San Francisco, August 1977.

Genest, M., & Turk, D. C. A proposed model for behavioral group therapy with pain patients. In D. Upper & S. Ross (Eds.), *Behavioral group therapy.* Champaign, Ill.: Research Press, 1979.

Gentry, W. D., Shows, W. D., & Thomas, M. Chronic low back pain: A psychological profile. *Psychosomatics,* 1974, *15,* 174–177.

Gill, M., & Hoffman, I. G. Special issue: Psychotherapy process. *Cognitive Therapy and Research,* 1980, *4*(3), 271–306.

Girodo, M., & Wood, D. Talking yourself out of pain: The importance of believing that you can. *Cognitive Therapy and Research,* 1979, *3*(1), 23–34.

Glass, D. C. *Behavior patterns, stress, and coronary disease.* Hillsdale, N. J.: Lawrence Erlbaum, 1977.

Glass, D. C., Snyder, M. L., & Hollis, J. J. Time urgency and the type A coronary-prone behavior pattern. *Journal of Applied Social Psychology,* 1974, *4,* 125–140.

Goldfried, M. R. The use of relaxation and cognitive relabeling as coping skills. In R. R. Stuart (Ed.), *Behavioral self-management: Strategies, techniques and outcomes.* New York: Brunner/Mazel, 1977.

Goldstein, A. P., Heller, K., & Sechrest, L. B. *Psychotherapy and the psychology of behavior change.* New York: Wiley, 1966.

Gordon, W. A., Freidenbergs, I., Dillen, L., Hibbard, M., Wolf, C., Levine, L., Lipkins, R., Ezrachi, O., & Lucido, D. Efficacy of psychosocial intervention with cancer patients. *Journal of Consulting and Clinical Psychology,* 1980, *48*(6), 743–759.

Gottlieb, H., Laban, C. S., Koller, R., Madorsky, A., Hackersmith, V., Kleeman, M., & Wagner, J. Comprehensive rehabilitation of patients having chronic low back pain. *Archives of Physical Medicine and Rehabilitation,* 1977, *58,* 101–108.

Greenhoot, J. H., & Sternbach, R. A. Conjoint treatment of chronic pain. In J. J. Bonica (Ed.), *Advances in neurology: Pain* (Vol. 4). New York: Raven Press, 1974.

517

COGNITIVE
BEHAVIOR
THERAPY IN
HEALTH
PSYCHOLOGY

Grzesiak, R. C. Chronic pain: A psychobehavioral perspective. In L. P. Ince (Ed.), *Behavioral psychology in rehabilitation medicine: Clinical applications.* Baltimore: Williams & Wilkins, 1980.

Hammen, C. L., Jacobs, M., Mayol, A., & Cochran, S. D. Dysfunctional cognitions and the effectiveness of skills and cognitive–behavioral assertion training. *Journal of Consulting and Clinical Psychology,* 1980, *48*(6), 685–695.

Harrell, T. H., & Beiman, I. Cognitive–behavioral treatment of the irritable colon syndrome. *Cognitive Therapy and Research,* 1978, *2*(4), 371–376.

Heider, F. *The psychology of interpersonal relations.* New York: Wiley, 1958.

Heilbrun, A. B. Projective and repressive styles of processing aversive information. *Journal of Consulting and Clinical Psychology,* 1978, *46*(1), 156–164.

Hendler, N., Derogatis, L., Avella, J., & Long. D. EMG biofeedback in patients with chronic pain. *Diseases of the Nervous System,* 1977, *38*, 505–509.

Hirsch, C. Efficiency of surgery in low back disorders. *Journal of Bone and Joint Surgery,* 1965, *47A*, 991–998.

Holroyd, K. A., Andrasik, F., & Westbrook, T. Cognitive control of tension headache. *Cognitive Therapy and Research,* 1977, *1*(2), 121–134.

Homme, L. E. Perspectives in psychology: XXIV—Control of coverants, the operants of the mind. *Psychological Record,* 1965, *15*, 501–511.

Horan, J. J. "In vivo" emotive imagery: A technique for reducing childbirth anxiety and discomfort. *Psychological Reports,* 1973, *32*, 1328.

Horan J. J., Hackett, G., Buchanan, J. D., Stone, C. I., & Denchik-Stone, D. Coping with pain: A component analysis of stress inoculation. *Cognitive Therapy and Research,* 1977, *1*(3), 211–222.

Jenkins, C. D. Psychologic and social precursors of coronary disease. *New England Journal of Medicine,* 1971, *284*, 244–255, 307–312.

Jenkins, C. D. Recent evidence supporting psychologic and social risk factors for coronary disease. *New England Journal of Medicine,* 1976, *294*, 1987–1994, 1033–1038.

Jenkins, C. D. & Zyzanski, S. J. Behavioral risk factors and coronary heart disease. *Psychotherapy and Psychosomatics.* 1980, *34*(2-3), 149–177.

Jenni, M. A., & Wollersheim, J. P. Cognitive therapy, stress management training, and the type A behavior pattern. *Cognitive Therapy and Research,* 1979, *3*(1), 61–74.

Johnson, W. *People in quandaries: The semantics of personal adjustment.* New York: Harper & Row, 1946.

Jones, A. L., & Wolfe, S. L. Treating chronic low back pain: EMG biofeedback training during dynamic movement. *Physical Therapy,* in press.

Keefe, F. J., & Brown, C. J. Behavioral assessment of chronic low back pain. In F. J. Keefe & O. Blumenthal (Eds.), *Assessment strategies in behavioral medicine.* New York: Grune & Stratton, in press.

Kelly, G. A. Personal construct theory and the psychotherapuetic interview. *Cognitive Therapy and Research,* 1977, *1*(4), 355–362.

Kendall, P. C., & Kongeski, G. P. Assessment and cognitive–behavioral interventions. *Cognitive Therapy and Research,* 1979, *3*(1), 1–22.

Kendall, P. C., Williams, L., Pechacek, T. F., Graham, L. E., Shisslak, C., & Herzoff, N. Cognitive–behavioral and patient education interventions in cardiac catheterization procedures. *Journal of Consulting and Clinical Psychology,* 1979, *47*(1), 49–58.

Khatami, M., & Rush, A. J. A pilot study of the treatment of out patients with chronic pain: Symptom control, stimulus control and social system interest. *Pain,* 1978, *5*(2), 163–172.

Langer, E., Janis, I., & Wolfer, J. Reduction of psychological stress in surgical patients. *Journal of Experimental Social Psychology,* 1975, *1*, 135–166.

Ledwidge, B. Cognitive behavior modification. A step in the wrong direction? *Psychological Modification,* 1978, *85*, 353–375.

Leon, G. R. Cognitive–behavior therapy from eating disturbances. In P. C. Kendall & S. D. Hollon (Eds.), *Cognitive–behavioral interventions: Theory, research, and procedures.* New York: Academic Press, 1979.

LeShan, L. The world of the patient in severe pain of long duration. *Journal of Chronic Diseases,* 1964, *17*, 119–126.

Levendusky, P., & Pankratz, L. Self-control techniques as an alternative to pain medication. *Journal of Abnormal Psychology,* 1975, *86*(2), 165–169.

Levine, M. E. Depression, back pain, and disc protrusion: Relationships and proposed psychophysiological mechanisms. *Diseases of the Nervous System*, 1971, *32*, 41–45.

Luria, A. *The role of speech in the regulation of normal and abnormal behaviors.* New York: Liveright, 1961.

Mahoney, M. J., & Arnkoff, D. Cognitive and self-control therapies. In S. K. Garfield & A. E. Bergin (Eds.), *Handbook of psychotherapy and behavior change* (2nd ed.). New York: Wiley, 1978.

Meichenbaum, D. A self-instructional approach to stress management: A proposal for stress inoculation training. In I. Sarason & C. D. Spielberger (Eds.), *Stress and Anxiety* (Vol. 2). New York: Wiley, 1975.

Meichenbaum, D. *Cognitive-behavior modification: An integrative approach.* New York: Plenum Press, 1977.

Meichenbaum, D. Cognitive–behavior modification: The need for a fairer assessment. *Cognitive Therapy and Research*, 1979, *3*(2), 127–132.

Meichenbaum, D., & Turk, D. The cognitive–behavioral management of anxiety, anger, and pain. In P. Davidson (Ed.), *The behavioral management of anxiety, depression, and pain.* New York: Brunner/Mazel, 1976.

Melzack, R., & Wall, P. Pain mechanisms: A new theory. *Science*, 1965, *150*, 1971–979.

Millon, T. *Modern psychopathology.* New York: Saunders, 1969.

Mitchell, K., R., & White, R. G. The control of migraine by behavioral self-management: A controlled case study. *Headache*, 1976, *16*, 178–184.

Morris, R. J., & Suckerman, K. R. The importance of the therapeutic relationship in systematic desensitization. *Journal of Consulting and Clinical Psychology*, 1974, *42*, 148.

Murray, E. J., & Jacobson, L. I. Cognition and learning in traditional and behavior therapy. In S. L. Garfield & A. E. Bergin (Eds.), *Handbook of psychotherapy and behavior change* (2nd ed.). New York: Wiley, 1978.

Nesse, M., & Nelson, R. O. Variations of covert modeling in cigarette smoking. *Cognitive Therapy and Research*, 1977, *1*(4), 343–354.

O'Leary, K. D., & Wilson, G. F. *Behavioral therapy: Applications and outcome.* Englewood Cliffs, N. J.: Prentice-Hall, 1975.

Pande, S. K., Gant, J. J. A method to quantity reciprocal influence between therapist and patient in psychotherapy. In J. M. Schlien (Ed.), *Research in Psychotherapy* (Vol. 3). Washington, D.C.: American Psychological Association, 1968.

Pavlov, I. P. *Conditioned reflexes* (1927). New York: Owen, 1960.

Pechacek, H. F., & Danaher, B. G. How and why people quit smoking: A cognitive–behavioral analysis. In P. C. Kendall & S. P. Hollon (Eds.), *Cognitive–behavioral interventions: Therapy, research, and procedures.* New York: Academic Press, 1979.

Pecheur, D. Cognitive theory/therapy and sanctification: A study in integration. *Journal of Psychology and Theology*, 1978, *6*(4), 239–253.

Piaget, J. *The child's conception of physical causality.* Translated by Marjorie Worden. New York: Harcourt, Brace, & World, 1930 (Original French Edition, 1927).

Piaget, J. *The origins of intelligence in children.* (Margaret Cook, trans.) New York: International Universities Press, 1952 (Original French Edition, 1936).

Piaget, J. *Structuralism.* (Chaninah Maschler, Trans.) New York: Basic Books, 1971 (Original French Edition, 1968).

Reeves, J. L. EMG-biofeedback reduction of tension headache: A cognitive skills-training approach. *Biofeedback and Self-Regulation*, 1976, *1*, 217–225.

Rosenbaum, M. Individual difference in self-control behaviors and tolerance of painful stimulation. *Journal of Abnormal Psychology*, 1980, *89*(4), 581–590.

Rosenberg, M. J., Hovland, C. I., McGuire, W. J., Abelson, R. P., & Brehm, J. W. *Attitude organization and change: An analysis of consistency among attitude components.* New Haven, Mass: Yale University Press, 1960.

Rosenthal, T. L., & Zimmerman, B. J. *Social learning and cognition.* New York: Academic Press, 1978.

Roskies, E. Considerations in developing a treatment program for the coronary-prone (Type A) behavior pattern. In P. O. Davidson & S. M. Davidson (Eds.), *Behavioral medicine: Changing health lifestyles.* New York: Brunner/Mazel, 1980.

Roskies, E., & Avard, J. Teaching healthy managers to control their coronary-prone (Type A) behavior. In K. Blankenstein & J. Polivy (Eds.), *Self-control and self-modification of emotional behavior.* New York: Plenum Press , in press.

519

COGNITIVE
BEHAVIOR
THERAPY IN
HEALTH
PSYCHOLOGY

Roskies, E., Spevack, M., Surkis, A., Cohen, C., & Gilman, S. Changing the coronary-prone (Type A) behavior pattern in a non-clinical population. *Journal of Behavioral Medicine*, 1978, *1*, 201–216.

Rosomoff, H. L., Green, C., Silbret, M., & Steele, R. Pain and the low back rehabilitation program at the University of Miami School of Medicine. In L.K.Y. Ng (Ed.), *New approaches to treatment of chronic pain: A review of multidisciplinary pain clinics and pain centers.* NIDA Research Monographs, May, 1981, 92-111.

Rotter, J. B. *Social learning and clinical psychology.* Englewood Cliffs, N.J.: Prentice-Hall, 1954.

Rotter, J. B. Generalized expectancies for internal versus external control of reinforcement. *Psychological Monographs: General and Applied*, 1966, *80* (whole vol. no. 609).

Rotter, J. B. Generalized expectancies for problem solving and psychotherapy. *Cognitive Therapy and Research*, 1978, *2*, 1–10.

Rosenman, R. H., & Friedman, M. Modifying type A behavior pattern. *Journal of Psychosomatic Research*, 1977, *20*, 321–333.

Rozensky, R. H. The effect of timing of self-monitoring behavior on reducing cigarette consumption. *Journal of Behavioral Therapy and Experimental Psychiatry*, 1974, *5*, 301–303.

Rush, A. J., Khatami, M., & Beck, A. T. Cognitive and behavioral therapy in chronic depression. *Behavior Therapy*, 1975, *6*, 398–404.

Rybstein-Blinchik, E. Effects of different cognitive strategies in the chronic pain experience. *Journal of Behavioral Medicine*, 1979, *2*, 93–102.

Sanchez-Craig, M. Cognitive and behavioral coping strategies in the reappraisal of stressful social situations. *Journal of Counseling Psychology*, 1976, *23*, 7–12.

Schachter, S. The interaction of cognitive and physiological determinants of emotional state. In L. Berkowitz (Ed.), *Advances in experimental social psychology* (Vol. I). New York: Academic Press, 1964.

Schreber, F. M., Schauble, P. G., Eating, F. R. & Skovholt, T. M. Predicting successful weight loss after treatment. *Journal of Clinical Psychology*, 1979, *35*(4), 851–854.

Scott, D. S., & Barber, T. X. Cognitive control of pain: Effects of multiple cognitive strategies. *The Psychological Record*, 1977, 273–283.

Seer, P. Psychological control of essential hypertension: Review of the literature and methodological critique. *Psychological Bulletin*, 1979, *86*(5), 1015–1043.

Shapiro, A. P., Schwartz, G. E., Ferguson, D. L. E., Redmond, D. P., & Weiss, S. M. Behavior methods in the treatment of hypertension: A review of the clinical status. *Annuals of Internal Medicine*, 1977, *86*, 626–636.

Shipley, R. H., Butt, J. H., Horwitz, B., & Farbry, J. E. Preparation for a stressful medical procedure: Effect of amount of stimulus preexposure and coping style. *Journal of Consulting and Clinical Psychology*, 1978, *46*(3), 499–507.

Skinner, B. F. *Science and human behavior.* New York: Macmillan, 1953.

Skinner, B. F. Why I am not a cognitive psychologist. *Behaviorism*, 1978, *5*(2), 1–10.

Spanos, N. P., Barber, T. X., & Lang, G. Cognition and self-control: Cognitive control of painful sensory input. In H. London & R. E. Nisbett (Eds.), *Thought and feeling: Cognitive attention of feeling states.* Chicago: Aldine, 1974.

Spanos, N., Horton, C., & Chaves , J. The effect of two cognitive strategies on pain threshold. *Journal of Abnormal Psychology*, 1975, *84*, 677–682.

Spanos, N. P., Radtke-Bodorik, H. L. The effects of hypnotic susceptibility, suggestions for analgesic, and the utilization of cognitive strategies for the reduction of pain. *Journal of Abnormal Psychology*, 1979, *88*(3), 282–292.

Sternbach, R. A. *Pain patients: Traits and treatments.* New York: Academic Press, 1974.

Sternbach, R. A. Clinical aspects of pain. In R. A. Sternbach (Ed.), *The psychology of pain.* New York: Rowen Press, 1978.

Sternbach, R. A., Wolf, S. R., Murphy, R. W., & Akeson, W. H. Traits of pain patients: The low-back "loser." *Psychosomatics*, 1973, *14*, 226–229.

Stone, G. L., Hinds, W. C., & Schmidt, G. Teaching mental health behavior to elementary school children. *Professional Psychology*, 1975, *6*, 34–40.

Strickland, B. R. External expectancies and health-related behaviors. *Journal of Consulting and Clinical Psychology*, 1978, *46*(6), 1192–1211.

Suinn, R. Anxiety management training for general anxiety. In R. Suinn & R. Weigel (Eds.), *The innovative psychological therapies: Critical and creative contributions.* New York: Harper, 1975. (a)

Suinn, R. M. The cardiac stress management program for type A patients. *Cardiac Rehabilitation*, 1975, *5*, 13–15. (b)

Suinn, R. M. Type A behavior pattern. In R. B. Williams & W. D. Gentry (Eds.), *Behavioral approaches within medical treatment*. Cambridge, Mass.: Ballinger, 1977.

Suinn, R. M., & Bloom, L. J. Anxiety management training for pattern A behavior. *Journal of Behavioral Medicine*, 1978, *1*, 25–37.

Suinn, R. M., & Richardson, F. Anxiety management training: A nonspecific behavior therapy program for anxiety control. *Behavior Therapy*, 1971, *2*, 498–510.

Turk, D. C. *A coping skills-training approach for the control of pain: Training manual*. Unpublished manuscript, Yale University, 1977. (a)

Turk, D. C. Application of coping-skills training to the treatment of pain. In C. P. Spielberger & I. G. Sarason (Eds.), *Stress and anxiety* (Vol. 5). New York: Brunner/Mazel, 1977. (b)

Turk, D. C. Cognitive behavior techniques in the management of pain. In Foreyt & Rathjen (Eds.), *Cognitive behavior therapy*. New York: Plenum Press, 1978.

Turk, D. C. Coping with pain: A review of cognitive control techniques. In M. F. Feuerstein, L. B. Sach, & I. D. Turkut (Eds.), *Psychological approaches to pain control, in press*.

Turk, D. C., & Genest, M. Regulation of pain. The application of cognitive and behavioral techniques for prevention and remediation. In P. C. Kendall, & S. D. Hollon (Eds.), *Cognitive-behavioral interventions: Theories, research, and procedures*. New York: Academic Press, 1979.

Wilson, G. T. Cognitive behavior therapy: Paradigm shift or passing phase? In J. P. Foreyt & D. P. Rathjen (Eds.), *Cognitive behavior therapy: Research and application*. New York: Plenum Press, 1978.

Wolpe, J. *Psychotherapy by reciprocal inhibition*. Stanford, Calif.: Stanford University Press, 1958.

Wolpe, J. The systematic desensitization treatment of neuroses. *Journal of Nervous and Mental Disease*, 1961, *132*, 189–203.

Wolpe, J. *The practice of behavior therapy*. New York: Pergamon Press, 1969.

Zuckerman, M., Bushsbaum, M. S., & Murphy, D. C. Sensation seeking and its biological correlates. *Psychological Bulletin*, 1980, *88*(1), 187–214.

Hypnosuggestive Procedures in the Treatment of Clinical Pain
Implications for Theories of Hypnosis and Suggestive Therapy

THEODORE X. BARBER

The themes of this chapter are that (1) hypnosuggestive procedures can be effective in reducing pain and (2) these procedures should be incorporated into the armamentarium of all professionals who treat pain. I will first summarize representative studies that illustrate how hypnosuggestive procedures can be used and how effective they can be in the alleviation of surgical and postsurgical pain, back pain, headaches and migraine, cancer pain, burn pain, dental pain, and childbirth pain. Throughout this review, I will try to be directly helpful to health professionals by presenting verbatim examples of hypnosuggestive procedures that can be useful in treating acute and chronic pain.

Before I proceed, it may be appropriate to dispel three misconceptions that may already have arisen:

1. Although hypnosuggestive procedures can be useful in dolorology (treatment of pain), they should constitute only one part of the dolorogist's armamentarium. There are many different kinds of pain having different causes and characterized by different qualities (Melzack, 1980); there are also many different kinds of people who have each of the innumerable kinds of pain, and each person in pain should be treated uniquely by some combination of medical and psychological procedures (Barber, 1959).

THEODORE X. BARBER ● Department of Supportive Services, Cushing Hospital, Framingham, Massachusetts, 01701. This paper was presented at a series of workshops sponsored by Proseminar Institute during 1980. The writing of the paper was supported in part by a grant from Proseminar Institute.

2. Hypnosuggestive procedures *can* be a useful part of the dolorologist's treatment methods, but they may not be. They are useful when the patient *accepts* the suggestion—when he or she does not disbelieve or contradict the ideas (or suggestions) presented but instead has a positive attitude toward them and an expectant belief that they will become a reality. Hypnosuggestive procedures are most potent when the therapist relates so compassionately and lovingly with the patient and presents suggestions in such a sincere, meaningful way that the patient fully accepts the suggestions intellectually, emotionally, and in the depths of his or her being.

3. Although hypnosuggestive procedures include innumerable kinds of suggestions, nowadays they typically include suggestions of calmness and various kinds of direct and indirect suggestions for pain relief. However, no one suggestion or set of suggestions is a necessary part of hypnosuggestive therapy. Whether or not a procedure includes suggestions of numbness, of deep relaxation, or of entering hypnosis is not important in determining whether to view it as hypnosuggestive. What is important in labeling procedures as hypnosuggestive is that the therapist presents suggestions to the patient in the same *serious and expectant way* that he or she presents suggestions to individuals in a "hypnosis" situation, regardless of whether or not the patient has been exposed to anything that can be called a hypnotic induction procedure.

Since the term *hypnosuggestive* implies simply that the patient has received communications and ideas in the same serious and expectant manner that suggestions have traditionally been given in situations that were thought to involve hypnosis, the patient may or may not think of hypnosis as associated with the procedures, may or may not become passive or drowsy, may or may not become relaxed, may continually keep the eyes open or continually closed, and so on.

1. Hypnosuggestive Procedures in Surgery

It appears that in unusual situations, when no analgesic or anesthetic drugs are available, hypnosuggestive procedures may be sufficient to reduce anxiety and pain so that the surgery can be tolerated. This effect is illustrated by a report published by an Australian physician and surgeon—Drs. Sampimon and Woodruff—soon after the termination of World War II. During the war, Sampimon and Woodruff (1946), together with several thousand Australian soldiers, had been captured by the Japanese and were interned in a prisoner-of-war camp. When they ran out of all anesthetic and analgesic drugs, they still had many minor surgeries to perform on the soldiers. Since no drugs were available, they used hypnosuggestive procedures to reduce anxiety and pain. At first they used traditional approaches, repeatedly suggesting that the patient was entering a hypnotic state. They soon concluded, however, that even though some of the soldiers could not be hypnotized, the suggestions for relaxation and for distraction were sufficient to reduce anxiety and pain and all the soldiers underwent the operations successfully. Although the soldiers typically showed some signs of pain during surgery, all of them remained sufficiently calm for the operations to be performed. We can conclude from these data that when we are sufficiently motivated to undergo surgery without drugs, most of us (and possibly all of us) are able to do so provided that our anxieties and fears are reduced by suggestions that produce calmness and distract us from the painful stimuli.

Some years later, Lozanov (1967) in Bulgaria was asked to perform a herniorraphy on an elderly patient who could not be given medication. Lozanov did not attempt to hypnotize the patient; instead, he gave suggestions to distract the patient and found that the patient was able to undergo the surgery with minimal pain and discomfort.

Rausch (1980) recently discussed his use of self-suggestive procedures for his own major surgery (cholecystectomy). Since he had used hypnosuggestive procedures extensively with clients in his dental practice, he wanted to see to what extent he could use self-suggestive procedures for his own surgery and was prepared to take whatever risks might be involved. He utilized the following procedures (which he subsumed under the term *self-hypnosis*): the night before surgery, he first suggested relaxation to himself until he achieved a very calm, tranquil state; then he visualized a movie screen on which he saw himself go calmly and successfully through each step of the forthcoming surgical procedures. Focusing on feelings of confidence, absolute certainty of success, and elation, he went to sleep. Awakening in the morning, he felt refreshed and calm and did not experience fear or apprehension. When brought to the operating room (without premedication), he felt as if he were in a dream and asked everyone there to send him good "vibes" and to anticipate and expect total success. He then took himself mentally away ("dissociated himself") from the situation by focusing his attention on engrossing "music" that he vividly imagined ("hallucinated"). During the initial incision, when his blood pressure increased from 135 to 190 and his pulse from 82 to 115, he felt that his "consciousness expanded," that is, he felt much more aware of his bodily sensations and his surroundings than he ever had before. According to the observers on the operating team, he showed no tensing of muscles during the original incision, no change in breathing, no flinching, and no facial expression; however, one of the observers later told him that he "turned a funny color as if [he] were dead." As the operation proceeded, he continued to take himself away mentally from the situation by vividly imagining his favorite music; also, as he became aware of sensations from the surgical area, he would "cancel" each sensation by mentally directing an imagined force to the area. During the 1¼ hours of the operation, he perspired profusely, but his pulse and blood pressure stabilized and remained steady. Throughout the operation, his "critical faculty was active." For 16 hours after surgery, he kept drifting in and out of sleep and felt as if he were in a dream. After 16 hours, he "snapped back" and was discharged on the fifth day after the day of surgery.

Other studies, reviewed elsewhere (Barber, 1963; Barber, Spanos, & Chaves, 1974; Chaves & Barber, 1976; Chertok, 1977) also showed that hypnosuggestive procedures were sufficient, at least with some highly motivated patients, to reduce fear and pain enough for surgery to be performed without any medication. Although the patients tolerated the surgery, it does not follow that they did not experience any pain. Some of the patients at first stated that the surgery was not painful, but when questioned more intensively and especially when given "permission" to say exactly what they experienced, they typically stated that although they felt pain at times during the surgery it seemed far away and did not bother them.

These reports also indicate that surgery can be successfully performed with hypnosuggestive procedures alone when the suggestions make the patient more relaxed, more calm, less fearful, less attentive to painful stimuli and enable him or her to reinterpret the sensations as less painful or not painful. Although these changes involve alterations in attitudes, attention, and ways of perceiving and interpreting the situation, they do not involve hypnosis in the lay sense of the term (being "out of it," unaware, or under the control of the hypnotist).

To place these studies in proper perspective, it is necessary first to remove an important misconception. It is commonly assumed that as surgery proceeds deeper into the body, the pain becomes more and more excruciating. This is a fallacy. A series of investigations, summarized by Lewis (1942), showed that only certain parts of the body hurt when *cut*, primarily the skin and other external tissues such as the conjunctiva and mucous membranes of the mouth and internal tissues that overlie the organs (e.g., the dura mater, the periosteum, the pericardium, and the peritoneum). Most tissues and organs of the body *do not hurt when they are cut by the surgeon's scalpel, although they can hurt markedly when they are squeezed, pressed, burnt, pulled, or rendered ischemic.* In brief, although pain is experienced when the tissues and organs of the body are exposed to pressure, traction, ischemia, and so on, the surgeon's scalpel *per se* gives rise to pain only when it cuts the skin and other external tissues and a small number of internal tissues. The conclusion is that the surgical scalpel typically produces a tremendous amount of fear but much less pain than we commonly believe. Consequently, by minimizing the fear and producing distraction from or reinterpretation of the painful stimuli, hypnosuggestive procedures can be more effective in surgery than one might surmise.*

2. Postsurgical Effects of Hypnosuggestive Procedures

Surgical patients are typically anxious. They are often afraid of dying during the surgery, fear pain, or fear that they may be incurable. They often do not know what to expect after they enter the hospital; they may feel alone, isolated,

*Data summarized elsewhere (Barber, Spanos, & Chaves, 1974; Chaves & Barber, 1973, 1974a, 1976; Kroger, 1973) indicate that there are many overlapping variables between surgery performed with hypnosuggestive procedures and surgery with acupuncture as performed in China. Very few surgical patients in China (about 2% to 3%) have their operations with acupuncture; these highly motivated patients volunteer for acupuncture because they wish to be part of the avante garde or good Communists. (The remaining 97% or 98% of the surgical patients in China, of course, have their surgery with anesthetic and analgesic drugs.) Prior to acupuncture surgery, the patients typically undergo an imaginative rehearsal of the surgical procedures so that they know what is coming. To reduce anxiety, they are given sedatives prior to surgery. They are also given local anesthetics, such as procaine, in order to numb the skin where the incision will be made. During the surgery, the acupuncture needles are stimulated electrically so that they give rise to throbbing, radiating, boring, numbing, and searing sensations that can distract the patient from the surgical procedures. These and many other data reviewed elsewhere (Barber *et al.*, 1974; Chaves & Barber, 1973, 1974a, 1976; Kroger, 1973) suggest that, although other factors may also be involved, the total acupuncture situation, in the same way as the total hypnosuggestive situation, can be effective in producing relative calmness and reducing fear of surgery, in distracting the patient from the surgical procedures, and helping him or her interpret the sensations as tolerable or not painful.

and helpless. Within this context, hypnosuggestive procedures appear to be quite useful.

In several studies, anesthesiologists or surgeons trained in utilizing hypnosuggestions visited the patient the night before surgery and, with the patient's understanding and consent, gave (1) suggestions of deep relaxation and calmness which would begin now and would continue immediately prior to, during, and after surgery and (2) suggestions that after surgery the patient would feel he or she were awakening from a deep sleep, would feel hungry, would be able to eat normally, would be able to urinate and defecate without discomfort, would tolerate the catheters, and so on (Fredericks, 1978; Papermaster, Doberneck, Bonello, Griffen, & Wangensteen, 1960; Van Dyke, 1970). It is important to emphasize that these kinds of suggestions were not given in a rote or rigid manner but were tailored for the patient, were given sincerely and within the boundaries of normal realism of what the patient could experience if he or she were to remain maximally calm, and were given in the context of a close interpersonal relationship. Within recent years there has been a very strong trend to give similar kinds of suggestions for surgery much more informally, without utilizing any kind of hypnotic or formal procedures. J. C. Erickson (1979) has described how these kinds of informal suggestions—which he calls "covert hypnosis"—can be used easily and usefully with *all* surgical patients. Immediately before surgery, the anesthesiologist or surgeon liberally offers to the sedated patient suggestions for relaxation, comfort, ease, and safety "without hypnotic induction ceremonies or discussions about hypnosis *per se*." The patient is given additional quiet suggestions for a calm, relaxed nap, with the anticipation of later awakening in the recovery room feeling comfortable and pleased that the operation went so well and smoothly. Since auditory perception at times continues during general anesthesia, similar positive suggestions are given during the surgery. The same kind of informal suggestions are "reiterated during the period of arousal from anesthesia, with additional emphasis on postoperative concerns such as : comfortable breathing, easy voiding and a pleasant feeling of hunger." J. C. Erickson (1979) and the other investigators who have used suggestions with surgery patients (Fredericks, 1978; Papermaster *et al.*, 1960; Van Dyke, 1970) have reported that these procedures generally reduce preoperative anxiety, minimize postoperative discomfort, and lessen the consumption of analgesics in the immediate postoperative period.

A quantitative study of the effects of hypnosuggestions on surgical patients has been presented by Werbel (1963). The study was designed to determine to what extent hypnosuggestions can reduce the severe pain typically experienced during defecation by patients who have just undergone surgery for hemorrhoids. Prior to hemorrhoidectomy, Werbel assigned his 22 patients either to a hypnosuggestive treatment or a control treatment. The 11 patients who were exposed to the hypnosuggestive treatment were seen the evening before surgery, when they were given suggestions for deep relaxation, and told "You relax wonderfully well. You are an excellent subject. Therefore, there is no need for you to feel pain following surgery. . . . When you have your first bowel movement, be relaxed just as you are now and you need feel no pain. . . ." The 11 control patients had the same kind of surgery without being exposed to the hypnosuggestions. The first bowel movement following the hemorrhoidectomy was reported to be *painless* by 8 of the 11 patients (73%) who had received the hypnosuggestions and only 2 of the 11 (18%) in the control group. *Severe pain* was reported by none of the patients in the hypnosuggestive group and by 5 in the control group. (The remaining patients in each group reported moderate pain.) Werbel appropriately concluded from these and other data presented in his paper that at least some of the pain associated with bowel movements after hemorrhoidectomy is due to the expectation and fear of pain, which produces abnormal tension in the anal muscles, and that appropriate hypnosuggestions can reduce this fear, produce relaxation, and relieve the pain.

3. Hypnosuggestive Procedures in the Treatment of Back Pain

About 90% of back problems resolve themselves within a few weeks or months regardless of the type of treatment received. Although the small percentage of back problems that persist and become chronic can be due to one or more of a large number of possible causes—such as diseases of the spinal cord, neoplasms, arthritis, referred visceral or somatic pain, and compression and irritation of spinal nerves and spinal nerve roots (Bonica, 1953, pp. 743–753)—there is evidence to indicate that chronic low-back pain is most often due to muscle problems (Freese, 1974, pp. 213–216).

Ripley and Wolf (1947) found that when sodium amytal was given to patients with back pain, spastic muscles in the back would relax and the back pain would usually disappear. Similarly, when X-rays showed a definite compression of the spinal cord, in about 60% of the cases no abnormality was found when the spinal cord was opened, apparently because the general anesthesia used for the surgery produced a relaxation of the back muscles which allowed the disc to slip back into place (Simeons, 1961, p. 229). Also, in an important study with 65 individuals with back pain and 10 controls, Holmes and Wolff (1952) found that, in back pain subjects, threatening situations led to hyperfunctioning and a correlated reduction of blood supply (ischemia) in the muscles of the back. The ischemia, of course, would be associated with reduced oxygen to the tissues and concomitant pain (Good, 1951). In brief, since many chronic back pains are associated with sustained muscular contractions, we might expect that hypnosuggestive procedures that focus on producing sustained relaxation and calmness would be helpful.

A recent report by Crasilneck (1979) showed how hypnosuggestions can be used successfully for the control of back pain. He worked with a very difficult-to-treat population of patients with chronic back pain: 29 referrals who were addicted to or dependent on pain medication and who had had at least one unsuccessful surgical operation for their back pain. Crasilneck was unable to work with 5 of the 29 because they had a negative attitude toward the initial treatment, were deeply depressed, or were extremely masochistic. Of the remaining 24 patients, 16 reported an average of 80% relief from pain at least by the fourth session and 20 of the 24 reported an average of 70% relief by the sixth session. Of the 20 successful patients, 15 voluntarily discontinued pain medication and the remaining 5 were withdrawn from the medication by their physicians. The 20 patients who were markedly relieved of back pain resumed work at a realistic level.

Crasilneck's (1979) excellent results were associated with the following treatment. In the first session rapport was established, hypnosuggestive therapy was discussed, and—after it was evident that the patient had positive attitudes toward the treatment—Crasilneck suggested eye heaviness and eye closure. He then gave the patient a series of test suggestions (e.g., inability to open the eyes, numbness of a finger, and smelling a spicy aroma). The patient was told that the ability to experience what was suggested demonstrated "the power of your unconscious mind" and the "control of your mind over your body." Next, the patient was told, "Now, I give you the suggestion that as you blocked pain in your finger a few minutes ago, you can block the pain in your back. Nothing is beyond the power of your unconscious mind. You are going to block most of the pain. Most of the pain will come under control." Crasilneck stated that additional suggestions were given to control the pain, to reduce the need for medication, and to stimulate the desire to get well. During the second session, each patient was taught to give himself or herself suggestions of relaxation and suggestions for pain relief (self-hypnosis) and was encouraged to use the self-suggestions as frequently as necessary. The patients were seen for hypnosuggestive treatment daily during the first week, every other day during the second week, every third day during the third and fourth week, and then once a week for about 2 more months. Following this, the patients were seen whenever they wished. The patients were seen an average of 31 sessions over a period of about 9 months. During these many sessions, discussions at times focused on the psychodynamic meaning of the pain, the understanding of secondary gains, and the handling of life problems. It thus appears that Crasilneck's successful treatment approach included at least three important factors—hypnosuggestions, psychotherapy, and many patient–therapist contacts within an apparently close relationship; each of these variables may have played a role in achieving control of the chronic low-back pain.

Although Crasilneck obtained very good results, he had to spend a great deal of time over a long period with each patient. The treatment period might be shortened in future work with back pain by broadening the therapist's repertoire. For instance, hypnosuggestions might be included as one part of a broader treatment, such as that used by Gottlieb and his co-workers (Gottlieb, Strite, Koller, Madorsky, Hockersmith, Kleeman, & Wagner, 1977) in the succussful treatment of 72 chronic-back-pain patients; this broad treatment package included a therapeutic milieu designed for relaxation, socialization, and recreation, physical therapy focusing on reconditioning of muscles, a vocational rehabilitation program, and lectures pertaining to back pain. The lectures used audiovisual aids to inform the patients about the anatomy and physiology of the back, how stress plays a role in back pain, and the effects of lifting, nutrition, weight, and pain medications.

Additional useful procedures for chronic back pain can be derived from Shealy's (1976) approach, which includes a large dose of direct suggestions and self-suggestion training (which he labels as *biogenic* training) plus many other procedures that, in addition to whatever direct effects they may have on the pain, also affect it indirectly by keeping the patient busy and thus distracting him or her from the pain. These additional procedures, which also carry a component of implicit nonverbal suggestions that "Something useful is being done for your pain," include ice rubdowns, total body massage, whirlpool baths, and biking, walking, swimming, or other exercises.

An important fact that needs to be heavily underscored is that chronic pain is sometimes maintained because it has positive advantages for the individual. Fordyce (1976) and others have emphasized the large number of rewards or secondary gains that individuals can derive from their chronic pain, including the following: attention, sympathy, concern, and care; staying home legitimately from an unpleasant job; resting and avoiding other difficulties and distasteful or anxiety-provoking activities; reduced expectations from spouse and children; more "respect" from others; and workmen's compensation insurance or other monetary rewards. More subtle variables may also play a role in maintaining pain; for example, a close examination of family dynamics sometimes reveals a family member's motivations for supporting pain or disability (Pace, 1976, p. 68); at times, chronic pain may provide the individual with a feeling of martyrdom, a means of restoring self-esteem by attributing failures in coping and self-deficiencies to the pain, a concealed and indirect method of discharging hostile impulses toward relatives and others, a means of self-punishment for relieving guilt, and so on (Elton, Burrows, & Stanley, 1980).

A number of investigations (Purtell, Robins, & Cohen, 1951; Ziegler, Imboden, & Meyer, 1960) indicate that pain which is not traceable to a denotable pathology yet serves many psychological needs of the individual (at times such pain may be seen as a "conversion symptom" or as "hysterical" or "psychogenic" pain) is much more common than is generally assumed. Although the prevalence of such pain may be debatable, there is no doubt that a certain number of people find life so lacking in possible gratification that the "rewards" of chronic pain are greater than any other rewards from life that they can envisage (Wooley, 1980). In these instances, of course, the rewards of the pain may be so important to the individual that he or she may not "really" wish to be cured of pain (Sternbach, 1974). Successful therapy with such patients implies a deep and basic change in their evaluation of themselves and their life situation and the development of a new life-style as an alternative to their illness.

The percentage of chronic-pain patients who fall into the above pattern appears to be much smaller than the percentage whose pain appears to be related to resentment and guilt (Pace, 1976, p. 23) or to lack of self-esteem and feelings of worthlessness and depression (Diamond & Dalessio, 1978, p. 99; Elton *et al.*, 1980). Close observation of the chronic-back-pain patient, headache patient, migraine patient, and so on often provides clues of underlying depression such as collapse of self-esteem, sadness, fatigue, poor concentration, and sleep disturbances. Treatment of the depression—and other negative feelings-thoughts-emotions such as resentment, anger, and guilt—by cognitive therapy (Beck, Rush, Shaw, & Emery, 1979), behavioral therapy (Lewinsohn, 1974), antidepressant drugs, and so on can be usefully supplemented by hypnosuggestions that focus on (1) the client's positive personal qualities (e.g., "I can see you really care about people and that you're a kind, good person. . ."), (2) feelings of strength and well-being (e.g., and "As time goes on, you'll begin to notice more and more the strong, healthy energy that vibrates through your body and you'll begin to notice a feeling of being at ease, feeling good, feeling happy. . ."), (3) heightened ability to concentrate and to be aware and alert, and (4) calmness and restful relaxation prior to and during sleep (Barber, 1978, 1979a,b; Barber & Wilson, 1978; Hartland, 1971; Stanton, 1975, 1977).

4. Hypnosuggestive Procedures in the Treatment of Tension Headaches and Migraine

A small proportion of headaches (about 2% to 5%) are associated with an organic etiology such as brain tumor, subarachnoid hemorrhage, intracranial pressure, or hypertension. When such factors have been excluded by thorough medical examination, we commonly find that the headaches are associated with repressed or unrepressed negative thoughts-feelings-emotions that can be subsumed under such terms as grief, frustration, anxiety, depression, anger, and hostility (Diamond & Dalessio, 1978, p. 95). Therapy for most tension headaches, therefore, should include procedures that aim to help the client cope calmly and proficiently with the problems of life with minimal anger, anxiety, frustration, and so on.

Field (1979) utilized hypnosuggestive procedures with this aim in the brief therapy (four or five sessions) of 17 patients who had had headaches continually over many years and who had not been helped by medical interventions. The procedures included suggestions for relaxation and home practice of self-relaxation. The major part of the therapy, however, comprised discussions and hypnosuggestions that aimed to modify the negative attitudes and emotions underlying the headache, such as worry, depression, guilt, lack of self-confidence, and negative thinking. A 3-month follow-up of the patients conducted by an independent investigator showed that the brief therapy (four or five sessions) definitely reduced headache frequency and severity in 10 of the 17 patients (59%) and had totally relieved headaches in 5 of these patients (29%).

Although relaxation (produced by suggestions of relaxation or by progressive relaxation training, EMG biofeedback training, or other methods) is clearly more effective than placebos in relieving tension headache (Cox, Freundlich, & Meyer, 1975; Haynes, Griffin, Mooney, & Parise, 1975; Tasto & Hinkle, 1973), it is unlikely that it is simply the relaxation of muscles *per se* that is the effective factor. Despite previous reports to the contrary, there appears to be a low correlation between muscle tension *per se* and tension headaches (Blanchard, Ahles, Shaw, 1979); at times, headaches continue when head and neck muscles relax and, *vice versa*, these muscles may stay tense when the headache is relieved (Beaty & Haynes, 1979; Haynes *et al.*, 1975, Philips, 1977, 1978). It appears more likely that the tension underlying tension headaches is at times due to muscular tension *per se* and at times to the mental tension that is typically subsumed under such terms as *worry, depression, anxiety,* and *resentment.*

Holroyd and his coworkers (Holroyd, 1979; Holroyd & Andrasik, 1978; Holroyd, Andrasik, & Noble, 1980) concluded from a series of careful studies that patients can reduce the frequency and severity of their headaches by becoming aware of the very first minimal signs of a headache and then immediately changing their cognitions or behaviors so as to block the headache symptoms. These headache-blocking actions appear to include anything that helps the individual reevaluate the bothersome situation or stops him or her from worrying, feeling resentful, or engaging in other negative thoughts-feelings-emotions. Useful headache-blocking activities appear to include self-suggestions of calmness and relaxation, withdrawal from the bothersome situation, rational reevaluation of the problem that may underlie the headache, appropriate assertive behavior, distraction, self-suggestions not to anticipate catastrophies, various kinds of fantasy, and prayer. Hypnosuggestions can play a useful role here, as one part of a broader armamentarium, by providing the individual with a set of self-suggestions to be used at the first minimal signs of a headache; the self-suggestions could include suggestions for calmness and flowing with the situation, as exemplified by a recent study with migraine (Anderson, Basker, & Dalton, 1975) which is described below.

Migraines have more vascular involvement than tension headaches. In migraine there is a reduction in blood flow to the cerebral cortex during the prodromal phase and an increase of blood flow during the headache phase. In more general terms, autoregulation of the cerebral blood vessels is impaired during the prodromal and headache phases of migraine (Diamond & Dalessio, 1978). Subsequent to emotional stress or to other stimuli (e.g., specific foods), neurogenic vasospasm occurs at the innervated vascular system at the base of the brain; local metabolic tissue abnormalities include acidosis and anoxia. The noninnervated parenchymal arteries, responsive to local metabolic demands, next dilate and, if vasodilation is sufficiently great, the cranial arteries on the outside of the head also expand. The alteration in tone of the extracranial arteries provokes the liberation of multiple local chemical and vasoactive substances which produce edema, a lowering of pain threshold, and, eventually, pounding migraine headache (Diamond & Dalessio, 1978).

Although much more work is needed to delineate the precipitating factors in migraine clearly, it appears that emotional stress or negative thoughts and feelings may at times play a role (Adams, Feuerstein, & Fowler, 1980). Henryk-Gutt and Rees (1973) asked individuals with migraine to observe for a period of 2 months their emotional state and any unusual events coinciding with the onset of the migraine. Although the patients had difficulties carrying out this assignment, they were able to associate 54% of the migraines with emotional stress. Other studies, reviewed by Harrison (1975), indicate that unexpressed anger may be the most common negative emotion related to the onset of migraine.

The studies cited above indicate that hypnosuggestive procedures that aim to produce calmness and readiness to flow with life problems may have a significant effect in reducing the frequency and severity of migraine. A recent study carried out in England by Anderson, Basker, and Dalton (1975) supports this conjecture.

Anderson *et al.* worked with 47 new patients who reported that they had had recurrent throbbing headaches for at least one year and who met other strict criteria for classical migraine (e.g., unilateral headaches preceded by a visual or other sensory aura). Equal numbers of the patients were randomly assigned to two treatments, one involving hypnosuggestions and the other drugs that were typically prescribed for migraine in that medical setting. Four physicians worked on the project and each treated half his patients with the hypnosuggestive procedures and half with drug therapy. The drug-therapy patients were seen by the physicians once a month for 12 months and were asked to take 5-mg doses of prochlorperazine four times daily during the first month and thereafter twice daily. They were also provided with ergotamine to be taken at the first sign of migraine. The hypnosuggestive therapy patients were also seen monthly for a year, but during the first part of the year they participated in at least six sessions in which they were exposed to hypnosuggestive procedures that included (1) a "trance induction" procedure, presumably comprised of suggestions for relaxation together with suggestions to enter a hypnotic state, followed by (2) positive suggestions ("ego-strengthening") suggestions that the patient will be less tense, anxious, and apprehensive, less dependent, and more alert, energetic, happier, and so on (Hartland, 1971). Next, the patients were taught "self-hypnosis"; that is, they were instructed to give themselves daily suggestions of increased relaxation and decreased tension and anxiety. They were also instructed to use a self-suggestive procedure to avert an attack of migraine; at the first sign of migraine they were to massage their foreheads lightly and repeat silently to themselves statements such as, "Becoming more and more calm . . . more and more comfortable . . . as I stroke my forehead, I feel the comfort spreading."

As Table 1 shows, 43% of the patients treated by hypno suggestions reported no migraines during the last 3 months of therapy, as compared with 13% treated by drug therapy. As also shown in Table 1, the average number of migraines decreased markedly for the hypnosuggestive group but not for the drug therapy group, and the number of patients suffering very severe, incapacitating attacks of migraine dropped markedly in the hypnosuggestive group but did not drop at all (in fact, went up) in the drug group.

Since individuals receiving the hypnosuggestive treatment received more unique, intense, and close attention from their physician than the drug-therapy group, they probably had a stronger tendency to overemphasize the success of

Table 1. *Hypnosuggestive Therapy versus Drug Therapy of Migraine*[a]

Outcome	Hypnosuggestive therapy $n = 23$	Drug therapy (drochlorperazine + ergotamine) $n = 24$
Median number of migraines		
6 months prior to therapy	4.5	3.3
First 6 months of therapy	1.0	2.8
Second 6 months of therapy	0.5	2.9
Number of patients with incapacitating attacks		
6 months prior to therapy	13	10
First 6 months of therapy	4	13
Second 6 months of therapy	5	14
Patients reporting no migraine during last 3 months of therapy	10 (43%)	3 (13%)

[a]Adapted from Anderson *et al.*, 1975.

the treatment. Keeping this proviso in mind, we can interpret the results con-servatively as follows: apparently useful procedures that can be added to the armamentarium of all therapists who treat migraine include (1) suggestions of relaxation; (2) suggestions for decreased tension, apprehension, and anxiety and increased well-being; and (3) suggestions for calmness to be taught to the clients as self-suggestions with instructions to use them as soon as they become aware that a migraine is threatening. Of course, research is needed to determine whether these three components are equally useful in minimizing migraine or if one is significantly more useful than the other. Further investigations should also be conducted to test directly such hypotheses as the following:

1. A substantial proportion of migraine attacks are preceded by a period of resentment, anger, anxiety, frustration, and other negative thoughts-feelings-emotions.

2. An oncoming migraine can be minimized or blocked by blocking the negative thoughts-feelings-emotions which precede it.

3. The negative thoughts-feelings-emotions can be blocked by self-sugges-tions for calmness, peace, and tranquillity.

Additional studies are also needed to ascertain how hypnosuggestive pro-cedures can be integrated with other methods that have been shown to help migraine, such as desensitization, assertiveness training, cognitive strategies (e.g., rational thinking, imaginal modeling, and thought stopping), and take-home cassette tapes that the individual can use to practice and learn the procedures (Mitchell & Mitchell, 1971; Mitchell & White, 1977).

5. Hypnosuggestive Procedures for Cancer Pain

Lea, Ware, and Monroe (1960) demonstrated the usefulness of hypno-suggestive procedures in the control of intractable pain. Although they originally worked with 20 patients, they were able to evaluate their results with only 17. Of the 17 patients who were included in the results, 8 had pain associated with malignant disease and the remainder had long-continued pain associated with phantom limb, decubitus, spasmodic torticollis, and other ailments. The treating "physicians" (who were medical students) spent at least an hour introducing the idea of hypnosis as a possible method for relieving the pain. Of all the patients, 9 were then seen for 2 to 10 hours in hypnosuggestive therapy, 5 were seen for 11 to 19 hours, and the remaining 3 for more than 20 hours. Although the hypnosuggestions varied for each patient, apparently all were given nonau-thoritarian, permissive suggestions to enter a relaxed, hypnotic state. This was followed by suggestions that as they relaxed more and more, they would become more comfortable, and as they relaxed in the same way after the therapist left, they would feel less and less pain. The hypnosuggestive therapy did *not* help 5 of the 17 patients; of the 5 failures, one was addicted to morphine for 28 years and 3 of the remaining 4 had serious complicating psychiatric problems. Of the 17 patients, 12 showed definite reduction in their reported pain; the results with 3 of these 12 successful patients were excellent in that they no longer considered pain a problem and stopped all medication. The major findings in the study were as follows:

1. Better progress was made when the individual was highly motivated to use hypnosuggestions for pain control (e.g., when the idea originated with the patient or the patient was referred by his or her own respected physician).

2. Since the patients were typically afraid that any new procedure would deprive them of their pain-control medication, they had to be reassured that their medication would not be taken away.

3. Hypnosuggestive therapy was difficult and protracted when the patient derived much secondary gain from the illness.

4. A very positive "side-effect" of the hypnosuggestive therapy was that the nursing personnel often spontaneously reported that the patients showed an immediate improvement in their overall mental attitudes and behavior (usually following the first hypnosuggestive session); the patients were more relaxed, less demanding of time, less often asked for attention, and slept much better at night.

5. Whether or not the patient was able to enter "deep hypnosis" was not an important factor in determining the degree of pain relief. The authors note that "As a matter of fact, two of our best patients obtained only light to medium trances, and significant responses were noted in even the very lightest hypnoidal states" (p. 6).

6. The most important finding of the study was that it was difficult if not impossible to determine to what extent the reduction in reported pain was due to the hypnosuggestions and to what extent it was due to the "intense doctor–patient relationship" (which was an integral part of the hypnosuggestive therapy) and to the unusual amount of personal attention that the patient received from the therapist.

In an earlier investigation on the effectiveness of hypnosuggestive therapy in relieving pain in 12 cancer patients, Butler (1954) similarly reported that (1) most of the patients were helped by the hypnosuggestive therapy but (2) the close therapist–patient relationship was more important than the specific hypnosuggestions in reducing the patient's suffering. Butler stated that he "gave of himself to the patients." He saw the patients every day, sometimes several times per day, and each time he gave many hypnosuggestions for pain relief. As long as he kept up this intense effort, the patients did well—the majority were relieved of pain. However, as soon as he stopped seeing the patient, the pain would usually return. The most important observation in this study may have been that when hypnosuggestions were discontinued but the physician (Butler) continued to give the same amount of personal attention and support to the patients, the patients typically continued to show pain relief.

Other workers have also reported that in treating the pain of cancer or other kinds of intractable pain, the sincere attention from the therapist that is found in a warm therapist–patient relationship is much more important than the specific therapeutic procedures. Working with a large number of cancer patients, Laszlo and Spencer (1953) concluded that fear, anxiety, and increased psychological need for attention and support among terminally ill patients were often mistaken for pain and treated with narcotics; however, sincere attention and interest on the part of the therapist could by itself often relieve the psychological misery which was mistaken for pain. Also working with hospitalized patients with serious pain, Sacerdote (1980) noted that often the pain—which had a definite basis in cancer, emphysema, coronary insufficiency, or other pathology—nevertheless represented primarily a cry for sympathy, attention, and help. In working with such patients, Sacerdote (1966) also pointed out that "In reality formal [hypnotic] induction is not always necessary or desirable"; suggestions are sufficient if they are given in a meaningful, personalized way to the patient in a context of a close interpersonal relationship. However, Sacerdote (1980) has also emphasized that hypnosuggestive therapy with terminally ill patients "inevitably" leads to deep involvement of patient and therapist and that part of this intense relationship is due simply to the patient's realization that, at a time when everybody else spends less and less time with him or her, there is at least one person who is willing to spend more time.

This picture of hypnosuggestive therapy with terminal illness is drastically different from the lay notion that the hypnotist "hypnotizes" the patient and then simply suggests away the pain. The true picture is of a miserably unhappy patient with pain and discomfort lying in bed helpless and hopeless—feeling that there is nothing he can do and nothing that can be done for him. The hypnosuggestive therapist, who is often a very loving person, enters and offers the patient a truly giving relationship. At the very minimum, he or she cares about the patient, is willing to devote much time to the treatment, and suggests to the patient calming, useful things in a warm, caring manner. We should keep in mind that the patient has probably been in the hospital for some time and no one has talked to him or her in this intimate way. The helpful hypnosuggestive therapist does not come to the patient in a mechanistic way; instead, he or she appears as a professional who sincerely cares about the patient and is able to offer useful suggestions and methods for dealing with pain and discomfort. By showing that someone truly cares and that something *can* be done for the pain, the therapist reduces the patient's loneliness, fear, and hopelessness and thus also reduces the patient's discomfort (Barber, 1963; Cangello, 1962; Perese, 1961).

6. Hypnosuggestive Procedures with Burn Patients

Recovery from severe burns is typically accompanied by continual pain and painful procedures such as dressing changes and debridement of scar tissue. Also, hospitalized burn patients are commonly lonely, despairing, and worried about the future—how they will earn a living, how they will appear to others, and how they will relate sexually. Within this context of psychological misery, we would expect hypnosuggestive procedures to be especially useful (Schafer, 1975).

Working with burned children, Bernstein (1963, 1965) at first used rather formal hypnotic induction rituals. As he gained experience, however, he agreed with Barber (1963) that the important variable in ameliorating pain was "the close interpersonal setting in which the suggestions of pain relief are given" (Bernstein, 1965, p. 7). He concluded that "the hypnotic trance state" was not important. Instead, for burned children, suggestions for comfort and well-being—given by a prestigious and compassionate physician—were sufficient to control pain because they had the force or power that have been traditionally attributed to suggestions given under hypnosis.

In a recent study carried out in a burn unit, Wakeman and Kaplan (1978) divided their patients two groups, one that received hypnosuggestions together with medication and a control group that received only medication. The 22 patients assigned to the hypnosuggestion group were matched as closely as possible on such variables as age, sex, and extent of burns with the 20 patients assigned to the control group. The hypnosuggestive therapist spent equal time with the control patients and the hypnosuggestion patients. The time spent with control patients was "only verbally supportive in nature (i.e., talking about progress, family, physical therapy issues, etc.)." With the hypnosuggestion group, the therapist utilized various "induction" suggestions (e.g., relaxation, hand levitation, and hand lowering) followed by suggestions to transfer anesthesia from an uninjured hand to an injured body area, suggestions to become more comfortable by relaxing more and more, suggestions for well-being to continue after the session (e.g., "[you] can remain comfortable for a long time . . . you will find that sleeping is no longer a problem . . . without apprehensions . . . only calmness . . . and self-confidence"), and suggestions for optimism and improved self-esteem (e.g., "and as the days go by . . . you will find that your attention . . . [is] more and more focused . . . on your assets . . . your strengths . . . such as appreciation and pride in . . . your self-control . . . cooperation . . . intelligence . . . and inner fortitude . . . and more and more focused on what new . . . and exciting experiences lie ahead . . . and your renewed energy to get as much out of life as possible in the years to come. . ."). In addition, the hypnosuggestion patients were taught how to give themselves suggestions for relaxation, deep comfort, and total anesthesia and were instructed to use these self-hypnotic procedures when they were needed. The major dependent variable in the study was the frequency and size of doses of medication requested by the patients. During the entire study, the patients were allowed to request their own analgesic medication (injectable morphine, oral aspirin, or acetaminophen) up to a maximum allowable dose. During their hospital stay, the hypnosuggestion patients requested less than half the medication that was requested by the control group; on the average, the hypnosuggestion patients asked for about one-third of the allowable medication, whereas the control patients asked for about three-fourths. The authors reported that in addition to helping the patients, the hypnosuggestive procedures also had two "side-effects"—they helped the family of the burn patient feel more optimistic about their loved one's recovery, and they had a positive impact on the staff of the burn unit in "greatly enhancing their attitudes about themselves as more effective and interpersonally involved health care providers" (p. 11).

7. Hypnosuggestive Procedures for Dental Pain

In a carefully executed doctoral dissertation, Gottfredson (1973) showed that hypnosuggestions can be effective with a substantial proportion of individuals in making the pain of dental procedures tolerable without the use of local anesthetics such as procaine. In this experiment, 29 patients in a dentist's private office were asked to participate in an investigation to determine the effect of hypnosis on dental pain; 25 were willing to participate. These subjects were tested first on responsiveness to the 12 test suggestions that comprise the Stanford Hypnotic Susceptibility Scale (Form A; e.g., suggestions that their eyes are becoming heavy and are closing, that one arm is rigid and immovable, and that the two hands which are touching lightly are now moving apart). In two dental sessions, each subject received either hypnosuggestions or a chemical anesthetic in counterbalanced order. Gottfredson did not present details pertaining to the hypnosuggestions, but they apparently included suggestions of relaxation, suggestions to go into a deep sleep while still hearing the experimenter's voice, suggestions of numbness of the tooth or teeth that were to be treated, and suggestions to forget any pain experienced during the dentistry. The dental procedures included fillings, crown preparations, and extractions.

Of the 25 subjects participating in the study, 4 were unable to undergo the dentistry with hypnosuggestions; as soon as the dental treatment began, they requested chemical anesthesia. Another 7 subjects requested chemical anesthesia after the dental treatment had been under way for some time. The remaining 14 subjects (56%) were able to undergo their entire dental treatment with hypnosuggestions alone. Three-fourths of the "good" hypnotic subjects who had passed from 8 to 12 of the 12 test suggestions on the Stanford Scale underwent the dental procedures without the local anesthetic, as compared with 38% of the "medium" or "poor" subjects who had passed 0 to 7 suggestions on the Stanford Scale. The good subjects as well as the medium and poor subjects experienced more pain with the hypnosuggestions than with the chemical anesthetic. However, during the hypnosuggestion session, the good subjects reported less pain than the others ($r = .39$ between predentistry response to test suggestions and reported pain during dentistry with hypnosuggestions). In general, the good hypnotic subjects found the hypnosuggestions almost as useful for tolerating pain as the chemical anesthetic and were willing to undergo future dentistry with hypnosuggestions alone. Prior to the dental session, the subjects had been shown how to lift 1 to 10 fingers to indicate their "depth of hypnosis." They were then asked during the dentistry to indicate their depth, and this measure did not relate at all to their reported pain or their ability to complete the dentistry without the chemical anesthetic. In brief, Gottfredson's investigation indicated that, with a substantial proportion of subjects, hypnosuggestions can increase pain tolerance in dental situations and that this effect is more common with subjects who on a pretest showed they were very responsive to suggestions.

In another recent study (J. Barber, 1977), clients at 10 dental offices were asked by an "assistant to the dentist" either if they would like to be more relaxed or if they would like to try hypnosis. It is not clear from the report whether more than 100 clients were approached, but the report states that 100 participated. The experimenter then gave a series of hypnosuggestions that usually extended over a period of about 10 minutes. These suggestions included the following: repeated suggestions for comfort and relaxation ("Take four more very deep, *very comfortable* breaths . . . when you exhale, you can just *feel that relaxation beginning to sink in* . . . just imagine a staircase . . . just notice how much more comfortable and relaxed you can feel at each step as you go down the staircase. . ."); permissive suggestions for arm heaviness ("Perhaps your left arm feels a bit heavier than your right. . ."); permissive suggestions for amnesia ("I wonder if you'll decide to let the memory of these things rest quietly in back of your mind. . ."); suggestions to experience comfort later during the dentistry ("Your experience will seem surprisingly more *pleasant,* surprisingly *more comfortable,* surprisingly *more restful* than you *might expect* . . . with nothing to bother, nothing to disturb. . ."); and indirect suggestions to experience comfort and relaxation when given a signal during the dental treatment ("Whenever [doctor's name] touches your right shoulder, like this . . . you'll experience a feeling . . . perhaps a feeling of being ready to be even more comfortable. . ."). The clients were then aroused. After they appeared to be fully alert, the dentist began his treatment and apparently very soon afterward gave the client the cue to reinstate relaxation and comfort. The dental treatments included fillings, root canal treatment, crown preparations, and extractions.

J. Barber reported that of the 100 patients who participated, 99 were able to undergo the dentistry without local anesthetics. This is, of course, a very remarkable degree of success. Unfortunately, the experimenter did not ask any of the clients to report what, if any, degree of pain they experienced. The same set of hypnosuggestions (which J. Barber labeled as *rapid induction analgesia*) were also used in another investigation by a dentist (R. J. Disraeli) and "a majority" of the 60 patients underwent their dental treatment without a chemical anesthetic; in this follow-up investigation also, it appears that the clients were not asked how much pain they had experienced (Cohen, 1977). In brief, the data indicate that about 10 minutes of hypnosuggestions emphasizing comfort during the dentistry (plus the demand characteristics that were present in J. Barber's specific experimental–dental situation) were sufficient for practically all the participants to tolerate whatever dental discomfort and pain were present; however, we do not know how much pain and discomfort they experienced in the situation.*

The two studies described above (J. Barber, 1977; Gottfredson, 1973) are "artificial" in that an attempt was made with *all* dental clients to use *only* hypnosuggestive procedures, with no chemical anesthetics whatsoever. In "real life" dentistry, hypnosuggestive procedures would be used alone (without other medications) primarily with individuals who do not want or should not have chemical anesthetics. With most other individuals, hypnosuggestive procedures would be used (together with chemical anesthetics) in order to calm the patient. The data

---

*Judging from the thorough investigation by Gottfredson (1973), from a follow-up study mentioned by Orne (1980), and from many other investigations (reviewed by Barber, 1963, 1970; Barber *et al.*, 1974; Chaves & Barber, 1976), which probed into the effects of hypnosis on pain, we can surmise that some clients in J. Barber's study experienced significant discomfort and pain at certain times during the dentistry. We can also conjecture that factors such as the following may have prevented the latter clients from asking for a local anesthetic such as procaine or lidocaine: (1) apparently neither the "assistant to the dentist" nor the dentist ever stopped to ask the client if he or she was comfortable, was experiencing pain, wished to continue, would like procaine, and so on; (2) the client had agreed to the procedure which was supposed to produce comfort, the "assistant to the dentist" had given about 10 minutes of continuous effort communicating ideas of comfort and relaxation to the client, and the dentist had waited about 10 minutes for the client to become calm; (3) apparently without a break in continuity, the dental equipment was placed in the client's mouth and the work was begun; and (4) to interrupt the proceedings, the clients had to experience serious discomfort which they believed would continue, and in some way they had to attract the attention of the dentist and tell him to stop because they were hurting. Apparently, only one patient who experienced serious discomfort in this situation was assertive enough to overcome the pressure to remain quiet by calling a halt to the ongoing dental work and asking for a local anesthetic.

at present indicate that hypnosuggestions can be usefully combined with chemical anesthetics to reduce anxiety and to produce calmness and ease in the dental patient (Gerschman, Reade, & Burrows, 1980; Pollack, 1966).

Dentists should learn to give suggestions for calmness and relaxation to their clients at the same time as they are carrying out their other dental procedures; there is no compelling reason why they should stop their ongoing dental work to give suggestions. The suggestions "Take a deep, comfortable breath . . . calm . . . at ease . . . relaxed. . ." can be interspersed with the dentist's ongoing manual procedures.

Dentists should keep in mind that, during dental stress, some clients try to think of other things, try to relax, or try to carry out some coping strategy, whereas other clients anticipate catastrophe, and such negative ideation is associated with higher levels of reported stress and pain (Chaves & Brown, 1978). Dentists should consequently aim to reduce the clients' anxious thoughts by helping them view dental pain as what it actually is—unpleasant but harmless (Meichenbaum & Turk, 1976; Spanos, Radtke-Bodorik, Ferguson, & Jones, 1979). In addition to interspersing ongoing suggestions for calmness with ongoing manual procedures, dentists could also at times, utilize cassette tapes that they have previously prepared, giving repeated suggestions for deep relaxation. The cassette tapes, which would be used especially with clients who experience more serious discomfort, would be helpful both in emphasizing calmness and in distracting the client from the dental procedures.

8. Hypnosuggestive Procedures for Childbirth Pain

The principles of hypnosuggestive therapy for pain which we have delineated above also apply to the pain of parturition:

1. When it is said that hypnosis was used by an obstetrician, the term *hypnosis* virtually always refers to a large number of procedures and suggestions. The procedures may include lectures on childbirth and breathing exercises similar to those used in "natural childbirth" (Dick-Read, 1953), in psychoprophylaxis as used in the Soviet Union (Chertok, 1959), and in the "Lamaze method" as used in France and the United States (Lamaze, 1958). The hypnosuggestions, which are given in a series of prenatal training sessions, almost always include suggestions to enter a calm, comfortable, tranquil state. Other hypnosuggestions that are commonly included in the training sessions are suggestions for calmness and relaxation to be practiced at home ("self-hypnosis") and of numbness of an arm followed by suggestions to touch a painful area with the "numb" arm and to feel the numbness spreading. Other suggestions often used both in the training sessions and during confinement include suggestions that the contractions will be experienced as pressure (instead of as pain), direct suggestions that the contractions (or the episiotomy) will not be painful (Hartland, 1971), suggestions of numbness "from the waist down" (Cheek & LeCron, 1968), suggestions to displace the pain by clasping the hands together and then tightening them with each contraction (August, 1961), suggestions to separate oneself from one's body and to observe the labor or delivery from a distance (Coulton, 1960), and suggestions to remember later only the satisfying or positive events (August, 1961;

Coulton, 1960; Hilgard & Hilgard, 1975; Stone & Burrows, 1980). An additional useful procedure that is commonly used in the training sessions is an imaginative rehearsal of the forthcoming labor and delivery; for example, the mother imagines herself entering the hospital with "a feeling of relief and joyful anticipation"; she then practices visualizing herself in a pleasant environment while the "mouth of the womb" is opened by the rhythmic contractions. Later, she practices breathing deeply before each imagined contraction and then practices holding her breath and bearing down steadily throughout the duration of the imagined contraction, (Coulton, 1960). It can be expected that women who have in this way imaginatively rehearsed the events of labor and are thus informed of the timing and location of sensations will be more likely to be less anxious and more tolerant of whatever pain they experience (Stone & Burrows, 1980).

2. There is cross-cultural evidence and as well as data from our society indicating that two women who are apparently experiencing the same kind of pain sensations during childbirth can interpret the sensations very differently; one woman might interpret the sensations as excruciating and unbearable whereas the other might interpret them as easily tolerable. Hypnosuggestive procedures are generally effective in changing the patient's interpretation of the childbirth pain. Although only a small proportion—5% to 15%—of the mothers undergoing confinement with only hypnosuggestions report no pain at all (August, 1961; Kroger, 1979), the great majority of mothers are calmer during the confinement and report their childbirth experience in a much more positive manner (Davenport-Slack, 1975; Davidson, 1962; Furneaux & Chapple, 1964; Hilgard & Hilgard, 1975, chap. 6; Michael, 1952; Rock, Shipley, & Campbell, 1969; Schibly & Aaranson, 1966; Stone & Burrows, 1980).

3. In addition to experiencing more comfort with hypnosuggestions as compared to a control group (Davidson, 1962), the women also request fewer drugs and smaller doses of drugs during childbirth (August, 1961; Davenport-Slack, 1975; Gross & Posner, 1963). This reduced use of medication is, of course, very commendable for the health of the mother and especially that of the newborn (James, 1960; Moya & James, 1960; Standley, Soule, Copans, & Duchowny, 1974).

4. The effectiveness of hypnosuggestive procedures in increasing comfort and reducing medication during childbirth is due partly to the hypnosuggestions themselves and partly to other correlated variables, such as the additional attention and support given by the obstetrician to the mother.

5. Laypeople seem to assume that hypnosuggestive procedures obliterate pain because they induce a "trance" or a "hypnotic state" that is qualitatively different from a state of deep relaxation or calmness. The notion that a uniquely different state—"a deep trance state"—is *the* important factor in reducing pain and increasing comfort is simply wrong (Davidson, 1962; Winkelstein, 1958; Stone & Burrows, 1980). Hypnosuggestive procedures are generally effective in reducing childbirth pain and increasing comfort when the many different types of suggestions together with the total hypnosuggestive setting help the mother to reinterpret the uncomfortable or painful sensations as tolerable, not important, or "nothing to get bothered about." This reinterpretation of the sensations is closely associated with paying less attention to and focusing less on the sensations and also with a relative calmness–relaxation in the sense of not worrying about and not being especially anxious about the total childbirth situation.

During the past two decades a rather large number of studies have been conducted to evaluate the effects of hypnosuggestions on pain produced in the experimental laboratory. The experimental pain was usually produced either by immersing a limb in ice water, blocking off the blood supply to a limb and thus producing muscle ischemia or placing a heavy weight on a finger (Forgione & Barber, 1971). The pain produced in these experimental situations, of course, differed in many ways from the naturally occurring pain seen in the clinic. For instance, the experimental pain (but not the clinical pain) was present for a limited period of time preset by the experimenter and was standardized to be painful but not too painful for practically all individuals. Despite these and many other differences between experimental and clinical pain, studies on the effects of hypnosuggestions on pain carried out in the experimental laboratory have yielded results that are congruent with those obtained in the clinic. Although the differences between laboratory and clinic situations suggest caution in generalizing from one to the other, a review of the work conducted in experimental pain laboratories provides additional data that can help us understand how hypnosuggestions can affect naturally occurring pain. With these considerations in mind, let us briefly summarize some of the highlights of the more recent experimental laboratory work in this area.

1. *Contrary to the layperson's myth of hypnosis, subjects generally show as much pain reduction when given suggestions for decreased pain under waking conditions as under hypnosis.* In the first experiment in this series, Barber and Hahn (1962) worked with selected individuals who were highly responsive to suggestions. These good hypnotic subjects were exposed to painful stimulation (immersion of a limb in ice water) after they were randomly assigned to one of the following conditions: (1) a control condition, (2) an imagination condition (in which they were simply instructed, without any hypnotic induction, to imagine a pleasant situation during the painful stimulation), or (3) a hypnotic condition (in which they were given a formal hypnotic induction procedure together with suggestions of numbness of the limb). The imagined condition was as effective as the hypnotic condition in reducing pain below the level found under the control condition.* These results were confirmed in one part of a recent study by Spanos *et al.* (1979): when given identical suggestions for numbness, good hypnotic subjects

---

*As compared with the control condition, the instructions or suggestions for pain reduction given under the waking and hypnosis conditions were also equally effective in reducing two psychophysiological responses to the noxious stimulus (respiratory irregularities and forehead muscle tension). These psychophysiological data indicate that the suggestions were effective in reducing anxiety and fear of pain; however, they cannot be interpreted by themselves as indicating that pain was reduced. Reduction in psychophysiological responses such as respiratory irregularities, forehead muscle tension, skin conductance or resistance, blood pressure, and heart rate can be interpreted more appropriately as reduction in anxiety or fear of pain rather than a reduction in pain *per se* because of data such as the following: (1) subjects anticipating or imagining a forthcoming pain stimulus typically show as much increase in these psychophysiological measures as subjects who are actually exposed to the pain stimulus (Barber & Hahn, 1964; Hilgard & Morgan, 1975; Hilgard, Macdonald, Marshall, & Morgan, 1974; Levine, 1930) and (2) subjects who have received a local anesthetic and who are not experiencing pain show similar psychophysiological reactions to the threat of pain as nonanesthetized subjects (Bowers & Van der Meulen, 1972).

who had been randomly assigned to the waking condition showed as much reduction in reported pain as good hypnotic subjects who had been randomly assigned to the hypnosis condition.

Similar results have been obtained in four studies using unselected subjects (instead of selected good hypnotic subjects). Specifically, unselected subjects who were given suggestions of anesthesia under a waking condition showed as much reduction in pain as unselected subjects who were given the same suggestions for anesthesia after a hypnotic induction (Barber, 1969; Evans & Paul, 1970; Spanos, Barber, & Lang, 1974; Spanos et al., 1979).

In all of the studies mentioned above, subjects who were randomly assigned to a waking (nonhypnotic induction) treatment were as responsive to suggestion for pain reduction as those who were randomly assigned to a hypnotic induction treatment. However, in three experiments (Hilgard, Macdonald, Morgan, & Johnson, 1978; Spanos & Hewitt, 1980; Stacher, Schuster, Bauer, Lahoda, & Schulze, 1975) in which the same good hypnotic subjects were given suggestions for pain reduction once when not hypnotized and once when hypnotized, they generally showed somewhat more pain reduction in the latter condition. Stam and Spanos (1980) recently presented the following data that reconcile the results of the last three experiments with those mentioned in the preceding two paragraphs: (1) good hypnotic subjects are generally motivated to do well under the hypnosis treatment; (2) when good subjects are given suggestions for pain reduction under a waking condition (while knowing that they also have received or will receive the same suggestions under a hypnosis condition), they refrain from responding as well as they can to the suggestions under the waking condition in order to help themselves "do better" under the hypnosis condition; and (3) when good hypnotic subjects are given suggestions for pain reduction under a waking condition (while *not* knowing that they will later receive the same suggestions under a hypnosis condition), they show as much reduction in pain under the waking condition as they later show under the hypnosis condition.

2. *Several kinds of suggestions (given without hypnotic procedures) are generally effective in reducing laboratory pain.* Suggestions of numbness and also suggestions to imagine pleasant events were both effective in reducing pressure pain (Chaves & Barber, 1974b). In another experiment (Scott & Barber, 1977), subjects were given a number of suggestions (e.g., suggestions to dissociate themselves from the pain, to reinterpret the sensations as not painful, and to imagine that the stimulated part of the body was numb) and asked to use one or more of the suggestions to control the experimental (pressure) pain. These "cafeteria-style" suggestions were effective in raising pain tolerance 100% above the control level. Similar results in markedly raising pain tolerance were obtained in other experiments (Turk, 1975, 1977) in which subjects were shown both how to relax and how to give themselves self-suggestions for numbness, for dissociating from the pain, for reinterpreting the pain, etc.*

*An additional interesting finding in these studies (Turk, 1975, 1977) was that prior to their participation in the experiment, many subjects had reduced their pain by using one or more self-suggestion strategies (e.g., numbness, dissociation, distraction, or reinterpretation). These data indicate that we should first carefully question clinical patients regarding what strategies they have previously used successfully to control their pain, and then incorporate their successful strategies into our hypnosuggestions.

3. *Subjects who are highly responsive to various kinds of hypnosuggestions, such as suggestions that an arm is becoming light and is rising and suggestions to reexperience oneself as a child, also tend to be more responsive to suggestions that aim to reduce experimental pain.* In other words, as might be expected, responsiveness to suggestions for pain reduction is significantly correlated (about $r = .50$) with responsiveness to other suggestions that are traditionally used in hypnosis experiments (Evans & Paul, 1970; Hilgard, 1967; Hilgard & Hilgard, 1975, p. 68). McGlashan, Evans, and Orne (1969) arrived at a similar conclusion from an experiment that indicated that (1) subjects who are highly responsive to suggestions (good hypnotic subjects) show a more marked increase (than poor subjects) in pain tolerance when they are given suggestions to enter hypnosis plus suggestions of analgesia and (2) the good subjects (but not the poor subjects) typically block the pain by utilizing a process that seems to resemble suppression, repression, or denial of the pain.

Although there is a correlation between responsiveness to other suggestions and responsiveness to suggestions to reduce experimental pain, the correlation is rather modest (about $r = .50$), indicating that a substantial proportion of good hypnotic subjects do not reduce experimental pain when given suggestions to do so. This leads to an important question: Why are some subjects who are highly responsive to hypnosuggestions able to and others unable to respond positively to suggestions for pain reduction? Although much more research is needed before this question is answered definitively, it appears that relevant variables include subjects' previous history of experience with pain and their present attitudes to pain. For instance, in a recent study, Spanos *et al.* (1979) found that some of the subjects who were very responsive to other suggestions were able to and others were not able to markedly reduce pain when given suggestions of numbness. The good hypnotic subjects who were able to reduce pain differed from the good hypnotic subjects who were not able to reduce it primarily in that they approached pain without extreme worry, did not exaggerate the unpleasantness of the pain situation, and did not imagine the pain to be catastrophic.

4. *When subjects are given suggestions for pain reduction (in either a hypnosis or nonhypnosis condition), they typically (1) try to attend away from (distract themselves) from the pain (Spanos et al., 1979) and (2) try, when they attend to the pain, to reinterpret it as less bothersome, less painful, or less catastrophic (Brown, 1979).* How well they succeed in attending away from and/or reinterpreting the pain—and thus how well they succeed in reducing the pain—depends on many variables including their responsiveness to suggestions in general and their attitudes toward pain. This formulation also implies that (1) some subjects may succeed in totally attending away from and/or totally reinterpreting the pain, (2) other subjects will not succeed at all and will experience the pain normally, and (3) still others will partly succeed in attending away from and/or reinterpreting the pain part of the time during pain stimulation, while the remainder of the time they experience it more or less in its full intensity.

5. *Since some hypnotic subjects (and also some nonhypnotic subjects) have complex, multifaceted experiences, they can describe their experiences (including their experiences in pain experiments) in seemingly contradictory ways depending on how the interview instructions and questions are worded.* For instance, some subjects report that they experienced the hypnotic state as essentially the same as the waking state (when

asked if they experienced the states as the same); they also report that they experienced the two states as essentially different (when asked if they experienced them as different) because they actually did experience the two states both as similar in some important ways and different in others (Barber, Dalal, & Calverley, 1968). Similarly, we could predict that subjects who had both pain and nonpain experiences in a "hypnotic analgesia" experiment would focus more on either the painful or nonpainful aspects of their experiences depending on how the interview was conducted. A series of experiments by Hilgard and his associates (summarized by Hilgard, 1977, 1979), taken together with a recent experiment by Spanos and Hewitt (1980), appear to support this conjecture.

Hilgard and his associates worked with good hypnotic subjects who reported that they experienced little or no pain when they had received suggestions for hypnosis plus suggestions for analgesia. Later, the subjects were interviewed again, but this time they were told that they had a hidden part (a "hidden observer") that could give additional information pertaining to the pain they had experienced during hypnotic analgesia. When the experimenter asked to speak to their "hidden part," 50% of the good subjects now stated that they had also experienced the pain in its full severity.

Data presented subsequently by Spanos and Hewitt (1980) indicated that these seemingly contradictory answers are due primarily to subtle demands in the interview situation that lead the subjects to focus on different aspects of their complex experiences. The experimental procedures were essentially the same as those used by Hilgard with one subtle change: the instructions given to half of the good hypnotic subjects implied that their "hidden" part had experienced more pain than they had reported, whereas the instructions given to the other half of the good subjects implied that their "hidden" part had experienced less pain than they reported. The testimony elicited from these two sets of good subjects was congruent with the subtle changes in the wording of the interview; the former half of the good subjects reported more severe "hidden" pain and the latter half of the good subjects reported less "hidden" pain.

In both the Hilgard experiments and the Spanos and Hewitt experiment there is no indication whatsoever that the subjects were lying, kidding, or just saying anything to please the experimenter. It appears much more likely that they could report that they had experienced little or no pain and also that they had experienced severe pain because they had actually had both experiences (Barber *et al.*, 1968; Spanos & Hewitt, 1980). Whenever the subjects attended to the pain and did not reinterpret it, they experienced it as normally painful and could focus on this aspect of their experience when the interview led them to this aspect. However, the subjects also succeeded at times in not attending to the pain and/or reinterpreting it as nonpainful, and they could focus on this aspect of their experience if the interview pointed them in this direction.

10. "Good" Hypnotic Subjects and the Relief of Pain

Although none of the studies reviewed in this paper found that relief of pain was related to "depth of hypnosis," a number of clinical studies and experimental investigations found that hypnosuggestions were more effective in reducing pain in good rather than medium or poor hypnotic subjects. Why are hypnosuggestions for pain relief in general more effective with "good" subjects? The defining characteristic of such hypnotic subjects is their ability to respond relatively easily and quickly to suggestions such as the following: (1) suggestions to imagine and/or to feel a limb or part of the body become heavy, light, warm, cold, numb, or rigid; (2) age-regression suggestions ("You are sitting at a desk . . . it is the third grade. . ."); and (3) suggestions for auditory hallucination ("You hear the orchestra playing. . .") and for visual hallucinations ("Open your eyes and look at the cat in the corner of the room. . .") Despite the layperson's myth that individuals have to be "put under" or "put into hypnosis" before they can respond to such suggestions, the facts are quite different. Provided that their interest and cooperation has been obtained, good hypnotic subjects are able to respond to the types of suggestions mentioned above more or less in the same proficient way either (1) when they are "awake" (when no attempt has been made to hypnotize them) or (2) after they have been hypnotized (after they have been given and presumably have accepted suggestions to enter a hypnotic state). A number of important considerations pertaining to good subjects are as follows:

1. If a very strict criterion is used—namely, that the subject respond quickly, easily, and profoundly to virtually all the kinds of suggestions that have been traditionally associated with the term *hypnosis*—then only 2% to 4% of the population would meet this criterion. (This group was traditionally labeled as *somnambules*.) If the criterion is not so strict, allowing room for a less-than-perfect response to some suggestions, the number of good subjects may include 10% or even 20% of the population. The important point here, however, is that responsiveness to suggestions can be viewed as falling on a normal curve, with most people responding to some suggestions and fewer and fewer falling on the more extreme ends of very high or very low responsiveness (Barber & Calverley, 1963; Wilson & Barber, 1978).

2. For many years, investigators have sought to determine what personality characteristics differentiate good hypnotic subjects from other individuals. Several hundred investigations in this area, which have been summarized elsewhere (Barber, 1964; Hilgard, 1965; J. R. Hilgard, 1970; Spanos & Barber, 1974), found only one set of characteristics that consistently appear to separate good hypnotic subjects from the others: good subjects appear to be able to imagine and fantasize more easily and more vividly than the not-so-good subjects. In fact, a recent intensive study in this area (Wilson & Barber, 1980) that probed into the life histories of 19 very good female subjects (*somnambules*) found that *each* subject shared the same type of secret that she had previously divulged to no one; namely, that she had spent a large part of her life (at least 50% of her time) fantasizing, and the fantasized people and objects were "very real" (at more or less "hallucinatory" vividness, so that they could be seen, heard, touched, smelled, etc.). In brief, two considerations could explain why these individuals were very good hypnotic subjects: (1) to be rated as a very good subject, an individual has to be capable of "hallucinating" (i.e., seeing, hearing, feeling, experiencing whatever the hypnotist suggests) and (2) these subjects had had a lifetime of "secret" practice in fantasizing at more or less hallucinatory intensity and consequently had developed the ability to "hallucinate at will."

3. Good subjects can display their talent for responding easily to suggestions *whenever their interest and coopeation is obtained*. Despite the myths about the coercive aspects of hypnosis, such subjects do not first have to be hypnotized to use their

abilities and they do not have to respond to suggestions when they do not want to, when they do not trust the hypnotist, or when they have nothing to gain from responding in a particular situation.

4. Although good subjects have special abilities or talents for becoming absorbed in suggestions that involve fantasy and "hallucinatory" ability—e.g., suggestions for hand numbness, limb rigidity, age regression, and visual hallucination—it does not follow that they will respond so easily and quickly to suggestions to relieve their pain. First, many pains derive from tissue pathology that continues even when suggestions can remove some of the excess fear and anxiety associated with the pain. Second some pains are associated with many rewards or secondary gains, and the suggestions will be limited in effectiveness until these rewards are minimized.

5. Although hypnosuggestive procedures are generally more effective in relieving pain in good hypnotic subjects, it does not follow that they are ineffective with poor subjects. On the contrary, they can be just as effective, but they may sometimes take more time or more effort on the part of the therapist. If the not-so-good hypnotic subject has a close relationship with the therapist, sees the therapist as utterly sincere, and finds the suggestions meaningful and useful, he or she will be receptive to the suggestions and—if they are recorded on an audiotape—to their repetition. By giving meaningful, useful suggestions, recording them on cassette tape, and asking the patient to listen to the tape regularly at home, the therapist can influence the ongoing feelings and cognitions (and thus the pain) of the not-so-good subjects about as much as those of the good subjects.

11. Recommendations for More Effective Hypnosuggestive Procedures

Although hypnosuggestions have been shown to be useful adjuncts to the dolorologist's armamentarium, it appears unlikely that they have been utilized in a maximally effective way. I believe that therapists can enhance the effectiveness of their hypnosuggestive procedures for pain control by enlarging or broadening their repertoire of (1) useful preliminary procedures, (2) useful verbal suggestions, and (3) useful nonverbal suggestions. Let us look at each of these aspects in turn.

11.1. Useful Preliminary Procedures

Before beginning the treatment of chronic pain, the therapist may wish to do the following:

1. Undertake a preliminary thorough interview that assesses the patient's thoughts-feelings-emotions prior to, during, and following previous painful episodes (Genest & Turk, 1979).

2. Ask patients to record the level or severity of their pain at specified times. By performing this task, patients can become more aware of how their pain is affected by various situations and by their own thoughts-feelings-emotions (Genest & Turk, 1979).

3. Ascertain the patient's individual way of responding to pain. It may be

helpful, in this regard, to ask the patient to respond to a standardized pain stimulus—e.g., the Forgione-Barber (1971) pain stimulator set at a low level of intensity. While determining pain threshold and pain tolerance, the patient can also be asked to give an account of what he or she is feeling and thinking at specified points during the pain stimulation. Afterward the patient can be asked to compare the experimental pain with his or her own pain. Although these procedures should be used with caution, they some times "provide a sense of the patient's thinking style, the components of his appraisal of pain and his ways of coping with it" (Genest & Turk, 1979, p. 257).

4. Additional information as to how patients cope with their pain can be obtained by suggesting to them that they reexperience a time when they were able to handle pain especially well and to report how they coped.

5. The hypnosuggestive procedures will probably be more effective if the therapist has conveyed to the patient during the preliminary period that, *although the pain hurts and is very real,* it is nevertheless enhanced by reactions such as worry, fear, unhappiness, increased muscular tension, reduced blood supply to the painful area and so on—and that these reactions can be reduced by hypnosuggestive procedures.

6. The therapist can enhance the effectiveness of hypnosuggestive procedures by first reducing "resistance to hypnosis." This resistance is most often a byproduct of the widespread layperson's myth of hypnosis, which contends that hypnotized individuals are "out of it" and "under the control of the hypnotist." There are two major ways to minimize this resistance. The first is simply *not* to define the situation to the patient as hypnosis. This is not difficult to do if the therapist uses only a small number of hypnosuggestive procedures as a limited part of a broader therapeutic armamentarium. For instance, suggestions for numbness or suggestions for calmness and relaxation can usually be defined and accepted by the patient as exactly what they are—as attempts to produce numbness, calmness, or relaxation for relief of pain. However, if many hypnosuggestive procedures are utilized or if other factors in the situation will lead the patient to define the procedures as hypnosis, it is very important for the therapist to reduce resistance to hypnosis by explaining the many ways that the myth of hypnosis is simply wrong and demonstrating to the patient in a careful step-by-step manner what hypnosuggestive procedures actually involve; for example, therapists may model or demonstrate for their patients how they themselves can experience calmness by suggesting "calm . . . at ease . . . absolutely calm" aloud softly to themselves and how they can also experience some degree of hand warmth or hand numbness by giving themselves suggestions softly but aloud for hand warmth or hand numbness.

11.2. Useful Verbal Suggestions

As emphasized previously, when it is said that hypnosis was used to treat pain, what is meant is that various types of suggestions (ideas or communications) were given to the pain patient in a serious and expectant manner. Hypnosuggestive therapy is effective to the extent that the patient accepts and utilizes the suggestions, and the extent of the patient's acceptance is dependent on many variables, including the relationship between the therapist and the patient as well as the denotations and connotations of the suggestions. The art of hypnosis, therefore, is not, as the myth holds, the art of "putting the patient under" but rather of presenting suggestions that are maximally meaningful, acceptable, and useful for the patient. Of course, it goes without saying that different suggestions are effective with different patients: one patient will be more responsive to direct suggestions for pain reduction, another will find suggestions for deep relaxation more useful, a third will be more proficient at using suggestions for numbness, a fourth will respond successfully to suggestions to dissociate from the pain, and so on. To determine which suggestions are most effective with a specific patient, we should be prepared to utilize various kinds of suggestions while, at the same time, carefully noting both verbal and nonverbal feedback from the patient (Sacerdote, 1980, p. 433). The hypnosuggestions included in the repertoire of the pain therapist should cover a broad range and could include, for example, the following:

1. Suggestions for deep relaxation, especially when given together with the suggestion that the relaxation will reduce the discomfort and pain, appear to be useful with a large number of pain patients (Sacerdote, 1977, 1980). These kinds of suggestions can be given in many complex ways, but they could also be given simply, as follows: "Calm . . . absolutely calm . . . at peace . . . so relaxed.... Taking a deep breath and, while breathing out slowly, relaxing completely . . . calm . . . at ease . . . relaxed," and so on.

2. A second set of suggestions, which can be viewed as extensions of those described above, inform the patient that he or she can reduce or block pain by going into a "hypnotic state" or a "trance state." In this case, the suggestions, which may begin with "Calm . . . relaxed . . . at peace," may continue with suggestions of "going deeper and deeper," "becoming drowsy and sleepy," and "as you go deeper and deeper into the hypnotic state, you feel more and more comfortable. . . ." The goal of these kinds of suggestions (which are worded in the same way as the suggestions that were used in some traditional "hypnotic induction procedures") is to produce a profound reduction in attention and active thought processes. To the extent that the patient can reduce attention to internal and external stimulation, to the same extent we might hypothesize that attention to pain would be reduced. Although this technique is useful, especially for bedridden patients, it also has limitations; for example, most pain patients are rarely in environmental situations where no demands are placed upon them and they can allow themselves to reduce their attention drastically. Consequently, the effective hypnosuggestive therapist utilizes the "deeper and deeper" suggestions for control of pain selectively, despite the myth of hypnosis (which assumes that the hypnotist relieves pain to the extent that he or she "puts the patient in a deep trance").

3. Some hospitalized pain patients who have received suggestions that they are becoming "more and more drowsy . . . sleepy . . . [and are] going into a restful, comfortable sleep" could be given a supplementary set of potentially useful suggestions that, as they go to sleep, they experience beautiful, wonderful, or exciting dreams. These dream suggestions can be especially useful with bedridden patients. The patients can be given individualized cassette tapes that include both the "drowsy . . . sleepy" suggestions and the suggestion to dream, and they can be instructed to utilize the tapes during periods of severe discomfort.

4. Although the first set of suggestions we listed above—the suggestions for deep relaxation—appear to be useful for various kinds of pain, I will venture to predict that future research will show that suggestions for "active relaxation" are more useful with certain kinds of pains such as back pain, headache, and migraine. Active relaxation (or "flowing with the situation") involves relaxation in terms of peace of mind while engaging in day-to-day activities—not worrying, not aggravating oneself over the undesirable behavior of others, not anticipating catastrophes, letting go of resentments and negative thoughts such as, "I can't stand this," "It shouldn't be happening to me," and "This isn't fair—what did I do to deserve this?" Suggestions to be at peace with and to flow with all life situations can be given after the therapist and patient have reached agreement that it is possible to fully accept (not be bothered by) unchangeable things we do not like (Barber, 1978). To arrive at this basic principle of happiness and to begin to put it into practice, it is usually necessary for the therapist to present himself or herself as a model and to guide the patient slowly and patiently to accept ideas such as the following: (a) Life has problems. All individuals experience many things in their life that they dislike intensely, such as deaths of parents, siblings, lovers, children, and friends; blindness, deafness, and crippling injuries; illnesses and diseases; loss of job or economic security; unwanted behaviors on the part of parents, spouse, children, and co-workers, etc. Although we cannot escape serious problems and cannot avoid experiences that are extremely undesirable, we *can* change the way we interpret and react to unwanted events. Individuals who have learned to live happily expect such problems and, although they do not like them, are not greatly surprised when they come and are set to accept them. (b) Well-functioning individuals are set to accept everything that comes in life—the good, the neutral, and the bad. When unwanted events arrive, they first work hard to determine whether the events can be changed. When they can be changed significantly by the individual's actions, the individual makes the greatest possible effort to change them. However, the characteristics of people and the nature of unwanted events (such as accidents, illnesses, and deaths) can rarely be changed once they have occurred. In this case, individuals who have learned to live well accept the events as part of the ongoing drama of their life which is outside of their control. *Accepting* (not fighting, not becoming upset about) everything that is undesirable but unchangeable in life is not the same as *liking* everything in life. On the contrary, it implies simply that when people or events cannot be changed, then becoming upset over them or "making ourselves sick about them" affects only us and does so in a hurtful way; it does not significantly change the unwanted characteristics of the person or the events. (c) Practically everyone virtually always assumes that he or she *has* to become bothered, upset, unhappy, miserable, and so on over everything undesirable that is encountered in life. This extraordinarily common assumption is simply wrong; some people do not let themselves feel miserable, guilty, or resentful about things they cannot change (Maslow, 1954); other individuals who have been seen in therapy (Ellis, 1962; Meichenbaum, 1977) have learned to face the unwanted events of life calmly, without making themselves miserable.

When patients have arrived at the point where they believe that this kind of "active relaxation" or "flowing with the situation" is *at least possible* for them, they can be given suggestions that can help them move towards the goal (e.g., "Feel yourself now listening to your [hypercritical] mother . . . you remain calm . . . at peace . . . peacefully, calmly observing the situation . . . letting it all flow. . ."). Although it is very difficult for some patients to arrive at this point and others can arrive there only after a series of therapy sessions, it is also sometimes surprising to find patients who quickly adopt this viewpoint and, as a result, gradually but definitively change their lives.

5. Although suggestions for hand anesthesia are rather commonly used in hypnosuggestive therapy, it seems to me that they are rarely presented as effectively as they could be. From my experience, their effectiveness can sometimes be enhanced by first asking the patient to gently rub ice cubes (covered by a cloth) over the surface of the hand to acquire a clear feeling of the kind of numbness that is to be produced by suggestions. Later, the anesthesia suggestions that are given to the patient can be made more potent by describing vividly and yet individually for each patient various kinds of numbness (e.g., numbness due to the ice, to procaine, or to the hand "falling asleep") that the patient has previously experienced. Typically, after the patient has begun to experience some degree of anesthesia, he or she is asked to place the "numb" hand over the area of discomfort or pain and to feel the numbness spreading.

6 and 7. Two additional sets of suggestions that are related to the suggestions for hand numbness are suggestions for hand warmth and for hand coldness. Prior to giving these suggestions, it is sometimes useful to ask the patient to actually place his or her hand in pleasantly warm or pleasantly cold water. Later, when receiving suggestions for hand warmth or hand coldness, the patient is guided to remember and reexperience in imagination the water of the appropriate temperature. When the patient experiences some degree of warmth or cold, suggestions are given to "transfer" the warmth or cold to the back, head, leg, or other area of pain.

8. With some pain patients, I have also found it useful to suggest that as they breathe in deeply, they will feel "energy" or "light" or "vibrations" or the "spirit of Jesus" or the "light of God" going to the area of pain and bringing comfort. Of course, suggestions worded in this way affect pain only with those patients who have favorable attitudes toward these concepts.

9. Another suggestion I have found useful, especially with hospitalized patients with intractable pain, is the suggestion to age-regress to a time when life was pleasant or at least not painful or threatening. When used for control of pain, the goal of age-regression is to distract patients from their pain by helping them recall, feel, and reexperience an earlier, happier time in life. If elementary school has pleasant connotations for the patient, suggestions can be given to "feel yourself becoming small and tiny . . . hands small and tiny . . . sitting at a big desk . . . feel the chewing-gum underneath the desk . . . smell the paste . . . the erasers . . . the eraser dust . . . the chalk . . . see the blackboards in the classroom. . .". Similarly, if the patient's wedding was a pleasant experience, suggestions can be given to regress to the day of the wedding and to reexperience each event during the day, during the honeymoon, and so on. Age-regression suggestions need not be given in a "literal" manner—patients in pain can be told, for example, to place themselves within an idealized childhood when everything is as they would have liked it to be.

10. I have also found other suggestions useful in helping pain patients "dissociate," "distract," "detach," or "distance" themselves from pain. For example, they can be given various kinds of suggestions to have an out-of-body experience—suggestions that they feel their spirit or their astral body leaving their physical body or that they may imaginatively experience themselves relaxing in a chair in the corner while at the same time they are observing their body "over there" (Sacerdote, 1980). (When this kind of "separating oneself from the pain" is used in an ultimately proficient way, it can give rise to an amazing control over pain. For instance, Green and Green (1977, p. 235) have described a man who can remain calm while he places the burning end of a cigarette against the inside of his forearm because he separates himself from his arm by thinking of his arm as an object "out there"). If the philosophy or interests of the patient allow it, various other suggestions can be used to produce "dissociation" or "distraction"; for instance, patients who are interested in experiencing "past-life regression" can be given suggestions that "It is now 1832 . . . look at your hands . . . feet . . . clothes," and so on.

11. With acute-pain patients, I have also found useful suggestions are based on the Zen Buddhist premise that fighting an undesirable situation (such as pain) only makes it worse and that accepting the undesirable situation is the best way to overcome it. Patients who are able to agree with this premise can be given suggestions that as they experience the pain without fighting it, it will lose its hurt, it will become just a thing-in-itself—a sensation (which does not have the quality of pain). Along similar lines, Meares (1968) pointed out that it is possible to experience "nonpainful pain," to experience pain as a not-pleasant sensation without the "hurt" in it, by maintaining a very calm attitude toward the pain and experiencing it in its pure form without any interpretation or "psychical embellishment." By setting himself to experience pain in this way—calmly and in its pure form—Meares himself on three occasions had teeth extracted without medication and without significant discomfort.

12. Since it appears that the severity of chronic pain can decrease when the patient feels lovable, loved, and loving, (Bennett, 1980) suggestions given sincerely and with feeling, such as the following, can be helpful with selected patients: "As the days go on, you'll become more and more aware of how lovable, loved, and loving you are. You'll feel more and more all of the lovableness that flows through your being, and all the love you are receiving, and all the love that flows from you to others. You'll feel so good, so at ease, so alive as you experience your love flowing out to every person that you meet. All the love that is so deep in your being will come forth. And as you become more and more aware of how lovable you are, you will feel the love from people around you and will become more and more aware of their love coming, flowing toward you. . . ."

13. Also useful at times are direct suggestions that the pain is going away or suggestions that state the same thing indirectly, e.g., suggestions that the patient is feeling more and more comfortable. Of course, direct suggestions for pain reduction should be used cautiously, after carefully considering the secondary gains and the psychodynamics that might underlie the pain.

In any one therapy session, the pain patient can be given only one or two of the hypnosuggestions described above or he or she can be given a series of these hypnosuggestions. At the present time, we do not have any evidence showing that one order of presentation of these suggestions is any better than any other. However, I have found in my own clinical work that the effectiveness of the hypnosuggestions can often be enhanced by (1) recording the suggestions on a cassette tape when they are first presented to the patient and (2) asking the patient to listen to the tape at specified times later, while "letting the suggestions go deep into your subconscious mind" (Erickson, Rossi, & Rossi, 1976). After the patient has listened to the cassette tape for a week or more, the therapist can ask the patient to give the suggestions to himself or herself first softly aloud and then silently without utilizing the tape. In other words, the therapist proceeds to remove the patient's dependence on the therapist and on the tape by shifting the procedure to self-suggestions, with the memorized or remembered suggestions on the tape serving as a model.

Before the end of this discussion of verbal suggestions, it should be reemphasized that other factors *associated* with the suggestions may be more important in ameliorating pain that the suggestions themselves. For instance, the suggestions may indirectly help the patients feel that they are not utterly helpless but have some potential control over the pain. (One of the best-established facts in dolorology is that individuals can tolerate more pain when they *believe* they can exercise some control over the pain (Bowers, 1968; Melzack & Perry, 1975; Staub, Tursky, & Schwartz, 1971). Furthermore, the specific suggestions are often less important than the patients' attitudes towards the suggestions and their beliefs that the suggestions are useful for them. Also more important than the specific suggestions may be the patients' feelings that something effective is being done for their pain and/or their feeling that a professional cares enough about them to devote much time and effort to relating closely with them (Bernstein, 1965; Butler, 1954; Lea *et al.*, 1960; Sacerdote, 1980).

11.3. Useful Nonverbal Suggestions

Textbooks on clinical hypnosis (Crasilneck & Hall, 1975; Hartland, 1971; Hartman, 1980; Kroger, 1979; Kroger & Fezler, 1976; Meares, 1960; Miller, 1979; Schneck, 1965; Spiegel & Spiegel, 1978; Wolberg, 1948a,b) focus heavily on verbal suggestions and tend to neglect the potency of nonverbal suggestions. It is, of course, well known that when a physician prescribes an ineffective drug or placebo for the patient, he or she is at the same time giving the patient the potentially potent and effective nonverbal suggestion, "This pill or drug will relieve your pain" (Beecher, 1955). It is, however, less well known that the pain-relieving effects of many apparently "physical" procedures (e.g., heating pads, ice treatments, gravity traction for back pain, massage, laying on of hands, transcutaneous nerve stimulation, biofeedback, acupuncture, and even surgery) may at times be due to their effectiveness in communicating to the patient the powerful nonverbal suggestion that "This potent physical procedure will heal you and relieve you of your pain" (Barber, 1980). Although there is suggestive evidence that some physical treatments (e.g., rubbing ice on the skin between the thumb and index finger) may relieve pain in another area of the body by a direct physical route (Melzack, Guité, & Gonshor, 1980), there is also strong evidence that other physical treatments (e.g., mammary artery rerouting surgery for anginal pain) actually exert their effects by the nonverbal suggestion route.*

During recent years there has also been an interesting controversy pertaining to the extent to which the relief of pain by acupuncture is due to nonverbal suggestions. The data can be interpreted in various ways. For instance, one interpretation (Melzack & Dennis, 1978) is that acupuncture relieves pain by the same principle of "counterirritation" or "hyperstimulation" that may underlie the effects of many traditional folkremedies (mustard plasters, ice packs, cupping, and blistering the skin). Another interpretation which has become popular in recent years is that acupuncture causes the release of the brain's own opiate-like substances (endorphins, enkephalins, etc.), which relieve pain naturally. Although some experimental studies seem to support the latter interpretation (Chapman, Wilson, & Gehrig, 1976; Cheng & Pomeranz, 1979), others contradict it (Hassett, 1980).

Another possible interpretation is that, although acupuncture *may* exert its effects partly through counterirritation and partly through its ability to release natural opiate-like substances, it nevertheless exerts some (or much) of its pain-relieving effects through a nonverbal suggestive effect. Data supporting the latter interpretation were presented by Knox, Handfield-Jones, and Shum (1979), who found that acupuncture by itself did *not* reduce pain (produced by immersion of a limb in ice water); however, it did reduce pain when it was given together with the suggestion or expectation that it would do so. Another important finding in this study was that, although suggestion plus acupuncture was effective in reducing pain, the same suggestion plus placebo was ineffective. One interpretation of these results is that although acupuncture by itself may be insufficient to relieve pain, it can make the suggestion that pain will be relieved more believable and thus more effective. The patient might more strongly accept the suggestion that pain will be relieved when he or she sees serious therapists earnestly fixing long needles in place, feels the unusual sensations produced by the needles themselves, and then experiences even more unusual sensations when electricity is applied to the needles.

Another study (Katz, Kao, Spiegel, & Katz, 1974) indicates that acupuncture for relief of chronic pain may be effective almost exclusively only with individuals who are highly responsive to hypnosuggestions. Of 13 individuals rated as rather unresponsive to hypnosuggestions, only 1 (8%) reported partial relief of pain with acupuncture. Of 36 individuals rated as very responsive to hypnosuggestions, 31 (86%) reported either nearly complete relief of pain (19 individuals) or partial relief (12 individuals).

An investigation by Lee, Andersen, Modell, and Saga (1975) also indicates that acupuncture for the treatment of chronic pain may be primarily a nonverbal

*Some years ago surgeons attempted to relieve angina pectoris by rerouting the mammary arteries to bring more blood to the heart. In a controlled surgical study, angina patients were given a "placebo" operation; that is, under anesthesia, an incision was made into the skin so that the patient incorrectly believed later that the operation had been performed. The results indicate that the effective factor in relieving angina was the patient's *belief* that the operation had been performed, not the operation itself (Gross, 1966, p. 139).

suggestive therapy. These investigators gave 979 acupuncture treatments to 261 patients with chronic pain. At a 4-week follow-up, 35% of the patients reported 50% or more reduction in the intensity of their pain, but just as many of the patients who were helped had received the suggestive acupuncture treatment (needles placed in random control points) as had received the actual acupuncture treatment (needles placed in the proper meridian locations).

The results of the Katz *et al.* (1974) and Lee *et al.* (1975) investigations were confirmed in three other experiments (Gaw, Chang, & Shaw, 1975; Kepes, 1976; Moore & Berk, 1976) showing that "suggestive or placebo acupuncture" was as effective as actual acupuncture and individuals who were independently rated as most responsive to hypnosuggestions showed the greatest degree of pain relief when they were exposed either to the false or the real acupuncture.

12. Overview: Hypnosuggestive Approaches to Pain

Before concluding, it appears appropriate to delineate a number of general principles of modern hypnosuggestive approaches to pain control that may have been lost in the details of this paper:

1. When it is said that hypnosis was used in pain therapy, what is meant is that various types of suggestions (ideas or communications) were given to the pain patient in a serious and expectant manner in an effort to ameliorate the pain. The suggestions may have included, for instance, suggestions of numbness, suggestions intended to distract the patient from the pain, direct suggestions for pain reduction, and suggestions for mental calmness and relaxation.

2. The art of hypnosis is not, as the myth holds, the art of "putting the patient under trance" but rather the art of presenting suggestions that are maximally meaningful, acceptable, and useful for the patient. The effectiveness of hypnosuggestions in ameliorating pain is dependent not on "how deeply the patient is hypnotized" but on the meaningfulness of the suggestions to the patient, the nature of the patient's pain, the characteristics of the patient and of the therapist, and the quality of the relation between the patient and the therapist.

3. The total experience of pain includes at least two components: (a) sensations that are meant to warn the individual that something undesirable is happening in some tissue or organ of his body and (b) the individual's *interpretation* of these (pain) sensations. A fact of utmost importance in understanding pain and in treating pain is that there are wide individual differences in the interpretation of pain sensations; the same intensity of sensation will be interpreted as quite tolerable or not especially bothersome by one person and as utterly intolerable by another.

4. If an individual is lonely, or feels unloved or unlovable, or is depressed, he or she is likely to interpret pain sensations within this total context of unhappiness as unbearable or intolerable. Also, if the individual fears the pain or fears the consequences of the illness that may underlie the pain, he or she may continually focus on it and think about it and thus magnify its painfulness. On

the other hand, if the individual feels loved and lovable, is living fully, and does not magnify about the pain, he or she may give little attention to it, disregard it, and not be especially bothered by it.

5. Since the interpretation of pain sensations is such an important part of the total pain experience, hypnosuggestive procedures can play an important role in pain control. Hypnosuggestions are effective in ameliorating pain when they help the patient (a) attend to other things and thus be distracted from the pain, (b) remain calm and thus not worry about and not be anxious about the pain, and/or (c) reinterpret the sensations as tolerable or not important. Although these effects of hypnosuggestions involve alterations in attention and ways of perceiving and interpreting the situation, they do not involve hypnosis or trance in the lay sense (being "out of it," relatively unaware, and under the control of the hypnotist).

6. The effectiveness of hypnosuggestive procedures in ameliorating pain is due only partly to the hypnosuggestions themselves and other correlated variables such as the additional attention and care given by the therapist to the patient; it is also partly due to the patient's growing belief that he or she is not a helpless victim of the pain but has some potential control over it.

13. References

Adams, H. E., Feuerstein, M., & Fowler, J. L. Migraine headache: Review of parameters, etiology, and intervention. *Psychological Bulletin*, 1980, *87*, 217–237.

Anderson, J. A. D., Basker, M. A., & Dalton, R. Migraine and hypnotherapy. *International Journal of Clinical and Experimental Hypnosis*, 1975, *23*, 48–58.

August, R. V. *Hypnosis in obstetrics.* New York: McGraw Hill, 1961.

Barber, J. Rapid induction analgesia: A clinical report. *American Journal of Clinical Hypnosis*, 1977, *19*, 138–147.

Barber, T. X. Toward a theory of pain: Relief of chronic pain by prefrontal leucotomy, opiates, placebos, and hypnosis. *Psychological Bulletin*, 1959, *56*, 430–460.

Barber, T. X. The effects of "hypnosis" on pain: A critical review of experimental and clinical findings. *Psychosomatic Medicine*, 1963, *25*, 303–333.

Barber, T. X. Hypnotizability, suggestibility, and personality: V. A critical review of research findings. *Psychological Reports*, 1964, *14*, 299–320.

Barber, T. X. *Effects of hypnotic induction, suggestions of anesthesia, and distraction on subjective and physiological responses to pain.* Paper presented at the annual meeting of the Eastern Psychological Association, Philadelphia, April 1969.

Barber, T. X. *LSD, marihuana, yoga, and hypnosis.* Hawthorne, N.Y.: Aldine, 1970.

Barber, T. X. *Positive suggestions for effective living and philosophical hypnosis* (cassette tape). Medfield, Mass.: Medfield Foundation, 1978.

Barber, T. X. *Hypnotic suggestions for weight control and smoking cessation* (cassette tape). Medfield, Mass.: Medfield Foundation, 1979. (a)

Barber, T. X. *Hypnotic and self-hypnotic suggestions for study-concentration, relaxation, pain control, and mystical experience* (cassette tape). Medfield, Mass.: Medfield Foundation, 1979 (b)

Barber, T. X. *Medicine, suggestive therapy, and healing: Historical and psychophysiological considerations.* Framingham, Mass.: Cushing Hospital, 1980.

Barber, T. X., & Hahn, K. W., Jr. Physiological and subjective responses to pain producing stimulation under hypnotically-suggested and waking-imagined "analgesia." *Journal of Abnormal and Social Psychology*, 1962, *65*, 411–418.

Barber, T. X., & Calverley, D. S. "Hypnotic-like" suggestibility in children and adults. *Journal of Abnormal and Social Psychology,* 1963, *66,* 589–597.

Barber, T. X., & Hahn, K. W., Jr. Experimental studies in "hypnotic" behavior: Physiological and subjective effects of imagined pain. *Journal of Nervous and Mental Disease,* 1964, *139,* 416–425.

Barber, T. X. & Wilson, S. C. Hypnotic inductions, mental relaxation, and permissive suggestions. (Cassette tape). Medfield, Mass.: Medfield Foundation, 1978.

Barber, T. X., Dalal, A. S., & Calverley, D. S. The subjective reports of hypnotic subjects. *American Journal of Clinical Hypnosis,* 1968, *11,* 74–88.

Barber, T. X., Spanos, N. P., & Chaves, J. F. *Hypnosis, imagination, and human potentialities.* Elmsford, N.Y.: Pergamon, 1974.

Beaty, E. T., & Haynes, S. N. Behavioral intervention in muscle-contraction headache: A review. *Psychosomatic Medicine,* 1979, *41,* 165–180.

Beck, A. T., Rush, A. J., Shaw, B. F., & Emery, G. *Cognitive therapy of depression: a treatment manual.* New York: Guilford, 1979.

Beecher, H. K. The powerful placebo. *Journal of the American Medical Association.* 1955, *159,* 1602–1606.

Bennett, Avis. Personal communication, Sept. 16, 1980.

Bernstein, M. R. Management of burned children with the aid of hypnosis. *Journal of Child Psychology and Psychiatry,* 1963, *4,* 93–98.

Bernstein, M. R. Observations on the use of hypnosis with burned children on a pediatric ward. *International Journal of Clinical and Experimental Hypnosis,* 1965, *13,* 1–10.

Blanchard, E. B., Ahles, T. A., & Shaw, E. R. Behavioral treatment of headache. *Progress in Behavior Modification,* 1979, *8,* 207–247.

Bonica, J. J. *The management of pain.* Philadelphia: Lea & Febiger, 1953.

Bowers, K. S. Pain, anxiety and perceived control. *Journal of Consulting and Clinical Psychology,* 1968, *32,* 596–602.

Bowers, K. S., & Van der Meulen, S. *A comparison of psychological and chemical techniques in the control of dental pain.* Paper presented at the meeting of the Society for Clinical and Experimental Hypnosis, Boston, October 1972.

Brown, J. M. *Cognitive activity, pain perception and hypnotic susceptibility.* Paper presented at the annual meeting of the American Psychological Association, New York, September 1979.

Butler, B. The use of hypnosis in the care of the cancer patient. *Cancer,* 1954, *7,* 1–14.

Cangello, V. W. Hypnosis for the patient with cancer. *American Journal of Clinical Hypnosis,* 1962, *4,* 215–226.

Chapman, C. R., Wilson, M., & Gehrig, J. Comparative effects of acupuncture and transcutaneous stimulation on the perception of painful dental stimuli. *Pain,* 1976, *2,* 265–283.

Chaves, J. F., & Barber, T. X. Needles and knives: Behind the mystery of acupuncture and Chinese meridians. *Human Behavior,* 1973, *2* (9) 19–24.

Chaves, J. F., & Barber, T. X. Acupuncture analgesia: A six-factor theory, *Psychoenergetic Systems,* 1974, *1,* 11–21. (a)

Chaves, J. F., & Barber, T. X. Cognitive strategies, experimenter modeling, and expectation in the attenuation of pain. *Journal of Abnormal Psychology,* 1974, *83,* 356–363. (b)

Chaves, J. F., & Barber, T. X. Hypnotic procedures and surgery: A critical analysis with applications to "acupuncture analgesia." *American Journal of Clinical Hypnosis,* 1976, *18,* 217–236.

Chaves, J. F., & Brown, J. M. *Self-generated strategies for the control of pain and stress.* Paper presented at the annual meeting of the American Psychological Association, Toronto, August 1978.

Cheek, D. B., & LeCron, L. M. *Clinical hypnotherapy.* New York: Grune & Stratton, 1968.

Cheng, R., & Pomeranz, B. Electroacupuncture analgesia could be mediated by at least two pain-relieving mechanisms: Endorphin and non-endorphin systems. *Life Sciences,* 1979, *25,* 1957–1962.

Chertok, L. *Psychosomatic methods in painless childbirth: History, theory, and practice.* New York: Pergamon Press, 1959.

Chertok, L. Dynamics of hypnotic analgesia: Some new data. *Journal of Nervous and Mental Disease,* 1977, *165,* 99–109.

Cohen, S. B. Editorial: On experiencing pain. *American Journal of Clinical Hypnosis,* 1977, *19,* 135–137.

Coulton, D. Hypnosis in obstetrical delivery. *American Journal of Clinical Hypnosis*, 1960, *2*, 144–148.

Cox, D. J., Freundlich, A., & Meyer, R. G. Differential effectiveness of EMG feedback, verbal relaxation instructions and medication placebo with tension headaches. *Journal of Consulting and Clinical Psychology*, 1975, *43*, 892–898.

Crasilneck, H. B. Hypnosis in the control of low back pain. *American Journal of Clinical Hypnosis*, 1979, *22*, 71–78.

Crasilneck, H. B., & Hall, J. A. *Clinical hypnosis: Principles and applications*. New York: Grune & Stratton, 1975.

Davenport-Slack, B. A comparative evaluation of obstetrical hypnosis and ante-natal childbirth training. *International Journal of Clinical and Experimental Hypnosis*, 1975, *23*, 266–281.

Davidson, J. A. Assessment of the value of hypnosis in pregnancy and labour. *British Medical Journal*, 1962, *2*, 951–953.

Diamond, S., & Dalessio, D. J. *The practicing physician's approach to headache* (2nd ed.). Baltimore: Williams & Wilkins, 1978.

Dick-Read, G. *Childbirth without fear*. New York: Harper & Row, 1953.

Ellis, A. *Reason and emotion in psychotherapy*. New York: Lyle Stuart, 1962.

Elton, D., Burrows, G. D., & Stanley, G. V. Chronic pain and hypnosis. In G. D. Burrows & L. Dennerstein (Eds.), *Handbook of hypnosis and psychosomatic medicine*. New York: Elsevier/North Holland, 1980.

Erickson, J. C. III. Hypnotic strategies in the daily practice of anesthesia. In G. D. Burrows, D. R. Collison, & L. Dennerstein (Eds.), *Hypnosis 1979*. New York: Elsevier/North Holland, 1979.

Erickson, M. H., Rossi, E. L., & Rossi, S. I. *Hypnotic realities*. New York: Halsted-Wiley, 1976.

Evans, M. B., & Paul, G. L. Effects of hypnotically suggested analgesia on physiological and subjective responses to cold stress. *Journal of Consulting and Clinical Psychology*, 1970, *35*, 362–371.

Field, P. B. *Stress reduction in hypnotherapy of chronic headaches*. Paper presented at annual meeting of American Psychological Association, New York, September 1979.

Fordyce, W. E. *Behavioral methods for chronic pain and illness*. St. Louis: Mosby, 1976.

Forgione, A. G., & Barber, T. X. A strain-gauge pain stimulator. *Psychophysiology*. 1971, *8*, 102–106.

Fredericks, L. E. Teaching of hypnosis in an overall approach to the surgical patient. *American Journal of Clinical Hypnosis*, 1978, *20*, 175–183.

Freese, A. S. *Pain*. New York: Putnam, 1974.

Furneaux, W. D., & Chapple, P. A. L. Some objective and subjective characteristics of labor influenced by personality, and their modification by hypnosis and relaxation. *Proceedings of the Royal Society of Medicine*, 1964, *57*, 261–262.

Gaw, A. C., Chang, L. W., & Shaw, L-C. Efficacy of acupuncture on osteoarthritic pain. *New England Journal of Medicine*, 1975, *293*, 375–378.

Genest, M., & Turk, D. C. A proposed model for behavioral group therapy with pain patients. In D. Upper & S. Ross (Eds.), *Behavioral group therapy, 1979*. Champaign, Ill.: Research Press, 1979.

Gerschman, J. A., Reade, P. C., & Burrows, G. D. Hypnosis and dentistry. In G. D. Burrows & L. Dennerstein (Eds.) *Handbook of hypnosis and psychosomatic medicine*. New York: Elsevier/North Holland, 1980.

Good, M. G. A general theory of pain. *Anesthesia & Analgesia*, 1951, *30*, 136–150.

Gottfredson, D. K. *Hypnosis as an anesthetic in dentistry*. Unpublished doctoral dissertation, Brigham Young University, 1973.

Gottlieb, H., Strite, L. C., Koller, R., Madorsky, A., Hockersmith, V., Kleeman, M., & Wagner, J. Comprehensive rehabilitation of patients having chronic low back pain. *Archives of Physical Medicine and Rehabilitation*, 1977, *58*, 101–108.

Green, E., & Green, A. *Beyond biofeedback*. New York: Delacorte Press, 1977.

Gross, H., & Posner, N. A. An evaluation of hypnosis for obstetric delivery. *American Journal of Obstetrics and Gynecology*, 1963, *87*, 912–920.

Gross, M. L. *The doctors*. New York: Random House, 1966.

Harrison, R. Psychological testing in headache: A review. *Headache*, 1975, *15*, 177–185.

Hartland, J. *Medical and dental hypnosis* (2nd ed.). Baltimore: Williams & Wilkins, 1971.

Hartman, B. J. *A system of hypnotherapy*. Chicago: Nelson-Hall, 1980.

Hassett, J. Acupuncture is proving its points. *Psychology Today*, 1980, *14* (7):81–89.

Haynes, S. N., Griffin, P., Mooney, E., & Parise, M. Electromyographic biofeedback and relaxation instructions in the treatment of muscle contraction headaches. *Behavior Therapy*, 1975, *6*, 672–678.

Henryk-Gutt, R., & Rees, W. L. Psychological aspects of migraine. *Journal of Psychosomatic Research*, 1973, *17*, 141–153.

Hilgard, E. R. *Hypnotic susceptibility.* New York: Harcourt, Brace & World, 1965.

Hilgard, E. R. A quantitative study of pain and its reduction through hypnotic suggestion. *Proceedings of the National Academy of Sciences*, 1967, *57*, 1581–1586.

Hilgard, E. R. *Divided consciousness: Multiple controls in human thought and action.* New York: Wiley, 1977

Hilgard, E. R. Divided consciousness in hypnosis: The implications of the hidden observer. In E. Fromm & R. E. Shor (Eds.), *Hypnosis: Developments in research and new perspectives* (2nd ed.). Hawthorne, N.Y.: Aldine, 1979.

Hilgard, E. R., & Hilgard, J. R. *Hypnosis in the relief of pain.* Los Altos, Calif.: Kaufmann, 1975.

Hilgard, E. R., & Morgan, A. H. Heart rate and blood pressure in the study of laboratory pain in man under normal conditions and as influenced by hypnosis. *Acta Neurobiologicae Experimentalis*, 1975, *35*, 741–759.

Hilgard, E. R., Macdonald, H., Marshall, G. D., & Morgan, A. H. The anticipation of pain and pain control under hypnosis: Heart rate and blood pressure responses in the cold pressor test. *Journal of Abnormal Psychology*, 1974, *83*, 561–568.

Hilgard, E. R., Macdonald, H., Morgan, A. H., & Johnson, L. S. The reality of hypnotic analgesia: A comparison of highly hypnotizables with simulators. *Journal of Abnormal Psychology*, 1978, *87*, 239–246.

Hilgard, J. R. *Personality and hypnosis: A study of imaginative involvement.* Chicago: University of Chicago Press, 1970.

Holmes, T. H., & Wolff, H. G. Life situations, emotions, and backache. *Psychosomatic Medicine*, 1952, *14*, 18–33.

Holroyd, K. Stress, coping and the treatment of stress-related illness. In J. R. McNamara (Ed.) *Behavioral approaches in medicine: Application and analysis.* New York. Plenum Press, 1979.

Holroyd, K., & Andrasik, F. Coping and self-control of chronic tension headache. *Journal of Consulting and Clinical Psychology*, 1978, *46*, 1036–1045.

Holroyd, K. A., Andrasik, F., & Noble, J. A comparison of EMG biofeedback and a credible pseudotherapy in treating tension headache. *Journal of Behavioral Medicine*, 1980, *3*, 29–39.

James, L. S. The effect of pain relief for labor and delivery on the fetus and newborn. *Anesthesiology*, 1960, *21*, 405–430.

Katz, R. L., Kao, C. Y., Spiegel, H., & Katz, G. J. Pain, acupuncture, hypnosis, In J. J. Bonica (Ed.), *International symposium on pain: Advances in neurology* (Vol. 4). New York: Raven Press, 1974.

Kepes, E. R. A critical evaluation of acupuncture in the treatment of pain. *Advances in Pain Research and Therapy*, 1976, *1*, 817–822.

Knox, V. J., Handfield-Jones, C. E., & Shum, K. Subject expectancy and the reduction of cold pressor pain with acupuncture and placebo acupuncture. *Psychosomatic Medicine*, 1979, *41*, 477–486.

Kroger, W. S. Acupuncture analgesia: Its explanation by conditioning theory, autogenic training , and hypnosis. *American Journal of Psychiatry*, 1973, *130*, 855–860.

Kroger, W. S. *Clinical and experimental hypnosis* (2nd ed.). Philadelphia: Lippincott, 1979.

Kroger, W. S., & Fezler, W. D. *Hypnosis and behavior modification: Imagery conditioning.* Philadelphia: Lippincott, 1976.

Lamaze, F. *Painless childbirth: Psychoprophylactic method.* London: Burke, 1958.

Laszlo, D., & Spencer, H. Medical problems in the management of cancer. *Medical Clinics of North America*, 1953, *37*, 869–880.

Lea, P., Ware, P., & Monroe, R. The hypnotic control of intractable pain. *American Journal of Clinical Hypnosis*, 1960, *3*, 3–8.

Lee, P. K., Andersen, T. W., Modell, J. H., & Saga, S. A. Treatment of chronic pain with acupuncture. *Journal of the American Medical Association.* 1975, *232*, 1133–1135.

Levine, M. Psychogalvanic reaction to painful stimuli in hypnotic and hysterical anesthesia. *Bulletin of the Johns Hopkins Hospital*, 1930, *46*, 331–339.

Lewinsohn, P. M. A behavioral approach to depression. In R. J. Friedman & M. M. Katz (Eds.), *The psychology of depression: Contemporary theory and research.* Washington, D.C.: Winston-Wiley, 1974.

Lewis, T. *Pain.* New York: Macmillan, 1942.

Lozanov, G. *Anaesthetization through suggestion in a state of wakefulness.* Proceedings of the 7th European Conference on Psychosomatic Research, Rome, September 1967.

Maslow, A. *Motivation and personality.* New York: Harper, 1954.

McGlashan, T. H., Evans, F. J., & Orne, M. T. The nature of hypnotic analgesia and placebo response to experimental pain. *Psychosomatic Medicine,* 1969, *31,* 227–246.

Meares, A. *A system of medical hypnosis.* Philadelphia: Saunders, 1960.

Meares, A. Psychological mechanisms in the relief of pain by hypnosis. *American Journal of Clinical Hypnosis,* 1968, *11,* 55–57.

Meichenbaum, D. H. *Cognitive behavior modification.* New York: Plenum Press, 1977.

Meichenbaum, D. H., & Turk, D. C. The cognitive–behavioral management of anxiety, anger, and pain. In P. O. Davidson (Ed.), *The behavioral management of anxiety, depression and pain.* New York: Brunner Mazel, 1976.

Melzack, R. Psychological aspects of pain. In J. J. Bonica (Ed.), *Pain.* New York: Raven Press, 1980.

Melzack, R., & Perry, C. Self-regulation of pain: The use of alpha-feedback and hypnotic training for the control of chronic pain. *Experimental Neurology,* 1975, *46,* 452–469.

Melzack, R., & Dennis, S. G. Neurophysiological foundations of pain. In R. A. Sternbach (Ed.), *The psychology of pain.* New York: Raven Press, 1978.

Melzack, R., Guité, S., & Gonshor, A. Relief of dental pain by ice massage of the hand. *Canadian Medical Association Journal,* 1980, *122,* 189–191.

Michael, A. M. Hypnosis in childbirth. *British Medical Journal,* 1952, *1,* 734.

Miller, M. M. *Therapeutic hypnosis.* New York: Human Sciences Press, 1979.

Mitchell, K. R., & Mitchell, D. M. Migraine: An exploratory treatment application of programmed behaviour therapy techniques. *Journal of Psychosomatic Research,* 1971, *15,* 137–157.

Mitchell, K. R., & White, R. G. Behavioral self-management: An application to the problem of migraine headaches. Behavior Therapy, 1977, *8,* 213–222.

Moore, M. E., & Berk, S. N. Acupuncture for chronic shoulder pain. *Annals of Internal Medicine,* 1976, *84,* 381–384.

Moya, F., & James, L. S. Medical hypnosis for obstetrics. *Journal of the American Medical Association,* 1960, *174,* 2026–2032.

Orne, M. T. Hypnotic control of pain: Toward a clarification of the different psychological processes involved. In J. J. Bonica (Ed.) *Pain,* New York: Raven Press, 1980.

Pace, J. B. *Pain: A personal experience.* Chicago: Nelson-Hall, 1976.

Papermaster, A. A., Doberneck, R. C., Bonello, F. J., Griffen, W. O., & Wangensteen, O. H. Hypnosis in surgery: II. Pain. *American Journal of Clinical Hypnosis,* 1960, *2,* 220–224.

Perese, D. M. How to manage pain in malignant disease. *Journal of the American Medical Association,* 1961, *175,* 75.

Philips, C. A psychological analysis of tension headaches. In S. Rachman (Ed.), *Contributions to medical psychology* (Vol. 1). Oxford: Pergamon Press, 1977.

Philips, C. Tension headache: Theoretical problems. *Behavioral Research and Therapy,* 1978, *16,* 249–261.

Pollack, S. Pain control by suggestion. *Journal of Oral Medicine,* 1966, *21,* 85–95.

Purtell, J. J., Robins, E., & Cohen, M. E. Observations of clinical aspects of hysteria. *Journal of the American Medical Association,* 1951, *146,* 902.

Rausch, V. Cholecystectomy with self-hypnosis. *American Journal of Clinical Hypnosis,* 1980, *22,* 124–129.

Ripley, H. S., & Wolf, S. The intravenous use of sodium amytal in psychosomatic disorders. *Psychosomatic Medicine,* 1947, *9,* 260–268.

Rock, N., Shipley, T., & Campbell, C. Hypnosis with untrained, nonvolunteer patients in labor. *International Journal of Clinical and Experimental Hypnosis,* 1969, *17,* 25–36.

Sacerdote, P. The uses of hypnosis in cancer patients. *Annals New York Academy of Sciences,* 1966, *125,* 1011–1019.

Sacerdote, P. Applications of hypnotically elicited mystical states to the treatment of physical and emotional pain. *International Journal of Clinical and Experimental Hypnosis,* 1977, *25,* 309–324.

Sacerdote, P. Hypnosis and terminal illness. In G. D. Burrows & L. Dennerstein (Eds.), *Handbook of hypnosis and psychosomatic medicine.* New York: Elsevier/North Holland, 1980.

Sampimon, R. L. H., & Woodruff, M. F. A. Some observations concerning the use of hypnosis as a substitute for anesthesia. *Medical Journal of Australia,* 1946, *1,* 393–395.

Schafer, D. W. Hypnosis on a burn unit. *International Journal of Clinical and Experimental Hypnosis,* 1975, *23,* 1–14.

Schibly, W. J., & Aaronson, G. A. Hypnosis: Practical in obstetrics? *Medical Times*, 1966, *94*, 340–343.

Schneck, J. M. *The principles and practice of hypnoanalysis.* Springfield, Ill.: Charles C Thomas, 1965.

Scott, D. S., & Barber, T. X. Cognitive control of pain: Effects of multiple cognitive strategies. *Psychological Record*, 1977, *27*, 373–383.

Shealy, C. N. *The pain game.* Millbrae, Calif.: Celestrial Arts, 1976.

Simeons, A. T. W. *Man's presumptions brain: An evolutionary interpretation of psychosomatic disease.* New York: Dutton, 1961.

Spanos, N. P., & Barber, T. X. Toward a convergence in hypnosis research. *American Psychologist*, 1974, *29*, 500–511.

Spanos, N. P., Barber, T. X., & Lang, G. Effects of hypnotic induction, suggestions of analgesia, and demands for honesty on subjective reports of pain. In H. London & R. E. Nisbett (Eds.), *Thought and feeling: Cognitive alteration of feeling states.* Chicago: Aldine, 1974.

Spanos, N. P., & Hewitt, E. C. The hidden observer in hypnotic analgesia: Discovery or experimental creation? *Journal of Personality and Social Psychology*, 1980, *39*, 1201–1214.

Spanos, N. P., Radtke-Bodorik, H. L., Ferguson, J. D., & Jones, B. The effects of hypnotic susceptibility, suggestions for analgesia, and the utilization of cognitive strategies on the reduction of pain. *Journal of Abnormal Psychology*, 1979, *88*, 282–292.

Spiegel, H., & Spiegel, D. *Trance and treatment: Clinical uses of hypnosis.* New York: Basic Books, 1978.

Stacher, G., Schuster, P., Bauer, P., Lahoda, R., & Schulze, D. Effects of relaxation or analgesia on pain threshold and pain tolerance in the waking and in the hypnotic state. *Journal of Psychosomatic Research*, 1975, *19*, 259–265.

Stam, H. J., & Spanos, N. P. Experimental designs, expectancy effects, and hypnotic analgesia. *Journal of Abnormal Psychology*, 1980, *89*, 751–762.

Standley, K., Soule, A. B. III, Copans, S. A., & Duchowny, M. S. Local–regional anesthesia during childbirth: Effect on newborn behaviors. *Science*, 1974, *186*, 634–635.

Stanton, H. E. Ego-enhancement through positive suggestion. *Australian Journal of Clinical Hypnosis*, 1975, *3*, 32–36.

Stanton, H. E. Utilization of suggestions derived from rational–emotive therapy. *International Journal of Clinical and Experimental Hypnosis*, 1977, *25*, 18–25.

Staub, E., Tursky, B., & Schwartz, G. E. Self-control and predictability: Their effects on reactions to aversive stimulation. *Journal of Personality and Social Psychology*, 1971, *18*, 157–162.

Sternbach, R. A. *Pain patients: Traits and treatments.* New York: Academic Press, 1974.

Stone, P., & Burrows, G. D. Hypnosis and obstetrics. In G. D. Burrows & L. Dennerstein (Eds.), *Handbook of hypnosis and psychosomatic medicine.* New York: Elsevier/North Holland, 1980.

Tasto, D. L., & Hinkle, J. E. Muscular relaxation treatment for tension headaches. *Behavior Research & Therapy*, 1973, *11*, 347–349.

Turk, D. C. *Cognitive control of pain: A skills-training approach.* Unpublished master's thesis, University of Waterloo, 1975.

Turk, D. C. *A coping skills–training approach for the control of experimentally produced pain.* Unpublished doctoral dissertation, University of Waterloo, 1977.

Van Dyke, P. B. Some uses of hypnosis in the management of the surgical patient. *American Journal of Clinical Hypnosis*, 1970, *12*, 227–235.

Wakeman, R. J., & Kaplan, J. Z. An experimental study of hypnosis in painful burns. *American Journal of Clinical Hypnosis*, 1978, *21*, 3–12.

Werbel, E. W. Use of posthypnotic suggestions to reduce pain following hemorrhoidectomies. *American Journal of Clinical Hypnosis*, 1963, *6*, 132–136.

Wilson, S. C., & Barber, T. X. The Creative Imagination Scale as a measure of hypnotic responsiveness: Applications to experimental and clinical hypnosis. *American Journal of Clinical Hypnosis*, 1978, *20*, 235–249.

Wilson, S. C., & Barber, T. X. *Vivid fantasy and hallucinatory abilities in the life histories of excellent hypnotic subjects ("somnambules"): Preliminary report with female subjects.* Paper presented at the annual meeting of the American Association for the Study of Mental Imagery, Minneapolis, June 1980.

Winkelstein, L. B. Routine hypnosis for obstetrical delivery. *American Journal of Obstetrics and Gynecology*, 1958, *76*, 153–159.

Wolberg, L. R. *Medical hypnosis: I. The principles of hypnotherapy.* New York: Grune & Stratton, 1948. (a)

Wolberg W. R. *Medical hypnosis II. The practic of hypnotherapy.* New YorK: Grune & Stratton, 1948. (b)

Wooley, S. C. Editorial: Phoning in sick (and tired). *Psychosomatic Medicine,* 1980, *42,* 233–235.

Ziegler, F. J., Imboden, J. B., & Meyer, E. Contemporary conversion reactions: A clinical study. *American Journal of Psychiatry,* 1960, *116,* 901–909.

23

Patient-Centric Technologies
A Clinical-Cultural Perspective

SANDRA M. LEVY AND JAN HOWARD

The concept of medical technology generally refers to tools and skills that are doctor-centered. Discussion tends to focus on "hard" technologies and hardware (for example, radiation and life-support systems rather than "softer" modalities more directly related to human skills). Doctor-centric technologies are controlled by physicians in several important ways: access to their use is at the discretion of doctors; knowledge of how and when to use them is also controlled by doctors or their authorized extenders; and they tend to be utilized in what Goffman (1961) terms the "workshops of physicians," that is, hospitals.

Because of the emphasis on doctor-centric technologies, patients are viewed as subordinate performers in health care systems. Clinical psychologists as well as other health care providers easily lose sight of the patient as an independent agent—as an actor—except, of course, in a problematic sense (for example, as a refractory noncomplier with treatment regimens). Health professionals tend to be unaware of patients as autonomous people with qualities and inherent capacities that cannot, by their very nature, be transferred to another. Such capacities include the subjective assessment of one's own physical discomfort, the interpretation of disease, the presentation of oneself for health care, the giving of consent for medical procedures, and the implementation and potential modification of regimens as they are incorporated into one's own life-style and needs. The powers that inherently reside in the patient's personal sphere are not usurpable by another—not by the physician, the psychologist, or any other health professional.

An awareness and appreciation of the patient's autonomy and what this

SANDRA M. LEVY AND JAN HOWARD ● Behavioral Medicine Branch, National Cancer Institute, National Institutes of Health, Bethesda, Maryland 20205.

entails would increase understanding of the dual nature of the health delivery process. That is, the "delivery" process is not merely a unilateral laying on of hands but by its very nature it requires partnership and alliance with the patient. A general awareness of this would also enable providers of care to capitalize on patients' potentials in order to maximize the effective delivery of service as well as to increase the human and ethical quality of care.

Lack of appreciation for the power inherent in the patient's role has two consequences. First, the view of the patient as a dependent, less than autonomous entity—in short, as less than a fully functioning human within a network of activity and exchange—leads to *ineffective* health care. Prescriptions are given that are not heard and advice is offered that is not followed. What has been prescribed or advised remains unintegrated into the patient's ongoing stream of consciousness and behavior.

The second effect caused by ignorance of the patient's capacities and power is the establishment of a dehumanized health care context. Howard (1975) has analyzed the sources of dehumanization as well as potential sources of human-ization within the present health care system. Modern technology, including the complex hardware of emergency wards and intensive care units, fosters the view of patients as objects to be done to rather than subjects to be considered in their own right. Fragmentation and specialization within medical and other profes-sional schools leads to a loss of appreciation for patients as persons. "When patients are seen as summations of *ad hoc* disease entities rather than as whole persons with interrelated or conflicting problems and needs, the focus is narrow, compartmentalized, and disease- rather than person-oriented" (p. 62).

In contrast, the fundamental source of humanization within the health care context is the recognition of the subjectivity and inherent worth of the patient as person. Howard (1975) developed what she referred to as an "ideology" of patient care which includes an appreciation for human autonomy and self-responsibility as well as freedom of choice and consent.

This chapter focuses on the contribution of the patient as an active agent in the health care process. The domains of patient expertise will be examined and techniques that build upon inherent patient capacities will be discussed. Such an analysis of the dual reality of the health care context—the patient's as well as the provider's reality—will, we hope, lay the foundation for optimizing the quality of health care.

1. The Domains of Patient Power

Five domains of patient expertise—experiential, integrative, initiative, in-formative, and implementive—are discussed here as separate domains, but clearly they are interactive and inseparable. For example, the patient experiences a symptom (chest pain), integrates the experience into his or her ongoing reality and sense of self, and—depending on the construction of reality placed on the shifting experience—initiates activity that may lead to health care. At any point during the health care process, the same patient may give or withhold consent for particular procedures and may, in fact, wrest control of the treatment process—covertly or overtly—from the hands of the professionals concerned with the patient's care. For the purpose of this analysis, however, we will view each domain of competence as distinct and will trace implications for health care delivery in terms of the character of each separate domain.

1.1. Experiential Expertise

The tools of health professionals permit them to measure certain parameters of bodily functioning. These assessments facilitate diagnosis and treatment. To a greater or lesser degree, however, providers of care also find it necessary to consult patients in determining their health or illness status and the appropriateness of possible therapy regimens.

The need for patient involvement is partly a result of incomplete medical records. When patients move from doctor to doctor, any particular record may show large gaps in continuity or a virtual absence of history. Even the records of primary care physicians are often incomplete. National data banks (Spingarn, 1974) with decentralized computer terminals may alleviate the missing-data problem, but they will never substitute for the experiential expertise of the patients themselves.

For some categories of symptoms (for example, low-back pain) practitioners may be entirely dependent on the subjective evaluations of their patients. Objective measures such as X-rays, blood tests, and so on may not be at all helpful in identifying the problem. As Foley (1979) pointed out in her discussion of pain syndromes in cancer patients, for certain types of metastatic disease the experience and report of pain is the earliest diagnostic sign of disease spread. For example, in bony metastases to the cervical vertebrae or to the base of the skull, "[pain] is the earliest complaint often preceding neurologic signs and symptoms by several weeks, and documentation with plain X-rays is often difficult" (p. 63).

The experience and report of pain, and more generally the role of the complaint related to physical symptoms, has been a subject of discussion and clinical research in recent years. This research has included interest in the reliability and validity of reports of pain within and between patients. Thus, Petrie (1967) summarized a series of studies revealing individual differences in pain tolerance (but not pain threshold) based on perceptual tendencies to "reduce" or "augment" incoming stimuli. Petrie speculated that these differences in tolerance for pain and suffering were due to differential ways of experiencing the environment and that these experiences varied according to the defensive, perceptual modulation by the person. Individuals who tended to reduce or "damp down" incoming sensations also tended to be less sensitive to danger signs of pain, less concerned with problems of health, and less likely to engage in prophylactic health measures. Hence, such individuals would be least likely to present themselves to health care givers at the earliest signs of disease and pain.

Within the patient–centric model that is being adopted here—which includes the view of medical care as a dual, shared process between consumer and specialist—the notion of patients as consultants is an attractive one. This is true because the patient is the only participant–observer of the disease process in question and because, as Foley (1979) noted, the complaint is often the earliest manifestation of serious disorder. But Petrie's work as well as more recent studies (Rosenbaum, 1980) suggest that the consultant is not totally reliable in the sense that a measuring instrument would reliably register physical phenomena. Not only do differential perceptual tendencies play a role in tolerance for symptoms but social and cultural factors (Igun, 1979) as well as the patient's personal history (Bakan, 1980) alter the interpretation of symptoms and the course of complaint.

This cognitive interpretation of symptoms will be the focus of the next section, concerned with integrative experience. However, it should be noted here that self-assessment and reporting of physical status have been shown to be influenced by a number of factors. These include recent life events, associated distress levels, age, socioeconomic status, and long-standing attitudes towards one's own health. Illustrative are Mechanic's (1980) findings from a longitudinal study of adults who had first been observed when they were children. He looked at the relationship between frequency of symptom reporting in the previous three months and childhood illness patterns. The factors explaining most of the variance in reported symptoms were current subjective reports of poor health and current psychological distress. Mechanic theorized that parents may influence a child's later absorption in bodily feelings and cues by reinforcing a body-monitoring orientation. The extent to which this bodily vigilance is realized in later life depends on the actual occurrence of illness as well as adverse life events and associated distress.

Future improvements in medical technology may make patient self-perceptions less crucial, but it is doubtful that the experiential world of the healthy or ill person will ever be irrelevant to competent diagnosis and management of care. Patients are obviously not completely objective observers (nor are health experts, for that matter), but they are the only actors in the health care system who can be participant–observers from the vantage point of the one who complains. Casting patients in the role of consultants may elevate their status in provider–patient relationships, with positive effects on patient dignity. As Leventhal (1975) points out, "... continued participation in a treatment situation as a less-than-equal partner can erode the patient's self-esteem, and enhance feelings of worthlessness and dehumanization" (p. 140).

1.2. Integrative Expertise

Patients are status carriers who incorporate within their psyches the vast array of expectations relevant to the various positions they occupy and roles they play. They are the ones who must integrate the multitude of physical as well as interpersonal systems that influence their health and illness behavior. In this sense they occupy a central vantage point in terms of their total experience.

This is not to say that patients are always the best evaluators of their life events. They may be biased, irrational, and confused regarding the milieus in which they operate. By definition, however, each patient is the critical link in the chain or chains that constitute the self.

The patient's ability to comprehend the relevance of illness for the whole self can be observed most clearly among the chronically ill, who literally have to live with their disease or disfunction. To "live with" illness means that the patient as the central organizer of his or her life adapts that life to the altered condition brought on by physical disease. Continuity of the problem over time and the fact that illness travels with the role player rather than the role vests it in the patient's total self and makes escape impossible. Yet different subsystems in the patient's universe may be differentially affected by illness. In a particular situation, the problem may be manifest or latent in terms of its impact on behavior.

Where illness states are acute, or in the earliest stages of developing chronic disorders, the integrative process related to the disease may be minimal or nonexistent. Cassell (1976), who systematically analyzed the character of patients' symptom reports to physicians, described what he referred to as a "distancing" of disease by these patients. In the language used to describe their complaints, symptoms and the associated organ as well as the potential disease processes were typically characterized as an "it"—as something foreign and other than the self. Although this tendency is theoretically interesting, it also has clinical import.

The proper interpretation of symptoms, leading to prompt and appropriate help-seeking behavior, is in large part a function of the social context within which the symptom is experienced. The social context involves the immediate environment, which colors the interpretation of developing symptom patterns, and the cultural setting within which the individual developed. Culture provides the basis for learned interpretation of health signs and possible solutions for health problems (Igun, 1979).

Fabrega (1979) has developed an ethnographic model of illness behavior that encompasses the individual's own interpretation of physical signs, the macroculture that supplies meaning to symptoms as well as solutions for the control of disease, and the possible neurological encoding of cultural significance that links social context and disease behavior. The various factors that influence the structure of illness behavior range across the levels of systems within which the individual functions (microneurological systems to macrocultural systems). At the subjective level of interpretation, bodily stimuli are experienced and are interpreted conceptually.

This interpretation of experience and whether or how the incipient illness is integrated into the self-system has important clinical implications. For example, Levy (1982) analyzed the cognitive construction that a sample of male patients imposed on symptoms associated with a developing myocardial infarction. There were wide individual differences in the extent to which these symptoms were validly interpreted. Moreover, delay in seeking help was associated in large part with the character of the construction placed upon the developing symptom pattern. Patients who delayed the longest (up to 18 hours in one case) were those who had had previous heart attacks and yet still failed to "retrospectively reconstruct" or fit their new infarction into their life history. That is, those who failed to make sense of what had happened to them physically and who continued to fail to integrate their physical status into their personal biography also tended to behave inappropriately in terms of their altered cardiovascular status. (The inability of these patients to integrate physical experience into their total lives was not significantly related to their intellectual capacity.)

In Cassel's (1976) discussion of symptoms and organs as being conceived of as separate from the self, he suggests the use of language as a therapeutic tool to reduce this distancing tendency. If, in fact, language functions as a final shaper of reality (Merleau-Ponty, 1962), then the fostering of particular language patterns might alter the individual's construct of his or her personal reality. The question of health care techniques that take into account patient characteristics and prerogatives will be the specific focus of concern in a later section of this chapter. The sharing of medical wisdom and the place of language will be addressed more fully at that point.

In a somewhat speculative vein, Fabrega (1979) hypothesizes that the surface appearance as well as the type and structure of behavior associated with diseases (for example, behavior typical of a heart attack—chills, "cold sweat," and altered sensorium) may be partly dependent on the kind of "reading" that the temporal–frontal cortical areas make on lower subcortical and brain stem changes. "Such a reading is hypothesized to be based on the meaning of cultural symbols that initially played a role in programming the brain" (p. 574). Teasing apart behaviors which are universal manifestations of a particular physical disorder from those that may vary cross-culturally bears on the question of the social shaping of neurologically encoded meaning which then becomes reflected in illness behavior. In Schwartz's (1980) discussion of behavioral medicine and systems theory, he points out that humans function as systems that are inseparately linked to other systems within and without the organism. "Processes at one level can modulate processes at another. This realization is crucial. Processes at the cellular level can influence behavior; conversely behavior can influence physical disease. The important point to remember is that complex interactions occur both *within* every level and across levels" (p. 28). The mechanisms of translation from culture to cell remain the unknown for biobehaviorists to unravel.

Returning to the immediate point, patients cognitively interpret and integrate their illness experience. This process happens willy-nilly as a characteristic of human functioning. But motives can be shaped by learning alternative constructions for experience. "Physiological states in human beings give rise to purposes when they are harnessed to conceptual schemes" (Lindesmith & Strauss, 1975, p. 159). Obviously, individuals cannot express purposes or rationalize behavior in terms that they have not learned. In the dual process of health delivery, it remains in large part the responsibility of the expert provider to give the patient linguistic and conceptual tools for the proper interpretation of health-relevant experience.

1.3. Initiator Expertise

In our health care system, access generally depends on patient initiative. The ethics of most health professions constrain solicitation of requests for service. This posture is changing somewhat as more and more emphasis is placed on outreach programs and patient "reminders." But it is still assumed that potential patients or their representatives must take the initiative in bringing providers and recipients of care together.

Certain institutions may require applicants, employees, or inmates to have their health or illness status confirmed and certified by a health professional if they are to become or remain members in good standing (Parsons, 1951; Waitzkin & Waterman, 1974). Even in these situations, however, the lay persons involved must initiate the interaction with health professionals by appearing at sick call, scheduling an examination, and so on.

It is also important to recognize that the continuation of provider–patient relationships generally depends on patient initiative, especially in the case of outpatients. Inpatients may find themselves in a more passive position. Once they have been institutionalized, voluntarily or involuntarily, they may lose their prerogatives to initiate interactions with health professionals. Follow-up visits and more routine contact may be totally at the discretion of providers.

For this reason an inpatient focus is more doctor-centric than an outpatient perspective. When they are housed in the workshops of physicians, patients lose some of their autonomy. The magnitude of the loss depends in part on the status of the patients involved and their capacity or incapacity to leave the institution. Lower-income patients in nursing homes may have virtually no power to initiate visits with their doctors, who may schedule appearances on a routine basis and examine every patient in the institution during one visit. In contrast, wealthy inpatients may have considerable leverage over the visiting habits of their physicians.

Taking the initiative in health care should, therefore, be regarded as a role obligation of patients-to-be, outpatients involved in ongoing care, and certain categories of inpatients. To be a competent initiator of action vis-à-vis medical systems requires a special expertise that cannot generally be usurped by health professionals. Although some practitioners play the role of patient advocates, channeling care seekers through the complexities of medical systems, most patients are on their own, especially if they are ambulatory.

Somewhat analogous to the initiator role is the lay-referral role played by many patients. As Freidson has observed (1960), lay persons have a unique function in the referral network, directing other lay people toward, back toward, or away from certain practitioners in their mental file. They serve in a triage capacity in the first instance of another's need or as validators or negators of medical advice their peers have received elsewhere.

The lay-referral role is one set of behaviors that can be duplicated by health professionals. But for the very reason that they are professionals, they are bypassed by lay persons who prefer a more familiar folk assessment of the situation. In Igun's (1979) cross-cultural study of health-seeking behavior, the participation of significant others in lay diagnosis and referral was an inseparable part of the treatment strategy. Because the individual's illness disrupted role behaviors within the entire family context, the family members assessed the appropriateness of treatment sources, initiated treatments, assessed a particular treatment's effectiveness, and altered treatment sources where they felt it was warranted.

Levy's (1982) study analyzing the experience of undergoing a heart attack traced the cognitive construction of a new perceptual reality—the dawning realization that the person was no longer in an everyday, familiar mode but in a different reality status involving a life-threatening event. Over time, this new reality of cardiac crisis ultimately entailed social consequences, and necessarily so if the individual was to survive. That is, the experience tended to be transitive in the sense that others were verbally or behaviorally called on to intervene as the individual gradually or suddenly lost energy as an independent agent. In fact, as several analysts (Hackett & Cassem, 1969; Moss, Wynar, & Goldstein, 1969) have pointed out, social others play an important role in the final decision to ask for expert help. It would seem reasonable to assume that an interaction may occur between the individual's dawning awareness of what is happening to him or her and the confirmation of this new definition by others in any position to react to the stress:

> I got dizzy. I got up to go into the house . . . I got up out of the chair and I fell down. I couldn't stand. I wasn't sure if I was having angina. My wife called the voluntary ambulance . . . I guess I was white as a ghost. Two girls came with the ambulance, and they thought they should take me in. I said okay.

> About five o'clock—six o'clock . . . before supper . . . I had another attack. We both decided after a few minutes that it was my heart.

> I was by myself. I got help from next door. It was a half hour before I got anybody. I insisted that I go home, even though they wanted to take me to the hospital. My family—my brother, sister, and wife—insisted I go to the hospital. I didn't go in until my family physician advised me that it was the only thing to do.

This last phase of helplessness and giving up of total autonomy can be very difficult. The only subject in that study who died during hospitalization repeatedly said during his interview, "I tell myself that sergeants never get sick. . . . I've been a pusher all my life." Another patient reported: "It occurred to me that I was having a heart attack. . . . I was having pain for a long time. This went on for 30 to 40 minutes. But somebody else called the ambulance . . . I never asked." At some point the social world intrudes, if only to discover a death that has already occurred. Even then the event is inherently social in the sense that others—spouse, coroner, police, the media, and so on—interpret the death and give it meaning.

In a recent article by Alonzo (1979), the author developed the point that illness and pathology may not be reported because people are able to *contain* signs and symptoms within socially defined situations. Examples of factors that allow the individual to contain symptoms of illness include engrossment in ongoing activity, other sources of explanation for disordered behavior (e.g., the aging process), and available resources that enable one to remain in the everyday situation despite decreased ability to function.

Finally, even when a person initiates health-seeking behavior, the actual appeal for treatment may have to be legitimatized (Albert, 1980). In order to be taken seriously, patients tend to present complaints as "obvious for the seeing" rather than as cognitive constructs that were developed over time. "Patient understanding of physical problems involves a process of construction that, in the end, results in an event being seen to be obvious from the outset, rather than construed and understood over the course of its discovery" (p. 243). For Albert, treatment becomes an achievement for the patient. Self-evidence of the problem is what "opens the doors of emergency rooms" and makes treatment warrantable. "The product, in this case a treatable disfunction, is often a simulation of the 'real' professional item. It is arrived at by quite different methodological processes, not by diagnostics but by contexting it in everyday structures" (p. 250). Albert points out that this differential process of arriving at a diagnostic endpoint is not due to the patient's inability to grasp medical facts but rather to the "constitutive differences between the lay and professional enterprises" (p. 250).

That is, the process of arriving at the negotiated treatment reality is radically distinct for the lay and professional people involved.

In discussing the concept of initiator expertise, we have focused on the patient's role in initiating contact with health care systems. We could have adopted a broader perspective. Once a patient has asked for help, initiative is also required in implementing treatment strategies. As mentioned earlier, this is especially true in the outpatient setting, but even inpatients (except the most debilitated) are capable of creating counterrealities and of thwarting or enhancing treatment plans. For heuristic purposes, we have considered this type of initiative to be a different manifestation of behavioral autonomy, to be discussed below.

1.4. Informative Expertise

The power of consent to medical procedures and experimentation rests with the patients or their legal representatives. According to current rules and regulations, that consent must be informed and voluntary. Information and the freedom to act on it provide the bases for decision-making power.

In the diagnostic and therapeutic situation, the meaning of *informed consent* is more open to interpretation than in the research context, where federal regulations have defined the concept rigorously. Candidates for medical research must be specifically informed about procedures and purposes, risks and benefits, alternative options, their right to terminate participation without prejudice, and their right to question the staff regarding procedures (DHEW, 1978 a,b). They must also be advised whether treatment or monetary compensation will be provided if injuries occur during the research (*Federal Register*, 1978).

The voluntary aspect of informed consent has been defined by DHEW as the "free power of choice without undue inducement or any element of force, fraud, deceit, duress, or other form of constraint or coercion" (DHEW, 1978b). Obviously, a well-informed patient is less vulnerable to fraud and deceit than an uninformed one, but knowledge does not guarantee freedom of choice. This freedom is also a function of the patient's cognitive and emotional disengagement from the subtle inducements, constraints, and pressures that frequently characterize doctor–patient relationships. Disengagement is particularly difficult when consent must be given during times of stress.

Assuming informed consent to be more than a paper-signing ritual, patients are vested with a domain of competence and control independent of health professionals. The processing and internalization of information relevant to the potential risks and benefits of alternative modes of care requires a special expertise on the part of patients. To assess rationally the pros and cons of available options when one is anxious, fearful, and vulnerable to persuasion is a difficult task at best (Cassileth, Lupkis, Sutton-Smith, & March, 1980; Gray, 1975; Hassar & Weintraub, 1976; Schultz, Pardee, & Ensinck, 1975), but patients are nevertheless obligated to perform it on their own behalf. The only way they can be legitimately excused from the informed consent process is to be proved legally incompetent.

There is perhaps an ethically ambiguous state where patients are conscious and not judged to be incompetent to give consent but where the situation makes rational judgment and decision making nearly impossible. For example, Smith (1974) analyzed the process of seeking consent in an emergency situation from cardiac patients who were asked to undergo a cardiac catheterization procedure. He found that at the time these consents were needed, the majority of patients could have been classified functionally with mental incompetents or children. Nevertheless, consent had to be obtained, and for the most part the process made a mockery of the intent of the law. Smith argues that under circumstances such as these, the observance of "reasonable care" (the converse of the "do no harm" dictum), with responsibility for the patient's welfare resting solely on the physician's judgment, would fulfill the clinical investigator's responsibility to the patient. "The formal requirement of (patient) consent, on the other hand, may allow precisely what the physician is morally forbidden to do; stifle the spirit of a law by observing it to the letter" (p. 403).

Where the exigencies of the moment make meaningful informed consent impossible, patients or their guardians may strike a provisional compromise with the powers that be. They may elect to join a trial or begin a therapeutic regimen on a temporary basis with the implicit or explicit understanding that they will reevaluate their participation when they are more capable of being rational and detached. Obviously, provisional participation is possible only where the therapy or procedure is ongoing and revocable. Radical surgery would not be a case in point; neither would cardiac catherization in the example given earlier. On the other hand, it could be argued that every consent in long-term clinical trials is provisional because the patient always has the option to withdraw. One's commitment to participate is never binding in a contractual sense (Fletcher, Branson, & Freireich, 1979; Levine & Lebacqz, 1979).

According to the literature, informed consent in ideal terms is rarely achieved. Although patients have a right and duty to choose treatment for themselves, they appear to have considerable difficulty understanding and remembering basic facts about the procedures involved, even those to which they have given consent (Epstein & Lasagna, 1969; Gray, 1975; Hassar & Weintraub, 1976; Howard, DeMets, & BHAT Research Group, 1981; Kennedy & Lillehaugen, 1979; Leeb, Bowers, & Lynch, 1976; Robinson & Merav, 1976). However, there is evidence to suggest that the average patient is capable of comprehending and retaining this information if he or she has a reasonable opportunity to digest and absorb it (Woodward, 1979). To maximize that opportunity, curious patients and their families may profit from an active personal quest for relevant facts about the studies or procedures in question (Bergler, Pennington, Metcalfe, & Freis, 1980; Howard, DeMets, & BHAT Research Group, 1981).

Some recent research (Krantz, Baum, & Wideman, 1980; Schain, 1980) has addressed the issue of individual differences in information seeking related to patients' typical coping styles. The findings reported by Schain suggest that patients do better when the amount and quality of information they receive is consistent with their coping strategy. Before they underwent a painful gynecological examination, patients were categorized as "monitors" (information seekers) or "blunters" (stoic, uninquisitive participants). Half the patients in each group were given either high or low levels of information regarding the medical procedure, and subsequent distress levels were measured. Results showed that for monitors, high information reduced pain during the procedure and hostility afterward, but it increased anxiety before and after the examination. On the other hand, blunters showed greater psychological benefit when they were given minimal information. This latter condition was associated with less anxiety, depression, discomfort, and psychophysiological arousal before and after the examination.

Although these are only preliminary findings from an ongoing study, they at least raise the issue of whether there should be some attempt to take into account the coping strategies of individual patients and to gear the information process accordingly. Obviously, enough information has to be imparted to allow the patient a considered choice, but the need to know is probably not uniform across patients. What is no more than informative for one person may be cognitively overwhelming for another.

Efforts are being made to enhance the decision-making competence of patients through formal and informal safeguards, as exemplified by institutional review boards and ombudsmen. These organizational structures buttress the autonomy and power of patients vis-à-vis health practitioners by mandating that experienced third parties enter the decision-making context as impartial referees or allies of the patient. Professional third hands make it possible for patients to function within the bounds of their own competence without having to digest and evaluate information that only professionals can readily comprehend.

The judicial system also plays a critical role in protecting patients and putting the concept of informed consent into operation. In carrying out these functions, the courts appear to be guided by their perceptions of what reasonable, average people need to know to make informed choices (*Truman vs. Thomas*, 1980). The patient who is not average may be offered individualized protection through judicial mandates that recognize unique concerns and the need to tailor disclosures accordingly.

In essence, the doctrine of informed consent is a doctrine of self-determination for patients. The traditional paternalistic role of health practitioners is being defined as illegal and immoral if it perpetuates a monopoly of knowledge and stifles patients' independence. Under certain conditions, health providers may know better than patients what is in the patient's best interest—what "gamble" he or she should elect. But modern rules and regulations forbid health professionals to implement their insight, benevolence, and will except by convincing the patient of the wisdom of their perspective. Trust in the physician is not an acceptable substitute for informed consent. Patients have the right to include trust—or its antithesis—in their decision-making equation, but they must do so of their own free will. At the very least, intentional choice is an ideal toward which continual strides must be made. In the final analysis, consent rests with patients, because they are the only ones who have a patient's stake in the consequences.

1.5. Implementive Expertise

Health professionals have essentially no power to control the deleterious behavior of patients outside the walls of medical workshops. Professional expertise is irrelevant in this larger world unless it is transferred in some manner to the actors involved. Astute health practitioners try to socialize patients to their professional set of norms regarding health and illness behavior. But the extent to which patients internalize these norms is highly variable (Leventhal, 1975). Acceptance appears to depend on ingredients of the professional–patient relationship, the patient's level of education, and a host of other factors relevant to motivation, uncertainty, and the character of the medical problem.

In direct care giver–patient relationships, patients remain free to "turn off" the interaction at any time or implicitly or explicitly to negotiate the outcome. Korsch, Gozzi, and Francis (1968) found that the report of patient satisfaction following visits with health care providers was a direct function of the professional's friendliness, provision of clear-cut explanations, and ability to consider the patient's expectations for the visit. Based on a content analysis of the professional–patient interactions, a critical point within the interviews seemed to be reached when the expert repeatedly failed to hear the patient's question. At that point, most patients simply "turned off" the interaction and stopped listening themselves.

Some investigators (Emerson, 1975; Scheff, 1975) have emphasized the power of professionals in the interviewing and examining context due to the differential status of providers and patients. However, patients rarely if ever give up their autonomy entirely, and they may manipulate the treatment situation in a covert fashion to maintain control of the process with some degree of comfort. This is illustrated in Hayes-Bautista's (1976) study of Chicano patients, whom he asked to remember the character of their last medical treatment. He then abstracted tactics that these patients used for modifying the treatment plan according to their own wishes. These tactics included what Hayes-Bautista called *convincing* and *countering* moves, coupled with *countermanaging* tactics by the professionals, and finally levels of *bargaining* that took place. Among the convincing tactics were leading questions to alert care givers to situational aspects that had not been taken into account as well as demands for treatment modification and threats to terminate therapy. Examples of countering tactics included augmenting the treatment regimen with additional home remedies or deliberately reducing dosage levels without the knowledge or agreement of the health professional.

When the expert became aware of these attempts by patients to control the care delivery process, countermanaging tactics were utilized. These included attempts to convince the patient with overwhelming professional knowledge and experience or asking the patient "as friend" to do the care giver a favor by complying with the treatment regimen. Not infrequently, bilateral bargaining was entered into, with some modification of treatment being allowed. The professional regarded some cooperation on the part of the patient as better than none.

In this same vein, Albrecht (1977) studied a sample of dental patients and concluded that the ensuing diagnosis and treatment plan was the result of a negotiating process. Dentists and patients frequently had different agendas and perspectives with respect to the importance of some diagnostic outcome (malocclusion, for example). What was treated—and how—was the result of a bargain struck by symbiotic partners in this health care context.

Although the issue of independence and patient autonomy is of clear importance in outpatient settings, the autonomy of inpatients takes on a more subtle character. Certainly the lives of inpatients are more circumscribed and constricted. Their limited geographical mobility, the absence of family and friends to intervene on their behalf, and the greater severity of their illnesses make them more vulnerable and dependent. Even inpatients, however, have some control over their destinies. They are not simply puppets who perform in accord with provider expectations. This is clearly illustrated in Goldstein's (1971) study, where the patients tended to behave as passively ill in order to be taken care of, while the staff "pushed for" independence of functioning. Yet there was an unspoken agreement between staff and patients that as long as the patients were "good," the staff would not be "mean" and withhold basic social sustenance from them.

Strauss (1978), in a chapter concerned with the silent bargains between staff and patients on geriatric wards, amplifies Goldstein's clinical observations. Due to lack of funding and inadequate personnel, these elderly patients tended to be managed on a tight schedule, although they were frequently in pain and were also socially isolated. The silent bargain to which Strauss refers involved the willingness of these patients, in return for small favors and social contact, to tolerate pain at intervals so as to fit their needs into a staff routine. Strauss describes this mutual negotiation process in some detail, and certainly interactions of this nature are important to examine, both as a one-way behavioral shaping process and as a two-way social exchange.

The concept of treatment compliance as typically conceived in the research literature recognizes the capacity of patients to be autonomous. Compliance is defined as "the extent to which a person's behavior (for example, taking medications, following diets, or changing life styles) coincides with medical or health advice" (Haynes, Taylor, & Sackett, 1979). One of the most consistent findings in the compliance literature is that the physician–patient relationship is significantly associated with the degree of patient cooperation. Continuity of care and empathic communication patterns between physicians and their patients tend to increase patient compliance. A certain mutuality in the relationship and an acknowledgement of the patient as an autonomous actor or agent would also seem to be implied in such findings.

In one study of pediatric cancer patients (Smith, Rosen, Trueworthy, & Lowman, 1979), it was found that older adolescent outpatients were significantly less likely to take their oral prescriptions of prednisone than were younger patients. The author speculated that the nature of the side effects—weight gain and skin blemishes—may have been particularly salient for that age group. Their noncompliance in this case was based on a refusal to initiate activity because of significant problems in integrating poor body image into their self-concept and relationships with peers. For these patients, the meaning of potential recurrence of cancer had to be understood within the context of their social lives at that point.

Patient autonomy is an inherent characteristic of patients as persons and is pervasive across health care contexts. Appreciation for patient power may force health professionals to take into account the patient's perspective and openly negotiate a workable treatment plan. Alternatively, if this awareness and openness of communication is missing, a unilateral plan of action may be adopted by the patient as the one who has the greatest investment in the care process and its outcome. Thus, of course, the dual nature of the bargaining process will be lost, subsumed by the patient's autonomous decisions in his or her own behalf.

2. Patient-Centric Technologies—Unilateral and Shared

In this chapter, the term *technology* is being used in its broadest sense. Webster's second definition of the word is "a technical method of achieving a practical purpose." In this case, of course, the practical purpose is health care. The methods for achieving that end, taking into account the inherent patient capacities detailed above, range from patient technologies entirely separate from professional health care providers to technologies shared by professionals and patients. Clearly, following from what has been said earlier, health care technologies can never exist entirely apart from patient influence, even if they are directly controlled by health professionals.

2.1. Unilateral Technologies

The concept of patient-centric technology distinguishes a particular set of instruments and practices from those within the doctor-centric category. Access to these technologies and the knowledge and skills required for their use are controlled by patients; utilization usually takes place within the workshops of patients—in their homes, jobs, recreational milieu, and therapeutic communities dominated by lay people.

Unlike those of doctor-centric technologies, tools in the workshops of patients tend to be soft rather than hard and oriented toward chronic illness rather than acute care. Some instruments and devices could be considered hardware (for example, artificial limbs, hearing aids, dialysis units, oxygen machines, telephones, and thermometers). But at the present stage of their development, patient-centric technologies are primarily focused on personal and interpersonal skills rather than instrumentation, and behavioral science is more relevant than physics, chemistry, or engineering.

In the five areas described above, technologies that capitalize on the exclusive expertise of patients are beginning to emerge. Thus, we see an increasing interest in peer self-help groups and interactional techniques that emphasize empathic skills and comprehensive care of whole persons. Men and women with a vast assortment of chronic illnesses, from alcoholism to breast cancer, have joined therapeutic forces mutually to exploit common problems, perspectives, and experiences. Patients at high risk of developing lethal and disabling disorders such as coronary disease are also grouping together to help control self-destructive behavior patterns.

Algorithms for self-care are enhancing the medical sophistication of adults and children in their day-to-day activities and are rationalizing processes of self and lay referral (Vickery & Fries, 1976). Healthy people and the chronically ill are learning to diagnose, monitor, and treat their own symptoms and to call for appropriate professional help selectively when their lay experience needs confirmation and assistance. For example, the practice of breast self-examination (BSE) for cancer detection has increased women's ability to distinguish normal from potentially malignant breast tissue (Hall, Adam, Stein, Stephenson, Goldstein, & Pennypacker, 1980). There is evidence that the practice of BSE leads to earlier detection of breast cancer (Foster, Lang, Costanza, Worden, Haines, & Yates, 1978; Greenwald, Nasca, Lawrence, Horton, McGarrah, Gabriele, & Carlton, 1978) and that earlier detection (and hence earlier treatment in the disease trajectory) is associated with better disease outcome (Wilkinson, Edgerton, Wallace, Reese, Patterson, & Priore, 1979; Worden & Weisman, 1975). Survival rates for women with diagnosed breast cancer who practiced BSE are currently being evaluated (Foster, 1981), but the presumption at this point is that, when transferred to the lay public, this technology does enhance survival.

More generally, self-care enthusiasts in the feminist movement are claiming and staking out jurisdictions of diagnosis and treatment traditionally reserved for doctors (Ruzek, 1978). These women are formulating ideologies and tactics that protect their lay-oriented technologies from professional dominance and cooptation. Their right to purchase and use the hardware of the medical establishment (for example, a speculum) has been challenged, but their softer technologies involving education and indoctrination may be less susceptible to professional scrutiny and control.

Self-help and peer-help groups are exploding onto the health care scene, although the notion of mutual aid is as old as humanity itself (Lieberman, Borman, and Associates, 1979), and some additional caveats need to be made with respect to their usefulness for patients. Some recent analysts (Gartner & Riessman, 1977; Kronenfeld, 1979) have begun to assess implications for health care inherent within the peer-help movement. For example, one potential result of placing responsibility for the patient's welfare onto the patient is the possibility of blaming the victim. By emphasizing *self*-help as a means of improving one's welfare, these approaches may tend to divert energy away from the structural and system-oriented transformations that are necessary to deal with many sources of illness (such as environmental pollution).

Gartner and Riessman (1977) elaborate on this idea in discussing dangers inherent in the professionalization of patients. In seeking to "service" themselves and their fellow sufferers as they were once "serviced" by professional helpers, patients tend to deal less with causes of a current disorder and more with symptoms and cures for it. As professionalized clients, they are more concerned with how they feel or who is helping rather than what works, "They do not look to causes (environmental factors, economic disturbances, genetic endowment, and individual and group behavior), but to what makes them feel better. . . . They apply professional solutions as a reflex and thus are only as effective or appropriate as the professionals they mimic. In actuality, they expand professional hegemony and constitute a political illusion" (p. 124).

Another potential danger in the peer-led health movements is the perpetuation of inequities in health care delivery. When neighborhood paraprofessionals become key agents in developing self-help approaches for underserved populations, "the poor may get self-help, while the rich get professional services") (Gartner & Riessman, 1977, p. 123).

Of course, there then remains the empirical question of peer-group efficacy in achieving health aims. As Kronenfeld (1979) points out, groups like those represented by the women's health movement have provided no data suggesting improvement in health status for their members. In fact, there is currently a dearth of careful investigations regarding the process and outcome of peer-led health efforts—who these various groups help and how (Levy, 1979).

Although self-care within a peer-help process is not a panacea for the ills of the health care system, self-help groups can play an important role within the process of health care delivery. They can function as patient-advocate forces (as parents of retarded children have in the past) as well as supplying individual health care support. Despite the dangers of encapsulation, these groups can also act as a stimulus for social change, potentially affecting the nation's health in a positive direction.

2.2. Shared Technologies

Verbal and nonverbal communication—but primarily the former—provide a link between the professional's world and the patient's perspective.

The communication involved in the process of obtaining informed consent is legally mandated, but mandates are merely points of departure. Attempts to effectuate the decision making power of patients in experimental and nonexperimental situations have highlighted the need for new and improved technologies in this area. Social scientists have identified forces in the environments of medical research that undermine the possibility of informed voluntary consent (Barber, 1976; Gray, 1975). These findings make clear the patients' vulnerability to professional paternalism, and they spell out parameters of decision-making autonomy (for example, signing consent forms at home instead of in the hospital). What we also see emerging are algorithms for informed consent that specify the kinds of information to be shared with patients as well as the sophistication or simplicity of the language involved.

The level of difficulty of the language used in consent forms is an important consideration in any discussion of comprehension. Morrow (1980) analyzed the readability of forms used in a larger study of the process of informed consent. He concluded that the readability level more closely resembled that of the *New England Journal of Medicine* than of the popular press. Since only about 25% of the U.S. population has any college education, this finding was interesting indeed. Morrow suggested that, at the least, forms should be written in short declarative sentences and that patients should review them for clarity and readability as such forms are developed.

In addition to algorithms concerned with the language of the consent process, techniques are being developed for conveying the idea of probability and uncertainty and for identifying conditions that require the presence of guardians as ombudsmen. As these algorithms are further refined, tested, and applied, candidates for medical experimentation will become more cognizant of their options and less vulnerable to persuasion.

More basic perhaps than formal communication is the broader concept of sharing professional wisdom and developing a partnership between patients and care givers. In the process of perfecting their own technologies, patients will have to wrest certain kinds of power from doctors and gain access to certain kinds of tools. At a minimum they must share the power conferred by knowledge. Physicians can no longer act like high priests who, as "insiders," have a monopoly over enlightenment. Women's collectives and other self-help groups are teaching lay people communication skills that can facilitate egalitarian dialogues with health professionals (Ruzek, 1978).

Trained peers may actually be better teachers of patients than physicians, because doctors learn to impart their wisdom to colleagues, not lay people. Fox (1975) believes this posture is changing—that the "new" medical student is motivated to converse with the patient in a language both understand. According to Waitzkin and Waterman (1974), the quality and quantity of information exchanged in such dialogues will vary with the social positions of the patients involved. Working-class patients apparently have a more restricted (less elaborated) code of communication than the middle class. If this is true, lower-class patients may need to learn a different technology of communicating with doctors than they now employ; in dialogues with these patients, doctors may need to adapt and respond to a different communicative style than they use themselves.

Thus, in the area of soft technologies, jurisdictional boundaries are fuzzier than for the hard tools. Because soft technologies relate to personal and interpersonal skills, multiple participants are often involved. To maximize the quality of their health care, patients will have to maximize the quality of their relationships with doctors in a middle land that intersects and connects the exclusive domains of physicians and patients. In this middle land, sharing the use of a technology is not necessarily to usurp it or to part with power.

It is, in fact, possible that in sharing with patients certain technologies such as knowledge, physicians may enhance rather than diminish their power. Since patients control their own destinies outside the workshops of physicians, the only way health professionals can influence those destinies is to transfer some of their wisdom to patients. In this way they can also combat and neutralize the power of vested interests such as drug companies and equipment manufacturers who continuously propagandize patients. Analogously, since doctors have certain skills and tools at their disposal that patients cannot begin to duplicate, the only way patients can appropriately exploit those technologies is to share with physicians the products of their own areas of competence, such as their experimental and integrative expertise.

In recent years, various aspects of the communication process between patients and professionals have been studied empirically (Roter, 1977; Stiles, Putnam, James & Wolf, 1979; Waitzkin, 1979). Waitzkin found that although the average time spent in information transmission from physician to patient was actually $1\frac{1}{3}$ minutes, the professionals considerably overestimated this figure (mean time estimates equaled $7\frac{1}{2}$ minutes). However, they underestimated the patient's desire for information. (Women patients and those with poor prognoses received more information, while working class patients received significantly less information than the middle class.) Roter (1977) found that when patients were trained to ask questions, the patient–provider interaction was characterized by negative affect, anxiety, and anger. This latter finding suggests that, as in any transition period where role responsibilities are shifting, conflict can occur.

Perhaps, through techniques to be discussed later, professionals can be trained to accept assertive patients who, by their questioning, demand a collaborative alliance.

In a more differentiated analysis of the expert–patient interview process, Stiles and his colleagues (1979) measured three interview characteristics—attentiveness, acquiescence, and presumptuousness. Patient satisfaction, assessed by postinterview questionnaire, was positively correlated with physician acquiescence (allowing the other's viewpoint to determine the course of conversation); but this was true only during the conclusion of the interview, not during the history-taking or examination components. Patients were also more satisfied when they expressed themselves in their own words during the history taking and when the experts were more informative at the conclusion of the interview. The point to be drawn from this study is that the process of collaboration between patient and professional may be a shifting and complex process. More refined and systematic scrutiny of this exchange, such as that carried out by Stiles and his associates, would appear to be warranted.

Finally, communication of wisdom on the part of the professional may have clinical implications. As Cassel (1976) suggested, language can be used therapeutically to help the patient integrate symptom experience into his or her sense of self. Again, however, the caution must be raised that there are individual differences in the need to know. Thus, the prediction of information coping styles—represented, for example, in the work of Krantz *et al.* (1980) remains an important clinical research objective.*

2.3. Emergent Inventory of Patient Tools and Skills

A complete inventory of existing and potential instruments and practices in the patient's domain is impossible at this time. The doctor-centric/hard technology bias tends to tunnel the vision of observers and root them in the past rather than the future. The characteristics of patient-centric and middle-land technologies are still to be determined as patients become more autonomous partners in health care relationships.

Yet it is reasonable to assume that any typology of patient technologies will include the following tools and skills in addition to many more: monitoring devices such as portometers and thermometers; communication devices such as telephones; communication techniques that direct conversation to relevant areas, reduce extraneous noise, and magnify the clarity of interpersonal expression; algorithms that guide self-care and signal the need for professional assistance; various levels of medical knowledge that rationalize behavioral control and expedite dialogues with health professionals; protagonists and intermediaries who

*In considering shared technologies, we have focused primarily on processes of communication that can link professionals and patients in collaborative endeavors. Our perspective reflects the clinical orientation of this chapter and the fact that communication is the key to partnerships that reach beyond diagnostic and therapeutic settings. Amalgamations of providers and consumers of care can also take the form of structures and alliances that yield power in the political arena. They can become instruments of social change to modify modes of health care delivery and sources of disease within the larger society.

buttress the power of patients and facilitate access to needed resources; organizational and interactional skills that enhance the capacity of patients to identify relevant peers, inspire a consciousness of kind, and profitably exploit that common identity.

Approaches that augment the patient's capacity to experience and integrate ongoing reality into the self-system, such as cognitive–behavioral techniques (Mahoney, 1974; Marlatt, 1976; Stuart, 1977), are part of this emergent inventory of patient-centric technologies. For example, Johnson and Leventhal (1974) reported the results of a study involving patients who were about to undergo an endoscopic examination. This is a rather painful, unpleasant experience involving the swallowing of a fiberoptic tube and retaining it for 15 to 30 minutes. Patients must be awake for the procedure and follow instructions. The investigators developed a preparatory message that described the probable sensory experience generated by the endoscopic examination. A second message delivered to a comparison group was developed to maximize patients' ability to perform the behavior requested by the physician. The sensory description was expected to eliminate idiosyncratic interpretations of the experience and to reduce emotional response, while the behavioral instruction was expected to reduce gagging and time for tube swallowing.

Group differences in outcome showed that patients in the sensory-description condition alone had more stable heart rates and required significantly less tranquilizing agents than control patients who received neither message. This manipulation also reduced gagging, but it had no effect on time for tube passage. In contrast, the group that received both sensory and behavioral information had a reduction in gagging but an increase in time for tube passage. This latter effect was due to the patients' opportunity to control their own rate of swallowing.

Cognitive–behavioral manipulations such as these build on patients' inherent capacities to imagine, predict, and exercise self-control. They can thus be viewed as tools that augment existing skills of individuals. Other techniques described in the literature recently could also be viewed as augmenting the patient's inherent skills (Currie & Renner, 1979; Davis, 1980). With respect to the context of treatment, Davis reported the results of a demonstration effort to convert an inpatient rehabilitation ward into a learning environment. Techniques such as goal setting, public goal-setting commitment, and patient modeling of the behavior change process for other patients were used to capitalize on patients' skills in that context.

The exercise of patient prerogatives, including consent form review and collaboration in form preparation, is consistent with a general view of the patient as assertive within the health care context. In Roter's (1977) study of lower-income predominantly minority patients, she randomly assigned subjects to an experimental group that was taught how to ask questions of professionals during an interview. This training involved the modeling of persistent behavior if questions were not answered or answers were not understood. Although, as indicated earlier, experimental patients were viewed more negatively by health care providers and were less satisfied postinterview than the control group, they demonstrated a higher ratio of appointment keeping during a 4-month follow-up period. It would seem that one effect of increasing the patients' perceptions of their own power of initiative was a collaborative engagement with the care process. As Kronenfeld (1979) has suggested, providers of care may need to develop more tolerance for aggressive patients. Perhaps a realization of the positive effects of assertiveness—greater engagement with the care process and increased compliance—may make patient inquisitiveness easier to bear.

Any inventory of patient tools and skills should include political technologies that make medical systems more accessible to patients and more responsive to their needs. These political practices may be pursued by individuals or by collectivities of patients. They may simply be personalized manipulations that cut through bureaucratic red tape and beat impersonal systems out of their inertia and uniform modes of action. They may also be collective forces that wrest shares of power from the medical establishment. And, perhaps, the idea of political technology should include the process of alienation that pulls the disenfranchised away from orthodox medical systems toward self-help groups such as the family. However, it is important to consider the caveat offered by Gartner and Riessman (1977) with respect to loss of power through fragmentation. "While there is an enormous role for deinstitutionalized local participation and small group forms, these must be integrated with changes of national scope. Small is beautiful only if it is a part of what is large and functional" (p. 122).

Sidel and Sidel (1976) have developed the notion of a *dual* role for self-help groups as alternatives to traditional care services. These groups must do more than deal with people with particular medical problems. They must also assume the responsibility of humanizing professionals. An example of this is provided by Gartner and Riessman (1977) in their discussion of the Center for Independent Living (CIL). Originally founded at Berkeley by handicapped students, this organization has grown in membership and performs multiple advocacy and training functions for disabled persons (sex counseling, financial advocacy, health care training, etc.). In this case, the humanizing of professionals (as well as the general public) involves securing civil rights for the handicapped as well as providing them with access to health care and behavioral opportunities.

More generally, Geiger (1975) views the rise of consumerism as a major source of humanization of health care. The organization of lay people to share with professionals the management of human services helps to promote a power balance by "requiring professionals to interact with and have some accountability to the organized lay public" (pp. 34–35). Of course, professionals do not always give up or share their power willingly.

For the most part, the consumer movement in health care has been expressed in self-help groups of one variety or another. The views of these groups toward the professional community vary, ranging from active rejection to coordination of services. Gartner and Riessman (1977) developed a series of models for professional involvement with lay groups, ranging from professionals functioning as coproviders of service and trainers of paraprofessionals to being referral sources for patient follow-up support and providers of consultation services.

Levy (1978) conducted a national survey concerned with how self-help groups are viewed by professionals. He reported that although the majority of professional respondents believed that peer groups could play a role in the delivery of service, only 31% believed that the probability was high that their agencies would be interested in integrating their services with such groups. In recent years, the medical profession and federal government have paid attention to groups such as DES Action, the national organization concerned with the effect of diethylstilbestrol on the offspring of women for whom the drug was prescribed during pregnancy. But we are still some distance from a truly collaborative and balanced professional–consumer health delivery system.

3. Health Care Delivery as a Bidirectional Process

In spite of emergent trends, patient-centric technologies can be considered embryonic at best. Their development is comparable to doctor-centric technologies at the stage when laying on hands was essentially the only tool in the physician's kit. Doctors are partly to blame for the retarded growth of patient technologies. They control access to critical diagnostic and therapeutic techniques and, as noted above, have been reluctant to share that power with patients.

This reluctance to share and collaborate with patients has implications for the training of professionals. Increasingly, articles are appearing in the professional literature (Bertman & Krant, 1977; Innes, 1977) addressing the professional's lack of empathy with patients coupled with insufficient communication skills. Poole and Sanson-Fisher (1979) reported findings from two studies which showed that medical students at the beginning of their training were able to empathize accurately with the patients only minimally and did not improve with the passage of time. In one experimental condition, "empathy training"—modeled on a Rogerian approach—was introduced in a workshop context. Premedical students who received the training showed a significant improvement in listening and communication skills by comparison with a control group that did not participate in the workshop. Although this study had some methodological weaknesses (for example, the treatment and control groups were not comparable in terms of professional experience), the results suggest the possibility of building a collaborative potential into professional training. In the course of this training, it may be important for health professionals to realize that patients differ in their emotional needs and in the capacity to manage their side of the partnership.

We recognize, of course, that professionals have an expertise and knowledge base, developed from long years of specialization, that cannot be transferred to patients or coopted by them. In fact, the findings from one study (Howard & Tyler, 1975) suggest that patients fare worse medically when they are too much in charge of their own care. Perhaps the appropriate conclusion is that patients and care givers are equal but different partners in the health delivery process. To ignore the power of either partner is to risk compromise or failure in the practice of health care.

Finally, from a social and environmental perspective, individuals alone—or small groups of individuals banded together—cannot assume total responsibility for altering sources of disease within the environment. Government policy affecting national priorities for health maintenance must be affected at the highest levels of administration. Groups of individuals can act as powerful lobbies to this end, but for radical groups there exists the danger of preciousness and isolation that may cause them to withdraw from the larger scene and "do their own thing."

The pervasive tendency to overemphasize personal power and responsibility is reflected in the following quotation from a noted cancer researcher: "In the immediate future . . . the greatest benefits [for cancer prevention] will depend on personal action, whereby an individual controls his personal environment and that of his family" (Higgenson, 1976). This position is a valid one, but only in part because there are severe limits to the effectiveness of individual action. Even the partnership between patient and professional that has been the focus here, building on the patient's capacity for autonomy, needs to be expanded into linkages between lay power vested in collections of individuals and the macrosocial order. Schwartz's (1980) discussion of systems theory as it applies to health care is relevant here. All levels of systems—from culture to cell—are linked, with power vested at every level. This chapter has focused on the patient's domain of competence within the structure of power.

ACKNOWLEDGMENTS

We would like to express appreciation to Leon H. Levy for his thoughtful editorial comments in the preparation of this chapter.

4. References

Albert, E. Appealing for treatment: A cognitive analysis of hospital emergency patients. *Social Science and Medicine,* 1980, *14A,* 243–251.

Albrecht, G. The negotiated diagnosis and treatment of occlusal problems. *Social Science and Medicine,* 1977, *11,* 277–283.

Alonzo, A. Everyday illness behavior: A situational approach to health status deviations. *Social Science and Medicine,* 1979, *13A,* 397–909.

Bakan, D. *Belief in chronic pain.* Paper presented at Twelfth Banff International Conference on Behavior Modification, Banff Alberta, Canada, March 1980.

Barber, B. The ethics of experimentation with human subjects. *Scientific American,* 1976, *234,* 25–31.

Bergler, J. H., Pennington, A. C., Metcalfe, M., & Freis, E. D.: Informed consent: How much does the patient understand? *Clinical Pharmacology and Therapeutics* 1980, *27,* 435–440.

Bertman, S., & Krant, G. To know suffering and the teaching of empathy. *Social Science and Medicine,* 1977, *11,* 239–644.

Cassel, E. Disease as an "it": Concepts of disease revealed by patients' presentation of symptoms. *Social Science and Medicine,* 1976, *10,* 143–146.

Cassileth, B. R., Lupkis, R. V., Sutton-Smith, K., & March, V.: Informed consent: Why are its goals imperfectly realized? *New England Journal of Medicine* 1980, *302,* 896–900.

Currie, B. & Renner, J. Patient education: Developing a health care partnership. *Postgraduate Medicine,* 1979, *65,* 177–182.

Davis, M. The organizational, interactional and care-oriented conditions for patient participation in continuity of care: A framework for staff intervention. *Social Science and Medicine,* 1980, *14A,* 39–61.

D.H.E.W. *Protection of human subjects.* OPRR Reports: Code of Federal Regulations: (45 CFR 46). National Institutes of Health, Public Health Service, U.S. Department of Health, Education, and Welfare, Rev. January 11, 1978a.

D.H.E.W. Beta-blocker heart attack trial: Guidelines for obtaining informed consent. *DHEW Publication* No. (NCI) 78-1603. National Institutes of Health, Public Health Service, Department of Health, Education, and Welfare, 1978b.

Emerson, J. Behavior in private places. Sustaining definitions of reality in gynecological examinations. D. Brisset & C. Edgly (Eds.), *Life as theatre*. Chicago: Aldine Press, 1975.

Epstein, L. C., & Lasagna, L. Obtaining informed consent: Form or substance. *Archives of Internal Medicine* 1969, *123*, 682–688.

Fabrega, H. The ethnography of illness. *Social Science and Medicine*, 1979, *13A*, 565–576.

Federal Register, 43 (51559), Nov. 3, 1978.

Fletcher, J. C., Branson, R., & Freireich, E. J. Ethical considerations in clinical trials: Invited remarks, *Clinical Pharmacology and Therapeutics*, 1979, *25*, 742–746.

Foley, K. Pain syndromes in cancer patients. In J. Bonica & V. Ventafridda (Eds.), *Advances in pain research and therapy* (Vol. II). New York: Raven Press, 1979.

Foster, R. *Breast cancer detection by breast self-examination.* (Grant NIH-CA 26363), 1981

Foster, R. S., Jr., Lang, S. P., Costanza, M. C., Worden, J. K., Haines, C. R., & Yates, J. W. Breast self-examination practices and breast-cancer stage. *New England Journal of Medicine*, 1978, *299*, 265–270.

Fox, R. Is there a "new" medical student? *The Key Reporter*, 1975, *40*, 2–4.

Freidson, E. Client control and medical practice. *American Journal of Sociology*, 1960, *65*, 374–382.

Gartner, A., & Riessman, R. *Self-help in the human services.* San Francisco: Jossey-Bass, 1977.

Geiger, H. The causes of dehumanization in health care and prospects for humanization. In J. Howard & A. Strauss (Eds.), *Humanizing health care*, Chicago: Aldine Press 1975.

Goffman, E. *Asylums.* New York: Anchor Books, 1961.

Goldstein, S. A critical appraisal of milieu therapy in a geriatric day hospital. *Journal of the American Geriatric Society*, 1971, *8*, 693–699.

Gray, B. H.: *Human subjects in medical experimentation.* New York: Wiley, 1975.

Greenwald, P., Nasca, P. C., Lawrence, C. E., Horton, J., McGarrah, R. P., Gabriele, T., & Carlton, K. Estimated effect of breast self-examination and routine physician examinations on breast-cancer mortality. *New England Journal of Medicine*, 1978, *299*, 271–273.

Hackett, T., & Cassem, N. Factors contributing to delay in responding to the signs and symptoms of acute myocardial infarction. *American Journal of Cardiology*, 1969, *24*, 651–658.

Hall, D., Adams, C., Stein, G., Stephenson, H., Goldstein, G., & Pennypacker, H. Improved detection of human breast lesions following experimental training. *Cancer*, 1980, *46*, 408–414.

Hassar, M., & Weintraub, M. "Uninformed" consent and the wealthy volunteer: An analysis of patient volunteers in a clinical trial of a new anti-inflammatory drug. *Clinical Pharmacology and Therapeutics*, 1976, *20*, 379–386.

Hayes-Bautista, D. Modifying the treatment: Patient compliance, patient control, and medical care. *Social Science and Medicine*, 1976, *10*, 233–238.

Haynes, B., Taylor, D., & Sackett, D. (Eds.), *Compliance in health care. Baltimore: The Johns Hopkins University Press, 1979.*

Higgenson, J. A hazardous society? Individual versus community responsibility in cancer research. *American Journal of Public Health*, 1976, *66*, 759–366.

Howard, J. Humanization and dehumanization of health care: A conceptual review. In J. Howard and A. Strauss (Eds.), *Humanizing health care.* New York: Wiley, 1975.

Howard, J., DeMets, D., & BHAT Research Group. How informed is informed consent? The BHAT experience. *Controlled Clinical Trials*, 1981, *2*, 287–303.

Howard, J., & Tyler, C. Comments on dehumanization: Caveats, dilemmas, and remedies. In J. Howard & A. Strauss (Eds.), *Humanizing health care*, New York: Wiley, 1975.

Igun, V. Stages in breast-seeking: A descriptive model. *Social Science and Medicine*, 1979, *13A*, 445–456.

Innes, J. Does the professional know what the client wants? *Social Science and Medicine*, 1977, *11*, 635–638.

Johnson, J., & Leventhal, H. Effects of accurate expectations and behavioral instructions on reactions during a routine medical examination. *Journal of Personality and Social Psychology*, 1974, *29*, 710–718.

Kennedy, B. J., & Lillehaugen, A. Patient recall of informed consent. *Medical Pediatric Oncology*, 1979, *7*, 173–178.

Korsch, B., Gozzi, E., & Francis, V. Gaps in doctor–patient communications: Doctor–patient interaction and patient satisfaction. *Pediatrics*, 1968, *42*, 855–871.

Krantz, D., Baum, A., & Wideman, M. Assessment of preferences for self-treatment and information in medical care. *Journal of Personality and Social Psychology* 1980, *39*, 977–990.

Kronenfeld, J. Self-care as a panacea for the ills of the health care system: An assessment. *Social Science and Medicine.* 1979, *13A*, 263–267.

Leeb, D., Bowers, D. G., Jr., & Lynch, J. B. Observations on the myth of "informed consent." *Plastic and Reconstructive Surgery*, 1976, *58*, 280–282.

Leventhal, H. The consequences of depersonalization during illness and treatment: An information-processing model. In J. Howard & A. Strauss (Eds.), *Humanizing health care*. New York: Wiley, 1975.

Levine, R. J. & Lebacqz, K. Some ethical considerations in clinical trials. *Clinical Pharmacology and Therapeutics*, 1979, *25*, 728–741.

Levy, L. Self-help groups viewed by mental health professionals: A survey and comments. *American Journal of Community Psychology*, 1978, *6*, 305–313.

Levy L. Processes and activities in groups. In M. Lieberman & L. Borman (Eds.), *Self-help groups for coping with crisis*. San Francisco: Jossey-Bass, 1979.

Levy, S. The experience of undergoing a heart attack: The construction of a new reality. *Journal of Phenomenological Psychology* 1982.

Lieberman, M. Borman, L., and Associates, *Self-help Groups for coping with crisis*. San Francisco: Jossey-Bass, 1979.

Lindesmith, A., & Strauss, A. A sociological conception of motives. In D. Brisset & C. Edgley (Eds.), *Life as Theatre*. Chicago: Aldine, 1975.

Mahoney, M. *Cognition and Behavior Modification*. Cambridge, Mass.: Ballinger, 1974.

Marlatt, G. Alcohol, stress, and cognitive control. In I. Sarason & C. Spielberger (Eds.), *Stress and anxiety*. Washington, D.C.: Hemisphere Publishing Company, 1976.

Mechanic, D. The experience and reporting of common physical complaints. *Journal of Health and Social Behavior*, 1980, *21*, 146–155.

Merleau-Ponty M. *Phenomenology of perception*. London: Routledge & Kegan Paul, 1962.

Morrow, G. *Studies on the utility and readability of informed consent forms*. Paper presented at the American Psychological Association Meeting, Montreal, September 1980.

Moss, A., Wynar, B., & Goldstein, S. Delay in hospitalization during the acute coronary period. *American Journal of Cardiology*, 1969, *24*, 659–665.

Parsons, T. *The social system*. New York: Free Press 1951.

Petrie, A. *Individuality in pain and suffering*. Chicago: University of Chicago Press, 1967.

Poole, A., & Sanson-Fisher, R. Understanding the patient: A reflective aspect of medical education. *Social Science and Medicine*, 1979, *13A*, 37–93.

Robinson, G., & Merav, A. Informed consent: Recall by patients tested postoperatively. *Annals of Thoracic Surgery*, 1976, *22*, 209–212.

Rosenbaum, M. Individual differences in self-control behavior and tolerance of painful stimulation. *Journal of Abnormal Psychology*, 1980, 581–590.

Roter, D. Patient participation in the patient provider interaction: The effects of patient question asking on the quality of interaction, satisfaction, and compliance. *Health Education Monographs*, 1977, *5*, 281–297.

Ruzek, S. *The Women's health movement: Feminist alternatives to medical control*. New York: Praeger, 1978.

Schain, W. Patients' rights in decision making: The case for personalism versus paternalism in health care. *Cancer*, 1980, *46*, 0177–0183.

Scheff, T. Negotiating reality: Notes on power in the assessment of responsibility. In D. Brisset & C. Edgly (Eds.), *Life or Theatre*. Chicago: Aldine Press, 1975.

Schultz, A. L., Pardee, G. P., & Ensinck, J. W. Are research subjects really informed? *Western Journal of Medicine*, 1975, *123*, 76–80.

Schwartz, G. Behavioral medicine and systems theory. *National Forum*, 1980, Winter, 25–30.

Sidel, V., & Sidel, R. Beyond coping. *Social Policy*, 1976, *1*, 67–69.

Smith, H. Myocardial infarction—Case studies of ethics in the consent situation. *Social Science and Medicine*, 1974, *8*, 399–404.

Smith, S., Rosen, D., Trueworthy, R., & Lowman, J. A reliable method for evaluating drug compliance in children with cancer. *Cancer*, 1979, *43*, 169–173.

Spingarn, N. *Confidentiality*. Report of the Conference on Confidentiality of Health Records, Key Biscayne, November 1974.

Stiles, W., Putnam, S., James, S., & Wolf, M. Dimensions of patient and physician roles in medical screening interviews. *Social Science and Medicine*, 1979, *13A*, 335–341.

Strauss, A. *Negotiations: Varieties, contexts, processes, and social order.* San Francisco, Jossey-Bass, 1978.

Stuart, R. *Behavioral self-management: Strategies, techniques, and outcome.* New York: Brunner/Mazel, 1977.

Truman v. Thomas: 27 California, 3rd 285, June 1980.

Vickery, D., & Fries, J. *Take care of yourself: A consumer's guide to medical care.* Reading, Mass.: Addison-Wesley, 1976.

Waitzkin, H. Medicine, superstructure and micropolitics. *Social Science and Medicine,* 1979, *13a,* 601–609.

Waitzkin, H., & Waterman, B. *The exploitation of illness in capitalist society.* Indianapolis: Bobbs-Merrill, 1974.

Wilkinson, G., Edgerton, F., Wallace H., Reese P., Patterson, J., & Priore, R. Delay, stage of disease, and survival from breast cancer. *Chronic Disease,* 1979, *32,* 365–373.

Woodward, W. E. Informed consent of volunteers: A direct measurement of comprehension and retention of information. *Clinical Research,* 1979, *27,* 248–252.

Worden, J., & Weisman, A. Psychosocial component of lagtime in cancer diagnosis. *Journal of Psychosomatic Research,* 1975, *19,* 69–79.

Author Index

Subject Index